AN

ARCHAIC DICTIONARY:

BIOGRAPHICAL, HISTORICAL,

AND MYTHOLOGICAL.

AN

ARCHAIC DICTIONARY:

BIOGRAPHICAL, HISTORICAL,

AND MYTHOLOGICAL;

FROM THE

EGYPTIAN, ASSYRIAN, AND ETRUSCAN

MONUMENTS AND PAPYRI.

BY

W. R. COOPER, F.R.A.S., M.R.A.S.,

Secretary to the Society of Biblical Archæology.

" FUIMUS."

Multæ terricolis linguæ, cœlestibus una.

LONDON:

SAMUEL BAGSTER AND SONS,

15, PATERNOSTER ROW.

1876.

REPUBLISHED BY GALE RESEARCH COMPANY, BOOK TOWER, DETROIT, 1969

Library of Congress Catalog Card Number 73-76018

———◆———

"The blessing of him that was ready to perish came upon me: and I caused the widow's heart to sing for joy."—Job xxix. 13.

———◆———

TO

STEPHEN EVANS, Esq.,

OF OLD CHANGE, LONDON,

THIS VOLUME IS GRATEFULLY DEDICATED

BY

W. R. Cooper

Barnsbury, June, 1876.

TO THE READER.

IN this short Dictionary, or rather Index of Names, for the most part either new or uncommon, no attempt has been made to claim for the work the character of completeness; the very nature of the facts which it embodies and the materials from which they are obtained, renders this impossible. Not a week passes by without producing some fresh authority upon Archaic history supplying additional personages to be enumerated and new events to be recorded. The very knowledge of this defect for some time deterred the author in his compilation, which he has only been persuaded to continue to its present form by the sheer necessity of making some such Index for his own use, which he then conjectured would by a little further trouble be acceptable to other students also. Hence, in contradistinction to the usual practice of authors, he has endeavoured to say as little, instead of as much as he well might, upon every person or place cited, preferring simply to relate those facts concerning them which are only to be derived from the results of recent scholarship, and which are not at present found either in a Classic or a Biblical Dictionary; therefore it is that many proper names, really of Archaic date are wholly omitted, such as those of the Patriarchs and the Prophets of Israel, the Demi-gods, and Heraclidæ of Greece, and the Heroes of Rome. All that is known about these latter personages can be found in standard works of reference, written in a more critical style. Further, also, as in the early ages with which the author has chiefly concerned himself, there was either no settled system of chronology, or else no consensus of opinion exists among scholars as to the equation of their systems with the data of modern science, no attempt has been made to affix other than Dynastic dates, and the student is left to place every event at the period assigned to it, by the chronological theory which he himself prefers. Finally, many of the reigns and subjects included in this list abound with original discrepancies, and inconsistencies, with these also the author does not concern himself; the statements which he makes, are in almost every instance, those of the monuments themselves, which in our present state of knowledge it would be ridiculous to attempt to correct. The reader is entreated to bear all these circumstances in his kindly consideration, to accept the work for what it is worth, as a substitute, till a better can be obtained, and a supplement to the ordinary school dictionaries, and to aid the author in the preparation of a superior edition if it should it ever be required, by communicating to him any omissions which he might be willing to supply, or any improvements or additions which he can suggest.

ARCHAIC DICTIONARY.

INTRODUCTION.

THE compilation of a Dictionary like the present is a work which it is difficult either to commence or to complete with any degree of satisfaction. The materials are, with apparent inconsistency, at once so scanty and so abundant, so uncertain and yet so indisputable, are spread over so wide an area, and are yet obtainable from so few sources, that every entry must be to a greater or less extent a tentative one, and every discrepancy accepted as veracious, till it is either confirmed or confuted by the results of subsequent interpretations. The ancient inscriptions, which are our only authorities for the history of their own times, are provokingly imperfect and unintelligible for the purposes for which they are now required. They recount the names and titles of the kings and officers with a monotonous verbosity, while the names of places conquered, and of monarchs rendered tributary, are written either in obscure ideographs, or imperfectly phoneticised syllables. From the want of a fixed era, and the general use of a moveable calendar, there is little accuracy in the dates of events described, even when, which is a rare occurrence, any years are mentioned. In many inscriptions the single object has been to cover so many square yards of mural space with eulogy of the reigning sovereign. When the events of his own life were insufficient for this purpose, a few years' actions from the annals of his predecessor were recklessly appropriated to his own; when on the other hand the symmetry of the design required it, or the space was limited, the succession of years was utterly disregarded, and the paragraphs were arranged to suit the ideas of the architect, and not to minister to the necessities of the historian; to magnify the glory of the king, whose successor would frequently erase his inscriptions, although that proceeding was denounced by the most awful curses. The portrait of the sovereign, and the great events of his reign were made to recur with tedious frequency, and sometimes the history of his actions is written across the dress which he wears, and at other times it is scattered over the background of the figure regardless of picturesque effect. The effect of this inversion upon the paragraphs themselves would be to produce such a confusion of sentences as the Decalogue would exhibit, if it were to be set up with the longer and shorter commandments arranged so as to alternate or balance each other without any regard to the sense of the words, or attention to the sequence of the ideas, to be conveyed to the mind of the reader. Not unfrequently also, the alteration or enlargement of a royal residence necessitated the destruction of a part of the inscribed slabs, and when that was the case, no care was taken to render the series complete by the reinscription of another slab in the place of that which was destroyed.

In the smaller official documents, those which were inscribed upon the foundation Cylinders or Timins of baked clay, a similar disregard of accuracy existed; the tablets were written by various scribes, who although copying from the same materials, differed widely from each other as to the manner in which they used them, and often omitted sentences which there was not room to crowd into the last lines of a column, or repeated an unimportant phrase to avoid a blank space on the monument. On the literary tablets, more especially those which were religious or mystical, two languages were generally employed, the Accadian original, and the later Assyrian translation; but even in that case the bilingual nature of the record does not render it easier of translation, for the Assyrian terms are often adaptations of the older Accadian words, and occasionally even substitutions of other ideas; and in almost every instance the two versions while substantially agreeing as to their purport, yet present so many differences of detail as to leave just those points unsettled, which to the modern critic or historian are of the highest value, and the uncertainty regarding which undermines all his premises, and vitiates all his conclusions.

Another source of error and annoyance is to be found in the fact that many of the recorded inscriptions bear in themselves the evidence of a credulous untrustworthiness, an orientalism of expression which renders it impossible that all their statements should be received as the witness of historical truth. When it is gravely stated that a monarch like Assurnazirpal makes an inroad into a country, and captures its capital city, together with 1200 surrounding towns; then after a few days' march besieges and destroys a second great walled city, and ruinates another 1000 or 800 towns, and this statement is repeated with little variation in describing the conquest of a country only a few hundred miles in extent; it immediately becomes obvious that there has been a reckless perversion of facts, and that even if the thousands of towns were the veriest hamlets of a crowded metropolis, there would still have been employed a considerable degree of bombastic exaggeration. Hence the names of persons and places, and the details of political events, have to be simply stated as they are found recorded; they can neither be reconciled with reason or with themselves, and dangerous and ridiculous above all would it be for an historian writing after a lapse of thirty centuries, to endeavour to synchronize or adapt them. They must wait till time which has preserved and revealed these writings, shall have subjected them to the analysis of comparison.

Although these remarks are intended to apply chiefly to the cuneiform inscriptions, they are equally true of the hieroglyphic literature also; for the Egyptian papyri, many of which were buried in the tombs of their possessors, and were never intended to be read, are often most perfunctorily written, and copied with the most heedless inaccuracy the one from the other. Phrases which were never entirely intelligible even to the most careful reader, become on these papyri a mere chaos of fragmentary sentences and heterogenous signs, among which the name and titles of the deceased, and those of the local deity which he worshipped, are often alone distinguishable; even the more exactly written MSS. are full of contractions and notes, which the course of ages has rendered undiscoverable.   The degrees of filiation in the family lists are often hopelessly confused owing to the habit of the scribes of comparing the affinities of all the deceased to the various mystical relationships which prevailed among the Egyptian divinities.   Almost every priest is a " royal father," and every wife is a "royal daughter," or "divine sister," while her deceased husband is equally an Osirian or one of the race of gods.   The same turn of writing which prevails to this day on our churchyard grave-stones and mural tablets, was prevalent in the minds of the writers of the funereal stele.   For eulogy and inaccuracy, poverty of expression and vulgarity of style, for their want of variety, and their pious frauds upon the characters of the dead, the lapidary inscriptions of Egypt and England run parallel, and if the future historian of the British empire were confined for his materials chiefly to the grave-stones of the dead, then the history that he would write of the people of Great Britain would be only• a little more reliable and more fragmentary than that which we are able to redecipher of the history of Egypt.   There is one remarkable exception however, such an historian might rely upon finding *our* mouments only defaced by time ; but the stelè of the Nile have three times suffered the most deliberate mutilation and erasure of divine and personal names, and each time at the dictates of a religious impulse, in the XVIIth, the XVIIIth, and the XIXth Dynasties.   Hence there are irrestorable lacunæ in their monuments, and portions of their history which can only be conjecturally replaced.

The information which contemporary monuments themselves do not contain can never be supplied by Greek or Roman authors, who were the most speculative of theorists, and the most credulous of historians. The voluptuous Greek and the avaricious Roman never thought that any other nation could have a history or an antiquity comparable to their own ; they were the sole Autochthœne, the others were merely barbarians, outer foreigners ; the rest of the world to them were ignorant and profane. With equal pride, the Egyptians termed the Asiatics and Europeans in return, "the vile, the impure;" and thus enveloped in the clouds of their own prejudices, neither people could see, or could have respected had they seen them, the excellencies of the other. Besides this drawback, it must be remembered that to the classical writers, the cuneiform and hieroglyphic inscriptions were as much a mystery as till lately they were to ourselves. All the knowledge concerning these countries that the ancients collected, they had to obtain from second or even third-hand sources, and to adapt them to the tastes of their countrymen by the addition of interpretations and glosses of their own. The treatise of Plutarch, *De Iside et Osiride*, about as faithfully represents the ideas of the Egyptian priests, as Jacob Bryant's Arkite theories and Deucalion myths do the Izdubar Legends of Assyria. The Hierarchs of Amen-Ra had a contemptuous pride in misinforming their scornful conquerors upon the tenets of their religion, for compared to them " you Greeks are children;" and they were equally indifferent whether the Hellenes regarded their Isis the mother of the gods as Kybele, or as Hera ; they acted on the old rule of the Mediæval writers : " They like to be deceived, let them be deceived." Furthermore, it must not be forgotten that any priest who should have told his conquerors that their own deities were of Hamitic origin, would have met the same fate as would have befallen any Israelite in the XIIth century, who should have dared to plead in defence of his murdered brethren at York, that the founder of the religion of his oppressors was himself a Jew.

When it is considered on what perishable materials the records of the past are written, on brittle earthenware and fragile papyrus which scarcely bears unrolling, it is not wonderful that apart from the errors in the original texts, there should also arise very many others from the destruction of portions of the documents, and the incrustation and obliteration of the edges of others. In some instances the tenor of the inscription has been such that the missing portions have been safely restored ; but in the majority of cases, the omissions have had to remain unsupplied. Occasionally, of the more important documents, duplicate copies have been found, and thus a standard text has been collected; while again, inscriptions which were imperfect in one language have been supplemented by contemporaneous notices in the records of another. Especially in the Assyrian and Babylonian inscriptions, of which a synchronous history extending over many years exists, and during the XXVIth Dynasty the same advantage in a smaller degree takes place with the Egyptian and Assyrian; and thus sometimes the meaning of a difficult passage has been restored by a reference to a contemporaneous document. This has been noticeably the case with the Assyrian contract and sale tablets; which are often accompanied by an endorsement in Phœnician to render the property, be it slave or goods, easier of exchange among the Semitic nations conterminous to Assyria; and the Phœnician characters having survived the hands of time and violence, have often preserved names and dates which since they were written in the more angular cuneiform characters have crumbled away. In the royal mural texts the most valuable adjunct to the interpretation of an inscription has been the pictorial illustration which accompanies it, and which instructs the mind by an universal language, with a reality that the most fervid rhetorician could never hope to equal.

Year after year, it might almost be written month by month, new tablets and MSS. are discovered, more satisfactory interpretations are made, and doubtful readings explained and expunged. A very short time will now suffice to place in our hands a wealth of literature, of which Berosus only knew one isolated section, Pliny and Trogus Pompeius had only heard the name. The invaluable aid of comparative philology and mythology, sciences of which Plato scarcely dreamt, and Livy disregarded, will enable us to reconstruct on an imperishable basis, the history of the Archaic world; to add to the list of the illustrious, multitudes of heroic men, great kings, merciful legislators, learned men, and noble women also, who gloriously filled their stations in the ages past, and whose memories shall have their palingenesis in the days to come. When no longer to examples drawn from Greek and Roman history shall we point the aspirations of our young in the normal schools of the future, but shall be able to exhort them to deeds of personal courage by the heroism of a Rameses and an Anebni; to bravely contend against contending fate, like Merodach Baladan of Babylonia, and Muthon of Tyre ; shall exhort them to serve their country with the fidelity of the Egyptian chancellor Bai, and to resign themselves to the apathy of the grave, old in wisdom and years like Pentahor, proudly lamented like Menepthah the Egyptian, or Assurbanipal the glorious king of Assyria.

From the consideration of the texts themselves, it is now necessary to explain, somewhat in detail, how those texts have been utilized for the requirements of this dictionary.

I. In the first place, the information contained in the work is based upon the Archaic inscriptions, Accadian, Assyrian, Egyptian, or Etruscan, alone, with scarcely a reference to the statements made by the classical writers. Hence all the names which occur in Ancient as distinct from Archaic history, have been rigidly excluded, except in those very rare instances where an isolated fact on an inscription concerning a Greek or Roman personage required the insertion of the name. Hence also the exceeding brevity of the statements which are given concerning many kings, deities, and heroes, whose actions are familiar to every student. Indeed, had an attempt been made to combine the two wholly different sources of information into the history of the life of one person, it would have been very difficult, if not impossible, to avoid rewriting much of what has been more exhaustively and ably collected by Murray, Smith, and Lempriere. However, as no real student will ever consult this Archaic Dictionary without these standard works of reference being examined also, it is to be hoped that the brevity and selection of the materials in this work will be the less inconveniently felt.

II. The occasional contrarieties of translation of the various texts, and the discrepancies of the texts themselves, have been already mentioned. It has been deemed safest in this instance to leave these sources of information as they are ; hereafter, the increase of knowledge and the addition of more materials will almost entirely remove this difficulty ; and should the dictionary reach to more editions than the first, these corrections will duly find their place in it, either at the hands of the author, or at those of a subsequent editor.

III.   There will be, moreover, found a considerable redundance in the matter of the variant etymologies of proper names.   This also is a defect, but it is one which after very careful consideration it has been deemed safest to leave unamended.   Owing to the different systems of interpretation adopted by the earlier and later students, and the various vocalic powers given by them to the characters of the inscriptions containing proper names, characters which are often purely ideographic, and have no exact phonetic equivalents, it has unavoidably arisen that the most divergent forms of spelling have been given as the rendering of the name of the same individual.   Some of these variant forms are now known to be wrong, but inasmuch as the books in which these revisions are contained are scanty and but little known, there was no other method left to show the student who had only one or two works, that the Sesertesen and Osirigesen of Sharpe, the Usertesen of Lepsius, and the Osirtasen of Birch and Mariette, were one and the same monarch, than to insert the different readings as cross references, and to give the fullest account of the person under the best known etymon, even where that one was not the most correct.

IV.   Another cause of the many cross references, which would otherwise have been objectionable, is the fact that the Egyptian and Assyrian names were frequently translated, and not transliterated, or else were written down phonetically by the different historians, and thus it has been often extremely difficult to identify the individuals meant in the inscriptions; and this was more particularly the case when the Assyrian or Egyptian names contained the titles of their own deities.   In that case the Hebrew writers from conscientious scruples, almost invariably parodied or changed them; as, for example, Mephibosheth, which means "Mouth of reproach," for Mephibaal, "Mouth of Baal;" Ishbosheth, "Man of shame," for Ithbaal, "Man of Baal;" Coniah, "Strength of the Lord," or "God appointed," for Jeconiah ; and Babel, " Confusion," for Babilu, "Gate of God." When they were simply translated, however, the case of the names was but little better ; and an analogous instance is afforded us in the present day by the French geographers, who in their lists of towns write Chapelle Blanc for Whitechapel, and Vienne for Wien, Plaisance for Piacenza, and Anvers for Antwerp ; and in modern history, Vilainton for Wellington, and "Le bon Docteur Noir," for Mr. Christopher Davis, the late negro surgeon of St. Bartholomew's Hospital. Pauncetto, an Italian nickname, rendered Mr. Littlebelly, Petropolis for St. Petersburg, and Death for D'ath, among ourselves, are also exactly parallel instances.

V.   Another unavoidable difficulty, though this refers more to the philologist than the general reader, is that many names which are spelt with similar letters in the English alphabet, and thus appear to be related to each other, are really written with totally opposite signs in the original text, by which their real dissimilarity is perceptible at a glance. This is more especially the case with the Egyptian titles; and it was attempted to remedy the defect by the use of certain diacritical signs, as in the excellent *Egyptian Grammar* of Mr. Renouf, and if the Egyptian language only were to have been thus dealt with, the matter would have been simple enough ; but unfortunately the dotted and apostrophised letters t, t, h, s, $ç$, a', etc., do not represent uniformly the same sounds in Egyptian, Arabic, Assyrian, and Sanscrit, and therefore their adoption would in the end have led the way to a more hopeless, because more apparently scientific confusion. The explanations which are occasionally given of the proper names, so far as they can be ascertained, will in some degree point out the differentiation, when they appear in other respects to be similar. See as an instance of this, the royal names, Aahotep, "Great peace ;" and Aahhotep, "Peace of the god Aah," where the guttural h makes the sole difference of meaning, as in the Hebrew name Sarai, altered by revelation into Sarah, "Princess ;" and Abram to Abraham, "Father of nations." For the rest it is to be hoped that many of the readers of this book will themselves be led to become students of the Archaic languages, and will restrain their brilliant theories of comparisons by recollecting that in

philology the very appearance of an analogy should be received
as an indication of a statement to be mistrusted, and that next to
statistics no science is more abused, more misleading, and more un-
fixed than comparative etymology.

VI.   The extraordinary length, sometimes extending to twelve
syllables, of the ancient names should also be noted ; but that also
is an unavoidable inconvenience, arising from their being in most instances compound adjectives, or honorific epithets, of which " Praise
God Barebones;" " Fight the good fight of faith;" "Valiant for truth;"
of the Puritan days; and " Strong i th'arm;" and " Go-to-bed;" of
the present day, are examples among proper names; and Pen-y-
cwm cuick, corrupted into " Penny come quick;" and Weston on
the sea, translated into " Weston super mare;" among villages, are
modern instances.   These and such similar phrases, for names they
can scarcely be called, when undivided by hyphens, like many of the
German and Welsh names of towns, must lead to an apparently
unpronounceable word, such as the following Welsh and German
instances :   Llansaintffraidglanconwy,   " Ecclesiastical   District   of
St. Ffraid, on the banks of the river Con;" Llanfairmathafarnei-
thaf, " E. D. of (St.) Mary, of the outermost Math-farn;" Llan-
fairpwllgwyngyllgogerbwllllantysiliogogo, " E. D. of (St.) Mary, of the
white-hazel pool, somewhat near to the pool in the E. D. of (St.)
Tysilio of the cave ;" and the German title, Hauptzollrevisiongepäcks-
bureauaufseher, "Chief-custom-revision-baggage-office-controller."   It
is, therefore, probable that in the Archaic times when such long names
were understood, certain portions of them were suppressed, as is the
third person plural of the French, or condensed as the names Meagher
and Cholmondely, pronounced respectively Marr and Chumly, are
among us.

VII.   The same reason will also explain why in a few cases entirely
different translations of the same name have been given.   When the
true syllabic division of a compound word has to be guessed, it is often
possible to explain it by a reference to some widely varying roots, and
yet for each interpretation to be presumably correct; as an instance of
this take the common English village name Kingswell, which may be

thus divided and explained with equal accuracy, "*Kings-well*, the well of the King, probably so named from the sainted King Edgar, who may have caused it to have been dug for the supply of the pilgrims to the Abbey Church, where his tomb remains; *King-swell*, the fop king, probably named in derision of the dandy English monarch, George IV., who is said to have passed through the village on his way to Brighthelmstone. Swell is an obsolete Archaism for an over-dressed person." *Archaic Dictionary of England and Wales*, A.D. 2075 ! !

VIII. Although the contents of the work are almost entirely limited to the personages of Archaic history, yet for the purpose of drawing attention to certain interesting points in comparative mythology, a few names of Aryan, Zend, and Scandinavian deities and heroes have been inserted. A very few however are mentioned, and these are intended rather to indicate certain points of contact between all the primæval religious systems, than to follow the argument up; they are designed simply to remind the student of the existence of certain initial dogmas, and to suggest subjects for comparison and examination, as the study of the Archaic monuments afterwards developes itself.

IX. Of very many of the people whose names are here contained, it can only at present be written that they filled such and such offices, and were the children of such and such parents, that they died and were buried. It is the old epitaph revived, "Colas était vive, Colas est mort." Still, despite this scantiness of information, it was necessary to include those names in an Archaic Biographical Dictionary, because the fact that the offices which those unknown personages held, were at one time of high importance, and therefore they were entitled to be now recorded. Modern history preserves the names of many Lord Chancellors, Marshals, and Mayors, who were men of considerable mark in their day, although they now are disregarded. So it is with the Egyptian and Assyrian officials, if nothing else is at present obtainable from their obituaries, we are yet able to ascertain the rise and antiquity of certain offices, and the growth of peculiar institutions, which, when arranged in the light of other similar inscriptions, are material aids to the philosopher in the reconstruction of ancient history. "A royal councillor," "one of the council of thirty" before the time of Abraham, a "keeper of the women," a "governor of a province," a "keeper of the signet," "chief of the bowmen," etc., all point out the existence of certain political ideas of the highest interest and importance. Often indeed the title survived the office, as those of "Apostolic Curser," "Head Falconer," "King's herbwoman," have now, but the retention of the names marks an era in the life of the nation when the offices ceased to exist. The existence of an office analogous to that of a tribune of the people in the court of a despotic sovereign, of a kind of elective franchise in an hierarchy ruling by the most absolute of divine right, the appointment of a "captain of the fleet" in a kingdom which had no sea navy, and of a "keeper of the chariots" of a country where cavalry could not act, are all points deserving of consideration, possessing sufficient notice to justify the insertion of even a greater crowd of apparently unimportant names.

X. Some exception may perhaps be taken to the utter absence of any expression of horror on the part of the compiler, at the savage deeds of the sovereigns whose actions he has been obliged to record, but the omission was intentional. Nothing is more prejudicial to a right comprehension of the moral characters of ancient heroes, than to form a judgment of their acts by the moral standard of our own later times. The statute books of the Plantagenet and Stuart period, contain enactments which would now be characterized as atrocious; English history even of recent times abounds with wars, massacres, and brutalities, which we are far from attributing to the personal disposition of the generals or statesmen under whom they took place; much more therefore does this apply to the Egyptian and Assyrian warfare. Their enemies were to them not only Gentiles or barbarians, but "impure, vile," and scarcely deserving in their system of belief any consideration whatever. The Assyrian monarch committed all his cruelties to the entire satisfaction of his gods Assur or Bel. Timour of India, or Rajah-rajah of Ceylon, would have done the same. Was not a Te Deum composed to glorify the carnage of Dettengen? Were not "thanks offered to Almighty God for putting an end to the great rebellion" at the butchery of Culloden?

The province of an historian, and more especially of a compiler of annals, is to relate the events themselves as his authorities recorded them, without reflections and without criticism. Manners and customs are the result of the development of a religious feeling which could at all times reconcile the greatest inconsistencies with the most sincere integrity. To reflect upon the defilement of boys and women by the soldiers of Assurnazirpal, would be inconsistent to the descendants of the *civilizers* of the Indies. The impalement of Aym and Abyate by the Assyrian soldiers 4000 years ago, cannot well be deemed monstrous by us, whose great grandfathers slaughtered and mutilated their own relations and affixed the bloody members to the walls of Temple Bar. It would be somewhat tartuffian to censure the negro raid of Thothmes III. as barbarous, when a great officer acting as a mercenary, receives honour for suppressing slavery by annexing a negro country to a despotic power ; and the bastinadoing of Paneba and the robbers must be passed over without censure, since we have ourselves retained the lash in the royal army, and after allowing it to fall into disuse, have restored the punishment of flogging for the thieves of the XIXth century.

XI. Apart from all other reasons also, the very names themselves are to an historical student possessed of considerable significance. The prevalence of certain surnames under certain Dynasties, and on the other hand their entire omission in others, the introduction of the names and titles of Semitic deities into compound, as Atenefra Bentanath, Egyptian epithet names, which took place under the XVIIIth, XXVIth, and later Dynasties, the use of the Divine titles both as *pre*fixes, and *suf*fixes, as in Raneferka, Neferkara, Merira, Thothmes, Hathorisis, Amense, etc., in a concrete form, as well as in an expanded one, the peculiar adjectives applied to the attributes of the deities, as Ranefer, "the good Ra," and the indifferent manner in which these epithets were used, all being so contrary to the practice of the contiguous nations, these and many others are among the points of interest to the philologist and historian. To compare our own customs with those of the Egyptians and Assyrians, while such names exist as Godfrey, Godwin, and Christopher, forms in which the most sacred of epithets are combined, yet we have no instance of the title of either member of the Christian Trinity being used as a personal name by itself alone, much less should we apply such an epithet to an animal or a stick. The encyclopedists did indeed succeed in marking their intense disregard of sacred things, by naming a special size of paper *Jésus*, and we have with a singular disregard of reverence called one of our chief Colleges at Cambridge, "Jesus ;" but these are the exceptions which justify the rule, and establish the converse proposition. In Egypt, on the other hand, the holy name Ra is found as borne alike by a king, a priest, and a private individual; a dog is called Senb; and Isis, Thoth, Amen, and Pthah, are all names of different officials, many of whom were not even priests. The use of the names of male deities as applied to women, and of feminine ones as borne by men, is a peculiarity of which modern continental history furnishes an example, as in Marie de Macmahon, and all Catholic children male or female who are devoted to the service of the Virgin Mary, and the almost pedigree names of the members of the royal house of Bourbon. The substitution of the figure of the deity Ra in the names which originally began with that of Set, as Setra, Setineckht; the obliteration of that of Amen, in Amenhotep, and all similar nomina under the XVIIIth Dynasty, and the substitution of the Greek Apollo for the Egyptian Horus in the Ptolemaic period, are things which, trivial in themselves, deserve a record, as pointing out the depth of religious or political feeling in the various revolutions of ancient times; and consequently, therefore, where these changes are indicated, even in names, and names only of whom nothing more is known, then for the purposes of comparison and analysis, despite their brevity or tautology, those changes must be noted, and those names must be preserved.

XII. Having at so great a length written to explain, if not to apologise, for so much that has been inserted, it almost approaches the nature of a contradiction to have to express regret for what has been unavoidably left out. To the compiler, if not to the reader, the work appears starred with omissions and defects; it resembles an intricate pattern on an Indian fabric, which has become so faded and rent by the action of time and malice, that the colours are only in part discernable, and the sequence of the design interrupted at almost every point. To quit the metaphor, however, it was found simply impossible at one attempt, to include the thousands of official names which are to be found on the stele, and in the cabinets and papyri, of English and continental collections, both public and private. The far larger part of these materials have never been carefully examined or published. The bulk of them are without any date, or indications by which a date could be approximately assigned; others would have to be compared with a tedious comparison, since it may often happen that the coffin of an individual is in one collection, his stele in another, his mummy, or what remains of it, in a third, and his trinkets, or canopic vases in a fourth. This has happened in the case of the bodies of Rameses III., Seti Menepthah, Queen Aahotep, and many other lesser dignitaries. Hence, only a like labour of many years can suffice to show definitely what objects are duplicate relics of the same individual, and what relationship an Unnefer in the Louvre has to an Unnefer in the Leyden or the British Museum. This also implies the work of more than one hand, the research of more than one scholar; still as it has been before stated, every year, nay every month, leads to the greater accumulation of materials, and the greater accuracy, it must not be said, completion, of the work; and if only the reader will bear these considerations in mind, and will send to the author any observations which may arise within him in using the work, then he will greatly assist in rendering each edition less faulty than the last, and be himself a partaker of what, undertaken in the midst of much business and greater weakness, has been a labour of pain and pleasure, of weariness and of pride.

XIII. Finally, the thanks of the compiler should be expressed in the warmest terms to those eminent scholars who have rendered him assistance in the work. To the Rev. A. H. Sayce, who not only has overlooked the proof sheets, but has contributed all the articles bearing on the history and mythology of Etruria and several of the longer Assyrian ones also, the most grateful thanks of the compiler are due; to Dr. Birch, who has generously assisted by his corrections and advice; to George Smith, who has allowed the free use of the advance sheets of his Assyrian Canon; to William Greenwood Hird; to Joseph Bonomi; to William Boscawen; and to numerous correspondents, hearty and honourable thanks are due. Whatever of accuracy or of interest the Dictionary possesses, it mainly owes to them; its faults and omissions are the work of a less practised hand. To Robert Bagster, who has gone over the revises with a technical eye, and superintended the arrangement of the slips, a tiresome and ungraceful office, the compiler desires to offer his sincere thanks; and in conclusion, to those who use this work in the spirit in which it was written, neither captiously censuring its defects, or deriding its difficiences, thanks by anticipation be accorded for their courteous reception of this the first register of six thousand once famous and till now forgotten names, whose history lies in their epitaph, "*fuimus.*"

ARCHAIC DICTIONARY.

───◆───

A.

A. "Water."

A mystical pool, near the celestial Nile. It is figured in the Vignette to the CXth Chapter of the Ritual of the Dead.

A.

An Egyptian measure; it was equal to twenty-six centilitres.

AA.

An Egyptian adjective, meaning "old" or "great," commonly used in the proper names of the Ancient and Middle empires, or from the IVth to the XVIIIth dynasties.

AA. "Old men."

The name of an Egyptian deity, worshipped in the town of Aat.

AA.

A city and the second nome of Lower Egypt, called by the Greeks Latopolis. It was sacred to the worship of the goddess Bast, or Bubastis.

AA.

One of the demons who accuse the soul of the deceased in the Hall of the two Truths.

AAA.

The chief of the signet-bearers in the land of Kens, in the Court of King Aspalut of the XXVth dynasty.

AAAATAMAD.

The Egyptian name of an unidentified town in Palestine.

AAAB.

The name of an island in the first nome of Upper Egypt.

AAAB.

An Egyptian gentleman, the son of Kherab. His period is unknown, except that it was between the XIIth and XVIIIth dynasties.

3

Aaani.

The Egyptian name of the ape, and more especially of the sacred Cynocephalus baboon, which was adored as the living emblem of the god Thoth.

Aaasiri.

A common Egyptian designation of the town of Busiris.

Aaauasasu.

The title of a royal house in Ethiopia, in the time of the XXVth dynasty.

Aabau.

An Egyptian officer; the son of Rames. He lived in the time of the XVIIIth dynasty.

Aah. "The Moon."

The Egyptian name of the god who was called by the Romans Lunus. He was represented as an Ibis-headed man, with the lunar horns and disk upon his head : or else, as a man kneeling on one knee, and supporting a disk above his head with both hands.

Aah.

The Egyptian name of an unidentified town.

Aahartais.

An Egyptian lady, the wife of Nakhons. *See* Nakhons.

Aahehu.

The Egyptian name of an unidentified town.

Aahenru.

The name of the Elysium of Osiris, in the Ritual of the dead.

Aaheru. "The Chief of Terrors."

One of the mystical deities of the Egyptian Hell.

Aahhotep. " Peace of Aah, *or* the Moon."

The queen of Kames, king of Egypt, and mother of Aahmes, the first monarch of the XVIIIth dynasty. Her golden jewellery at the Museum of Boulaq is the chef d'œuvre of Egyptian art, and is unequalled for elegance by anything except the Etruscan goldwork.

Aahhotep.

The wife or consort of Amenhotep I., of the XVIIIth dynasty.

Aahlu.

The Egyptian name for the plains of Elysium, of which the valley of Balot formed a part.

Aahmas.

The queen-consort of Thothmes I. of the XVIIIth dynasty.

Aahmas.

A royal nun, or Pallacide, in the reign of Amenhotep I. of the XVIIIth dynasty.

Aahmer.

The *Pehu*, or frontier town of the ninth nome of Lower Egypt.

Aahmes.　"Born of the Moon," *or* "Moon-born."

An early Egyptian proper name. It is sometimes written, but wrongly, with one A ; and was by Dr. Leemans and the Dutch Egyptologists transcribed as Oohmes, which see.

Aahmes I.

The son of Kames, king of Thebes. He completed the expulsion and subjugation of the Hykshos invaders, and was the first king of the XVIIIth dynasty. He carried on several other wars, and subdued the Nubians of Ethiopia, taking to wife their Princess Nofretari. This union gave rise to the claims of the Egyptian kings to the crown of Nubia. Aahmes re-established the original worship of the gods, opened the country up to commerce, and made public roads throughout the empire. He reigned more than twenty-two years. The horse and wheeled chariot were first used in his reign.

Aahmes II.

The son of a humble family : he was a native of the city of Siouph. He was an officer in the court of Uahprahet, king of Egypt, who sent him to quell an outbreak among the people. He acquitted himself with so much address, that he was unanimously crowned king in the place of his master, who was deposed, and though at first treated with consideration by Aahmes, was yet finally strangled in prison, to appease the wrath of the people. Anxious to consolidate his right to the throne, Aahmes married Anknas, the daughter of Psametek II., of the Saite dynasty. He made peace with the Cyrenians, and took to wife also Ladike, the daughter of Kritoboulos, the Cyrenian. He cultivated the arts of merchandise and agriculture with much success, and was universally beloved by his people. Towards the close of his reign, the Persians under Cambyses, sought for a pretext to enter Egypt, and they found it at last in the policy of Aahmes, whose daughter was demanded in marriage by the Persian monarch. The king of Egypt, unwilling to degrade his only child to the condition of a secondary wife, sent instead of her Nitetis, the daughter-in-law of his predecessor, Uahprahet, and the last descendant of Psametik I. When Cambyses discovered this fraud, he prepared for the invasion of and conquest of Egypt ; but ere his armies reached the Delta Aahmes died, after a long reign of forty-five years. He was the Amasis of the Greeks. Aahmes II. was succeeded by his son, Psametik III., in whose reign the final conquest of Egypt took place ; after which the empire ceased till the time of the Ptolemies, under the Roman suzerainty.

AAHMES.

A great Egyptian naval officer and general, under Aahmes, the first king of the XVIIIth dynasty. He was born at Eilethyia, and defeated the Hykshos fleet on the waters of Tanis, now Lake Menzaleh. He was honourably rewarded by the king, and three times received the *askh*, or collar of gold, as an official acknowledgment of his bravery.

AAHMES.

The son of King Aahmes I., of the XVIIth or XVIIIth dynasty.

AAHMES.

The brother of Antef, a great Egyptian governor and commander, in the XIIth dynasty, which see.

AAHMES.

An architect or superintendent of public works, in the reign of an unnamed king of the XVIIIth dynasty.

AAHMES.

A scribe of the royal treasury. Period uncertain.

AAHMES MITAMUN.

The sister of Amenhotep I., of the XVIIIth dynasty.

AAHMES NEBTTU.

A daughter of Amenhotep I., of the XVIIIth dynasty.

AAHMES PENNEBENUT.

A subordinate prince, in the reign of Amenhotep II., of the XVIIIth dynasty.

AAHMES SIPIRI.

A son of King Amenhotep I., of the XVIIIth dynasty.

AAHMU.

A Syrian people, who took refuge in Egypt in the XIIth dynasty, and who were for some time considered by Egyptologists to have been really the patriarch Jacob and his family.

AAHNARU.

A name of the Egyptian Hades, the same as Aahlu, in the CXLIXth chapter of the Ritual of the Dead.

AAHNT.

The Egyptian name of an unidentified town.

AAHOTEP.   "Great peace," *or* "Peace of Aah," (the Moon).

The daughter of an early Egyptian king; but of what king it is not known. *See also* Aahhotep.

AAHTB.

An unidentified Egyptian district.

AAI.

An Egyptian captain in the XIXth dynasty, probably under Ramesis II. His wife's name was Uernara.

AAKET.

An unidentified ancient Egyptian town, in the reign of King Assa-Tatkera.

AAKHEPERKA.

The armour-bearer of Thothmes I., of the XVIIIth dynasty.

AALEK.

The Egyptian name of the Island of Philæ, in Upper Egypt.

AALIM. "The Fish Town."

The Egyptian name for the town of Elim, which is often mentioned in Hebrew history.

AALTAAI.

The Egyptian name of a town in Palestine, which is now called Tell Arad.

AALU.

The Egyptian name of an unidentified town.

AALUNA.

The Egyptian name of an unidentified town in Palestine.

AALUNA.

Another name of the Egyptian Elysium. *See* Aahlu.

AAM

One of the mystical deities of the Egyptian Ritual of the Dead.

AAMATER.

The Egyptian name of an unidentified town.

AAMU. "People."

An Egyptian word, applied indiscriminately to any of the Semitic nations or tribes with whom they were at war. It was derived from the Semitic noun "*am*," which means "people" also.

AAMU.

An Asiatic people contiguous to Egypt, who were first subdued by King Pepimerira, of the VIth dynasty, and repeatedly attacked afterwards by the later kings.

AANEBS.

An Egyptian city, situated near the site of the modern Damietta, in the Delta.

AANEFER.

The Egyptian name of an unidentified town.

AANEKHTOU.

The name of an Egyptian workman, who was punished for swearing "by the life, the august," which were the titles of Pharaoh.

AANEN.

A town in the Memphite nome; possibly the same as Tanen, which see.

AANHU.

A class of Egyptian workmen.

AA-N-PA.

An Egyptian official title, generally rendered "chief of the house," or major-domo.

AANSA.

The Egyptian name of a country at present unidentified.

AAPE.

Another form of the name of the Egyptian town called Panopolis by the Greeks.

AARA.

The Egyptian name of the town called by the Greeks, Heliopolis.

AARERT.

The Egyptian name of an unidentified town.

AARKARK.

The Egyptian name of a people in Nubia.

AAS.

A mystical deity of the Egyptian Ritual of the Dead.

AASAA.

The Egyptian name of an unidentified Asiatic country.

AASENA.

An unidentified Egyptian (?) town.

AASH.

The name of a mystical deity, in the XCVth chapter of the Ritual of the Dead.

AASKHAU.

The Egyptian name of the town called by the Greeks, Xois.

Aat.

An Egyptian adjective, signifying "great"; a frequent prefix to the names of towns and buildings. The final T is the feminine article. *See also* Aa.

Aataat.   "Great House."

The name of an early Egyptian city, near to the town of Memphis.

Aatab.

The Egyptian name for the town of Abaton on the Island of Philæ. It was sacred to the deity Horus.

Aataka.

The Egyptian name of an unidentified district, from whence anciently copper was obtained.

Aatam.

A town in the fourth nome of Upper Egypt.

Aatam.

The ancient Egyptian name of the town now called Medinet Habu. It is famous for the great palace temple of Rameses III. of the XIXth dynasty, a portion of which was afterwards used as a Christian church in the IVth century.

Aatefnut.   "Great Tefnut."

The Egyptian name of an unidentified town, sacred, as its name implies, to the goddess Tefnut.

Aatensha.

Another name of the Egyptian town called Prosopis by the Greeks ; it was sacred to the crocodile-headed deity Sebek.

Aathakat.

A town on the Saitic branch of the Nile. It was sacred to the deity Hapi, the Nile.

Aatkabh.

Another name of the Egyptian town generally called Abu, and by the Greeks, Elephantine.

Aatrant.

A city in Upper Egypt, the site of which is unknown.

Aatur.

Another name of the Island of Philæ, in Upper Egypt ; it was sacred to Osiris and Horus.

Aaturt.

The Egyptian name of an unidentified country.

AAU.   "Old One."

An epithet of Osiris in the LXXVIIIth chapter of the Ritual of the Dead.

AAUTA.

The Egyptian name of an unidentified country.

AB.   "The Pure."

The lowest sacerdotal order in the Egyptian priesthood.

AB.

An early Egyptian monarch of the VIth dynasty, whose place in the lists is not known.

AB.

The title of Amen Ra in his attribute of Amen the generator.   Khem and Horus were also called generators, and were represented ithyphallically.

AB.

An Egyptian name of the Island of Elephantine.

ABA.

The royal scribe of an unnamed Egyptian queen, of the XXVIth dynasty.

ABAA.

The chief priest of the altar of Amen Ra, in the XVIIIth dynasty.

ABAALISABA.   "Lords of Sheba."

The generic title of the nobility of the kingdom of Sabæa, in South-western Arabia.

AB-AB-GAR.   "Fire that makes Fire."

The Accadian name of the month Abu, which see.

ABAKARU.

A name given to a variety of hunting-dog, used by the ancient Egyptians, resembling the modern Spitz breed.

ABALAA.

The Egyptian name of a transjordanic town, the Abile of the Greek writers, and the Abel of the Hebrews.

ABAUR.   "Great Third."

A mystical spirit, mentioned in the XLIInd chapter of the Ritual of the Dead.

ABBA-UDDU.   "Father of Light."

The Accadian name of the month Dhabitu, which see.

ABDAI.

A Syrian prince. He was the father of Caleb, king or suffete of Tyre. *See* Caleb.

ABDAMELEK.

The name of a chief officer in Idalion, in the isle of Kypros (Cyprus), about B.C. 400.

ABDANAI.

A country rendered tributary by Samas-Rimmon, king of Assyria. Its situation is uncertain.

ABDASTORETH. "Servant of Ashtoreth."

King of Tyre. He succeeded his father, Baaleazar, and was slain by the four sons of his nurse, after a reign of nine years. With him perished the dynasty of Hiram. After his death the throne of Tyre was for fifty-one years occupied by various usurpers, till the accession of Ethbaal, or Ithobalus, the priest of the goddess Ashtoreth.

ABDELEIN.

A Tyrian. The father of Muthon III. and Gerashtoroth, co-kings or suffetes of Tyre.

ABDILIHITI.

King of Arvad, one of the tributaries of Sennacherib.

ABDIMILKUTTI.

King of Zidon. He made alliance with Sandari, king of Sisu, and revolted against Esarhaddon, who, however, marched against Zidon and destroyed it, putting to death all its principal men, and settling a large number of captives from other places in it, under an Assyrian general. He then beheaded Abdimilkutti and Sandari.

ABDSHEMS. *Surnamed* "Sheba."

The son of Yashdjob, king of Yemen. He regained the provinces lost by his father's inactivity, and uniting all the petty kings of Yemen under one sceptre, reduced to slavery the Adiler, who had fled to Hadramaut in the time of Yarub. He built great works in the city Mareb, which till then had been called Sheba, and was succeeded by his sons, Himyer and Kahlan.

ABDSHEMSASLAM.

An eunuch in the court of Tobba Sharahbil, king of Saba. He and his brother Marthad erected a great temple at Abyan to Yatha and the local deities of the Himyarites.

ABEBA.

A great officer and favourite of Ati, an Egyptian king of the VIth dynasty.

ABERIOU.

A captive Syrian people, who were at one time supposed to have been the Jews. *See* Aperiou.

ABET.

An Egyptian sculptor of the XIIth dynasty. He was the son of the sculptor Nefera and his wife Astekhu. His own wife was named Hathorisis, an uncommon example of the use of two deities in an Egyptian proper name.

ABHA. *Or* ABHT.

The Egyptian name of a country which was inhabited by a race allied to the negroes.

ABHIRA.

A country near the mouth of the Indus ; one of the traditional sites of the Ophir of the Hebrew writers.

ABIANES.

King of the Medes. He succeeded Articarmin, and reigned thirteen years.

ABIBAAL. " Father of Baal," *or* " My Father is Baal."

King of Tyre. He succeeded his father, Hiram I., but no particulars of his reign are known. He was succeeded by his son, Hiram II.

ABIBAAL.

King of Berytus (Beirout), to whom Sanchoniathon dedicated his philo-theosophical writings.

ABIBAAL.

One of the ten competitors for the crown of Arvad, on the death of King Yakinlu.

ABIBAHEL.

King of Samaria. He was one of the tributaries of Esarhaddon.

ABIL.

An Amalekite tribe, who settled in the district of Yathrib, in South-western Arabia.

ABILKISU. " Son of Kisu."

An early Chaldean king, possibly belonging to the IInd dynasty of Berosus.

ABILSIN.

An early Babylonian king, of whom nothing is known.

ABIMELEK. " My Father is the King."

One of the competitors for the throne of Arvad, after the death of Yakinlu.

ABITIKNA.

One of the cities near Armenia which unsuccessfully revolted against Sargon II., who sent its inhabitants into slavery into Palestine and Phœnicia.

ABIYATEH.

The son of Tehar.   An Arabian officer, to whom, together with his brother Aimu, Vaiteh, king of Arabia, committed the charge of his army sent to assist in the rebellion of Saulmugina against Assurbanipal. He materially aided in the revolt of Babylon, but was starved into submission, and surrendered himself to Assurbanipal.   In the meantime, Vaiteh having been conquered, a second prince of the same name took the throne of Arabia ; and Abiyateh, breaking his allegiance, accepted a share of the kingdom, and aided Vaitèh II. to fight against Assyria. After a prolonged warfare, he was a second time defeated by Assurbanipal, and sent prisoner to Assyria, where he was flayed alive.

ABKAT.

A city in Upper Egypt.   Its site is unknown.

ABL.

The Egyptian name of an unidentified country in Palestine.

ABLANATHAN.

A common name on the Greco-Egyptian Gnostic gems.

ABMUT.   "Thou art our Father."

The Egyptian name of a people inhabiting the Upper Nile.

ABNUNAKI.

An Accadian city ; the Mullias of the Assyrians.

ABOT.

The Egyptian name for a city and nome in Upper Egypt, called by the Greeks " Thinites."   It was sacred to the deity Anhur.

ABOTIS.

An Egyptian town in the Hypselite nome.   It was sometimes called Absi.

ABSAFU.

The Egyptian name of an unidentified Asiatic country.

ABSAK.

The ancient name of the city of Abusimbel in Nubia.   It is and was famous for its stupendous cave temple, executed by the orders of Rameses II. of the XIXth dynasty.

ABSARDON.   "Father of Sardon."

A Phœnician deity, the local god of Wara, on the Western coast of Sardinia.

ABSI.

Another form of the name of the Egyptian town Abotis.

ABSIA.

In Chaldean astronomy, the name of an unidentified star.

ABSKHENT.

The Egyptian name of a country in the Soudan or Nigritia.

ABSQEB.

The Egyptian name of a country to the North of the peninsula of Mount Sinai.

ABT.

The Egyptian name of the Lunar disk, as a separate object apart from its divinity. *See also* Aah and Atin Ra.

ABTU.

One of the mythological fishes of the Egyptian mysteries.

ABTU.

The Egyptian name of a people on the Upper Nile, who are mentioned in the Inscription of Unas, of the VIth dynasty.

ABU.

The name of the Chessmen or Latrunculi of the Egyptians. *See* Sent.

ABU.

The Egyptian name of the elephant.

ABU.

The city of Elephantine, in Upper Egypt, where Thothmes III. built a temple to the deity Khnum, the creating spirit.

ABU. "Horns."

The name of a mystical deity in the LXIVth chapter of the Ritual of the Dead.

ABU.

The fifth month of the Assyrians. It was sacred to the goddess Allat, "the Queen of the Spear," and was called by the Accadians, Ababgar, "fire that makes fire." It answered roughly to our July.

ABUSHAREIN.

The modern name of the ruins of a city which was founded by Zursin, king of Babylonia, and where most of his inscriptions have been found.

ABUSIMBEL.

See Ipsambul and Absak.

ABUSKHAU.

A mythical personage in chapter XXXI of the Ritual of the Dead.

ABYAN.

A son of Himyar, or Himyer, who gave his name to the district of Abyan, in South-west Arabia.

ABYATE.

Another form of the name of the great Arabian chief, Abiyateh, which see.

ABYDOS.

A town in Middle Egypt, called formerly "This." It was the chief of the burialplaces of Osiris.

ACANTHON.

An Egyptian city, in the Memphite nome of the Heptanomos.

ACCAD.

Nipur was Calneh, in Accadian, "the city of Bel." Accad was a *district* of South-eastern Chaldea, in which the Accadai or "Highlanders" settled. It was opposed to Sumir (or Sungir, or Shinar) of which Nipur was a city. Mr. Smith reads Agane as Agade, and identifies it with a city of Accad; but I know of no other Assyriologist who agrees with him.--A. H. Sayce.

ACCALU.   "The Devourer."

One of the dogs of Marduk, which was made into a god by the Assyrians.

ACERBAS.

The traditional name of the husband of Queen Dido. He was properly called Zicharbad, which see.

ACHARYA.

The Hindu term for a spiritual teacher or preceptor.

ACHECHU.

One of the mystical deities of the Egyptian Ritual of the Dead.

ACHEM.

See Sept Achem, an Egyptian deity, worshipped at the town of Sept-hor.

ACHEN.   "Recluse."

An Egyptian title, applied to the ladies of the royal harem.

ACHENCHERES.

The Greek name of an Egyptian king, which is supposed to have been the same as Khuenaten, the heretical surname of Amenophis IV.

ACHERI.   "Enemy."

The name of a mystical animal which was symbolical of evil in the Egyptian mythology.

ACHERRES.

The name of two Egyptian kings of the XVIIIth dynasty according to the Greek lists. They are not certainly identified.

Aches.

A king of the IIIrd Egyptian dynasty. He reigned forty-two years.

Achitu.

A town in Assyria, where Xathrites vainly endeavouring to rouse up the Assyrians against the Medes their conquerors, was slain by Vomises, the general of Darius Hystaspes.

Achmeir.

The modern name for the city and nome in Upper Egypt which was called by the Greeks Panopolis.

Achoris.

The Greek form of the Egyptian royal name Hakar, which see.

Achsuf.

One of the mystical deities of the Ritual of the Dead.

Achsurus.

A Persian royal name; by some historians thought to have been intended for that of Ahasuerus.

Achzib.

The Hebrew name of the city called by the Assyrians, Akzibi, which see.

Acis.

A river-god, the tutelary deity of the town of Acium, in Sicily.

Acoris.

A chief town in the Cynopolite nome of the Heptanomos. It is now called Tehnah.

Acraganes.

An Assyrian royal name (quoted by Syncellus from Ctesias; Eusebius writes it Ocrazapes). It is supposed by some writers to have been another form of the name of Assurbanipal.

Acrocephalic.   "Highheaded."

A term employed by Anthropologists to denote a skull which in a degree exceeds the height of the average skulls of a race or class.

Acu.   *See* Agu.

The Chaldean name of the moon, when spoken of astronomically.

Ad.

A people of South-western Arabia, who are mentioned as impious in the Koran. They are supposed to have been the Sabeans.

AD.

In Arabian history, the grandson of Ham. He had one thousand wives, four thousand sons, and lived twelve hundred years. He populated nearly all Yemen, founded the tribe of Ad, and was succeeded by his sons, Shedid and Shedad.

ADADANU.

A king of the country of the Asatai, who paid tribute to Samas Rimmon, or Samsivul, king of Assyria.

ADAR.

An Assyrian deity, the god of the thunderbolt and storm-cloud. He was called "The Sun of the South," and was also the deity of physical power, the analogue of the Herakles of the Greeks. He was frequently called also Bar and Ninip.

ADAR PILESER.   "Adar the son of the sanctuary," *or* " Adar protects his son."

Another form of the Assyrian royal name, Ninipallassar, which see.

ADAR PILESER.

An Assyrian king, the successor of Belkudurussur. It is supposed that he was partly under allegiance to the kings of Egypt ; but nothing is definitely known of the state of Assyria at that period. *See* Ninipalassar.

ADASI.

The father of an early Assyrian king named Belbani. He was one of the ancestors of Sargon II.

ADAVAS.

A city and people in the mountains of Mesopotamia. It was subdued by Assur-risilim, king of Assyria, and finally conquered by Tiglath Pileser I.

ADD.

The Egyptian name of the Palestinian district inclosed between Hebron, Ascalon, and Joppa.

ADDARU.

The twelfth month of the Assyrian year. It was dedicated to the seven great gods, and was called by the Accadians, Sekisil, "sowing of seed." It answered roughly to our February.

ADDUMU.

The capital city of that district in Arabia which bordered on Assyria. It was conquered by Esarhaddon, and was the Dumah of Hebrew writers.

ADIA.

A city in Assyria which supported the rebel Assurdainpal, in his revolt against his father, Shalmaneser II.

ADIACRAS.

A king of the Libyans, who assisted king Uahprahet in his war against the Cyrenians, which ultimately led to the dethronement and death of the king of Egypt.

ADILE.

A tribe in Mesopotamia, which was conquered by Tiglath Pileser II.

ADINI.

The son of Dakuri, a Chaldean prince who paid tribute to Shalmaneser I., king of Assyria.

ADINI.

A prince of the land of Bit Adini. *See* Ahuni.

ADINNU.

A city of Hamath, which was conquered by Shalmaneser II.

ADITES.

A Hamitic race ; one of the two great nations by whom the peninsula of Arabia was early peopled. *See* Amalika.

ADITES.

In Shemitic history, the name of the first mythical dynasty of Arabian kings.

ADITYA'S.

In Hindu mythology twelve deities created by the great deity Indra, out of the twelve months of the year.

ADIUR. " Devoted to Ur."

A mythical Chaldean king, referred to by Sargon II. as the founder of the dynasty. He may have been the Alorus of the Greeks. (G. Smith).

ADIYA.

Queen of Arabia, and wife of Vaiteh I. She went with her husband to his invasion of Palestine, and though for a time successful, was ultimately defeated, Vaiteh being sent a prisoner to Nineveh, where Assurbanipal caged him among his hounds, Adiya sharing the same ignominious captivity.

ADJAI.

The Egyptian name of an unidentified Syrian town.

ADLILA.

A town in Mesopotamia, which was besieged and destroyed at different times both by Sibir, king of Babylon, and Assurnazirpal, king of Assyria.

ADMATA HAKHODESH. " Holy Land."

The name given by the later prophets in Hebrew history to the country of Palestine.

ADNAN.

A king of the Hejaz, who, attempting to stop the inroads of Nebu-chadnezzar in Arabia, was by him defeated at the battle of Dhat Irak, and compelled to fly into the mountains, where he died.   He was suc-ceeded by his son, Maad.

ADONIBAHAL.   " My Lord Baal."

One of the ten competitors for the crown of Arvad, after the death of King Yakinlu.

ADRAHASIS.

A man of Surippak, and son of Ubara-Tutu.   The patriarch to whom, according to the Deluge Tablet, the gods revealed the secret of the im-pending deluge, and who erected an ark accordingly, whereby he and his family and sevens of all clean beasts were saved.   His name, when transposed, is believed to be the origin of the Greek name, Xisuthrus. Its meaning appears to be, "shut up in a box or ark," from the two characters signifying " enclosed," and " box," respectively.   In Accadian he is called Tam-zi (Tammuz), " The Sun of life."

ADRAMMELEK.

Probably the Hebrew form of the Assyrian royal name, Assur-Mulik, or Adar-malcu, which see.

ADRANA.

Another name of the strong fort of Istalli, which see.

ADULMA.

The Egyptian name of the town of Adullam in Palestine.

ADUNUBAHAL.

King of Sizana, one of the confederacy of Syrian kings who were de-feated by Shalmaneser II.

ÆACES.

Son of Syloson, king of Samos.   He revolted against his sovereign in chief, Darius, the Mede.

ÆL.

In Scandinavian mythology the name of the nectar which departed heroes drank in the Walhalla, from the hands of the goddess Freyia.

ÆON.

In Phenician mythology, the son of Colpias and Baau (Bohu or Chaos), the two primæval deities. He and his brother Protogonos were the earliest created mortals.   Æon was the first to discover the use of fruit as food.

ÆSAR.

The Etruscan name of the Supreme Being.

Aetes.

The son of Aetes, Priest of Alexander and the gods Soteres (the Saviour gods) under Ptolemy V.; one of the priests meeting at Memphis, who set up the trilingual decree commonly called the Rosetta stone.

Aethrapaiti.

The Persian title of high priest.   *See also* Mobed and Magupaiti.

Aevonu.

A Toda deity, of whom little is known.

Af.

In Egyptian mythology the mystical name of the sun in the lower hemisphere, or Hades.

Afaf.

An Egyptian name for the crocodile.   *See also* Temsuh.

Afki.

A mystical name in the LXIVth chapter of the Ritual of the Dead.

Afrs.

The Egyptian name of an unidentified town.

Agane.

A city in Babylonia, founded by the mythical king Sargon I., who peopled it with the mixed races whom he carried off in his various wars. Here he established a palace, named Ekiamizallak, and a national library, the remains of which have not yet been recovered.

Agdites.

An Arabian people who came from Yemen about the third century, A.D., and introduced pure Arabic into the Amalekite nations of Arabia Petrea.   They were also called Ghassanites.

Agiel.

In Cabalistic mythology the Intelligence of the planet Saturn.

Agisa.

An obscure officer who was raised to the throne of Babylon on the death of Sargon II.   He only reigned a month, at the end of which time he was slain by Merodach Baladan, who had himself been deposed by the king of Assyria, and who was again driven into exile by Sennacherib, the son of Sargon II., who defeated him at the battle of Kisu.

Agni.

The Vedic name of the Supreme Being under the character of the deity of fire.   The analogue of the Hephæstus of the Greeks.

Agron.   " The Fugitive."

In Lydian mythology the founder of the Lydian dynasty of the Heraklidæ.   The name being Assyrian, he has been conjectured to have been a fugitive Assyrian prince.

Agu.

Another form of the name of the Accadian Moon-god, Acu, which see.

Agukakrimi.   " The Moon the Maker of Brilliance."

An early Babylonian king, the son of Tassigurubar. He was a great warrior, and recovered some images of the deities Marduk and Ziratbanit, which had previously been carried away to the land of Hani. He also restored the temple of Bel at Babylon, enlarged the Babylonian territory, and colonized the land of Asnunnak, an unknown district.

Aguragas.

An early Babylonian king of the Kassite dynasty. He was the son of Ummiahzirita. Nothing else is known respecting him.

Agus.

The father of Matihil, a Syrian prince, which see.

Agus.

The father of Aram, a petty Syrian chief, conquered by Shalmaneser II.

Ah.

The Egyptian name of an unidentified country.

Ah.

The Egyptian name of a town near Esne.

Ah.

A name of the Egyptian god Lunus ; more properly written Aah, which see.

Ah.

The eponymy of the eighteenth day of the lunar month.

Ah.

An unknown Egyptian medicine.

Ahab.   Assyrian, Akhabbu.

The son of Omri, who reigned over Israel twenty-two years. He married Jezebel, daughter of Ethbaal, king of Zidon, and introduced the worship of Baal and Ashteroth into Israel, persecuting the prophets and worshippers of Yahveh (Jehovah). He is the first Israelite king mentioned in the Assyrian inscriptions, having been defeated by Shalmaneser at Karkar (Aroer), in B.C. 854, along with the other allies of Benhadad, of Damascus, to whose aid he had brought a force of 10,000 men. Ahab had been attacked twice by Benhadad, and once besieged in vain in Samaria. In the second invasion he had defeated the Syrians at Aphek ; the result being a league between the two countries, the restoration of the Israelitish cities taken by Benhadad, and a permanent

4*

Israelite embassy in Damascus. Ahab met his death at Ramoth-Gilead, which he had attacked and endeavoured to take from the Syrians, then weakened by the defeat of Karkar. Ahab was weak and luxurious, and a great builder. Jericho was rebuilt in his reign.

AHAB.

The *Pehu* of the twenty-second nome of Upper Egypt. *See* Pehu.

AHABBU.   *Or* Akhabbu.

The Assyrian form of the Hebrew royal name Ahab, which see.

AHAKEFAH.

The Egyptian name of an unidentified country.

AHARRI.   "The West." In Accadian, Mar-Tu; "The path of the setting sun."

The name by which Phenicia is known in the Assyrian inscriptions.

AHEHU.

An uncertain Egyptian town, sacred to the deity Samtati.

AHEM.

The *Pehu* of the seventh nome of Upper Egypt.

AHFUR.

The Egyptian name of an unidentified town.

AHHOTEP.   " Fields of Peace."

A mystical locality in the Egyptian mythology, mentioned in the Ritual of the Dead. *See also* Aahhotep, " Peace of Aah."

AHI.

An Ethiopian town, held for Rameses VI., by Pannu, prince royal of Ethiopia.

AHI.

A mystical divinity, called also, " Lord of the Heart." He is mentioned in the CLth chapter of the Ritual of the Dead.

AHI.   " Assistant."

A title of the Egyptian deity Horus, as the performer of the religious rites called the Assistances of Horus to his father Osiris.

AHIMELEK.   " Brother of the King."

One of the ten competitors for the throne of Arvad, after the death of king Yakinlu.

AHIMILKI.

King of Ashdod. He was one of the tributaries of Esarhaddon.

AHIT.

An Egyptian sacerdotal office, holdable by both sexes. Its duties are not exactly known. *See also* Ahi, of which this name is the feminine form.

AHIT.

An Egyptian sacerdotal office, generally rendered priestess.

AHIYABABA.

An inhabitant of Bit Adini, who slew the viceroy of the king of Assyria at Suru. He was taken captive by Assurnazirpal, and flayed alive.

AHIZUHINA.

A city or country in Mesopotamia, governed by Nergal-uballid, in the reign of Tiglath Pileser II.

AHLAMI.

A people in the mountains of Mesopotamia, who were subdued by Assur-risilim, king of Assyria.

AHMES.

A priest of the god Khonsu of Thebes, in the reign of Amenhotep I. of the XVIIIth dynasty. His wife's name, like his own, was Ahmes.

AHMES.

A royal personage of the XVIIIth dynasty, the son of the lady Tallau. He must not be confounded with Ahmes or Aahmes the king.

AHMES.

An Egyptian officer, and chief of the soldiers in the period of Darius. His father's name was Psabenhor, and that of his mother, Taapenha.

AHMESSEKER.

A royal steward in the XXVth dynasty. He was the son of the steward Psametikkhu.

AHMESSENETUAHBRA.

An Egyptian officer who was *smer*, commandant of the palace, commandant of the temples, keeper of the throne, commandant of the gates, and chief of the councils of the king. His mother's name was Tapera. He lived about the time of Uaprahet I. of the XXVIth dynasty.

AHMUR.

A town in the third nome of Upper Egypt.

AHRA.

An Egyptian priest. The time when he lived and the deity to whose worship he was devoted, are unknown.

AHRIMAN.

In Zendic mythology the great malevolent principle: the author of all evil, physical and moral; the enemy of mankind, and the constant but not eternal antagonist of Ahuramazda. He was sometimes considered to have been the same as Afrasiab, which see.

AHSANA.

A city in Babylonia, which was conquered by Samsivul or Samas Rimmon III., king of Assyria, towards the close of his reign.

AHSENUT.

A place in the twenty-first nome of Upper Egypt.

AHSERA.

The son of Ullusunu, king of Minni. On ascending the throne, he broke the treaty of tribute with Assyria, and plundered some of the border towns. Upon this, Assurbanipal, king of Assyria, assembled a large army at the town of Duran, to invade Minni. Ahsera made an attempt by a slight surprise to rout the Assyrian army; but he was completely defeated, and fled in haste to his capital city, Izirtu; and when that surrendered, to the fortress of Istatti or Adrana, leaving his troops to be slaughtered by the victor at Izirtu. He was unable to resist the forces of Assurbanipal, although ably assisted by his general, Raidisadi, and his people revolting from him, he and all his family but one, were massacred, and his body treated with great ignominy. His son Valli succeeded him, and made peace with Assyria.

AHSHU.

A place in the twenty-second nome of Lower Egypt.

AHTAMER.

The *Pehu* of the fourteenth nome of Lower Egypt.

AHTI.

An Egyptian goddess, having the head of an uræus and the body of an hippopotamus. She was one of the Typhonic or malevolent deities.

AHU.　*Or* AHA.

The Egyptian name of the " House of the King," or palace.

AHU.

An Egyptian deity; another name of the god Atum or Tum, the setting sun.

AHUNI.

The son of Adini, and king of Lahlahte and of the territory of Bit Adini, in Mesopotamia. He submitted himself and his country to Assurnazirpal, king of Assyria; but after his death rebelled, and vainly attempted to resist the arms of Shalmaneser II., by whom he and his army were utterly defeated after several battles, and all his allies were dispersed.

AHURA.

An Egyptian princess, the daughter of Merinebpthah, an unidentified Egyptian king. She is one of the heroines of the ancient romance called the Story of Setnau. She married her brother Pthahneferka, by whom she had a son, named Merhu.

Ahura.

The Iranian name of the Supreme Being. A short form of the following name.

Ahuramazda.   "Wise Spirit."

The great and beneficent creator of good in the Zendic mythology. He was called also " The Good Spirit," and he has been considered as in some points resembling the Assyrian deity Merodach. The world was created by him for the residence of mankind, and all the good angels were made by him also. His chief mission, however, was to preserve the human race and to defeat the evil being, Ahriman. His name is often contracted into Ormazd.

Ai.

An Egyptian priest, or " Divine Father " in the XVIIIth dynasty.

Ai.

The wife of Mentuhotep, a state officer, and mother of Mentuhotep the general in chief of the armies of an unnamed king of Egypt, of the XIIth dynasty.

Ai.

An Egyptian king, of the XIIIth or XIVth dynasty. He was the successor of Rahotep.

Ai.

The royal secretary of King Atefnuter Ai, of the XVIIIth dynasty. He married a lady named Ti.

Ai.   *Or* Atefnuter Aui.

A king of Egypt during the troublous time which followed the revolution and death of Amenhotep IV., of the XVIIIth dynasty, to whom he was fan-bearer and groom of the royal stud. Being regarded as an heretic by his successors, his tomb was opened, and his name and inscriptions erased by order of one of the kings of the XIXth dynasty.

Aia.

The butler of an unnamed Egyptian king. He had a son, Khamtair, who held the like office with himself, and his mother, Taka, and wife Anub, were both priestesses of Amen.

Aialla.

A Nabathean town, conquered by Assurbanipal in the second Arabian war.

Aiari.

The chief priest and *saru* of Pthah, in the reign of Menepthah II., of the XIXth dynasty.

Aichtab.

An unidentified country in Africa, to the South of Lower Egypt.

AIEMAPT.

Another form of the name of the god Imouthes, which see.

AIKAMARU.

The son of Ammihitah of Vas, a Mesopotamian chief, who during the reign of Assurbanipal attacked and completely destroyed all but one man of the Nabatheans.

AIKHE.

An Etruscan male divinity, who is represented on an Etruscan mirror accompanying the deities Euturpa, Altria, and Thalna.

AIKHENLKA.

The Egyptian name of a country near the Soudan, in Upper Egypt.

AIMENAMUN.

According to some Egyptologists another form of the name of Seti Menepthah I. of the XIXth dynasty.

AINA.   *And* AININI.

The Egyptian name of the two springs of Beersheba in Palestine, between Hebron and Rehoboth.

AINAU.

A town in the East, where Rameses III. built a great reservoir, sunk in the earth thirty cubits deep, surrounded by a wall, with quays and doors of cedar wood and bronze. This place has been supposed to have been the Beersheba of Hebrew history.

AININI.

The Egyptian name of an uncertain Syrian city.

AIONS.

A mystical divinity, who is mentioned in the CXLth chapter of the Ritual of the Dead.

AIPAK-SINA.

An Elamite deity, of whom nothing is known, and whose statue was taken captive by Assurbanipal, king of Assyria.

AIRAMMU.

King of Edom, one of the tributaries of Sennacherib.

AIRU.

The second month of the Assyrians; sacred to the deity Hea. Its Accadian name was Khar-sidi, "The propitious Bull." It answered roughly to our April.

AIRYANEM-VAEJO.

In Zendic philosophy the early seat of the Aryans, in the valley of the Hindu Kush.

AIT.

A town in Egypt. It was sacred to Isis and Horus; its site is unidentified.

AIULN.

A country in Palestine. The Ajalon of Hebrew writers.

AJ-DAHÂKA. "Biting Snake."

The Ahi or "Serpent of Darkness" of the Rig-Veda. He is called Zohak by Firdusi.

AJTAHAGA.

The Median form of the royal name read by the Greek historians as Astyages.

AKA.

One of the mystical deities of the Ritual of the Dead.

AKAITAU.

A desert country near the gold mines, now called Gebel Ollaki, where Rameses II. ordered a well to be dug for the use of the labourers there, and called the well after his own name, Meriamoun Rameses.

AKAIUSHA.

The name by which the Achæans, or Greeks, were known to the Egyptians; whom they invaded with many allied tribes. They were defeated by Menepthah II. of the XIXth dynasty.

AKALKAR.

The Egyptian name of a district near Ethiopia.

AKAMA.

The Egyptian name of an unidentified mountain in Asia.

AKANTI.

The Egyptian name of an unidentified Assyrian fortress.

AKAR.

A mystical name of a region of the Egyptian Hades, which is mentioned in the Ritual of the Dead.

AKAR.

A mystical reptile, called the "Viper of Set" in the XCIVth chapter of the Ritual of the Dead.

AKARIT.

Another form of the name of the Assyrian fortress Akanti, which see.

AKARKHENTKATS. "Wise one keeping her place."

The name of the third of the mystical cows, or Hathors, of Egyptian mythology.

Akbaru.

A king of Napiatu, in Arabia, who paid tribute to Esarhaddon, by whom he was put to death.

Akela.

The mother of Tahrarka or Tihrak, the third king of Egypt of the XXVth dynasty.

Aken.

A country in Nubia, at present unknown.

Aker.

The father of Pantena the Egyptian governor of the South or the Ethiopian provinces. *See* Pantena.

Akerti.   *Or* Akourit.

A Syrian city, which was besieged and captured by Amenhotep II. of the XVIIIth dynasty.

Akesh.

A town in Ethiopia, which was famous as having been the birthplace of Shabaka I. of the XXVth dynasty.

Akh.   " Intelligence."

In Egyptian mythology one of the five component parts of the human being. It was also sometimes called Khu.

Akhekh.

In Egyptian mythology one of the names of the mystical Serpent of Evil.

Akhem.

The sacred name of the Mummied Hawk. It was an emblem of the deity Sokari, or rather of the Memphite dwarf deity, Pthah-Sokari-Osiris.

Akh es samain.   " Brother of the Heavens."

An Arabian deity, worshipped at the city of Irdah.

Akhimit.

The brother of Azuri king of Ashdod. His brother Azuri, having refused to pay tribute as usual to the king of Assyria, Sargon II., he deposed him, and placed Akhimit on the throne instead. At that the people revolted, and in their turn dethroned him, and made a man named Yaman, who was not of the blood royal, king. This led to the siege of Ashdod by Sargon, who carried off Yaman into captivity, together with very many of his subjects, replacing them by people from other parts of his dominion, and reducing the state to the condition of an annexed province of Assyria. The siege is mentioned in Isaiah xx. I.

AKHIRAMU.

An Assyrian officer in the court of Esarhaddon. He was a holder of the two sceptres, apparently at the same time with Neboatsib, which see.

AKHLE.

The Etruscan name of the mythical hero who was called Akhilles by the Greeks.

AKHUVITR. *Or* AKHVIZR.

An Etruscan goddess, who is represented as clothed like Alpanu, with the addition of a star behind her head. *See* Alpanu.

AKHVISTR.

An Etruscan divinity, generally represented as a nude, winged youth, with a long fillet in his hand, and an attendant upon Turan and Atunis (Adonis).

AKINA.

A country to the South of Egypt, at present unidentified.

AKITA.

A district to the South of Egypt, towards Nubia, where the ancient gold mines were situated.

AKKABARINA.

An Elamite city, which was destroyed by Sennacherib, king of Assyria.

AKKERKUF. *Or* TEL ASWAD.

A city in Babylonia, where Kurigalzu II. or III., king of Babylonia, erected the temple of Bit-ugal, in honour of the god Bel.

AKKI.

A Babylonian husbandman, who discovered the infant king Sargon II. when he was abandoned by his mother on the river Euphrates. He nourished the child, who by his care became in after years king of Babylonia.

AKKU.

A Phenician city, which was conquered by Sennacherib, king of Assyria, on his first invasion of Palestine. It was the Accho of Hebrew writers.

AKOMANO. "The Evil Spirit."

In Zendic mythology the first of the evil Darvands, which see.

AKOURIT.

A town in Mesopotamia. *See* Akerti.

AKSAKABA.

The Egyptian name of an uncertain Syrian city.

AKSAPH.

The Egyptian name of a country in Palestine, which is at present unidentified.

AKTES.

An Egyptian king of the Vth dynasty.

AKTI.

The Egyptian name of the country of Akkad in Chaldea.

AKTIS.   " The Sunbeam."

The son of Helios, the sun. A mythical hero who was said by the Rhodians to have been the first astronomer.

AKTRA.

The Egyptian name of the town of Gadara, in Cœle Syria.

AKUSAA.

An Egyptian goddess, the wife of the god Tum, " The setting Sun."

AKZIBI.

A Phenician city, which was conquered by Sennacherib, on his first invasion of Palestine. It was the Achzib or Ecdippa of Hebrew history.

AL.   Or EL.   " God."

The name of the supreme deity of the ancient Nabatheans. He was the universal deity of Palestine and Phenicia.

ALAGUNI.

In Hindu mythology one of the four heavenly streams which flow from the palace of Brahma and unite to form the Ganges.

ALALA.

Another form of the name of the goddess Allat. She was one of the forms of Ishtar.

ALAM.   " The Shadow," or " The Image."

In Babylonian astronomy the name of the deity Marduk as the planet Mercury in the month Chislev.

ALAMLUK.

King of Sabœa in Arabia. He succeeded Wathil, the son of Himyar, and was succeeded by his son, Shammir.

ALAMUN.

A district to the north of Assyria, conquered by Tiglath Pileser I.

ALAPAROS.   " Bull of Light?"

The second antediluvian king of Babylon, according to the list preserved by Berosus.

ALAPI.

The Assyrian name of the Winged Human-headed bulls, which were used to guard the entrances of the palaces, and beings similar to which were believed to have had real existence at the mythical time of Izdubar. They were also called Kirubi, whence the cherubim of Hebrew writers.

ALATAKKI.

An Accadian city the site of which is not known.

ALATH.

In ancient Nabathean mythology the feminine form of the local deity Elga, which see.

ALB.

In Scandinavian mythology the spirit of the night, or the nightmare; the succubus of the Mediæval writers.

ALDEBARAN.

A bright star in the eye of the constellation "the Bull." It was adored as a divinity by the people of Sabæa.

ALEXANDRIA.

The modern name of the city which took the place of the Egyptian city and nome of Sai Mehit. It was founded by Alexander the Great, B.C. 332, and rapidly increased in importance till its wall became six miles in circumference. It contained the tomb of Alexander, the state palaces of the Greco-Egyptian Ptolemies, a museum, temple of Serapis, and one of the largest libraries of the ancient world. Its harbour with its pharos or lighthouse, which was 550 feet high, was unequalled; and the trade of the city extended to the whole of the Roman Empire. Alexandria suffered severely in the wars between Julius Cæsar and Pompey; was nearly ruined by an earthquake, in A.D. 365, in which 60,000 persons perished, and was captured, and its library and public buildings destroyed, by Amru, the general of the Saracen Caliph Omar, on the twenty-second of December, A.D. 640.

ALEXANDROSCHŒNE.

The Greek name of the Phenician town which was called by the natives Ous, which see.

ALFADER.   " Father of all."

In Scandinavian mythology the name of the Supreme Being, as the creator of gods, giants, and men.

ALGAT.

The Egyptian name of an unidentified Asiatic country.

ALGUM.

A precious wood, much referred to in Hebrew and Egyptian history. It was probably the camphor wood of modern carpentry.

ALI.   Or WALI.

In Scandinavian mythology the son of Odia and Rindr. He slew the wicked giant Hödhr, to avenge the death of the beautiful Baldur, the beloved of gods and men.

ALILAT.

An ancient Arabian goddess. She was possibly a form of the moon.

ALLABRA.

A kingdom near Armenia, which unsuccessfully revolted against Sargon II., by whom it was ravaged and annexed to Assyria.

ALLAH.   "God."

The ancient as well as modern name of the Supreme Deity among the Arabs of the Hejaz.

ALLAH TAALA.   "The Supreme God."

An ancient title of the Deity among the pre-koranic Arabs.

ALLAMU.

A Chaldean name of the deity Nergal, which see.

ALLAT.

An Arabian goddess, worshipped at the town of Tayf, near Mecca where she was represented as a shapeless stone.

ALLAT.

An Assyrian goddess, one of the many forms of Ishtar, called "The Queen of the Spear," or "Divining Rod." The month Abu, or July, was sacred to her.

ALLU.

The Seven Stairs to the abode of Osiris, which are mentioned in one of the mystical chapters, the CLXIVth, of the Ritual of the Dead.

ALLUL.

One of the twelve Stars of the West in Chaldean astronomy.

ALLUPH.

The chief of one of the Edomite tribes. There were originally ten. These chiefs were called dukes by the Hebrew writers.

ALMAKAH.

A principal deity of the Himyarites of South-western Arabia.

ALMELON, or Sippara.

The third antediluvian king of Babylon, according to Berosus.

ALMOSHTARI.

The planet Jupiter. He was adored as a divinity by the ancient Arabians.

ALO.

The Egyptian name of an unidentified city in Ethiopia.

ALOHNIM.   "The Gods."

The name of a group, or possibly triad, of Sidonian divinities, to whom temples were erected by Eshmonazer II., king of Sidon.

ALOROS.   "Ram of Light?"

The first antediluvian king of Babylon. *See* Alorus, of which, according to Berosus, this name was an abbreviation by the Greeks.

ALOZZA.

An ancient Arabian deity, who was worshipped at Nakhla, near Mecca. ·

ALPAN.

An Etruscan goddess, who waits upon Turan or Venus. She is winged, with earrings and necklace, and two palm-branches, which she strikes together. She may be compared with the Greek Graces.

ALPANU.   *Or* ALPNU.

An Etruscan goddess, with coronet, earrings, tunic, and mantle, and a star behind her head, who is represented on one mirror as embracing the goddess Akhuvitr, on another as embracing the goddess Thanr, and on a third as attracting the love of a youth called Famu.

ALSWIDR.   "Swift."

In Scandinavian mythology the name of one of the two horses of the sun.

ALT.

The Egyptian name of a simple chain or necklace. It must not be confounded with the official collars called Uskh or Mna, which see.

ALTÆGU.

A city in Palestine where Sennacherib gave battle to the armies of the kings of Egypt and defeated them utterly. It was the Eltekon of Hebrew writers.

ALTAKHSAS.

The Egyptian form of the Persian royal name Artaxerxes.

ALTRIA.

An Etruscan goddess, answering to the Greek Graces. She was represented as a nude and beautiful woman, with a crown and necklace, and generally in the company of Thalna and Euturpa (Euterpe).

ALULU.

The Egyptian name of the grape, and also of the grape vine.

ALU SA ACCADDI.

An Assyrian generic geographical title, meaning " Cities of Accad."

ALU SA IRTSITU.

An Assyrian generic geographical title, meaning "Cities of the Earth."

ALU SA NAPALKUTU.

An Assyrian generic geographical title, meaning " Foreign Cities."

ALU SA SUMIRU.

An Assyrian generic geographical title, meaning " Cities of Sumir."

ALZI.

A district in the Upper Euphrates, which was usurped by the Hittites till their overthrow by Tiglath Pileser I.

AM. " Devourer."

A demon of the Egyptian Hades, who is mentioned in the Ritual of the Dead.

AM.

The name of the *Pehu* of the seventh nome of Upper Egypt.

AM.

An Egyptian palace, meaning more particularly a residence with a paradisus, park, or garden, as in the East.

AMA.

An Egyptian lady, the daughter of the chief Tesamen, which see.

AMA.

A queen-mother of the XIth dynasty. Her place is supposed to have been between Mentuhotep III. and Rasanchka.

AMABT.

A class of Egyptian priests.

AMADA.

A town in Nubia, where Amenhotep II. of the XVIIIth dynasty built a temple in honour of the gods Harmachis and Amun, to perpetuate a record of his victories over the peoples of Mesopotamia and Assyria.

AMADAAI.

The name by which the Medes were known to the Assyrians under Shalmaneser III.

AMADANI.

A district of Chaldea, by the head of the Tigris. It was conquered and devastated by Assurnazirpal.

AMAKHAR.

The king of the city of Kharmisandai, or Harmisanda, on the borders of Assyria, who paid tribute to Samas Rimmon, or Samsivul III., king of Assyria.

AMAKHU.

Another name of the city of Sah. It was called Hermopolis by the Greeks.

AMALIHA.

An Assyrian governor, the name of whose district is lost. He was the eponym of the year 782 B.C., the last of the reign of Vulnirari III.

AMALIKA.

An Aramæan or Semitic people. One of the two great nations which formed the early population of Arabia. *See* Ariba, and Adites.

AMAM. "The Devourer."

One of the mystical monster deities of the Egyptian Hell.

AMAMAS.

The king of Kingüstilinzamar, or Cingistilinzakharai, a district bordering upon Assyria. He was rendered tributary by Samas Rimmon, or Samsivul III. king of Assyria.

AMANA.

A Syrian town, near to the Lebanon range of mountains in Upper Palestine. *See* Ammana.

AMANUS.

The modern name of Mount Hamanu, from whence Shalmaneser II. obtained timber for his buildings in Assyria.

AMAR. *Or* AMAUR.

The Egyptian name of the country of the Amorrheans.

AMARAGU. "Effulgence of Agu."

An early Accadian monarch. *See* Agukakrimi.

AMARDAKI.

The Accadian name of the city which was called by the Assyrians Marad. Its site is not well known.

AMARI.

An Ethiopian people, who were conquered by Rameses III. of the XIXth dynasty.

AMARSIN.

An early Babylonian monarch who reigned at Ur.

AMARUD. "The Circle of the Day."

The Accadian name of the deity Marduk, the son of Hea. *See also* Silikmulukhi.

AMASHTORETH. "Mother of Ashtoreth."

A Priestess of the goddess Ashtoreth at Sidon. She was the wife of Tabnith, king of Sidon, and the mother of Eshmonazer II.

AMASIS.

The Greek form of the Egyptian royal name Aahmes, or Ahmes, which see.

Amatnim.

An early Babylonian king, the predecessor of Sargina or Sargon II. Nothing else is known respecting him.

Amatu.

A people in Mesopotamia, who were conquered by Tiglath Pileser II., king of Assyria.

Ambaris.

Son of Hulli, or Xulli, king of Tubal. He succeeded his father by the favour of Sargon II., notwithstanding which he revolted against the king of Assyria, who had even given him his own daughter in marriage, with the province of Cilicia as a dowry. Enraged at such conduct, Sargon attacked Ambaris after a delay of some years, and sent him into slavery.

Amelagar of Sippara.

According to Berosus, the fifth antediluvian king of Babylon.

Amem.

An Egyptian lady, the wife of Enantef the overseer of the altar of a deity, probably Osiris, in the reign of Amenemha II. of the XIIth dynasty.

Amememhasenb.

An Egyptian gentleman, the son of Ape. Among the members of his family were two Negroes. His period is unknown, except that it was between the XIIth and XVIIIth dynasties.

Amempsin of Larsan.

According to Berosus, the eighth antediluvian king of Babylon.

Amemu.

An inferior Egyptian deity, who was represented as a man with the head of a sparrow-hawk.

Amen.

An overseer of the workmen of the royal palace of an unnamed king of Egypt.

Amenaa.

An Egyptian functionary of the XIIth dynasty. He was called a *Senes*, an unintelligible title.

Amenagarsal.

An Assyrian city on the river Tigris. Its site is at present unknown.

Amenamen.

A mystical title of the deity Amen Ra, in the CLXVIth chapter of the Ritual of the Dead.

Amenankhnas.

The wife of King Tutankhamen, of the XVIIIth dynasty.

Amenaru.

An officer in the court of Queen Ameniritis of the XXVth dynasty. His sarcophagus and mummy are in the British Museum.

Amenei.

. A royal scribe, in the reign of Osirtesen I. of the XIIth dynasty.

Amenei.

A royal scribe, in the reign of the grandson of Antefaker, a king of the XIth dynasty. *See* Antefaker.

Ameneman.

The chief librarian of the royal palace at Thebes, in the reign of Rameses II. of the XIXth dynasty.

Amenemant.

An Egyptian priest, the father of the priest and governor Basu, which see.

Amenemap.

A priest of Amen Ra, in the reign of Ai, or Atefnuter Ai, or Aui, king of the XVIIIth dynasty.

Amenemap.

The son of the legal and royal officer Piai, of the XVIIIth dynasty. He was also surnamed Apui.

Amenemap.

The son of the preceding. He was a priest of the deity Ptah.

Amenemap.

A great Egyptian officer, in the XVIIIth dynasty. He was prophet of the goddess Uertheku, and Athlophore or standard bearer at the right hand of the king, besides holding other offices apparently mystical. He had a son who was named like himself, Amenemap. *See* Athlophore.

Amenemap.

A royal scribe, of the XIXth dynasty. His father's name was Piai, and that of his mother Khaa.

Amenemapet.

The viceroy or royal prince of Ethiopia, in the reign of Seti I. of the XIXth dynasty.

Amenemapet.

A prince of Kush, or Ethiopia, in the reign of Rameses I. of the XIXth dynasty. Probably the same as the foregoing.

Amenemapet.

A son of Rameses II. of the XIXth dynasty.

5*

AMENEMEF.

A priest of Amen, and father of Khonsmes the spondist of Amen Ra, *See* Khonsmes.

AMENEMHA I.

The first king of the XIIth Egyptian dynasty. He ascended the throne in troublous times, conquered the Magui, and built a great palace at Heliopolis. He is supposed to have been attacked by conspirators in his ninth year, after which he reigned jointly with his son and successor, Osirtasen I., for seven years longer. He is the first Egyptian king who is recorded to have hunted the lion and the crocodile. The kings of this line are called Amenmai Thori by Sharpe in his History of Egypt.

AMENEMHA II.

A king of the XIIth dynasty. He succeeded Osirtasen I., and continued the Southern wars of Egypt. He reigned at least forty-four years, but little is recorded of the events of his reign.

AMENEMHA III.

The greatest king of the XIIth dynasty. He conceived the grand project of saving Egypt from the dangers alike of draught and inundation, by converting the low land, now called the Fayoum, into a vast reservoir of fresh water. The lake thus constructed was known to the Greeks as the lake Mœris. It had an area of 10,000,000 square metres, and a portion of it still forms the swamp called Birket Kerun. He also built two pyramids beside it, for the burial of himself and his wife ; and is said further by the Greeks to have constructed a famous labyrinth, of which the remains existed in the time of Diodorus Siculus.

AMENEMHA IV.

An Egyptian king of the XIIth dynasty ; the successor of Amenemha III. He continued the works at the mines of the Wady Magara, near Sinai, and he and his sister were buried in the pyramids of Amenemha III.

AMENEMHA.

A royal scribe, whose monument is in the Leyden Museum. Period uncertain, probably of the XVIIIth dynasty.

AMENEMHA.

The brother of Senbu a priest of Osiris. His period is uncertain.

AMENEMHEB.

A great officer in the army of Thothmes III. of the XVIIIth dynasty, whom he accompanied in all his Syrian invasions, and whose life he saved from the attack of an infuriated elephant. He was present at a battle before Nineveh, and was afterwards made captain of the royal barge at Thebes. *See* Shataemuaa.

AMENEMHEB.

The chief of the temple of Amen Ra. He was the son of Hentateh, a noble priestess of Amen. Period uncertain.

AMENEMHEB.

The chief of the grooms of an unnamed king of the XVIIIth dynasty. He had a son named Hui.

AMENEMHEBI.

A keeper of the . . . . of the House of Pthah. His wife was named Kairimon. The period when he lived is uncertain.

AMENEMHET.

A royal scribe, chief of the region of Tenti, and overseer of the House of Osiris. He married the royal lady Benkasi. Period uncertain.

AMENEMHOTEP.

A royal scribe of the White House (Memphis). Dynasty uncertain, but of the Second Empire.

AMENEMSOU.

A royal scribe in the palace of Osirtesen I. of the XIIth dynasty.

AMENEMUA.

One of the thirteen sons of Rameses II. of the XIXth dynasty.

AMENENHEB.

A prince of Kush, in the reign of Rameses II. of the XIXth dynasty.

AMENHEMEIF.

The auditor of the dwelling (domestic residence) of Thothmes IV. of the XVIIIth dynasty. He had a sister named Eiri.

AMENHEMOFT.

The overseer of the palace gates of Thothmes IV. of the XVIIIth dynasty. He had a sister named Schemouth.

AMENHEMTI.

An Egyptian gentleman, whose statue is in the Leyden Museum. Period uncertain, probably that of the Middle Empire.

AMENHERATF.

An Egyptian, the son of the functionary Heknofre and his wife Mautmai, of the XVIIIth dynasty.

AMENHESEMIF.

A prince and officer of the court, in the reign of his father, Rameses II. whom he assisted to defeat the Negroes in his first campaign. He died before his father, as indeed did also all his twelve brothers and many of his sisters.

AMENHIKHOPSEF.

A son of Rameses II. of the XIXth dynasty. He died before his father.

Amenhiunamif.

A son of Rameses II. He died before his father.

Amenhiunumif.

A son of King Herhorsiamun, of the XXIst dynasty.

Amenhotep I.   "Peace of Amen."

A king of the XVIIIth dynasty. He first reigned under the regency of his mother, Nofretari; afterwards he subdued the Shashu, who are supposed to have been the Bedouin Arabs, and also some of the petty kings of Palestine. He reigned thirteen years, and was succeeded by his son, Thothmes I. He was the Amenophis of the Greek historians.

Amenhotep II.

The successor of Thothmes III. His reign being disturbed by a revolt of the people of Mesopotamia, he invaded that country, and besieged the city of Nineveh. In the town of Takhisa, the site of which is unknown, he killed seven kings with his own mace, cut off their heads, and tied their bodies upon his war-galley, finally hanging them upon the walls of Thebes. He also re-subdued the Shashuous and the Phenicians. He reigned not less than seven years, and was succeeded by Thothmes IV.

Amenhotep III.

The successor of Thothmes IV. He was a great warrior, invading and subduing in succession Ethiopia, Mesopotamia, Assyria, and the Soudan, which latter country he attacked solely for the purpose of obtaining Negro slaves, of whom in one combat he killed and captured 1052. Being also a great hunter, chiefly of lions, in one of those expeditions he became acquainted with a tribe of Japhetic borderers, the daughter of the chief of whom, a lady named Taia, he afterwards married. Amenhotep III. was further a great builder and restorer of the ancient temples, and following the example of an earlier Egyptian sovereign, Amenemha, of the XIIth dynasty, he constructed in his eleventh year a great reservoir, 3000 cubits long and 600 broad. Towards the close of his reign he associated his son, Amenhotep IV., with him in the empire, and he cannot have held the throne of Egypt for a less period than thirty-six years. A stupendous temple was erected by him in the desert, with two colossal figures before it; one of these, the larger of the two statues, afterwards became the vocal Memnon of Greek history. *See* Shamy, and Memnon.

Amenhotep IV.

The son of Amenhotep III., with whom, for a few years, he reigned jointly under the governance of Queen Taia, his mother. He was apparently of weak intellect, although he is said to have maintained the empire of his father. The sole worship of Aten Ra, the Solar Disk, was forcibly introduced by him, accompanied with a more than usually slavish adoration of himself. He changed his own name into that of Khu en Aten, "Glory of the Solar Disk," and, in concert with his mother, disgraced all the officers and priests of the established religion, and founded a new capital at Alabastron, now Tel el Amarna, in Upper Egypt. According to one historian, Lenormant, he had seven daughters, who fought in their chariots beside their father in the predatory wars which were then common. His weakness of character and violence of temper combined, brought on a revolution, which led to the dethronement, and probably death, both of his mother and himself, after a reign of certainly more than six years. His wife was named Nefertitai. The death of Amenhotep was followed by a period of considerable disorder, and under his successor, Horus, the original worship of the Egyptian gods was revived, and that of Aten Ra degraded to its former subordinate position, the temple at Tel el Amarna pulled down to construct that of Amen Ra at Karnak, and the capital city itself removed, and its site destroyed. *See* Taia and Aten Ra.

Amenhotep.

A son of Thothmes IV. of the XVIIIth dynasty.

Amenhotep.

A prince of the blood royal, in the reign of Amenhotep II.

Amenhotep.

A subordinate Egyptian governor or prince, in the reign of Amenhotep II. of the XVIIIth dynasty.

Amenhotep.

A prince of Kush, in the reign of Amenhotcp III. of the XVIIIth dynasty.

Amenhotep.

A prince of Kush, in the reign of Tutankhamen, of the XVIIIth dynasty.

Amenhotep.

An Egyptian officer of the XVIIIth dynasty. He was a royal scribe, favourite of the king, and custodian of the granaries of the North and South.

Amenhotep.

An Egyptian lady, the wife of Unsu the steward or treasurer of Amenhotep III. This is an instance of a male name being applied to a woman.

Amenhotep.

A royal scribe, and "favourite of the king" of one of the monarchs, probably an Amenhotep, of the XVIIIth dynasty.

Amenhotep.

A royal scribe, the overseer of the (royal) house, and chief of the city of Memphis. Period uncertain, probably of the XVIIIth dynasty.

AMENHOTEP.

An Egyptian officer of the XVIIIth dynasty. He was surnamed Hui. His father's name was Amenmes, and that of his mother Nubnofre.

AMENHOTEP.

A son of Rameses II. of the XIXth dynasty.

AMENHOTEP.

A high priest of Amen Ra, in the reign of Rameses IX. of the XXth dynasty.

AMENHOTEP.

An Egyptian priest, who was overseer of the temple of Pthah, and overseer of the prophets of the temple of Pasht, or Sekhet, at Memphis. His mother's name was Toutouka. The period when he lived is uncertain.

AMENHOTEP.

An Egyptian architect. He was son of the architect Senna. The time when he lived is uncertain.

AMENHOTEP.

The chief of the land surveyors of Amen Ra. The period when he lived is uncertain.

AMENHOTEP.

A priest and prophet of the gods Amen and Month, in the XVIIIth dynasty. His double sarcophagus is in the Leyden Museum.

AMENHOTEP.

A priest, who was called "a singer at the gate of Amen." Period uncertain, probably of the XVIIIth dynasty.

AMENHOTEPHAPU.

An Egyptian prince of the blood royal, in the reign of Amenhotep II., of the XVIIIth dynasty.

AMENHOTEPTETUNAFHAPU.

A prince of the Nekheb, or South country, *i.e.* Syene, near Ethiopia, under Amenhotep II.

AMENI.

The son of King Osertesen or Sesertesen I. of the XIIth dynasty.

AMENI.

A great Egyptian officer, called *Suten Rekh*, or "royal father," of the XIIth dynasty. His wife's name was Hotep, "peace," the daughter of a chief whose name is not given. He had a son named Pthahsankh, "Pthah, who makes to live," and a daughter named like her mother, Hotep.

AMENI.

The son of an Egyptian functionary named Antefaker and his wife Hotept. He lived probably in the XIIth dynasty.

AMENI.

The superintendent of the works in the temples of Upper and Lower Egypt, in the reigns of Amenemha I. and II. of the XIIth dynasty. He was the son of the chief Tauuer and the lady Meristekhu.

AMENI.

The name of two of the sons of Antef, a great officer in the court of one of the kings of the XIIth dynasty.

AMENI.

The son of Apa. He was a priest of Osiris, in the XIIth dynasty.

AMENI.

Certain Egyptian amulets, in the shape of a right angle or carpenter's square. They were generally wrought in Hæmatite or black stone, and are often found with the mummies ; their symbolical meaning is unknown.

AMENI.

The chief of the embalmers of an unnamed king of the XVIIIth dynasty. His wife's name was Hathorse, and his daughter's Pthahse, He had also a son who was named like himself, Ameni.

AMENI.

A great Egyptian general and officer of state, in the reign of Osirtasen I. of the XIIth dynasty. He conquered the people of Kush, protected the Egyptians during a great famine, and administered the government of the province of Sah, in Upper Egypt, with great prudence. He was buried in a tomb at Beni Hassan.

AMENIANTEFAMENEMHA.

An Egyptian monarch, apparently of the XIIth dynasty. His place in history is however a little uncertain.

AMENIRITIS.

The sister of Shabaka king of Egypt, and regent of Egypt during the reigns of three of the sovereigns of the Ethiopian or XXVIth dynasty. She ruled wisely and with much popularity, and married Piankhi II., with whom she governed Ethiopia as joint sovereign.

AMENIRITIS.

The chief of the hunters of Amen. Period unknown, but subsequent to the XIXth dynasty.

AMENISENB.

An Egyptian official, in the reign of Osirtesen I. of the XIIth dynasty. His father's name was Uaemkau. Little is known concerning Amenisenb, except that he lived on till the time of the Hykshos invasion.

Amenkemhasurara.

A sacred scribe, in the reign of a king Amenemha, of the XIIth dynasty.

Amenkherkhent.

The mystical name of the second gate of the city of Thebes, in Upper Egypt.

Amenkno.

A gatekeeper of the temple of Amen Ra. Period uncertain.

Amenmeit.

A priestess of the god Amen Ra. Her statue is in the Leyden Museum. Period uncertain.

Amenmer.

The general prenomen of many of the Egyptian kings, from the XXIst to the XXVIth dynasties.

Amenmerassetkhert.

The prenomen of Takelothis I., of the XXIInd dynasty.

Amenmerbastseuasarkon.

A prenomen of Osorkon, or Uaserken II. of the XXIst dynasty.

Amenmerermes.

The prenomen of a king named Rameses, whose place in the lists is not known.

Amenmerinut.

A king of Egypt of the XXVIth dynasty, the successor of Rutamen on the throne of Ethiopia, at Napata. Encouraged by a prophetic dream, he successfully invaded Upper Egypt, and on entering Lower Egypt was opposed by the kings of the Delta, especially Pakrur, king of Pisabti. He gave battle to and defeated them all, and received their presents and submission, returning in safety to Ethiopia before the Assyrian army had arrived in Egypt to avenge his inroad. No further particulars of his reign are known. He was succeeded by Piankhi II.

Amenmerpamai.

The prenomen of King Pamai, a monarch of the XXIInd dynasty.

Amenmersasa.

The prenomen of Sheshank II. of the XXIInd dynasty.

Amenmersebastaser.

The prenomen of Sheshank III. of the XXIInd dynasty.

Amenmerusarkon.

The prenomen of Osorkon I. and II. of the XXIst dynasty.

AMENMES. "Born of Amen."

An Egyptian scribe, whose monument is in the Leyden Museum. The period when he lived is uncertain.

AMENMES.

A son of King Aahmes I. of the XVIIth or XVIIIth dynasty.

AMENMES.

An Egyptian functionary, the father of Amenhotep, surnamed Hui, an officer of the XVIIIth dynasty.

AMENMES.

An Egyptian functionary, of the XVIIIth dynasty.

AMENMES.

An unassigned early Egyptian royal name.

AMENMESES. "Son of Amen."

A prince of the royal family of Rameses II., whose exact period is not known. He is supposed to have ascended the throne during the domestic disturbances which followed that monarch's decease, and he left the throne to his son Sipthah, who reigned as Merenpthah II.

AMENMESESHIKUAS.

An Egyptian king of the XIXth dynasty. His filiation is uncertain.

AMENMESSU.

According to Lepsius, a king of Egypt in the XIXth dynasty, between the reigns of Menepthah I. and II.

AMENNAANKA.

A mystical title of the deity Amen Ra, in the CLXVIth chapter of the Ritual of the Dead, or the Chapter of the Boat.

AMENNAKHTI.

A priest of Amen Ra, probably in the XVIIIth dynasty. He was the son of the priest of Amen-harhemneb, Pihoroër.

AMENNATAKARUTI.

A third mystical title of the deity Amen Ra, in the CLXVIth chapter of the Ritual of the Dead.

AMENNEKHT.

An Egyptian officer, the auditor of justice in the tribunal of Amenhotep I. or II. of the XVIIIth dynasty. His wife's name was Scharei.

AMENNOFRE. "Amen the good."

A son of the royal prince and priest of Amen Eopou. He lived before the XVIIIth dynasty.

AMENNOT.

An unassigned early Egyptian royal name.

AMENOPHIS.

The Greek form of the Egyptian royal name Amenhotep, which see.

AMENOPHIS.

An Egyptian king, whose history as it is transmitted to us by the Greek writers is inconsistent with that of any recorded Amenhotep. The Jewish historian Josephus attributed the oppression of the Israelites and the Exodus to a monarch of this name; but his conjecture is not supported by historical testimony. If there were any basis for the theory, it would be derived from the strongly Semitic form of worship introduced by Amenhotep IV., or Khuenaten, which see.

AMENOPHIUM.

The name given by the Greek writers, to the great temples at Thebes, which were erected by Amenhotep III. of the XVIIIth dynasty, and of which there now remain only the two mutilated colossi, which are called by the Arabs Shamy and Damy. *See also* Memnon.

AMENPARUIUSAKA.

A mystical title of Amen Ra, in the CLXVIth chapter of the Ritual of the Dead.

AMEN-RA. "Amen, the Sun; or the Self-existent." "The Hidden."

The supreme being of the Egyptian mythology considered as an abstract entity; all the other deities, even Ra himself, being but emanations from him. He was chiefly adored at Thebes, in Upper Egypt, and his worship was repeatedly overthrown and restored in Egypt during the principal dynasties. *See* Apophis, Amenhotep IV., and Arsu.

AMENRAHERSEF.

A son of Herhorsiamun, of the XXIst dynasty.

AMENRASNETEMHETSTPN.

The prenomen of Nekhtanebo I. of the XXXth dynasty.

AMENRUT.

The Egyptian form of the Persian royal name Amyrtæus, of the XXVIIIth dynasty.

AMENRUTA.

A mystical title of the deity Amen Ra, in the CLXVIth chapter of the Ritual of the Dead.

AMENSE.

The son of Sennu the royal scribe and lieutenant of an unnamed king, at the close of the XVIIIth dynasty.

AMENSE.

An Egyptian king, of the XVIIth dynasty.

AMENSE.

An Egyptian lady, the sister of Senbu a priest of Osiris, whose period is uncertain.

AMENSERFAU.

The sacred name of the first gate of the city of Thebes, the capital of Upper Egypt.

AMENSET.

A sister of Amenhotep I. of the XVIIIth dynasty.

AMENSET.

A sister or daughter of Amenhotep III. of the XVIIIth dynasty.

AMENSIDSJAANKH.

An Egyptian scribe. His funereal stèle is in the Leyden Museum. Uncertain period.

AMENT.

The feminine form of the divine name Amen, "the Hidden."

AMENT.

A Theban goddess. She was a form of the goddess Maut the wife of Amen Ra, and was represented as wearing the sacred red crown.

AMENT.

The Egyptian name for the city and nome in Lower Egypt, which was called by the Greeks the Lybian. It was sacred to the worship of , the goddess Hathor, "the Lady of Horns." *See* Hathor.

AMENTA.

A mystical place mentioned in the Ritual of the Dead.

AMENTAKEHAL.

A hereditary Ethiopian princess, and the wife of Tirhakah, or Tihrak, of the XXIVth dynasty. She was the mother of King Urdamani, which see.

AMENTEMHA.

An Egyptian gentleman. His period is uncertain, save that it was after the XIIth and prior to the XVIIIth dynasties.

AMENTHES.

The Grecised form of Rhotamenti, the mythological title of Osiris as judge of the dead in Hades, which see.

AMENTI.   " The Hidden."

In Egyptian mythology the general name of the underworld or Hades, including the lower heaven or Aahlu, "fields of peace," with its twenty-one gates, Kerneter, "good place," Rusta, or purgatory, and hell. It was under the special governance of the setting sun as Osiris Rhotamenti the judge of the souls of the dead, of Horus, and the funereal deities. The great Hall of the Two Truths was there, and in it the examination of the soul of the deceased took place. There were also the fifteen gates of the House of Osiris, and the fourteen Abodes of Hell. Amenti had its rivers both of separation and punishment, in that respect resembling the Hades of Greek mythology, which was doubtless copied from it. It is fully described in the great collection of funereal rituals called the Ritual of the Dead, and it was often spoken of as the country of the words of truth, and the happy land of Osiris. Owing to the graves of the Egyptians being mostly excavated in the mountains on the western bank of the Nile, the terms "land of the west," and " the hidden land," became synonymous, and the present name of the village of Erment is derived from that of one of the chief cities near the ancient Necropolis. For further details *see* Aahlu, Atum, Horus, Kerneter, Rhotamenti, Rusta, and "The Book of the Lower World."

Amentotankhatra.

The prenomen of the Ethiopian king Ergamenes.

Amentuankh.

Another form of the Egyptian royal name Tutankhamen, which see.

Amenuahsu.

An Egyptian naval commander, and chief of the royal fleet of an un-named king of the XVIIIth dynasty.

Amenuahsu.

An Egyptian priestly officer, called "the Receiver of the House of Life." He was the son of Semut, and lived probably in the XIXth dynasty.

Amenurbau.

The sacred name of the third gate of the city of Thebes in Upper Egypt.

Ameresk.

A country in the highlands of Armenia, called also Elasi, which was rendered tributary to Egypt by Thothmes III.

Ameretat.   " Immortality."

In Zendic mythology the name of the sixth of the heavenly Amshas-pands, which see.

Amersis.

The name of an Egyptian king of the XVIIIth dynasty, according to the Greek lists. He is not certainly identified.

Amerys.

A very late Greco-Egyptian proper name, which occurs on the stèle of the Ptolemaic period.

Amesaospentao.

The Zendic name of the heavenly beings who were called Amshaspands by the Persians, which see.

Amestris.

The wife of Xerxes, king of Persia. By some writers she is supposed to have been the Esther of Hebrew history.

Amgarrun.

The name of the city of the tributary king Padi, whose detention by Hezekiah, king of Judah, brought on the invasion of Palestine by Sennacherib. It has been read as Migron by some Assyriologists, and Ekron by others. *See* Padi and Hezekiah.

Amh.

In Egyptian mythology the Exit Gate of the funereal region of Amenti or Hades.

Amhi.

The name applied to the city of Memphis, as the chief city on the West bank of the Nile in the region of the tombs.

Amida.

A famous city, near the head waters of the Tigris, which was repeatedly attacked by the different kings of Assyria. One of the first to conquer the district was Vulnirari or Rimmon Nirari III. It was then invaded and ravaged by Assurnazirpal, who took its chief Ilani a prisoner, and slew many of the garrison. The conqueror carried 3000 captives to Nineveh, beheaded 600 of the soldiers, placing their heads in two heaps by the city gate, and crucified or impaled 400 of the chief citizens on the walls. After this siege it was annexed to the kingdom of Assyria, and in the reign of Shalmaneser VI. (Smith's Shalmaneser IV.), was governed by a viceroy or Pasha, named Merodachbaluzur. Amida subsequently shared in the destruction which befell the Assyrian Empire, but during the Sassanian period revived again and occupied an important position in early Christian history. It is still called by the inhabitants Kar Amid, " Castle of Amida," and is generally known to European travellers under the name of Diarbekr.

Amidassi.

Brother of Assurliha, king of Karalla. On the death of Assurliha at the hands of Sargon II., the people raised his brother to the throne. He continued the war of the revolted chiefs against the king of Assyria, but without any success, and his kingdom was ruined by Sargon and his army.

Amika.

A chief of the district of Lamua, who fled from the armies of Assurnazirpal, king of Assyria, who conquered and annexed his territory.

Amilanu.

A tablet writer or official scribe, in the reign of Gamilsin, king of Babylonia. He is the earliest scribe whose name is thus recorded.

AMKHENT.

The Egyptian name of the Heracleopolite or twenty-second nome of Upper Egypt. *See* Seft.

AMKHU.

An Egyptian religious title applied to a young man upon his entering upon maturity, generally in connection with the worship of some deity.

AMLATU.

A tribe in Mesopotamia, who were conquered by Tiglath Pileser II.

AMMAH.

In Egyptian mythology the name of the Gate of the Dead, or of Hades, from whence, according to the Ritual of the Dead, the souls of the deceased went out on their way to heaven.

AMMALI.

A city near the river Turnat, which was conquered by Assurnazirpal.

AMMANA.

A district or city near Lebanon in Northern Palestine, which was conquered by Tiglath Pileser II. It was the Amana of Hebrew history.

AMMANAS.

An unidentified Himyaritic divinity. He was probably a patron of agriculture, as a portion of the produce of·the fields and herds was offered to him.

AMMANKASHIBAR.

An Elamite deity, of whom nothing is known.

AMMAS.

A city near Armenia, conquered by Dayanassar the Tartan for Shalmaneser II.

AMMAT.

An Assyrian measure of length. *See* Suklu.

AMMATGAGAR.

The same as the *soss* in Assyrian metrology, only in this case it was used as a superficial measure equal to 360 square yards.

AMMAVAS.

A Mesopotamian people who had revolted from, and were re-subdued by Tiglath Pileser I.

AMMENEPTHES.

Another form of the Egyptian royal name Amenophis, or Amenhotep, as written by the Greek historians.

AMMENON.

According to Berosus, the fourth antediluvian king of Babylon.

AMMERES.

According to the Greek lists, the name of an Egyptian king of the XIIth dynasty. He has not yet been certainly identified.

AMMERES.

According to the lists of the Greek historians, the name of a late king of Egypt.

AMMIBAHLA.

A chief prince who was tributary to Assurnazirpal. He was murdered by another chief named Buramanu, and his death was cruelly avenged by the king of Assyria.

AMMIDIKAGA.

An early Babylonian king, a successor of Hammurabi. Nothing else is known respecting him.

AMMIHITAH.

A chief of Vas in the land of Armenia. He was the father of Aikamaru the destroyer of the Nabatheans. *See* Aikamaru.

AMMOCHISTA.

A petty kingdom in the Island of Kypros, or Cyprus, which paid tribute to Esarhaddon, king of Assyria.

AMMONIUS.

The father of Cleopatra the wife of Soter. He was the archon of Thebes in the reign of the Emperor Trajan.

AMMULADI.

King of Kedar. He joined Vaiteh I. in his invasion of Palestine against Assurbanipal, king of Assyria, who defeated him and sent him to Nineveh, where he caged him among his hounds, together with Vaiteh and his queen Adiya.

AMNTMER. *Or* AMENTMER.

The *Pehu* of the eighteenth nome of Lower Egypt.

AMORŒUS.

The name given by Ctesias to Queen Tomyris the Amazon, by whom Cyrus was defeated, slain, and his body treated with indignity.

AMPEH.

The twenty-first nome of Upper Egypt. It was called by the Greeks Arsinoites the Lower.

AMPKA.

The Egyptian name of an unidentified town.

'AMRAN.

An Himyaritic city in South-western Arabia.

AMSET.

The mystical name of one of the planks of the Boat of Souls, in the XCIXth chapter of the Ritual of the Dead.

AMSET.

One of the seven great spirits in the Ritual of the Dead, see also the other funereal and Canopic deities.

AMSET.

The Carpenter, a son of Osiris, and also one of the four genii of the dead who were offered by the deceased to make an atonement for his sins, and to whose care the different viscera of the embalmed body were committed. He is generally represented in the form of an ovoid vase with a human head as a cover; on the vase is often a prayer to the goddess Isis on behalf of the deceased.

AMSHASPANDS.

In Zendic mythology the names of the six " immortal saints," a series of genii created by Ahura Mazdu to assist him in the government of the world. Their names were Vohumano, Asovahisto, Khsathsovairyo, Spentaarmaiti, Haurvatat and Ameretat, which see.

AMSHOIR.

The censer of the ancient Egyptians. It was generally made in the form of a human hand and arm holding an open patera, in which the fire for the perfume was laid.

AMT.

One of the mystical demons, called " the Devourer of the Dead," in the Egyptian purgatory. He had the head of a crocodile, the forepart of a lioness, and the hind quarters of an hippopotamus. *See also* Apet.

AMTEN.

A great Egyptian governor in the reign of King Snefru of the IIIrd dynasty. He had charge of many of the chief nomes of Lower Egypt. His tomb, formerly at Abouseir, has been removed bodily to the Museum of Berlin by Dr. Lepsius.

AMTIHU.

The Egyptian name of a people who are by some writers supposed to have been the Edomites.

AMU.

The name of the third, or Libyan, nome of Lower Egypt. This name must not be confounded with Aamu, which see.

AMUHIA.

The Assyrian form of the Median royal name Amytis, the Queen of Nebuchadnezzar, which see.

AMUKEHAK.

The Egyptian name of an unidentified country to the North of Egypt.

AMUKKAN.

The father of Kinziru, the last king of Babylonia under the ancient dynasty. Nothing is known respecting him.

AMUN.

Another form of the Egyptian divine name Amen when it was used as a prefix; all the following titles may as well be written with an *e* or an *u*, the significance being the same. *See* Amen.

AMUNHIKHOPSEF.

The surname of Rameses X. of the XXth dynasty.

AMUNHIKHOPSEF MIAMUN.

The surname of Rameses V. of the XXth dynasty.

AMUNHIKHOPSEFNUTERHIKTEN.

The surname of Rameses VI. of the XXth dynasty.

AMUNIRITIS.

A priestess of Amen, and the wife of an obscure Egyptian or Ethiopian king named Kashto, of the XXIVth dynasty.

AMUNMAI THORI.

The form adopted by Sharpe and some other Egyptologists for the royal name Amenemha, which see.

AMUNNEBKETTOTI.

A wife of Amenrut or Amyrtæus, one of the Greco-Persian monarchs of the XXVIIIth dynasty.

AMUNTA.

A feminine form of the great deity Amen Ra. She was sometimes called Tamun.

AMUNTIKHET.

The wife of Taharka, or Tirakah, the third king of the XXVth dynasty.

AMUT.

The Egyptian name of an unidentified town.

AMYNUS.

In Phenician mythology a son of the deity Agrotus. He is said to have taught men to construct villages and to rear cattle.

AMYRTAIOS I.

A petty king of Egypt under the Persian dynasty. Aided by Inarus, king of Lybia, he revolted against his master, Artaxerxes, king of Persia, by whom he was after a six-years' struggle subdued and driven into the Delta. Inarus was impaled, and Thannyras placed upon the throne of Lybia, and Pausiris on that of Egypt.

6*

Amyrtaios II.

King of Egypt under the XXVIIIth dynasty, after the Persian conquest. He was the only king of that dynasty, and no particulars of his life and reign are known.

Amytis.

The daughter of Vakistar, king of Media. She married Nabukuduruzur, king of Assyria, and greatly improved the city of Babylon by her artistic influence. The hanging gardens were considerably augmented by her orders, although she was not the inventor of the idea, as similar groves existed at Koyunjik, the palace of Assurbanipal.

An.

The hieroglyphic name of the city of Hermonthes in the South, as Heliopolis was the An of the North, of Egypt.

An.

The capital city of the nome of the same name in Lower Egypt.

An.

The twenty-first nome of Lower Egypt. It was sacred to the worship of the deity Horus. Its site is not yet identified.

An.

The Egyptian name of the city of Denderah, in Upper Egypt. It was sacred to the deities Sebek and Athor, and the great temple there is the most perfect of any remaining in Upper Egypt.

An.

An early Egyptian king of the Vth dynasty, of whom little or nothing is known.

An.

An Egyptian monarch, who reigned at the close of the XIIIth or the beginning of the XIVth dynasty. Little or nothing is known respecting him.

An.   "Scribe."

The name of the Egyptian writers or clerks. They were also called Skhai.

An.   Or Un.

The Egyptian name of the city and nome of Heliopolis, in Northern Egypt. It was situated in the thirteenth nome, and was sacred to the god Atum.

An.   "A Star."

The phonetic value of the cunieform character which represented both a star and the idea of deity.

An.

The surname of Ra-en-user, an Egyptian king of the Vth dynasty.

AN.

The Egyptian name of a funereal column erected over the tombs of strangers, or enemies slain in battle.

AN.

A son of Amenemap, a priest of Amen, in the period of the XVIIIth dynasty. His wife's name was Raa.

ANA.

The first king of the VIIth Egyptian dynasty.

ANA.

An Egyptian lady, the wife of Aker, and the mother of Pantina governor of the South. *See* Pantina.

ANAA. "The Great An."

An early Egyptian name of the city of Tentyris or Denderah. *See also* An.

ANAA.

An Egyptian monarch of the XIth dynasty. He is only known from his name occurring on a list of the kings of Egypt in the Abbot Papyrus.

ANAHID.

The Armenian name of the Assyrian goddess Anaitis, under which title she was worshipped in Armenia.

ANAI.

A royal priestess, or Pallakist, of the XVIIIth or XIXth dynasty. *See* Merian.

ANAI.

A royal scribe of the XIXth dynasty. He was one of the great family of Uermu, which see.

ANAITIS.

A Semitic goddess of a warlike character, somewhat approaching the Bellona of classic mythology. She was represented as a naked woman standing on a lion, and sometimes on a crocodile, holding a spear or bow, and wearing a peculiar crown formed of tall feathers. Her worship was introduced into Egypt probably about the time of Rameses II. after his Syrian victories, one of his daughters, Bentanath, being named after the goddess.

ANAITIS.

A feminine form of the great deity Mithra, as introduced into the Median religion when corrupted from Zoroastrianism. She was in some respects analogous to the Mylitta of the Babylonians, which see.

ANAKUNADASHARRUASSHUR.   " I the Great King of Assyria."

A name supposed by Greek writers to have been that of the father of Assurbanipal. It was really only the common title of the Assyrian kings.

ANAKYNDARAXES.

A patronymic given by Greek historians to Assurbanipal, being a corruption of his Assyrian title Anakunadasharruasshur, " I the Great King of Assyria."

ANAMAT.

An Egyptian city of which Bakennifi, chief of the troops under Piankhi Meramon, was the lord.

ANAR.

Another form of the name of the Scandinavian deity Onar, which see.

ANASCH.

The scribe of the treasure of the deity Anhurschu, and of the goddess Tafne, at the temple of Thinis.   His mother's name was Iseueri ; she was also a priestess of Tafne.

ANASERU.

An unidentified Semitic people who dwelt in the neighbourhood of Lower Egypt.

ANASIEH.

The modern name of the city and nome in Upper Egypt which was called by the Greeks Heracleopolis.

ANAT.   *Or* ANATU.

The feminine Sacti of the Assyrian deity Oannes.   She was the wife of Anu, and the impersonation of passive reproductive matter.   Her chief title was " The Lady of Death and Life."   Under the name of Anaitis she was worshipped by the Egyptians, in which case she was regarded as a feminine form or wife of the god Reseph.

ANAUA.

A royal scribe of the city of Memphis in the XIXth dynasty.

ANAUKAS.

The Egyptian name of a district near to Tahi, which see.

ANAUKAS.

The Egyptian name of a city of the Upper Rotennu, which was believed by some to have been Cilicia.

ANAUKASA.

A strong fortress of the Rotennu in the land of the Tahai, in Northern Syria, which was taken by Thothmes III. of the XVIIIth dynasty, in his ninth campaign.

ANDARIA.

A people in the mountains of Mesopotamia, who were subdued by Assurrisilim, king of Assyria.

ANDER.

In Zendic mythology the second of the wicked Darvands. He was considered by them to be the same deity as the Indra of the Vedas, but of an opposite or evil character.

ANDRON.

The chief city of the Andropolite nome in Lower Egypt.

ANDROPOLIS.

A nome of Lower Egypt, West of the Nile. Its chief city was Andron.

ANDUANKI.

The Accadian name of the city of Assan in Elam.

ANEBNI.

A son of king Ratukhnumamen of the XVIIth dynasty.

ANEBNI.

A royal son, whose name occurs among a list of princes in the reign or Hatasu, queen of Egypt in the XVIIIth dynasty. He may have been a younger brother of that queen, but his exact filiation is unknown.

ANEBOS.

The form in which the name of the city of Nipur is recorded as that of a king, by the historian Moses of Khorene.

ANEM.

The Egyptian name of a precious stone which is at present un-identified.

ANEMENABU.

The Egyptian name of the sacerdotal panther's skin worn by the chief priests of Khem. *See* Anmautf.

ANEMHER.

An Egyptian deity which was worshipped in the city of Arma.

ANEPOU.

The name of the elder brother of Satou, and one of the heroes in the ancient Egyptian romance of " The Tale of the Two Brothers."

ANGA.

The collective name of a series of treatises derived from the Hindu Vedas. They are called respectively the Siksha, the Kalpa, the Vyakarana, the Chhandas, the Jyotisha, and the Nirukta, which see.

ANGIRAS.

In Hindu mythology certain deities emanating from Brahma, to whom he committed the power of creation. Other similar deities were Atri, Bhrigu, Daksha, Marilshi, Narada, Palaha, Pilastya, and Warishka.

ANGYRON.

A chief town of the Aphroditopolite nome. It was situated on the Western bank of the Nile, in the Heptanomos.

ANHAHORRAU.

The brother of the probably fabulous Prince Pthah-neferka in the Egyptian romance called "The Story of Setnau."

ANHESMEN.

The third nome of Upper Egypt.

ANHU.

The capital of the nineteenth nome of Lower Egypt.

ANHUR.   "That which brings to Heaven."

An Egyptian deity who is always represented as in a marching attitude, and robed with a long dress. He wears a headdress of four plumes, with the usual uræus serpent of celestial deity. He holds a cord in his hands, which is supposed to symbolise one of the forces of the universe. He was a form also of the solar god Shu, and in that character he had for his consort the goddess Tefnut, the Heavenly Cow. He was the Anouris, or Egyptian Mars, of the Greek writers. Anhur was chiefly worshipped in the city and nome of Abot, which was situated in the Eastern bank of the Nile, in the Thebaid, and was afterwards called by the Greeks Thinites. (Pierret and Birch).

ANHURMES.

An Egyptian priest of the deity Anhur. He had a wife named Tomeri, and a son named Smento. One of his daughters was named Hatscheps, or Hatasu, after the great Egyptian queen of that name of the XVIIIth dynasty.

ANHURNEKHT.

The brother of Anhurse, a great scribe in the XIIth dynasty.

ANHURSE.

A great Egyptian scribe of the civil order, who together with his family of seventy people, was attached to the worship of the deity Anhur at Abydos in the XIIth dynasty.

ANI.

The superior of the writers and a priest of Ptah, in the XIXth dynasty.

ANI.

A priestess of Isis, and the mother of Khemmes, a royal scribe of Rameses III.

Ani.

A royal scribe, principal *Heb*, and chief of the temple of (Osiris?) in the reign of an unnamed king of the XVIIIth dynasty.

Ani.

A prince of Kush, and state officer, under Seti Menepthah I., and Rameses II., of the XIXth dynasty.

Ani.

The ancient Egyptian name of the city of Emeh.

Ani.   "Sea."

The Egyptian name of the twentieth or Arabian nome of Lower Egypt. It was also called Septhor, and was sacred to the deity Sept Achem.

Aniei.

An Egyptian functionary whose *Shabti* or votive mummy figure is in the Leyden Museum.

Anima.

The son of Tetenhor. He was a priest of the deity Anhur. Period uncertain, but subsequent to the XIXth dynasty.

Animals, Sacred.

The system of Zoolatria, or animal worship, was said to have been introduced into Egypt by King Kekau of the IInd dynasty; and the chief of the sacred animals and reptiles which were adored either as incarnations of, or servants of, the various deities, were—

The Bull Apis ; sacred to Osiris.
The Bull Mnevis ; sacred to Osiris.
The Bull Pacis ; unknown.
The Cat ; sacred to Bast.
The Cobra, or Uræus Serpent ; sacred to all the deities.
The Cow; sacred to Athor.
The Crocodile; sacred to Sebek.
The Cynocephalus Baboon ; sacred to Thoth.
The Eel ; sacred to Atum.
The Fish Latus ; sacred to Isis.
The Frog ; sacred to Haket.
The Hippopotamus ; sacred to Thoeris.
The Ibis ; sacred to Thoth.
The Jackal ; sacred to Anubis.
The Lapwing; sacred to Osiris.
The Lion; sacred to Sekhet.
The Ram ; sacred to Pthah and Khnum.
The Scarabeus Beetle; sacred to Kheper Ra.
The Scorpion ; sacred to Selk.
The Sparrow-Hawk ; sacred to Horus.
The Shrewmouse ; sacred to Buto.
The Vulture; sacred to Maut.—(Pierret and Birch.)

ANIT.

Another form of the name of the goddess Hathor, or Athor, "The Lady of Horns."

ANIU.

One of the mystical deities of the Egyptian Ritual of the Dead.

ANKA.

A minor Egyptian goddess. She was the wife of Khnum the creating spirit, and was the Anucis of the Greek writers.

ANKAF.

An early Egyptian city, the site of which is not known. It was sacred to the goddess Nushem.

ANKARAMA.

A daughter of Takelot II. of the XXIInd dynasty.

ANKH.

The overseer of the cars of the palace of Amenemha I. of the XIIth dynasty. He was the son of the lady Hathorset.

ANKH.

The overseer of the chariot stables of Amenemha III. of the XIIth dynasty. His mother was named Hathorset.

ANKH. "Life."

The name given by the Egyptians to the emblem in the form of a handled cross, somewhat resembling the Tau or St. Anthony's cross. The cause of its significance is unknown, but as an emblem of life it is always borne in the hands of the gods, and symbolically laid on the lips of the mummy to revive it, or poured over the king at his mystical baptism. As an hieroglyphic, it is simply the determinative of all things relating to the ear. It is the most common of all the Egyptian symbols.

ANKH, UZA, SENB. "Life, Health, Strength!"

The formula with which most Egyptian royal documents were concluded. It was analogous to the "Vivat Rex" of the Latins.

ANKHAM.

A peculiar sacred flower in the Egyptian mythology. It was probably the lotus.

ANKHAREOUTEF.

A royal scribe in the court of Rameses II. of the XIXth dynasty.

ANKHATEFS.

An Egyptian lady, the mother of Osirtesen-pepa, or Topareh, of the XIIth dynasty.

ANKHES.

The wife of Sekherta an Egyptian "functionary of the interior," in the XIIth dynasty.

ANKHESENAMEN.

The wife of King Tutankhamen, one of the last monarchs of the XVIIIth dynasty.

ANKHESENATEN.

A daughter of Amenhotep IV. of the XVIIIth dynasty.

ANKHFKHONS.

A priest and spondist of Amen Ra, in the XVIIIth dynasty. His outer sarcophagus is in the Leyden Museum, and the inner one, together with his mummy, in the Museum of Rome.

ANKHHAPI.

A priest of Pthah of Memphis, and of the King Snefru, who was there adored as a deity. He was the son of Horimhotep and the lady Satbou. The period when he lived is unknown.

ANKHHAPI.

An Egyptian priest, the son of Aairiaa. The period when he lived is uncertain.

ANKHHAPI.

A priest of Apis, the son of Imhotep. He lived in the Ptolemaic and Roman period.

ANKHHAPI. "The Living Apis."

A musician of Osiris, in the first century A.D. His coffin and mummy are in the British Museum.

ANKHHAPIMES. "Son of the Living Apis."

A prophet or priest of the temple of Amen Ra. Dynasty uncertain, but of the Middle Empire.

ANKHHI.

An Egyptian lady, the mother of Psametek priest of Pthah, and the deity Nefer Atum.

ANKHHOR.

A priest of the bull god Apis. Period uncertain.

ANKHHOR.

A priest of Apis. He was the son of Paduenra. His period is not precisely known.

ANKHHOR.

An Egyptian priest and prophet of the god Month. He was the son of Hor and the lady Samonth. Period uncertain. His double arcophagus and mummy are in the Leyden Museum.

ANKHHOR.   " The Living Horus."

One of the rebellious chiefs of Lower Egypt, who ultimately submitted to Piankhi-Meramon, of the XXIInd dynasty.

ANKHKAROAMAT.

A daughter of Takelot II. of the XXIInd dynasty.

ANKHNAS RANOFREHET.

An Egyptian princess, the daughter of Psametik II. She married the usurper Aahmes, who treated her with much consideration and honoured her as the chief of his wives.

ANKHPIEOI.

An Egyptian gentleman, whose votive statue is in the Leyden Museum.

ANKHPISKHE.

The father of the priest and overseer of Amen, Einamen-nefriboni, which see.

ANKHSAMTAUI.

The father of Paseenpthah, a priest of Apis, in the reign of Sheshank IV. of the XXIInd dynasty.

ANKHSAPENAP.

The granddaughter of Piankhi II. of the XXVIth dynasty.

ANKHSEN RANOFREHET.

See Ankhnas.

ANKHSEPUNTEPET.

A lady of the blood royal of Panki, or Piankhi, an obscure king of the XXIVth dynasty.

ANKHSNEF.

An Egyptian functionary, the son of the master Djobbons, and the lady Tikar. A figure of Horus, dedicated by him to that divinity, is in the British Museum.

ANKHTA.   " City of Life."

A sacred quarter of the city of Memphis.

ANKHTA.

An Egyptian lady, the mother of the great officer Samtatitafnekht, which see.

ANKHTAKELOT.

The chief of the choristers of the goddess Maut, in the reign of an unnamed monarch of the XXVIth dynasty.

ANKHU.

The keeper of the great barge of the god Pthah-Sokari-Osiris. His period is unknown, except that it was after the XIIth and before the XVIIIth dynasty.

ANKTA.

The name of the sixth, of the seven mystical Halls of Osiris, in the Ritual of the Dead.

ANKU.

An Egyptian lady, the second wife of Uah a private gentleman and father of Senbu priest of Osiris. *See* Senbu.

ANMAIMA.

The Egyptian name of a country in Asia, which is not certainly identified.

ANMAUTF.

The name of an high sacerdotal dignity, the emblem and vestment of which was a panther's skin, and the long lock of hair peculiar to the god infantile Horus. The title is said to mean literally, "Husband of his Mother." It was specially connected with the worship of the Ithy-phallic god Khem.

ANMENT.

The Egyptian name of the city of Hermonthis, in the Thebaid of Upper Egypt. It was the capital of the seventh, or Hermonthite, nome.

ANMER.

The *Pehu* of the third nome of Lower Egypt.

ANMERUTHER.   " Salt Lake of the Sea."

A mystical lake near the heavenly Nile in Hades. It is figured in the Vignette to the CXth chapter of the Ritual of the Dead.

ANMLA.

The Egyptian name of an unidentified foreign country.

ANMUTF.

A mystical epithet applied to the Eye of Horus in the CXXXVIIth chapter of the Ritual of the Dead.

ANNA.

The queen of Sebekhotep II. of the XIIIth dynasty.

ANNAMIM.

The earliest settlers in the valley of the Nile. They were the Anu of Egyptian history.

ANNAP. "GOD."

The Turanian word for the idea of Deity in the abstract. It was derived from *An* "a star."

ANNEKE.

An Egyptian lady. She was the wife of Nakhtankh, which see.

ANNOUB.

One of the Hykshos kings of Egypt, of whose reign no particulars are known. He was probably the Anōn of the Greek writers.

ANNU.

The *Un* of the eighth nome of Lower Egypt.

ANNUMER.

The *Pehu* of the fifteenth, or Bubastite nome, of Lower Egypt. It was sacred to the goddess Hathor.

ANNUMER.

The *Pehu* of the second, or Latopolite nome, of Lower Egypt. It was sacred to the goddess Bast.

ANNUNNACI.

In the magical texts the name of certain Assyrian deities, the offspring of the deity Anu or the Sky. They inhabited the lower world, and were called the deities of the earth.

ANON.

The Greek form of the Hykshos-Egypto royal name Annoub, which see.

ANOS.

In Greco-Babylonian mythology the son of Kissare and Assaros, and the first member of the Divine Triad. His analogue was the Anu of the Assyrians. *See* Anu.

ANOUBAPION.

A proper name which occurs in the very lowest or Greco-Roman time of Egyptian history.

ANOUKE.

An Egyptian warlike goddess, possibly of Syrian origin, represented as a woman with a spear in her hand, and with a peculiar crown formed of high feathers curving outwardly from a white bonnet upon her head. She was the third member of the great Nubian Triad, and her worship dates to the period of Osirtesen III. of the XIIth dynasty. Her festival took place on the 28th day of Paophi and the 30th of Athyr.

ANP.

One of the sacred names of the ram deity Mendes.

ANPUTELEPTUF.

An uncertain Egyptian deity of the Greco-Egyptian period. *See* Anpu.

ANQT.

Another form of the name of the Egyptian goddess Anouke.

ANQTTITE.

A daughter of Sebekhotep III. of the XIIIth dynasty.

AN-RES. "Southern An."

The Egyptian name of the city and district of Hermonthis in Upper Egypt.

ANRN.

An uncertain Egyptian goddess.

ANRTA.

The Egyptian name of an unidentified Asiatic country.

ANRTU.

The Egyptian name of the town in Palestine which was called Anrata by the Hebrew writers

ANRU.

The Egyptian name of the funereal fields, or public Necropolis, near Memphis.

ANRU.

A name of the Egyptian Elysium, which occurs in the Ritual of the Dead.

ANRUTF. "The Sterile."

The Egyptian name of one of the mystical regions of Hades. It is described in the XVIIth chapter of the Ritual of the Dead. *See also* the following.

ANRUTF.

The Northern gate of the House of Osiris, in the Egyptian Karneter.

ANSAB. "Statues."

The name given by the Koranic writers to the sacred stones or Bœtylia, which were worshipped, and anointed with oil, by the ancient Arabians. *See* Bœtylia.

ANSAPATA.

An Elamite deity of whom nothing is known, except that it was one of those whose statues were carried off by Assurbanipal on his conquest of Elam.

Ansata. *Or* Crux Ansata.

The handled Tau cross. The emblem of life, which was always held in the hands of the Egyptian deities. The nature of the object, and the reason of its symbolism are unknown. *See* Ankh.

Ans Ra.

A mystical name of a divinity in the XLIInd chapter of the Ritual of the Dead.

Ant.

The Egyptian name of the city which was called by the Greeks Cœnopolis.

Ant.

The *Mer* of the ninth, or Canopic nome, of Lower Egypt. It was sacred to Osiris.

Ant.

The *Pehu* of the second, or Latopolite nome, of Lower Egypt.

Anta.

The Egyptian name of an unidentified town.

Anta.

A warlike Egyptian goddess, who is generally represented as wearing a white mitre similar to that of Osiris, ornamented with two feathers, and brandishing a kind of battle-axe in her left hand while she holds a spear with her right. She is very rarely represented on the Egyptian sculptures, and is not found before the time of Amenhotep I. of the XVIIIth dynasty. She was properly a Syrian or Asiatic goddess. *See also* Anaitis, etc. (Pierret.)

Antaemnekht. "Anaitis in Her Strength."

The name of the favourite hound of Rameses II. who accompanied his master in his battles.

Antæopolis.

The capital city of the Antæopolite nome. It is now called Gou.

Antæopolis.

The twelfth nome of Upper Egypt. Its Egyptian name was Douf, and it was sacred to the worship of the god Horus.

Antæopolites.

A nome in the Thebaid to the East of the river Nile; its chief towns under the Greek dominion at least, were Pesla, Hieracon, Isram, Mutham, and Antæopolis.

Antarta.

The Egyptian name of one of the goddesses of the Khita, the Hittites of Jewish history.

ANTARUBA.

In Chaldean astronomy the name of an unidentified fixed star.

ANTASSURA.   " Upper Sphere."

In Chaldean astronomy the name of an unidentified fixed star. .

ANTEF I.

An Egyptian king of the XIth dynasty, of whom nothing is as yet known.   This monarch and his successors are thought by some Egyptologists to have been merely petty kings reigning in the Thebaid, contemporaneously with the monarchs of the XIIth, XIIIth and XIVth dynasties.   These kings are also often called Entef and Enentef.

ANTEF II.   *Or* ANTEFAA.   "Antef the Great."

The brother of king Antef I., a monarch of the XIth dynasty.   He was a great hunter, and his tomb in the Asasseef is remarkable for its containing representations of four distinct species of Egyptian hounds which were used in the chase ; but there are no records of his reign and acts.

ANTEF III.   *Surnamed* HARMIHA ; *Prenomen*, RACHEPERAPUERMA.

The fifth king of the XIth Egyptian dynasty.   In this dynasty all the kings bore the names of Antef and Mentuhotep alternately.   Little is known respecting him, except that he was the brother of Antef II.

ANTEF IV.   *Prenomen*, RANEBKHEPER.

An Egyptian monarch of the XIth dynasty, the successor of Mentuhotep II.   His place is uncertain, and he is only mentioned in the Abbot papyrus.

ANTEF.

A great Egyptian officer in the XIIth dynasty.   He was first lieutenant of the king, and governor of the city of Tanis and the district of Abydos. He executed some important government works, and is stated to have been famous for his clemency and impartiality.   He also took charge of the armies of Egypt, and invaded and subjugated a country whose name is lost, but which was probably on the coast of Syria.   His monumental inscription records his virtues and their rewards in a style of considerable eulogy, and he appears to have held his various offices for a long time.   He had a brother named Ahmes, and a son Teti.

ANTEF.

The son of an Egyptian named Antefaker and his wife Hotept.   He probably lived in the XIIth dynasty.

ANTEF.

An high Egyptian officer and *Sam*, the son of Setmena, in the reign of Osirtesen I. of the XIIth dynasty.   He had two wives, named respectively Sethathor and Merit, and several sons named Usertesen, Nebkau, and Sebektu, and also a daughter Setamen.   Antef was called on his funereal inscription, " He who seeks the poor in their distresses."

7

ANTEF.

A son of Merri, the Egyptian superintendent of canal and public works in the reign of Osirtesen I. of the XIIth dynasty.

ANTEFAKER.

An Egyptian officer probably of the XIIth dynasty. His wife's name was Hotep, by whom he had a son named Osirtesen, and five other children.

ANTEFAKER.

A royal scribe in the reign of Osirtesen I. of the XIIth dynasty. He married a lady named Kekou.

ANTEFAKER.

The son of Bennekheb, an Egyptian lady of the XIIth dynasty, who together with all her family was attached to the worship of the crocodile god Seb.

ANTENAU.

The Egyptian name of a people who were associated with the Tahennu in Upper Mesopotamia. *See* Tahennu, *and* Rotennu.

ANTEOPOLIS.

The Greek name for the city and nome in Upper Egypt, which was called by the Egyptians Sheshotep.

ANTHAQT.

The Egyptian name of an unidentified town.

ANTHEMUSIA.

A principal city on the great state North road from Babylon to the Euphrates.

ANTHMERTEN.

The Egyptian name of an unidentified town.

ANTI.

A peculiar kind of incense or gum which was procured from Arabia, it was indeed the chief article of commerce imported into Egypt from that country.

ANTI.

A nomadic people inhabiting the country between Kush and the Thebaid. They were also called the Petti on the Egyptian monuments.

ANTINOE.

A chief town in the Antinoite nome of Middle Egypt ; it was also called Besa. The Egyptian name was Dimast.

ANTINOITES.

An eighth nome which was added to the Heptanomos by the Emperor Hadrian. Its chief towns were, the Speos Artemidos, now called Beni Hassan famous for its early tombs, and Antinoe or Besa.

ANTIPHRA.

A Libyan city on the West of the Lake Mareotis.

ANTKHU.

The Egyptian name of an unidentified precious stone.

ANTNMU.

The Egyptian name of an unidentified town.

ANTU.

A mystical locality in Egyptian mythology.

ANTUI.

The Egyptian name of an unidentified district.

ANU.

In Assyrian mythology the first great deity of the upper triad, Anu, Elu or Bel, and Hea, or Heaven, Earth, and Hades. His residence was in the upper or seventh heaven, which was called the heaven of Anu, and was symbolized by an emblem resembling a Maltese cross, which was often worn round the necks of the Chaldean kings. As the god of heaven, he was called " The God of Heaven," "Anu the King, The Great God, The God of the World, The Chief of the Gods, and Father Anu." The Assyrians regarded him more in the light of the Zeus of the Greeks as a divine and benevolent personality. The Accadians, on the other hand, looked upon him simply as the Spirit or fetisch of Heaven, in which case he was called Anna, or still more simply Na. His wife Anu, or Anatu, was simply a feminine form of himself. She was the goddess of life and death, and the Anaitis of the Egyptians. *See* Anaitis. (Boscawen.)

ANU.

Another form of the name of the earliest inhabitants of the valley of the Nile. They are considered by some writers to have been the Annamim of the Hebrew authors.

ANUA.

A royal scribe and priest of Pthah at Memphis, in the XIXth dynasty.

ANUB.

A priestess of Amen, and the wife of the chief butler Aia, which see.

ANUBIS.

In Egyptian mythology the chief of the gods of the dead. He was called "The Son of the Cow" or of the goddess Nephthys, and he was generally represented as a jackal-headed man, or as a jackal resting upon the top of an open tomb, having a collar or ribbon round his neck, with a sceptre between his paws, and with the flabellum of the god Khem behind him. In this latter form he most frequently occurs on the funereal pectorals of the XIXth dynasty. He was, as the peculiar deity of the dead, the guardian of the mummied body, and the president of the embalmers; and as his office, like that of Horus, led him to drive away evil spirits from the deceased, he was also called like him, "The Conqueror of the Enemies of his Father Osiris." Anubis was also in some degree analogous to the Hermes Psychopompos of the Greek, inasmuch as he was the guardian of the way of life, and, together with Horus, escorted the souls to Hades. In the earlier papyri, and in the Ritual of the Dead, Anubis assumed several important characters; but his cultus gradually declined before the increase of that of Horus and Amen Ra, till after the XXVIth dynasty, when he appears to have been again regarded as a form of Horus, both as the avenger of Osiris and the justifier or redeemer of the dead. His name is more properly written according to the hieroglyphic system, Anpu or Anepu. The jackal was his sacred animal.

Anugas.

A city of the Rotennu between Egypt and the Euphrates. Site unknown.

Anuketmatma.

A daughter of King Sebekhotep II. of the XIIIth dynasty.

Anuktata.

A princess of Egypt. She was the daughter of Sebekhotep II. of the XIIIth dynasty, by his wife Anna.

Anunit.

A star which was identified by the Assyrians with the goddess Ishtar, the daughter of the Moon-god Sin.

Anunit.

An Assyrian or Chaldean goddess worshipped by the early monarchs. She has been supposed to have resembled the Venus of the Greeks. *See also* Anaitis.

Anup. "Anubis."

A city and nome in Upper Egypt, which was called by the Greeks Cynopolis. It was sacred to the worship of the deity Anubis.

Anupenkau.

The chief of the gates, secretary of the king, premier officer of the palace, and *smer* of an unnamed monarch of the Vth dynasty.

Anurta.

The Egyptian name of the river Orontes, in Upper Syria.

Anysis.

A nome in Egypt which, according to Herodotus, was held by the Calasirian class of warriors.

Anzan.

A province of the ancient empire of Elam. It was situated upon the Persian Gulf.

Ao.

An Assyrian deity called "The Intelligent Guide, the Lord of the Visible World, the Lord of Knowledge, Glory and Life." His most usual symbol was a serpent. In concert with the other great divinities the city of Dursharyakin (Khorsabad) was dedicated to Ao by Sargon II. *See also* Vul, and Hea.

Ao.

According to Wilkinson, the name of an uncertain Egyptian deity, sometimes called Moui. He was represented as a kingly figure with an upright feather on his head.

Aos.

In Greco-Babylonian mythology the son of Kissare and Assaros another third member of the first divine triad. By his wife Dauke he was the father of the demiurgus Bel.

Aouaa.

The form used by some Egyptologists for the name Iuaa, the father of Queen Taia.

Aoura.   *Or* Balot.

A beautiful valley in the Elysian Fields of the Egyptians, which had to be passed through by the deceased before his trial, by Osiris and the forty-two assessors.

Aoutou.

The Egyptian name of an unidentified Syrian city near Tyre, on the sea coast of Palestine.

Ap.

The Egyptian name of an Asiatic country which is not at present certainly identified.

Ap.

One of the Egyptian names of the Cynocephalus Baboon, which was sacred to the god Thoth. *See also* Aani.

Ap.

The Egyptian name of a pyramid or tomb generally.

Apa.

The father of Ameni the priest of Osiris, in the XIIth dynasty, which see.

Apa.   "Fly."

An Egyptian amulet, representing the flying scarabeus, an emblem of the Sun and of Pthah Sokari Osiris. It was often wrought in blue porcelain and attached to the coverings of mummies. These and also ring scarabæi are first found on the little fingers of mummies prepared at the time of the XIIIth dynasty. At the time of the XVIIIth and subsequent dynasties they came into occasional use for mummies of important and rich persons. This custom prevailed through the subsequent dynasty, was more common at the time of the XXVIth, and became universal in the time of the Ptolemies. Some of the amulets exhibit high polish and finish but the Egyptians appear to have experienced considerable difficulty in engraving minute hieroglyphics on hard stone. Various materials were employed, such as green jasper, felspar, serpentine, basalt, schist, and a dark soapstone or steatite. The Apa are of larger size than the scarabæi used for finger-rings or other personal adornment, and are sometimes three or more inches in length. The inscription on these amulets is one of the chapters relating to the heart, found at the end of the LXIVth chapter of the Ritual, and the formula was ascribed to different periods, as that of Heshetp, or Usaphais, a king of the Ist dynasty, and the period of Menkara, a monarch of the IVth dynasty. It was supposed to have been written by the finger of the god Thoth himself on a brick of glazed earth, sandstone, or some other material in blue letters, and to have been found by the prince Hartataf, on a tour made by him, to examine the temples. This inscription was considered only fit for the chaste and pure, and the scarabæus on which it was inscribed was placed over the heart; it was dipped in some essence, and the chapter repeated over it. The object of the charm was to preserve the heart, in which the soul was supposed to reside after death, from destruction or decay. The scarabæus itself also indicated the idea of self-existence, or the changes or phases or transformations, through which the soul passed in the future state. The name of the person for whose mummy the Apa were made is generally, but not always, inscribed in the text. (Birch.)

APA. *Surnamed* KHUT HOTEP.

A sacred scribe and priest of Pthah. Period uncertain.

APA.

The father of a private Egyptian of the family of Senbeb, which see.

APACHNAS.

According to the Greek lists an early Egyptian king of Bubastis. He has not yet been certainly identified.

APANDA.

King of the Medes. He reigned, at first jointly with his father Astyages, and afterwards alone, for thirty years.

APANT.

A city in Egypt. It was one of the chief places where Sebek, the crocodile deity was worshipped.

APAP.

The simpler form of the name of the evil serpent Apophis, which see.

APAP.

An Egyptian officer, the father of the priest gardener Sarenen, of the XVIIIth or XIXth dynasties. *See* Sarenen.

APASON.

In Greco-Babylonian mythology the son of Sige, the primitive mother and father of the gods by his wife Jauthe. Apason was derived from the Accadian Apsu " the deep," which see.

APASTATAUK.

The king of Vila, a district bordering upon Assyria. It was invaded and rendered tributary to Nineveh by Samsivul or Samas Rimmon III.

APATIMILIKU.

The Kypriote form of the personal name Abdamelek, which see.

APEIUM.

The name of the great temple at Memphis, where the sacred living bull Apis was enshrined and worshipped.

APENTEK.

The Egyptian name of an unidentified Asiatic country.

APEPI I.

A king of the Hykshos dynasty, of whose reign no particulars are known.

APEPI II.

A king of the Hykshos dynasty, under whose government the patriarch Joseph is, by the larger number of Egyptologists, believed to have entered Egypt. He was a wise and politic king, and his court was almost entirely Egyptian. Towards the close of his reign he by force introduced the sole worship of the Syrian deity Set or Sutech, and commanded Tiakken or Raskenen Takuna, king of Thebes, one of his vassals, to set an example of adoration. This the native Egyptian king refused to do and a war of resentment was the consequence, a war which continued during the life of Apepi, and ended in the expulsion of the Shepherds and the restoration of the old dynasties. A beautiful bust of this monarch has been recently found in making the excavations for the Suez Canal, and it is now the chief ornament of the Boulaq Museum. Apepi was the Apophis of the Greeks.

APER.

An unidentified town in one of the Saitic nomes of Lower Egypt.

APERHEB.

Among the Egyptians, the name of the festival of the twenty-first day of the lunar month.

APERIU. *Or* ABERIU.

A captive people who were employed by Rameses II. of the XIXth dynasty, in the construction of his great city, Pa Ramessu, or Tanis, near Heliopolis. They were at one time considered to have been the Israelites in bondage; but inasmuch as the same people were also employed by Thothmes III. of the XVIIIth dynasty in the erection of his great buildings at Thebes, that identification has been generally abandoned.

APERU.

An Hieratic order in the Egyptian temples, analogous to that of the novices in Catholic convents.

APET.

An Egyptian goddess who was represented under the form of an upright hippopotamus with long pendant breasts, generally leaning upon a peculiar cross-like instrument, which has been regarded as a sign of protection. She appears to have been substituted for the goddess Maut in the lower times of the empire, and her titles were " The good Nurse," " The Great One who bears the Gods," " The Great Mother of him who is married to his Mother," *i.e.*, the Ithyphallic Horus. She was also under the title of " The great Ta Ouer " or Thoueris, represented as an avenging deity, having a lion's head and armed with a long straight knife, in which character she was called " The Nourisher of those who approach to the flames (of hell)." *See also* Thoeris. (Pierret.)

APHERU. " Guide of the Roads."

In Egyptian mythology a name of the divine jackal Anubis. He worshipped in the city and nome of Chesfchent.

APHERUMES. "Son of the god Apheru."

An Egyptian functionary. The period when he lived is uncertain.

APHERUMES.

An Egyptian king of the XIIIth dynasty, of whom nothing further is known.

APHOBIS.

According to Mr. Heath another form of the name of the early Egyptian writer called Pthah Hotep, or Pthah-ases, which see.

APHRODISIA.

A petty kingdom in the Island of Kypros or Cyprus, which paid tribute to Esarhaddon.

APHRODITOPOLIS. " City of Aphrodite, *or* Venus."

The Greek name for the city and nome in the Fayum or Upper Egypt, which was called by the Egyptians Tsets, and Chev. It was sacred to the worship of the goddess Hathor.

APHRODITOPOLIS.

Also the Greek name of the city and nome of Sebets, in Upper Egypt.

APHTHIS.

A nome in Egypt, which according to Herodotus was held by the Calasirian class of warriors.

API.

A son (?) of Amenemap, a priest of Amen Ra, of the XVIIIth dynasty.

APIA. " Earth."

According to Herodotus, the name of a Scythian deity, answering to the Tellus of the Greeks.

APIKANT.

One of the early Egyptian names of the town of Athribis.

APINAMA. " The Bull-like Founder."

The Accadian name of the month Arakh-samna, which see.

APINANA. " Foundation."

In Chaldean astronomy the name of an unidentified fixed star.

APIRAK.

An early Babylonian city, the site of which is not known; it was possibly the same as Karrak or Nisinna.

APIS. Or HAPI.

The bull deity of Memphis, in Lower Egypt, an incarnation of Pthah the creative deity. He was said to have been born of a cow, which was impregnated by a stroke of lightning from heaven. He was black in colour, with a white mark on his forehead, a mark like a half-moon on the back, and a lump of flesh in the form of a scarabeus under his tongue. He was only allowed to reign for twenty-five years, when he was drowned in a cistern. The temple where he was worshipped in great splendour was the Apeium, and that excavated to contain the sarcophagi of defunct Api was called the Serapeum. This latter temple has been discovered in recent years ; and a series of tablets of the priests of Apis have been found therein, ascending from the period of the XVIIIth dynasty to the time of the Ptolemies, and thus a very important series of data for the construction of Egyptian history has been obtained. When worshipped during life he was venerated as Hapi Ankh, " the living Apis," and when adored as a divinity after death, he was called Hapi Osiri or Ser-Apis, the Osirian (dead) Apis.

APIS.

A chief town of the first Mareotic nome of Lower Egypt. It was also called Taposiris.

APITUS. " She who is on the Hill."

An Egyptian goddess who was worshipped in the city of Tuaa, in the Oxyrhynchite or eighteenth nome on the Western side of the Nile in Middle Egypt.

APMATENU.

An Egyptian deity, who was generally represented with a jackal's head and holding the *Uas* or Cucufa staff, the emblem of a divine life. He was another form of the deity Apheru.

APOLLINOPOLIS.

The second nome of the Thebaid in Upper Egypt, its ancient name was Teshor, and its chief city was Teb, now called Edfou. It was sacred to the god Horus, " the rising sun." The nome is now called by the Arabs, Qoos.

Apollonius.

A Greek name which seems to have taken the place of that of Horus as a proper name in the latest periods of Egyptian history. (De Rougé.)

Apophis.

The Greek form of the royal name Apepi, the last of the Hykshos kings of Egypt, which see.

Apophis.

In Egyptian mythology the name of the great serpent of evil inhabiting the lower world, whose office it was to seduce the souls of the deceased into error or forgetfulness as they crossed the waters of the infernal Nile, on their way to the Kerneter or Egyptian paradise. To protect the souls of the justified from this terrible enemy, they were accompanied by the deity Horus, and strengthened by the goddess Nut with the water of life and heavenly food. The terrible ordeal once passed, and the soul of the deceased acquitted by the Osiris and the forty-two assessors in the Hall of the Two Truths, they afterwards assisted the benevolent Horus to fight against and conquer the serpent enemy, who was then brought captive to the throne of Ra, the Sun deity, tortured with knives, bound with ropes, and eventually slain. *See also* Horus, and Ra.

Apra.

A Syrian town, mentioned in the Egyptian papyri. It is supposed by some to have been the Ophrah of Hebrew history.

Apries.

The Greek form of the Egyptian royal name Uahprahet, the Hophra of the Jewish writers, which see.

Apro.

The name of an Egyptian funereal ceremony, called the "Opening of the Mouth."

Apronadius.

The Greek form of the Assyrian royal name Assurnadinmu, which see.

Aps.

The Egyptian name of an unidentified district in the Soudan in Upper Egypt.

Apsaras.

In Hindu mythology a number of heavenly virgins, 600,000,000 in all, whose office it was to solace the gods and the souls of departed men.

Apsu.   "The deep."

The Accadian word from which the name of the Greco-Babylonian deity Apason was derived.

APT.

The Egyptian name of the hippopotamus.

APT.

The Egyptian sacred name of the city of Thebes, whence the title of Amen Ra, Amenenapt or "Amen who is in the Apt," *i.e.* Thebes.

APTA.   "The Horn of the World."

The Egyptian name of the Southern extremity of the world.   The idea intended to be conveyed is similar to that in the names of Capes Finisterre and Lands End.

APTERA.   "Guide of the Road."

A name of the god Anubis, as conductor of the souls on the road to the lower world, and under which title he was worshipped in Thebes.   *See also* Anepu.

APTMER.

An unidentified Egyptian city, which was vainly held by the rebel chiefs against Piankhi Meramon of the XXVIth dynasty.

APTU.

An old Egyptian name of the city of Thebes.   It is merely another inflection of the sacred name Apt.

APU.

The son of an Egyptian king, but of what king it is not known.

APU.

The wife of Sennofre, and the mother of Bekenamun, a royal scribe and state officer of one of the kings of the XVIIIth dynasty.

APU.

The wife of Uetu, the chief of the Keneb.   *See* Uetu.

APU.

An Egyptian lady, the mother of Penteni the priest of Anhur, and wife of Tatai who was a priest of Anhur likewise.

APUI.

The son of the royal officer Piai, of the XVIIIth dynasty.   He was more generally called by his surname Amenemap.

APUTA.   *Or* AKUPTA.

The Egyptian name of an unidentified town in Palestine.

AQ.

The *mer* or reservoir, of the fourth, or Saite nome, of Lower Egypt.   It was anciently called Sai-Res, and was sacred to the worship of the goddess Neith.

AQAUASA.

The Egytian name of the town and country of Achaia.

AQER.

One of the mystical serpents of Egyptian mythology.

AR.

An Egyptian land measure or square. It was another form of the Aroura.

ARA.

The wife of Thothmes IV. of the XVIIIth dynasty.

ARABIAN NOME.

The name applied by the Greeks to the city and nome of Sept Achem, the twentieth nome of Lower Egypt. Its chief town was Phacusa East of the Nile. The deities specially worshipped there were Horus under the figure of a sitting hawk with two upright plumes on his head, and the goddess Sekhet under the name of Soupt Sekhet. *See also* Soupt.

ARACHOSIA.

A great city on the Southern road from Babylon to India. It was more famous in early mediæval than in Archaic history.

ARACHOTIA.

A rich district of Persia, which was bravely held for Darius Hystaspes by the Satrap Vibanus.

ARADUS.

See Areta.

ARAKH-MAKRU.   "The Incidental Month."

The intercalary month of the Assyrian year. It was sacred to the deity Assur, and was called by the Accadians Sedir, "Dark (Month) of Sowing." It was the Ve Adar of the Jews.

ARAKH-SAMNA.   "The Eighth Month."

The eighth month of the Assyrian year. It was sacred to the god Marduk, and was called by the Accadians Apinama, "The Bull-like Founder." It answered roughly to our October.

ARAKHTU.

The Assyrian name of the river Araxes, a confluent of the Euphrates. It was called by the Accadians Gukhande. It runs in a deep valley towards Arabia, and is conjectured to have been the Gihon of the Hebrew writers which compassed the whole land of Cush.

ARAKHU.

A Babylonian prince, the son of Haldita. He claimed himself to have been Nabukuduruzur, the son of Nabonahid, and revolted against Darius Hystaspes, by whose general, Intaphres, he was defeated, and the city of Babylon again taken by assault.

ARAM.

A king of Ararat, who was conquered, together with his people, by Shalmaneser II.

ARANA.

The Egyptian name of the district in Palestine which was called Eglon by the Hebrew writers.

ARASTI.

The chief of the city of Ammali, near the river Turnat, or Tornadotus. He was conquered by Assurnazirpal.

ARAT.

A consort of Thothmes IV. of the XVIIIth dynasty.

ARATTU.

A Syrian town, which was conquered by Thothmes III. of the XVIIIth dynasty.

ARAUTA.

The *Mer* of the twelfth, or Ka-she nome of Lower Egypt.

ARAZIAS.

A kingdom in Media, where Munirzuarta its chief, and 1070 of his warriors were slain by Samsivul or Samas Rimmon III.

ARBACES.

A Median chief, who combined with the Susianian chiefs to overthrow Nineveh in the reign of Assuracus. He was successful in his revolt, and established a republic in Media, over which he was the chief governor for twenty-eight years. He was succeeded by Mandauces. (Lenormant.)

ARBACHA.

A city or district of which Assurituduri was prefect under Tiglath Pileser I. and Sargon II.

ARBAHA.

A city in the South of Assyria, which supported Assurdainpal in his revolt against his father, Shalmaneser II.

ARBAKI.

A city (in Mesopotamia?) which was conquered, together with 250 other towns subjacent, by Assurnazirpal.

ARBASTUTANIF.

A daughter of King Takelothis I. of the XXIInd dynasty.

ARBASUTANIFU.

A daughter of King Amenrut, of the XXVIIIth dynasty.

ARBELA.

A chief city in the mountains East of Assyria, which was famous for being the favourite residence of the goddess Ishtar, and was often re-built by the Assyrian monarchs. *See* Ishtar.

ARBELUS.

The form in which the name of the city of Arbela is preserved as that of a king in the history of Moses of Khorene.

ARCHANDRON.

A chief city in the Hermopolite, or the fifteenth nome, of Upper Egypt.

ARCHENANUS.

A Greek name in the canon of Ptolemy, which is supposed to have been a corrupted form of that of Sargon II.

ARDARA.

A king of the country of the Ustassai, who paid tribute to Samas Rimmon, or Samsivul III., king of Assyria.

ARDASARI.

The king of Surdira, a district East of Assyria, which was conquered by Dayan-Assur the Tartan of Shalmaneser II.

ARDATES.

According to Berosus the Greek name of the father of the hero of the Flood. *See* Ubaratatu.

ARDORACH of Sippara.

According to Berosus the seventh andediluvian king of Babylon. *See* Enedareschus.

ARDSHIR.

A Persian form of the royal name Artaxerxes, which see.

ARDUSIN.

An early king of Babylonia, the son of Kudur Mabuk, under whom he reigned as Viceroy in Babylonia. He erected a great wall around the city of Ur to prevent the invasions of the nomadic tribes, and built several temples to the Babylonian divinities. His name is now read as Eri Agu, or Rim-Agu.

ARDYS.

Son of Gyges, king of Lydia. He presented his submission to Assur-banipal, king of Assyria, who confirmed him on the throne of his father.

AREOS. *Or* ARSU.

Another form of the name of the Syrian rebel Arsu or Aarsu, who introduced monotheism into Egypt at the death of King Sipthah of the XIXth dynasty. He reduced the gods to the condition of men, and no more offerings were made in their temples. His insurrection was put an end to by Seti-Nekht, the father of Rameses III.

ARERETH.

The Egyptian name of an unidentified people on the Upper Nile.

Areta.

The Egyptian name of a country which was conquered by Thothmes III. It was probably the land of Aradus.

Argana.

A city of Hamath, which was conquered by Shalmaneser II.

Argisteus.   *Or* Aegisteus.

King of Idalion, in the Island of Kypros or Cyprus.   He was one of the tributaries of Esarhaddon.

Argistis.

King of Ararat, the son of Minua, king of Ararat or Armenia.   He induced Mutallu, king of Kummutha or Commagene, to revolt against Sargon II., but when the Assyrians approached he deserted both his friend and his kingdom, and fled from his country, which was ravaged and annexed by the Assyrians.   Recovering from this defeat he greatly enlarged the kingdom, even in turn invading Assyria for that purpose. This led to a long war with Shalmaneser III., who compelled him to retire into the mountains as a tributary, after a conflict extending over eight years.

Arhall.

The Egyptian name of an unidentified Asiatic country.

Ari.

An Egyptian title, meaning properly Guardian, but sometimes rendered on the funereal inscriptions, " Companion " or " Citizen."

Ari.

The Egyptian name of the country of Arya, or Bactria, the sacred home of the Aryan races.

Aria.

A Greco-Egyptian priestess, the daughter of Diogenes.   She was a Kanephorus of the goddess Arsinoe Philadelphus, the daughter of Ptolemy Philadelphus, who was worshipped at Memphis, in the reign of Ptolemy V.

Aria.

The Greek name of the district in Persia called Karoyu, which see.

Ariazantus.   " Men of Aryan Race."

The second great caste of the Medes, the Arizanti of the Greek historians.

Ariba.

The first and most ancient inhabitants of Arabia.   They were divided into two great families or nations, the Adites and the Amalika.   The first were a Hamitic, and the second a Semitic, people.

ARIEL. *Or* ERILI.

King of Soli, in the Island of Kypros. He was one of the many Grecian tributaries of Esarhaddon.

ARIENKHUT.

A royal officer and priest of Osiris, and *Smer* of the palace of an early unnamed king of Egypt, probably of the time of the XIth or XIIth dynasty.

ARIHEB.

The Egyptian name of an unidentified town, which is supposed to have been the Pharbœtus of the Greek writers.

ARIL.

The name of an Etruscan deity, who bears the heavens on his shoulders. His analogue was the Atlas of Greek mythology.

ARIMA. *Or* ARIMAI.

A country near Media, bordering upon Assyria, which was rendered tributary by Samsivul or Samas-Rimmon III.

ARIOCH.

An early Palestinian king of Ellassar, who fought with the king of Sodom. His name has not yet been found upon the monuments, unless it is non-Semitic; it appears to be the same as Eriacu, "Servant of Acu," the Moon-god. Arioch was at one time supposed to have been the same as Urukh, the early monarch of Babylonia, which see.

ARIRANTESF.

An uncertain Egyptian deity, who was worshipped in the Greek period.

ARIRGI.

A district to the North of Assyria, which was conquered by Tiglath Pileser I.

ARISE.

The Egyptian name of an unidentified town.

ARISTAGORON.

A Kypriote functionary, who is mentioned in a votive inscription to the god Pandoseris, in behalf of his son, in the Cesnola collection.

ARIT.

An Egyptian constellation, one star in which has been thought to have been β Andromedæ. (Renouf.)

ARIU.

The seventeenth or Cynopolite nome of Upper Egypt. Its ancient name was Samhut, and its chief city was sacred to the worship of the dog-headed god Anubis, whence the Greek name of the nome was derived.

ARIURU.

An Egyptian feminine name commonly used under the Saitic or the XXVIth and XXVIIIth dynasties.

ARIZAGI.

A city in Syria, which was conquered by Tiglath Pileser I.

ARIZANTI.

The Greek form of the Median name Ariazantus, which see.

ARKAM.

A later group of Amalekite tribes who settled in Tayma and the Eastern part of Arabia Patrea. They were expelled from Arabia by the Jorhamite tribes.

ARKAM.

The official title of the kings of the Arkam, a tribe of the Amalekites.

ARKAMUN.

An Ethiopian king. He lived in the reign of Ptolemy Philadelphus, and was the Ergamenes of the Greeks. The sanctuary at Dakkeh in Nubia was constructed by him.

ARKEBEMRO.

The Egyptian name of the city of Heraclea.

ARKENKHEREL.

The name of an unidentified Ethiopian king, probably of a very late period.

ARKHATE.

An Etruscan divinity, who was represented as an old bald-headed man in a cloak, who warns Famu against the blandishments of the goddess Alpanu.

ARM.

A people of the South of Egypt, who were conquered by Rameses II. of the XIXth dynasty.

ARMA.

A city in Upper Egypt. Site unknown.

ARMA.

The Egyptian name of the town of Elymais.

ARMÆUS.

The name erroneously given by Diodorus Siculus, and the Greek authors, to the king of Egypt by whom the great pyramid was erected. *See also* Cheops, Chufu, and Chemmis.

ARMANNU.

A deity of the Susians, of whom nothing is known. It may have been the secret name of the god Susinak, which see.

ARMATHEN.

The Egyptian name of an unidentified Asiatic country.

ARMENIA.

A kingdom in Asia which was repeatedly attacked by the Assyrians, more especially under Shalmaneser II. *See* Veduri.

ARMPAKH.

The Egyptian name of an unidentified district which is supposed to have been situated in Palestine.

ARNAFGESF.

The mystical name of one of the planks of the Boat of Souls in the XCIXth chapter of the Ritual of the Dead.

ARNEBASKENIS.

Probably a Greek form of the name of Aroeris the elder Horus.

ARNUTHA.

Another Egyptian name of the river Orontes in Northern Syria.

AROER.

A city in Palestine which was called by the Assyrians Qarqar.

AROERIS.

The Greek form of the name of Harsiesi or Arnebaskenis, the elder Horus.

ARP.

The Egyptian name of the country which was called Arupe by the Greek writers.

ARP.

The general name of wine among the ancient Egyptians.

ARPAD.

A city near Damascus, of which Zazai was the archon under Sennacherib.

ARPAESIS.

A goose feeder of Elephantine, in the reign of the Emperor Trajan, A.D. 116. His name was the old Egyptian Harseisis.

ARPARPHESEP.

The Egyptian name of the city and nome of Takens.

ARPHAXAD.   " Border of the Chaldees."

A people dwelling near to Chaldea, from whom the Hebrews were in later times descended.

ARRAFA.

The name of the female diviners of the ancient Arabians of the North of the Peninsula. They belonged to a distinct tribe and held their office by hereditary succession, and they possessed the guardianship and right of service of various local temples. The male diviners were called Kahiu, which see.

ARRAT.

An Assyrian measure of capacity, eight of which went to the *log*, which see.

ARREX.

The Egyptian name of the city of Edessa, in Mesopotamia. It was reputed to have been founded by Nimrod, and was famous for its theological school in the fifth century, A.D. It is now called Orfat by the Arabs.

ARRPAKH.

The Egyptian name of the district of Arrapachitis.

ARS.

The name of a mystical personage who is mentioned in the CIIInd chapter of the Ritual of the Dead.

ARSA.

The Egyptian name of an Asiatic country or town, which is supposed by some writers to have been the city of Assur in Assyria.

ARSACES.

A noble Parthian, who revolted against Antiochus Theus, king of Syria, whose troops he defeated, B.C. 254, and afterwards making himself king of Parthia, established the dynasty of the Arsacidæ. He reigned for four years, and died B.C. 248. He was succeeded by Tiridates or Arsaces II., who carried on the wars with the Seleucidan kings, who at last recognised the empire of Parthia as an independent state, in the reign of Artabanus I., or as he was more generally called Arsaces III. The dynasty continued till the death of Artabanus IV. or Arsaces XXVIII., the last of the line, in battle with Artaxerxes or Ardashir I., the founder of the Sassanian monarchy. (Haydn.)

ARSAPHES.

The Greek form of Harscheft, a surname of Osiris.

ARSES.

A governor of Egypt after the Persian conquest. Little is known from the monuments respecting him.

ARSES.

An early king of Persia. He was made king by the great general Bagoas, who then revolted against him and assassinated him, placing Darius Codomanus on the throne, B.C. 336.

ARSHADA.

A city of Arachosia, where Vibanus, the satrap of the country under Darius Hystaspes, put to death the chiefs of the army sent against him by Veisdates the rebel king.

ARSINOE.

A daughter of King Ptolemy Neus Dionysius, and the sister of Queen Cleopatra, by whose orders she was assassinated, B.C. 41.

ARSINOE PHILADELPHOS.

A daughter of Ptolemy Soter, and the sister of Ptolemy Philadelphus. She was adored as a goddess at Memphis under Ptolemy V.

ARSINOE PHILOPATOR.

The sister of Ptolemy Philopator, and the daughter of Ptolemy Euergetes I. She was adored as a goddess at Memphis, under Ptolemy V.

ARSINOIS.   Upper and Lower.

The Greek name for the cities and nomes in Upper Egypt, which were called by the Egyptians Neha-chent, sacred to the god Sebek, and Neha Pehu, sacred to the goddess Hathor respectively. (Lenormant.)

ARSINOITES.

A province of Lower Egypt, anciently called Tashe, " Country of the Lake," on account of its containing the great lake and pyramids of Mœris and his queen. Its principal town was Crocodilopolis, and was sacred to the crocodile-headed deity Sebek. Arsinoites was probably the twenty-first nome of Lower Egypt. *See also* Amenemha. (Pierret.)

ARSIYANIS.

A mountain district of Minni, which was ravaged by Assurbanipal after the fall of Akhsera, the king of the country.

ARSU.   *Or* AREOS.

The name of a great Syrian chief who invaded the Delta of Egypt during the disputes between the successors of Merenpthah I. He overthrew the established religion of the country, degraded the deities to the condition of mere men, connected the commerce of Egypt, and loosening the bands of allegiance set all the nation in revolt. After some years of anarchy, he was dethroned by the tact and bravery of Prince Seti-Nekht, who aided by the native clergy expelled the Syrians, reversed their alterations, and restored the kingdom to order and prosperity.

ART.

The name of a district in Thebes which included the temples of Karnak and the Ramasseion.

ARTABARDES.

A general of Darius Hystaspes, by whom he was sent to subdue the revolt of Veisdates, the pseudo Bardes, whom he twice defeated and then sent captive to his master, who had the rebel king impaled at Chadidia. *See also* Vahyazdata.

ARTÆUS.

According to Ctesias, a king of the Medes. He succeeded Abianes, and reigned forty years.

ARTAMES.

A Perso-Egyptian court official in Egypt during the reign of Xerxes king of Egypt and Persia.

ARTASIRARI.

A king of a district in Nahri, who paid tribute to Samas Rimmon, king of Assyria.

ARTAXERXES I. LONGMANUS.

King of Persia upon the assassination of his predecessor, Artabanus, B.C. 465. He has been supposed to have been the Ahasuerus of the Hebrew writers. His name occurs several times in the Hieroglyphic inscriptions of Egypt, but his real place is in Classic history.

ARTEMIDOS, SPEOS.

See Speos Artemidos, and Antinoites.

ARTEMISIA.

The wife of her brother Mausolus, and queen of Caria, in Asia Minor. She reigned with great prudence, and upon the death of her husband she erected a splendid pyramidal tomb over his remains, calling it after his name a Mausoleum, B.C. 352. The building was for many years one of the so-called seven wonders of the world, and its ruins are now in the British Museum, together with the statues of Artemisia and Mausolus which adorned the entrance. The Mausoleum has since become remarkable from the circumstance that an alabaster vase, having the name of Xerxes engraved upon it in Cuneiform characters, was found among the debris a few years ago.

ARTEMISIUM.   " Temple of Artemis, *i.e.* Diana."

The scene of a great naval battle between the Greeks and the Persians, under Xerxes, B.C. 480, where the Egyptian sailors and ships conducted themselves with great bravery.

ARTICARMIN.   *Or* ARTUKAS.

King of the Medes. He succeeded Sasarmin or Sosarmus, and reigned thirty years according to Ctesias, but fifty according to the results of recent scholars.

ARTIHOR.

The *Uu* of the tenth, or Aphroditopolite nome, of Upper Egypt.

ARTIMER.

A place in the eleventh nome, or nome of Kashebs, of Lower Egypt.

ARTIMPASA.   " The Noble Lady."

According to Herodotus, the name of a Scythian goddess answering to the heavenly Venus of the Greeks.

Artines.

King of the Medes. He succeeded Artæus, and reigned twenty-two years. (Ctesias.)

Artinu.

The Egyptian name of an unidentified Asiatic country.

Artu.

The Egyptian name of the town of Aradus in Palestine.

Aru.

An Assyrian measure of capacity, nine of which went to the *log*, which see.

Arua.

A king of the country of Cindutausi, who paid tribute to Samas Rimmon.

Aruhaba.

A mystical region mentioned in some copies of the CLXIVth or extra chapter of the Ritual of the Dead.

Arum.   *Or* Aram.

The son of Agus, a petty Syrian chief who was conquered by Shalmaneser II.

Aruna.

The Egyptian name of an unidentified district, which is supposed by some writers to have been the Mœonia or Ilion.

Arunata.

The Egyptian name of the river Orontes in Northern Syria.

Arunr.

The Egyptian name of an unidentified town in Palestine.

Arusias.

A city of Minni, which was destroyed by Assurbanipal, king of Assyria, after the defeat of its king, Ahsera.

Arutaikasataika.

A mystical title of Amen Ra, in the CLXVIth chapter of the Ritual of the Dead.

Arvanel.

In Zendic mythology the sacred river from which the first created human beings drank.

Arwakr.   " Wakeful."

In Scandinavian mythology the name of one of the two horses of the sun.

Aryaman.

The Aryan name of the Supreme Being.

Aryandes.

The Persian Viceroy of Egypt under Darius Hystaspes.   He was put to death by his master on a suspicion of high treason.

Aryanem Vaēdjo.

In Iranian mythology the name of the original birthplace of the human race.

Aryaratha.

According to the consensus of Japhetic traditions, the name of the birth-place of mankind.

Arza.

A small town between Egypt and Palestine on the river of Egypt, which was conquered by Esarhaddon and annexed to Assyria.

Arzania.

A river of Armenia, near to which Seduri, king of Armenia, was utterly defeated by Dayan Assur, the Tartan of Shalmaneser II.

Arzanibu.

A Mesopotamian people who were conquered by Tiglath Pileser I.

Arzuhina.

A Babylonian city where for a time Maruduknadinahi, or Merodach-iddin-akhi, was defeated by Tugulti Palesar I., king of Assyria.

As.

The literal reading of the Hieroglyphic name of the goddess Isis.

As.   "Isis."

A daughter of Amenhotep III. of the XVIIIth dynasty.

As.

The Egyptian name of an unknown town which is mentioned as existing in the reign of King Cheops, of the IVth dynasty.

As.

A daughter of Rameses VI. of the XXth dynasty.

Asa.

An Egyptian officer of the VIth dynasty, who was priest of Bast, priest of the Pyramid of Tat Asu the tomb of King Teta, royal scribe, keeper of the treasury, and *Smer*, and *Heb*, of the reigning monarch, whose name is unknown.

ASA.

The grandson of Rehoboam, king of Judah. He formed an unsuccessful league with Benhadad, king of Syria, B.C. 940. *See* Azechamen and Uaserken I.

AS-AAN. " Abundance of Rain."

The Accadian name of the eleventh month Sabadhu or Sebat, which see. It answered roughly to our January.

ASAFAI.

An idol in the form of a man, which was erected in the place of a sacred stone or Bœtylia on the hill of Safa, near Mecca, about A.D. 300.

ASANI.

A district in South-east Assyria, which was conquered by Tiglath Pileser I.

ASARDIN.

According to the old chronologers, a king of Babylon, who reigned about B.C. 680. He was probably the same as the rebel king Assurdayan, which see.

ASATAI.

A people who were rendered tributary by Samas Rimmon king of Assyria.

ASB.

A mystical divinity. He is called the brother of Isis and Osiris in the LXIXth chapter of the Ritual of the Dead.

ASB.

Another form of the name of the town of Haasb, which see.

ASCHSEPSEN.

A devotee of Apis. He was the son of Pemeskhemet, in the reign of Amasis II. of the XXXIst dynasty.

ASEI.

See Uashesha.

ASEIOHIAMENTI.

An Egyptian priest, and the auditor of an unnamed divinity. The period when he lived is uncertain.

ASEN.

In Scandinavian mythology the name of the benevolent, or good deities.

ASENHEIM.

In Scandinavian mythology the name of the heavenly region where the gods resided ; its principal city was Asgard, which was supposed to have been the centre of the world.

ASENNU.

A private Egyptian gentleman, in the time of the XVIIIth dynasty. *See* Tutu.

ASER.   *Or* ASEZ.

The sea or lake of the eighteenth nome, or nome of Chrud-chen, of Lower Egypt.

ASERA.

The title of an Etruscan goddess, who is armed with a hatchet. *Aisera* occurs in Etruscan inscriptions; and *Æsar*, according to Suetonius meant "a god."

ASERYMUS.

One of the many usurpers who occupied the throne of Tyre after the murder of Abdashtoreth, the last of the house of Hiram.

ASES.

The Egyptian name of an unidentified town.

ASESA.

The second king of the VIIth Egyptian dynasty.

ASESKAF.

An Egyptian king of the IVth dynasty. He was the immediate successor of Menkara, and was the Asychis of Manetho.

ASESKAFANKH.

A great functionary in the reign of an early king of Egypt in one of the first six dynasties. His tomb is one of the most important of all which are excavated in the great Pyramid Hill.

ASESKARA.

An Egyptian king of the Vth dynasty.

ASGARD.

In Scandinavian mythology the name of the capital city of Asenheim, the dwelling-place of the gods. It was supposed to have been situated in the centre of the world, and to contain golden palaces with gates of precious stones. The central part of the city was called Gladsheim.

ASGUZA.

A petty kingdom near Media, which was subjugated by Esarhaddon, king of Assyria.

ASHARIAH.

The son of Tabeal, an obscure pretender to the crown of Judah, put forward by Rezin of Damascus and his allies, in opposition to Ahaz. He was utterly defeated, together with his adherents, by Tiglath Pileser II. He was called in Hebrew history, "The Son of Tabeal" only, his true name is preserved in the Cuneiform inscriptions. This name rests solely on the reading of Dr. Oppert, whose views are much controverted.

ASHDOD.

A great town in Philistia, which was frequently the chief of a revolt against the kings of Egypt and Assyria, by one of the latter of whom it was completely conquered. *See* Akhimit.

ASHER.

The Egyptian name of the fruit of the Heglyg tree.

ASHERRU.

A mystical abode of the gods in the Ritual of the Dead.

ASHMUNAZEER.

Another form of the Phenician royal name Eshmonazer, which see.

ASHTARCHEMOSH.

A deity of the Moabites, probably a female or Androgynous form of the god Chemosh.

ASI.

The Egyptian name of a country in Palestine, to the North of Aradus, between the Orontes and the sea. It was rendered tributary to Egypt by Thothmes III. in his fortieth year.

ASIA.

The king of Dayeni, near the Euphrates. He submitted to Shalmaneser, king of Assyria.

ASK.　　"Oak."

In Scandinavian mythology the name of the first men created out of the trees growing by the seashore. *See also* Ymir.

ASKH.

A splendidly jewelled and enamelled golden collar, or torque, which was often bestowed by the Egyptian kings upon their officers as the reward of personal valour in war.

ASLU.

An Assyrian measure of length, and the name of the six double hours into which the day and night were respectively divided. *See* Casbu.

ASMATARTA.

A wife of Rameses III. of the XIXth dynasty.

ASMIR.

The Egyptian name of a precious stone which is at present unidentified. It has been conjectured by some writers to have been the emerald, and by others, corundum, or emery.

ASMUN.

A Chaldean city on the Persian Gulf. It was called by the Accadians Nitukki.

ASNAPPAR.

An Assyrian royal name, so written by the Hebrew historians. It is supposed to have been the same as Assurbanipal.

ASNEFER.

The Egyptian name of a town which is at present unidentified.

ASNOFRE.

The wife of Menepthah I. of the XIXth dynasty.

ASNOFRE.   "The Good Isis."

A daughter of Rameses II. of the XIXth dynasty.

ASNOFRE.

A wife of Rameses II. of the XIXth dynasty.

ASNUNNAK.

A country colonised by Agu-kak-rimi, an early Kassite king of Babylonia.   Its locality is not known.

ASOKA.

A famous king of Maghada, in Lower India.   He was the grandson of Chandragupta or Sandracottus, and was early converted by the disciples of Sakya Munya to the religion of Buddha, which he formally adopted as the national faith at the great council of Palibothra, about B.C. 250, sending his brother Mahindo and his sister Sangamitta to convert the Ceylonese. Later on in his reign he issued a series of political edicts, which he had engraved upon the sides of several great *Lats* or pillars, from the Jumna to the Ganges, and from Cuttack to Guzerat.   These inscriptions are the first dated monuments in Indian history, and they are remarkable for the sanctity with which they invest every species of life, even to that of the vegetable creation. The grandest architectural remains of the Buddhist period date from his reign, which also marked an era in Indian chronology.

ASOR.

In Hindu mythology the name of a race of evil spirits, who are always addicted to sorcery.

ASOVAHISTO.   "The Pure Better One."

In Zendic mythology the second of the heavenly Amshaspands, which see.

ASPALUT.

A king of Egypt, in the Ethiopian period, or the XXVth dynasty. Nothing is certainly known concerning him.

ASPASTATAUK.

A king of the country of the Huilai, who paid tribute to Samas Rimmon, king of Assyria.

ASPURTA.

A king of Ethiopia, of about the time of the XXVIth dynasty. His wife Madsenen was a priestess of Amen Ra.

ASQALNA.

The Egyptian name of the town of Ascalon, in Philistia.

ASRA.

The literal reading of the name of the god Osiris. It is more generally written Hesirei.

ASROMIAMUN.

The name of an unidentified Ethiopian king. The period when he lived is uncertain.

ASSAN.

A town or district in Elam, which was called by the Accadians Anzan.

ASSA-TATKERES.

The eighth and last king but one of the Vth dynasty. Like his predecessors, he carried on the mining operations at Sarbout el Khadem, in the peninsula of Mount Sinai, and was the father of Pthah Hotep, the earliest known writer of proverbs.

ASSAYA.

A district in Mesopotamia, which paid tribute to Assurnazirpal, king of Assyria.

ASSESSORS.

The name given by Egyptologists to forty-two judges, who each in the Hall of Judgment interrogate the soul of the deceased respecting different crimes which he may have committed, from which crimes he is able to absolve himself by repeating the so-called negative confession of the CXXVth chapter of the Ritual of the Dead. The deceased is then in turn declared by the assessors to be justified, and after undergoing various transformations, he passes into the highest heaven of the spiritual world.

ASSETH.

According to the Greek lists, the name of an early Egyptian king of Bubastis. He has not yet been certainly identified.

ASSHURABAMER.

According to Lenormant, whose view is not now maintained, the last king of the first empire of the Assyrians. He was defeated by the king of the Hittites, and lost the whole of the external provinces of Assyria. The discontent excited among his subjects at this disaster led to a conspiracy, by which he was dethroned, and the principal traitor, Belkatirassur, placed on the throne.

Asshuradinna.

According to some early Assyriologists, the true reading of the Assyrian royal name Esarhaddon, which see. *See also* Asshuriakhidiun.

Asshurbalat.

Another reading of the Assyrian royal name Assur-ubalid, which see.

Asshur-nadin.   "Asshur giveth."

The eldest son of Sennacherib, king of Assyria. He was made king of Babylon by his father, upon the defeat of Merodach-baladan, but soon died, and was succeeded by the rebel Irigibel, which see.

Asshur-rish-ishi.   "Assur possesses a Head."

Another reading of the Assyrian royal name Assur-ris-ilim, which see.

Assoros.

In Greco-Babylonian mythology the brother and husband of Kissare, and father of the first divine triad, Anos, Illinos, and Aos. His analogue was the Assur of the Assyrians with his wife Serua.

Assu.

The Egyptian name of an unidentified Asiatic country.

Assuan.

The modern name of the ancient town of Syene, which was one of the Southern boundaries of Egypt, and from whence the greater part of the granite used in the Egyptian temples was quarried. It was famous for its temple of Isis-sothis, or the Dog-star personified as a goddess, and from which temple it seems probable that the national astronomical observations were taken.

Assur.

In Hindu mythology another name of the evil spirits who were called Asvarna, which see.

Assur.

In Archaic history the general name of the empire of Assyria. The original seat of the Assyrian people when they migrated from Babylonia was a tract on the river Tigris, between the latitudes 35º and 37º, being a territory extending about one hundred miles from North to South, and about seventy miles from East to West. During the best period of the empire, Assyria proper extended from latitude 35º to 38º and longitude 40º to 45º, embracing the countries on the East of the Tigris as far as the mountain ranges of Media, reaching on the South to below the junction of the rivers Tigris and Zab, on the West extending to the banks of the Khabour, and spreading its Northern boundary as far as the mountains now called Jebel Djudi.   About the 7th century B.C. the subject districts of Assyria included Lydia, Cyprus, and Egypt on the West, Elam and part of Media on the East, and Babylonia and part of Arabia in the South, an extent of territory which was always with difficulty held together, and the strain to secure which ultimately dismembered the empire. The chief cities of Assyria were Assur, the ancient, and for many years the only capital ; Calah, a large city situated about twenty miles to the South of Nineveh ; Reson, a city lying between Calah and Nineveh ; and lastly Nineveh itself, the later capital of the country, and the one best known to the Greek and Hebrew writers. The ecclesiastical centre of the country appears to have been Arbela, the favourite city of the goddess Ishtar in later times, and Assur the residence of the god Assur, the father and king of the gods, and father of the Assyrians. (Smith.)

ASSUR.

The great Deity of the Assyrians, the King and Father of the gods, and therefore not included in the mythological genealogies of the Assyrians. He was called "The God who created Himself," and his chief temple was dedicated to Sadimatati, or the "Mountain of the World."

ASSURACHERIB.

Another form of the name of the great Assyrian king Sennacherib, which see.

ASSURACUS.   Or SARACUS.

According to the Greek writers, the name of the last king of Assyria.

ASSUR-AKHI-IDDIN.   "Assur gave Brothers."

The true form of the Assyrian royal name which is more generally written Esarhaddon, which see.

ASSUR-BANAI-UZUR.   "Assur, protect my Offspring."

The chief of the palace of Shalmaneser II. and eponym of the years B.C. 856 and 817. The chief event in which latter year was an expedition to Bale.

ASSUR-BANI.   "Assur my Creator."

The governor of Calah, in the reign of Sargon II. He was eponym of the year B.C. 713, the chief event in which was a warlike expedition into the land of Media and Tubal.

ASSUR-BANI-PAL.   "Assur, create a Son."

The Sardanapalus of the Greeks, was made co-regent of Assyria with his father, Essar-haddon, in B.C. 670, and became sole king, B.C. 668. He was a great patron of literature, and institutor of the great library of Kouyunjik, passionately fond of hunting, but cruel, sensual, and effeminate. At the beginning of his reign, Egypt revolted ; but Tirhakah's army was routed at Car-banit, in the Delta, and Egypt reconquered. A second revolt soon afterwards broke out, but was promptly repressed, and Necho, satrap of Sais, carried to Nineveh, though shortly afterwards released. Rud-Ammon, Tirhakah's successor, again drove the Assyrians out of Egypt ; but his success was short, Egypt had again to submit, and Thebes was sacked (see Nahum iii. 8). Tyre, the siege of which had been begun by Essar-haddon, now submitted, as well as the kings of Tubal and Cilicia ; and Gyges of Lydia sent tribute to Nineveh. The Minnians, Medes, and Elamites were also successfully attacked. But, in B.C. 660, Psammitikhus, the son of Necho, with the help of Gyges, shook off the Assyrian yoke, and under the conduct of Saul-mugina, Assur-bani-pal's brother and satrap of Babylonia, and of Umman-igas and Tammaritu, kings of Elam, a general revolt broke out throughout the whole empire. Elam had already suffered much from Assyria a few years before, in the reign of Teumman ; civil war, however, now broke out there, and the Elamites had to make peace with Assyria. Babylon, Sippara, Borsippa, and Cuthah were taken, and Saul-mugina burnt himself. The Arabians and Nabatheans were compelled to return to submission, an Assyrian army being marched into the heart of Arabia, and the revolted cities of Palestine were severely punished. Taking advantage of a fresh civil war, Assur-bani-pal now sent an army into Elam, which ravaged the country, destroyed Shushan and other cities, and made Elam a dependency of Assyria. Ardys, son of Gyges, thereupon sent tribute to Assur-bani-pal. The date of Assur-bani-pal's death is uncertain. (Sayce.)

Assur-basa.

A garrison city, established by Tiglath Pileser II. at the foot of Mount Naal, between Assyria and Armenia.

Assur-bel-kala. " Assur (is) Lord of all."

A king of Assyria, son of Tiglath-Pileser I., who invaded Babylonia and conquered the successor of the Babylonian king Maruduk-sapikzurrat, whose name is unknown.

Assur-bel-nisi. " Assur (is) Lord of Men."

An early king of Assyria, who executed an amicable treaty with Kara-indas, king of Babylonia, as to the boundaries of their respective kingdoms, in the fifteenth century B.C.

Assur-bel-ukin. " Assur established the Lord."

A more correct reading of the Assyrian name Assurbeluzur, which see.

Assur-bel-uzur.

The governor of Kirruri, in the reign of Rimmon-nirari III. He was eponym of the year B.C. 797, the chief event in which was an expedition to Manzuat.

Assur-bel-uzur.

The governor of Calah, in the last year of the reign of Shalmaneser III. He was eponym of the year B.C. 772, the chief event in which was an expedition to Hadrach.

Assur-dainanni. " Assur, judge Me."

The Rabsaki of Tiglath Pileser II., who sent him to subdue the Eastern provinces of Media, which he successfully accomplished, bringing back much spoil to Assyria. He was governor of Mazamua, and eponym of the year B.C. 733, the chief event in which was a warlike expedition to Damascus.

Assur-dain-pal. "Assur, judge the Son."

The eldest son of Shalmaneser II. He incited the people of Nineveh to revolt against his father, who had offended them by the removal of the Assyrian court to Calah ; and he soon had a following of twenty-seven cities with their respective governors. His brother, Samas-Rimmon III., however, reduced the tribes to their allegiance before the death of Shalmaneser II., which took place soon after. Nothing is known as to the death of Assur-dain-pal.

Assur-dan I. "Assur is Judge."

An early king of Assyria, the son of Ninip-pileser, who in the reign of Zamama-zikiriddina invaded and plundered the country of Babylonia, and began the reconstruction of the temples of Anu and Rimmon at Assur, which were erected by Samas-Rimmon II. He died, however, before he had time to do more than pull down the structures.

Assurdan II.

A king of Assyria. In his reign the empire began to revive from the long period of depression into which it had fallen after the death of Assur-rabu-amar. He was succeeded by Rimmon-nirari II.

Assurdan III.

The successor of Shalmaneser III. Early in his reign he began to attack Damascus and Babylonia, making several expeditions also to Media and Syria. Towards the close of his reign a great rebellion arose, headed by the people of the old capital Assur. The revolt reached over six years, and was rendered remarkable by the appearance of a great eclipse, that of the 15th June, B.C. 763, which was regarded as an evil omen. The energies of Assurdan enabled him, however, to conquer the rebellion, and a peaceful period of two years succeeded, after which he died, having reigned eighteen years. His successor was Assur-nirari II.

Assur-danin-sarri. "Assur the Strengthener of the King."

An Assyrian officer in the court of Esarhaddon. He was one of the officials who were called "Holders of the Two Sceptres." *See* Nebo-atsib.

Assurdayan.

Another form of the Assyrian royal name Assurdan, which see.

Assur-ebil-ili. "Assur is Lord of the Gods."

The son of Assurbanipal. He may have succeeded Bel-zikir-iskun on the throne of Assyria, and after a short and troubled reign been attacked by Nabopalassar, the former general of the king of Assyria, but who was at that time king of Babylon, and his son Nabukuduruzur. The two rebels, aided by Necho, king of Egypt, destroyed the city of Nineveh, and the king himself gathering his wives and treasures together, burnt himself to death in his palace ; thus the Assyrian history of Assyria terminated. Assurebilili was possibly the Saracus of the Greek historians.

ASSUREDILILANI.   "Assur is Arbiter (?) of the Gods."

See Bel-zikir-iskun, to which king this name probably belongs.

ASSUR-IZKA-DAIN.   "Assur judges Crimes."

An Assyrian officer whose titles are lost.   He was eponym of the last year of Shalmaneser IV., B.C. 720, the chief event in which was a warlike expedition to Palestine.

ASSUR-LIHA.

King of Karalla.   He revolted against Sargon II., who defeated him, and then had his city burnt, and himself flayed alive.

ASSUR-LIHHIS.

The name formerly given by the French Assyriologists to Assur-Nirari, king of Assyria.

ASSURLIKKISH.

A king of Assyria, under whom, according to some Assyriologists, the original empire was overthrown by the Medes.   The point is open to considerable doubt, and the monarch in that case would have been Assur Nirari II., which see.   All Assyriologists agree in making Tuklat Palesir II. his successor.   *N.B.*—This name is retained for reference although the view is now abandoned by Assyriologists.

ASSUR-MAKHIR-NISI.   "Assur the Presenter of Men."

The governor of Arbaha, in the reign of Rimmon-nirari III. and eponym of the year B.C. 803, the chief events in which were a warlike expedition to " over the sea," and the visitation of a pestilence.

ASSUR-MULIK.   "Assur who causes to march."

A younger son of Sennacherib, and the heir to the throne on the death of his brother Assurnadin.   He occupied a splendid palace at Nineveh, specially erected for him by his father.   Notwithstanding which, he conspired with his brother Nergal-Sharezer and assassinated his father.   This act at once cost him the succession, as his younger brother Esarhaddon at once ascended the throne, and he had to take refuge in the land of Armenia, which was always at war with Assyria.   He was the Addramelek of the Hebrew writers.

ASSUR-NADIN-AKHE.   "Assur gives Brothers."

The successor of Iriba-Rimmon, king of Assyria.   Nothing is known respecting him.

ASSUR-NAZIR-PAL.   "Assur protects (his) Son."

A great king of Assyria.   He was the son of Tugulti-Ninip II. and nearly the whole of his reign of twenty-five years was spent in wars undertaken to enlarge the kingdom of Assyria, these wars being characterised with more than usual cruelty on the part of the victor.   His first wars were against the bordering states of North Assyria, then the Eastern provinces of the Tigris.   After conquering all his opponents, and impaling or flaying alive the chiefs of the conquered cities, he marched into Syria, and warred as far as the Mediterranean sea, where he received tribute of the Phenicians and the coast towns. Returning to Nineveh, he rebuilt the chief temples of that city, and also the city of Calah, which had been founded by Shalmaneser I. and had been destroyed during the reigns of the weak monarchs who succeeded him. He then constructed a preserve of wild animals for the chase there, and afterwards excavated a canal from that city to the river Zab. He was also a prudent but merciless legislator, and was succeeded by his son, Shalmaneser II.

ASSUR-NIRARI I.   " Assur my Helper."

An early ruler of Assyria, of whom little is known. He was the father of Nebo-dan.

ASSUR-NIRARI II.

He succeeded Assurdan III. and began his reign with an expedition against Hadrach in Northern Palestine, and in the second year of his monarchy to Arpad. A period of inaction ensued, followed by a revolution, the particulars of which are not known, but it ended in the destruction of the dynasty, and the accession to the throne of the usurper Tiglath Pileser II.

ASSUR-RABU-AMAR.

A king of Assyria, one of the successors of Samas-Rimmon II. In his reign the king of Aram or Syria reconquered the whole of the region of the Euphrates from the Assyrian empire.

ASSUR-RIS-ILIM.   " Assur, Head of the Gods."

An early Assyrian king. He was the son of Mutaggil-Nebo, whom he succeeded, and again restored the power of the Assyrian empire, which was falling under the Babylonian aggressions, by conquering the various tribes in the North and North-east of Mesopotamia. He was further a great builder, and was succeeded by his son Tiglath-Pileser I.

ASSUR-SALIMANNI.   " Assur gives me Peace."

The governor of Arbaha, in the reign of Tiglath Pileser II. He was eponym of the year B.C. 735, the chief event in which was a warlike expedition to Ararat.

ASSUR-SEMUANI.   " Assur, hear me (?)."

The governor of Kalzi in the reign of Shalmaneser IV. He was eponym of the year B.C. 724, the chief event in which was a warlike expedition to a country whose name is lost.

ASSUR-TAGGIL.   " Assur gives Confidence."

The Tukulu of Rimmon-nirari III., and eponym of the year B.C. 806, the chief event in which was a warlike expedition to Arpad.

ASSUR-UBALID.   " Assur gives Life."

An early king of Assyria, whose daughter Muballidat-Serua, married a king of Babylonia, but what king is not known.

ASSURUBALID.

According to the French Egyptologists another form of the Assyrian royal name Asshurubalat, which see.

ASSUR-ZIKUR-ESIR. "Assur directs (his) Man."

An early Patesi or chief lord, a ruler of Assyria, who first assumed the title, "King of Countries," and who was engaged in a controversy or dispute with Kharbi-sipak, king of Babylonia. He is sometimes called Niniptugultu Assur.

AST.

The Egyptian name of the sacred fruit of the Persea almond tree. It was one of the trees which was considered as a tree of life, and on the fruit of which the goddess Sofkh wrote the name of the king. It is now extinct in Lower Egypt.

AST.

The Egyptian name of an unidentified town, possibly the Ἄστυ of Greek writers.

AST.

The Egyptian name of an unidentified Asiatic country.

ASTABORAS.

An Ethiopian river which runs into the Nile near to the Island of Meroe in Upper Egypt.

ASTALENEN.

The Egyptian name of a country opposite to Nubia.

ASTARETENHEB.

An Egyptian lady, of whom nothing is known except that she had a sister named Iseret. Her name possesses an interest as containing that of the Syrian goddess Astarte, whose worship was introduced into Egypt after the conquest in Palestine of Thothmes II. of the XVIIIth dynasty.

ASTARTUS.

One of the many usurpers who occupied the throne of Tyre after the murder of Abdashtoreth, the last king of the house of Hiram.

ASTEKHU.

The mother of Abet an Egyptian sculptor of the XIIth dynasty.

ASTEN.

A name of the Ibis-headed deity Thoth, by which he was venerated in the temple of Denderah.

ASTES.

A mystical Egyptian divinity mentioned in the XVIIth chapter of the Ritual of the Dead.

ASTLIK. (ISTAR?).

The daughter of Xisuthrus according to Moses of Chorene, and the sister of Zirvan, Titan, and Japethostes, whom she reconciled to each other after a war which had broken out between them on account of the arrogance of Zirvan, the eldest brother of the protogiants, which see.

ASTMURSA.

The Egyptian name of a town situated on the banks of the Astabaras.

ASTVADERETA. "Existing Truth."

One of the three prophets descended from Zarathustra, by whom the evil principal was to be finally destroyed.

ASTYAGES.

King of the Medes. He succeeded Astybares, and reigned jointly with his son Apanda twenty years. (Ctesias.)

ASTYBARES.

King of the Medes. He succeeded Artines, and reigned forty years. (Ctesias.)

ASUR.

A Dedanite tribe who alone remained in Arabia when the Arkamites were expelled by the Jorhamites. They founded the district of Asur in Southern Arabia.

ASURA. "The living Spirit."

The name of the Supreme Being among the Indians of Hindustan. It was probably the origin of the Assur of the Assyrians.

ASURAMEDHAS.

The Sanscrit form of the name of the good Supreme Deity of the Zendic faith, Ahuramazda or Ormuzd, which see.

ASUU.

The Egyptian name of an unidentified country.

ASVAHEDHAS.

The name of the noblest sacrifice to the Supreme Deity in Vedic times. The victim was always a horse, as being the animal most useful to man. This custom continued in Scandinavia to the advent of Christianity, and among the Scythian nations to a still more recent period.

ASVARNA. "The Sleepless."

In Hindu mythology the name of the wicked spirits which surround and work evil to mankind. Their chiefs were named Bhuta, Basmagut, etc. They were also called Assur.

ASVINS.

In Vedic mythology the two deities of the morning and evening twilight. These Hindu gods were the origin of the Dioscuri of the Greeks.

ASYCHIS.

According to the Greek writers, a wise and beneficent king of Egypt who regulated the law of mortgages. He is supposed by some to have been Osirtasen III. under his divine name of Rashaken.

AT.

An Egyptian title corresponding to that of "chief" or "prince."

AT.

A town in the ninth, or Panopolite nome, of Upper Egypt. It was sacred to the deity Min.

ATA.

A king of the Ist dynasty, of whom nothing else is known except that his name occurs on the second Table of Abydos.

ATA.

An Egyptian lady, who was perhaps the daughter of Sutenrekh-Ata a king of the Vth dynasty.

ATAHAT.

An Egyptian district situated on the great road from Coptos to the Red Sea.

ATAHUTI I.

The son of Menes, king of Egypt, of the Ist dynasty. He built a palace at Memphis, and wrote several books on medicine, and is said by the Greeks to have introduced the practice of cutting for the stone. He is called by some writers Athothes.

ATAHUTI II.

The third king of Egypt of the Ist dynasty, of whom nothing is yet known.

ATAI.

An island or country to the South of Egypt. It is not yet certainly identified.

ATAI.

The Egyptian name of an unidentified Asiatic country.

ATAI.

Another name of the city called Busiris by the Greeks.

ATAIUHAI.

A lord of Coptos, by whom the Hieroglyphic inscriptions at El-Hama-mat were set up in the reign of Darius Hystaspes. Possibly the same as the following.

ATAIUHI.

A Perso-Egyptian officer, the son of Artames. He held a high position in Egypt under the reigns of Xerxes and Artaxerxes, kings of Egypt and Persia.

ATAKA.

A place which was famous in the time of Rameses III. for its bronze foundries. It was perhaps the Athak of Hebrew history.

ATAKHERAMEN.

An Ethiopian king, whose place is uncertain.

ATAMEN.

A town to the West of the Delta, near the site of the modern village of Terraneh.

ATAMENNUTERHEKTEN.

The surname of Rameses VII. of the XXth dynasty.

ATARED.

In ancient Arabian mythology the name of the planet Mercury, adored as a divinity.

ATARGATIS.

A Syrian goddess, also called Derketo. Herodotus identifies her with Aphrodite Urania. She presided over love and generation, and was regarded as the begetter of the universe, and also as a feminine form of the deity Hadad. Her chief temples were at Hierapolis (Mabig) and Askalon. She was born of an egg that had descended from heaven into the Euphrates, though the Syrian version of the legend was that she had been a woman who had thrown herself into a lake, and there been transformed into a goddess after giving birth to Semiramis. She was represented with the head and body of a woman, and the tail of a fish, and her worshippers consequently abstained from eating fish. Atargatis was chiefly worshipped at Askalon.

ATARMATU.

A country to the South of Egypt not certainly identified.

ATARUAMTERHEMUTRANU.   " Names never revealed."

The name of a mystical deity who is mentioned in the CLXVth chapter of the Ritual of the Dead.

ATAVISM.

A term used by modern anthropologists to describe the tendency which exists in a race or tribe to revert occasionally to the characteristics of the primitive type.

ATCHIDU.

A district of Armenia (?) where the army of Dadarses the rebel was defeated by the army of Darius Hystaspes under Vomises for the fourth time. *See* Tigra and Zoza.

ATEF.

An Egyptian title, signifying "father." It was often used in the composition of proper names.

ATEF.

The mother of Nunnu, an Egyptian officer in the XVIIIth dynasty.

ATEFAAMEN.

A son of Rameses II. of the XIXth dynasty.

ATEF AMEN.   "Father of Amen."

A son of Rameses II. of the XIXth dynasty.

ATEF CROWN.

The crown generally worn by Amen Ra. It consisted chiefly of two upright ostrich feathers beside a tall white cap, with the ram's horns, uræi and solar disk in front. It was supposed to represent the kingdom of Egypt, the white cap signifying light, the two feathers truth, the uræi serpents royalty, the ram's horns generative power, and the solar disk divinity. It is repeatedly mentioned in the Ritual of the Dead, and represented on the bas-reliefs, colossi, and statuettes. (Pierret.)

ATEFKHENT.

A town in the thirteenth or Upper Lycopolite nome of Upper Egypt. *See* Chefschent, and Apheru.

ATEFNEBMA.

The father of Merira, an Egyptian captain of the XVIIIth dynasty.

ATEFNOFRE.

The brother of the scribe Horemkhu, which see.

ATEFNUTER AI.

A king of Egypt in the XVIIIth dynasty; one of the disputed successors of Amenhotep IV.

ATEFTE.

The name of an unidentified nome in Nubia.

ATEH.

An unidentified city in Egypt, situated in one of the Northern nomes.

ATEKHRAMUN.

An unidentified Ethiopian king.

ATEM.

The name of the mother goddess of time in the CLXVth chapter of the Ritual of the Dead.

ATEMMER.

A place in the seventh, or Phathyrite nome, of Upper Egypt. *See also* Seshesh and Hathor.

ATEN-NEFRU.   "The most lovely Disk."

The name under which the special worship of the solar deity Aten Ra was introduced to the Egyptians by Amenhotep III., at the instigation of his queen Taia.

ATEN RA.

The name of the deity of the Solar Disk, who was originally one of the minor deities of the Egyptian mythology. He was represented as a solar disk giving forth rays, each of which terminated in a hand holding the cross of life. In the time of Amenhotep IV. the wife of that monarch, Queen Taia, attempted to make absolute and universal the worship of Aten Ra, whom she maintained to be the same as the Syrian deity Adon Ra, or Adon-ai. The king at first slowly introduced the new form of deity under the name of Aten-nefru, and then gradually declared the sun under that name to be the supreme deity alike of Egypt and its dependencies, and to carry out this plan he closed the temples of the older divinities, degraded their priests, and ultimately removed the capital of the empire to a new site at Tel el Amarna. This total subversion of the natural religious principles, and the unwise haste with which it was accompanied, led to a revolution which resulted in the overthrow of the XVIIIth dynasty and the degradation of Aten Ra. There is in many points a considerable resemblance between some of the rites of the worship of Aten and the ceremonial observances of the Jewish nation. In both systems there was no visible representation of the Supreme Being : there were altars of incense, burnt sacrifice, and more remarkable still, a table of shewbread in both. The plans of the temples were very similar to each other, as also were the robes of the officiating priests. Whether there ever was such a strong affinity between them as to imply the existence of one common origin cannot now be well ascertained ; certain it is that the troubles of the Jews in Egypt appear to have synchronised pretty closely with the religious disturbances which followed the death of Queen Taia. (Lenormant.)

ATESHGAHS.

The Zendic name of the fire temples of Ahuramazda.

ATETA.

A king of the Ist dynasty, whose name is given on the second Table of Abydos. *See also* Teta, which is another manner of reading the same name.

ATH.

The *Uu* of the nineteenth, or Aphroditopolite nome, of Upper Egypt. *See* Tsets.

ATHAANKHTSENBT.

A priest of Apis. He was the son of Nofretumirihotep, and he lived in the time of the XXVIth dynasty.

ATHAL.

An Arabian mountain in the Neged or South country. It was the Jetur of Hebrew writers.

ATHENEGOZMÆA.

The Greek form of the name of an unidentified Nabathean goddess.

ATHHETSA.

The Egyptian name of an unidentified town.

ATHLOPHOROI.

The Greek name of the standard-bearers of the Egyptian kings. Their duty was to carry the emblems of victory before the monarch. Their Egyptian title has not yet been found on the monuments.

ATHOTES.   *Or* ATHOTHES.

A most ancient king of Egypt, who, according to the Greek historians, invented the Hieroglyphic system of writing. The statement is probably derived from the Egyptian tradition of the invention of letters by the god Thoth, from whose name Athotes, or Athothes seems to have been derived. *See also* Atahuti.

ATHOTHES.

The successor of Menes, and second king of Egypt. *See* Athotes and Teta.

ATHRIBIS.

A city and nome in Lower Egypt at the head of the Delta, which according to Herodotus was held by the Calasirian class of soldiers. The chief town of the nome was anciently called Hataheriab, and it was sacred to the god Harkhentkat, and the goddess Khouit, who was a form of Hathor. On the disruption of the Egyptian empire the nome was established as a petty kingdom by the Assyrians under the Icosarchy. It was also called by the Egyptians the city and nome of Ka.

ATHTOR DHU KABDH.   "Athtor of the East."

An Himyaritic deity, worshipped at the town of Main, in South-western Arabia.

ATHTOR DHU YAHRAK.

Another and a local name of the Himyaritic deity Athtor.

ATHU.

The Egyptian name of the city of Natho, in the Delta.

ATHYR.

The third month of the Egyptian sacred year. It began about the 18th of September.

ATI.

An Egyptian functionary of the XIXth dynasty.

ATI.

A city and nome, the ninth, of Lower Egypt. It was sacred to the worship of Osiris, and was probably the Greek Canopus.

ATI.

The first king of the VIth Egyptian dynasty. He reigned thirty years, and was assassinated by his guards. He was the Othoes of the Greeks.

ATIM.

The mother of Mentuhotep IV., of the XIth dynasty.

ATIMER.

The *Pehu* of the second, or Latopolite nome, of Lower Egypt.

ATIMY.

Among the ancient Greeks the act of excluding any person from holding a public office by a disqualifying decree.

ATINMERIT.

An Egyptian queen, possibly a daughter of Amenhotep IV., as her husband, whose name is not yet known, succeeded that monarch on the throne of Egypt.

ATMA.

The Egyptian name of a country, which is by some Egyptologists supposed to have been Edom.

ATMOO.

Another reading of the name of the Egyptian deity Atum, which see.

ATNIKU.

A Mesopotamian people, who were conquered by Tiglath Pileser I.

ATONATIUH.   " The Sun of the Waters."

The name given in Mexican mythology to the first age of the world, which was terminated by a deluge.

ATRI.

In Hindu mythology certain deities emanating from Brahma, whom he invested with the power of creation.

ATRINES.

The son of Opadarmes.   He raised an insurrection in Susiana against Darius, and became king of Susia.   He was attacked and brought prisoner to Darius, who slew him.

ATRMEHIT.

The *Mer* of the twenty-first nome of Lower Egypt.

ATTAMITU.

The commander of the archers in the army of Ummanigus, king of Elam, in his war against Assurbanipal.   He was slain in the battle, and his head sent to Nineveh.

ATU.

A place in the ninth nome of Upper Egypt.   *See also* Ati.

ATU.

The Egyptian name of an unidentified Asiatic country.

ATU.

A priest of Amen Ra. The period when he lived is uncertain.

ATUM.   *Or* ATMOO.

The Egyptian deity of the setting sun or darkness. He was called "the sun who reclines himself," and was represented as an erect human figure, wearing a crown composed of an expanded lotus surmounted with four upright feathers, like those on the crown of Amen Ra. He was specially adored at Heliopolis in Lower Egypt.

ATUMA.

A district in South-east Assyria, which was conquered by Tiglath Pileser I.

ATUNA.

A kingdom near Armenia, tributary to Sargon II., who added to it the kingdom of Sinuhta as a reward for the fidelity of its king Matti, which see.

ATUR.

The *Mer* of the sixth, or Tentyrite nome, of Upper Egypt.

ATUR.

The *Pehu* of the eleventh, or Anteopolite nome, of Upper Egypt.

ATUR.

The *Mer* of the twenty-first, or An nome, of Lower Egypt.

ATUR.

An Egyptian measure of length, corresponding to the stadium of the Greeks.

ATUR.

An Egyptian name for the papyrus plant, *Cyperus Nilotica.*

ATUR.   " River."

The local name of the ancient port of the capital city of Thebes in Upper Egypt.

ATUR.

The name of one of the principal branches of the Nile, in Lower Egypt, or of a locality situated on its coast.

ATURNTAMEN.

An unidentified place to the East of Elephantine, in Upper Egypt.

ATUT.

Another form of the Egyptian royal name Athothes, which see.

AUA.

The wife of Amenemapt, a priest of Amen Ra, in the reign of Ai or Atefnuter Ai, a king of the XVIIIth dynasty.

AUAIT.

An uncertainly identified Egyptian goddess.

AUAU.

The Egyptian name of a species of hunting-hound, which was much used in the XVIIIth and XIXth dynasties.

AUAUAIT.

An unidentified country to the South of Egypt.

AUDHUMBLA.

In Scandinavian mythology the mystic cow on whose milk the giant Ymir was suckled. Compare the Egyptian myth of Tefnu.

AUDR.

Another form of the name of the Scandinavian deity Udr.

AUFAA.

A priest of Apis, in the XXVIth dynasty. The son of the priest Schedsnefer and the lady Nesmaut.

AUFAA.

A priest of the deity Maut. Period uncertain.

AUFNA.

An Egyptian monarch of the XIIIth dynasty.

AUFRER.

An Egyptian officer, the father of the governor Nesahor, which see.

AUI.

See Ai, *or* Atefnuter Ai. A king of Egypt in the XVIIIth dynasty.

AUI.

A choristress of the goddess Bast. She was the sister of an officer named Pthahmai, and lived probably at a late period.

AUI.

An Egyptian lady, the wife of Titia the chief of the scribes of Amen Ra, in the reign of Thothmes III.

AUKHEPERU.

Priest of Apis. He was the son of Pakhrua and the lady Hathorhat. The period when he lived is uncertain.

AUNTUM.

The Egyptian name of an unidentified Asiatic country.

AUPA.

The Egyptian name of an unidentified district in Upper Syria.

AUR.

A common Egyptian epithet name of the river Nile.

AURAUAAKARUSAANK.

The name of a mystical cow, who is adored in the CLXIIIrd chapter of the Ritual of the Dead.

AURAVADASPU.

An early Bactrian king, of the Keanian dynasty. He was the father of Vistaspa, who introduced the Zendic faith into Bactria, and was called Lohrasp by the Persian writers of the Middle Ages.

AURERA.

An Egyptian royal lady in the XIIth dynasty, the mother of Prince Bebe, which see.

AURERI.

The Egyptian form of the name of the Roman emperor Verus as emperor of Egypt in the XXXIInd dynasty.

AURKA.

An unidentified country to the South of Egypt.

AUSIM.

The modern name for the Egyptian city and nome of Latopolis or Aa, which see.

AUSTRI.   " East."

In Scandinavian mythology one of the four horns which supported the vault of heaven when the gods made the sky out of the skull of the giant Ymir.

AUT.

An Egyptian god.   He was simply the idea of "triumph" personified as a deity.

AUTENISU.

An unidentified country mentioned in the Egyptian inscriptions.

AUTHU.

The Egyptian name of a district between Sarepta and Tyre, on the sea-coast of Palestine.

AUTIYARA.

A province of ancient Media, which is named in the Behistun inscription of Darius Hystaspes.

AUU.

A priest of Osiris, and *Smer* of the palace of an unnamed monarch of the VIth dynasty.

Av.

A mystical deity who is represented as Criocephalic with the solar disk on his head, holding a viper in his left hand, and the Ankh cross in his right, while the folds of the serpent Mehen are over his head and around him. He was a form of the deity Khnuphis, and is figured in the Book of the Lower World. (Deveria).

Avalokita.   "The Manifested."

A Sanskritic title of the Supreme Being as a revealer of himself to man.

Avaris.

A town on the Bubastic branch of the Nile. It was anciently called Ha-ouar and was fortified by King Setipeti Nubti, and made the capital of the Shepherd Empire of the XVIIth dynasty. It has, according to M. Chabas, been wrongly considered to be Tanis, and was more probably near Pelusium on the site of the ruins called Tel el Her.

Avatar.

In Hindu mythology the name given to each of the ten incarnations of the preserving deity Vishnu.

Avil kush.   "Man of Kush."

The probable true form of the name of the mystical Chaldean king who was called by the Greeks Evechous.

Avun.

A personage of Etruscan mythology. He is represented on a mirror as a warrior armed with a spear, in company with the male Turan.

Awani Aoton.

A great festival held by the Hindus, in the month of August, in honour of the god Siva.

Awzal.

The modern name of the province and town in Yemen which was probably the Uzal of Hebrew writers.

Aya.

A Mesopotamian people who were conquered by Tiglath Pileser I.

Aym.

Another form of the Arabian name Aimu, which see.

Ayurveda.

A commentary on the Hindu system of medicine derived from the Rigveda.

Aza.

The son of Irranzi, king of Minni. He was slain by his subjects, and his body thrown over a cliff with great ignominy, because of his fidelity to Sargon II. his suzerain, against whom all the kings of Armenia had revolted except himself.

Azalla.

A people of Mesopotamia who paid tribute to Assurnazirpal.

Azapirani.   *Or* Atzupirane.

An ancient Babylonian city by the banks of the Euphrates, which was famous as being the birthplace of the half mythical Sargon I.

Azau.

A king of Kirzan, who was conquered by Shalmaneser II.

Azech Amen.

A king of Ethiopia, probably of the ancient royal house of Seti I., which had long maintained a precarious dignity at Napata in Southern Egypt.   He invaded and conquered Egypt in the reign of Uaserken I., and was proceeding further to conquer Palestine also, when he was defeated on the borders of Judah by King Asa, who at Zephath utterly routed his army, and by compelling him to retreat into Ethiopia, freed Egypt from his dominion also.   No further particulars of his reign are known.

Azial.

An Assyrian chief who set up as governor of the town of Suru in the place of Ahiyaba its king, who was flayed alive by Assurnazirpal, king of Assyria.

Azibahal.

One of the ten sons of Yakinlu, king of Arvad.   On the death of his father Azibahal and his brothers all contested the right of succession, but they agreed to refer the decision to Assurbanipal, king of Assyria, their suzerain, by whom Azibahal was declared the lawful successor, and the other princes were dismissed with rich presents.

Aziluth.

In Cabalistic mythology the general name of the ten personal emanations of the Supreme Being, of which the Sephiroth formed the first triad, viz. " The Lord of Spirits," " The Lord of the Elect One," and " The Lord of the other Powers."

Aziz.   " The Powerful."

In ancient Nabathean mythology a deity whose character and attributes are uncertain.

Azlam.

The name of the blunt arrows used by the ancient Arabians in the art of divination.   *See* Kehana.

Azotus.

A frontier town in Syria, which was besieged and captured by Psametik, king of Egypt, after a siege of twenty-nine years.

Azrak.

An Amalekite tribe who settled in the district of Yathrib in South-western Arabia.

Azriyahu.

The Assyrian form of the Hebrew royal name Azariah, which see.

Azu.

A king of Gozon who was conquered by Shalmaneser II.

Azuri.

King of Ashdod. He was tributary to Assyria, but refusing to pay his arrears to Sargon II., he was by that monarch deposed, and his brother Akhimit put on the throne. *See* Akhimit.

Azutappa.

A border town of Mesopotamia conquered by Tiglath Pileser I.

B.

BA.

An Egyptian deity who was worshipped at the town of Bakhtan.

BA. "The Soul."

In Egyptian mythology one of the five component parts of the human being. *See* Akh, Kha, Khaba, etc. It was represented as a human-headed bird, often with the cross of life in its claws.

BA.

The Egyptian name of the metal iron. It is sometimes written Baa, Baaenepe, and Bet.

BAA. "Bronze Vessels."

The use of bronze vases, called by the Egyptians *baa, baaenta,* or *khenemt,* from the earliest times, is proved by the discovery of statuettes, arms, and vessels of this material, some of which bear inscriptions as old as the VIth Egyptian dynasty. The number of utensils wrought in bronze is very numerous, consisting of jugs or ewers, with long spouts for pouring out water, washing vases or basins, of the shape of the flower of a water-plant, small jugs, *khenems,* with spout for holding oil, cauldrons with handles, libation vases, the bowl and end of the handle of the *amshoir* or censer, and situlæ or buckets with handles, for holding water in the temples : these latter are often represented in Ptolemaic works of art as being held in the hands of the goddess Isis. Many little votive baskets or buckets have in relief the figures of the god Amen-Horus, Khem or Mentu, and other deities, adored by a worshipper. Bowls for drinking were also sometimes made of bronze. The bronze vessels of the Egyptians were remarkably well made, and are generally fairly preserved. (Birch.)

BAAENEPE.

One of the Egyptian names of the metal iron.

BAAL. Assyrian, BILU.

A Semitic word, meaning "Lord," which was applied to a god as a term of adoration. Hence the plural, Baalim, in the Old Testament is equivalent to "gods." We hear of Baal-Berith, Baal-Peor, Baal-Gad (the god of fortune), Baal-zebub ("The Lord of Flies"), Baal-Khamman or Ammon (the sun as "Lord of Heat"), Bel-samen (*Baal-shemaim,* "The Lord of Heaven"), etc. In Assyria, Merodach, the patron deity of Babylon, was usually called Bel-Merodach, and was distinguished as "The Younger Bel" from "The Old Bel," Bellithon (*Baal-éthan*), the

10

creator of the universe. The latter was Bel, Bêlus, *par-excellence*, and answered to the Accadian *Mul-ge* or "Lord of the Underworld." Bel-Merodach was a form of the Sun-god, and so was identical with the Phenician Baal (Bel-samen and Bel-Ammon). Human sacrifices were offered to the Phenician Sun-god Baal, and he was represented by the *khamman*, an upright stake or pillar of stone (erroneously translated "image" in the Authorised Version). At Tyre, Baal, there called Melkarth, or "King of the City," had two pillars, one of gold and one of smaragdus, or emerald, in front of his temple (comp. 1 Kings vii. 21). The organised worship of the Phenician Baal was introduced into Israel by the marriage of Ahab with Jezebel. The Canaanite Baal and Baalim worshipped before the time of Samuel were Sun-gods, but not the special state-gods of Phenicia. With Baal were conjoined Ashtoreth (Assyrian, Istar), the Moon-goddess, and Ashera (wrongly rendered "grove" in the Authorised Version), the goddess of fertility, who was represented by an upright pillar. Bel-Merodach, originally the Sun, came afterwards to be identified with the planets Jupiter and Mercury.

BAALIM.

In Phenician mythology the names of certain minor deities emanating from Baal. They were the eponymous, or local deites, of certain towns. *See* Baal-Sidon, etc.

BAAL-CHON.

A title of the Phenician deity Baal, as "The Preserver of All Things."

BAAL-HAMON.   "Burning Baal."

A form of Baal as the national deity of the town of Carthage, to whom human victims were burnt alive.

BAAL-HERMON.

The name of the divinity Baal as the local deity of Mount Hermon.

BAAL-JARHI.   "Baal of the Moon."

In ancient Nabathean mythology a form of the national deity Baal.

BAAL MOLOCH.

A title of the Phenician deity Baal, as "The Destroyer."

BAAL-PISGAH.

The name of the deity Baal as the local divinity of the town of Pisgah.

BAAL-SAMIN.   *Or* SAMEM.

The name of the deity Baal as the deity of the sun or heavens. *See* Samas.

BAAL-SIDON.

The name of the divinity Baal as the local deity of the city of Sidon.

BAAL-TAMAR.

A local name of the Phenician deity Baal. The town of which he was the eponymous is uncertain.

Baal-Tars.

The name of the divinity Baal as the local deity of the city of Tars.

Baal-Thammuz.

A title of the deity Baal, as the deity of procreation. He was called also, Adon or "Lord."

Baal-Tsur.

The name of the deity Baal as the local divinity of Tsur.

Baal-Zebab.

The name of the deity Baal as the Lord of regenerated things, or of life from the dead.

Baal.

A Tyrian who after the fall of Tyre was raised to the honour of kingship, as a vassal to Babylonia, by Nebuchadnezzar the conqueror. He reigned ten years, and was then deposed in a popular revolt.

Baalator.

King of Tyre. He came to the throne on the deposition (?) of the cosuffetes, Muthon III., and Gerashtoreth. He reigned one year, and then he was dethroned, and was succeeded by Meherbaal, who was placed on the throne by the king of Babylon.

Baaleazar I.

King of Tyre. He succeeded his father·Hiram II. He reigned seven years, and was succeeded by his son Abdashtoreth, which see.

Baaleazar II.

The king of Tyre. He was the son of Ethbaal, that priest of Ashtaroth who terminated the Tyrian anarchy by usurping the throne himself. He reigned only six years, and was succeeded by his son Mathan.

Baali.

The king of the city of Upri, in the Island of Kypros (Cyprus). He was one of the tributaries of Esarhaddon. Another form of the name of Upri was Puzus, and also Aphrodisia, which see.

Baalitsapuna.

An Egyptian sanctuary near Mount Kasios. It is supposed by some Egyptologists to have been the Baalzephon of Hebrew history.

Baalram.

A Kypriote nobleman who erected a temple at Idalion, or Cyprus, to the Phenician deity Reshep Mikal.

Baalsyllech.

The father of Ecnibaal, the king or suffete of Tyre. *See* Ecnibaal.

10*

BAAU.   " Night."

In Phenician mythology the primæval goddess Night, the wife of Colpias, wind, and the mother of Æon and Protogonos, the two first mortals, which see.

BABA.

Certain executioner deities of the Ritual of the Dead. There were many such inhabiting the Egyptian hell ; and they had generally the heads of various savage animals, and held swords in their hands. They were the Βέβων of Plutarch and the Cabereii of the Greek mythologists.

BABARURAI.

A country near Media, which was conquered by Samas-Rimmon or Vulnirari, king of Assyria.

BABDUNA.

An early Babylonian city which was destroyed by Sargon or Sargina I. Its site is not at present identified.

BABDUR.

An Elamite city, on the borders of Babylonia. It was conquered by Sargon II. in his war with Sutruknanhundi, king of Elam.

BABEL.

The name of a Ziggurat or tower which was built by the early post-diluvians as a protection against another deluge. It was destroyed by the gods by night as fast as the sons of men built it up by day. It is said to have been 272 feet square, and to have been erected in seven stages analogous to the temple of Vul or Bel at Borsippa, which was erected by Nebuchadnezzar, and the ruins of which are indeed still considered to mark its site. The name of the tower was originally Babilu, "Gate of the Gods," which was misrendered by the Hebrew writers Babel, "Gate of Confusion."

BABERU.

An Egyptian name of the town of Babel or Babylon, in Chaldea.

BABI.

In Egyptian mythology another name of the mystical spirit Rubi, which see.

BABILAT-NUKHSI.   " Stream of Gladness."

An ancient name of the river Tigris in Lower Babylonia.

BAB-ILU.   "The Gate of (the God) Ilu."

The Babylonian name from whence, by an ironical alliteration, the name of Babel, "Gate of Confusion," was derived by the Hebrew historians.

Babios.

The form in which the name of the city of Babylon is preserved as that of a king in the annals of Moses of Khorene.

Babite.

The capital city of Zaboul, king of Dagara, where he was defeated in battle with great loss by Assurnazirpal, king of Assyria.

Babmouth.

An Egyptian lady, the mother of Psenio, which see.

Babylon.

The great central city of the early empire of Babylonia. In its first appearance in history it occupies the position simply of one of the towns of the associated tribes of Mesopotamia, who were called by the Egyptians the Rotennu. Tradition ascribed to the national god the first erection of the walls of Babylon, but the Cuneiform inscriptions give that honour to Hammurabi, one of the earliest monarchs of Babylonia. He not only raised the town to the position of a capital city, but considerably strengthened and adorned it, excavating a canal from it to the river Tigris, on the banks of which it was situated, calling the canal " The Delight of Men." Subsequent monarchs still further enlarged the city and built a number of magnificent temples, one of which, that of Bel, was long one of the wonders of the world. To Sammuramat, the queen of Vulnirari III. and the Semiramis of the Greeks, was due the construction of the massive walls, 360 stadia long or more than 40 miles, by which the city was enclosed, as also the great quay and royal palace. Nebuchadnezzar still more adorned and strengthened the capital; and his father Nabopalassar caused the hanging gardens and terraced walks to be executed, to please his wife, Amytis. After the fall of the first Assyrian empire Babylon became practically the chief city of the world, and when it was finally destroyed by the Persians under Darius it possessed a splendour and wealth which has never since been equalled. The chief ruins of the city now are the mounds which go by the name of Hillah, after the name of Hillat, one of its ancient districts. The mounds were first described by Mr. Claudius Rich in 1818, and opened by M. Botta in 1842, since which time they have been repeatedly explored and a new world of history brought to light. With respect to its magnitude, Babylon is considered by Mr. Bonomi to have covered an area of 225 square miles, while that of London (in 1869) was only 114 ; on the other hand it did not contain more than 700,000 inhabitants as against the 3,000,000 of the capital of England. Other particulars concerning Babylon will be found under the names Hammurabi, Nebuchadnezzar, Amytis, Bit, Bel, Borsippa, etc.

Babylon.

A town in Egypt near to the present site of Old Cairo. According to Diodorus Siculus it was founded by a large number of Assyrian and Chaldean prisoners who were working in the quarries near Memphis, and who, being unable to submit to the excessive hardships imposed upon them, revolted, and possessing themselves of a strong fortress already existing there, defied the army of Sesostris (Rameses II.) and harassed the neighbouring country. After having in vain attempted to subdue them by force, the king of Egypt was obliged to make an agreement with them. He accorded them a general amnesty and left them in possession of the fortress which they had seized, and which they therefore named after the capital city of the empire from whence they came, Babylon. The event was probably historical but there is no record of it in the Egyptian inscriptions. The town was afterwards famous in Hebrew history as the resting place of the tribes who were driven out of Palestine by Nebuchadnezzar.

BABYLONIA.

One of the earliest and greatest empires of Archaic history. It is supposed to have been founded by an Hamitic or Cushite race anterior to the time of the VIth Egyptian dynasty. The first historical notice of the country which exists shows that it was divided between two races, the Sumir and the Accad, who spoke two different languages, the one Turanian and the other Semitic. The Turanians or original Cushites appear to have been the inventors of the Cuneiform system of writing, but they were early subjugated by the Semitic peoples who blended together with them. The chief cities of Babylonia were Nipur, the earliest seat of power and for many centuries the centre of the national religion, Eridu, Ur, Karrak, Urukh (Erech), Larsa, Sippara, Zergulla, and Agane. The early history of Babylonia is unknown, all the great temples having been built by the predecessors of Hammurabi, the first conqueror and king of the Kassite dynasty, by whom the city of Babylon, the ultimate capital of the empire, was founded. After the destruction of the Assyrian monarchy, between which and that of Babylon there were continual wars in one of which Babylon was itself destroyed, Nebuchadnezzar raised the restored empire of Babylonia to an unrivalled degree of glory, and it continued the chief nation of the world till the fall of Babylon under Cyrus and Darius, B.C. 518. Under the Persian conquerors many attempts were made by the native princes, especially Merodach-baladin III., to regain their independence, but always in vain. The new dynasty of the Seleucidans completed the commercial ruin of the country, and in the time of Pliny Babylon was a desert, and the empire of Bel and Nebo parcelled out into a series of subordinate Roman provinces. *See also* Agane, Sargon, Merodach-baladin, and Nebuchadnezzar.

BADNUB.

The Arabic name of the ancient Egyptian city Penub, which see.

BÆTYLIA.

In ancient Arabian mythology the name of certain sacred stones, originally ærolites, worshipped in Phenicia and all over India and Arabia ; of which the black stone of the Caaba at Mecca is an example. This stone-worship has been thought by some writers to have been probably a rude form of Linga cultus.

BAGABARTA.

Another form of the name of the great deity of Armenia, Bagamazda, which see.

Bagamar.

An Elamite deity, of whom nothing is known.

Bagamazda.

The supreme deity of Armenia in the time of the ancient Assyrians. The name can also be read as Bagabarta.

Bagdadu.

The original name of a famous city in Babylonia which is now called Bagdat. It occupied a prominent place in the Saracenic history of the Dark Ages, and was for many. centuries one of the principal seats of learning in Asia.

Bagdatti.

The leader of the great Armenian rebellion against Sargon II. He caused Aza, king of Minni, to be slain for his fidelity to the king of Syria, who in return, when he had put down the great revolt, had him flayed alive over the same place where he had slain his master.

Bagistan.

A country in Mesopotamia, which is supposed to have been the Bakhtan of later Egyptian history.

Bagmasti.

A famous Armenian goddess, the consort of the deity Haldi. She was worshipped at Muzazin, in Ararat. Her temple, together with that of Haldi, was plundered and burnt by Sargon II., king of Assyria, who carried her statue into captivity.

Bah.   " The Inundation."

A mystical divinity, who is mentioned in the CXLth chapter of the Ritual of the Dead.

Bahaka.

The name of a species of white hunting hound, called also Mahut. It was used in the earlier Egyptian dynasties, and is represented in the tomb of Antefaa of the XIth dynasty.

Bahal.

King of Tyre. He was one of the tributaries of Esarhaddon. His name is sometimes written Baal.

Bahalhanun.

One of the ten competitors for the crown of Arvad, after the death of their father, King Yakinlu.

Bahali.

A Phenician city, conquered by Vulnirari III., or Rimmon-Nirari, B.C. 804.

BAHALIZABUNA.

The Assyrian name of the Syrian city of Baalzephon. It was conquered by Tiglath Pileser II.

BAHALMALUK. "Baal the King."

Another of the ten competitors for the throne of Arvad after the death of King Yakinlu.

BAHALYASHUB.

Another of the ten competitors for the crown of Arvad, after the death of King Yakinlu.

BAHBAIT.

An Egyptian town on the site of the ancient Sebennytus. It was called by the Greeks Isidis. It was famous for its grand granite temple of Hathor, which was erected by Ptolemy Philadelphus.

BAHILU.

Queen of Idilu, a petty kingdom in Arabia, which was conquered and annexed to Assyria by Esarhaddon.

BAHLIRASI.

The name of a city or district on the coast of the Mediterranean, where Shalmaneser II. carved an image of himself in the rock, to record his victories. The place is now called Nahr-el Kelb or the Dog River.

BAHU.

An Accadian synonym of the name of the Assyrian goddess Gula, the "Lady of Death."

BAI.

A great chancellor of Egypt in the court of Merenpthah I. By his influence after that monarch's death, the usurper Sipthah and the princess Tauser were acknowledged as joint sovereigns over the land of Egypt at the city of Chev, and the legitimate heir of the crown, Prince Seti, afterwards Seti II., was made to acquiesce in their accession. Nothing further is yet known of his life or acts.

BAI.

The name of a special priesthood, which was attached to the worship of the god Apis. It was held by hereditary descent, but its duties and ceremonies are as yet unknown. It was probably sacrificial, as it is hieroglyphically expressed by a knife.

BAI.

A priest of Apis, in the reign of Tirhakah, of the XXVth dynasty.

BAI.

A keeper of the bulls of Amen Ra. The period when he lived is uncertain.

BAIENNETER.

The third king of the IInd Thinite dynasty of Egypt. Having no male heir, he introduced a law by which the succession of the crown devolved to his daughter. He reigned forty-seven years, and was the Binothres of the Greek historians.

BAILU.

The queen of Ikhilu, an Arabian country. She was conquered and put to death by Esarhaddon, king of Assyria. *See* Bahilu.

BAÏN. "Illustrious."

The name of an order of military nobles in the Sabæan kingdom of Yemen in Arabia.

BAIUM.

A royal fortress of the kingdom of Sabæa, near to the city of Zafar.

BAK.

An Egyptian prince of the blood royal of the XVIIIth dynasty. He was the son of the lady Tauau, and the brother of an Aahmes who does not however appear to have been the king of that name.

BAKAA.

The father of Rere, an important officer of state in the reign of Seti I. of the XIXth dynasty.

BAKANA.

The name of a Libyan tribe, which was subjugated by Rameses III. of the XIXth dynasty.

BAKASU.

A kind of short two-edged dagger, which was used by the ancient Egyptians. It was generally made of bronze, with a handle either of gold, silver, or ivory.

BAKAT.

An Egyptian lady who was raised to the rank of a princess upon her marriage with Nehara, a great prince in the time of the XIIth dynasty.

BAKENKHONSU.

A first prophet of Amen, and the chief architect of Thebes, under the reigns of Seti I. and Rameses II. of the XIXth dynasty. He appears to have been one of the most important officers of his time.

BAKENNIFI.

An Egyptian officer, who was the chief of the troops under Piankhi Meramon of the XXVIth dynasty. He was also governor of the city of Anamat.

BAKENRANF.

A chief priest or *Sam* and governor of a district in the reign of Psametik I. of the XXVIth dynasty. His tomb at Sakkarah is one of the most beautiful and important in existence for its magical and liturgical texts.

BAKENRANF.

A king of Egypt of the XXIVth dynasty. He was the son of Tafnekht, or Thnephactus. He was a wise and brave but unfortunate king ; and several miracles, such as the prophecy of a monstrous double ram, are said to have happened in his reign. He was conquered by Sabako, king of the Ethiopians, who burnt him alive after he had reigned six years. He was the Bocchoris of the Greeks.

BAKHDI. " Bactria."

In Zendic mythology the name of the third resting-place of the Iranians, after their exile from Aryanem-Vaedjo, which see.

BAKHEN.

An Egyptian town, the site of which is unknown. It was sacred to the deity Ba.

BAKHEPERUNEB.

The prenomen of King Tutankhamen, of the XVIIIth dynasty, which see.

BAKHTAN.

A country in Mesopotamia, which has been supposed to have been the Bagistan of Classic history. One daughter of the king of that country married Rameses XII., king of Egypt : and another, the princess Bentaresh, was possessed by a demon who was only expelled from her by the presence of the sacred ark of the deity Khonsu, of Upper Egypt. *See* Rameses XII.

BAKRANS.

An Egyptian lady, of the family of Bocchoris, or Bakenranf. Her mummy and sarcophagus are in the British Museum.

BAKURNRO.

A queen of Egypt, the wife of King Amenmeses, who was one of the last monarchs of the XIXth dynasty.

BALA.

A city near Armenia, which combined with Urza, king of Armenia, against Sargon II., who conquered it, and sent its inhabitants into slavery into Palestine and Phenicia.

BALADU.

The governor of Sibaniba, in the reign of Vulnirari III. He was eponym of the year B.C. 787, the chief events in which were an expedition to Matai, and the consecration of a new temple to the god Nabu.

BALASI.

An early Chaldean astronomer, some observations by whom have been preserved. The name is the same as that which is rendered Belasis by the Greek historians.

BALASU.

A Chaldean nobleman. He was the father of Nabusalim king of the Dakkusi, which names see.

BALBASU. "Bel is to be."(?)

The name of an early Assyrian tax collector. *See* Kaptiya.

BALDUR.

In Scandinavian mythology the beautiful and bright god of the summer season. He was slain by treachery by Loki a wicked demon, by means of an arrow taken from the mistletoe tree. At his death the deities and all nature wept.

BALOT. *Or* AAHLU.

In Egyptian mythology another name for the Elysian valley of Aoura, which see.

BALTILISHUR.

An Elamite city, which was destroyed by Sennacherib.

BAMBYCE.

An Aramæan city, the site of which is now called Kalessi. It was the Hierapolis of the Greek writers.

BANA.

The son of Kala. He was an Assyrian tax collector at Warka, in the reign of Cambyses.

BA-N-DED.

Another form of the name of the Egyptian sacred ram deity Mendes.

BANTANATH. "Daughter of Anaitis."

The daughter of Rameses II., king of Egypt of the XIXth dynasty. From her being named after a Semitic deity her mother was probably one of the foreign or hostage wives of Rameses. She became a queen, but of what country or who she married are as yet unknown. She was at one time supposed, but wrongly so, to have been a wife, as well as a daughter, of her father.

BAR.

Another form of the name of the Assyrian deity Ninip. He was called also Adar and Ussur by the early Assyriologists.

BARA.

A king of the country of Ginzinai, who paid tribute to Samas Rimmon.

BARABUR.

A district rendered tributary to Assyria by Samsivul or Samas Rimmon III.

BARGA.

A city of Hamath which was conquered and annexed to Assyria by Shalmaneser II.

BARSIP. *Or* BORSIPPA.

A town in Babylonia famous for the great temple of the god Bel, which rose in seven spheres, and the summit of which was coated with gold. It was erected towards the close of his reign by Nabukuduruzar II., king of Babylon. *See also* Borsippa.

BARTABBA.

In Chaldean astronomy the name of an unidentified fixed star.

BARTABBADUDU. "The Doubly Little."

In Chaldean astronomy the name of a star or planet which is not yet certainly identified.

BARTABBAGALGAL. "The Doubly Great."

In Chaldean astronomy the name of a famous star or planet of the West, which has not yet been certainly identified.

BARU.

An Assyrian measure of capacity, ten of which went to the *log* or *lagitu.*

BARUIR.

A king of Armenia who combined with the Medes and Persians to destroy Nineveh. In this he was successful, and then uniting all the petty Armenian kingdoms under one government, he became their sovereign on the fall of the Assyrian empire. Baruir reigned more than forty years, towards the last of which his kingdom was ravaged by Tiglath Pileser II. He was succeeded by his son Urtsa. (Lenormant.)

BARUKATATAU.

A mystical name of the Osirian deceased when fully glorified. It occurs in the CLXIIIrd chapter of the Ritual of the Dead.

BASA.

A priest and chief of an unascertained Egyptian town. He was the son of the priest Amenemant. The period when he lived is unknown.

BASHU.

The name of a town in Egypt which was sacred to the deities Osiris and Sekhet. Its site is at present unidentified.

BASMAGUT.

In Hindu mythology an evil spirit who wrought ill to mankind. He is said to have destroyed himself in his intense wickedness.

BASOUI.

An Egyptian priestly dress made out of a large piece of white cloth, with a broad fringe along the outer hem. It is often found accompanying the mummies of the XIXth dynasty, and was sometimes sixteen feet long by two wide. It may have been that which was called in the papyri the " Robe of Sanctification."

BAST. *Or* BUBASTIS.

A goddess who was worshipped in the second, or Latopolite nome, of Lower Egypt. *See* Bubastes and Sekhet.

BASTPADUSE.

Another form of the Egyptian royal name Petubastes, which see.

BATA.

The name of the younger brother who was the victim of falsehood and jealousy in the ancient Egyptian romance called the " Tale of the Two Brothers," which was written in the reign of Rameses II. His name is sometimes read Satou.

BATA.

A great mystical serpent who is called " The Soul of the Earth," in the LXXXVIIth chapter of the Ritual of the Dead.

BATAANTA.

See Bantanath or Bentanat, a daughter of Rameses II. of the XIXth dynasty.

BATANA.

A short stick used by the ancient Egyptians, with which domestic servants were frequently chastised by their masters.

BATH.

An Hebrew measure of capacity, equal to 7½ gallons.

BATTA.

King of the Lydians. He was the father of King Maurmaiu, who was lost in the battle of the Greeks when they invaded Egypt against Menepthah II.

BATZU.

An Arabian territory which was ravaged by Esarhaddon, who put to death eight of its sovereigns, including two queens.

BAU.

An Egyptian gentleman of the XIIth dynasty. His father was named Mentuhote, his mother Sebekaa, and his sons Usertesen and Ameni.

BAUENHAR.

An early Egyptian town, over which the deity Khnum presided. Its site is not known.

BAUT.

An Egyptian deity who was worshipped at the town of Parsha.

BAZU.

A district in Arabia which was conquered and plundered by Esarhaddon, king of Assyria. It was probably the Buz of Hebrew writers.

BAZZUTA.

A king of the country of the Taurlai, who paid tribute to Samas Rimmon, king of Assyria.

BEBE.

The son of an Egyptian king of the XIIth dynasty, probably Rasebaknefru.

BEGBE.

The modern name of the town which was called by the ancient Egyptians, Senem.

BEGELMIR.

In Scandinavian mythology the last of the ice giants. He escaped destruction in the blood of Ymir, wherein all his brethren were drowned, by building a ship in which he and his wife took refuge. After the reconstruction of the earth he then re-peopled it.

BEHNESA.

The modern name of the eighteenth nome and city in Upper Egypt, which was called by the Greeks, Oxyrhynchus.

BEHNI.

The Egyptian name of a town in Nubia near to Philæ. It was famous for a brick temple to Ra or the sun, which was erected there by Thothmes III. of the XVIIIth dynasty.

BEHRA.

In Hindu mythology the name of a sacred lake near the residence of Brahma. It had the properties of a fountain of perpetual youth.

BEIT. "Castle."

The name applied in the kingdom of Sabæa to the castled towns of the vassal lords in contradistinction to those erected by the king, which were called Hedjar.

BEIT ALLAH. "House of God."

The name given by Mahomet to the great temple or Caaba at Mecca, when he adopted it as a sacred place of pilgrimage.

BEITOUALLY.

The modern name of a village in Nubia, where Rameses II. caused a temple to the deities Ra and Khnum to be excavated in the living rock; and upon the walls of the inner chambers of which he had all his victories described, with a series of magnificent bas-reliefs illustrating them.

BEK.

An Egyptian officer. The first squire, and chief of the grooms of Rameses II. of the XIXth dynasty.

BEKENAMEN.

The royal scribe, and royal favourite of one of the monarchs of the XVIIIth dynasty, but of what monarch it is not known. His father's name was Sennofre, and his mother's name Apu.

BEKTAMUN.

The daughter of an unidentified Egyptian king.

BEKTATEN.

A daughter of Amenhotep IV. of the XVIIIth dynasty.

BEKTENHAK. " Servant of the King."

An official Egyptian title, which was applied to ladies of rank who were in personal attendance at the royal palace.

BEKTMUT.

A daughter of Rameses II. of the XIXth dynasty.

BEKTUERNURO.

The wife of Amenmeses, king of Egypt, in the XIXth dynasty.

BEL.

The great national deity of the Babylonians, as Assur was of the Assyrians. He was one of the deities of the first triad, consisting of Anu, Hea, and Bel, and in Accadian his name was written Engi. He was also called Elu, or Ilu, in which form he takes a prominent position in the Izdubar Legends, and more generally Bilu, whence the Greek name Bel. His chief titles were " The God of the World," that is of the affairs of the world, " Determiner of Destinies," and " Father of the Gods," in this case the term gods being applied to the stars. He is now considered to represent the great deification of physical power, and he was the presiding deity of the moving heavenly bodies. Hence, therefore, the great astronomical work of Sargon I. was called Namar-Bili, " The Illumination (or the eye of) Bel." In the ancient mythical tablet recording the war of the gods, Sin, the moon, Shamas, the sun, and Ishtar, the queen of the stars, are called his children. In the Deluge Legend, Bel is the chief god by whom the destruction of mankind is effected, and he was the only deity who murmured at Harisadra being saved; as a punishment for which offence he was shut out of heaven and no offerings were made by the patriarch to him. Bel is continually represented as taking council of the wise and benevolent Hea, and generally his characteristics were those of force and wrath, rather than of wisdom or love.   The consort of Bel was the goddess Bilat, or Belat, who was a goddess of reproductive nature and a feminine form of himself, in which latter character she was also a goddess of war.   Bel was represented on the sculpture under the figure of a king, wearing a tiara crested with bulls' horns and a sceptre as the emblems of power.   *See also* Baal.   (Boscawen.)

BELATSUNAT.

An early queen of Babylonia, the first recorded in Archaic history She was succeeded by her son Singasit.

BELBALAD.

The Tartan of Samsivul IV. and eponym of the year B.C. 815, the chief events in which were an expedition to Deri and "the great god to Deri went."

BELBALIDINA.

The general of Nabubalidina, king of Babylonia.   He marched to the relief of the people of the Suru, who had revolted from the Assyrian subordination ; but he was defeated together with his allies by Assur-nazirpal, king of Assyria.

BELBANI.

An early king of Assyria.   He was the son of a man named Adasi, and was one of the ancestors of Sargon II.

BELBASA.

King of the Gambuli.   He assisted Urtaki, king of Elam, in his invasion of Babylonia, and was with him defeated by Assurbanipal.

BELBASANI.

The governor of Siphinis in the reign of Vulnirari or Rimmon Nirari III.   He was eponym of the year B.C. 792, the chief event in which was an expedition to Hupuskia.

BELDAAN.

The Rabbitur of Assurnirari II.   He was eponym of the year B.C. 750, in which year it was recorded that there was "peace in the land."

BELDAAN.

The governor of Calah in the reign of Tiglath-Pileser II.   He was eponym of the years B.C. 744, the chief event in which was an expedition to Zimri, and 734, in which year took place an expedition to Palestine. He may have been the same officer as the Rabbituri Beldaan.

BELDAAN.

The chief of the palace of Vulnirari or Rimmon Nirari III., and eponym of the year B.C. 808, in which year took place an expedition to Minni or Ararat.

BELDAGON.

A form of the deity or demiurgus Bel, as the creator of life from the waters. He was represented as a divine being, half man and half fish, and he was practically the same deity as Oannes, or Dagon, which see.

BELEMURANNI.

The governor of Rezeph in the reign of Tiglath Pileser II. He was eponym of the year B.C. 737, the chief event in which was an expedition to Media.

BELESIR

The chief of the palace of Shalmaneser III. He was eponym of the year B.C. 778, the principal event in which was an expedition to Ararat.

BELESIS.

The Greek form of the Chaldean proper name Balasi, which see.

BELGUR.

The king of Zibara, who was conquered by and paid tribute to Samsivul or Samas Rimmon III. After ravaging the country, the king of Assyria set up his own statue in the capital city of Zibara, in token of his conquest.

BELHARRANBELUZUR.

The chief of the palace of Tiglath Pileser II. He was governor of Gozan, and eponym of the year B.C. 741, in which year commenced a three years' war with Arpad, and B.C. 727, when there was another warlike expedition to a country the name of which is lost.

BELIBNI.

A Chaldean officer who took captive and surrendered Tammaritu, king of Elam, to Assurbanipal.

BELIBNI.

A Babylonian officer who had been educated at the court of Sargon II., and who was placed on the throne of Babylon by Sennacherib after the defeat of Merodach-baladin, at the battle of Kisu.

BELILAI.

The governor of Arbaha in the reign of Assurdan III. He was eponym of the year B.C. 769, the chief event in which was an expedition to Ituha.

BELITARUS.

The Greek form of the Assyrian royal name Belkatirassu, which see.

BELKAPKAPU.

An early king of Assyria, who is also said to have been the founder of the Assyrian monarchy, a statement which has been repeated in the Cuneiform inscriptions of several early monarchs.

11

BELKATIRASSU.   " Bel has strengthened my hand."

The superintendent of the royal gardens of the kings of Assyria. In the decline of the Assyrian power he raised a conspiracy, and dethroned his master, thus becoming himself king of Assyria. He thus founded a new line of kings, and was the Belitarus of the Greeks. (Lenormant.)

BELKUDURUZUR.

An early Assyrian monarch. He was the son of Tugultininip, and was killed by Vulpalidinna, king of Babylonia, who threw off his allegiance to the Assyrians.

BELLABARISRUK.

A noble Chaldean, who is supposed to have been chief of the Magi. He headed a conspiracy, and temporarily usurped the throne of Babylon in the reign of Nabukuduruzur.

BELLABARISRUK.

The son and successor of Nergalsarussur, king of Babylon. He was only an infant, but was, so it is asserted by the Greek historians, put to death by the Chaldean lords on account of his vicious propensities. He was the Laborosoarchod of Berosus. (Lenormant.)

BEL-LUDARI.

The governor of Bile in the reign of Tiglath Pileser II. He was eponym of the year B.C. 730, in which year there was peace in the land.

BELLUSH.

Another form of the Assyrian royal name Belnirari, or Vulnirari.

BELNIRARI.

An early king of Assyria, the son of Asshurubalat. Taking advantage of a revolution in Babylonia, he marched an army into that country, and for a time conquered it. *See* Vulnirari.

BELQZABAT.

The governor of Mazamua in the last year of the reign of Samsivul or Samas Rimmon IV. He was eponym of the year B.C. 811.

BELSADUA.

The governor of Dihnun in the reign of Assurdan III. He was eponym of the year B.C. 756, in which year there was peace in the land.

BELSAMILICAPI.

A very early Babylonian king. He was one of the ancestors of Vulnirari I., but nothing else is known respecting him.

BEL-SAMU.

An early Chaldean king who reigned at Zirgulla. He was called by the Turanians Va-anna ; nothing else is known respecting him.

BELSARANNI.

The prefect of the city of Kurban, under Sennacherib.

BEL-SARRA-UZUR.   " Bel protect the King."

The son, and, at the fall of the empire, joint king of Babylon with his father, Nabonidus. He reigned but for a very few years, as immediately after the defeat of the Babylonians by Cyrus, king of Persia, Babylon was blockaded and taken after a short siege, in which Bel-sarra-uzur was slain. Soon after that his father, who had abandoned the throne by flying to Borsippa, surrendered to the Medes and Persians, by whom he was sent into exile into Carmania, where he died ; and the second Babylonian empire ceased to exist. Belsharussar or Bel-sarra-uzur was the Belshazzar of Hebrew history. (Lenormant.)

BELSHAZZAR.

The governor of the city of Kisesim. He revolted against Sargon II., by whom he was captured and led into slavery, and the name of his city changed to Karmasmasu.

BELSHAZZAR.

The Hebrew form of the Chaldean royal name Bel-sarra-uzur, which see.

BELSILALANI.

The prefect of the city Karchemish, the Carchemish of Hebrew writers, in the reign of Sennacherib.

BELSTA.

In Scandinavian mythology the daughter of the giant Bölthorn, and the wife of Borr, the son of the first man.

BEL-SUMILI-KAPI.

An almost mythical king who was reputed to have been the founder of the Assyrian monarchy. His name is only met with in an inscription of Vulnirari or Rimmon Nirari I.

BEL-SUM-ISCUN.

An early Chaldean astronomer, and a chamberlain of state, some observations by whom have been preserved.

BEL-TAGGIL.

The governor of Isana, in the reign of Assurdan III. He was eponym of the year B.C. 758, the chief events in which were an expedition to Guzana, and a subsequent peace in the country.

BELTANAGBAL.

According to the early Assyriologists, another form of the Assyrian royal name Vulnirari, which see.

BEL-TARZI-ANVA.

The governor of Calah, Hamidi, and some other cities, in the reign of Rimmon-nirari III. He was eponym of the year B.C. 798, in which there was an expedition to Zimri. He dedicated four small statues of the god Nebo, in gratitude for the preservation of the life of the king and the queen Sammuramat : two of these statues are now in the British Museum.

BELTIS.   *Or* BELAT.

In Babylonian mythology the sister and consort of the deity Bel. She was the goddess of war as well as of nature, and was called "The Mother of the Gods." According to Herodotus, every woman living in Babylon was compelled to prostitute herself to a stranger in the temple of Beltis once in her life. Her analogue was the Mylitta of Greek mythology.

BELZARBI.

A form of the deity Bel, to whom a temple was erected at Babylon by Nabukudaruzur or Nebuchadnezzar.

BEL-ZIKIR-ISKUN.

A King of Assyria. He succeeded Assurbanipal, but his relationship to him is not known. He was simultaneously attacked by Phraortes king of Media, Psammetichus king of Egypt, and the revolted chiefs of Babylon. By the aid, however, of his general, Nabopolassar, he defeated the Elamites and subdued the Babylonians, whilst himself repulsed the Medes at the battle of Rhages, where their king was slain. The Medes soon recovered their position, and the king of Assyria was only delivered from his foes by an incursion of the savage Scythians into Media, and afterwards into Assyria, where they allied themselves with him for a time, but after his death, and indeed at the close of his reign, plundered and ravaged the country. Bel-zikir-iskun was succeeded by Assur-ebil-ili, the son of Assurbanipal.

BENAIBARQA.

A Phenician city which was conquered by Sennacherib on his first invasion of Palestine. It was the Beneberak of Hebrew writers.

BENAT-ALLAH.   "Daughters of God."

In ancient Arabian mythology the name of a multitude of inferior deities of the feminine gender. Their characteristics are not certainly known.

BENATEHHOR.

A priest of Amen Ra, in the country of Uas, in the time of Necho II. of the XXVIth dynasty.

BENDIDI.

The Assyrian name for the Egyptian city of Mendes, which was raised into a separate kingdom under the Assyrian Icosarchy under Esarhaddon.

BENEBERAK.

The Hebrew name of the Phenician city Benaibarqa, which see.

BENEMBA.

The wife of Tahutnefer, a sacred scribe of Amen Ra, in the XVIIIth dynasty.

BENHADAD I.

King of Syria, and the son of Hadad, the king of Edom or Idumea.

BENHADAD II.

The son and successor of Benhadad I., king of Syria. He was the leader of the Syrian confederacy against Shalmaneser II., whom he encountered, together with his allies, with an army of between 80,000 and 90,000 men. The king of Assyria, however, defeated them all at Qarqar, but was unable to pursue his victory, owing to his own severe losses. Benhadad was more successful in his wars with Omri, king of Samaria, whom he compelled to pay tribute.

BENHADAD III.

A king of Damascus. He was three times defeated by Jehoash, king of Israel, who recovered from him the cities taken by his father. He had but a short reign, and was succeeded by Mariah, the last independent king of Damascus.

BENHIDRI.

The Assyrian form of the Syrian royal name Benhadad, which see.

BENI-HASSAN.

A town in Middle Egypt which was formerly called Speos Artemidos. It was famous for its extensive and beautifully decorated tombs, and especially one, that of Khnumhotep, a great officer in the court of Osirtesen I. of the XIIth dynasty. In it are represented some of the most graphic details of Archaic Egyptian life, as well as the famous scene of the arrival of the thirty-seven Aahmu bringing tribute to Egypt, who were at one time believed to have been the Hebrews under Jacob. From the peculiar columns in the entrance to the excavations the form and principle of the Grecian Doric is thought to have been derived. *See* also Khnumhotep and Sekhet.

BENIHASSAN.

See Speos Artemidos, Khnum Hotep, and Sekhet.

BENKAEI.

A royal Egyptian priestess, the wife of Amenemhet the chief of the region of Tenti and overseer of the House of Osiris. She lived probably in the time of the Old Empire.

BENNEBENSKHAUF.

A priest of Khem, and chief of the auditors of an unnamed Egyptian queen, probably of the Bubastic period or XXVIIth dynasty.

Bennekheb.

An Egyptian lady who was attached to the worship of Seb the father of Osiris, in the XIIth dynasty. The worship of that deity was not at that time common in Egypt. Her husband or son was named Antefaker.

Bennu.

The sacred bird of Osiris, probably a kind of lapwing. From its being supposed to accompany the soul through its journeys in the lower life, it was gradually accepted as its emblem, the emblem of its resurrection. It was further also a symbol of a period of time, the great cycle of 1265 years, which gave rise to the Grecian fable of the phœnix.

Bennu.

In Egyptian astronomy the name of the planet Venus, whose phases as a morning and an evening star were supposed to symbolise death and the resurrection. (Brugsch.)

Bent.

The name of the Egyptian harp. It was often of great size, and had no vertical pillar ; the number of strings ranged from four to twenty-two. There were great varieties of form adopted in its construction.

Bentaresh.

The name of a younger daughter of the king of Bakhtan. She was possessed by a demon who was only expelled from her body by the presence of the sacred ark of the deity Khons of Thebes, which was sent out of Egypt for that purpose by her brother-in-law, Rameses XII. of the XXth dynasty.

Bentehhor.

A priest and scribe in the temple of Amen Ra. The time when he lived is uncertain.

Bentmut.

A sister of Amenhotep IV. of the XVIIIth dynasty.

Bentres.

The earlier name of the princess Ranofru, the wife of Rameses XII.

Bentreshpu.

An Egyptian lady. Her name is of Syrian origin. *See also* Astaret-enheb.

Beon.

According to the Greek lists, the name of an early Egyptian king of Bubastis. He has not yet been certainly identified.

Berenice.

A daughter of Ptolemy Soter II. She was generally called Cleopatra. She succeeded her father, and reigned for six months, at the end of which she was assassinated by her cousin Alexander II., B.C. 80.

BERENICE.

A daughter of Ptolemy Auletes. She deposed her father, and reigned in Egypt conjointly with her sister Tryphena for a year, and then by herself for two years longer. She was slain by the Roman general Gabinius, and Ptolemy Auletes was restored to the throne, B.C. 55.

BERENICE.

The daughter of Antigonus, king of Asia Minor, the second queen of Ptolemy Soter I., and the mother of Ptolemy Philadelphus, B.C. 311.

BERENICE.

The wife of Euergetes I.

BERENICE.

The wife of Ptolemy Philomater III.

BERENICE EUERGETES.

The daughter of Ptolemy Philadelphus. She was adored as an Egyptian goddess in the city of Memphis under Ptolemy V.

BERENICE CHRYSOS.

An Egyptian seaport on the Red Sea, 150 miles from the town of Coptos, having stations at regular intervals on the road leading to it through the desert.

BEREZAT.

In Zendic mythology a holy mountain, in the centre of the earth, from whose side flows the sacred river Arvanel.

BEROSUS.

A Chaldean priest, who translated the annals of his country into Greek about B.C. 276, when he dedicated the work to Antiochus Soter. His records were at one time disputed, but they have to a great extent been confirmed by the Assyrian monuments and tablets, especially since the discovery of the so-called Izdubar Legends by Mr. G. Smith.

BERUTH.

In Phenician mythology the wife of the primæval deity Eliun, or Hypsistus.

BES. *Or* BESA.

A warlike and savage deity of Arabian origin ; when introduced into Egypt he was regarded as a form of Typhon or Baal. He was represented as a short man with deformed legs, and a hideous face with a protruding tongue ; with his right hand he generally brandished a sword over his head, upon which was a high crown of erect feathers curving outwardly. Round his loins was a panther's skin, the tail hanging down between his legs. Besa was also the special god of dancing, and of the female toilet, and hence his figure continually occurs upon mirrors and perfume bottles. His analogue has been thought to be the Siva of the Hindus.

BESA.

Another name of the Greco, or rather Romano-Egyptian town or Antinoe, which see.

BESSA.

A peculiar kind of terra cotta bottle, made by the Alexandrians. The body of the vessel resembled the head of the god Bes.

BET.

An Egyptian name of the metal iron. *See* Ba and Baaenepe.

BETESWAMY.   "God of Sport."

A Badaga deity who was supposed to inhabit the forests of the Neilgherriés in Hindustan.

BETH-AKHIADANNA.

An Elamite city which was destroyed by Sennacherib.

BETH-AKHLAMI.

An Elamite city which was destroyed by Sennacherib.

BETH-AMMON.   "House of Ammon."

A town in South Palestine which was conquered by Vaiteh I., king of Arabia, on his conquest of Palestine against Assurbanipal.

BETH-AMUKKAN.

A city of Elam, which was destroyed by Sennacherib.

BETH-ANATH.   "House of Anaitis."

A Syrian town which was conquered and fortified by Seti I. of the XIXth dynasty.

BETH-ARRIBI.

An Elamite city which was destroyed by Sennacherib.

BETH-ASSUTSI.

An Elamite city which was destroyed by Sennacherib.

BETH-BUNAKI.

An Elamite city which was destroyed by Sennacherib.

BETHDAGON.

See the Phenician name Bitdaganna.

BETHEL.   "House of God."   *Also* BETHU-EL, Greek, Βαιτυλος.

In Phenician mythology the name given to certain sacred stones, which were probably ærolites, in which the divine essence was supposed to dwell. They were analogues to the Bætylia of the Prekoranic Arabs, and possibly also to the Linga of the Hindus.

BETH-IMBIAH.

An Elamite city destroyed by Sennacherib.

BETH-IMDIRA.

An Assyrian city which revolted to Assurdan, the rebel, and was after-wards re-conquered by Samas Rimmon or Samsivul III.

BETH-KATPALANI.

An Elamite city which was destroyed by Sennacherib.

BETH-QAMUL.   " House of the Camel."

A town in Moab which was erected by Mesha, king of Moab. It is remarkable for being mentioned on the stele now called the Moabite Stone.

BETH-QITSI.

An Elamite city which was destroyed by Sennacherib.

BETH-RISIYA.

A city of Elam which was destroyed by Sennacherib.

BETH-SALATAKKI.

A city of Elam which was destroyed by Sennacherib.

BETH-SHEAL.

The Egyptian name of an uncertain Syrian town.

BETH-TUPHAR.

The Egyptian name of an uncertain Syrian town.

BETH-UBIAH.

An Elamite city which was destroyed by Sennacherib.

BETTA.

An officer called a "walker" in the XIIIth dynasty. His funereal inscription is obscure.

BHAVANI.

In Hindu mythology the goddess mother of the Trimurti or the three deities Brahma, Vishnu, and Siva. Her attributes varied in different parts of India according to the name of the local goddess in whom she was venerated.

BHRIGU.

An Hindu deity. *See* Angiras.

BHUMASSER.

In Hindu mythology the name of a terrible giant who was overcome by the god Krishna, who liberated from his power 16,000 princesses, and then married them all himself.

BHUTA.

In Hindu mythology the name of an evil spirit. *See* Asvarna.

BIAZI.

In Chaldean astronomy the name of an unidentified star.

BIBAN EL MOLUK.

A great valley, waste and narrow, between the Libyan mountains at the back of the city of Thebes in Upper Egypt. It was and is famous for its containing the deeply excavated tombs of the kings of Egypt, chiefly of the Ramesside period. There are however also there the great tomb of Amenhotep III., and of several Egyptian queens. Perhaps the finest tomb of all is that of Seti-menepthah I., which was first opened by Belzoni in 1815, and which has since been repeatedly described, and its antiquities illustrated. According to tradition there are yet remaining several other grand sepulchres in the neighbourhood, but their site has not yet been discovered.

BICHERES.

According to the Greek lists the successor of Ratheris, king of Memphis. He has not yet been certainly identified.

BIENECHES.

. The eighth king of Egypt, and the last monarch of the first Thinite dynasty. He reigned twenty-six years.

BIENRA.

In Egyptian mythology the name of the deity of the soul of the sun, adored under the form of a kneeling ram.

BIFROST.

In Scandinavian mythology the name of the rainbow which was considered to be a bridge from earth to heaven, only to be crossed by the good spirits.

BII.

An unidentified Egyptian district. It was probably situated near Memphis.

BIIRKHU.

The Assyrian form of the Egyptian royal name Bakenranf or Bocchoris, which see.

BIKRAN.

A town in Palestine, which was conquered and added to his dominions by Mesha, king of Moab.

BIL.

In Scandinavian mythology the child of Wedfonar, and one of the two spots on the moon's face.

BIL. "The Lord."

A Himyaritic deity. He may probably have been the Bel of the Chaldeans.

BILALA.

A deity of the Susians, of whom nothing is known.

BILDAYAN.

The Rabbituru under Assur Nirari, or Vulnirari, king of Assyria.

BILE.

A city or district in Mesopotamia which was governed by an Assyrian chief named Bel-ludari, in the reign of Tiglath Pileser II.

BILIMMIANI.

The Tartan of Assyria during the first years of the sole reign of Sennacherib.

BILIT.

The Assyrian feminine Sacti of the god Bel. She was called "The Mother of the Gods," and was the Mylitta of Greek mythology. *See* Beltis, or Belat.

BILIT TAAUTH. "Mother of the Gods."

A Chaldean goddess, to whom a temple was built at Ur by Urhammu, king of the Chaldeans.

BILKUMMI. "Lord of the Palace."

The title of an Assyrian officer of state, who probably had custody of the royal household.

BILNIMIKI. "Lord of Mysteries."

A frequently occurring title of the Assyrian deity Hea, the god of the underworld.

BILSIDI.

The prefect of the palace under Shalmaneser III.

BILSUNU.

The prefect of the city of Khindana, in the reign of Assurbanipal.

BILZI.

A town near Karchemish, conquered by Samas Rimmon III., king of Assyria.

BINEBTAT.

An Egyptian deity adored under the figure of a kneeling ram. His title was the spirit lord of Tattu.

BINLIKKISH.

Another reading of the Assyrian royal name now accepted as Vul-nirari or Rimmon-nirari, which see.

BIN-NIRARI I.

Another form of the Assyrian royal name Vulnirari, which see.

BINOTHRES.

The Greek form of the Egyptian royal name Baienneter, which see.

BINRA.

A son of King Aahmes I. of the XVIIth dynasty.

BIR.   "Vermillion."

In Chaldean astronomy the name of one of the twelve stars of the West.

BIRADJIK.

The modern name of the Assyrian territory which was anciently called Bit-Adini.

BIRDADDA.

Another form of the name of Birvul, king of Arabia.

BIRIZ-KHADRI.

A king of the Medes, whose district was overrun and his towns demolished by Assurbanipal, king of Assyria.

BIRTU of Kar Bel-matati.

An Aramean city which was conquered by Tiglath Pileser II.

BIRTU of Labbanat.

An Aramean city which was conquered by Tiglath Pileser II.

BIRTU of Sarragitu.

An Aramean city which was conquered by Tiglath Pileser II.

BIRUTU.

A town in South-east Assyria conquered by Assurnazirpal.

BIRVA.

In Chaldean astronomy the name of an unidentified star.

BIRVUL.

A king of Arabia, conquered and led into captivity by Assurbanipal in his war with Vaiteh.   He was also called Birdadda.

BISIRA.

The king of Arima, a district bordering upon Assyria, rendered tributary by Samsivul III.

Bisirain.

A king of the country of the Arimai, who paid tribute to Samas Rimmon, king of Assyria.

Bit. "A House" *or* "Temple."

This common prefix in Assyrian names is indifferently spelt Bit, Bet, and Beth. The latter name is the Hebrew, and the first the Assyrian form.

Bit-almas.

A temple erected in Agane, by Sargina I., and rebuilt by Nabonidus II., the last king of Babylon.

Bit-amukkani.

A temple erected in Sape, by Kinziru, the last king of Babylon. It was destroyed by Tiglath Pileser II.

Bit-anna. "House of Heaven."

The name of a great temple to the goddess Anunit, erected by Urukh, king of Ur, at Erech, and subsequently enlarged by his successors.

Bit-daramsemu.

A temple erected in Larsa, by Rimsin, an early king of Babylonia.

Bit-dianisi. "House of the Judge of men."

A temple to the deity Shamas, the sun, erected by Nebukuduruzzar II.

Bit-eser. "Temple of Uprightness."

The Chaldean general name of the temples of the god Adar.

Bit-galzib.

The name of a temple erected at Larsa, by Sindinna, an early Chaldean king.

Bit-gilsa.

A temple erected at Ur, to the goddess Ninmarki, by Dungi, king of Babylonia.

Bit-ginablungani.

A temple erected at Ur, by Gungunnu, king of Babylonia.

Bit-harris.

A temple erected at Ur, by Dungi, king of Babylonia.

Bit-hausa.

A temple erected at Zirgulla, by Ardusin, king of Babylonia.

Bit-ilahat.

A castle near Sana, in Sabæa, dedicated to the goddess Ilahat.

BIT-ILILANI. " House of the Gods."

A famous temple in Palestine not quite identified.

BIT-KERIB.

A temple built at Urukh or Warka, by Singasit, an early Babylonian king.

BIT-KHILIANI.

A temple erected at Ur, by Gungunna, king of Babylonia.

BIT-KIBA.

A temple erected at Urukh, by Singasit, an early Babylonian king.

BIT-KUR. " Temple of the Country."

The name of a temple of the deity Bel.

BIT-MAKHTILLA. " House of Height."

A temple of the deity Anu, where situated it is not known.

BIT-MEKIT.

A temple at Nipur in honour of the goddess Nana. It was restored by Libitanna or Libitnana, king of Babylonia.

BIT-MINUNI.

The name of a temple erected at Larsa, by Sinidinna, an early Chaldean king.

BIT-NERGAL. " House of Nergal."

Another name for the temple of Bitsaresir, erected at Ur, by Urukh and his son Dungi.

BIT-NURKINUGAL.

A temple erected to the deity Ur, at Ur, by Gungunnu, king of Babylonia.

BIT-PARRA.

A temple erected in Ridu or Eridu, by Ardusin, an early king of Babylonia.

BIT-RUBMAH.

The name of a temple erected at Larsa, by Sinidinna, an early Babylonian king.

BIT-RUBMAH.

A temple erected at Ur, by Kudur-Mabuk, king, and his son Ardusin, viceroy, of Babylonia.

BIT-SAGGAL.

A temple erected at Babylon in honour of the deity Marduk, by Hammurabi, the founder of the new capital. This temple was often enlarged and rebuilt by the subsequent kings of Babylonia.

BIT-SAHALLA.

A temple erected in the royal city Sape, by Kinziru, the last king of Babylonia. It was destroyed by Tiglath Pileser II.

BIT-SARESIR.

A temple erected at Ur, by Urukh, king of Babylonia, and completed by his son Dungi. It was called also Bitnergal.

BIT-SARNA.

A temple erected at Ur, by Ardusin, an early king of Babylonia.

BIT-SIDDA.

A temple or town in Babylonia, which is mentioned in an inscription of the time of Dungi, but of which nothing is known.

BIT-SIGABI.

A temple erected at Ur to the deity Ur, by Zursin, king of Babylonia.

BIT-SILANI.

A temple erected in the royal city of Sarrapanu by Nabusabsi, king of Babylon. It was plundered and destroyed by Tiglath Pileser II., king of Assyria.

BIT-TIMGAL.

A temple erected at Ur, by Urukh, king of Babylonia.

BIT-UDDAIMTIZ.

A temple erected in Larsa, by Rimsin, an early Babylonian king.

BIT-UGAL.

A temple erected to the god Bel, by Kurigalzu II. or III., king of Babylonia, at a place now called Akkerkuf.

BIT-ULMAS.

A temple to the goddess Anunit, at Sippara, which was restored by Sagasaltiyas, king of Babylonia.

BIT-ZIDA.

A famous Assyrian temple built, or more properly rebuilt, by Cyrus, king of Persia.

BIT-EDIE. "House of Eternity."

The Assyrian name for Hades.

BIT-ERIBUS. "House of Darkness."

An Assyrian name for Hades.

BIT-ADINI. "Temple of Adini."

A territory in Mesopotamia now called Biradjik. It was conquered by Assurnazirpal, king of Assyria. *See* Ahiyababa.

BIT-AHLAMI.

An Elamite city destroyed by Sennacherib.

BIT-BARRA.

A city of Illipi, conquered and added to Assyria by Sennacherib, after the revolt of Ispabara.

BIT-DAGANNA. "House of Dagon."

A Phenician city conquered by Sennacherib on his invasion of Palestine. It was the Bethdagon of the Hebrew writers.

BIT-HAMBAU.

A town in the land of Zimri, conquered by Tiglath Pileser II.

BIT-IMDUR.

An Assyrian mountain city which supported Assurdainpal in his revolt against his father Shalmaneser II.

BIT-KILAMZAH.

A town of the Yasubigalla, North of Elam, conquered by Sennacherib, and by him rebuilt as an Assyrian garrison town.

BIT-KUBATTI.

A city of the Yasubigalla, conquered by Sennacherib, and annexed to Assyria.

BIT-MATZAMANA.

A town near Armenia conquered by Dayan Assur, the Tartan for Shalmaneser II.

BIT-RISIYA.

An Elamite city destroyed by Sennacherib.

BIT-SANGIBUTI.

A town in the land of Zimri, conquered by Tiglath Pileser II.

BIT-TAMARTI. "House of observation."

The name of the royal observatory of the ancient city of Agane.

BIT-TUTU. "House of Tutu."

A city in Chaldea where the Babylonian chief, Suzub, made a last and unavailing stand against the subjection of his country to Sennacherib.

BIT-YAKIN.

A district in Southern Babylonia, which was overrun and plundered by Sennacherib after the expulsion of Merodach-baladin, and the defeat of Suzub the patriot.

BIT-ZITTE.

A city of Phenicia, conquered by Sennacherib on his first invasion of Palestine.

BITHIAH. "Daughter of Jehovah."

In Hebrew history a daughter of an Egyptian king, whom an Israelite chief, named Mered, took to wife. Nothing is discovered concerning her as yet in Egyptian history.

BIT-NUR.

In Accadian mythology the general of Adar, the champion of the gods, and the favourite of Bel. He was chiefly invoked for the protection of pregnant women, and for the maturity of the embryo.

BOCCHORIS. *Surnamed* The Wise.

The Greek form of the Egyptian royal name Bakenranf, which see.

BODAGL.

An Amalekite tribe settled in the district of Yathrib in Arabia.

BODASTORETH I.

King of Tyre, one of the successors of Pümelion. He is only known from a notice on a Phenician inscription.

BODASTORETH II.

The son and successor of Bodastoreth I., king of Tyre. He was on friendly terms with a local king of Sidon, whose name is not known.

BŒTHOS.

The Greek form of the name Butau, which see.

BOKTNASSAR.

The Arabian form of the Chaldean royal name Nabukuduruzur.

BORSIPPA.

The name of a great temple in seven spheres, which was called also Val-saggatu. It was built by Nebuchadnezzar on the site of an earlier building which the Babylonians believed to have been the traditional tower of Babel. *See also—*

BORSIPPA.

The name of a Babylonian city, meaning either "The Town of the Root of Languages," or "The Town of the Dispersion of Tribes."

BOUER.

A scribe of the royal archers of an Egyptian king. Period uncertain.

BOUTO.

The Greek name of the city and nome of Chrud-Pehu, in Lower Egypt. *See also* BUTO.

BOZRAH.

An Edomite city near Jebel, now called El Busaireh. It must not be confounded with the Bozrah of the Hauran, which is also mentioned by Hebrew writers.

BRACHYCEPHALIC.   "Short-headed."

A term used by modern anthropologists to describe a species of skull in which the length is inferior to the breadth.

BRAGI.

In Scandinavian mythology the god of Oratory and Poetry.

BRAHASPATI.

In Hindu mythology the name of the planet Jupiter and one of the Vedic deities.

BRAHMA.

In Hindu mythology a beneficent and great deity, from out of whose body all human and divine souls emanated by a process of volition, and to whom they must finally return. Every sect of Hindûism has its particular views of the nature and attributes of this supreme divinity, who is also adored by the Buddhists under another theory.

BRAHMADICAS.

In Hindu mythology the nine companions of Brahma. They were the earliest patriarchs.

BRAHME.

In Hindu philosophy the abstract principle of deity and entity as an eternal impersonality.

BRAHMIN.

The highest caste in the Hindu system, created from the head of the deity Brahma.

BRAMAPATNAM.

The dwelling of the great Hindu divinity Brahma, on the summit of Mount Meru; from the four gates of which issued the four streams of which the Ganges is composed.

BRATHU.

In Phenician mythology one of the early giants, children of Phos and his brethren, after whom Mount Brathu was named.

BUBA.

The father of Bubu, chief of Kirhi, which see.

Bubastic Dynasty.

The historical name of the kings of the XXIInd dynasty whose seat of empire was at Bubastis.

Bubastis.

Another form of the name of the Egyptian goddess Bast, the peculiar deity of the Latopolite nome.

Bubastis.

A town in Lower Egypt, now called Tel Basta, the seat of empire of the XXIInd Egyptian dynasty. Also anciently called the city and nome of Habu. From this city Psametik I. enlarged a canal begun by King Seti, to open a way from the Nile to the Red Sea. The work was stopped by an unfavourable oracle after 120,000 men had been worked to death in the excavations.

Bubastis.

A nome in the Delta of Lower Egypt, which was held by the Calasirian class of soldiers. Its principal city was Bubastis, which was sacred to the goddess Bast.

Bube.

An Elamite city destroyed by Sennacherib.

Bubi.

A city of Elam, destroyed by Sennacherib; probably the same as the the preceding.

Bubu.

The son of Buba. He was chief of the town of Kirhi, on the Upper Tigris, which he vainly defended against Assurnazirpal, king of Assyria, by whom he was taken prisoner and flayed alive.

Buccaboo.

A common Cornish word of affright. It is said to be derived from an Aryan noun meaning " Deity." (Lach Szyrma.)

Buddahu.

An Arabian kingdom, which was ravaged, and its king, Habanamru, put to death by Esarhaddon, king of Assyria.

Buddha.

The great Hindu deity and reformer, and the originator of the Buddhistic religion. He was a real personage, named Sakya-Muni, which see.

Budibahal.

One of the ten competitors for the crown of Arvad, after the death of King Yakinlu.

12*

Budii.

The Greek form of the name of the Medo-Persian caste Budiya, which see.

Budil.   *Or* Pudil.

An early king of Assyria.   He was the father of Vulnirari I. and was a great conqueror.   He built the first royal palace of Assyria.

Budiya.   *"Adscripti Glebæ."*

The name of the fifth great caste of the Medes.   It was composed of serfs, and was the Budii of the Greek historians.

Buduil.

King of the Ammonites, and one of the tributaries of Sennacherib. His name is sometimes written Peduil.

Bulludhu.

An early Chaldean astronomer, some prognostications by whom have been preserved.

Bunasi.

A city in the mountains of Nizir, conquered by Assurnazirpal.

Bundehesh.

The name of a Pehlevi translation of a lost Zendic work upon the creation, one of the sacred books of the Parsees.

Bunu.

One of the twenty petty kingdoms into which Egypt was divided after the Assyrian invasion under Esarhaddon.

Buramanu.

The chief of the city of Sinapu.   He raised a revolt against Ammibahla, the Syrian governor, and slew him ; but his master, Assurnazirpal, conquered the town, and flaying Buramanu alive, fastened his skin on the city wall.   The rest of the rebels were allowed to purchase their pardon.

Burante.

A king of the country of Yazbuk, in Northern Syria, conquered by Shalmaneser II.

Burdada.

A Median chief, who at first attempted to resist Tiglath Pileser II. on his invasion of Media; but he was compelled to flee for his life, and was in the end captured by the Assyrians.   Their treatment of him is not recorded.

Bure.

In Scandinavian mythology the first man, whose three grandchildren, Odin, Vili, and Ve, killed Ymir, the frost giant, from whose body they made the earth. *See* Ymir.

Burnaburyas I.

An early king of Babylonia. He succeeded Milisihu, and must not be confounded with the later Babylonian monarch of the same name.

Burnaburyas II.

Another early king of Babylonia. He made a treaty with Buzur Assur, king of Assyria, and repaired several of the temples at Urukh and Larsa, which had fallen into decay.

Buruta.

An Elamite city; destroyed by Sennacherib.

Busæ.

The Greek form or the name of the Median caste Buza, which see.

Busiris.

A nome in the Delta, which was held by the Hermotybian class of warriors. Its chief city was Pa-osiri-neb-Tattu, " House of Osiris, Lord of Tattu," to whom it was dedicated.

Busutu.

A city of Minni, destroyed by Assurbanipal, after the defeat of Ahsera, king of Ararat.

Butau.

The first king of the IInd Thinite dynasty of Egypt. In his time an earthquake took place, which destroyed many people, at Bubastis. He reigned thirty-eight years, and was called by the Greeks Bœthos.

Buto.

An Egyptian goddess, chiefly worshipped in the city and nome of Bouto, in Lower Egypt, which was named after her.

Buvalu.   " The Giant."

An epithet applied by the Chaldeans to the mythical hero Izdubar, adored as a deity.

Buz.

A district in Arabia, probably that known to the Assyrians as Bazu, which see.

BUZA.   " Natives."

The third great caste of the Medes; the Busæ of the Greek historians.

BUZUR-ASSUR.

An early king of Assyria, of whom little is known.

BUZUR-SA-DI-RABI.

The pilot of the ark of Adrahasis in the Chaldean legend of the deluge.   *See* Adrahasis.

C.

CAABA.

The great sacred temple at Mecca, containing the black stone which fell from heaven, and the well called Zemzem. It is one of the oldest sites of stone, or Bætylia worship, in existence.

CAB.

An Hebrew measure of capacity, equal to three pints.

CABASA.

The chief town of the Cabasite nome of Lower Egypt.

CABASITES.

A nome of Lower Egypt, West of the Phetnitic branch of the Nile. Its chief town was Cabasa. It was sacred to the worship of Horus, and its ancient name is unknown.

CABIRIM. "Powerful Ones."

In Phenician mythology the name of the seven planets considered as deities.

CACMUKU.

The Chaldean name of a great festival, in many respects analogous to the Saturnalia of the Romans. *See* Sacees.

CADIMIRRI. "Gate of God."

The Accadian name of the city of Babilu, or Babylon.

CÆSAR, CAIUS JULIUS.

The conqueror of the world. Born B.C. 100; assassinated B.C. 44. His chief monumental connection with Egypt is the insertion of his name in the royal cartouches. His, like many other great names, ha' a more fitting place in a Classic Dictionary.

CÆSARION.

The son of Cleopatra VI. and Julius Cæsar. He was the last of the Ptolemies, and the sacred ceremonies attending his birth form the principal subject of the inscriptions in the temple of Hermonthis. Cæsarion was also called Ptolemy XVIth.

CAGAGILGATI.

In Chaldean astronomy the name of the Pole-star as a god.

CAICNA.

The Phenician name of the city called by the Greeks Laodicea, and by the modern Arabs, Oum el Awamid.

CALAMUS.

One of the Phenician cities of the Triapolis, which see.

CALASIRIANS.

One of the two great divisions of the warrior class in Egypt. They were distributed over the following nomes or districts ;—Thebes, Bubastis, Aphthis, Tanis, Mendes, Sebennytus, Pharbæthus, Thmuis Onuphis, Anysis, Mycephoris, and Athribis, furnishing in all 250,000 men.

CALEB.

The son of Abdai. He was king or suffete of Tyre for six months after the death or deposition of Baalsyllech, which see.

CALIYA.

In Hindu mythology the name of a great evil serpent, who was ultimately overcome and crushed by the god Vishnu in his incarnation as Krishna.

CALMATI.

In Chaldean astronomy the name of an unidentified star.

CALNEH. "The Dwelling of Oannes."

One of the four most ancient cities of the world, and a capital of Chaldea. It was called also Ur in the Cuneiform inscriptions. Its sacred names were "The City of the God who watches over the Moon," and "The City of the House of the World." It is now called Mugheir.

CALNO.

The Hebrew name of a Syrian town called by the Assyrians Kullani.

CAMASPATES.

A Median general of Darius Hystaspes, who defeated and took prisoner the usurper Sitratachmes.

CAMBYSES.

The son of Cyrus, king of Persia. He ascended the throne about B.C. 529, soon after which he successfully invaded Egypt, and established the first Persian dynasty. At his first conquest he testified much respect for the religion and customs of the Egyptians, and caused himself to be initiated into the Isaic mysteries ; but afterwards being unsuccessful in battle, and believing that the people hated him, he changed his demeanour towards them, and ridiculing their religion, and especially the worship of Apis, caused their temples to be rifled and the bull god himself slain. There is no direct reference to this event in the Hieroglyphic texts, except a statement that under Cambyses, or Kambish as he was called, "a great calamity afflicted the entire country." A few years after this occurrence the king died B.C. 521. The name of Cambyses is found in the Assyrian texts also, but his more proper place is in the annals of Classic history.

CAMILLUS.

According to a fragment of Callimachus, the Etruscan Mercury. Servius says that youthful priestesses were called *Camillæ*. The attendant minister of the Flamen Dialis at the sacrifices was named *Camillus*.

CANDACE.

See Cleopatra surnamed Candace, the wife of Soter, and the mother of the lady Sensaos.

CANDACE.

See Kandake.

CANEPHOROI.   " Basket Bearers."

An Egyptian sacerdotal office generally held by women, whose duty it was to carry in baskets upon their heads the fruit and food of the sacred animals to whose worship they were devoted. The same office was also known in Greek mythology, and it lingered on till the IIIrd and IVth centuries of the Christian era.

CANOPIC VASES.

These vases made of alabastar, calcareous stone, porcelain, terracotta, and even wood, were destined to hold the soft parts or viscera of the body, embalmed separately and deposited in them. They were four in number, and were made in shape of the four genii of the Karneter or Hades, to whom were assigned the four cardinal points of the compass. The body of the vase was that of the genius, and the head mortised into it was the cover. The names and order of these genii were Amset, human-headed, the first genius, and the body of his vase held the stomach and large intestines. Hapi, the second, cynocephalus ape, held the small intestines ; Tuautmutf, the third, jackal-headed, held the lungs and heart ; and Kabhsenuf, the fourth, the liver and gall bladder. They were separately embalmed, were made into oval packets and placed in the vases. These vases were either plain, with the name of the genius which they represent, or with a particular formula, ending with the name of the deceased. The formulæ were speeches respectively made by Isis, Nephthys, Neith, and Selk on behalf of the deceased. The vases were placed in boxes with partitions, then set on sledges and drawn to the sepulchre with the other funereal apparatus. In the vignettes of the Ritual, chapter LXXXIX, and in the paintings of the coffins, they are represented placed under the bier on which the mummy is laid. They are found in the tombs in different positions, sometimes at the corners or angles of the coffins, in niches in the walls of the sepulchral chamber, or in the boxes with partitions in which they were taken to the sepulchre. Only the richer persons had these special receptacles, the viscera being often made into separate packets disposed close to the mummy, and covered with the bandages. Many fine examples of these vases in arragonite or oriental alabaster and calcareous stone are exhibited on the upper shelves of the walls of the North and South Egyptian Galleries of the British Museum. (Birch.)

CANOPUS.

A Greco-Egyptian deity in the form of a human-headed vase, really that of the funereal god Amset, one of the four infernal deities who had charge of the viscera of the dead.

CANOPUS.   "Conops *or* Canopy."

The Greek name of the Hermopolite city and nome in Lower Egypt, called by the Egyptians Ati.

CANOPUS.   Decree of.

This stèle was discovered in the excavations at the ruins of San in 1866. It contains a long triliteral text in Greek, Hieroglyphic, and Demotic, analogous in character to that on the Rosetta Stone, the system of interpretation of the Egyptian language derived from which it amply confirms. The decree itself is dated in the ninth year of Ptolemy III. and Euergetes I., and it describes the honours which were to be rendered to the king, the queen, and an infant princess whom they had lost ; its most important subject is practically the announcement of a rectification of the calendar by the introduction of five additional days, which were to be festivals of the gods Euergetes, to complete the solar year. This change was to take place at the rising of the star Sothis, on the 1st of the month Payni, *i.e.* 18th July, and it thus introduced a leap year into Egyptian astronomy B.C. 238, or more than two centuries prior to the official introduction of the leap year into Alexandrian chronology by the Emperor Agustus, B.C. 25. (Sharpe.)

CAPA.

An Assyrian city which revolted to Assurdan, and was reconquered by Samas-Rimmon.

CAPISCANE.

A fortress in Arachotia, where Vibanus the Satrap of the country, defeated the troops sent against him by Veisdates, the rebel king of Persia, and thus testified his allegiance to Darius Hystaspes.

CAPIUS.

In Phenician mythology a giant, one of the children ot Phos and his brethren. Mount Capius received its name from him.

CARDUNIAS.

The original name of Lower Chaldea. *See* Gandunias.

CARTOUCH.

The name given by the French Egyptologists to the elongated ring, or signet, within which the Hieroglyphic characters of the royal names are enclosed. Those of the earliest monarchs are the simplest, and those of the Ptolemaic period the most complex of the series.

CARUCASSI.

A people who under their king Kastasite assisted Nabopalassar to destroy the Assyrian empire. They were probably the inhabitants of the district now called Caucasia.

CASBU.

The six divisions into which the day and night were divided by the Babylonians. The Assyrians called the same divisions Aslu.

CASSIUM.

An Egyptian city on the Arabic frontier towards Palestine.

CAVEH.

In Arabic mythology a blacksmith of Ispahan, whose two sons having been slain to feed the snakes of Zohak, he incited the people to revolt, and slaying the demon monster, established a new dynasty. *See* Zohak.

CAYL.

The Himyaritic title of the great nobility who were vassals to the king.

CECHOUS.   *Or* KHAIECHIS.

The Greek form of the Egyptian royal name Kakau, which see.

CENE.

A chief town in the Heracleopolite nome of the Heptanomos.

CERCASORA.

A chief city of the Latopolite nome, West of the Nile, in Lower Egypt.

CHABARAS.

A river in Mesopotamia, which rising in Mount Marius, flows into the Euphrates at Carchemish, separating Assyria from Aramea.

CHABRIAS.

The admiral of the Egyptian fleet under Nekhtarhebi. He was unsuccessful in repulsing the invasion of the Persians under Artaxerxes II., but they were ultimately defeated and expelled at the battle of Mendes by Nekhtarhebi himself.

CHADIDIA.

A town in Persia where Veisdates, the rebel king, was together with his principal officers impaled and put to death by Darius Hystaspes.

CHAFKEM.

The son of an early Egyptian king. The period when he lived is uncertain.

CHAIRES.

The sixth king of the IInd Thinite dynasty of Egypt. No acts are recorded of his reign, which lasted seventeen years.

CHALAOS.

The form in which the name of the city of Calah is preserved as that of a king by Moses of Khorene.

CHALKI.

A city or district of which Assurbani was prefect under Tiglath Pileser I I. and Sargon I I.

CHAMÆL.

In Cabalistic astronomy the angel of the planet Mars.

CHANDRAGUPTA.

A great Hindu monarch, the grandfather of Asoka, by whom Buddhism was made the state religion. He was the Sandracottus of the Greeks. *See* Asoka.

CHARTUMMIN.

The name by which the Egyptian Rekhgetamen, or doctors of magic, were referred to in Hebrew history.

CHEFREN. *Or* KHEFRENES.

The Greek form of the royal name Shafra, which see.

CHEMMIS.

A nome in Upper Egypt held by the Hermotybian class of soldiers.

CHEMMIS.

The name erroneously given by Diodorus Siculus to the founder of the great pyramid of Gizeh. *See* Armæus and Chufu.

CHEMOSH.

The chief deity of the Moabites, to whom human sacrifices were offered, and in whose honour the Moabite stone was erected by Mesha, king of Moab, the contemporary of Jehoshaphat, king of Judah.

CHEMOSH-GAD.

A king of Moab. He reigned thirty years, and was succeeded by his son Mesha, who enlarged the kingdom, and rebuilt many of the towns which had fallen into decay.

CHEM-TAT-EF.

The son of an early Egyptian king.

CHENALOPEX.

The species of goose which was worshipped as a sacred animal at Thebes, in Upper Egypt.

CHENERES.

A king of the IInd Thinite dynasty of Egypt, of whom nothing is recorded.

CHENOBOSCIUM.

A chief town in the Panopolite nome, of the Thebaid of Upper Egypt.

CHEOPS.

The Greek form of the royal name Khufu, which see.

CHEPHETS.

Another name of the Phenician deity Pothos, which see.

CHESF-CHENT.

The Egyptian name for the city and nome in Upper Egypt, called by the Greeks Lycopolis the Upper. Sacred to the deity Apheru.

CHESF-PEHU.

A city and nome in Upper Egypt, called by the Greeks Lycopolis the Lower. It was sacred to the deity Hathor.

CHEV.

The Egyptian name for the city and nome near the Fayum, called Aphroditopolis by the Greeks. Here the great chancellor Bai caused the usurper Septhah and his queen Tauser to be proclaimed joint-sovereigns of Egypt after the death of Merenpthah I., to the temporary exclusion of Prince Seti, the heir apparent and brother of Queen Tauser. The nome was also called the Thmute by the Greeks. It was sacred to the worship of the goddess Hatmei, or Truth.

CHHANDAS.

An ancient Hindu treatise, dealing chiefly with the prosody and versification of the sacred Vedas.

CHINZIRUS.

The Greek form of the Babylonian royal name Kinziru, which see.

CHIRABU.

The Egyptian name of the city of Haleb, or Aleppo, which see.

CHNOUBIS.

The Gnostic form of the divine energic spirit of the Egyptian mythology. The Gnostics generally represented this deity under the form of a lion-headed serpent with a glory of seven rays inclosing the letters of his name.

CHŒREUM.

A chief city in the Hermopolite nome of Lower Egypt.

CHOIAK.

The fourth month of the Egyptian sacred year. It began about the 18th of October.

CHOSMASBELUS.

See Shamash-Bel.

CHRUD-CHEN.

A city and nome in Lower Egypt. Its site and the deity to which it was sacred are not known.

CHRUD-PEHU.

A city and nome in Lower Egypt, the Bouto of the Greeks. It was sacred to the worship of the goddess Buto.

CHUFU.

Another Greek form of the name of the Egyptian king who is called Cheops, Khufu, and Chofo.

CHUN-ABT.

A city and nome in Lower Egypt, called by the Greeks Heroopolis. It was sacred to the worship of the deity Horus.

CHUSIS.

A chief town of the Hermopolite or fifteenth nome of Upper Egypt. It is now called Cosseah.

CIARA.

A king of the city of Karsibutai, who paid a tribute of horses to Samas-Rimmon, king of Assyria.

CIBBUBU.

In Chaldean astronomy an unidentified fixed star.

CIMARUSAI.

A country near Media which was rendered tributary by Samas Rimmon, king of Assyria.

CIMMERIANS.

See the Gimirri.

CINDCARBU.

A deity of the Susians of whom nothing is known.

CINDUTAUSAI.

A country which was rendered tributary by Samas-Rimmon, king of Assyria.

CINGISTILINZAKHARAI.

A country near Media, which was rendered tributary by Samas Rimmon, king of Assyria.

CINNELADANUS.

The name given by the Greek authors to Esarhaddon, king of Assyria.

CINUCAI.

A country near Media, which was rendered tributary by Samas Rimmon, king of Assyria.

CIPABARUTACAI.

A country near Media, which was rendered tributary by Samas Rimmon, king of Assyria.

CISILIVU.

Another form of the name of the Assyrian month Cuzallu, which see.

CIT.

The Sun-god of the Cassites of Amardia.

CLEOPATRA.

A queen of Egypt. She was the daughter of Ptolemy Epiphanes, and married her brother Ptolemy Philomater about B.C. 170, and on his decease she again married her second brother Ptolemy Physcon B.C. 146, by whom she was soon repudiated.

CLEOPATRA.

A queen of Egypt, and daughter of Ptolemy Philomater, by whose orders she was forcibly married to her uncle and father-in-law, Ptolemy Physcon, on his repudiation of her mother. On the death of her husband she became co-sovereign with her son Ptolemy Soter II. B.C. 117, and then quarrelling with him drove him from the throne, and and placed her second son Alexander in his stead, who in return caused her to be put to death about B.C. 89.

CLEOPATRA BERENICE.

A queen of Egypt, and daughter of Ptolemy Soter II. *See* Berenice.

CLEOPATRA. *Surnamed* TRYPHENA.

A queen of Egypt. She was the wife of Ptolemy XIII., daughter of Ptolemy Neus Dionysius, and sister of the following Cleopatra.

CLEOPATRA.

A queen of Egypt, and the most famous of her race in history. She was the daughter of Ptolemy Auletes, and was born about B.C. 69. On his death she became sole queen, and then married her eldest brother Ptolemy, who was put to death by Julius Cæsar, who reconfirmed her position on the throne. She then married her second brother, also named Ptolemy, but growing tired of him caused him to be poisoned, and then visited Rome. Her further career belongs to Classic history. She died B.C. 30.

CLEOPATRA.

An Egyptian lady, the daughter of Ammonius, and the wife of Soter, archon of Thebes. Her mummy and sarcophagus are in the British Museum.

CLEOPATRA CANDACE.

A Greco-Egyptian lady, the daughter of Ammonius, and wife of Soter by whom she was the mother of the lady Hathorsetdsjatho, or, as the Greeks called her, Sensaos, which see.

CLYSMA.

A town at the opening of the Bay of Heroopolis. Its site is now occupied by the town of Suez.

CO.

A Greco-Egyptian town in the Cynopolite nome of the Heptanomos.

COCHABIEL.

In Cabalistic mythology the spirit of the planet Mercury.

CODAR EL AHMAR.

In Arabic history a wicked man of Thamud, who slew the sacred camel of Saleh, and thus caused the destruction of the tribe of Thamud. He is supposed to have been the Chedarlaomor of Hebrew writers, but that is not likely. *See* Kudurlagamar and Saleh.

CODAYA.

A town in ancient Arabia, between Mecca and Yathrib. Sacred to the worship of the goddess Monat.

CŒNE.

One of the chief towns of the Coptite nome of the Thebaid in Upper Egypt.

CŒNOPOLIS. "Supper City."

The Greek name of an Egyptian city properly called Ant.

COFERMARLON.

The Egyptian name of an uncertain Syrian country or town.

COLOSSI.

The Egyptians were remarkable beyond any other nation for their gigantic statues of deities, kings, and symbolic animals, of which the sphynx is a unique example. These immense works of art were generally wrought in monolith, and were brought to their position simply by the use of the roller and lever, conjoined with the united efforts of many hundred men. The following are the chief isolated statues which remain, those which are wrought in the solid rock and form the façade of the great temple of Abusimbel, being properly architectural features : Amenhotep III., XVIIIth dynasty, at Thebes, a pair, one of them being the vocal Memnon ; Rameses II., XIXth dynasty, several at Mitrahenny, at Luxor and Karnak, besides the four at Abusimbel ; Rameses III., XIXth dynasty, at Medinat Habu. Others of smaller size, but still colossal, are those of Sebekhotep III., XIIIth dynasty, at the Louvre ; and also another of a still earlier period, upon the face of which Amenhotep III. has had his own name cut, although the statue itself is of the XIIth dynasty. (Pierret.)

COLPIAS. "Wind." (?)

In Phenician mythology the primæval deity of the wind, who with his wife Baau or night begot Æon and Protogonus, the first mortal men.

COMMAGENE.

The name given in later history to the district of Kummuha, which see.

CONE.

A peculiar kind of headdress in the shape of a cone was often used by the Egyptian women of high rank under the XVIIIth and XIXth dynasties. These ornamental cones were generally painted in white or yellow, and were often decorated with wreaths of flowers. The headdress has been supposed to have a religious as well as a state significance, inasmuch as in the paintings in the tomb of Khaemha, a priest is represented as placing one of these cones on the head of a functionary who is being introduced to King Amenhotep III. (Pierret.)

CONOSCONCOLEROS.

A title erroneously applied by the Greek historians to the king Assurbanipal. It is a corruption of Kunusskunkilassur, "I the King, Vicegerent of the god Assur," a usual Assyrian title.

CONTRA-APOLLON.

A chief town in the Thebaic nome of Upper Egypt.

CONTRA-COPTOS.

A chief town in the Tentyrite nome of the Thebaid in Upper Egypt.

CONTRA-LATON.

A chief town in the Thebaic nome of Upper Egypt. The town was more anciently called Chnubis.

CONTRA-OMBOS.

A chief city in the Apollinopolite nome of the Thebaid. It was situated, as its name implies, on the opposite bank of the river Koum Ombos.

CONTRA-SYENE.

A town in the Apollinopolite nome of the Thebaid, opposite to Syene.

COPTOS.

The chief city of the Coptite nome. It was situated at the termination of the roads from the Red Sea to the river Nile, and from its early Christian bishopric the Egyptian Christians were named Copts.

COPTOS.

The Greek name for the city and nome in Upper Egypt, in the Thebaid, East of the river Nile. Its chief town was Coptos, called by the Egyptians Harti.

COR.

A Hebrew measure of capacity equal to 75 gallons.

CORTE.

A Greco-Egyptian town in the Dodecaschœnon, a district of Nubia.

COSSÆANS.

A Hamitic or Cushite people dwelling in Susiana. They were the the Kossi of the Cuneiform inscriptions.

COSSEAH.

The modern name of the Greco-Egyptian town Chusis, which see.

Coxcox.

The name given in Mexican mythology to the patriarch, who together with his wife Xochiquetzal, escaped the deluge by constructing a boat of cypress wood.

Crux Ansata.

See Ansata.

Cucufa.

The name of the peculiar staff which was called *Uas* and was held by the Egyptian deities.   It had the head of an unknown animal on the top, and a peculiarly shaped hook at the other end.   The extremities were generally made of bronze.

Cukhia.

In Chaldean astronomy the name of an unidentified star.

Curium.

A petty kingdom in the Island of Kypros, which paid tribute to Esarhaddon.

Cuzallu.   *Or* Cisilivu.

The ninth month of the Assyrian year.   It was sacred to the god Nergal, and was called Ganganna, "the very cloudy," by the Accadians. It answered roughly to our November.

Cyganaca.

A city in Persia.   It was the birthplace of the impostor Martius.

Cynocephalus.   "Dog-headed."

A species of baboon (*Simia Hamadryas*), venerated by the Egyptians as sacred to the deity Thoth.   He was supposed to preside over the balance of the souls in the hall of judgment, because all his members were equal, *i.e.* terminated in hands.   He was also the emblem of the hour meter, because, if Greek writers are to be believed, he urinated at precisely equal intervals twelve times a day.   He was also one of the guardians of the infernal regions, and one of the genii of Amenti.

Cynon.

An island city on the Nile in the Cynopolite nome of the Heptanomos.

Cynopolis.   "City of Dogs."

The Greek name for the city and nome in Upper Egypt, called by the Egyptians Anup.

Cyrus.

The Greek form of the name of the great Persian conqueror Kurush, which see.

D.

DAANS.

The seventh of the ten great tribes of Persia. They were a nomadic or shepherd caste.

DABOOD.

The modern name of the town of Parembole in Nubia, which see.

DABU-BEL.

The governor of Amida in the reign of Assurdan III. He was eponym of the year B.C. 762, the chief event in which was a revolt in the city of Assur.

DABU-SAR-ASSUR.

The *great* Tukulu of Sargon II. He was eponym of the year B.C. 717, the chief event in which was an expedition to Carchemish.

DABU-ZILLI-ESAR.

The governor of Assur in the reign of Sargon II. He was eponym of the year B.C. 716, the chief event in which was an expedition to Minni and Media.

DADARSES.

A brave general of Darius Hystaspes, who sent him three several times into Armenia and Media to repress the insurrections which had arisen there, and in which mission he was blockaded by the Medes, and delivered by the army of his co-officer Vomises, which see.

DADIL.

A king of Colchis. He paid tribute to the Assyrians under Tiglath Pileser I.

DADILU.

The king of Kaska, a petty Syrian state which paid tribute to Tiglath Pileser II.

DADKERA.

The French form of the name of the Egyptian king Assa-Tatkera of the Vth dynasty.

DADOES.

A Persian officer, the father of Megabyzus, an officer and friend of Darius Hystaspes.

13*

DAG. "Day."

In Scandinavian mythology the son of Nott (the night), by her third husband Dellingr. She rode on a mythical horse named Skenfaxi, whose mane lit up the heaven and the earth.

DAGARA.

A district in South-eastern Assyria which revolted against Assurnazirpal, who only conquered it after some years' resistance. The capital city was Babile. *See* Zabvul.

DAHE.

A Persian race who were completely destroyed and reduced to the vilest slavery by Sennacherib, king of Assyria. They are supposed to have been the Dahi of Greek, and the Dinaites of Hebrew writers.

DAKAN.

An Assyrian deity worshipped by Assurnazirpal. He was probably the Dagon of the Hebrew writers.

DAKHE. *And* DAKHOS.

In Greco-Babylonian mythology two mysterious ancestors of the gods. They were the issue of Apason and Tauthe. *See also* Davke.

DAKKE.

The modern name of the Greco-Egyptian town of Pselcis, in the Dodecaschœnon.

DAKKURI.

A Chaldean tribe inhabiting the deserts West of Babylon. They plundered the province after the death of Sennacherib, and were severely punished for it their king Samasibni being burnt alive.

DAKSHA. "The Wise."

A Vedic title of the Supreme Being as the divinity of wisdom and powerful will.

DAKSHA.

An Hindu deity of creation. *See* Angiras.

DAKURI.

See Adini.

DALTA.

The king of Illipa, an Elamite prince tributary to Sargon II. On his death the throne being disputed between his two nephews Nibe and Ispabara, the kingdom was again torn by a war between the Assyrians, who came to the help of Ispabara, and restored him to the throne, and the Elamites under Sutruk Nanhundi, who assisted Nibe, but in vain, they being defeated at Marubisti.

Damastes.

The king of Curium in the Island of Kypros. He was one of the tributaries of Esarhaddon.

Damdamusa.

An Assyrian settlement on the Tigris. The inhabitants were attacked by the people of Haziluha, another Assyrian town also, but were delivered, with great cruelty however, by Assurnazirpal.

Damos.

The king of Ammochosta, in the Island of Kypros. He was one of the tributaries of Esarhaddon.

Damunu.

A tribe in Mesopotamia, conquered by Tiglath Pileser II.

Damy.

See Memnon, Shamy, and Amenhotep III.

Danai. *Or* Tena.

The name of some islands in the Mediterranean Sea, rendered tributary by Thothmes III.

Danawas.

In Hindu mythology the name of a race of evil spirits, who were always at war with the deity Indra.

Danni-Devaru. "Cold-water Gods."

A title given by the Badagas of India to the Mahalinga idols, which were supposed to enable their priests to walk upon hot coals as if they were cold water.

Dantesula.

An Elamite city, which was destroyed by Sennacherib.

Danukobi.

In Hindu mythology the name of the sacred bathing-place of the god Vishnu.

Daon of Sippara.

According to Berosus, the sixth antediluvian king of Babylon.

Dapinu.

In Chaldean astronomy one of the names of the planet Mercury.

Dapinu.

The name of the deity Marduk as the planet Mercury in the month of Tammuz.

Dapour.

The Egyptian name of an uncertain Syrian town.

DARIA.

A people in Mesopotamia, who were conquered by Tiglath Pileser I.

DARIAH. " The Brilliant."

The planet Venus, adored as a goddess by the ancient Nabatheans.

DARIDA.

In Hindu mythology a huge giant, who challenging the god Siva to fight, was defeated by that divinity's daughter, Vadrakale.

DARIGA.

A city in Assyria, which supported Assurdainpal in his revolt against his father, Shalmaneser II.   It was re-conquered by Samas-Rimmon.

DARIUS I., HYSTASPES.

A noble Persian, the son of an officer named Hystaspes.   Together with six other noblemen he conspired against the usurper Smerdis and slew him, and then afterwards prevailed upon his confederates, by force and artifice, to yield to him the crown of Persia, B.C. 521.   His principal feat was the conquest of Babylon after a ten months' siege, B.C. 518, soon after which he granted permission to the Jews who had been taken captive by Nebuchadnezzar to return to Jerusalem, and otherwise showed them great favour.   He next divided his empire into nineteen satrapies or provinces, and having invaded India, constituted it a twentieth district.   Unsuccessful in his war with the Scythians, he crossed into Europe, carrying all before him, leaving to his general, Megabazus, the conquest of Greece.   He then conquered the Islands of the Mediterranean, reduced Chalcedon, besieged and captured the city of Byzantium, and introduced a regular system of tribute and taxation from the subject provinces for the support of his government.   After this he added the kingdom of Egypt to his dominion, that country being already tributary to the Persian crown, and having done that, turned his whole attention to the reduction of Greece.   At Ephesus he defeated the Ionians, B.C. 499, and recovered Cyprus, and a second time became victor over the Ionian fleet at Miletus, B.C. 494.   His general, Mardonius, with a large army and navy having invaded the main land of Greece, and being repulsed, B.C. 491, Darius sent a second and more powerful body of soldiers and foreign auxiliaries to the war ; but his soldiers were signally defeated at the famous battle of Marathon, B.C. 490.   This disastrous accident excited the king of Persia to form a third and still larger army for the subjugation of the Grecians and their allies, in the midst of the preparations for which he died suddenly, B.C. 485.   The principal Cuneiform monuments of Darius Hystaspes are the famous trilingual inscription on the rocks at Behistun, recounting his accession to the throne of Persia and his wars with the Babylonian rebels, and the equally well-known inscription on his tomb at Nakhshi Rushtam, in both of which he attributed his victories to the Persian deity Ormuzd, whose worship he forcibly introduced into his conquered territories.   There also exist many contract and official Cuneiform tablets, dated in the various years of his reign ; but they contain few or no historical notices.   In Egypt the longest Hieroglyphic inscription executed during his power is a hymn to the deity Amen Ra, on the walls of the temple of Amen in the oasis of El Khargeh, but it contains no historical reference or even a date. Other inscriptions are found on the rocks at El Hamamat, on several of the later temples, and many incidental allusions on the funereal stèle of the Egyptian officers of the Persian dynasty, notably at the Louvre and Turin, and the Apis stèle from the Serapeum. Despite all these data and the very complete biographies of Darius which have been left us by the Greek historians, there are many points in his history which it is at present impossible to understand, and many contradictory and chronological difficulties which are yet irreconcilable.

DARIUS II., NOTHUS.

An illegitimate son of Artaxerxes II. He was made king of Persia after the death of the usurper Sogdianus, B.C. 424. He made war with the Ionians, and died B.C. 405. Like his ultimate successor Codomanus, he is only incidentally mentioned in the Archaic inscriptions.

DARIUS III., CODOMANUS.

King of Persia, B.C. 336. He was placed on the throne by the Eunuch Bagoas, who afterwards becoming his enemy, attempted to poison him. He was defeated by Alexander the Great at the battle of Arbela, and was murdered by Bessus, governor of Bactria, B.C. 331.

DARIUS THE MEDE.

According to the Book of Daniel, the conqueror of Babylon under, or jointly with, Cyrus. He has been considered by some historians to have been the same as Cyaxares, the son of Astyages, by others to have been Darius Hystaspes, and by some still more recent Assyriologists, as a mythical, or at all events an unhistorical, personage. A few years' further researches into the yet unexamined tablets and stèles of the various museums of Europe will probably lead to an approximate settlement of the place in history of Darius the Mede.

DARVANDS.

In Zendic mythology six evil spirits created by Ahrimanes, in opposition to the Amshaspands of Ahuramazda. Their names were Akomano, Ander, Saurva, Nasatyas, Taric, and Zaric. These were mostly the same as the deities of the Vedas, only changed into demons by the Zends.

DATEBIR.

A country in Chaldea, conquered by Samsivul, or Samas-Rimmon, king of Assyria.

DAVCINA.

An early Chaldean goddess, the wife of Hea, and the mother of Marduk. She has been supposed to represent the earth in a female form, as Hea was the god of the waters. Her analogue was the Phenician goddess Bohu. *See* Davke.

DAVKE. "The Female Earth."

In Greco-Babylonian mythology the wife of Aos, and the mother of the demiurgus Bel. She was also called Davcina.

DAYAN.   "Judge."

The name of the Assyrian legal functionaries who decided causes in the gates of the temples and palaces.   There was always the right of appeal from their decision to the king.

DAYAN-ASSUR.   "Assur is Judge."

A great general or Tartan in the army of Shalmaneser II.   He was sent against Seduri, king of Armenia, whom he defeated ; after which he subjugated the tribes of Patesia, and two years later entered the kingdom of Minni, defeating the king Udaki, and the next year, passing into Persia, conquered the various tribes bordering upon Assyria.   He returned through Halman and Simisi, and came back to Assyria just upon the close of the life of Shalmaneser.

DAYANI.

A people of the Nairi, inhabiting the district of the Upper Euphrates. Their king, Seni, submitting to Tiglath Pileser I., his life was spared and his dominions restored to him as a vassal of Assyria.

DAYAN-SAME.   "Judge of Heaven."

The Babylonian name of the Pole-star.

DAYENI.

A country near the Euphrates, conquered by Shalmaneser II.

DAZDAUPIRA.

The Persian form of the name of the officer of Darius who was called by the Greeks Zophyrus.

DEDAN.

A district in Arabia now represented by the Island of Daden, one of the Bahrein Isles.   *See* Dihtan.

DEDAN.

A tribe of Joktanite Arabs, not to be confounded with the Dedan of of the Bahrein Isles.

DEID.   *Or* DIDO.

The wife of Batta king of the Lydians, and mother of King Maurmaiu, who was lost in battle fighting against Menepthah II.

DEIR-EL-BAHARI.

A small but beautiful, limestone and partly rock hewn temple, near Thebes, which was erected by Queen Hatasu of the XVIIIth dynasty, after the conquests in Arabia.   It had an avenue of sphynxes, terminated by two obelisks, and the interior walls of the court and sanctuary were covered with pictures representing the queen of Egypt in male costume fighting among the Arabs, receiving their queen a prisoner, and superintending the embarkation of her fleet.   The text which accompanies these pictures is of the highest value, and has furnished modern historians with some most important details as to the internal organisation and naval resources of Egypt at the best period of the XVIIIth dynasty.   *See* Hatasu, *and* Thothmes II. and III.

Deir-el-Medineh.

A small temple near to Medinet-Habu in Upper Egypt. It was of a very late period, having been begun by Ptolemy Philopater, and completed by his successors.

Dejoces.

The Greek form of the Median royal name Diakku, which see.

Dejoces.

, A governor of Minni, who revolted against Sargon II. at the instigation of Ullusumue, king of Minni.

Dejoces.

The son of Phraortes. He was an able legislator, and united the whole of the independent tribes of Media under one government. He reigned for fifty-three years, and was succeeded by his son Phraortes or Fravartis.

Del-e-astartus.

One of the many usurpers who for a short time occupied the throne of Tyre after the death of Abdastoreth the last of the house of Hiram.

Dellingr.

In Scandinavian mythology a descendant of Asen, the third husband of Nott, by whom he had the deity Dag, which see.

Demavend.

The modern name of the district called by the Iranians Varena.

Demeter.

In Grecian mythology the goddess of the generative power of the earth. The Ceres of the Romans. *See* Parthivi Mutar.

Denderah. *Or* Tentyra.

A magnificent temple, on the roof of which an Arab village has been built. It was begun by Ptolemy XIII., but the edifice itself was only a restoration on a larger scale of the ancient Theban temple of the goddess Hathor. The sculptures are specially interesting to historical students, and the most reliable contemporary portraits (coins excepted) of Cleopatra VI. and her son Cæsarion are found upon the interior walls.

Dennu.

An ancient Egyptian official title which was applied to persons holding very different offices, and which is therefore now generally rendered "chief," or "director." "Great Dennu of Egypt" was a title given to Rameses VII. in a papyrus which is now in the Museum of Turin.

Deri.

A city in Babylonia, which was attacked by Samsi-Vul III., king of Assyria, during a great religious processional festival in honour of the great god of Deri.

DERKETO.

See Atargatis.

DERUSIÆANS.

The fifth of the ten great Persian tribes. They were an agricultural caste.

DEVA.

The Vedic name of Deity in an abstract sense.

DEVAS.

In Zendic mythology a species of evil manes, created by Ahrimanes in opposition to the Yazatas of Ahuramazda. They were the representatives of the Devas of the Veda, but endowed with opposite qualities.

DEWETAS.

In Hindu mythology certain good spirits who worked for the weal of the human race. They were also called Ghandharvas.

DHAMAR. "The Protector."

A Himyaritic deity, a form of the god Il.

DHAMARALI-BAYYIN.

A king of the Himyarites, about the first century A.D. He was succeeded by Kariba-il-watr-yahanam.

DHAMARALI-DHARAH.

King of the Himyarites, about B.C. 80. He was succeeded by Yadail-Watr.

DHANUVEDA.

An ancient commentary on the Hindu Yajus-Veda, treating of military tactics.

DHARAH. "Excellent."

An order of military nobles in the Sabæan kingdom of Yemen.

DHARBITU.

The tenth month of the Assyrian year. It was sacred to the god Papsucul, and was called by the Accadians Abba-Uddu, "The Father of Light." It answered roughly to our December.

DHARMA-SASTRA.

An ancient Hindu treatise on the civil and canon laws, chiefly based upon the four Vedas. It was one of the greater Sastras, which see.

DHASI.

The altar considered as the seat of the deity in Vedic mythology.

DHAT-ANVAT.

The sacred date tree near Mecca, worshipped by the ancient Arabians.

DHAT-BAADAN.   " Lady of Baadan."

An unidentified Himyaritic goddess.

DHAT-BADAN.

A Himyaritic goddess, of whose attributes and offices nothing is known.

DHAT-HAMI.   " Lady of the Sacred Enclosure."

An unidentified Himyaritic goddess.

DHAT-HAMIN.

A Himyaritic goddess, of whose attributes and offices nothing is known.   Perhaps the same as Dhat-Hami.

DHAT-IRAK.

A place near Mecca, the site of the battle between Nebuchadnezzar and Adnan, king of the Hejaz, in which the latter was defeated, and his people carried captive to Babylon.

DHATAR.   " The Creator."

A Vedic title of the Supreme Being as the divinity of creation.   *See also* Ivashtri.

DHAVATA.   " The Fire."

The Sanskrit name of the Scythian goddess Tabiti, which see.

DHU-ANUSCOUR.   " The Vultures Man."

A surname of Lokman, king of the Adites, so called because on account of his piety he was given to live the duration of life of seven vultures.   *See* Lokman.

DHU-KHOLOSA.   " Lord of Kholosa."

An unidentified Himyaritic deity, to whose shrine at Tebala, annual pilgrimages were undertaken, a custom terminated by Mahomet.

DHU-L-CALAT.

An Arabian deity worshipped at Sendad, near the Euphrates.

DHU-MAHDAM.

The father of the Arabian martyr prophet Shoaib, which see.

DHU-RIASH.   " Lord of Riash."

A Himyaritic prince who usurped the throne of Sabæa after the death of Yafar.   He was succeeded by the rightful king Noman, son of Yafar.

DHU-SAMAWI.

A Himyaritic male deity, of whose attributes and offices nothing is known.

DHU-SHAMAWI.   " Lord of the Heavens."

A Himyaritic deity.   The analogue of the Baal-hamin of the Phenicians.

DHU-SHARA.   " Lord of Seir."

The true name of the Nabathean deity Dulshara, which see.

DHURNAT.

A Chaldean river.   The Tornadotus of Classical writers.

DIAHBINA.

A city in the district of Yalman subdued by Samas-Rimmon, king of Assyria.

DIAITHEMIS.

A Kypriote who is mentioned on a votive inscription to Apollo in the Cesnola collection.

DIAKKU.

A Median chief whose policy united the various tribes of Media into one powerful kingdom after the death of Assurbanipal.   He was the Dejoces of the Greeks, and was succeeded by his son Phraortes.

DIAN-NISI.   " Judge of Men."

A title of the deity Shamas among the Assyrians.   It has been compared with the Dionysius of the Greeks.

DIARBEKER.

The modern name of the city and district which was called Amida by the Assyrians.

DIAR-THAMUD.   " Country of Thamud."

In Arabic history that part of Arabia which was inhabited by the Horites of the Hebrew writers.

DIBBAT.

The Chaldean name of the seven chief stars, among which the sun and moon were reckoned.   The Dibbat was the name of an animal famous for its bright eyes ; it has not been identified, but has been conjectured to have been the lynx.   (Sayce.)

DIDI.

See Taiti.

DIDO.   " The Fugitive."

A title assumed by Elissa, queen of Tyre, when driven from her kingdom by the cruelty of her brother Pümeliun, she sailed to found the city of Kiryath-Hadeschath or Carthage.   *See* Elissa.

DIESPITER.

The Archaic form of the name of the Roman deity Jupiter.

DIHIBINA.

A Chaldean city conquered, together with 300 others, by Samsi-Vul, or Samas-Rimmon, king of Assyria.

DIHNUM.

A city between the Euphrates and Tigris which supported Assurdainpal in his revolt against his father Shalmaneser II.

DIHTAN.

A small kingdom in Arabia, which was conquered for the first time by the Assyrians under Esarhaddon. It may have been the Dedan of Hebrew writers.

DIHUTANI.

An Arabian kingdom, conquered, and its queen Yapaa slain, by Esarhaddon. It may have been the same as the preceding.

DILALA.

An Elamite deity, of whom nothing is known.

DILBAT.

The Babylonian name of a planet supposed to be Venus.

DILGAN. *Or* ICU.

In Chaldean astronomy a name of the planet Jupiter, as one of the twelve stars of the West. *Also—*

DILGAN. "The Star of Babylon."

The Accadian name of the planet Mercury, as one of the forms of the god Marduk.

DILME.

In Chaldean astronomy the name of an unidentified star.

DIMAMAI.

A country rendered tributary by Samas-Rimmon, king of Assyria.

DINAITES.

A Persian people mentioned in Hebrew history, supposed to have been the same as the Dahe, which see.

DINTASHAANTARBITKARSHA.

An Elamite city, destroyed by Sennacherib. *See also—*

DINTASHADUMIAN.

An Elamite city, destroyed by Sennacherib.

DINTASHAZULIA.

An Elamite city, destroyed by Sennacherib.

DINTURKE.

An Accadian name of the city of Babylon.

DIOGENES.   " God-born."

A Greco-Egyptian priest (?) the father of Aria, the Canephoros of the goddess Arsinoe-Philadelphus, at Memphis, under Ptolemy V.

DIOLCOS.

One of the false mouths of the river Nile.

DIOSCURI.

The two twin deities, the Sons of the Morning, who were called Castor and Pollux by the Romans.   They held the reins of the horses of the sun.   *See* Asvins.

DIOSPOLIS.   " City of the Gods."

The Greek name for the Egyptian city and nome called Tsam, which see.

DIPTI.

An early Amardian or Cassite deity.   His attributes are not known.

DIR.

A name of the deity Marduk.   *See* Makru.

DIRKI.

The Accadian name of a city or district called by the Assyrians Diru, and at present named Duair.

DIRNACUS.

A king of the country of the Marruai, who paid tribute to Samas Rimmon, king of Assyria.

DIRRI.

A district and people by the head of the Tigris, who were conquered by Assurnazirpal.

DIRU.

The Assyrian name for a city or district called by the Accadians Dirki.   Its modern name is Duair.

DISI.

An Assyrian astronomer in the reign of Esarhaddon.

DISK, WINGED.

The winged disk, with pendant crowned uræi, carrying the cross of life. An emblem which was always placed over the doorways to the Egyptian temples, was supposed to represent the progress of the sun in the heavens from the East to the West. As a form of the solar deity it was a symbol of the god Horus likewise, and was regarded by the Egyptians as the protecting or benevolent spirit, the Agathodæmon of the Greeks. Its analogue was in some respects the Ferohir of the Assyrians, and perhaps the Spirit of the Sun of the Cabalists.

DIVS.

The Persian name of the evil beings or manes called Devas by the Zends. *See* Devas *and* Yazatas.

DJAHLAH.

A noble Himyaritic chief of the house of Mudad. *See* Maad.

DJARAOU.

The Egyptian name of an unidentified Syrian city.

DJASIM.

The collective name of a number of Amalekite tribes, who settled in the district of Yathrib, in Arabia.

DJEMSHID.

In Iranian history, the mythical hero who led the Aryan tribes in their first emigration to Asia, and who taught them the arts of civilization. He is said, however, to have taught them idolatry also. His real name was Yima-Khacta.

DJENDIB.

A king of the Arabs, who sent 100 camels as tribute to Shalmaneser VI. at Damascus.

DJONDA.

In Arabic history, a wicked king of the Thamudites, who was destroyed together with his people, by the word of the prophet Saleh.

DJOTBONS.

The father of the priest Ankhsnef, which see.

DODECARCHY.

After the invasion of Egypt and the pillage of Thebes, by Assurbanipal, king of Assyria, about B.C. 640 (?), and the flight of Urdameni, the son-in-law of Tirhakah, twelve of the great chiefs of the Delta established themselves as independent monarchs, in the same manner as an icosarchy had been introduced in B.C. 668 by Esarhaddon. These chiefs continued to reign for some years, and reduced the provinces of Lower Egypt to a condition of weakness and distress: one of their number, however, named Psametik, the Psammetichus of the Greeks, having married Ameniritis, a princess of Thebes, assumed the crown of Egypt, and partly by policy, partly by force, terminated for a time the Egyptian dodecarchy, by becoming sole king of Egypt in the XXVIth dynasty.

DODECASCHŒNON.   " Seventy Miles."

A province of Southern Egypt, in Nubia, between the first and second cataracts, including Philæ, Parembole, Tzitzi, Taphis, Talmis, Tutzis, Pselcis, Corte, and Hierosycaminon.   It embraced an area of seventy miles around.

DOLICHOCEPHALIC.   " Long or Bean-headed."

A term applied by modern anthropologists to that class of skull which is both long and narrow, in regular proportion.   *See* Macrocephalic *and* Brachycephalic.

DOOMAT-EL-JENDEL.

An Arabic province, supposed to have been the Dumah of Hebrew writers.

DOORGA.   *Or* DURJA.

A Hindu goddess, a form of Parvati the consort of Siva, in her attribute of the avenger.

DOUN-SE-PA-NEFER.

A devotee of Apis, in the time of Amasis II.   He was the son of Ouzahor and the lady Khaskhem.

DRAH-ABOUL-NEGGAH.

The modern name of the most ancient portion of the Necropolis of Thebes.   It contains the tombs of the sovereigns of the XIth dynasty, down to the commencement of the XVIIIth.

DROPICANS.

The ninth of the ten great tribes of Persia.   They were a nomadic, or shepherd caste.

DSHAINAS.

A Hindu sect whose creed is a combination of Buddhism and Brahminism.

DSJAHO.

A form of the Hieroglyphic name Saho, some Dutch Egyptologists using the sound *dsj* for the Egyptian character representing *sah*. *See* the following examples.

DSJA-KHONS.

The father of the priest of Amen, Pesahi, which see.

DSJA-TA-BAF-ANKH.

The father of Pebamen, a functionary in the temple of Amen-Ra, which see.

DSJOT-KHONS.

A priestess of Amen Ra.   Period uncertain.

Dsjot-men.

A spondist of the temple of Amen.   Period uncertain.

Dsjot-month.

A spondist of Amen, and prophet and overseer of the sacred scribes of the god.   Period uncertain.

Dsjot-month.

A priest and scribe of the temple of Amen Ra, in the time of Amenhotep II. or III. of the XVIIIth dynasty.   His sarcophagus and mummy are in the Leyden Museum.

Duair.

The modern name of the Assyrian city or district called Dirki.

Duban.

The Assyrian name of a city or district called by the Accadians Dur-ank-i.   Its site is not known.

Dubutna.

A king of the Patina, a tribe inhabiting the Northern part of the river Orontes, which paid tribute to Assurnazirpal.

Dugab.

An official title among the Babylonians.   The nature of the office is not certainly known.

Dujsiati.

A country in Arabia rendered tributary to Esarhaddon.

Dulshara.   " Lord of Mount Seir."

In ancient Nabathean mythology the great national solar deity.   He was compared by the Greek writers to the Greek deity Dionysos.

Dumah.

The Hebrew name of the Arabian capital city Addumu, which see. *Also* Doomat-el-Jendel.

Dunanu.

A tribe in Mesopotamia, who were conquered by Tiglath Pileser II.

Dunanu.

The last king of the Gambuli.   He was taken captive by Assurbanipal against whom he had revolted, and made to enter Nineveh with the head of his ally Tiumman king of Elam, hung to his neck, after which he was flayed alive.

Dungi.

An early king of Babylonia, son and successor of Urukh, whose buildings he completed and enlarged.

14

DUNI.

A Chaldean district, from whence all the lower empire was named. It has been compared with the Eden of Hebrew history.

DUNNI-SHEMESH.

An Elamite city destroyed by Sennacherib.

DUNNUSAIDU.

The phonetic name of the Babylonian monarch Dungi, king of Ur.

DUNNUSAIDU.

A Babylonian city founded by Dungi, king of Ur.

DUN-PA-UDDU.

The Assyrian name of the planet Mercury during the month Nisan.

DUR.

An Elamite city destroyed by Sennacherib.

DUR-AHISU. (?)

A Babylonian city on or in a river, which was conquered by Samsi-Vul or Samas Rimmon, king of Assyria.

DUR-AN.

An Assyrian city on the borders of Minni where Assurbanipal collected his forces before defeating Ahsera, the king of that country.

DURAN.

⌐he governor of the Assyrian cities which were reconquered from the Elamites by Sennacherib.

DUR-ANK-I.

The Accadian name of a city or district called Duban by the Assyrians. Its site is not known.

DUR-ASSHUR-AKH-IDDIN. "Fortress of Esarhaddon."

The name given by the Assyrians to the city of Memphis in Lower Egypt after its conquest by Esarhaddon.

DUR-ASSUR. "Castle of Assur."

See Dur-i-assur.

DUR-ATHURA.

A Babylonian city on the river Surappi, taken by Sargon II. on his invasion of Babylonia.

DUR-BALADH. "The Fortress of Life."

An Assyrian city which revolted to Assurdan, and was reconquered by Samas-Rimmon.

Dur-banit.

The name given by the Assyrians to the city of Tanis in Egypt, after its conquest by Esarhaddon.

Dur-bil-mat-i. " Fortress of the Lord of the Land."

The Assyrian name of the city of Sais in Egypt, after its conquest by Esarhaddon.

Dur-i-assur.

The governor of Tushan in the reign of Tiglath Pileser II. He was eponym of the year B.C. 728, in which year "the king took the hands of Bel," *i.e.* held a festival to that deity. *See* Dur-Assur.

Dur-i-galzu.

Another form of the Babylonian royal name Kurigalzu, which see.

Dur-kurigalzu. " Castle of Kurigalzu."

A great fortress on the Northern frontier of Chaldea, towards the Assyrians, built by Kurigalzu. It was for more than fifteen centuries the key of the country.

Dur-la-dinna.

A Chaldean town belonging to the Dakkuri. It was conquered by Sargon II. in his war with Merodach-baladin, king of Babylon.

Dur-papsukul.

A city of the Accadians which was destroyed, together with 447 surrounding cities, by Samas-Rimmon, king of Assyria.

Dur-sargina. " Castle of Sargina."

A city founded by Sargon or Sargina I., the mythical king of Babylonia.

Dur-sargina.

An Assyrian city founded by Sargon II., king of Assyria, in imitation of that erected by his ancestor, the mythical Sargon, after whom he was named. The ruins are now called Khorsabad, and from them many splendid historical slabs have been obtained.

Dur-tila.

An Assyrian city which supported Assurdainpal in his revolt against his father Shalmaneser II.

Dur-u.

An Elamite city which was destroyed by Sennacherib.

Dur-undasi.

An important Elamite city conquered by Assurbanipal, in his war with the usurper Ummanaldas, king of Elam.

Dur-yakin.

A town in Lower Chaldea, founded by the father of Merodach Baladin I., who was there defeated with great loss by Sargon II., king of Assyria.

Dusares.

The Greek form of the name of the Nabathean deity Dulshara, which see.

Duvara.   " Gate."

The name of the royal palace in old Persian history. It was inaccessible to all but a chosen few, and was the origin of the title " Sublime Porte," which is still in use in Turkey as the name of the palace.

Duzi.   " The Son of Life."

The first husband of the goddess Ishtar, who descended into Hades in search of him. He was the same as Tamzi and the Tammuz of Hebrew history.

Duzu.

The fourth month of the Assyrians, sacred to the god Adar. It was called Sukulna, " Seizer of Seed," by the Accadians, and it answered roughly to our June.

Dyauspiter.

In Vedic literature a title of the deity Indra, from whence the Diespiter, or Jupiter, of the Romans was derived.

E.

EALDEAKI.

An Accadian city, the site of which is not known.

EATE.

An Egyptian officer, whose monument is in the Leyden Museum. Period uncertain.

EBIH.

A Chaldean city or district, conquered by Samsi-Vul, or Samas Rimmon, king of Assyria.

ECBATANA.   *Or* AGBATANA.

The capital city of the empire of Media. It was founded about B.C. 710, by the chief Dejoces, the first king of the Medes, and it soon attained a position of strength and importance. According to Herodotus, whose statement is borne out by the existence of a similar style of architecture in Assyria, the city was built on a hill, having the royal castle in the centre, and being surrounded with seven walls, each of them adorned with coloured tiles (in reference to the seven planets of the Median religion), the two innermost walls being coated with plates of silver and gold respectively. In process of time the city became one of the most important capitals in Asia ; but it received a severe blow in the destruction of the Magi within its walls by Darius Hystaspes, to commemorate which an annual feast called the Magophonia was instituted. The great extent of the empire of Darius necessitating a more central seat of government, he founded the city of Susiana, in Persia proper, for that purpose, after which the importance of the Median capital of Ecbatana steadily declined; it still however remained a great city, although no longer a metropolis, and it preserved a degree of splendour down to the Christian period.

E-CI.   " Mound City."

An old Accadian name of the city of Babilu, or Babylon.

ECNIBAAL.

A king or suffete of Tyre. The son of Baalsyllech. He reigned for two months only during the anarchy which followed the death of Baal, the king placed on the throne by Nebuchadnezzar.

EDALI.

The Kypriote form of the name of the town which was called Idalium by the Greeks.

EDDAS.

In Scandinavian mythology the sacred poetical books, several of which remain to us in a more or less corrupted condition.

EDFU.

The modern name for the city and nome of Apollinopolis, called by the Egyptians Teshor. The most ancient name of this town was Teb. The great temple of Edfu is one of the most stately and best preserved, Karnak and Tentyra excepted, in Upper Egypt. It was dedicated to the god Horus, and was built on the same plan as that of Tentyra, by Nekhtarhebi II. of the XXXth dynasty. The interior walls are covered with a series of mythical inscriptions relative to the legend of Horus and a series of dialogues with the divinity and the royal founder. A great number of towns and other geographical sites are mentioned in the Hieroglyphics, together with the usual inflated lists of donations to the temple and its priests.

EGIDES.

The name given by the French Egyptologists to certain little shields, often wrought in silver or gold, in the shape of the collar called the *Askh*, and having the head of the goddess Sekhet, or Bast, at the top. These ornaments were often hung on the upraised prows and stems of the solar and sacred boats, and were also wrought in cornelian and other hard stones, to be worn as amulets : their mythological use is not known. The Egides were formerly called the Shields, or Ægis, of Pasht.

EGOTOS.

A Kypriote whose name occurs on a votive inscription in the Cesnola collection.

EGYPT.

The oldest and most mysterious of all the empires of antiquity, and the mother of Archaic history. It was anciently called Khem, a word supposed to signify "black ;" it was also called in the hieroglyphics "The Country of the Sycomore," and "The Country of the Fig." Its earliest traditions are themselves lost in the traditions of mythology, and its latest monuments are anterior to Ancient or Classic history. Geographically Egypt is a narrow strip of country, about 400 miles long and about five broad, being simply the shores of the river Nile hemmed in between lofty mountains on the one hand, and a series of sterile deserts on the other. Occupying at the Delta the North-eastern corner of the great continent of Africa or Lybia, it is joined to Asia by the Isthmus of Suez, is bounded on the North by the Mediterranean Sea, on the East by the Isthmus and the Red Sea, and on the South by Nubia, beyond Syene, the limits of Egypt proper. In the time of the principal dynasties, Egypt was divided into two kingdoms : that of Upper Egypt, of which the capital city was Thebes, and Lower Egypt, of which the seat of empire was the city of Memphis, by some writers considered to have been the original starting place of Egyptian civilisation under Menes. In the period between the XIIIth and XVIIIth dynasties, took place the terrible incursion which was long remembered as the Hykshos invasion, and on the termination of which the second period of Egyptian history commenced, and the importance of the empire culminated under Thothmes I. and III., and Hatasu the queen, of the XVIIIth dynasty, at which time Palestine, Mesopotamia as far as Nineveh, South-western Arabia, Nubia, and Cyprus, and some of the smaller islands of the Mediterranean Sea were included in the dominions of the king of Upper and Lower Egypt. The XIXth dynasty under the Ramesside monarchs, the second of whom was the Sesostris of the Greeks, maintained, if it did not witness an enlargement of these conquests ; but in the XXIInd and subsequent dynasties the power of Egypt declined, till the accession of the Ethiopian monarchs, the chief of whom was Pianki Meramen. Internal wars and consequent political weakness succeeded, and Egypt was conquered by Esarhaddon, and the lower empire was broken up into a congeries of twenty petty kingdoms, called the Icosarchy, and on the invasion of Assurbanipal, a few years later, that number was reduced to a dodecarchy of twelve princes. These again were absorbed by the Persian or XXVIIth and XXXth dynasties, the last king of which was Nechtarhebi II., under whose successor Amasis or Aahmes II., the Egyptian empire finally fell to pieces, and Egypt remained a subject territory, following the fluctuations of the Persian court under Darius and his successors till the time of Ptolemy Lagus, the founder of the Ptolemaic dynasty, which furnished a line of sixteen Greco-Egyptian sovereigns, nominally Egyptian till the death of Ptolemy Cæsarion XVI., the son of the famous Cleopatra VI. ; after which Egypt was annexed to the Roman empire, and its history passed from the region of Archaic into the boundaries of Classic or almost modern history. The subject of Egyptian chronology is obscure even beyond the powers of comparative conjecture, the accession of Menes, the first historical king, being made to range from B.C. 5004 to 2000, and it is yet an unsettled point whether any, and if so which, of the dynasties were contemporaneous, and how far even the astronomical calculations of the Egyptian priests are to be relied upon prior to the reign of Tirhakah, the contemporary of Hezekiah, king of Judah. *See also* the appendices for the tables of Egyptian dynasties, mythology, and the genealogy of the Ptolemaic kings ; *also* Menes, Apepi, Amenemha III., Thothmes II., Rameses II. and III., Piankhi, Amasis, etc.

Ehe.

An uncertain Egyptian goddess, represented as a woman with a cow's head, perhaps a form of the deity Hathor. (Wilkinson.)

Ehoou.

The Egyptian deity of the Day. He was generally represented as wearing the Pschent, together with the long lock of hair falling on the right side, as worn by the god Horus. (Wilkinson.)

Ei-amen-nef-neb-oui.

An overseer of the priests of the temple of Amen. His father was named Ankhpiskhe, and his mother Sakhons. His triple coffin and mummy are in the Leyden Museum.

EILETHYA.

A chief town in Upper Egypt, which was sacred to the worship of the goddess Seben.

EINHERIAR.

In Scandinavian mythology the name applied to the souls of heroes slain in battle, upon their entrance into the Walhalla.

EIRENE.

A Greco-Egyptian lady, the daughter of Ptolemy. She was a priestess of the goddess Arsinoe Philopater, at Memphis, in the reign of Ptolemy V.

EI-USKH.

A priest of Pthah-Sokari-Osiris, in the reign of Rameses III. He was the son of Pthahmes, a priest of the same deity likewise.

EKATE.

A king or deity who is mentioned in the Kypriote inscription of Dali.

EKI.

The Accadian name of several cities or districts whose sites are not known.

EKIAMIZILLAK.

The name of the palace erected at Agane by Sargon I. or Sargina.

EKIM.

The Assyrian form of the name of the class of evil spirits who were called by the Accadians Gigim.

EL.   " The God."

A name of the Phenician deity Hadad, which see. He was the analogue of the Ilu of the Babylonians.

ELAMU.

The Semitic or Assyrian name of the district now called Khuzistan.

ELANI.

A district North of Assyria, conquered by Tiglath Pileser I.

ELASI.

See Ameresk.

ELBS.

In Scandinavian and Teutonic mythology, a species of mischievous genii of two kinds, elbs of light and elbs of darkness. The latter were chiefly interested in the metallic riches of the earth, and they formed a numerous company, having their own king. They were analogous to, if not the same as, the gnomes.

ELEPHANTINE.

A town in the extremity of Upper Egypt, now called Gezret Essouan, the seat of the VIth Egyptian dynasty. It was famous for its granite quarries.

ELGA. "The Lofty God."

A title of the deity El among the ancient Nabatheans. In that form his feminine counterpart was the goddess Alath.

ELIADAD.

A Syrian general who took the city of Damascus from the Jews by a surprise, and gave the crown to his son Rezon, the Rezin of Hebrew history.

ELIMIEL.

In Cabalistic mythology the intelligence of the moon.

ELISSA.

The daughter of Mathan, king of Tyre. She was left by her father's will queen of Tyre, conjointly with her brother Pümeliun. The people however, deposed her from her rights, and she then married Zicharbaal, the high-priest of Ashtaroth, who was assassinated by order of the king. Elissa on this raised an insurrection, together with 300 of the principal nobility, but she was overpowered by the democratic or popular party, and voluntarily quitted Tyre, together with her adherents. To do so she seized the shipping in the port, and conducted her friends to the North African shore, where she founded a city called Kiryath-Hadeschath, or "The New Town," taking herself the epithet of Dido, or "The Fugitive." The name of her city became afterwards softened by the Greeks into Carachedon, and by the Romans into Carthage.

ELIUN.

Another name of the Phenician deity Hypsistus, which see.

ELKAIS.

The modern name for the city and nome in Upper Egypt, called by the Greeks Cynopolis.

EL-KARGEH.

The modern name of the ancient town Hibe, the capital of the great Oasis in the Libyan desert; famous for its ancient temple of Amen Ra.

ELLASAR. "City of Assur."

The name by which the Chaldean city of Larra, or Larsa, is mentioned in Hebrew history.

ELLAT-GULA.

Queen of Babylonia. She was the last sovereign of the dynasty of Sargina I. Nothing is known respecting the events of her reign.

ELLINZAS.

A city of Illipa conquered and enlarged by Sennacherib, who named it Karu-sennacherib, and added it as a fortress to the empire of Assyria.

ELLIPI.

A region near Ispahan in Persia, which was conquered by Vulnirari III.

ELTEKON.   *Or* ELTHECA.

The Hebrew name of the city called by the Assyrians Altaqa, or Altægu, which see.

ELULI.

King of Tyre, about B.C. 726.   He began his reign by reducing an insurrection which had arisen in the town of Kitium, in the Isle of Kypros.   Soon after that he was attacked by Sargon, king of Assyria, and though abandoned by all the other Phenician kings, he held out Tyre to the last, even when the metropolis on the main land joined with Sargon.   In the end the king of Assyria abandoned the siege, after a blockade of five years.   When Sargon left, Eluli found himself still in distress by the loss of all the Phenician settlements; and soon afterwards Tyre was attacked again by Sennacherib, who having conquered all Palestine forced the Tyrians to submit, and Eluli abandoning the defence fled in despair.   A man named Ethbaal was then raised to the throne by Sennacherib, and he paid tribute as a vassal and dependent upon Assyria.

ELUNI.

A people in the mountains of Mesopotamia, who were subdued by Assurrisilim, king of Assyria.

EMBLA.

In Scandinavian mythology the name of the first woman, who was created by Odin and his brother deities after the death of Ymir.

EMPE-ANKH.

The father of Harsaf a spondist of Thoth, which see.   His wife's name was Teti-ma-nefer.

EMSAH.   TEMSAH.   " A Crocodile."

The Egyptian name for the city and nome called by the Greeks Tentyris, sacred to the worship of Isis.

EN-ANTEF.

The overseer of the altar of Osiris (?) in the reign of Amenemha II.   He was the son of the lady Ranfankh, and he married a lady named Ameni. All the members of his family were either named Antef or Enantef.

ENCI.   " The Earth."

Another form of the name of the Accadian deity Hea, which see.

ENEMESSAR.

The name by which Shalmaneser IV. was known to the writer of the book of Tobit.

ENGUR.

The king of the city of Tsibarai, in Girubbunda.   He paid tribute to Samas-Rimmon or Samsi-Vul, king of Assyria.

ENIEL.

The king of Hamath, conquered by Tiglath Pileser II.

ENNA.

An Egyptian scribe in the reign of Rameses II. He was the author of the romantic story called " The Tale of the Two Brothers," which was written for the amusement of the young king.

ENNA-ENNA.

A royal scribe in the reign of Amenemha I. of the XIIth dynasty.   He was the author of an historical work called " The Instructions of Amenemha I. to his son Osirtesen," which has been often published.

ENSKERK.

The granddaughter of Tetet, an early Egyptian king.

ENSKERKA.

The grandson of Tetet, an early Egyptian king.

ENTARIUSH.

An Egyptian form of the Persian royal name Darius, which see.

ENTEF.

Another form of the Egyptian royal name Antef, which see.

ENTEMASMUR.   " Tip of the Tail."

In Chaldean astronomy one of the seven stars of the week.

ENTENAMASLUR.

In Chaldean astronomy an unidentified fixed star.

ENZUNA.   " Lord of Wisdom."

In Accadian mythology the eldest son of the god Mulge.   He was probably the Sin or Moon-god of the Assyrians, which see.

EOEA.

A priest of Pthah.   His period is uncertain.

EOERI.

An Egyptian officer, an " Overseer of the House," whose monument is in the Leyden Museum.   Period uncertain.

EOPEI.

An Egyptian lady, an assistant of the deities Amen and Hathor. Period uncertain.

EOPEII.

A royal scribe attached to the palace of Memphis. He was the son of the scribe Heti, and grandson of the scribe Meresoure. Period uncertain.

EOS.

In Grecian mythology the goddess of the Dawn. She was represented as a beautiful woman with a crown of light and rosy finger nails.

EPAPHOS.

In Greco-Egyptian mythology the son of Io, and the first king of Egypt. He had a daughter called Lybia, from whom the district so named derived its title.

EPARNA.

A prince or king of Patusarra in Media. He was conquered and taken captive to Nineveh, by Esarhaddon, king of Assyria.

EPHAH.

A Hebrew measure of capacity, equal nearly to one English bushel.

EPIPHI.

The eleventh month of the Egyptian sacred year. It began about the 16th May.

EPITERETAI.

The receivers of the Egyptian inland taxes under the Ptolemies. They replaced the *Merismoi* or publicans, whose conduct was nationally unsatisfactory.

EPIZI.

Certain mountains near to Media, where the people fled for shelter from the invasion of Samsi-Vul or Samas-Rimmon III., king of Assyria.

EPONYM.

An Assyrian officer analogous to that of Consul among the Romans. Each year the king nominated a magistrate, whose sole duty it was to give his name to the year in the chronological records. The highest officers of the crown had this right during the early years of a reign, the king himself being the eponym of the year of his accession. The next years were named after the Commander-in-chief, or Tartan, the Chief Eunuch, the Minister of State, and lastly the Governor of the Country, after which the king selected the eponym from the other great officers of state at his pleasure.

ERATU.   "Pregnant Women." (?)

In Chaldean astronomy an unidentified star.

ERECH.

A capital of Chaldea, and one of the four earliest cities of the world. The site of many great temples and of the famous library of Tiglath Pileser. It was the Orchœ of the Greeks, and is now called Warka by the Turks.

ERGAMENES.

See Arkamun, an Ethiopian royal name.

ERIBMEGALI.   "Descent of Great Waters."

In Chaldean astronomy an unidentified star.

ERIDUKU.

The Accadian name of the city Eridu.

ERINU.

The Assyrian name of the cedar tree.

ERISINNI.

The eldest son of Vaali or Baali, king of Minni. He was sent by his father to convey his submission and a good tribute to Assurbanipal, king of Assyria, after his subjugation of the country.

ERISU.

The king of Salamis, in the Island of Kypros. He was one of the tributaries of Esarhaddon.

ERMENIHOTEP.

The brother of Ameni the superintendent of the works of Amenemha I. and II. of the XIIth dynasty.

ERPA-HA.

An Egyptian title, answering to that of Royal Chancellor.

ERVIL.

The modern name of the Assyrian city Arbela, which see.

ESDUSARABE.

The governor of Gozan, in the reign of Assurdan III. He was eponym of the year B.C. 763, the chief events in which were a revolt in the city of Assur, and an eclipse of the sun in the month Sivan.

ESHMONAZER I.

A king of Sidon, of whom little is known.

ESHMONAZER II.

King of Sidon, the son and successor of Tabnith the son of Esh-monazer I. He built many temples at Sidon, and he received from Nebuchadnezzar, king of Babylon, a portion of the destroyed kingdom of Judah as an addition to his own. The inscription on the coffin of Eshmonazer, now in the Museum of the Louvre, is the longest Phenician inscription at present known.

ESMUN.

In Phenician mythology the name of the eighth planet. As a personage he was an invisible deity, and approached nearest to the Sun-god Baal-samin.

ESNEH.

The modern name for the Egyptian city and nome which was called by the Greeks, Latopolis, and by the Egyptians, Ten.

ESSAR-HADDON.   ASSUR-AKH-IDDINA, " Asshur has given brothers."

The younger and favourite son of Sennacherib, who succeeded his father, January, B.C. 680, after defeating his two elder brothers at Khani-rabbat, on the upper Euphrates. He rebuilt Babylon, conciliated the people, and proclaimed himself king of Babylonia, reducing various tribes in its neighbourhood.   Zidon, which had revolted, was destroyed; and the kings of Palestine and Cyprus voluntarily submitted themselves.   The Kimmerians were attacked in the North, and forced to march towards Asia Minor, and Cilicia was once more reduced to obedience.   The Medes were also subdued, and an expedition sent into the deserts of Arabia, which penetrated 900 miles into the heart of the country.   Egypt was next conquered, and divided into twenty satrapies, Tirhakah being driven into Ethiopia.   Tyre was also besieged, and Manasseh, king of Judah, carried captive to Babylon. Esar-haddon associated his son, Assur-bani-pal, with him in the government on the 12th of Iyyar (April), B.C. 670, and died two years later (B.C. 668).

ESUS.

The name of the Supreme Being among the Celts.

ETHÆOS.

The Greek form of the name of an unidentified Nabathean deity.

ETHAUSVA.

The Etruscan goddess who aided women in childbirth, she was the analogue of the Greek goddess Eileithyia.

ETHBAAL I.   " Man of Baal." (?)

A king of Tyre, of whom next to nothing is known.   His name is the Ithobalus of the Greek writers.

ETHBAAL II.

A Tyrian who was raised to the throne of Tyre, after the conquest of the island by Sennacherib, and the forced abdication of the king Eluli, which see.

Ethbaal III.

King of Tyre. He united with Uaprahet, king of Egypt, against Nebuchadnezzar, king of Babylon, who, having driven the Egyptian army into Egypt without even daring a battle, attacked and blockaded Tyre. For thirteen years the siege lasted, "till every head was made bald and every shoulder peeled," and then Tyre fell, and its importance thus finally destroyed, Ethbaal and his family being carried away captives into Babylon. After this Nebuchadnezzar raised a native named Baal to the titulary honour of tributary king of Tyre.

Ethbaal.

Another form of the Sidonian royal name Tubahal, which see.

Ethiopia.

An independent country to the South of Egypt, called Noub by the Egyptians, Milukha by the Accadians, and Kusu by the Semitic Assyrians. It was early annexed to the Egyptian empire by the marriage of Aahmes I. with the princess Nofretari of the XVIIIth dynasty.

Etura. "House of Rest."(?)

In Chaldean astronomy an unidentified fixed star.

Etymander.

The Greek name of the district anciently called Hœtumat, which see.

Euisidosses.

The king of Idalion, successor of Pythagoras, in the fourth century B.C.

Euturpa.

The Etruscan form of the name of the muse Euterpe of the Greeks.

Evagoras I.

A king of Salamis, in Kypros (Cyprus). He reigned from B.C. 410 to B.C. 375.

Evagoras II.

A king of Idalion, or of Kition and Idalion, about B.C. 353.

Evagreton.

A Cretan who with his wife, Mnestasa, is mentioned in a Kypriote inscription in the Cesnola collection.

Evechous.

A mythical Chaldean king, the founder of the Ist Chaldean dynasty. His name is at present only to be met with in the lists of Berosus: it was possibly Avil-Kush.

Evelthon.

A king of Salamis, in Kypros (Cyprus), about the fourth century B.C.

EVIL-MERODACH.   *Or* AVIL-MARDUK.   " Man of Marduk."

The son and successor of Nabukuduruzur on the throne of Babylon. He reigned only two years, when he was assassinated by his brother-in-law Nergalsarussur, the son of the usurper Bellabarisruk.

EVRPHIA.

A female figure, who is represented on an Etruscan mirror as dancing before Faün.

EZAMA.

A mountain people on the borders of Media and Susiana, conquered by Sennacherib.

F.

FAI-BOK-RA-NEF.

A prophet priest of the temple of Amen, probably in the XXVth dynasty.

FAI-HON.

An overseer of the gatekeepers of the royal palace. Period uncertain.

FAI-HOR-OUSER.

An Egyptian gentleman, the husband of the lady Sotemeit, the son of the lady Setakarf, and father of the prefect of the palace Ratoker, in the XXVIth dynasty.

FAI-IRI-EI.

A royal scribe, whose monument is in the Leyden Museum. Period uncertain.

FAI-ITEN-HEMH-BAI.

An Egyptian priest, the son of the lady Pthahmeit. His splendid funereal inscription is in the Leyden Museum.

FAI-NOFRE.

An Egyptian royal scribe, whose monument is in the Leyden Museum. Period uncertain.

FAI-NOFRE-BAI.

A prophet or priest of Osiris, in the reign of Rameses III. of the XIXth dynasty.

FALLHOFNER.

In Scandinavian mythology the name of one of the horses of the gods.

FAMU. *Not* THAMU, *as Gerhard.*

A deity who is represented on an Etruscan mirror. *See* Alpanu.

FARAM-YANHAB.

A Himyaritic king of Saba and Dhu-Raidan, in South-west Arabia. He reigned jointly with his sons, Il Sharah-Yadhab and Yadail-Bayyin.

FAÜN.

According to Corssen the Etruscan Orpheus. He was represented on mirrors as seated on a rock and playing a lyre, with laurel crown and necklace. A female, with crown, necklace, tunic, and mantle, is at his side, called Rutupis, Rodôpis according to Corssen.

15

FAYOUM.

The modern name for a province in Upper Egypt, which was called by the Greeks the Upper and Lower nomes of Arsinöe. Its ancient name was Rehoun.

FENT.

The surname of the Egyptian princess Uuhetu, of the XIIIth dynasty, which see.

FENT-HEMP-AMENTI.

The title given by some early Egyptologists to the deity Osiris in his form of Osiris-Rhotamenti, which see.

FENT-KAUS.

The daughter of an early unknown Egyptian king.

FERIDUN.

The grandson of Djemshid. He was raised to the throne by the people of Ispahan, who, at the instigation of Caveh the blacksmith, had slain the monster Zohak, which see. His real name was Thraetaona.

FERVERS.

In Zendic mythology the third rank of celestial deities, being the souls of every object that had life, to which therefore prayers were offered. A species of celestial manes. (Lenormant.)

FIPEKE.

The name of an Etruscan lion-headed monster, with water flowing from his mouth, and an upturned urn beneath him, who was combated by Herakles. Gerhard believed him to represent the Hydra; Corssen, more probably, a water-imp.

FIRAMODOR.

The goddess of the earth, or the general powers of nature, among the Anglo-Saxons. Her analogue was the Demeter of the Greeks.

FIRKIN.

A Grecian measure of capacity, equal to eight gallons.

FLABELLIFERI.

The bearers of the great fan or flabellum of feathers, two of which were borne before the Egyptian monarch upon state occasions.

FOLKWANG.

In Scandinavian mythology the name of the residence of the goddess Freyia, in the sacred city of Asgard. Her palace there was called Sessrummir, which see.

FORSETI.

In Scandinavian mythology the son of Baldur and Nanna. He was the heavenly peacemaker.

Fravashis.

Certain fetichistic spirits who were worshipped by the early inhabitants of Media.

Freyia.

In Scandinavian mythology the goddess of love. Her name was sometimes written Frua or Früa.

Freyr.

In Scandinavian mythology the god of sunshine, rain, and fruitful weather.

Fricka.

Another form of the name of the Scandinavian goddess Friga, which see.

Friga.

In Scandinavian mythology the wife of Odin. Her name was sometimes written Fricka.

Frua.

Another form of the name of the Scandinavian goddess Freyia, which see.

Fufluns.   *Or* Fuflunu.

The Etruscan Bacchus, after whom was probably named the city of Pupluna or Populonia. Objects dedicated to him were termed *Fuflunsl*, or *Fuflunl*, "belonging to Bacchus."

Fulla.

In Scandinavian mythology a goddess, the sister and companion of the goddess Freyia. Her name was also sometimes written Volla.

G.

GABAL.

A Syrian city which is supposed to have been the town called by the Egyptians Kapaon.

GAB-GAB-NIKI.

The Accadian name of a city or district whose site is not known.

GABRIEL.

In Cabalistic astronomy the angel of the moon.

GAD.   "Good Fortune."

The Phenician name of the star Jupiter.

GADATAS.

According to the Greek historians a conspirator who, together with Gobryas, slew Laborosoarchodus, king of Babylon.

GADES.

A city in Spain which was conquered by Nabukuduruzur. It is now called Cadiz.

GADYTIA.

A district of Arachotia, in Persia, where Vibanus, the Satrap, a second time defeated the army sent against him by Veisdates, the rebel king of Persia. *See* Vibanus.

GAGA-MAKHERU.

Another name of King Menkera of the IIIrd dynasty.

GAGI.

A Median prince, the chief of the Saki. *See* Sarati *and* Paraza.

GAHAL.

The father of Suzub, a brave Babylonian rebel. *See* Suzub.

GAH-ANBAR.   "Gathering of Time."

In Zendic mythology the name of the first period of creation, in which Ahuramazda created the heavens.

GAH-EIATHREM.

In Zendic mythology the name of the fourth period of creation, that of the trees and plants.

GAH-HAMESPTHMEDEM.

The name of the sixth and last of the Zendic periods of creation, in which Ahuramazda created man.

GAH-MEDIAREH.

The name of the fifth Zendic period of creation, that of the animal world.

GAH-MEDIOSHEREM.

In Zendic mythology the name of the second period, in which Ahuramazda continued the work of creation. *See* Gah-anbar.

GAH-PETESHEM.

In Zendic mythology the name of the third period of creation, in which Ahuramazda created the earth.

GAHUPANI.

A petty kingdom in Arabia, which was ravaged for the first time and its king Nikharu put to death by Esarhaddon.

GAL.   " The Great."

The astronomical name of the deity Marduk as the planet Mercury in the month Sebat.

GALLAMTA-UDDUA.   " He who goes forth in Strength."

A Chaldean name of the deity Nergal or Allamu.

GALLI.

The ancient name of the priests of Phrygia.

GALLU.

The Assyrian name of the class of evil spirits which were called by the Accadians Telal, which see.

GAMA.

The Egyptian name of the papyrus reed *Cyperus Papyrus*. *See* Papyrus. *See also—*

GAMA.

The Egyptian name of the papyrus root which was cooked as a vegetable by the Egyptians.

GAMAR.

One of five chiefs who incited the Lybians to revolt against Rameses III.

GAMIL-NANA.   " Benefit of Nana."

The name of an Assyrian tax collector at Warka, in the reigns of Cambyses and Nabonidus.

GAMIL-NINIP.   " Benefit of Ninip."

An early king of Babylonia who reigned at the city of Nisinna.

GAMIL-SIN. "Benefit of Sin."

An early king of Babylonia who reigned at Ur. Nothing else is known respecting him.

GAMIL-SIN. "Benefit of Sin."

A city in Babylonia, which was called after the early monarch of that name.

GANA-SUTI-CANU.

A city of Datebir, conquered, together with 200 of the adjacent cities, by Samsi-Vul, king of Assyria.

GANDHARVAS.

The horses of the sun in Vedic mythology, symbols of the fierce rays of Surya.

GANDH-ARVA-VEDA.

An ancient commentary derived from the Hindu Samaveda, treating of the subject of music.

GANDU.

An Assyrian or Babylonian, the father of the earliest writer of Cuneiform tablets at present recorded.

GANDUNIAS. "The Enclosure of Duni."

The original name of the kingdom of Lower Chaldea. The name Duni has been compared with the Eden of Hebrew history.

GANESA-PULEAR.

In Hindu mythology the son of Siva, and the god of wisdom. He was represented as a human being with an elephant's head.

GANGA.

In Hindu mythology the sacred river Ganges, incarnated as a deity.

GANGAMMA.

A river deity, venerated by the Todas and Badagas.

GAN-GAN-NA. "The Very Cloudy."

The Accadian name of the month Cuzallu, which see.

GANNANATI.

A country conquered by Vulnirari or Rimmon-Nirari III., king of Assyria.

GANRUBAI.

The prefect of Quazi under Sennacherib.

GAR.

An Assyrian measure of length, the same as a *Ribu*, which see.

GARARAI.

A queen of Egypt and Nubia, in the reign of Nut-amen, or Nut-mei-amen of the XXVIth dynasty.

GARSALE.

The royal city of Marudukbaladsuiqbi, king of Babylon, which was conquered, together with 200 of the adjacent cities, by Samsi-Vul or Samas-Rimmon, king of Assyria.

GARU. *Or* TARU.

The frontier town of Egypt towards Syria, on the left bank of the Nile. It was probably the Heroopolis of the Greeks.

GAU. "Robbers."

A kind of game of chess among the ancient Egyptians. It was played on the same board as the Sent, which see.

GAUGAMA.

A state in Northern Syria, conquered by Tiglath Pileser II.

GAUTMAR.

One of five chiefs who incited the Lybians to revolt against Rameses III.

GAZA.

A famous town on the borders of Egypt and Palestine. It was conquered and plundered by Tiglath Pileser II., and its king Hanun driven to make peace.

GEBAL. " Tomb of the God."

The second capital of the Sinites of Phenicia, who afterwards deemed it their most important city. It was said to contain the sepulchre of Tammuz, the Adonis of the Greeks. *See* Tamzi.

GEBELEIZES.

Another name of the great deity of the Getæ, called Zalmoxis, which see.

GEDJEMUGASHURIN.

In Hindu mythology a great giant who conspired against the gods, and who was overpowered by Ganesa, the son of Siva.

GEF. " Corn."

The name of a mystical pool near the heavenly Nile. It is figured in the vignette to the CXth chapter of the Ritual of the Dead.

GEFION.

In Scandinavian mythology a virgin goddess, the guardian of the youth of virgins.

GENUS.   *And* GENEA.

The first earthly children, the son and daughter of Æon and Protogonos. They were the first to worship the deity whom they venerated in the sun. Their children were Phos, Pur, and Phlox, which see.

GEOS.

The Greek form of the Egyptian royal name Teos, which see.

GER-ASHTAROTH.

The son of Abdelim. He and his brother Muthon III. were co-suffetes or kings of Tyre. *See* Muthon III.

GERDA.

In Scandinavian mythology the wife of the god Freyr.

GERMANIANS.

The sixth of the ten great Persian tribes. They were an agricultural caste.

GERRHA.

The name of the peculiarly worked square shields which were used by the Khitæ or Hittites.

GERROM.

An Egyptian city on the sea-coast between Arabia and Palestine.

GET.

The Egyptian name of the Olive fruit.

GET.

The name of the Egyptian amulet in the shape of a buckle. It was usually made of red jasper.

GETA.

An Egyptian god. He was the principle of "eternity" deified.

GHANDHARVAS.

In Hindu mytholgy another name of the good spirits called also Dewetas, which see.

GHASSANITES.

Another name of the Arabian people who were more generally called Agdites, which see.

GHAZA-HADJ.

A son of Abdshems, king of Yemen. He was more generally called Himyar, which see.

GHIFAR.

An Amalekite tribe who settled in the district of Yathrib, in Arabia.

GHUMDAN.

A royal fortress of the kingdom of Sabæa, near Sana.

GIAMMU.

The king of a district on the river Belichus. He attempted to resist the progress of Shalmaneser II., but was murdered by his subjects in order that they might make peace with the king of Assyria. His cities were Killala and Tulsaabilahi.

GIGARTUS.

One of the Phenician cities of the Triapolis, which see.

GIGIM.

In Accadian mythology the name of a class of mysterious evil spirits who afflicted mankind. They were called by the Assyrians Ekim.

GIHON.

In Hebrew tradition a river of Paradise. It is considered by Aryan scholars to have been the Oxus.

GIMIRRI.

A people who, together with the Scythians, ravaged Assyria and Media at the downfall of the Assyrian empire. They were the Cimmerians of Classic history.

GIMTU.

A Philistian city conquered by Sargon II. after the defeat of Yaman, king of Ashdod. It was also called Gnirzo.

GINDIBUH.

An Arabian chief who entered into a Syrian confederacy against Shalmaneser II., bringing a force of 1000 camels to aid his allies, who were all defeated by the king of Assyria.

GINGIA.

A district bordering on Assyria, which was rendered tributary by Samsi-Vul or Samas-Rimmon III.

GINGINAI.

A country near Media (?) which was rendered tributary by Samas Rimmon, king of Assyria.

GINKHIDAI.

A country rendered tributary by Samas-Rimmon, king of Assyria.

GINKHUKHTAI.

A country rendered tributary by Samas-Rimmon, king of Assyria.

GINNUNGAGAP.

In Scandinavian mythology a great chaos, or rather void space, bounded on the North side by the cold region Niflheim, and on the South by the warm district Muspelheim. Out of the drops coming from twelve rivers which flowed from Niflheim into Ginnungagap, coming into contact with the heat of Muspelheim, the first giant Ymir was created. *See* Ymir.

GINZINAI.

A country rendered tributary by Samas-Rimmon, king of Assyria.

GIÖLL.

In Scandinavian mythology a river which separated the land of shades from earth. It was crossed by a bridge of gold.

GIRDADI.

A king of the people of Assaya in Mesopotamia, who paid tribute to Assurnazirpal.

GIRTABKABI.   " The Double Sword."

In Chaldean astronomy an unidentified fixed star.

GISDHUBAR.   " Mass of Fire.'

Another form of the name of the mythical hero Izdubar, which see.

GISTA.

A king of the country of Abdanai, who paid tribute to Samas-Rimmon, king of Assyria.

GIZILBUNDA.

A district near Armenia destroyed in a great part by Samsi-Vul or Samas-Rimmon III.

GJEL.

In Scandinavian mythology the name of one of the horses of the gods.

GLADR.   " Spirited."·

In Scandinavian mythology the name of one of the horses of the gods.

GLADSHEIM.

In Scandinavian mythology the central part of the city of Asgard, the capital of the gods. *See* Asenheim.

GLENR.

In Scandinavian mythology the husband of Sol, the sun.

GNA.

In Scandinavian mythology the messenger of the goddess Frigge.

GNIRZO.

A town in Philistia, conquered by Sargon II.   *See* Gimtu.

GNO.

An Egyptian priest or assistant of the temple of Amen Ra.   Period uncertain.

GNOMES.

In Scandinavian mythology a mystic nation of dwarfs who guarded the metallic treasures of the earth.   *See* Elbs.

GOBAL.

A maritime district in South-west Arabia.   It was the Obal of Hebrew writers.   *See also* Tamna.

GOBRYAS.

A Babylonian conspirator.   *See* Gadatas.

GOG.

Probably the Hebrew form of the name of Gugu, or Gyges, king of Lydia, which see.

GOIM.

A people who were conquered by Budil, king of Assyria.   They were called also the Quti.

GOMATES.

A magian of the city of Pissiachadu.   He raised up an insurrection against Darius Hystaspes, calling himself Bartius, the son of Cyrus, the brother of Cambyses.   He for a short time obtained the throne, but was afterwards deposed and slain by Darius, who restored the Zoroastrian religion, which had been overthrown by Gomates.

GOORU.

In Buddhist mythology a travelling priest, whose special duty was the education of the young in matters of faith.

GOR.

In Scandinavian mythology the god of the month of harvest.

GOU.

The modern name of the Greco-Egyptian town of Antæopolis.

GRABATUSA.

The charioteer of Khitasira, king of the Hittites.   He was killed in the battle of Kadesh by Rameses II.

GRAPHIEL.

In Cabalistic mythology the intelligence of the planet Mars.

GRITHA.

In Scandinavian mythology one of the wives of Odin.

GRYDAT.

In Scandinavian mythology another of the wives of Odin.

GUBAL.

A North-Syrian state, which was conquered by Tiglath Pileser II.

GUBARUWA.

The Persian name of the officer and friend of Darius Hystaspes who was more generally called Gobryas.

GUD-E-A.

An early Chaldean king, ruling at Zirgulla. He was a great builder; but nothing else is known respecting him.

GUGU.

The Assyrian form of the name of Gyges, king of Lydia, which see.

GUKHANDE.

The Accadian name of the river Arakhtu, or the Araxes, a confluent of the Euphrates, which runs toward Arabia.

GULLINBURSTI.

In Scandinavian mythology the name of the horse which drew the chariot of the goddess Freyia.

GULLTOPP. " Golden Tress."

In Scandinavian mythology the name of the horse of Heimdall.

GULUSU.

A tribe in Mesopotamia, conquered by Tiglath Pileser II.

GUN-GUN-NU.

An early Babylonian king who reigned at Ur. He was possibly the son of Ismidagan. He is recorded as the builder of several temples at Ur.

GUNULAHMI.

A people who were conquered by Budil, a very early king of Assyria.

GURRU.

An Assyrian measure, used in the tonnage of ships. It is not exactly known to what it would have been equal.

GURUMU.

A tribe in Mesopotamia, who were conquered by Tiglath Pileser II.

GUSHTASP.

The Persian form of the name of Hystaspes, which see.

GUSUR.

One of the names of the Assyrian deity Marduk.

GUTI-UKI.

The Accadian name of the Babylonian city Guti.

GUZUNE.

An Assyrian city on the borders of Minni. It was conquered by Ahsera, king of Minni, who was soon afterwards defeated by Assur-banipal.

GYGES.

An officer of Candaules, king of Lydia ; he murdered his master, married his wife, and usurped the throne, thus founding the dynasty of the Merm-nadæ. He reigned from B.C. 687 to 653 (so Gelzer), and was the co-temporary of Archilochus, Simonides of Amorgos, Terpander, and the Homer of Euphorion. In consequence of a dream he sent embassies and tribute to Assur-bani-pal, including two captive Kimmerian chiefs. His aid enabled Psammitikhus to revolt successfully from Assyria ; but the Kimmerians soon afterwards invaded Lydia again, and he was slain in battle. His son, Ardys, again submitted to Assyria. Gyges was a benefactor of the Delphic oracle, and the old folk-tale of underground treasures and a ring which rendered the owner invisible attached itself to him. He is called Gugu in the Cuneiform inscriptions, and Gog in the Old Testament.

GYLLER.   "Golden." ·

In Scandinavian mythology the name of one of the horses of the gods.

H.

HAAS.

A mystical divinity or spirit, who is mentioned in the XLth chapter of the Ritual of the Dead.

HAB.

The sacred name of the ibis as the messenger of Thoth.

HAB.

The Egyptian name of the pickaxe or hand plough which was generally placed in the hands of the *Shabti* mummy figures.

HABAN.

The father of Yanzu, king of Zimri, which see.

HABANAMRU.

The king of Buda or Budahu, a kingdom in Arabia. His country was ravaged and himself put to death by Esarhaddon, king of Assyria.

HABBAR.

A high-priest of Melkarth, who became king or suffete of Tyre. He reigned for six months after the death or deposition of Caleb, and upon his own death or resignation, two joint suffetes were elected, named Muthon and Gerashtaroth, which see.

HABINI.

The king of Tel-Abni, a petty state of Mesopotamia, which submitted to Assurnazirpal.

HABITZU.

A King of Kadasiha or Kadesh, a district in Arabia. He was conquered and put to death by Esarhaddon.

HABU.

A city and nome n Lower Egypt, called Bubastis by the Greeks. It was sacred to the worship of the goddess Hathor.

HADAD. " The Only One."

The name of the Supreme Being in Phenician mythology. He was sometimes called El and Jaoh, the last in a mysterious sense.

HADATTA.

A Nabathean town where the army of Assurbanipal were compelled to rest themselves in the war with the Arabian and Nabathean rebels.

HADJAR-EL-ASWAD.

The name of the sacred black stone in the great temple of Mecca. It is supposed to have been originally an ærolite or Bætylia.

HADURA.

In Arabic history a tribe inhabiting the province of Yemen, which was called Rass. They were idolaters, and slew the prophet Shoaib, the son of Dhu-mahdam, who was sent to convert them. They were in consequence destroyed for their impiety.

HAGAR. *Or* HAKAR.

The Hieroglyphic form of the name of a king of the XXIXth Egyptian dynasty who was called Achoris by the Greeks. He joined Evagoras, king of Kypros, in his war against Artaxerxes II., and was defeated by him B.C. 393. He reigned eight years.

HAGARANU.

A tribe in Mesopotamia who were conquered by Tiglath Pileser II.

HAGIEL.

In Cabalistic mythology the intelligence of the planet Venus.

HAIASDAN.

The primitive name of ancient Armenia.

HAIDALA.

A mountain city of Elam, whither Khudurnanhundi fled for refuge from the army of Sennacherib, who was compelled by the stress of winter weather to retreat, leaving the king of Elam to die there in peace about three months afterwards.

HAK.

The Egyptian name of a kind of razor, which was shaped like an adze with a wooden handle.

HAK.

A city and nome in Lower Egypt, the Heliopolis of the Greeks, sacred to the deity Atum or Atmoo, the god of the setting sun.

HAK.

The mystical name of one of the planks of the boat of souls, in the XCIXth chapter of the Ritual of the Dead.

HAKA.

An Egyptian officer who was at one and the same time chief of the worship of Apmateku, captain of the soldiers, royal *Heb*, and governor of a town whose name is lost. He lived about the time of the Vth dynasty, and was succeeded by his son Pthah-ases, who held the like dignities.

HA-KA-PTHAH.

A name of the city of Memphis in Lower Egypt.

HAKE.

An uncertain Egyptian deity, much resembling Harpakrut, which see.

HAKER.

A mystical viper in the fourth abode of Osiris, who is mentioned in the CLth chapter of the Ritual of the Dead.

HAK-HEB.

A sacred town in Upper Egypt, where the god Horus was born and brought up by his mother Isis.

HAKOR.

The Egyptian form of the royal name of the second king of the XXIXth dynasty, which was written Achoris by the Greeks.

HALAKAMIR.

A king of the Himyarites about the first century A.D. He was succeeded by Yadail-Bayyin.

HALBUDA.

A mountain people on the borders of Media and Susiana, who were conquered by Sennacherib.

HALDI.

The great deity of the people of Ararat in the city of Muzagir. His shrine was plundered and his statue taken into Assyria by Sargon II., who thought thus the more effectually to break the power of the Armenian confederation. On the king of Assyria attacking the town, Urzana the king, with all his treasures, fled to the mountains, leaving the city an open prey. Himself escaped, but his wife, family, and the temple treasures fell into the hands of Sargon.

HALDIA.

An Armenian deity, the local god of the city of Musassir on lake Van, probably another form of the preceding deity.

HALDILE.

A petty kingdom in Arabia, subdued for the first time by Esarhaddon, king of Assyria.

HALDITA.

A Babylonian chief, the father of the rebel Arakhu, which see.

HALLUDUS.

An early Elamite king. His statue was brought to Nineveh by Assurbanipal, after the Elamite conquest by the Assyrians.

HALULE.

A city on the Tigris where Sennacherib defeated in one terrible battle Suzub and Merodach-baladin, kings of Babylonia, and Ummanmiman, king of Elam.

HALZIA.

A city of Minni, destroyed by Assurbanipal after the defeat of Ahsera.

HAMA.

In ancient Arabian mythology a species of screech owl, which flying round the tombs of the dead, kept them informed as to what went on among their relations in this world. These birds were also called Sada.

HAMANU.

A range of mountains to the North of Palestine, where Shalmaneser II. obtained timber for his palaces in Assyria. The place is now called Amanus.

HAMARANI.

A tribe in Mesopotamia, who were conquered by Tiglath Pileser II.

HAMARKI.

The Accadian name of a town or district, the site of which is not known.

HAMATA.

The Assyrian governor of the city of Suru, by the people of which he was killed. His death was terribly avenged by Assurnazirpal.

HAMIEL.

In Cabalistic astronomy the angel of the planet Venus.

HAMKA.

The Egyptian name of the red jasper stone, which was much used for the manufacture of amulets.

HAMMU.

In Egyptian mythology a kind of spirits who were often represented as adoring the rising sun.

HAMMURABI.

An usurper king of Babylon, of Kassite origin. He defeated Rimsin, king of Larsa, and erected a capital city at a place then called Dindur, the name of which he changed to Bab-ili, the "Gate of God," the Babylon of history. He erected or rebuilt a great temple there, called Bit-saggal, to the god Merodach, and dug a great canal named Hammurabi-nuhus-nishi, "Hammurabi the Delight of Men." He then erected many great temples and a splendid palace, which was afterwards repeatedly restored by his successors on the throne of Babylon. He also built a palace at Kilmed, near Bagdat, and a great tower to the deity Zamana near Hymer. Hammurabi further embanked the river Tigris with a great wall, to restrain the inundations. The length of his reign is not known.

HAMMURABI-NUHUS-NISHI. "Hammurabi the Delight of Men."

The name of the great canal excavated at Babylon by Hammurabi.

HAMSET.

A royal personage of the Vth dynasty. He was the son of Kaa, the chief of the royal works of a king of that period.

HAN. "The Vase."

A game of skill among the ancient Egyptians. It was played by two people, having a number of pieces of terra cotta or ivory, which moved on a circular board marked with concentric lines. Its rules are unknown.

HAN-ANKH-EF.

A son of King Nofre-hotep, of the XIIIth dynasty.

HANANU.

An Assyrian governor, in the reign of Sargon II. The name of his district is lost; but he was the eponym of the year B.C. 701, the chief event in which was an expedition to Palestine.

HANAZIRUKA.

A king of the Medes, who was defeated with the loss of 2,300 of his men, his capital city, and 1,200 villages, by Samsi-Vul or Samas Rimmon III.

HANDUR.

A district bordering on Assyria, rendered tributary by Samsi-Vul or Samas-Rimmon III.

HANEBU.

The Egyptian name for the Ionians or Greeks.

HANEN.

Another form of the Egyptian name for the land of Ionia.

HANHAR.

A title of an Egyptian deity corresponding to the Ares of the Greeks. He was also called Onouris and Anhur, which see.

HANI.

A king of Samala, in Mesopotamia. He came to the assistance of Ahuni, king of Lahlahte, against Shalmaneser II., by whom he was utterly routed.

HANIRABBAT.

A district West of Assyria, near the Upper Euphrates, which submitted without a battle to Tiglath Pileser I., and where in later times Esarhaddon defeated his two brothers, Assurmalik and Sharezer, and compelled them to fly into Armenia.

HA-NOFRE-T.

A daughter of Rameses-Miamun, of the XXth dynasty.

HANRUTA,

The Egyptian name of the Syrian river Orontes.

HANT.

An Egyptian lady, the wife of Urshu, the superintendent of the boatmen of Amen Ra.

HANUN I.

A king of Gaza, who paid tribute to Tiglath Pileser I.

HANUN II.

A king of Gaza. He attempted to defy Tiglath Pileser II., who defeated and drove him into Egypt, occupying and plundering the country; after which Hanun, unable to obtain assistance from Pharaoh, submitted and paid tribute to the Assyrians.

HANUN III.

A king of Gaza. He combined with Sibahe, king of Egypt, to resist the demands of Sargon II., king of Assyria, who met him at Raphia, on the borders of Palestine and Egypt, and utterly defeated him, carrying him a captive to Nineveh.

HANUT.

See Ha-shaat.

HAP.

An Egyptian city, the *Uu* of the fourth nome of (?) Upper Egypt.

HAPENTMAT.

The mother of King Snefru, of the IIIrd dynasty.

HAPI.

The mystical name of one of the planks of the boat of souls, in the XCIXth chapter of the Ritual of the Dead.

HAPI.

The Digger, one of the four genii of the dead. He was represented as a vase having a monkey's head as a cover. Upon the vase was often inscribed a prayer to the goddess Nephthys. *See* Amset, *and* Canopic Vases.

HAPI-ANKH. " The Living Apis."

The name under which the deity Apis was worshipped in the town of Ha-shaat, and at Memphis in Lower Egypt.

HAPIMOU.

The god of the Nile. He was generally represented as a very corpulent man, holding an altar with wild birds, and with his head crowned with lotus flowers and papyri. He was sometimes painted red, to represent the water of the Nile when muddy at the time of the annual inundations, or green, the usual shade of the water at the other seasons of the year.

HAPI-U.

An Egyptian gentleman, the father of the lady Set-ap, which see.

HAPI-U.

The wife of Atef-neb-ma, and mother of Merira an Egyptian captain, which see.

HAP-MU.

The father of Ouaphres, or Uaprahet, which see.

HAP-TEK.

Another name of the Egyptian princess Mer-tetes, which see.

HAPU.

An Egyptian lady, the wife of Iri-sen-aker, an early Egyptian officer, which see.

HAQU-RA-NEB-MA.

A variant form of the prenomen Ra-ma-neb, of Amenhotep, III. of the XVIIIth dynasty.

HAR. " Horus."

A shorter form of the name of the deity Horus, sometimes also written Hor.

HAR.

A priest of the god Mentu. Period uncertain.

HARAKAITI.

The ninth resting-place of the Iranians after their exile from Aryanem Vaedjo, or the tenth abode of the Zends if that is included. It was the country of Arachosia.

HARAN.

A town in Yemen, whither Maad, the son of Adnan king of the Hejaz, was hidden by his father, after the battle of Dhat-Irak.

HAR-ANA-K-AF-SHAT.

The name of one of the mystical deities who is mentioned in the CLIVth chapter of the Ritual of the Dead.

HAR-AN-TAT-EF.

One of the titles of the deity Horus.

HAR-BAI.

A prophet and priest of Amen-Ra of Thebes. He married the princess Ti-nefer-hotep, and was the father of Horsonf, who was also a priest of Amen.

HAR-BENEN.

The father of Ra-kheper-ka, a priest of Osiris, which see.

HARBISIHU.

An early Babylonian king. He contended with Assur-zikur-esir, or Ezar, king of Assyria, a kingdom then rapidly rising into power.

HARDISPA.

A city of the Yasubigalla, which was conquered by Sennacherib and annexed to Assyria.

HAR-EM-HA.

A sculptor of the XIIth dynasty. His wife's name was Khet-ankh.

HAR-EM-HEB-I.

A son of Her-hor-si-amen, of the XXIst dynasty.

HAR-EM-HEB-I. *Or* HORUS HAREMHEBI. *Surnamed* "The Restorer."

The last monarch of the XVIIIth dynasty. Although originally brought up in the worship of Atin-Ra, he also adored the ancient, but rejected deity, Amen-Ra ; and upon his accession to the throne, or soon after, completed the revolution against the disk worshippers and their religion, which had begun at the close of the reign of Amenhotep IV., in whose court he formerly held office. He fought against and subdued the Kushite Negroes, and although at first only one out of eight rival kings in the different provinces of Egypt, he became before his death the sole monarch of both the Upper and the Lower countries. His queen, named Muts-natem, also exercised power in her own person of her sole right, and he was probably for a short time succeeded by her, after a reign of not less than seven years.

HAR-EM-HEBI.

An Egyptian officer of the XXVth dynasty, whose sarcophagus and mummy are in the British Museum.

HAR-EM-HUE-F.

One of the mystical demons of the Egyptian incantational mythology. It assumed the form of a snake, and was supposed to interpenetrate the souls of the deceased, and possibly of the living also.

HARGE.

A town in South Palestine, which was conquered by Vaiteh I., king of Arabia, on his invasion of Palestine against Assurbanipal.

HARHAR.

A district between Ellipi (Ispahan) and Assyria, conquered and annexed to Assyria by Vulnirari III.

Har-Hor. "Horus the Supreme."

The high-priest of Amen, in the reign of Rameses XII., and the first king of the XXIst dynasty. He assumed the command of the troops and the management of the public works, and on the death of Rameses XIII. he allied himself with the kings of Assyria, whom the Egyptians were no longer able to overpower, and resigning all right to the domination of Mesopotamia, usurped the throne of Egypt. He however conquered the Northern Syrians or Rotepnu. He took to wife a Semitic princess, and gave Assyrian names to all his children, none of whom succeeded him, his grandson, Painetem, coming next to the crown. *See* Painetem.

Har-hut.

The winged disk of the sun with two pendant uræi. It was the symbol of Horus, the protector, and the Agathodemon of the Greeks, or the Ferohir of the Assyrians.

Haria.

A Mesopotamian people, who were conquered by Tiglath-Pileser I., king of Assyria.

Harilu.

A tribe in Mesopotamia, who were conquered by Tiglath-Pileser II.

Har-im-hotep.

The father of Ankh-hapi, a priest of the deities Pthah and (king) Snefru, at Memphis. Period uncertain.

Har-khebu.

A priest of Apis, in the thirty-fourth year of Darius Hystaspes.

Har-khem.

The keeper of the royal house of the women of Seti I., of the XIXth dynasty.

Har-khent-skhem.

One of the seven mystical spirits who is mentioned in the XVIIth chapter of the Ritual of the Dead.

Har-machis.

A name given in Egyptian mythology to the solar deity Ra, when in the horizon. The setting sphinx was the symbol of this deity; and the great sphinx in front of the Pyramid of Cheops was in the earliest ages wrought out of the rock, in honour of the god. This statute was already an old one in the time of the IVth dynasty, and it was subsequently restored by Thothmes III. of the XVIIIth dynasty, who erected a temple between its paws.

Har-m-ankh-amen.

The overseer of the sacrificants of the temple of Amen, the husband of the lady Isi-em-kheb and the father of the lady Ka-ka, which see.

HAR-MENA.

A priest of the god Harhut of Edfu, in the XIXth dynasty. His mother's name was Senuer.

HAR-MI-HA.

The surname of the Egyptian king Antef III.

HARMISANDA.

A district on the borders of Assyria, which was rendered tributary by Samsi-Vul or Samas-Rimmon III.

HAR-NASCHT. " Horus in Victory."

An Egyptian priest and director of the Golden Hall of an unnamed king of the XVIIIth dynasty. His mother was named Ti-hathor.

HAR-NEM-ATA.

The Egyptian name of an uncertain Syrian town.

HAR-NET-ATEF.

A high-priest of the god Amen Ra, at Thebes. He was also an officer of high rank in the time of the XXVth dynasty. His sarcophagus and mummy are in the British Museum.

HAROERI.

A priest of the god Sennofer, which see. He lived in the XVIIIth dynasty.

HAROYU.

The fifth resting-place of the Iranians, after their exile from Aryanem Vaedjo. It was the Aria of the Greeks, and is now called Herat.

HARPAKRUT. " Horus the Child."

The infantile form of the deity Horus. He was represented as an infant, with a long lock of hair pendant over his left side, and with the fore-finger of his right arm pointing to his lips. In the time of the Ptolemies many of their eldest sons were represented under this divine form.

HARPASEBENSHA.

The Grecian form of a royal name of a monarch of the XXIst dynasty, but whom it is not certainly known. The name is only found in the lists of Manetho.

HAR-PI-RA.

An Egyptian deity. He was a form of the god Harpakrut, and was represented as wearing the solar disk and royal uræus.

HARPUSKIA.

A kingdom in Western Mesopotamia, which was conquered, together with its king Azau, by Shalmaneser II.

HARRISGALLA.

The name of a great wall which was erected round the city of Ur by Ardusin, king of Babylonia.

HARRU.

A kingdom to the East of Assyria, conquered by Dayan-assur, the Tartan of Shalmaneser II.

HAR-SAF.

A royal scribe of the city of Memphis, in the reign of Rameses II.

HAR-SAF.

A spondist of the god Thoth. His father was named Empe-ankh and his mother Teti-ma-nefer. The period when he lived is uncertain.

HAR-SAM-TOUI.

A title of the god Horus, as the uniter of the two kingdoms of Upper and Lower Egypt under one sceptre.

HAR-S-ANKH.

An Egyptian gentleman of rank, of the XIIth dynasty. His mother's name was Sebek-hotep and one of his sisters was named Isis.

HAR-SCHEFT.

A surname of the deity Osiris. It was the Arsaphes of the Greeks.

HAR-SHAF.   "Terrible Face."

An Egyptian epithet, early applied to the god Khnum.

HAR-SI-AMEN.   "Horus, Son of Amen."

A name of the deity Horus, in his character of a son of Amen Ra.

HAR-SI-ESI.   "Horus, Son of Isis."

The father of Pouisis, and the husband of the lady Taterkat.

HAR-SI-ESI.

A priest of Amen, in the tenth year of Augustus Cæsar.

HAR-SI-ESI.

In Egyptian mythology the elder Horus. He was called Aroeris by the Greeks.

HAR-SI-ESIS.

The name under which the Egyptian deity Horus was worshipped at the city of Tsets in Upper Egypt.

HAR-SI-ESIS.

A king of Zab-nuti. He was one of the twenty petty kings of Egypt under the Assyrian Icosarchy.

HAR-T-ATEF.

The son of Menkara, king of Egypt. To him were attributed several mystical works and the discovery of the LXIVth chapter of the Ritual of the Dead.

HARTCHEA.

The form of the Armenian royal name Urtsa, as given by Moses of of Khorene.

HAR-TE-MA. "Horus the Executer of Justice."

A title of the deity Horus, when he was represented as slaying the enemies of the king.

HARTIS.

A city in Mesopotamia which submitted to Assurnazirpal.

HARUA.

The prime minister of the princess Amen-iritis, the daughter of Shabaka of the XXVIth dynasty.

HAR-UAH-ANKH-ANTEF.

An Egyptian monarch, of the XIth dynasty. Nothing is known respecting him, and his name is not placed in the regnal lists. *See* Antef.

HAR-U-PU-KA-KA-SHARU-SHA-BAU.

The name of a mystical deity mentioned in the CLXVth chapter of the Ritual of the Dead.

HARUSPICES.

The Etruscan soothsayers, who divined future events from the inspection of the entrails of victims ; an art afterwards introduced into Rome. *Haruspex* is not an Etruscan mutilation of the Greek ἱερόσκοπος, but is derived from the roots which have produced *hira*, " entrail," and *specio*, "to look at." The Etruscan equivalent (according to the bilingual inscription of Pisaurum) was *netsvis trutnut.*

HASAN.

A king of the city of Yathrib, in Arabia. He was a tributary of Esarhaddon, who imposed a heavy tribute on his son Yala, by whom he was succeeded. *See* Yathrib.

HA-SEBEK.

An Egyptian town, as yet unidentified. It was one of the two Crocodilopoli of the Greeks, being a place sacred to the god Sebek.

HA-SHAAT.

An Egyptian town, sacred to the worship of the deity Apis. It was also called Hanut.

HASIS-ADRA.

Another form of the name of the patriarch Adrahasis, which see.

HASSIMIR.

The viceroy of the country of Isbaggi, under Urukh, king of Ur.

HASU.

A Libyan tribe who were subjugated by Rameses III. of the XIXth dynasty.

HAT.

A town in Upper Egypt ; site unknown.

HAT-ANT.

The Egyptian name of the town called Antæopolis by the Greeks.

HAT-A-SU.   *Or* HATSHEPS.   " The First of Noble Ones."

A queen of Egypt of the XVIIIth dynasty.   She was the daughter of Thothmes I., and regent of the kingdom during the reigns of her brother, Thothmes II., and the earlier part of that of Thothmes III. She invaded the land of Ta-Neter or Arabia Felix, and Pount, Arabia Barbarica, bringing the queen of that country captive to Egypt.   She was the first to establish an Egyptian navy on the Red Sea, and she re-opened the turquoise mines at Wady Magara, which had been abandoned since the time of the Hykshos, and enlarged the temples of Ammon at Karnak and of Athor at Deir el Bahri.   The length of her reign and the time and cause of her death are at present unrecorded.

HAT-A-SU.

The name of the queen of Thothmes III.   Her history and relationship, if any, to the royal family are unknown.

HAT-ATHOR.

Another name of tne town of Tentyra, in Upper Egypt.

HAT-EI.

An Egyptian scribe, whose monument is in the Leyden Museum. Period uncertain.

HATEN-ASH.

The Hieroglyphic name of the cedar oil, which was much used as an unguent by the ancient Egyptians.

HAT-HESI.

A town in the Libyan nome, sacred to the goddess Isis.

HATHNA.

A young nude Satyr, who was represented on an Etruscan mirror as upturning an amphora, with a leopard on each side of him.

HAT-HOR.

An Egyptian goddess called "the Lady of Horns." She was supposed specially to preside over the birth of princes, the female toilette, and the production of precious stones. She was the local deity of the nome of Lower Arsinoe, in Upper Egypt, of the gold and turquoise mines at Wady Magara, and of the land of Pount in Arabia Felix. Her name was often written Athor. In common with the other goddesses her headdress was the solar disk resting upon the outspread horns, and she was represented on the monuments with the ears, and sometimes with the face, of a cow. The Egyptian queens were generally considered to be under her special favour.

HAT-HOR.

The father (?) of an unimportant Egyptian named Senbeb. His name is important as showing that the Egyptians used the names of their deities as proper names of persons without any alteration or combination.

HAT-HORS.

In Egyptian mythology seven deities, also called the seven cows, who attended upon the birth of children, and in a certain degree foretold their destinies. Their analogues were the Parcæ of the Greeks.

HAT-HOR-HAT.

An Egyptian lady, the wife of Pakhrua, and the mother of Ankh-kheper-ra, priest of Apis.

HAT-HOR-HET-AEI.

An Egyptian lady, the daughter of Petemet and the lady Hemsuisi. Her sarcophagus and mummy are in the Leyden Museum.

HAT-HOR-ISIS.

An Egyptian lady, the wife of the sculptor and architect Abet, of the XIIth dynasty. Her name is peculiar as containing those of two deities Hathor and Isis.

HAT-HOR-SE.

The father of Osirtesen, an Egyptian official in the reign of Amen-emha II. of the XIIth dynasty.

HAT-HOR-SE.

The wife of Ameni, the chief of the embalmers of a king of the XVIIIth dynasty.

HAT-HOR-SE.

An Egyptian lady, the wife of a private individual named Ta-ta, who probably lived in the XIIth dynasty.

HAT-HOR-SE.

An Egyptian lady, the sister of two private individuals of the XIIth dynasty, named Antef and Ameni.

HAT-HOR-SE-T.

An Egyptian lady, the mother of Ankh, the keeper of the cars of the palace of Amenemha I. of the XIIth dynasty.

HAT-HOR-SET-DSJATHO.

The Egyptian name of the lady Sensaos, which see.

HAT-HOR-SET-MONTH.

An Egyptian lady, the daughter of Neferpou and the lady Ketet. Her sarcophagus and mummy are in the Leyden Museum.

HATI.

In Scandinavian mythology the name of the wolf which by pursuing and seizing the moon caused eclipses. He was the son of the giant Hrodwitner, by the giantess Iarnwidr. *See* Sköll.

HATI.

An Egyptian emblem or amulet in the shape of a heart, generally wrought in red feldspar, jasper, or cornelian.

HATI-NOFRE. "Good Heart."

An Egyptian scribe, whose monument is in the Leyden Museum. Period uncertain.

HAT-KA-NEBTER. "Abode of the Universal Lord."

One of the mystical cows or Hathors of Egyptian mythology. She was called "the Universal Lord" (*sic*).

HAT-MEHI.

An Egyptian goddess, worshipped in the city and nome of Chev, in Lower Egypt.

HAT-MEHU.

A city in Upper Egypt. Its site is unknown.

HAT-MIT-RA.

The mother of Amenhotep II. of the XVIIIth dynasty.

HAT-NE-HAT.

Another name of the city of Tentyris, in Upper Egypt.

HAT-NUB.

The Egyptian name for the royal quarries at Ombos, in Upper Egypt.

HAT-NUT.

A town in Egypt sacred to the goddess Sekhet. Site unidentified.

HAT-RESHPU.

An Egyptian town, sacred to the goddess Reshpu or Reseph. Site unknown.

HAT-SCHEPS.   *Or* HAT-A-SU.

An Egyptian lady, the wife of the governor Titiu of the XVIIIth dynasty.

HAT-SCHEP-U.

An Egyptian lady, the daughter of Nunnu, an officer in the XVIIIth dynasty.

HAT-SCHEP-U.

A daughter of Anhurmes, the priest of the deity Anhur, in the XVIIIth dynasty.

HATU-KHNUM-AMEN.

A king of the XVIIth dynasty.

HA-UAR.

The Egyptian name of the capital city of the Hykshos, which the Greeks corrupted into Avaris.

HAUBAS.   " The Shining."

A Himyaritic solar male deity, of whose attributes nothing is known. He was probably a form of the god Il.

HAURVATAT.   "The Universe."

In Zendic mythology the fifth of the heavenly Amshaspands, which see.

HAVILAH.

In Hebrew tradition a country abounding with gold, believed by Aryan scholars to be the district of Darada near Cashmere, and thought by some Assyriologists to have been Ava in India.

HAYANI.

A king of Hindana in Mesopotamia, who paid tribute to Assurnazirpal.

HAZAEL.

A king of Damascus. He ascended the throne after murdering Benhadad II., and soon afterwards he was called to the defence of his kingdom against Shalmaneser II., who defeated him with a loss of 16,000 men and all his baggage. The king of Assyria then marched to the siege of Damascus, but abandoned it for want of time, and contented himself with wasting the land instead. *See Appendix*, Kings of Damascus.

HAZAIL.

A king of the Hedjaz in Arabia. He submitted to Sennacherib, who rendered him tributary to Assyria. He was succeeded by his son Vaiteh, which see.

HAZ-AQI-YAHU.

The Assyrian form of the Hebrew royal name Hezekiah, which see.

Haziluha.

A Syrian settlement at the head of the Tigris. The people revolted against the Assyrians, and were subdued by Assurnazirpal.

Hazu.

A district in Arabia conquered by Esarhaddon. It was probably the Uz of Hebrew writers.

Hbai.

The Egyptian name of the town of Isidis or Baibait.

Hea.

One of the most important of all the Assyrian gods, as he combines in his numerous titles the attributes of several Classic deities. His Accadian name was En-ki, or the "Lord of the World," (earth,) and his Assyrian name read phonetically Ea or Hea. He unites in his offices the attributes of Pluto (Hades), of Poseidon (Neptune), and of Hermes (wisdom). Hea, as the representative of the Greek Poseidon, was "Lord of the Abyss," *sar abzu*, and he was spoken of as Hea "who dwells in the great deep." In a list of his titles he is called "Lord of the Madudu or Sailors," and it was Hea who taught Hasis Adra how to build the ark, or ship (*elapu*), in which he sailed over the flood. In this character of the god of water and ocean, he was associated with a female deity Bahu, "The Void," who may be identified with the *bohu* of Genesis I. Hea held dominion over a large number of spirits who dwelt in the *abzu* or the deep. In the character of the Greek Pluto, or lord of Hades, Hea himself figured but seldom, but his consort Nin-ki-gal, "the Lady of the Great Land," appears very frequently. Hea as lord of Hades, had the name of Nin-a-zu, and his wife was called Nin-ki-gal wife of Nin-a-zu. But it was in the character of the god of wisdom, the "god who knows all things," that Hea figured most prominently; Nin-ni-mi-ki, "Lord of Wisdom," or as the Accadian expresses it, "the Lord of the Bright Eye." It was Hea alone who could deliver man from the various spells and curses with which the complicated system of Chaldean magic beset him. Hea also delivered Ishtar from the power of Nin-ki-gal, in the legend of her descent into Hades. Hea had for his female consort in his character of "Lord of Wisdom" the goddess Dav-kina, the female deification of the earth, who was probably only another form of Nin-ki-gal, and resembles the Classic Persephone or Proserpine; though perhaps Nin-ki-gal and Dav-kina may be better identified with Persephone and Ceres (Demeter), the "Mother and Daughter" of the Greeks. (Boscawen.)

Heabani.   "Creation of Hea."

A famous sage, who according to the Izdubar Legends dwelt in a cave by himself by the shores of a great river, and avoided all human society. He was renowned for his great wisdom, and was the chief friend and assistant of Izdubar in his various undertakings. He was represented as a monstrous being, half man and half bull, somewhat resembling the Minotaur or Pan of Greek mythology. After having rendered many services to Izdubar, he was killed by the bite of some poisonous insect, probably a fly, but his spirit was afterwards raised to earth again in answer to the earnest petitions and spells of his afflicted companion. The relation of Heabani to the deity Hea other than his name is uncertain, and the real character of the sage is itself not clearly defined, as the legends relating to his conflicts with the bulls, lions, and evil spirits, which so continually occur on the Babylonian cylinders, have not yet been fully translated.

HEA-EI.

An Egyptian royal scribe, probably of the XVIIIth dynasty.

HEA-MANNA.

A form of the Assyrian divinity better known as Nisroch-salmon.

HEA-MU-BASA. "Hea the Creator."

A governor of Amukkan. He joined the revolt of Saulmugina, and was severely punished for it after his defeat by Assurbanipal.

HEA-MUKIN-ZIRA. "Hea the Establisher of Seed."

An early Babylonian usurper, who succeeded Simmasihu, and reigned three months only.

HEB-I.

Another name of one of the seven mystical cows or Hathors of Egyptian mythology. *See* Hathors *and* Parcæ.

HEB-I.

A scribe of Amen-Ra. He was the son of Sen-mes, who filled the same office before him. The period when he lived is unknown.

HEB-N-T-ABT.

An Egyptian ecclesiastical festival held on the second day of the month.

HEBUNUROTANT.

The father of Rameses III. of the XXth dynasty. *See also* Seti-nekht.

HECATOMPYLON. "Hundred Gated."

An epithet applied to the city of Thebes by Homer. It is not supported by monumental evidence, unless by a figure of speech all the gates of the different temples in the city were implied in the phrase.

HEDJAR. "City."

The name applied in the kingdom of Sabæa to the royal castles and their suburbs. *See also* Beit.

HEH.

A port on the Upper Nile where Osirtesen III. of the XIIth dynasty set up his statue. Beyond this point no boats were permitted to pass.

HEH.

The Egyptian god of time.

HEH-EN-KHONSA.

An Egyptian judge.   Period uncertain.

HE-HOR-REI.

An Egyptian priest, the son of Pnei-hor.   Part of his tomb is in the Leyden Museum.

HEH-T.

·The Egyptian goddess of time, the consort or feminine form of the analagous deity Heh.

HEI.

A prince of Kush, in the reign of Amenhotep III. of the XVIIIth dynasty.

HEI.

A prince of Kush, in the reign of Tut-ankh-amen of the XVIIIth dynasty.   He may have been the same as the preceding.

HEI.

An overseer of the palace of an Egyptian king, probably one of the Amenhotep monarchs of the XVIIIth dynasty.

HEIDRUN.

In Scandinavian mythology the name of the sacred goat, from whose milk the souls of deceased heroes were fed in the Walhalla, which see.

HEIMDALL.

,In Scandinavian mythology the swift-eared watchman at the gate of heaven.

HEIMTHURSEN.

The giants who were born of the sweat of the frost giant Ymir.

HEK.

The Egyptian name of the beer made of red barley, a drink originally introduced from Asia.

HEK.

According to the lists a mythical or divine prehistoric king of Egypt.

HEK-AN.

A surname of the Egyptian king Rameses III.   Another form of—

HEK-AN-U.

A surname of Rameses III. of the XIXth dynasty.

HEK-NOFRE.

An Egyptian official of the XVIIIth dynasty. He had a wife named Maut-mai, and a son named Amen-her-h-atf. Nothing else is known respecting him.

HEL.   " Cover."

In Scandinavian mythology the goddess of the lower region or hell, and of death. She was the daughter of Loki, an evil giant, and was represented as an old woman, dirty and black visaged.

HELIOPOLIS.   "City of the Sun."

The name given by the Greeks to the city and district of An, in the Delta of Egypt. It was anciently called Hak.

HELIOPOLIS.

According to Berosus the Greek name of the ancient Chaldean capital city Sippara. It was founded by the Turanians or Cushites, and its ruins are now called Sufeira. *See* Babylonia.

HELL.

In Scandinavian mythology a horrible region in the lower world, where the souls of the wicked were punished. It had thirty-two, or thirty-seven, filthy rivers full of mire and dirt, in which the condemned had eternally to wade. In the midst was the dreadful hall called Nastrand, with a roof composed of venomous serpents, and having all its gates open to the bitter North. It was surrounded by the river Giöll, which was crossed by a golden bridge guarded by the virgin goddess Modgudhr.

HELTE.

A Badaga idol, the wife of Hirodea, which see.

HEM-AT-ROTA.

The mother of Rameses III. of the XXth dynasty. *See* Hiset.

HEM-BAI.

A prophet of Amen Ra, and keeper or scribe of the offerings of Amen. He was the son of the lady Tes-amen. Period uncertain.

HEM-NEF-HOR-BEK.

A priest of Osiris in the time of the XXIVth or XXVth dynasty.

HEM-SU-ISI

An Egyptian lady, the wife of Petemet, and the mother of the lady Hat-hor-het-aei, which see.

HEN.

An Egyptian lady, the sister of Senbu, a priest of Osiris whose period is uncertain, except that it was prior to the XVIIIth dynasty.

Henne.

The father of Papi, an Egyptian priest of Osiris, which see.

Hent-anu.

The mother of Rere, one of the principal officers in the court of Seti I. of the XIXth dynasty.

Hent-ateh. " Royal Favourite."

A pallacist and priestess of Amen Ra in the XVIIIth dynasty.

Hent-kherpu.

A princess of Egypt, daughter of Rameses II. of the XIXth dynasty.

Hent-nofre.

The wife of Niani, one of the commanders of the army of Seti I.

Heos.

The goddess Aurora, or morning, of Greek mythology. She was said to have been the mother of Memnon, a prince of the Negroes who took part in the Trojan war. Her usual epithet was Rhododactylos. *See* Eos.

Hept. " The Pools."

A mystical region of the Egyptian Ker-neter, which see.

He-ptha-r-esis.

King of Pizattikhurunpi, one of the twenty petty kings of Egypt who were established by the Assyrians, who called him Pakhunaniapi.

Hept-skhes.

A mystical Egyptian divinity, mentioned in the XVIIth chapter of the Ritual of the Dead.

Heracleopolis-parva.

See Herakleopolis.

Heraclius-soter.

See Tphous.

Herakleopolis.

An Egyptian city in the Sethroic nome of the Delta, which was conquered by Piankhi, king of Ethiopia and of Egypt, when he subdued the revolt of the princes under Taf-nekht. It was called also Heracleopolis-parva.

Herakleopolis-magna. " Town of Herakles (Hercules)."

A town in the Heptanomos or Middle Egypt, now called Ahnas el Medineh. It was the seat of empire of the IXth and Xth Egyptian dynasties.

Herat.

The modern name of the Persian district anciently called Haroyu, which see.

HERAUNTIC-AKSANA.

In Hindu mythology a fearful giant, by whom the world was hidden beneath seven other worlds, till the god Vishnu in the form of a wild boar rescued it.

HER-BEN.

An Egyptian civilian, the son of Apa.

HE-REREM.

A priest of Apis, the son of Padus, and grandson of the governor Hererem, of the XXIVth dynasty.

HE-REREM.

A governor of an Egyptian province in the XXIIIrd or XXIVth dynasty.

HER-HET-SU.

An Egyptian officer, the son of Gerger. He is only known from an inscription on an Apis tablet in the Museum of the Louvre.

HER-HOR-SI-AMUN.

The first king of the XXIst dynasty.

HERHUT.

In Egyptian mythology the emblem of Horus as the good spirit, represented as a winged solar disk, having two uræi pendant therefrom.

HERI.

A sacred scribe and priest of Pthah in the Ptolemaic period. His father's name was Ka-ankh.

HERI-BASET.

The father of Hor-imhotep, an Egyptian captain of the Ptolemaic period.

HERKHEBA.

A priest of Amen Ra. The time when he lived is unknown.

HERMINO.

In Teutonic mythology one of the three sons of Mannus the son of Tuisco, and the founder of one of the three great races of the Germans. *See* Istio.

HERMODUR.

In Scandinavian mythology the god who brought back the beloved Baldur from the realms of Hel

HERMOPOLIS MAGNA AND PARVA. "City of Hermes (Mercury)."

The Greek name for the Egyptian cities and nomes called respectively Un and Sah, which see. They held out under their king Namrut, against Piankhi, king of Ethiopia, who conquered them after a three days' siege.

Hermotybians.

One of the two great divisions of the warrior class in Egypt. They were distributed over the following nomes :—Busiris, Sais, Chemmis, Papremis, the Island of Prosopitis, and half of Natho. These districts furnished in all 160,000 men.

Heroopolis.   " City of Heroes."

The Greek name for the frontier town of Egypt towards Syria. It was probably the Egyptian city Garu, or Taru.   *See also* Chun-Abt.

Hertha.

In Teutonic mythology the goddess of the creative power of the earth. The Tella-Mater of the Romans.

Heru.

Another form of the name of the Scandinavian deity Tyr, which see.

Herusha.   " Inhabitants of the Desert."

A nomadic people, to the East of the Delta, who were conquered by Rameses III. They were an Arabian people, dwelling "in the sands," and were first subdued by King Pepi-Merira of the VIth dynasty.

Hese-men-aa.   " Strangler of Waters."

A mystical pool near the celestial Nile. It is figured in the vignette to the CXth chapter of the Ritual of the Dead.

Hesi.

The Egyptian name of the great goddess called by the Greeks Isis. She was the mother of Horus and the wife of Osiris.   *See* Isis.

Hesi-em-kheb.

Another form of the name Isiemchev, which see.

Hespu.   *Or* Heseps.

The fifth king of Egypt, and the son of Ounephes. He was the author of some sacred books, and was called by the Greeks Usaphaidos. He reigned twenty years.

Hes-ra.

The wife of Smen, a great captain of Thothmes IV. of the XVIIIth dynasty.

Het.

An early Egyptian astronomer, some observations by whom have been preserved.

Het-aai.

A scribe of the family of the priest Amenemheb, of the XIXth dynasty.

Het-het.

A mystical name of the seven great spirits of the Ritual of the Dead. They were also called Ket-ket.

Heti.

A royal scribe, the father of Eopeii, the royal scribe of the palace of Memphis.

Hetmas.(?)

A son of King Aahmes I., of the XVIIIth dynasty.

Hetp.   *Or rather* Hotep.   "Peace."

A pool of the heavenly Nile; figured in the vignette to the CXth chapter of the Ritual of the Dead.

Hetp.   "Bushel."

An Egyptian measure of capacity; quantity unknown.

Hetu.

The Egyptian name of the hyæna, which was occasionally used for food.

Hezekiah.   "Strong in the Lord."   In Assyrian, Hazaqiyahu.

The son of Ahaz. He reigned twenty-nine years over Judah, in conjunction with Moab, Edom, the Philistines, and Egypt, in B.C. 711. He revolted from Assyria (the fourteenth year of his reign), but was conquered and reduced to obedience by Sargon. He had previously received an embassy from Merodach-Baladan of Babylon, urging him on to this step. On the death of Sargon, he again revolted; and Sennacherib, in B.C. 701, punished him by devastating Judah, carrying away multitudes of men and cattle, and besieging him in Jerusalem "as a bird in a cage." He had vainly attempted to pacify the Assyrian king by releasing Padi, who had been handed up to him by the people of Ekron, and by the present of thirty talents of gold and 800 of silver, besides other treasures. The army sent against him, however, was miraculously destroyed, and Hezekiah spent the remaining five years of his life in peace.

Hibe.

The capital city of the great oasis in the Libyan desert. It is now called El Khargeh. It is famous for a temple of the deity Amen Ra, which must not be confounded with that in the oasis of Ammon further North.

Hieracon.

A chief town in the Apollinopolite nome of the Thebaid, in Upper Egypt.

Hieracon.

A chief town of the Antæopolite nome of the Thebaid, East of the river Nile.

Hierapolis.   "City of Priests."

The Greek name of the Phenician city Bambyce, which see.

HIERASYCAMINON.

A Greco-Egyptian town in the Dodecaschænon, a district of Nubia.

HIERATIC.

A less defined and more cursive a form of the Hieroglyphic script, from which it differs chiefly in the number of the characters employed being more limited, and of those characters themselves only the essential parts being indicated, the whole of the signs drawn in outline. The Hieratic script was principally used for state documents and scientific papyri, such as the great Harris papyrus of Rameses III. and the Ebers medical papyrus. It was rarely used for lapidary purposes ; and, owing to its varying very much in its beauty and accuracy with the care of the scribe, it is a very difficult style of Hieroglyphy to translate. Towards the Greco-Egyptian or Ptolemaic period, the Hieratic gave way to a still more cursive form of writing called the Demotic, which was corrupted from it ; but this latter form of character was never highly valued, and as it was only in use among the lower classes, and for the most ordinary purposes, it soon degenerated into a simply unintelligible scribble.

HIEROGLYPHIC.   " Sacred Writing."

The name given by the Greek writers to the peculiar script employed by the ancient Egyptians, which consisted chiefly of pictorial representations of various animate and inanimate objects, used either phonetically, syllabically, or as ideographs expressive of certain ideas. Of these, together with certain other signs which were used as determinatives of expressions or ideas, there were no less than 960 different forms, but no two of them were exactly analogous in appearance, and only a limited list was resorted to for ordinary purposes, the other varieties being employed chiefly for the sake of effect or differentiation. In sculptured monuments the Hieroglyphics are either in bas-relief or a kind of hollow-relief, cut below the surface, from a line to an inch deep, the outline alone being on the surface, and the details elaborately carved at the flat at the bottom, according to the requirements of the monument. This style of art, while it distinctly rendered the outline on the surface, by its giving all the details below, effectively protected the texts from the hazard of injury or the ravages of time. The coloured Hieroglyphs are also divisible into two distinct classes ; the monochromatic, and the polychromatic or those which rendered with more or less fidelity the colour of the objects they were intended to depict, employing blue for the heaven and celestial objects ; red for the sun, the earth, the tint of the Egyptian skin, and the clay from which mankind sprang ; yellow for the moon and objects of wood and brass ; green for trees, bronze, and herbage ; while animals were painted in their proper colours as nearly as the conventional style of art admitted, the lion yellow, the hippopotamus black, the wasp yellow, and fishes blue and red. It was in the scribe's power, and on those public monuments where the Hieroglyph became an architectural decoration he by no means neglected it, to make each Hieroglyph a little miniature of the object it represented, and the temple and the tomb alike glittered with the vivid colours of these pictorial arabesques. For the mass, however, of monuments, the scribes were less ambitious in the display of colour. On many coffins and objects where polychromatic Hieroglyphs are used, the scribe seems to have exhausted the resources of an ill-furnished palette, and to have placed inappropriate colours on different parts of the dress or form. As the great mass of coloured Hieroglyphs are in monochrome, or only relieved by a single colour, the polychromatic texts throw great light on the objects represented by many Hieroglyphs, which would otherwise remain obscure. The chief monochromatic colours were :— black, in fashion during the IVth and following dynasties, and still later for inscriptions incised on alabaster ; blue, the celestial and favourite colour of the Egyptians, very prevalent at all times, particularly during the XIIth and XVIIIth dynasties ; green, used under the XIIIth ; and yellow, which came into use at the close of the XVIIIth and continued till the XXth dynasty, the type of religious dissension or caprice. The disposition of the Hieroglyphics is very different, according to their employment. When used in isolated words explanatory of persons and objects represented, they are distributed promiscuously in the field, either in horizontal or vertical groups, or both combined. More careful inscriptions have them marshalled in vertical or horizontal lines, each being separated and defined by a broad straight line. One rule was always observed by the scribe : all animals and other objects which comprise the same group or sentence were made to face in the same direction. As a general practice, that of the characters facing to the right was preserved, agreeably to the genius of Semitic languages ; but there were many exceptions, due chiefly to artistic considerations. The Hieroglyphics were also generally read from the direction in which they faced. Thus, when all faced to the right, the reader commenced with the first object on the right ; when they faced to the left, with the first object on the left hand. (Birch, in Bunsen's *Egypt's Place in Universal History.*)

HIK.

A surname of Amenhotep III. of the XVIIIth dynasty.

HIK-MA-MI-AMUN.

The surname of Rameses III. of the XXth dynasty.

HIK-NEKHT.

An early Egyptian scribe. Period uncertain.

HIK-TEN.

A surname of Rameses III. of the XXth dynasty.

HIK-TEN-RES.

The surname of King Tut-ankh-amen of the XVIIIth dynasty.

HILDE.

In Scandinavian mythology the name of the chief of the goddesses of fate or Walküres, which see.

HILKA-BESHA.   "Go away, Evil One."

Two magical incantational phrases which were used by the ancient Chaldeans, and continued afterwards as a mystic formula by the Alchemists of the Middle Ages, to whom their meaning was unknown. (Lenormant.)

HILLAT. "The Profane City."

The name given by the Chaldeans to that quarter of Babylon which was peopled by the various captives taken in the wars of Nabukudur-uzur. The site is now called Hillah, which now includes the ruins of the whole city.

HIMI.

A district north of Assyria, which was conquered by Tiglath Pileser I.

HIMYAR. "The Red."

The son of Abdshems, king of Yemen. He founded the Himyarite dynasty, which gradually changed the name of the people of the country from Sabæans to Himyarites. The true name of Himyar was Ghazahadj.

HINDANA.

A kingdom or district in Mesopotamia which paid tribute to Assurnazirpal.

HINDANU.

A city in the Euphrates near to its junction with the Khabour, which was conquered by Assurnazirpal, king of Assyria.

HINDARU.

A tribe in Mesopotamia which was conquered by Tiglath Pileser II.

HINTHIAL.

The Etruscan word for "ghost" or "shade."

HIPPONON.

A chief town in the Cynopolite nome of the Heptanomos or Middle Egypt.

HIRAM I.

A king of Tyre, by whose assistance David, king of Israel, was enabled to collect materials to construct the royal palace of Jerusalem. He was succeeded by his son Abibaal.

HIRAM II.

King of Tyre. He was the son and successor of Abibaal, and according to the Greek historians the siege of Troy took place in his reign. The people of Kitium, in the Isle of Kypros, having rebelled against him, he attacked and subjugated them in person. Returning to Tyre, he almost re-built the city, and re-erected with extreme splendour the national temple of the deity Melkarth, which had been founded 1000 years before. He built also a temple to the sister deity Ashtaroth, and united the sacred island of Melkareth with the larger one of Tyre, which he then surrounded with embankments and high walls. He assisted Solomon, king of Israel, in erecting the temple of Jerusalem, in return for which that king victualled the Tyrian fleet. He also united with the Jewish king in sending a fleet to Ophir, and gave him one of his daughters in marriage. He reigned thirty-four years, and was succeeded by his son Baaleazar.

Hiram III. (?)

King of Tyre, the brother and successor of Meherbaal. He reigned in Tyre twenty years, during the last six of which he was the vassal of Cyrus, king of Persia. He was succeeded by his son Muthon IV.

Hiram.

Another king of Tyre. He was one of tne many Syrian princes who were subjugated by Tiglath Pileser II. after the battle of Khummuha.

Hiranu.

A town in Mesopotamia, which was conquered by Tiglath Pileser II.

Hirata.

An Arabian town conquered by Assurbanipal. It was the Hira of mediæval writers.

Hirataqaza.

A town in Southern Palestine, which was conquered by Vaiteh I., king of Arabia, on his invasion of Palestine against Assurbanipal.

Hiriadeva.   " Chief God."

The name of the sacred buffalo bull worshipped by the Todas of the Neilgherries.

Hiristu.

A people in the mountains of Mesopotamia, who were subdued by Assurrisilim, king of Assyria.

Hirodea.

A Badaga idol, of whom little is known.

Hise-t.

The mother of Rameses VI. of the XXth dynasty.

Hise-t.

The daughter of Rameses VI.

Hise-t.

An Egyptian lady, probably the mother of Rameses III. of the XXth dynasty. *See* Hem-at-rota, both these ladies being styled king's mother.

Hise-t.

A daughter of Amenhotep III. of the XVIIIth dynasty.

Hise-t-a-matrota.

A wife of Rameses III., king of Egypt, in the XXth dynasty.

Hiset-em-kheb.

The third wife of Osorkon II. of the XXIInd dynasty. *See also* Isi-em-chev.

Hise-t-nofre-t.

A daughter of Rameses II. of the XIXth dynasty.

Hise-t-nofre-t.

A wife of Rameses II. of the XIXth dynasty.

Hise-t-nofre-t.

The wife of King Seti-Menepthah I. of the XIXth dynasty, and the daughter of Rameses II.

Hisiarsah.

A Cuneiform form of the Perso-Greek royal name Xerxes.

Hiuki.

In Scandinavian mythology one of the two children of the moon. *See* Bil.

Hizaki.

An Accadian city, the site of which is not known.

Hlin.

In Scandinavian mythology a goddess who especially protected all persons whose lives were endangered.

Hnoss.

In Scandinavian mythology the daughter of the goddess Freyia. She was the goddess of beauty.

Ho-ankh.

A Greco-Egyptian lady, the wife of the priest Inhehemto, and mother of Nefer-hor-hemt-oou-en-ra.

Hobal.

An ancient Arabian divinity ; possibly a form of the Sun-god.

Hobs.

A title applied to the god Horus.

Hodhr.

In Scandinavian mythology the god of the dark winter. He was generally represented as being blind.

Hœtumat.

The tenth resting-place of the Iranians after their exile from Aryanem Vaedjo. It was the Etymander of the Greeks.

Hofhwarfnir.

In Scandinavian mythology the name of the horse of the goddess Gna.

Hoh.

An uncertain Egyptian goddess, having a serpentine (not an uræus) head. (Wilkinson.)

Homa.

The name given by the Iranian philosophers to the mystical water of life.

Hon.

An Egyptian measure of capacity, equal to 75 pints. It was the *Hin* of Hebrew writers.

Hon.

The modern name for the city and nome in Upper Egypt which was called by the Greeks Phathyros.

Honix.

Another name of the deity Vili, the son of Bör, and the brother of Odin.

Honover.

The creating word of the Supreme Being. It is personified as a deity in the Zendavesta. *See* Memra.

Hon-pthah.

The son of Pthah-hat-ankh-ef, and the great-grandson of Orsokon II. of the XXIInd dynasty.

Hon-t.

An Egyptian lady, the wife of Toti the flabellum-bearer of a king of the XVIIIth dynasty.

Hon-t.

A granddaughter of King Sebekhotep II. of the XIIIth dynasty.

Hon-t-kha-ra.

A daughter of Rameses II. of the XIXth dynasty.

Hon-t-khem-u.

The daughter of an Egyptian king, but of what king it is not known.

Hon-t-mit-heb.

A daughter of Amenhotep III. of the XVIIIth dynasty.

Hon-t-to-kheb.

A daughter of King Amenhotep I. of the XVIIIth dynasty.

Hon-t-to-neb.

An Egyptian lady, the wife of Kauta, the son of Amenemap, a priest of Amen Ra, in the reign of King Ai, of the XVIIIth dynasty.

Hont-usen.

A granddaughter of Tetet, an early Egyptian king.

HOPHIOAUEMES.

An Egyptian officer, the auditor and director of the palace of an unnamed king. (Leemans.)

HOPHIOOUENA.

An Egyptian priest, the chief of the prophets of Osiris (?) in the reign of Osirtesen I.

HOR.   *Or* HORUS.

An Egyptian gentleman, the son of Sent. He lived between the XIIth and XVIIIth dynasties.

HOR.

A scribe of the army of Amenhotep III. of the XVIIIth dynasty, and chief of the house of Queen Taia. His wife's name was Tabaret.

HOR.

An Egyptian officer, the son of Senma. He was priest of the goddess Ma and of the god Mentu, and also priest of the royal pyramid named Ka-nefer, in which Amenemha I. was buried. He died in the reign of Osirtesen I. of the XIIth dynasty.

HORA.

A royal scribe in the reign of Amenemha I. of the XIIth dynasty.

HORA.

A chief-priest of Amen Ra, director of the panegyries, and chief of a country unnamed, about the time of the XIXth dynasty. *See* Triaconterides.

HORA.

The royal scribe of Seti-Menepthah I. of the XIXth dynasty. His wife, Nofre-ari, was a priestess of Amen Ra.

HOR-EM-HEBI.   *Or* HAREMHEBI.

The royal scribe, favourite of the king, and great chief of the soldiers, of an unnamed monarch of the XVIIIth dynasty.

HOR-EM-KHU.

A royal scribe in the reign of Amenhotep I. of the XVIIIth dynasty.

HOR-EM-KHU.

Another form of the Egyptian sacred name Harmak-ra, or Harmachis, which see, *as also see* Sphynx.

HOR-HIUN-AMIF.

A son of Rameses II. of the XIXth dynasty.

HOR-IM-HOTEP.

An Egyptian captain under one of the Ptolemies. His father's name was Heribaset.

Horirem.

An Egyptian gentleman, the son of Outhor and the lady Tahart. His mummy and sarcophagus are in the Leyden Museum.

Hor-iri-aa.

A priest of Apis, in the time of Darius Hystaspes.

Horminuter.

The father of Taspu, a wife of Takelot I. of the XXIInd dynasty.

Hor-pet-u-ankhi I.

An obscure Egyptian king of the XXIst dynasty, of whom nothing but his name is known.

Hor-pet-u-ankhi II.

A king of the XXIst dynasty. He succeeded Pisem II., and was the last king of the dynasty.

Horsenedto.

An Egyptian deity, a form of the god Harpakrut, which see. (Wilkinson.)

Hor-shesu. "Servants of Horus."

In Egyptian mythology the name given to the early period of the rule of the gods upon earth.

Hor-si-hise-t.

The son of Prince Sheshank, son of Osorkon I. of the XXIInd dynasty.

Hor-son-f.

A prophet and priest of Amen Ra at Thebes. He was the son of Horhbai, a prophet of Amen Ra, and the lady Ti-nefer-hotep, a priestess of the same god.

Hor-ti.

The Egyptian name for the city and nome in Upper Egypt called by the Greeks Coptos. It was sacred to the deity Min.

Hortitif.

The son of an Egyptian king, but of whom it is not certainly known. *See* Hartatef.

Horus. (Cippus of Horus.)

The name given by Egyptologists to certain small stèle of a mystical nature, which were generally wrought in serpentine. and which always represented the deity Horus the child, as a naked boy, standing upon the backs of two crocodiles, which revert their heads, and holding in his hands a scorpion, a lion, two serpents, and a gazelle: to the right and left of him are generally two standards, dedicated to the two forms of the rising and the setting of the sun, and over the deity is the monstrous head of the god Bes, with his tongue protruding. The field of the stèle is generally filled with a magical formula, almost always badly written. The god Horus is called "The Old Man who becomes Young;" and from hence it is supposed that the idea is of the eternal youth of the victorious divinity at the time of death, or another form of expressing the resurrection, under the symbol of the rising sun. The crocodile could not turn his head; it was to the belief of the Egyptians a symbol of an impossibility: therefore, as the god was to grow young again, he trod that emblem under his feet, for he had triumphed over death, and had made the crocodiles of darkness (so described in the Ritual of the Dead) to turn back their heads. The monstrous head of the god Bes may have been intended to signify the destructive powers of nature, so that the ever young Horus might be supposed to complete the cycle of eternity in himself. There are a great number of these stèle in existence, and they were at one time thought to have had an astronomical significance, then again, by later scholars, to have been intended as amulets to protect the wearer or possessor from the attacks of dangerous animals; but the explanation above given by M. Chabas is accepted as being the most satisfactory.

HORUS.   *Or* HAR.

One of the most prominent of the Egyptian deities. He was the child of the great deity the sun in his semi-human form as Osiris, and of his wife and sister, the goddess Isis, as the celestial firmament, and was generally called Horus, the Saviour. In his *first* and highest office he was the sun in its mid-day power, and thus he was venerated as an hypostasis of the Sun-god Ra, by whose influence all nature existed, and who was himself the visible type of Amen Ra, the hidden and incomprehensible deity. In that character he was generally represented as a man with the head of a hawk, upon which was poised the solar disk. In his hands were the emblems of authority and life, and from his right eye were all good things created. As Horus-Ra he was frequently figured on the upper part of the Egyptian mummy cases, and on the amulets laid upon the head of the deceased. The hawk among birds, and the basilisk among reptiles were his emblems. In this, his first and most abstract character, Horus was identical with the Supreme Being himself. The *second* character of Horus was that of the avenger of the injuries of his father upon his uncle Seb or Typhon, who had at first reigned in Egypt conjointly with Osiris, but had afterwards quarrelled with and slain him, scattering his severed members all over the land of Egypt. To "Horus of Crocodiles," as the son of Osiris was called in that attribute, fell the duty of warring with Typhon, the evil spirit, and all his coadjutors, divine, demoniac, and animal. The *third* character of Horus was that of *Sneb*, or "The Redeemer," in which office he was the vicarious protector of the souls of the deceased in Hades, or the Kerneter. By him the deceased was introduced to Osiris in the Hall of the Two Truths, and at his entreaties the sins which the soul had committed were either atoned for or pardoned. Horus further transferred to the benefit of the deceased the various good offices which he had himself performed in behalf of his father, and more especially those ceremonial rites which were called the "Assistances of Osiris." By the aid of Horus, all the terrors of the rivers of Hades and the abodes of hell were dispelled, and the ultimate end of the Egyptian believer was to be assimilated to the character and deity of Horus the Redeemer. Horus was called in the Hieroglyphic texts the "Sole Begotten of his Father," "The God creating Himself," "Horus the beloved Son of his Father," "The Lord of Life," "The Justifier of the Righteous," and "The Eternal One." The kings of Egypt were always regarded as incarnations of Horus, as well as of the sun Ra, and hence one of their two royal cartouches was always designed to express that hypostasis and was called the Horus title.

HORUS.

A great military commander, of the XXVIth dynasty. He was the son of the lady Nefer-u-sebek. He had charge of the government of the Mendesian nome and was also governor of Heracleopolis, where he executed several important additions to the temples of the deities Atum and Osiris-Unnefer. He also took the presidency at the great festival of the goddess Sekhet, which was held on the fifth day of the month Pharmuthi.

HORUS.

A scribe of Amen Ra. He lived in the Saitic period.

HOR-UTA.

The granddaughter of Peteharpocrates, a royal scribe, which see.

HOSAH.

The Hebrew name of the Phenician city of Mahalliba-Usu, which see.

HOSEA. Assyrian, AU'SI and HUSIA.

The last native king of Israel who was appointed in the place of Pekah by Tiglath-Pileser, and who reigned nine years. He conspired with So, or Sibahe, of Egypt, to revolt from Assyria, and was accordingly deposed and imprisoned by Shalmaneser. Samaria was also besieged, and, after three years, taken by Sargon (B.C. 720), who carried away 27,280 of the inhabitants, appointed Assyrian governors over the city, and forcibly imposed tribute upon Hoshea.

HOSIT-EM-BENT.

An Egyptian lady, daughter of an officer named Osirtesen, which see.

HOSIT-EM-TOTH.

An Egyptian lady, the daughter of an officer named Osirtesen, and the sister of Hositembent.

HOTEP. "Peace."

An Egyptian lady, the wife of an officer named Osirtesen, who may have lived in the XIIth dynasty.

HOTEP.

An Egyptian lady of high rank, the daughter of a chief functionary, and wife of Ameni, an officer living in the time of the XIIth dynasty.

HOTEP.

The daughter of the preceding lady.

HOTEP-BESE-T.   " Peace of Bes."

An Egyptian lady, the mother of Pe-ankh-em-ta-nen.   Her mother was named Thothartais.

HOTEPHERS.

The grandson of Tetet, an early Egyptian king.

HOTEPHERS.

The daughter of an early Egyptian king, possibly of the family of Tetet.

HOTEPHETES.

A granddaughter of Tetet, an early Egyptian king.

HOTEP-HI-MAT.

A surname of Menepthah I., king of Egypt, in the XIXth dynasty.

HOTEP-PTHAH.   " Peace of Pthah."

The father of Zet-auf-pthah, priest of Apis, which see.

HOTEP-T.

An Egyptian lady, the wife of Antefaker, and the mother of Osirtesen, Antef, and Ameni; all private individuals, probably of the XIIth dynasty.

HOTEP-UI.

The son of an Egyptian officer named Osirtesen, and his wife Hotep.

HOUI.   Or HUI.

An Egyptian architect, whose votive statuette is in the Museum of the Louvre.

HOUTEOIRI.

A royal priest and scribe of the royal bowmen.   He was the son of a lady named Neitaker.

HOW.

The modern name of the city of Diospolis-Parva, in the Thebaid.

HPSELE.

The chief town of the Hypselite nome of the Thebaid.

HRASWELGR.

In Scandinavian mythology the name of the great eagle, or the winds, which sat on the North side of the skies.

HRIMFAXI.

In Scandinavian mythology the name of the horse of the goddess Nott (night), the foam from whose bridle caused the dew.

Hrodwitner.

In Scandinavian mythology the giant father of the wolf Hati, the enemy of the moon.   *See* Jarnwidr.

Hru-amen.

A commander of the troops of an unidentified Egyptian king of the XXVIth dynasty.

Htuabi.

A title of the deity Tum or Atum, in the LXXVIIIth chapter of the Ritual of the Dead.

Hu.

A mystical being mentioned in the CXth chapter of the Ritual of the Dead.

Hu.   " Taste."

An obscure Egyptian divinity who is named in the XVIIth chapter of the Ritual of the Dead.

Hud.

In Arabian history a prophet who was sent to convert the Adites from idolatry.   He preached without effect for fifty years during the reign of Khuldjan.   At last the entire people of the Adites having been punished by a drought, were miraculously slain by a tempest, except a few who had believed in Hud.

Hudun.

A city in Mesopotamia which submitted to Assurnazirpal.

Hugin.   " Thought."

In Scandinavian mythology one of the ravens which sat upon the shoulders of the great god Odin.

Hui.

The auditor of the palace of justice in the reign of a king of the XVIIIth dynasty.   He was a worshipper of the Syro-Egyptian goddess Katesch.

Hui.

The son of Amen-em-heb, the chief of the grooms of a king of the XVIIIth dynasty.

Hui.

An Egyptian officer, the keeper of the royal bark of Meri-Ra or Thothmes III. of the XVIIIth dynasty.

Hui.

The governor or viceroy of Ethiopia under Amenhotep III., to whose third successor Tut-ankh-amen, he sent a costly embassy, attended with a large retinue of Negroes.

18

Hui.

An Egyptian captain of the XIXth dynasty. Nothing else is known respecting him.

Hui.

A royal treasurer in the reign of Rameses II. of the XIXth dynasty.

Huilai.

A country near Media, which was rendered tributary by Samas-Rimmon, king of Assyria.

Huischera.

An Egyptian officer, the scribe of the treasury at Sais, in the XVIIIth dynasty.

Hukkurana.

A Nabathean city where Abiyateh the rebel was taken captive by the army of Assurbanipal.

Hula.

The chief of the Assyrian colony of Halziluha, near the head of the Tigris. He and his people attacked the Assyrian town of Damdamusa, but they were defeated by Assurnazirpal, who flayed alive their chief Hulai.

Hulli.

A Syrian nobleman whom Tiglath-Pileser II. placed on the throne of Tabal, instead of Varsarmi, the king, who had revolted from him.

Humai.

The lord or chief of Memphis in the reign of Thothmes III.

Humbanigash.

A king of Elam. He and Merodach Baladin I., and Urza, king of Ararat, combined against Sargon II., but without success, as Humbanigash was first of all defeated by the king of Assyria on the plains of Kalu.

Humba-undasha.

An officer in the Elamite army who betrayed the plans of Umman-minan and his allies to Sennacherib, thus securing an easy but sanguinary victory to the king of Assyria at the battle of Halule.

Humri.

The name by which Omri, king of Israel, is mentioned in the Assyrian inscriptions.

Humut.

A city in Babylonia which was conquered by Tiglath Pileser II., who enlarged it, built a palace there, and changed its name to Kar-Assur.

Huni.

The last king of the IIIrd Egyptian dynasty. He reigned twenty-six years, and was the Kerpheres of the Greeks.

Hunra.

A priestess of the goddess Nut in the XVIIIth dynasty.

Hupuskia.

The capital city of the district of Nairi, North of Assyria, which submitted to Assurnazirpal. *See* Nairi.

Huracca.

An Assyrian city which revolted to Assurdan, and was reconquered by Samas-Rimmon, or Samsi-Vul IV.

Hurantalu.

A town and fortress of the Rotennu, in Upper Syria. It was made tributary to Egypt by Thothmes III.

Hurarina.

A desert town in Nabathea, which was conquered by Assurbanipal in his second Arabian war.

Huras.

A city of Girubbunda, near the East of Parthia, which was destroyed, together with 600 of its garrison, by Samas-Rimmon, king of Assyria, its king Pirisat with all his family being taken captive in Nineveh.

Hurbasa.

An Egyptian chief who unsuccessfully revolted against Piankhi-Mer-amen of the XXVIth dynasty.

Husia.

The Assyrian form of the Hebrew royal name Hoshea, which see.

Husinna.

A small Syrian state which paid tribute to Tiglath Pileser II.

Hut.

The Egyptian name of the onion, a favourite article of diet in Egypt.

Hut.

The white crown of Upper Egypt. *See* Pschent.

Huta.   Sepulchral Tablets.

The funereal tablets, called *huta,* were used for the same purpose as tombstones and sepulchral monuments are at the present day, but they were distinguished by having been placed inside the tombs, and not outside and in the open air. They were of different materials, as granite, sandstone, alabaster, and limestone ; and of different sizes

and shapes, square, rectangular, and either pointed or rounded at
the top ; those of square shape often representing the entrance or
cornice of a tomb. At a later period (about the XXIInd dynasty,
or in the ninth and eighth centuries B.C.) wooden tablets, made of
sycamore, were substituted.   These tablets were generally rounded
above, and surmounted by a wooden figure of the *bai*, or soul, and
stand on a pedestal of two small flights of steps, into which they
are inserted.   They have been covered with linen, coated with plaster,
on which have been painted in tempera the vignettes, or pictures,
and inscriptions.   The principal subjects represented are the deceased
attended by his mother, wife, sister, or brethren, standing in adoration
to the boat of the Sun, or to the solar deities Ra, Sekar or Socharis
Tum, Atum or Tomos, and Osiris, either alone or accompanied
by his wife Isis, Nephthys, Anubis, Amset, Hapi, Tuautmutf, and
Kabhsenuf, and other sepulchral deities.   The texts accompanying these
scenes are the names and titles of the deities, and of the deceased,
usually placed in the scene along with them, and a larger inscription,
in horizontal lines of Hieroglyphics, placed under the scene, being a
proscynema, or act of adoration, to the principal deities, praying them
to confer the usual benefit of food, permission to pass from Hades, or
off the earth, and for the soul to go to heaven, or the empyreal regions.
Some inscriptions are also adorations, or hymns to the sun.   The
name of the deceased on these tablets was preceded by the title of
Osiris, into whose condition he was supposed to pass after death ;
but about 100 B.C., females began to have the title of *Athor*, or the
goddess of beauty, prefixed to their names.   Some of these tablets were
surmounted on the rounded top by the figure of a human-headed hawk,
emblem of the *bai*, or soul, which was fixed by a plug into the upper
rim of the tablet. (Birch.)

Huzirina.

An Assyrian city which supported Assurdainpal in his revolt against
his father Shalmaneser II.

Hyanes.

The Greek form of the name of the Satrap of Darius, who was named
Vivana, which see.

Hykshos.   (Hyk, " Ruler;" Shasu, " Shepherds.")

The name given by the Egyptians to the terrible Syrian invaders,
probably nomadic Arabs, who entered the country at the termination
of the XIIth dynasty.   They were a combination of the adjacent
Semitic tribes, and they overran and governed Egypt from the XIVth
to the XVIIth dynasty, introducing a new religion, new towns, and
new manners, and ruling with great cruelty, till their final subjugation
by Kames, the first king of the XVIIIth dynasty.   They are called on
the monuments Mena.   *See* Apepi, Set-i-pet-i-nubti, *and* Kames.

Hymir.

The modern name of the ancient Babylonian city of Kis, where
Hammurabi erected a tower, called " The Tower of the Country," to the
deity Zamana,

HYPHERNES.

The Persian form of the royal name which was written by the Assyrians as Eparna, which see.

HYPOCEPHALI.

Under the heads of some mummies were placed flat circular disks of linen covered with plaster, representing the pupils of the eyes of the sun, and inscribed with vignettes, and an inscription, or else bronze disks, on which the same was engraved. These amulets were placed under the heads of the mummies to produce, or renew, the vital warmth, *bes,* of the body, and represented the symbolic eye, or *uta,* of Shu or Horus. The scenes beheld were supposed to be in the pupil of the eye, while the outer band, or border, which contained an inscription, represented the iris. The principal subjects were: 1. The goddess Uta holding the lotus over the cow of Athor, Amen generator, the genii, or gods of the Amenti, and a scarab. 2. Khnum-Ra, or Af, in his boat, and another boat with the ape Kafi, a form of Osiris. 3. Amen-Ra bifrons, Ra and scarab in boat, and the boat with mummied hawk. 4. Khnum ram-headed; quadrifrons, adored by apes. These vignettes refer to the CLXIInd chapter of the Book of the Dead, or Ritual. (Birch.)

HYPSELITES.

. A Western nome of the Thebaid of Upper Egypt. Its chief town is now called Shob.

HYPSELOS.

The Greek name for the city and nome in Upper Egypt called by the Egyptians Tuf.

HYPSISTUS.   " The Most High."

In Phenician mythology an early deity, who was otherwise called Eliun.

HYPSURANIUS.

In Phenician mythology a giant and the son of Capius. He inhabited the city of Tyre, which indeed he founded, and quarrelled with his brother Usous, who was the inventor of clothing made from skins.

HYSTASPES.

The Greek form of the Persian name Kustaspi, which see.

I.

IATNAN.   *Or* YATNAN.

The Assyrian name of the Island of Kypros or Cyprus, in the Mediterranean Sea.

IBILSIN.

An early Babylonian king who reigned at Ur.   Nothing else is known respecting him.

IBIUM.

A chief town in the Oxyrynchite nome of the Heptanomos or Middle Egypt.

IBRAHIM.

The modern name of the city or district which was called by the Assyrians Kute.

IBT.

An Egyptian prefix, signifying " East."

ICSUDA.

One of the dogs of the deity Marduk, who was also made into a mythical god by the Assyrians.

ICU.

In Chaldean astronomy a name of the planet Jupiter as one of the twelve stars of the West.

IDADU.

An early Chaldean king ruling at Ridu.   Nothing else is known respecting him.

IDALION.

A capital city in the Island of Cyprus.   It was the Idalium of the Greeks, by whom it was consecrated to the worship of Aphrodite.   It was tributary to the Assyrians under Sargon, Sennacherib, and Esarhaddon.

IDILU.

A petty kingdom in Arabia, conquered for the first time by the Assyrians under Esarhaddon.

IDKU. "The Eagle."

In Chaldean astronomy one of the seven stars of the west.

IDUNN.

In Scandinavian mythology the wife of Bragi, the god of oratory. She was the goddess of immortality, and as such had no parents.

IG.

The Assyrian royal shekel, equal to 12 pennyweights.

IKA-SAMSU.

A king of Ekron. He was one of the tributaries of Esarhaddon.

IKATAI.

The Egyptian name of an unidentified Syrian city.

IKB-IBEL.

A city in Babylonia, where Merodach-baladin I. took refuge from Sargon II. before his complete defeat at the battle of Dur-Yakin.

IKH-ILU.

A petty kingdom in Arabia, which was ravaged, and its queen, Bailu, put to death by Esarhaddon.

IKK-ILU.

Another form of the Arvadite personal royal name Yakinlu, which see.

IKUL-ANU. "Palace of Anu." (?)

A temple erected to the deity Anu at Babylon, by Nabukuduruzur II.

IL. "God."

The Supreme Deity in the abstract, of the Sabæans. The Ilu of the Chaldeans.

ILA. Or IDA.

In Vedic mythology the daughter of the patriarch Menu, to whom she was born after the deluge, as a reward for his piety. She became the progenitor of the human race.

ILABU.

A city situated on an island in the Euphrates. It was conquered by Assurnazirpal.

ILANI.

A chief of the district of Amida, conquered by Assurnazirpal.

ILGI.

An early Chaldean monarch. He was the son of Urhammu. He completed the temple of the Moon-god Sin, which his father had begun at Ur. No other particulars of his reign are known.

ILKIYA.

The Archon of Damascus, under Sennacherib.

ILLIBU.

A kingdom in Mesopotamia which was rendered tributary to Assyria by Sargon II.

ILLINOS.

In Greco-Babylonian mythology the son of Kissare and Assaros, and the second member of the first divine triad. His analogue was the Ilu of the Assyrians. *See also* Anu *and* Bel.

ILLIPA.

An Elamite kingdom, governed by Dalla and his successor and nephew Ispabara, as a tributary of Assyria.

IL-MAKAH.   "The God that Hears."

A Himyaritic or Sabæan deity, who was more generally worshipped in Sabæa. To him was dedicated the principal temple at Mareb, in South-western Arabia.

IL-SHARAH.

A king of the Himyarites, about the first century B.C. He was succeeded (?) by Karibail.

IL-SHARAH-YADHAB.

A petty king of Saba. *See* Faram-Yadhab.

IL-TEBU.

One of the dogs of the deity Marduk, who was made also into a god by the Assyrians.

IL-TIM-ARBA.

An Elamite city destroyed by Sennacherib.

ILU.   "God."

The Assyrian Deity as an abstract entity. His residence was in the heavens, and the other divinities were emanations or personifications of him. *See also* Anu *and* Bel.

ILU-BA.

An early king of Assyria, of whom nothing is known. He was succeeded by his son, Iritak.

ILU-BIHID.

A king of Hamath. He was in no way related to the royal line, but contrived to usurp the throne by promising to deliver the country from the Assyrians, with the aid of Sibahe, king of Egypt. He was, however, defeated and captured at the city of Arva, by Sargon II., who had him flayed alive and his city burnt.

ILU-DARIA.

The Tartan of Assurbanipal, king of Assyria. He was ruler of the province of Lubdi, near Babylonia, and revolted against his master, siezing the district of Ubummi ; but while attacking the city of Kullimir, he was slain in a night sally of the besieged, and his head sent to Assurbanipal.

ILU-HILTI.

The king of Rure, a district to the North of Assyria, which was conquered by Shalmaneser II.

ILU-KASSAT.

An early Chaldean king, possibly belonging to the IInd dynasty of Berosus.

ILUKIYA.

An Assyrian governor, in the court of Vulnirari III. He was the eponym of the year B.C. 805, the chief event in which was an expedition to Hazazi.

ILULEUS.

The Greek form of the name of the Tyrian king Lulya, which see.

ILUS.   " Mud."

In Phenician mythology an elementary deity, the offspring of the energic wind, and the material chaos.

IM.

In Accadian mythology the name of the Assyrian deity Bin or Vul. the god of the atmosphere.

IMGURBEL.

The name of one of the great walls of Babylon, which was erected by Nabukuduruzur or Nebuchadnezzar.

IMGURBEL.

A city in Assyria which supported Assurdainpal in his revolt against his father Shalmaneser II.

IMHOTEP.

An Egyptian deity, and one of the first kings of Egypt. He was afterwards called the son of the god Pthah. He was an architect, and the reputed author of many mystical books of art and mythology. He was called by the Greek writers Torsorthrus.

IMHOTEP.

The son of the king and deity Imhotep of the IIIrd dynasty.

IMHOTEP.

An ancient Egyptian official. He was called the "Chief of the Secrets of the Place of Life," and chief of the soldiers. He lived probably about the period of the Vth dynasty.

Imhotep.

An Egyptian priest, the son of Isueri, in the XXVIth dynasty.

Imki.

The Accadian name of the city or district of Muru, whose site is not known.

Imouthes.

The Egyptian god of medicine and surgery, supposed to have been King Tseshortsa (Torsorthrus) under a deified name, or perhaps the god Imhotep.

Imsugilna.

In Chaldean astronomy the name of an unidentified fixed star.

Imu.

A Syrian people, mentioned in the Egyptian texts as subdued by Thothmes III. They have been supposed to have been the Emin of Hebrew history.

Inarus.

A petty king of Libya, whom, together with the Athenians, the Egyptians under Amyrtaius called to their aid against the Persians under Artaxerxes-Mnemon, from whom they had revolted. At first the Egyptians were successful, but eventually the Persians raised the siege of Memphis, drove Amyrtaius to the marshes of the Delta, and impaled Inarus, placing as Satraps, Thannyras on the Libyan throne, and Pausiris on that of Egypt. The struggle lasted six years.

Indra.

In Hindu mythology the title of the Supreme Being as the living power of heavenly fire and of lightning. He was called also Dyauspitar, the Diespiter or Jupiter of the Romans.

Ingnio.

One of the three sons of Mannus, and founder of one of the German races. *See* Istio.

Inkuki.

The Accadian name of a city or district, the site of which is not known.

Innin.

In Accadian mythology an evil demon, a species of Lemure or hobgoblin.

Innumau.

A fortress belonging to the Rotennu, which was conquered by Thothmes III., and its revenues given to the temple of Amen Ra.

Intaphres.

A general of Darius Hystaspes, who subdued the rebel Arakhu, which see.

IOL.

A Carthaginian settlement in Palestine, which was called in later times Cherchel and Cæsarea.

IÖRD.   "The Earth."

In Scandinavian mythology the daughter of the goddess Nott, "night," and her second husband Onar.

IOUERNUF.

A governor of a temple in the reign of Queen Aahmes Nofretari.

IOU-S-AAS.   "The Great One who comes."

An obscure and mysterious Egyptian goddess. She was the daughter of Ra, and was called the Queen of Heliopolis, a town in which she was worshipped. She was represented as wearing the headdress either of Isis or Hathor, and is rarely mentioned in the Hieroglyphic texts.

IPHKHARDESU.

The Assyrian form of the Egyptian royal name He-ptha-resis, which see.

IPSAMBUL.   Or ABUSIMBEL.

The modern name of an Egyptian town where Rameses II. built a great temple partly excavated out of the solid rock, on the walls of which he recorded his victories over the Khitæ or Hittites. See Abusimbel.

IRANZI.

King of Minni, a tributary of Assyria. Contrary to his wishes he was urged by his subjects to revolt against Sargon II., who defeated him, and destroyed his two principal cities, carrying off the inhabitants. He was succeeded by his son Aza, who was slain by his subjects for his fidelity to Assyria.

IRBASTUTANIFU.

A daughter of King Amenrut or Amyrtaius, of the XXVIIIth dynasty.

IRBASTUTANIFU.

The wife of King Amenrut or Amyrtaius, of the XXVIIIth dynasty.

IRBIE.

In Chaldean astronomy the name of an unidentified star.

IREM.

In Arabian history the name of the palace and gardens of Shedad, king of Ael. It was built in impious imitation of the garden of Eden, for which its founder was slain by heaven. Its site is now called Yerim.

IRHEHEMTO.

A priest and prophet of Pthah of Memphis, and father of Nofer-hor-hemt-oou-en-ra, priest of Arsinoe-Philadelphus, under one of the Ptolemies.

IRHULENA.

King of Hamath. He and Benhadad, king of Damascus, and Ahab, king of Israel, endeavoured to stop the conquests of Shalmaneser II. in Palestine. At the battle of Qarqar, however, the king of Assyria overcame and subdued all his opponents with a loss on their side of 20,500 men.

IRIBA-MARUDUK.

An early king of Babylonia, of whom nothing else is known than that he was the father of Maruduk-bal-idinna.

IRIB-BIN.

The successor of Shalmaneser II. Nothing is known respecting him, but that he was succeeded by his son (?) Assuridinaklie.

IRIGIBEL.

A rebel Babylonian chief, who usurped the throne of Babylon upon the death of Assurnadin, and was himself succeeded by another rebel. Mesisomordach, after a short reign of one year.

IRI-HAPI-EOO-ER.

An Egyptian, whose sarcophagus is in the Leyden Museum. He was the son of Khons-neb-ankh.

IRI-SEN.

An Egyptian officer the son of At. His place and period are uncertain.

IRI-SEN-AKER.

An uncertain Egyptian officer in the reign of a King Mentuhotep, probably of the XIth dynasty. His wife's name was Hapu, and his son's Mentuhotep. Nothing else is known respecting him.

IRITAK..

An early king of Assyria, of whom nothing is known, except that he erected a temple called the " House of Salvation," in memory of some deliverance afforded to himself. The site of the temple is unidentified.

IRITIS.

The brother of. Senbu, a priest of Osiris. His period is uncertain.

IRKALLA.

An Assyrian deity, whose residence was in Bit-edie, " The House of Eternity," or Hades.

IRMA.

A city near Damascus which was conquered by Tiglath Pileser II., on his way to assist Ahaz, king of Judah.

IRMIN.

An old Saxon deity. He is supposed to have been an analogue of the Scandinavian deity Tyr, which see.

IRQUANATA.

A Syrian kingdom, which was one of the confederacy against Shalmaneser II., by whom it was subdued.

IRRIYA.

A city of Babylonia, which was invaded and plundered by Assurdan, king of Assyria, in the twelfth century B.C.

IR-SAACCA-KI.

An Accadian generic title, meaning " Cities of Accad." *See* Alu-sa-accadi.

IR-SA-KI.

An Accadian generic name, meaning " Cities of the Earth." *See* Alu-sa-irzitu.

IR-SA-KI-EN-GIKI.

An Accadian generic title, meaning " Cities of Sumir." *See* Alu-sa-sumir.

IR-SA-KI-PAL-KI.

An Accadian generic geographical title, meaning " Foreign Cities." *See* Alu-sa-napalkutu.

IRSHUSIN.

An early Babylonian monarch, who reigned at Ur.

IRTIZATI.

A king of the country of Ginkhidai, who paid tribute to Samas-Rimmon or Samsi-Vul, king of Assyria.

IRUKA.

A mystical title of Amen Ra in the CLXVIth chapter of the Ritual of the Dead.

ISAFF.

A form of the solar deity who was worshipped in ancient Arabia.

ISAIC TABLET.

A famous monument of late Roman-Egyptian art, which is preserved in the Museum of Turin, and which has been published by Kircher, Montfaucon, and other writers, as an invaluable key to the Egyptian mythology and Hieroglyphics. It is now generally regarded as an impudent forgery. It is a piece of ornamental brazen work, of the time of Adrian, executed by a person who was ignorant alike of the language and the art of Egypt. " Upon a plaque of bronze, covered with silver, which sustains four lions, are represented three series of divinities, assembled at hazard. They are accompanied by symbolical figures and inscriptions completely denuded of sense, among which are some purely fanciful royal cartouches. In the centre of the tablet the goddess Isis, after whom the monument is named, is represented sitting on her throne under a shrine." (Pierret.)

ISANA.

A city or district of which Mitunu was the prefect under Sennacherib.

IS-ARTAIS.

A common Egyptian feminine name in the Middle Empire.

ISBAGGI. (?)

A country in Babylonia, which was ruled by a viceroy named Hassimer, in the reign of Urukh, king of Ur.

ISBI-BAR-RA.

An early Babylonian king, reigning at Karrak. Nothing else is known respecting him.

ISE-KHEB-AU.

An Egyptian lady, wife of the singer of Pthah-zet-pthah-auf-ankh, and mother of the chancellor Psametik, of the XXVIth dynasty.

ISERET.

An Egyptian lady, the sister of Astaret-en-heb, which see.

ISETAARI.

An Egyptian lady, the wife of the royal scribe and priest Peti-har-pe-khruti, which see.

ISEUERI.

A priestess or assistant in the temple of the goddess Tafne or Tefnu, at Touni or Thinis. She was the mother of Anasch, the scribe of the sacred treasury there.

ISEUERI.

The wife of Petiharpocrates, a royal scribe, which see.

ISH-MA-BAAL.　　"Man of Baal."

A king of Gaza. He was one of the tributaries of Sennacherib.

ISHTAR.

One of the chief deities of the Assyrians and Babylonians alike; although she was generically one of the deities of the second rank. She was the daughter of the Moon-god Sin, and was identified by the Chaldeans with the planet Venus. She was essentially a warlike goddess, and was called "The Goddess of Battles and of Victories," in which attribute she was often represented as giving a bow to the Assyrian king in token of his victories over his foes. She was also, as the goddess of reproductive nature, the keeper of all the treasures of the earth, and hence was figured as Allat, "The Queen of the Spear or Divining-rod." In another form of the same principle she was the goddess of sensual indulgence. She was the special protectress of Erech, and in her character of Anna, or Nana, of Nineveh, while she was distinguished also at Arbela, another great seat of her worship, as Ishtar of Arbela. Her offices, names, and attributes were very various, and there appears to have been two Ishtars, mother and daughter, one the great Nature-goddess, and one the heroine of one of the mythical legends, called "The Descent of Ishtar into Hades." There is a considerable amount of confusion yet remaining to be cleared away with regard to the relations of Ishtar to Davcina, Bilit, Ashtaroth, and Izdubar ; but generally the mythologies agree in making her the goddess most brought into contact with men and the under-world.

ISHTAR (of Arbela ; of Nineveh).

In Assyrian mythology Ishtar became divided into Ishtar of the morning star and goddess of war, and Ishtar of the evening star and goddess of love. In the latter character she was generally addressed as Bilit (Baaltis) or "Lady." This separation of the qualities originally ascribed to the same goddess was peculiar to the Assyrians and Canaanites. It remained unknown in Babylonia. (Sayce.)

ISHTAR-MU-KAM-ISH.

The chief keeper of the tablets of King Assurbanipal.

ISI-EM-CHEB.

An Egyptian lady, the wife of Har-m-ankh-amen, the overseer of the sacrificiants of Amen Ra ; and mother of the lady Kaka, which see.

ISI-EM-CHEV.

A princess of the royal line of Seti I., who married Ra-men-kheper, one of the princes of the usurping house of Har-Hor, of the XXIst dynasty.

ISI-EM-KHEB. *Or* ISIEMCHEV.

A priestess of Amen Ra, the daughter of the priest Mont-emha. Her votive statuette is in the Museum of the Louvre.

ISI-OER.

A priestess of Amen Ra, the daughter of the lady Khons-irites. The period when she lived is uncertain.

ISI-OER.

A priestess of Amen Ra. *See* Oer *and* Tentcheiat.

ISI-OER.

An Egyptian lady, the mother of the lady Ta-set-ta, a priestess of the god Ra.

ISIRIS.

The Greco-Phenician form of the name of the Egyptian deity Hesirei, or Osiris.

ISIS.

A queen of Egypt, of the Older Empire. Her tomb was broken open by robbers in the reign of Rameses IX.

ISIS.

A great Egyptian goddess, the second member of the second great triad, Osiris, Isis, and Horus. She was the queen and the personification of heaven, and the sister and wife of Osiris, whose members she sought throughout Egypt to collect and bury, when he was slain, and his limbs scattered, by his brother Set. She was generally represented as a beautiful woman, with full breasts and winged arms, and wearing a throne on her head; the throne, *hesi*, being the Hieroglyphic of her name. Isis was also often represented as wearing a disk between two cow's horns, and under that form she was almost always confounded with the goddess Hathor, while in the most ancient monuments of Egypt the cow was also her symbol. Sometimes again Isis was figured as standing upright, and with her arms, which were furnished with wings, covering the mummy of Osiris, or occasionally enfolding the statue of the king; and in that characteristic she was called "Isis the Protectress;" since she was thus supposed to be bringing the dead body of her husband to life. Sometimes, also, the goddess was figured as holding her hand upwards before her face, as in a posture of grief, during which position she was believed to pronounce the mystical evocations to the soul of Osiris. Astronomically, the spirit of Isis was placed in the star Sirius, which under the name of Sothis held an important position in the astrological and astronomical calendar of the Egyptians. *See also* Hathor, Osiris, and Horus.

ISIS.

The sister of Har-sankh, an Egyptian gentleman of rank in the XIIth dynasty.

ISI-TA-NEFER.

An Egyptian lady, a choristress of Amen Ra, and the wife of Ben-neb-en-skhauf, which see.

ISI-TEF-NASCHTI.

The father of Pihor, a priest of Amen Ra, which see.

ISIUM.

An Egyptian city in the Memphite nome of the Heptanomos, or Middle Egypt.

ISIUM.

A chief town of the Antæopolite nome in the Thebaid of Upper Egypt.

ISKANDER.

The Turkish form of the Greek royal name Alexander.

ISMI-DAGAN.   "Dagan Heard."

An early Babylonian king ruling over Nipur, Ur, and Karrak.

ISMI-DAGAN.

The earliest known king of Assyria. He was succeeded by his son, Samsi-Vul I., in the nineteenth century B.C.

Isminthians.

Probably an Etruscan title of the god Turms or Hermes.

Ispabara.

Nephew of Dalta, king of Illipa in Elam. His succession to the throne being disputed by his brother Nipe, he called in the assistance of Sargon II., who defeated Nipe and his allies, and confirmed his possession of the kingdom of Illipa as a tributary of Assyria.

Ispaki.

King of Asguzu, near Media. He attempted to invade Assyria, but was defeated and slain by Esarhaddon.

Ispimagu.

King of Taini or Thynis (Thínis?), one of the twenty petty kings of Egypt under the Assyrian Icosarchy.

Ispuni.

King of Ararat or Armenia. He was the son of Seduri, the improver of the kingdom, and was succeeded by his son Minua.

Issapri. *Or* Issabri.

An Assyrian city, which supported Assurdainpal in his revolt against his father, Shalmaneser II., and was reconquered by Samas-Rimmon.

Istar-duri.

The governor of Arbaha, under Sargon II. He was eponym of the year B.C. 714, the chief event in which was an expedition to Media, Ararat, and Muzazir.

Istar-duri.

The governor of Nisibin, in the reign of Shalmaneser III. He was eponym of the year B.C. 774, the chief event in which was an expedition to Ararat and Zimri.

Istar-nan-hun-di.

An early king of Elam. His statue was brought to Nineveh by Assurbanipal after the Elamite conquest.

Istar-su-mes-ses.

An early Chaldean astronomer. Records of the phases of Venus by him are preserved in the Cuneiform inscriptions.

Is-tat-ti.

A strong fortress in the kingdom of Minni, where for a short time Ahsera the king escaped from Assurbanipal, king of Assyria, who ultimately destroyed the city and fort. It was also written, by the Assyrians, Adrana.

Istio.

In Teutonic mythology one of the three sons of Mannus, and the father of one of the three races of the Germans.

ISTUNDA.

One of the many petty Syrian states which paid tribute to Tiglath-Pileser II.

ISUA.

A Mesopotamian people, conquered by Tiglath Pileser I.

ITHAMAR.

A king of the Sabæans, who paid tribute to the mythical hero Izdubar.

ITHUANDER. *Or* ETEANDROS.

King of Paphos, in the Island of Kypros. He was one of the tributaries of Esarhaddon and Assurbanipal.

ITNI.

A Mesopotamian people, conquered by Tiglath Pileser I.

ITTI.

King of Allabra. He, together with other Armenian kings, revolted against Sargon II., by whom he was conquered, and, with his wife and children, sent into slavery into Syria.

ITTI.

A king of Azalla, in Mesopotamia, who paid tribute to Assurnazirpal.

ITUHA.

A kingdom in Mesopotamia or Chaldea, which was several times invaded by Vul-nirari or Rimmon-nirari III., king of Assyria, and was finally conquered by Tiglath Pileser II.

ITUNI.

An Elamite officer who was sent by Tiumman, king of Elam, to make terms with Assurbanipal, king of Assyria, on the eve of the battle of Shushan. His mission was too late : the battle took place, the Elamites were completely routed, and Tiumman slain.

IUA.

A chief of the receipts of an unnamed Egyptian king, probably of the XIXth dynasty. His wife was named Maa.

IU-AA. " Great Arrival."

An unknown chief of a Japhetic people, whose daughter Taia became queen of Egypt by her marriage with King Amenhotep III., which see.

IU-IMA.

Another form of the name Imu, a people who were delivered up to Thothmes III. by the treachery of an Egyptian officer Tahutia.

Iu-iu.

An Egyptian official, the keeper of the treasury of a king of the XVIIIth dynasty. He was the son of the lady Tai.

Iu-iu.

The first priest of Osiris in the reign of Rameses II. He succeeded in that office his father Unnefer, which see.

Iu-na-maa.

A town and fortress of the Rotennu, which was made tributary by Thothmes III.

Iu-ru-ta-na.

The Egyptian name of the river Jordan in Palestine.

Iu-senb.

An Egyptian gentleman, the son of the lady Sekhet-hotep-et. His funereal stèle is important, as it contains the names of thirteen members of his family, all of whom held different offices, civil, ecclesiastical, and military, from which the non-existence of castes, in the true meaning of the word, in ancient Egypt has been proved. The period of Iu-senb is uncertain, but it was later than the XIIth and not so late as the XVIIIth dynasty.

Ivalush.

The rendering at one time adopted of the Cuneiform characters of the Assyrian royal name Vul-nirari.

Ivashtri.   " The Creator."

Another of the Vedic titles of the Supreme Being as the origin of creation. *See also* Pragapati *and* Dhatar.

Izdubar.   *Or* Gizdhubar.   " Mass of Fire."

According to the newly discovered Izdubar Tablets an early mythical Assyrian hero, who was probably a form of the solar deity. He was a great chieftain, and delivered the city of Erech when it was assailed by the giants. He had for his wife the goddess Ishtar, who proved unfaithful to him, and sent some monstrous bulls to destroy him. These animals he was enabled to slay by the assistance of his faithful friend and adviser the deified sage Heabani, who was ultimately killed by an unknown insect or reptile called a Tambukki. Izdubar afterwards becoming afflicted with a cutaneous malady, went by the advice of his boatman Urhamsi to seek the sage Adrahasis, who having survived the Deluge, was supposed to be able to cure him of his malady. Adrahasis complied with his request, and related to him in considerable detail the legend of the flood. Upon returning to Erech Izdubar set up a monument in memory alike of his cure and of the story related by his benefactor, and then by the aid of enchantment had the soul of Heabani raised up to commune with him. Izdubar seems after these events to have become a king, but his history is so mixed up with a mythological series of legends that his real character is uncertain, as also are of course his parentage and date. As he had a chief companion named Zaidu, who was also a hunter, he may have been the same as the following—

IZDUBAR.

A very early Chaldean king called the " Powerful King." He was succeeded by his son Zaidu, " The Hunter."

IZIRTU.

The capital city of Ahsera, king of Minni. It was conquered by Assurbanipal, king of Assyria.

J.

JA.

An Egyptian title corresponding to that of mayor of a city.

JADIS.

An early Arabian Semitic race. *See* Tasm.

JAH.

The awful name of the Supreme Being among the Hebrews. It is a shortened form of Jehovah, or as it is now written Jahveh, "The Self-existent." As the proper name of the local deity of Judea, Jah often occurs in the Cuneiform inscriptions, as it does also on the Moabite Stone, where it is written Yaveh. This title must not be confounded with that of the Assyrian deity Yav, the inundater, who was a form of Anu.

JAH.

The Egyptian name of an unidentified Syrian city.

JANAIS.

According to the Greek lists an early Egyptian king of Bubastis. He has not yet been certainly identified.

JAOH. "*The* Being."

A mysterious or secret name of the Phenician deity Hadad, which see.

JAPHETOS.

According to the Greeks, one of the three sons of Xisuthrus. *See* Zervau.

JARNWIDR.

In Scandinavian mythology the giantess who was the mother of the two wolves, Sköll and Hati, which attack the sun and moon.

JEHU. Assyrian, YAHUA.

An officer in the service of Ahab, king of Israel. He was the son of Nimshi, and overthrew the dynasty of Omri and Ahab, and reigned twenty-eight years over Israel. He had been an adviser and friend of Ahab, whose family and descendants he afterwards murdered, wading to the throne through their blood. The stratagem by which he destroyed the worshippers of Baal and Asherah in one day is well known. One of the epigraphs of the Black Obelisk Inscription of Shalmaneser states that Jehu, wrongly called "the son of Khumri," or Omri, sent to Assyria, by way of tribute, "silver, gold, bowls of gold, vessels of gold, goblets of gold, pitchers of gold, lead, sceptres for the king's hand, and staves." The tribute was probably sent in B.C. 842, after the defeat of Hazael of Syria, by Shalmaneser. Hazael afterwards conquered all the Israelitish territory on the East of the Jordan.

JERUSALEM.

A famous city of central Palestine, the early history of which is unknown. It was probably a stronghold of the Jebusites in pre-historic periods, and as such it was wrested from them by the suffete Joshua, soon after the Jewish conquest of Canaan. The complete subjugation of the city was however, apparently only accomplished by David, who thenceforth made it the capital of his kingdom. The history of Jerusalem is almost the history of the Jewish nation, and it therefore does not properly belong to an Archaic dictionary. On the Cuneiform inscriptions of Assyria the sieges of the city by Sennacherib and Nebuchadnezzar are given in some detail with particulars which do not occur in the Jewish record of the events; indeed the Assyrian monarchs seem to have regarded the Hebrew nation as always a tributary one, except perhaps during the reign of Solomon. The invasion of the city under Pul or Phul is at present one of the chief difficulties in the matter of Archaic chronology, no king of Assyria having yet been found who either bore that name, or if he had a similar one, who entered Palestine. The conquest of Jerusalem by Shishank or Shishak of the XXVIth dynasty, is recorded on the inscriptions of Karnak, and the Babylonian attack, and ultimate destruction of the capital, are confirmed by the annals of Nebuchadnezzar. The account of the siege of Bethulia and Palestine by Holofernes, and the death of that general, as related in the book of Judith, is now generally accepted as a patriotic romance ; but the subsequent restoration of the temple and palaces by the Persian kings, and the presents made to the city by the Greco-Egyptian Ptolemies, are all matters of Classic history. The conquest of Palestine by Esarhaddon and Assurbanipal, and in still earlier times, the triumphal marches of Thothmes II. and Rameses II. and III. into Mesopotamia, either did not directly affect Jerusalem, or are not referred to in the inscriptions. Few cities have been more often ruined and rebuilt than the capital of the Jewish empire, not less than seventeen complete conquests being known, from the time of Joshua to that of Mahomet Ali. Though at all times a small town, it was capable of being defended by a small garrison, or from its excellent system of wells and conduits of protecting a large body of people ; hence the apparent discrepancy in the accounts of the numbers slain in its various conquests is reconcilable with the truth of history, and with the extent of a capital city at no time more populous than a modern suburb of London or Paris, or broader than half a mile from wall to wall.

JETUR.

An Ishmaelite settlement mentioned by Hebrew writers. It was in the province of Mount Athal in the Neged.

JIDDAH.

A seaport of the Jorhamite Arabs in the Hedjaz.

JINN.

In ancient Arabian mythology a series of spiritual beings whom men were able to control by the power of magic.

JORHAM.

The son of Djahla, of the royal line of Mudad. His daughter Maana married Maad, king of the Hedjaz. *See* Maad.

JORHAM.

A Joktanite race by whom the Arkam and Katoora were expelled from Arabia. *See* Arkam.

JYOTISHA.

An ancient Hindu astronomical treatise, derived chiefly from, and explaining, the system of the sacred Vedas.

K.

KA.

A city and nome in Lower Egypt, called by the Greeks Athribis; sacred to the deity Horus.

KA. "Touch."

An obscure Egyptian divinity, named in the XVIIth chapter of the Ritual of the Dead.

KA.

A daughter of Amen-em-ap, a priest of Amen Ra, in the XVIIIth dynasty. She had also a sister named Ta-na-ra.

KA. "Existence."

In Egyptian mythology one of the five component parts of the human being. *See* Khaba, Akh, Sah, *etc.*

KAA.

An Egyptian amulet, in the form of a staircase or series of steps, alluding to the XVIth chapter of the Ritual of the Dead, where the god Shu is described as standing upon the stairs in the land of Suten-Khem. These amulets were generally wrought in green porcelain.

KAA.

The chief of the royal works of a king of the Vth dynasty, and probably the father of the royal chief Hamset, which see. There was also another functionary of this name about the same period.

KA-ANKH. "The Living Bull."

The father of Heri, a sacred scribe and priest of Pthah, in the Ptolemaic period.

KA-ARI.

A mystical title of Amen Ra in the CLXVIth chapter of the Ritual of the Dead.

KABH.

The Egyptian name of the water-bottle from which libations were poured on the altars of Ra and other gods.

KABHSENUF.

The mystical name of one of the planks of the boat of souls, in the XCIXth chapter of the Ritual of the Dead.

Kabhsenuf.

The Bleeder ; one of the four genii of the dead. He was represented as a vase with a hawk's head as a cover. On the vase was often inscribed a prayer to the goddess Selk, and its contents were the mummied liver and gall bladder.

Kadasiha.

A district in Arabia, which was ravaged and its king Habitzu put to death by Esarhaddon.

Kadesh. " The Holy."

A town in Syria, near to which Rameses II. defeated Khita-sira, king of the Hittites, with great slaughter, together with all his allies and many of their principal men. *See* Rameses II. *and* Khita-sira.

Kadesh.

A petty kingdom in Arabia, conquered for the first time by the Assyrians under Esarhaddon.

Kadesh.

A strong city on the Orontes, in Upper Palestine, which was chosen by the Assyrians as the place wherein to meet Thothmes III., and to tender their submission and offer hostages after the battle of Megiddo.

Kadjarti.

An Assyrian mythical hero, who is said in the Egyptian inscriptions to have been chief of Assur, and to have fought with some monstrous hyænas in the land of the Shashus.

Kadu-malka. *Or* Qavus-Malka.

Another form of the name of that king of the new kingdom of Edom who was contemporary with Tiglath-Pileser II.

Kadu-muh.

Another form of the name of a king of Edom who was contemporary with Esarhaddon, king of Assyria.

Ka-en-nets.

The grandson of Tetet, an early Egyptian king.

Kafh-en-ma-nofre.

A high Egyptian functionary, whose titles have been lost. His statue is in the Leyden Museum.

Kahaka.

A people confederate with the Libyans and Maxues, who were defeated by Menepthah II. The race became soon extinct, and who the people were is not known.

Ka-harus-apu-saru-ma-hakar-uma.

A mystical title of the goddess Bast, in the CLXVth (a supplemental) chapter of the Ritual of the Dead.

KA-HEB.

A city and nome in Lower Egypt, sacred to the deity Osiris. Its site is not yet known.

KAHI.

An uncertain Egyptian goddess, probably some country personified.

KAHIN.

The name of the diviners of the ancient Arabians. The office was frequently hereditary. The female diviners were called Arrafa.

KAHLAN.

The son of Abdshems. From him were descended the nomadic and desert tribes of Sabæa in Yemen.

KAHTAN.

The father of Yarub, the conqueror and destroyer of the Arabian kingdom of Yemen.

KAIKASHA.

A tribe of the Libyans, subjugated by Rameses III.

KAIKAUS.   *Or* KAIKHOSRU.

The Persian form of the Bactrian royal name Kava-Us, which see.

KA-KA.

An Egyptian lady, the daughter of the priest and overseer of Amen Horm-ankh-amen and the lady Isi-em-cheb. Her double sarcophagus and mummy are in the Leyden Museum.

KAKA.

The Egyptian name of the fruit of the Doum Palm (*Cucifera Thebaica*).

KAKA.

A king of Egypt of the Vth dynasty. His name at present is only found in some of the royal lists.

KAKAU.

The Cechous of the Greeks. The second king of the IInd Thinite dynasty of Egypt. He introduced animal worship into the country, that of the bull Apis at Memphis, Mnevis at Heliopolis, and the ram Ba-en-tattu at Heliopolis. He reigned thirty-eight years.

KAKE.

An Egyptian nobleman, probably of the Vth dynasty.

KAKE.

A king of the Vth dynasty. He must not be confounded with the preceding name.

KA-KEM.

A city and nome in Lower Egypt, sacred to the bull deity Apis. Its site is not yet known.

KAKHRA.

The twelfth resting-place of the Iranians after their exile from Aryanem Vaedjo, which see. It is supposed to have been the district now called Khorassan.

KAKI.

A king of Harpuskia, in Western Mesopotamia. He was conquered by Shalmaneser II.

KAKIA.

A king of Nairi, in Northern Assyria. He was conquered by Shalmaneser III.

KAKKARAYA.

The god of vomiting ; a Badaga deity.

KAKKI.

A king of Sinuhta. He refused to pay tribute to Sargon II., who made war against him, and capturing his chief city, took him, his wife, and family captives into Assyria, and set Matti, king of Atuna, on the throne instead.

KAKMI.

A kingdom which revolted against Sargon II., by whom it was subdued.

KAKSIDI. "Creator of Prosperity."

In Chaldean astronomy one of the seven stars of the week. *And also—*

KAKSIDI.

In Chaldean astronomy one of the twelve stars of the West.

KAL. KALAU, *and* KALU.

The names of a mystical region in the fourteenth abode of Osiris, mentioned in the CLth chapter of the Ritual of the Dead.

KALABSHE.

A town in Nubia, the vulgar or profane name of which was Talmis. It had a famous temple, erected by Amenhotep II. of the XVIIIth dynasty, which was never however completed. The Hieroglyphics on the walls have in many cases been only indicated by the pencil in red outline, and have not been sculptured ; but the bas-reliefs, which were apparently first executed are numerous, and still remain in excellent preservation. The figures of animals, especially of dogs, which are found there on the decorations are remarkable for their characteristic conventionality.

KALDILI.

A country in Arabia which was rendered tributary by Esarhaddon.

KALESSI.

The modern name of the Phenician city Bambyce, which see.

KALLISTEUS.

The Greek name of the Egyptian confectionery or cake called Kelushta, which see.

KALLU-KAMBA-RAYA.   "Stone Pillar God."

A Badaga deity, of whom little is known. It was probably a Bætylia.

KALPA.

An ancient Hindu treatise, dealing chiefly with the due performance of the ceremonies prescribed in the sacred Vedas.

KALTITSULAYA.

An Elamite city which was destroyed by Sennacherib.

KALU.

A plain country, South of Assyria, where Sargon II. defeated Humbanigash, king of Elam, in a pitched battle.

KALZI.

A city or district which was governed by Assursimuani, in the reign of Shalmaneser VI. (or IV.—Smith.)

KAMA.

The Hindu god of love. He was represented as a boy holding a bow and arrows, and riding on a parrot.

KAMANU.

An Elamite city which was destroyed by Sennacherib.

KAMAS.

A royal lady or consort in the reign of Aahmes I. of the XVIIIth dynasty.

KAMASHALTA.

King of Moab. He was faithful to Assurbanipal, and conquered Ammuladi, king of Kedar, on his invasion of Palestine, in concert with Vaiteh I., king of Arabia. He then sent the king of Kedar in chains to Nineveh.

KA-MAT-EF.   "Bull of his Mother."

An epithet applied to the Egyptian kings and to heroes, who were always compared to the largest animals of their country. The phrase might be better rendered, "Valiant Son of his Mother." *See* Horus.

KAMBATET.

An Egyptian form of the Persian royal name Cambyses.

KAMES.

A Theban monarch of the XVIIth dynasty, the son of Tiakken. He carried on the war begun by his father against Apepi, the Hykshos king, and his son Aahmes terminated the struggle by expelling the Hykshos dynasty. He was called Tsafento, " Sustainer of the World," a title which has been compared with the Zaphnath-Paaneah of Hebrew history. His reign was a short one.

KAMI.

A kind of balsam which was used as an unguent by the Egyptians.

KAMON.

A Syrian city which was conquered by Rameses II.

KAMOSH-NADAB.

Another form of the Moabite royal name Kemosh-natbi, which see.

KAMRAN.

An Elamite city which was destroyed by Sennacherib.

KAMSA.

In Hindu mythology a great and cruel king of India, who persecuted the deity Khrishna, by whom he was at last slain.

KAMU. " Black."

The name of a species of Egyptian mastiff. *See* Pahates.

KAMUR. "Egypt."

A mystical divinity who is mentioned in the LXIVth chapter of the Ritual of the Dead.

KAN.

The Assyrian name of the *Calamus Aromaticus*, "the sweet cane" of Hebrew writers.

KANANA.

The Egyptian form of the name of the land of Canaan.

KANDAKE.

A queen of Ethiopia, whose daughter was conquered by the Romans. She was the Candace of Greek writers. *See* next name.

KANDAKE.

A queen of Meroe in Ethiopia, who twice attacked the Romans when they established their power in Upper Egypt, but who was defeated by Gallus, B.C. 22.

KANEBTI. "Curly Haired."

Certain North Egyptian officials, whose duties are not quite understood; they met Thothmes III. with presents and tribute after his Syrian conquest. They may have been the inhabitants of Canopus.

KA-NEFER. "Good Bull."

The name of the royal pyramid wherein Amenemha I. of the XIIth dynasty was buried, and where he was worshipped. *See* Hor.

KA-NEFER.

The inspector and keeper of the registers of a king of the Vth dynasty. He was of royal birth.

KAN-MA-GARRI. "Book of Worship."

The lost prayer book of the Assyrians. (Fox Talbot.)

KAN-MAMITU. "Book of the Mamit."

A lost book on Assyrian magic. (Fox Talbot.)

KAN-MIKRI. "Book of Prayer."

A lost book of the Assyrian Ritual. All these are mentioned in the catalogue of an Assyrian library on a tablet which is now in the British Museum. (Fox Talbot.)

KAN-NUNAI.

The governor of Kalzi in the reign of Sargon II. He was eponym of the year B.C. 703.

KAN-RA.

The surname of Khem-mes, a royal scribe of Rameses III.

KAN-TA.

A son of Amen-em-ap, a priest of Amen Ra, in the reign of Ai, one of the disputed kings of the XVIIIth dynasty. His wife's name was Hont-to-neb, and that of his son Neb-nofre.

KAN-TAP-SAR-TI. "Book of Explanations."

A lost book of commentaries on the Assyrian religion. (Fox Talbot.)

KAN-TILITE. "Book of Praise."

The lost psalter of the Assyrians. (Fox Talbot.)

KANU.

An Assyrian measure of length, composed of six *ammat*. It was equal to ten feet.

KAPADA.

A district in Media, where the army of Darius Hystaspes encamped after the defeat of the impostor Phraortes.

KAPAON.

The Egyptian name of a Syrian city, which is supposed to have been Gabal.

KAPTIYA.

The son of Bal-basu. He was a tax collector at Warka under the reign of Cambyses.

KAPU.

An Assyrian city which supported Assurdainpal in his revolt against his father Shalmaneser II.

KAPUR.

A king of the Mashuash, who was killed at the head of his army in the war between the Egyptians and Libyans, in the eleventh year of Rameses III.

KAR.

A mystical region of Amenti, which is mentioned in the CXXXVIth chapter of the Ritual of the Dead.

KARA-BEL.

An early king of Babylonia. He was the successor of Burnaburyas I., which is all that is known concerning him.

KARADJEH-DAGH.

The modern name of Mount Masius in Armenia.

KARA-HARDAS.

An early king of Babylonia, and the son-in-law of Assur-u-balid, king of Assyria. His subjects, aided by the Kassi, revolted against and slew him, and placed a man of low origin, named Nazibugas, on the throne.

KARA-INDAS.

King of Babylonia and of the Kassi. He made an amicable agreement with Assur-bel-nisu, king of Assyria, as to the extent of their respective dominions.

KARAKAMASHA.

The Egyptian name for the Syrian town of Carchemish, where Thothmes III. defeated and rendered tributary to Egypt the people of Mesopotamia. It was also one of the forty Asiatic cities conquered by Rameses III. of the XIXth dynasty.

KAR-ALLA.

A kingdom near Armenia, which unsuccessfully revolted against Sargon II.

KARAMENTONEN.

A chief of the signet bearers to King Aspalut, of the XXVIth dynasty.

KAR-ASSUR.

A city in Babylonia, founded upon the ruins of an older town, which was destroyed by the Assyrians under Tiglath Pileser II., in their first invasion of the land.

KAR-ASSUR-NAZIR-PAL. "The Fort of Assurnazirpal."

A fortress built by Assurnazirpal, king of Assyria, on the left bank of the Euphrates.

KAR-ASU.

The Assyrian geographical name of the district of Upper Euphrates.

KARBANA.

A city in Middle Egypt where the Mashuash established themselves, and were defeated by Rameses III.

KAR-BAT.

The capital city of the district of Halehazta, in Zagros, near Elam. It was subdued by Assurbanipal, and its king Tandai carried prisoner to Nineveh.

KARBUKEF.

One of the seven mystical spirits who are mentioned in the XVIIth chapter of the Ritual of the Dead.

KARCHEDON.

The Greek form of the name of the Tyrian settlement Kiryath Hadeschath or Carthage, which see.

KAR-DUNIAS.

The ancient name of Babylonia in the Cuneiform inscriptions.

KARIABETTARAYA.

A Badaga idol, invented to commemorate a good native whose benevolence was unbounded.

KARIARAYA.

A Badaga deity, worshipped under the form of an old rusty knife.

KARIBAIL-BAYYIN.

A king of the Himyarites about the first century A.D. He was succeeded by Samahali-Yanaf II.

KARIBAIL-WATR-YAHANAM.

A king of the Himyarites about the first century A.D. He was succeeded by Samahali-Yanaf.

KAR-MAHA.

A tribe in Mesopotamia which was conquered by Tiglath Pileser II.

KAR-MAS-MASU.

A city formerly called Kisesim, but which was thus renamed by its conqueror Sargon II.

KARMES.

A king of Tamissus, in Cyprus. He was one of the tributaries of Esarhaddon.

KARMIBASHA.

An Elamite city which was destroyed by Sennacherib.

KARNAK.

The capital of Egypt in the period of the Middle Empire. The oldest monuments of this stupendous city of giants date from the time of Osirtesen I. of the XIIth dynasty, before the arrival of the Hykshos invaders, and while the city was simply a great place in Upper Egypt. The principal edifices are, however, those of the monarchs of the XVIIIth, XIXth, and XXth dynasties ; although, as those buildings fell into decay they were repaired and often enlarged by the subsequent monarchs, who added their own cartouches, often to the destruction of the names of the original builders. The following, according to Mariette Bey, are the most interesting of the Pharaonic ruins :—1. The great Hypostyle Hall, or the Hall of Columns, which was originally constructed by Amenhotep II. of the XVIIIth dynasty, but altered and covered with Hieroglyphics by Seti I. of the XIXth dynasty. There are in all 134 standing and six fallen columns in this hall, those in the centre having the form of the stem and flower of the expanded papyrus and being seventy feet high and eleven in diameter. 2. The enormous historical bas-reliefs on the exterior wall to the North of the Hypostyle Hall, relating to the campaigns of Seti I. in Eastern Asia. 3. The bas-reliefs on the exterior of the Southern wall of the same chamber. These represent the events of the campaign of Shiskak I., of the XXIInd dynasty, in Palestine. 4. Another inscription and bas-relief, at a right-angle to this, on which are recorded the conquests of Rameses II. against the Hittites ; being a part of the famous text which is now called the Poem of Pentaour. 5. The lofty obelisk of Hatasu and Thothmes III. of the XVIIIth dynasty. This is 105 feet high. 6. To these must be added the great geographical lists of conquered towns which submitted to Thothmes III. of the XVIIIth dynasty, and which comprise nearly the oldest itinerary of the Holy Land and parts of Mesopotamia and Asia. In the whole, the sacred inclosure at Karnak extended to a depth of 1170 feet, and it was connected with the city and royal palace of El Luxor by an avenue of sphynxes, by some accounts nearly two miles long.

KARO-AMAT.

The grandmother of Sheshonk I. of the XXIInd dynasty.

KARO-AMAT.

The first wife of Osorkon II. of the XXIInd dynasty.

KARO-AMUT-MIMUT.

A chief of the palace of Amen Ra, in the reign of Sheshonk I.

KARO-MAMA-MIMUT. *Or* KARUMMAMA.

The wife of Takelot II., the sixth king of the XXIInd dynasty.

KARO-MANA.

An Egyptian queen, the wife of either Takelut I. or II.

KARR.

The name of the ten halls of the damned in the Egyptian purgatory and hell.

KAR-RAK.

A city in Babylonia, called also Nisinna, which see.

KAR-RA-SAMAS.

The true name of the Babylonian town sometimes called Teara-Samas, which see.

KARRISLAKI.

An Elamite city destroyed by Sennacherib.

KAR-SARGON.   " Fort of Sargon."

The name given by Sargon II. to the city of Hur-Har, after he had reduced it to the condition of a subject town held by an Assyrian garrison.

KARSHA.

An Elamite deity, of whom nothing is known.

KAR-SHALMANESER.   " Fortress of Shalmaneser."

The name given to the city of Tulbursip, on the East of the Euphrates, by the Assyrians, after its capture by Shalmaneser II.

KARSIBUTA.

A small kingdom, probably near Armenia, which was rendered tributary by Samsi-Vul or Samas-Rimmon III.

KARTEK.   " Spark Holder."

An early Egyptian name of the goddess Thoeris, which see.

KAR-THISBE.

An Assyrian city, to which Sennacherib transferred the captive people of Kassi and Yatsubigalla, whom he conquered in his second campaign.

KARTO-NEN-AMEN.

A high-priest of Amen Ra, in the reign of King Aspalut, of the XXVth dynasty.

KARUM-MAMA.

See Karo-mama-mimut.

KAR-U-SENNACHERIB.   " Fort of Sennacherib."

The name given by Sennacherib to the city of Ellinzas, after he had conquered it from the rebel Ispabara, and rebuilt it as an Assyrian fortress.

KAS. "The Twins."

One of the Accadian names of the month Sivanu, which see.

KASAIKA.

A mystical name of Amen Ra, in the CLXVIth chapter of the Ritual of the Dead.

KASBU. *Or* ASLU.

An Assyrian measure of length, called a day's journey. It was composed of thirty *sosses*, or about fourteen miles.

KASCH-TA.

The father of Queen Ameniritis of the XXVIth dynasty, which see.

KA-SEM.

The Egyptian name of the Amazon stone, or emerald.

KA-SHE.

A city and nome in Lower Egypt. Its site, and the deity to whose worship it was dedicated, are not yet known.

KASHTO.

A king of the XXIVth dynasty. His position and filiation are uncertain.

KASIKYA.

A tribe of the Hittites who conquered the Assyrian district of Subasti, from whence they were expelled or defeated by Tiglath Pileser I.

KASMUT.

A high-priest of Amen Ra, in the reign of King Aspalut, of the XXVIth dynasty.

KASMUT.

A royal lady or mother in the reign of Amenhotep I. of the XVIIIth dynasty.

KASR. "Castle."

The modern name of the mound which denotes the ruins of the great temple of Bel, erected by Nabukuduruzur at Babylon.

KASSU-NADIN-AHU.

An early Chaldean monarch who succeeded the usurper Hea-mukin-ziru, and reigned six years.

KASTARITE.

A king of Carucassi (probably the Caucasus). In conjunction with Mamitarsu, king of the Medes, the Cimmerians, Minnians, and people of Saparda (Sepharad) on the Black Sea, he attacked Assyria, took many of its cities, and finally, with the help of Nabopolassar, destroyed Nineveh and the Assyrian empire. Kastarite is the Kyaxares of the Greeks. (Lenormant.)

Kastubili.

A chief of the country of Kazalla, who revolted against Sargina or Sargon I., who subjugated the country, and wasted it with fire and sword.

Kat.

A mystical divinity who is mentioned in the LXXVIIIth chapter of the Ritual of the Dead.

Kat.

The Egyptian ounce, ten of which made one *Ten* or pound. The *Kat* was equal to 140 grains troy.

Kat-b.

A priestess of the goddess Maut in the XXIInd dynasty. Her coffin and mummy are in the British Museum.

Katesch. " Sacred, Holy."

An Egyptian goddess of Syrian origin. She formed one of a triad with the deities Reschep and Anta.

Kati.

The king of Que, a Syrian district, which was conquered by Shalmaneser II. after he had several times invaded it.

Katoora.

A third and later division of the Amalekites, who settled about the district of Mecca in Arabia.

Katsiu. " The Ærolite."

An Aramæan deity, in the form of a stone, supposed to have fallen from the heavens. He was worshipped in the district of Hauran. *See* Bætylia.

Kau.

The name of a mystical divinity in the LXXXVth chapter of the Ritual of the Dead.

Kau-el-kebir.

The modern name for the city and nome in Upper Egypt which was called by the Greeks Anteopolis.

Kauib.

A son of King Tetet, an early Egyptian king.

Kava-kavata

A Bactrian monarch ; the founder of the Keanian dynasty. He was succeeded by his son, Kava-us. He was the Kai-Kobad of Persian history.

KAVA-US. *Or* KAVA-USRAVA.

A Bactrian king of the Keanian dynasty. He was the son of Kava-kavata, and was succeeded by his son, Kava-Usrava. He was the Kai Kaus of Persian writers.

KAVILAUL.

Among the Todas an inferior kind of ascetic, usually the servant of a Pàlaul, which see.

KEANIAN DYNASTY.

A powerful Bactrian dynasty, founded by Kava-Kavata. It was in the reign of Auravadaspa, the fifth king of this dynasty, that the Zendic religion was introduced into Bactria.

KEBTU.

The Egyptian name of the town of Coptos in the Thebaid.

KEBU.

The father of Tes-amen, which see.

KEFAT.

The name by which the Phenicians were known to the Egyptians.

KEFENNU.

An Egyptian functionary, " Chief of the House," in the reign of Amenemha III. of the XIIth dynasty.

KEFSCHEMSU.

An Egyptian overseer, whose statue is in the Leyden Museum. Period uncertain.

KEFT.

The modern name of the city and nome in Upper Egypt called Coptos by the Greeks.

KEHAK.

A Japhetic people from Northern Africa, who, together with the Greeks, invaded Egypt in the XIXth dynasty, and were defeated by Menepthah II.

KEHANA.

A species of divination by arrows, practised by the ancient Arabians. Seven blunt arrows, called Azlam, each having a particular mark, were placed in a bag, and one was then drawn out and the oracle read by the diviner. It was also a custom used by the Assyrians.

KEK.

The Egyptian god of darkness. (Wilkinson.)

KEKARA.

The royal scribe of the granaries, in the court of King Aspalut of the XXVIth dynasty.

KEKOU.

An Egyptian lady, the wife of the royal scribe Antef-aker, which see.

KEK-T.

The Egyptian goddess of darkness; the consort of the god Kek. (Wilkinson.)

KELESHIN.

The modern name of Mount Niphates, in Mesopotamia.

KELUSHTA.

A kind of confectionery among the Egyptians: a species of bread, moulded and painted. It was the Kallisteus of the Greeks.

KEMA.

A daughter of King Nofre-hotep, of the XIIIth dynasty.

KEMA.

The mother of King Nofre-hotep, of the XIIIth dynasty.

KEMAT.

An Egyptian sacerdotal title, generally applied to women, and rendered "Chantress," a singer or chorister of a god.

KEMES.

The son of an Egyptian king, but of what king it is not known.

KEMOSH-NATBI.   *Or* CHEMOSH-NATBI.

A king of Moab who tendered tribute to Sennacherib upon his first invasion of Palestine.

KEN.

An early Egyptian astronomer, some observations by whom have been preserved.

KEN-AMEN.

The son of the priest Amen-em-ap, of the XVIIIth dynasty.

KENS.

A nome in Nubia, which was sacred to Khnum-Ra.

KENUS.

A district in Nubia, rendered tributary to Egypt by Thothmes III. Probably the same as the preceding.

KENUST.

A town in Nubia, also called Kenous.

KEPHER.   "The Town."

A Tyrian settlement on the West coast of the Isle of Sicily, now called Solentum.

Keriath-aal.

The Egyptian name of an uncertain Syrian town.

Keriath-anab.

The Egyptian name of an uncertain Syrian town.

Ker-neter. " The Land of the Gods."

The Egyptian name for the Land of the Underworld, more generally applied to the purgatory, where the soul underwent various probationary trials and duties prior to its entering the Judgment Hall of Osiris, or the Hall of the Two Truths.

Kerpheres.

The Greek name for the king Huni, which see.

Kes-kes-t.

An Egyptian lady, the daughter of an officer named Osirtesen, which see.

Ketarayea.

A Torea idol, worshipped under the form of a golden nose-ring.

Ketet.

An Egyptian lady, the wife of Neferpou, and the mother of the lady Hathorset-month, which see.

Ket-ket.

In Egyptian mythology the name of the seven great spirits of the Creator. They were also called Het-Het. *See* Ma-antef-ef.

Kha. " Body."

In Egyptian mythology one of the five component principles of the human body. *See* Sah, *etc.*

Khaa.

The mother of a royal scribe named Amen-em-ap, which see.

Khaa.

The roya scribe of the royal table of Rameses II. of the XIXth dynasty.

Kha-ba. " Shade."

In Egyptian mythology one of the five principles of the human body.

Khabash.

A satrap or viceroy of Egypt, after the Persian conquest. He at first endeavoured to strengthen his country against the Persian fleet under Xerxes, but he was compelled to submit and furnish that monarch with an Egyptian contingent of 200 ships for the battle of Artemisium, B.C. 480.

KHABBATU. " The Plunderer."

In Chaldean astronomy a name of the planet Mars.

KHABUR.

The modern name of the ancient river Chaboras in Mesopotamia.

KHAEM-MIAMEN.

The surname of Rameses IX. of the XXth dynasty.

KHAEM-MI-AMEN-NUTER-HIKTEN.

The surname of Rameses XIII. of the XXth dynasty.

KHAEM-PE.

A priest of Pthah in the XVIIIth dynasty.

KHAEMT.

The son of Amenhotep II. of the XVIIIth dynasty.

KHAEM-UAS.

One of the many sons of Rameses II. of the XIXth dynasty. He was also called Choemat. His tomb was a splendid one near Thebes, and there are, in all the museums of Europe, numerous objects and Shabti figures which were taken from it.

KHAEN-SUAS.

A pallakist of Apis in the XXVIth dynasty.

KHAF-HOR.

A grandson of Tetet, an early Egyptian king of the Ist dynasty.

KHAF-RA-ANKH.

A grandson of Tetet, an early Egyptian king.

KHAF-RA-SIF.

Another grandson of Tetet, an early Egyptian king.

KHAFS-NOFRU.

The son of King Snefru of the IIIrd dynasty.

KHA-HEA. "The Fish of Hea."

The astronomical name of the deity Marduk, as the planet Mercury in the month Adar.

KHAI.

A royal scribe and director of the soldiers in the court of an unnamed king of the XIXth dynasty.

KHAI-BES. " City of Lamps."

An Egyptian city which was sacred to the goddess Bast, or Sekhet. Its site is unknown.

Khair.

An Egyptian gentleman, the father of a comparatively unknown individual named Nakht-ankh, which see.

Khak-hau.

A surname of Thothmes IV., of the XVIIIth dynasty.

Khalil-astoreth.

The father of a king of Sidon who was contemporary with Bodastoreth, king of Tyre. The name of the Sidonian king is lost.

Khalludus.

An early king of the Susians. He was the father of Sutruk-Nakhundi, a famous king of Elam.

Khalpirti.

Another form of the name Khapirti, which see.

Khalu.

See Kharu, a Syrian maritime people, who were conquered by the Egyptians.

Khamourabi.

See Hammurabi, of which this name is another form, used by the French Assyriologists.

Khamur.

A mystical region in the Egyptian Kerneter. It is mentioned in the LXXXVIIIth chapter of the Ritual of the Dead.

Khanatsiruca.

A king of the Matai or Medes, who was conquered, and 2300 of his soldiers slain, by Samas-Rimmon or Samsi-Vul III., king of Assyria, who also destroyed 1200 of his cities by fire.

Khanirabbat.

A town on the Upper Euphrates, where Esarhaddon, king of Assyria, defeated the rebellious army raised against him by his two elder brothers, Adram-melech and Nergalsharezer, which see.

Khanni-Cit.

An early king of Amardia. Nothing else is known of him, except that he was succeeded by his son Sutur-Cit.

Khanunu.

A king of Gaza, whose country was invaded by Sargon II., king of Assyria. He called to his assistance Shabatuk or Sibahe, king of Egypt, but he was, together with his Egyptian ally, utterly defeated by the Assyrians at the battle of Raphia.

KHAPIRTI.

The Accadian name of the province of Susiana.

KHARABU.

The Egyptian name for the district of Aleppo, which was rendered tributary to Egypt by Thothmes III.

KHA-RA-TA-NEK-HA.

The wife of Horus, and the mother of the royal scribe Peteharpocrates, which see.

KHARFESTER.

In Zendic mythology a series of wicked beings, who were expressly created to punish the crimes of mankind. They were destroyed in the Deluge by Tashter, the creative spirit.

KHARMISANDAI.

A city near Media, rendered tributary by Samas Rimmon, king of Assyria.

KHARSAK-KURRA.   "Mountains of the East."

The Chaldean name of the highlands of Media.

KHAR-SIDI.   "The Propitious Bull."

The Accadian name of the month Airu, which see.

KHAR-SI-YESU.

The Assyrian form of the Egyptian royal name Harsiesis or Aroeris, which see.

KHARU.   *Or* KHARUN.

The Greek Kharon, who was borrowed by the Etruscans to denote one of their demons of death. He was represented as armed with a mallet or hammer, and of a revolting appearance.

KHARU.   *Or* KHALU.

A maritime people on the coast of Syria, subdued by Seti I. of the XIXth dynasty.

KHARUI.

The Egyptian name of the town of Choloe.

KHARU-SATA.

The name of a mystical cow who is adored in the CLXIIIrd chapter of the Ritual of the Dead.

KHAS-KHEM.

An Egyptian lady, the wife of Ouzahor, and the mother of Douñ-se-pa-nefer, which see.

KHASSIKHU.

A king of the country of the Matsirausai, who paid tribute to Samas Rimmon or Samsi-Vul III., king of Assyria.

KHASU-EN-AMEN.

A priest of Apis, the son of Pa-se-nen-khons. His precise date is uncertain.

KHAT.

An Egyptian lady, the sister of the royal scribe Usur-ha, which see.

KHATA.

An Egyptian lady, the mother of Takiuata, which see.

KHATI.

An Egyptian officer. He was the son of an officer named Osirtesen and his wife Hotep.

KHATI-UER.

An Egyptian royal functionary. His period is unknown.

KHATIUER.

The father of the Egyptian officer Seuati, of the XIIth dynasty.

KHATKIRIBI.

The Assyrian name of the Egyptian city Athribis under the Icosarchy.

KHATUMA.

The Egyptian name of an unidentified Syrian city.

KHEBOTA.

An Egyptian festival which was held on the occasion of digging or manuring the ground.

KHELFUN.

A flat-nosed satyr, with crown, leopard's skin, and goat's tail, who on an Etruscan mirror is conjoined with Munthukh.

KHEM. *Or* HORUS-KHEM, "The Bull of his Mother."

This ithyphallic deity was generally represented as standing upright, with his right arm extended in the attitude of scattering seed, and having behind it the threshing instrument which is generally called a flagellum. His left hand and arm are closely enveloped in a thick robe, which swathes him like a mummy. His phallus is erected; and his head-dress consisted of two upright plumes similar to those of the deity Amen Ra; he wore a large and richly ornamented collar round his neck. Mythologically Khem represented the idea of divinity in its double character of father and son. As father he was called the husband of his mother, while as a son he was assimilated to the god Horus. He properly symbolised generative power, surviving death indeed, but submitting to a state of rigidity and inertion over which he could not triumph till his left arm was freed. In the CXLVIth chapter of the Book of the Dead, the deceased is said to exclaim, when his soul is reunited to his body, "that he has overcome his bandages, and that it is given him to extend his arm." Khem was also the symbolic deity of vegetable life, and it was probably in allusion to this theory that in a vignette to the Book of the Dead, the new birth of the deceased is represented by a tree growing out of his person while he lies upon a bier. The great festival of germination, in the Egyptian husbandry was held in honour of the god Khem, and it is fully figured on the walls of the palace temple of Rameses III. at Medinet Habu.

KHEM-HOTEP.   "Peace of Khem."

An Egyptian artist or painter of the XIIth dynasty.

KHEM-MES.   "Son of Khem."

The royal scribe of the place or palace of justice in the reign or Rameses III. of the XIXth dynasty. His mother Ani was a priestess of Isis, and his surname was Kan-ra.

KHEM-RA-N-SEM-KHEKH. "Prevailing by the Name in her Throat."

The name of the sixth of the seven mystical cows or Hathors or Egyptian mythology. *See* Hathors.

KHEN-EM-KHONSU.

A priest of Apis, in the reign of King Pa-mai of the XXIInd dynasty. *See* Pa-mai.

KHENEMS.

A peculiar kind of oil bottle used by the ancient Egyptians. It was generally made of bronze.

KHENI.

The Egyptian name of the town which is now called by the Arabs Silsilis.

KHEN-TA.

An Egyptian title of an uncertain nature, at present rendered "Functionary of the Interior."

KHENT-HESERT.

A title of the Egyptian deity Thoth.

KHENT-NOFRE.

An Egyptian district, the chief city in which was governed by Zadkhian, one of the chiefs who rebelled against Pianki-Meramen of the XXIInd dynasty.

KHENTUR.

A mystical region of the Egyptian Ker-neter which is mentioned in the XCIIIrd chapter of the Ritual of the Dead.

KHEP.

An Egyptian measure of length, equal to five digits.

KHEPER-RA.

The name of the god Ra in his character of the Producer and Sustainer of Life. In this form the scarabeus or sacred beetle of Egypt was his emblem.

KHER.

The Egyptian name for the district in Thebes which was appointed for the tombs and funereal offices of the dead.

KHER.

An Egyptian city which was held by the rebel chief Pa-bas against Piankhi Meramen of the XXIInd dynasty. It may have been the same as the preceding district.

KHER-AB.

The father of an Egyptian named Aaab, which see.

KHER-HEB.

The chief funereal priest who officiated over the ceremonies of the Kher. It is sometimes but erroneously rendered high-priest, as a general title.

KHER-MAUSER.

The name of a mystical cow who is adored in the CLXIIIrd chapter of the Ritual of the Dead.

KHERSH.   "Truss."

An Egyptian measure ; weight or quantity unknown.

KHERT-ASE.

Another form of the Egyptian name Sekherta, which see.

KHET-ANKH.

The wife of Har-em-ha, a sculptor (or perhaps an embalmer) of the XIIth dynasty.

KHET-EF.

The captain of the boatmen of Rameses II. of the XIXth dynasty.

KHET-UI.

A son of Hes-hor-si-amen, of the XXIst dynasty.

KHIDI.

A district in Susiana. Its locality is unknown.

KHIMUNI.

The Assyrian name for the Egyptian city called by the Greeks Panopolis, which see.

KHININSI.

The Assyrian name of the Egyptian city of Herakleopolis, which was established as a petty kingdom under the Assyrian Icosarchy.

KHIN-MAKH-NU.

An Assyrian city which revolted to Assurdan, and was reconquered by Samas-Rimmon for his father Shalmaneser III.

KHIRABU.

A town of the Hittites, which was sacred to its own local form of the god Sutekh.

KHIRAPUSAR.

The secretary of Khitasira, king of the Hittites. He was killed by the Egyptians at the battle of Kadesh.

KHIRTSINA.

A king of the Nahri; he was the son of Migdiara. He was subdued, and 300 of his cities destroyed, by Mulis-assur, the chief of the commanders of Samas-Rimmon.

KHIRUBU.

The Egyptian name for the Chalybes of Greek history. They combined with the Hittites against Rameses II., and were, together with their allies, utterly defeated and subjugated by him.

KHISASAP.

A town of the Hittites, which was sacred to its own local form of the god Sutekh.

KHITA.

A Canaanite people, the Hittites of Hebrew history, who were often at war with the Egyptians, and who were completely subdued by Rameses II. of the XIXth dynasty.

KHITA-SIRA.

A king of the Hittites. He was the son of Maur-sar and the grandson of Sepa-ru-ru, kings of the Khitæ. He raised a combination of Syrian kings against Rameses II., by whom he was utterly and disastrously defeated at the battle of Kadesh. He ultimately signed a treaty of peace with Rameses II. and gave him his daughter in marriage as a subordinate wife.

KHNEM.

The son of the royal lady Ata of the Vth dynasty. He was president of the agricultural works of King Suten-rekh-ata (?).

KHNENTA.

In Zendic mythology the eighth resting-place of the Iranians after their exile from Aryanem Vaedjo, which see. It is supposed to have been the country now called Kandahar.

KHNUM.   *Or* KNEF.

In Egyptian mythology the incarnation of the divine breath or spirit of Amen Ra. He was represented as a ram-headed deity, bearing the

Atef crown. His analogue was the Chnuphis or Chnoubis of the Gnostic heretics. Khnum was the chief deity of Nubia, where he was generally one of a triad with the goddesses Sati and Anouke. He was also called on the inscriptions " The Maker of gods and men as the soul of the sun, by whose warmth they were created." In that attribute he was often represented as sitting at the potter's wheel and fashioning the mysterious primal egg of human generation.

KHNUM-HOTEP. " Peace of Khnum."

The governor of Menat Khufu, in Upper Egypt. He was the son of a prince-governor named Nehara and of the princess Bakat. The mines at the Wady Megara were under his care, and a tribe of Syrian people called the Aahmu visited Egypt during a famine in his time. These were long supposed to have been the Israelites under Jacob. Khnum-hotep was buried in a sumptuous tomb at Beni Hassan, where his life and riches are recorded.

KHNUM-KHUFU.

See Khufu. The real name of the builder of the great pyramid.

KHNUM-REKHI. " Bringer of Joys."

An epithet or title of Rameses III. of the XIXth dynasty.

KHONS. *Or* KHONSO-PTHAH.

The great deity of Thebes who was specially worshipped by Rameses XII. He was represented as a mummy figure standing upright, wearing the plumes of Amen, and holding the sceptre, scourge, and emblems of life and strength. He must be distinguished from the eponymous Pthah of Memphis, who was represented as a deformed hydrocephalous dwarf.

KHONS-AF-ANKH.

An Egyptian priest whose mummy is in the British Museum.

KHONS-EM.

An Egyptian, whose sarcophagus and mummy are in the Leyden Museum. His titles are unintelligible from the obliteration of the Hieroglyphics relating them.

KHONS-HOTEP. " Peace of Khonsu.'

A priest of the house of King Amen-mei-hor-hem-neb, of the XVIIIth dynasty. His mummy and double sarcophagus are in the Leyden Museum.

KHONS-IRI-TES.

An Egyptian lady, who was the mother of Isioer, a priestess of Amen Ra.

KHONS-IRI-TES.

The keeper of the beasts (or sacred cattle) of Amen Ra. His period is unknown, but it was subsequent to the XIXth dynasty.

KHONS-MES. "Son of Khons."

A spondist of Amen, priest of the temple of Month, and scribe of the holy offerings at Thebes. He was the son of Amen-em-ef, a priest of Amen.

KHONS-MES.

An Egyptian gentleman whose statue is in the Leyden Museum.

KHONS-MES.

A spondist of Amen Ra and keeper of the White Hall of that god. He married the lady Ten-t-amen, and had a daughter named Ta-eiouih-ra, who, together with her mother, was also a priestess of Amen.

KHONS-NEB-ANKH. "Khonso, Lord of Life."

An Egyptian officer, who was the father of Iri-hap-ieooer, which see.

KHONSU.

A queen of Egypt, the daughter of Sebekhotep V. of the XIVth dynasty.

KHONSU.

The accountant of the granaries of Rameses II. of the XIXth dynasty.

KHONSU. *Surnamed* PARANNEFER.

A Flabellum-bearer of Amen Ra. Period uncertain.

KHONSUAIRITIS.

The superintendent of the granaries to King Aspalut, of the XXVth dynasty.

KHOPESCH.

A peculiar form of scimitar or curved sword, which was generally held in the hands of the Egyptian deities Amen Ra, Mentu, and Bar. It was also used as an emblem of valour.

KHOU.

The Egyptian name of the intelligence or consciousness of the soul after death, which ascended for a time into heaven, till its rehabilitation into the body after the last judgment and purgation.

KHRIM-MU-RA.

An unassigned early Egyptian royal name.

KHRISHNA.

In Hindu mythology the eighth incarnation of the deity Vishnu, in which form he was supposed to be the son of the shepherd Nanda, by his wife Ysodha. His adventures and doctrines form a cultus by themselves.

KHSATHSOVAIRYO.   "The Powerful King."

In Zendic mythology the third of the heavenly Amshaspands, which see.

KHSHAIRSHA.

The Egyptian form of the Persian royal name Xerxes, which see.

KHU.

An Egyptian amulet, representing the sun on the solar hill or horizon.

KHU.

The Egyptian name of the human intelligence, considered as a component principle of the body of man.

KHU-EN-ATEN.   "Glory of the Solar Disk."

The name which Amenhotep IV. adopted for his own after his forcible introduction of the monotheistic worship of Aten Ra into Egypt.

KHU-EN-PTHAH.

A priest who was attached to the worship of King Neferakara, of the Vth dynasty.

KHUFU.   *Or* KHNUM-KHUFU.

The first king of the IVth dynasty.   He fought against and conquered the Arabs of the peninsula of Mount Sinai, and erected the great pyramid which he called "The Splendour of Pyramids."   He founded the temple of Athor at Tentyris, and was said to have written a work called the "Sacred Book."   He was the Cheops of the Greeks, by whom he was said to have been an infidel.

KHUFU-MER-NUTER-U.

The grandson of Tetet, an early Egyptian king.

KHUFUT.

A granddaughter of Tetet, an early Egyptian king.

KHULDJAN.

In Arabian history a wicked king of the Adites, in whose reign the whole nation was destroyed.

KHUMBA.   *Or* KHUMBUNE.

A deity of the Susians, of whom nothing is known.

KHUMBANIGASH.

Another form of the Elamite royal name Humbanigash, which see.

KHUNDURAI.

A city near Media, rendered tributary by Samas-Rimmon, king of Assyria.

KHUNSU.

A consort of Antef III. of the XIth dynasty.

KHUNSU. *Or* KHONSU.

A daughter of Sebekhotep V. of the XIIIth dynasty.

KHU-OER.

A chief of the palace of an unnamed king of the XVIIIth dynasty.

KHUSARETH. "Harmony."

A Phenician goddess. She was the wife of Thuro, the deity of the written law.

KHUSE-MAKH.

In Chaldean astronomy one of the twelve stars of the West.

KHUT-HOTEP.

The surname of the sacred scribe Apa, which see.

KHUZABA.

In Chaldean astronomy the name of an unidentified star.

KHUZIRINA.

An Assyrian city, which revolted to Assurdan and was reconquered by Samas-Rimmon or Samsi-Vul.

KHUZISTAN.

The modern name of the district or town which was called Numki by the Accadians and Elamu by the Semites.

KIARI.

The king of a district called Karsibuta, possibly near Armenia. He paid tribute to Samsivul III.

KIBABA.

A king of Harhar. He revolted against Sargon II., who defeated him, and changed the name of his capital city to Kar-Sargon.

KIBIGANE.

The name of a canal which was excavated near Larsa, by command of Sin-idinna, an early Babylonian king.

KIBOTOS. "Ark."

The name given by the Phrygians to the city of Apamea, where they believed the ark of Deucalion to have rested.

KIDAH.

Another name of the ancient Arabian divining arrows, more generally called Azlam. *See* Kehana.

KIKUPAN.

A temple erected at Babylon "to the sovereign (queen) of the house of heaven," or the goddess Nana as the Moon-goddess.

KILITERU.

A king of the Hittites of Southern Syria, who led his people into Assyria, but was defeated and slain in the city of Seris by Tiglath Pileser I.

KIMARU.

A district bordering upon Assyria, rendered tributary by Samsi-Vul III.

KINABUA.

Governor of Tushi, in the reign of Vulnirari III. He was eponym of the year B.C. 795.

KINALU.

The capital of the district of Patina, on the Orontes. It was taken by assault by Dayan-assur, the Tartan of Shalmaneser II. ; and its king, Surrila, an usurper, committed suicide to avoid a terrible death.

KINDAKURBU.

An Elamite deity of whom nothing is known.

KINGIISTILINZAMAR.   Or CINGISTILINZAKHARAI.

A district bordering upon Assyria, which was rendered tributary by Samsi-Vul III.

KINUKA.

A district bordering upon Assyria, also rendered tributary by Samsi-Vul III.

KINZIRU.

A king of Sape and Babylonia, who attempting to resist Tiglath Pileser II.'s claim to complete Chaldean dominion, was by him besieged and put to death in his own city. He was a descendant of Amukkan, king of Sape, and was the Chinzirus of the Greek writers.

KIP-ABARATAKA.

A district bordering upon Assyria, which was rendered tributary by Samsi-Vul III.

KIP-ALMAS-DAKI.

The Accadian name of a city or district the site of which is not known.

KIP-KIPI.

The Assyrian name for an Egyptian city the site of which is not known, to which Rutamen, king of Egypt, fled after the battle of Memphis.

KIPRE.

A tribe in Mesopotamia which was conquered by Tiglath Pileser II.

KIPSI.

A noble Median. *See* Upas.

KIP-SU.

A mountain people on the borders of Media and Susiana, who were conquered by Sennacherib.

KIP-SUN.

An Assyrian city which supported Assurdainpal in his revolt against his father Shalmaneser II., and was reconquered by Samas Rimmon.

KIR-GIN-GUR-NA.   " The Errand of Ishtar."

The Accadian name of the month Ululu, which see.

KIR-HI.

A city on the Upper Tigris, which was conquered first by Tiglath Pileser I., and again by Assurnazirpal, who took Bubu its chief captive and flayed him alive.

KIR-RI.

The brother of Kati, king of Que.   Shalmaneser II. having conquered the district of Lamina and the city of Tarzi in Northern Syria, placed Kirri upon its throne as a vassal king.

KIR-RURI.

A city or district in Mesopotamia, which was governed by Napharili in the reign of Tiglath Pileser II.

KIR-SHAMASH.

An Elamite deity of whom nothing is known.

KIRTIARI.

The chief of the city and district of Larbusa in the mountains of Nizir. He was conquered by Assurnazirpal.

KIRUBI.

The name of the Assyrian winged human-headed bulls.   *See* Alapi.

KIRYATH-HADESCHATH.   "The New Town."

The original name of the Tyrian settlement which was founded by Queen Elissa in North Africa, and was generally called Carthage in Classic history.

KIRZAN.

A kingdom in the Western mountains of Mesopotamia, which was conquered by Shalmaneser II. and Assurnazirpal.

KIS.

A city in Babylonia, now called Hymir, where Hammurabi, king of Babylon, erected a tower to the deity Zamana.

KI-SE-SIM.

A city conquered by Sargon II., who led its chief Belshazzar into captivity, and then, placing an Assyrian governor over the city, changed its name to Kar-mas-mas-u.

KISH.

Another form of writing the name of the Babylonian town Kisu, which see.

KIS-KI.

The Accadian name of the Babylonian city Kisu, now called Hymir, which see.

KISSARE.

In Greco-Babylonian mythology the offspring of Apason and his sister wife Tauthe. Kissare by his sister Assaros was the father of the first triad of the gods Anos, Illinos, and Aos. *See* Anu.

KISU.

A town or district in Babylonia where Merodach Baladin I. was defeated and driven into exile by Sennacherib, after his short re-occupation of the throne of Babylon on the death of Sargon II.

KISU.

The king of Haldile, a petty kingdom in Arabia conquered by Esar-haddon.

KISURAKI.

An Accadian city, the site of which is unknown.

KIT.

A sister of Sekherta, an Egyptian officer of the XIIth dynasty.

KITION.

A capital city in the Island of Cyprus. It was called Kithium by the Greeks.

KITLALA.

A city near the river Belichus, conquered by Shalmaneser II.

KITZU.

A king of Kaldili in Arabia, who paid tribute to Esarhaddon, king of Assyria, by whom he was put to death.

KLUTHUMUSTHA.

The Etruscan form of the name of Clytemnestra, the faithless wife of Agamemnon.

KOCHOME.   " Black Bull."

The ancient name of the town of Sakkarah in Lower Egypt.

KOLPIA.   " The Wind."

In Phenician mythology the husband of Bahu, or the female earth. His name was also written Colpias.

KOMOS.

In Greek mythology the guardian of festivities.

KOSAI.

A leader or chief of the Beni-Koreish, about A.D. 500. He enlarged the town of Mecca, and rebuilt the Caaba, to do which he was obliged to cut down the sacred grove of date palms which surrounded it.

KOSSI.

See Cossæans

KOŸUNJIK.

The modern name of the mounds which occupy the site of the city of Nineveh.

KRITOBOULOS.

A nobleman of Cyrene, whose daughter Ladike became one of the wives of Aahmes II., king of Egypt.

KSHATRYA.

The military caste of the Hindus, who were said to have been created from the heart of Brahma.

KUA.

The name of the great oracle of Marduk at Babylon.

KUBAN.

A Nubian village, near to which were situated the ancient Egyptian gold mines, which were much worked by the kings of the earlier dynasties. It is famous from a stèle which was found there recently, in which Rameses II. in singular phraseology relates that there being no water in the locality, and the mines being about to be abandoned in consequence, he caused a well to be dug, "he spoke to the rock and the water flowed out." The actual site of the gold mines was at a place now called by the Arabs Wady Ollaki. They were explored by order of Mahomet Ali, but with little result as to the benefit to be derived from re-opening them.

KUDUR-LAGAMAR.   " Servant of Lagamar."

A king of Elam, whose name has very recently been found on the monuments. He was the Chedorlaomer of Hebrew history. (Boscawen.)

KUDUR-MABUK.

A Syrian or Elamite king, the son of Simti-Silhak, who governed Babylonia by his son Ardusin as viceroy. He is supposed to have been a descendant of Kudur-lagamar, the Chedorlaomer of Hebrew history.

KUDUR-NAN-HUNDI.

See Kudur-nan-khundi, king of Elam.

KUDUR-NAN-KHUNDI I.

An early Elamite king, so called by the Assyrians. He invaded Babylonia in the time of Bel-sumizzir, and carried away into Elam, from Erech, an image of the goddess Nana. It remained in Elam till it was restored to Nineveh by Assurbanipal, when he subjugated the country after a lapse of 1635 years.

KUDUR-NAN-KHUNDI II.

The son of Sutruk-Nankhundi, king of Elam. He was the opponent of
Sennacherib, who burnt many of his cities, and obliged him to retire
from his capital, Madaktu, to the mountains. He died suddenly, and
was succeeded by his brother, Umman-minan, B.C. 695.

KUDURRU.

One of the two sons of Ummanaldas, a former king of Elam, who
together with the sons of Urtaki, the late king, fled for refuge into
Assyria upon the accession of Tiumman.

KUKURU.

An Assyrian general, who recorded an eclipse or darkening of the sun
in the reign of Assurbanipal. (Fox Talbot.)

KULAL. " The Perfect."

A Himyaritic deity, a form of the god Il.

KULLANI.

A Syrian town, which was conquered by Tiglath Pileser II. It was
the Calno of Hebrew history.

KULLIMIR.

An Assyrian city besieged by the rebel Tartan Iludaria, whom the
inhabitants surprised and slew in a night sally, and then sent his head to
their sovereign Assurbanipal.

KULSU. *Wrongly read* KULMU.

An Etruscan Chaonian goddess, with buskins, and shears in one hand
and a flaming funeral torch in the other, who on a sarcophagus from
Chiusi is represented as issuing from the door of a tomb.

KUMBECEPHALIC.

The term used by Professor Daniel Wilson to denote the ante-bronze
period dolichocephalic type of skull. *See* Dolichocephalic.

KUMMU. " Palace."

A frequent affix to the names of towns in Assyrian geography.

KUMMUHA.

A city on the Euphrates, near to the sources of the Tigris, where
Tiglath Pileser I. defeated the invasion of the Hittites into Assyria,
under their king Kiliteru.

KUNALI.

The chief town of the petty Syrian kingdom of Unqi. It was destroyed
by Tiglath Pileser II., who afterwards re-established it as an Assyrian
garrison town.

KUNUSS-KUN-KIL-ASSHUR. "I the King Vicegerent of the god Assur."

An Assyrian royal epithet out of which the Greek writers fabricated
the name Conosconcoleros.

KUPHI.

A peculiar kind of incense used in Egyptian worship, the ancient receipts for making which are still preserved in the papyri.

KURBAN.

A city or district near Nineveh of which Bel-sar-anni was the prefect under Sennacherib. It revolted to Assurdan, and was reconquered by Samas Rimmon or Samsi-Vul for Shalmaneser II.

KURIBATTARAYA.   "Lord of Sheep."

A Kurumba deity.

KURIGALZU I.

A very early king of Babylonia, a successor of Hammurabi. Nothing else is known respecting him, but he must not be confounded with the later king of Babylonia of the same name.

KURIGALZU II.

A son of Burnaburyas II., who became king of Babylonia. Nothing is known respecting him.

KURIGALZU II. OR III.

A king of Babylonia, the son of Burnaburyas II., and very probably the same as Kurigalzu II. He built a city called Dur-kurigalzu, and restored many of the Babylonian temples. He also erected the temple of Bit-ugal in honour of the god Bel.

KURUSH.

The Persian form of the royal name called by the Greek historians Cyrus.

KURUSH.   Or CYRUS.

The grandson of Astyages, and the son of Cambyses, king of Persia, by his wife Mandane. Owing to the apprehensions of his grandfather that he might usurp the throne which he intended for his two other grandsons Khsathrita and Sithratakhma, (the Xathritas and Sithratach-mes of Herodotus), he was exposed on a desert mountain, where he was brought up by an herdsman of Astyages, who named him Agradates, but afterwards Kurush, in memory of a still-born son of his own. If the Greek historians are to be credited, certain romantic incidents led to the lad's discovery by his grandfather. He soon revolted against Astyages, who at last allowed him to go as Satrap with his father Cambyses into Persia, where he was eminently successful as a soldier. He then incited the Persians to rise against the Medes, who had overthrown the Zendic religion, and to re-establish the faith of Zarathustra or Zoroaster, B.C. 559. After this he made war with the Lydians, whom he defeated and annexed to his empire by the conquest of Sardis. He then, but with less success, attacked the cities of Greece, and afterwards marched into India. Having subdued that country, or at all events a portion of its Southern coast, he joined with Cambyses and besieged the city of Babylon, which fell before their armies, thus terminating the Chaldean empire, B.C. 538. About that time he granted permission to the Jews, who were then in captivity in Babylonia, to return to their own country and rebuild Jerusalem, which they did in great numbers, B.C. 536. After the reduction of all Chaldea, Kurush a second time invaded Lydia, the people having attempted to throw off his yoke, B.C. 546. He then led his armies against the Massagetæ, a Turanian or Turkish tribe inhabiting the Steppes to the North of the Jaxartes. At first he obtained the victory, taking captive Spargapises, the son of their Queen Tomyris, who killed himself for shame. A second engagement followed however, and in that after a long continued hand to hand fight, the king of the Persians was slain, and his head cut off and thrown into a bowl of human blood by Tomyris. After the battle the Persians obtained back the body of Kurush, and gave it a grand burial at Pasargadæ, and erected a splendid monument there, representing him as a glorified spirit, or one of the Amshaspands, with four large wings, and wearing the great Egyptian *Atef* crown of justification. Above his head hovers the image of his sovereign deity Ormuzd, and a short Cuneiform text simply tells the passer by : " I am Cyrus, the king, the Achæmenian." The tomb is now called by the Turks the tomb of the mother of Solomon.

KURUZZA.

A city near Damascus, which was conquered by Tiglath Pileser II. on his march to assist Ahaz, king of Judah.

KUSHITES.

The Classical appellation for the Negroes inhabiting Ethiopia, who were a continual source of annoyance to the Egyptian kings of the earlier dynasties. They were subsequently incorporated with the empire by Thothmes I.

KUSTASPI.

A king of Kummuha in Northern Syria. He combined with Sarduri, king of Armenia, and other kings, to resist the conquests of Tiglath Pileser II., but in vain, as they were all defeated at the battle of Kummuha, and rendered tributary to Assyria.

KUSU.

The Assyrian name of the land of Ethiopia.

KUTE.

The Assyrian name of a city or district called by the Accadians Teggabaki, the modern Ibrahim. It was conquered by Shalmaneser I. when he marched to the relief of his ally Maruduk-zikur-izkur, king of Babylon.

KUWERA.

In Hindu mythology the god of wealth.

KYAXARES.

A king of the Carucassi. *See* Kastarite.

Kylikomanteia.

The Classical name of a kind of divination by cups containing mystical sentences, a form of enchantment much practised among the Assyrians.

Kyphi.

An Egyptian sacred incense, the receipts for preparing which are still extant.

Kypranor.

Another form of the Kypriote royal name Pasicrates, or rather Stasicrates, which see.

Kytalos.

A peculiarly shaped staff, by which the Spartan kings and generals sent private messages to the Ephori. To use it a piece of paper was wound tightly upon the Kytalos, and the message was then written upon it. On unwinding the slip of writing the words would present no intelligible connection till the message was rewound upon a staff, the counterpart of the one upon which it was originally wound.

L.

LABARIS.

According to the Greek lists the name of an Egyptian king of the XIIth dynasty. He is said to have constructed the labyrinth, and is not certainly identified. *See* Amenemha III.

LAB-KI.

The Accadian name of the city of Urukh.

LAB-MAHKI.

An Accadian city, of which the site is unknown.

LABOROSOARCHOD.

According to the Greek lists a king of Babylon, the successor of Nergalsarussur. He is supposed to have been the infant king Bellabarisruk or Ulbasurkidina, which see.

LABTURI.

The son of Tubusi, king of Nahiri. He was the chief of the city of Uda, in Mesopotamia, a country which was conquered and annexed to Assyria by Assurbanipal.

LABYNETUS.

The Greek form of the Chaldean royal name Nabonahid, which see.

LACHISH.

A strong city in the South of Palestine, the people of which combined with Adonibezek and other petty kings to resist the entrance of the Hebrews into Canaan. They were, however, defeated by Joshua, and their country incorporated with the Jewish possessions. About B.C. 810 Amaziah, king of Judah, fled to this city for refuge from a conspiracy which had broken out against him; but he was followed and assassinated there. In about B.C. 698 Sennacherib, king of Assyria, invaded Judah, and taking Lachish, made it the depôt of his army while he summoned Jerusalem to surrender, and prepared another army for the reduction of Egypt; and it has been supposed that he remained there while the terrible destruction related by Isaiah took place. There is an interesting bas-relief in the British Museum, representing Sennacherib superintending the siege of Lachish, and giving orders for the destruction of the city.

Ladike.

A native of Cyrene, the daughter of Kritoboulos. She married Aahmes II., king of Egypt of the XXXth dynasty, who sought by that means to strengthen his influence with the Greeks, who had placed him upon the throne.

Laff.

A tribe of the Amalika who settled in the district of Yathrib.

Laga.

In Scandinavian mythology a goddess who was one of the wives of Odin.

Lagada.

A deity of the Susians of whom nothing is known.

Lagalaga.

A town in South-eastern Assyria, which was conquered by Assurbanipal.

Lagamar.

A deity of the Susians of whom nothing is known. *See* Kudur Lagamar.

Lagitu.

An Assyrian measure of capacity, called generally the *log*.

Lahiru.

A town in Mesopotamia, conquered by Shalmaneser I., on behalf of his ally Maruduk-zikur-izkur, king of Babylonia.

Lahlahte.

A city in Mesopotamia which was conquered by Shalmaneser II.

Lahua.

A tribe in Mesopotamia which was conquered by Tiglath Pileser II.

Laile.

The king of Yedih, in Arabia. On the invasion of Arabia by Esarhaddon he fled from the country, and the statues of the local gods were carried to Nineveh by the Assyrians. After the departure of Esarhaddon, Laile sent an embassy with presents and his submission to the king, imploring the return of his deities. These Esarhaddon accepted, and restoring the statues, made the king of Yedih king also of the land of Bazu.

Lakhiru.

A city of Elam which was destroyed by Sennacherib.

Lakshmi.

The Hindu goddess of love. *See* Radha.

LALAN. *Or* LARAN.

The Etruscan war-god. He was represented with youthful countenance, cloak, buskins, helmet, spear, sword and shield. His analogue was the Ares of the Greeks.

LALLA.

The king of a district called Millid, conquered by Shalmaneser II., king of Assyria.

LALUKNA.

A city which revolted against Sargon II., who conquered it and sent the inhabitants into slavery to Damascus.

LAMENTU.

The king of Chemmis in Lower Egypt. A petty Egyptian kingdom under the Assyrian Dodecarchy, which was the Panopolis of the Greeks.

LAMERSEKENI.

A captain of Piankhi, king of Egypt in the XXIInd dynasty. He and Poarma, another captain, were sent by the king to suppress the insurrection of Princes Tafnekht and Nimrod, which they accomplished.

LAMUA.

A district of South-eastern Assyria, which was the scene of many of the battles of Assurnazirpal.

LANHABBI.

An Arabian or Nabathean town, whither the remains of the army of Vaiteh II. fled, and where Aimu, the brother of Abiyateh was captured by the Assyrians.

LAODICE.

See Ladike. A Cyrenian lady, one of the wives of Aahmes II.

LAODICEA.

The Greek name of the Phenician town Caicna, which see.

LAQIPU.

The governor of Kalzi, in the reign of Assurdan III. He was eponym of the year B.C. 760, the chief event in which was a revolt in the city of Arbaha.

LARAN.

See Lalan.

LARANCHA.

A Chaldean city mentioned by Berosus. It is supposed to have been the same with Senkereh, which see.

LARBUSA.

A district in the mountains of Nizir in Armenia. It was conquered by Assurnazirpal.

Larra. *Or* Larsa.

The Assyrian name for the Chaldean city called Ellasar in Hebrew history. It was the Larancha of the Greeks, and the Senkereh of later writers.

Lars.   Etruscan, Larsh.

The title of an Etruscan noble or gentleman. The corresponding female title was Larthi, answering to " Madame."

Lasa.

An Etruscan divinity, of gentle aspect, who seems to have accompanied the departing souls as an attending Fate. He was represented as winged, with cap, earrings, necklace and buskins, and carrying in his hands a stylus, inkhorn, and paper.

Lasanau.

A country called " The Great Country," in the Cuneiform inscriptions. It was the birthplace of the great scribe Nebo-sar-ziltimu, the compiler of the standard astronomical work of the Chaldeans for Sargon I.

Lasa-rakuneta.

An Etruscan winged goddess who was represented with coronet, earrings, necklace, and shoes, and what may be either a box of cosmetics and pencil, or a stylus and inkhorn in her hand. *See* Lasa.

Lasa-sitmika.

A winged youth or deity with a staff, who is represented, on an Etruscan mirror from Volsinii, as standing beside Turan and Adonis. *See* Lasa.

Lasa-veku.

An Etruscan divinity who is represented on a mirror as standing before Minerva ; winged, with cap and buskins, and a green twig in the right hand. *See* Lasa.

Latopolis.   " City of Latona."

The Greek name for the Egyptian city and nome of Aa, in Lower Egypt, which see.

Latopolis.

The Greek name for the city and nome of Ten, in Upper Egypt.

Latrunculi.

The Roman name of the Egyptian game called Sent, which see.

Laz.

An Assyrian deity worshipped by Tiglath Pileser II.

Leather Bands for Mummies.

At the time of the XXth dynasty the mummies had occasionally a band of leather straps, about an inch broad, with an edge or binding.

They were spread at the ends, and were stamped, or embossed, at the extremities. They came into use at the time of the XXth dynasty, and continued under the XXIst and XXIInd dynasties. The principal subjects embossed were a king adoring the god Khem, or Amen-Horus, and the names of the monarchs of the dynasties.

LEHITAU.

A tribe in Mesopotamia which was conquered by Tiglath Pileser II.

LEINTH.

The Etruscan genius of life.

LEMANUEL.

In Cabalistic mythology the spirit of the moon.

LETHAM.

An Etruscan divinity, who was conjoined with Menerva and Tinia.

LETSETE.

In Scandinavian mythology the name of one of the horses of the gods.

LEUCAPIS.

A Libyan city on the West of the lake Mareotis. It was famous in the Ptolemaic period.

LEUCOS-PORTUS.

A Greco-Egyptian seaport on the Red Sea, also founded by the Ptolemies.

LIBANUS.

In Phenician mythology one of the early giants. The Lebanon and Antilibanus mountains were said to have been named after him. *See* Capius.

LIBIT-NANA.   " Work of Anunit."

A Babylonian king, the first ruler of Nipur, who restored the temple of Nana, called Bit-Mekit.

LIB-SI-ANNA.   " Shepherd of the Heavenly Flock."

In Chaldean astronomy one of the seven stars of the week.

LIDAN-GULA.   " Offspring of Gula."

An early Chaldean proper name.

LIDINI.

A petty kingdom in the Island of Kypros, which .paid tribute to Esarhaddon.

LIDUNNAMU.

A Chaldean of low origin, who was raised to office by Suzub the Babylonian rebel in the reign of Sennacherib, by whom he was defeated.

LIK-BA-GAS.

Another name of Urukh, the early Babylonian king.

LILITH.

An evil spirit, who the Arab writers say was the first wife of Adam, and that her children were the jins or devils. She is said to have had 784 children, as the letters of her name have this numerical value. Her name is found in the Assyrian inscriptions as Li-lit, "the black," an "evil spirit." She was said to have stimulated nocturnal impurities, and to have been more especially dangerous to married women at the birth of their first child, upon which occasion the Arabian nurses still throw stones at the foot of the bed to drive her away. (Boscawen.)

LIMU.

The Assyrian name of the officer who is now generally called an eponym, which see.

LIMU.

An Assyrian city which supported Assurdainpal in his revolt against his father Shalmaneser II.

LIMUR-PATIS-ASSUR.   "Dwelling of the Vicegerent of Assur."

The name given by the Assyrians to the city of Athribis in Egypt, after its conquest by Esarhaddon.

LINGAM.

In Hindu mythology an emblem of the masculine powers of nature, generally adored under the form of an upright stone, often in combination with the Yoni, which see.

LISHANA-SHEL-IMRANI.

A peculiar Hebrew or Targum dialect, used by the modern Jews of Kurdistan.

LITUI.

A peculiar curved line which was drawn by the Egyptians from the inner angle of the eye to the upper part of the cheek. It was always appended to the mystical eye amulets of Osiris or Horus.

LODUR.

Another name of the Scandinavian deity Ve, which see.

LOFE.

In Scandinavian mythology the goddess of love. She instituted the ceremony of matrimony.

LOG.

An Assyrian measure of capacity, containing ten *baru*, equal to nine *aru*, or perhaps equal to eight *arrat*.

LOHRASP.

The name given by the Persian mediæval historians to Auravadaspa, king of Bactria. *See* Auravadaspa.

LOKMAN.

In Arabian history the founder of the second great Adite nation. He reigned over the few who believed in the prophet Hud, and is said to have governed for a thousand years. He built a great dyke to restrain the mountain torrents by which the former Adites had been swept away, and there founded the city of Marib. The remains of the dyke and city still exist. He was surnamed Dhu-anuscour, and was succeeded by his son Lukagm. *See* Lukagm *and* Dhu-anuscour.

LOSNA.

The Latin Moon-goddess. Her figure is found on a mirror from Præneste, which is erroneously supposed to be Etruscan.

LUBAT.

The Chaldean name of the seven chief planets. *See* Dibbat.

LUBAT.

In Chaldean astronomy the planet Jupiter, so called from its brilliancy.

LUBAT-GUTTUV. "Furrow of Heaven," *i.e.* ecliptic.

In Chaldean astronomy a name of the planet Jupiter.

LUBAT-SUKUS. "Head Man."

In Chaldean astronomy a name of the planet Saturn.

LUBDI.

A city in the South of Assyria which supported Assurdainpal in his revolt against his father Shalmaneser II. It was also the seat of the rebellion of the Tartan Iludaria, which see.

LUBURNA.

A king of the people of Patina on the Orontes. He was a tributary of Shalmaneser II. His subjects slew him, and raised to the throne one Surrila, which see.

LUCUMO.

The title of Etruscan priests and princes. According to Festus, it properly meant "one possessed" or "inspired." He also ascribes to this word the origin of the name Luceres, given to one of the three tribes of Rome.

LUDIM. *Or* RUDIM.

In Hebrew tradition the son of Mizraim. He is considered by some Egyptologists to have given the title to the indigenous Egyptian race.

LUKAGM.

The son of Lokman. He was the second king of the revived empire of the Adites. Nothing certain is known respecting him.

LUKSAI.

A country which was rendered tributary by Samas-Rimmon or Samsi-Vul, king of Assyria.

LULA.

In Chaldean astronomy one of the twelve stars of the West.

LULLIMI.

A people in the mountains of Mesopotamia, who were subdued by Assurrisilim, king of Assyria.

LULYA.

A king of Tyre, who was tributary to Tiglath Pileser I. He was the Iluleus of the Greeks.

LUSUNA.

The king of the district of Harru, East of Assyria. He was conquered and his kingdom pillaged by Dayan-assur, the Tartan of Shalmaneser II.

LUT.

See Rut and Ludim.

LUXOR.

An Arab village on the Eastern bank of the Nile, situated amid the ruins of the great temples of Amen and Pthah, which were erected by the monarchs of the XIXth dynasty. The chief of the buildings are but little inferior to the grand edifices of Karnak, from which Luxor is distant about two miles. The plans of the temples are very irregular, owing to their having been originally erected on the shores of the river Nile, and partly upon a kind of quay inclosed between two windings of its stream. The oldest parts of the temple are of the date of the reign of Amenhotep III. of the XVIIIth dynasty. The great colonnade bordering the shore was erected by Horus, the restorer. The two colossi in front of the entrance pylon, and the lofty obelisks which accompany them, were set up by Rameses II.-Miamun. The internal buildings, now more or less in ruins, were the work of successive Pharaohs, from the period of the XIXth dynasty and that of Tirhakah and Psametik of the XXVIth dynasty, to Alexander the Great, all of whose cartouches are found upon the walls. Luxor was connected with the capital temples of Karnak at Thebes, by a grand avenue of crio-sphynxes a mile and a half long (Bonomi), terminated by obelisks and colossi, and its suburbs were surrounded with smaller avenues, temples, and ædiculi, now more or less covered with sand and debris.

LYBIAN NOME.

The Greek name for the third nome in Lower Egypt which was anciently called Ament.

LYCOPOLIS MAGNA AND PARVA. " Greater, and Lesser, City of Wolves."

The Greek name for the cities and nomes in Upper Egypt called respectively Chesf-chent and Chesf-pehu, which see.

LYCOPOLIS. " Wolf City."

See Siayut.

LYDUS.

A mythical hero, who with Tyrrhenus led the original Lydians by sea from Greece to the coasts of Italy.

M.

MA.   *Or* MAU, " The Cat."

An Egyptian epithet applied to the sun.   The reason for the use or the epithet is obscure.   (Renouf.)

MA.   " Truth."

A mystical divinity, the daughter of Ra.   She is mentioned in the CXLth chapter of the Ritual of the Dead.

MAA.

An Egyptian god.   He was the deification of sight.

MAA.

The wife of Iua, a chief of the receipts under an Egyptian king, probably of the XIXth dynasty.

MAA.

An Egyptian lady, the sister of the officer Tutu of the IVth dynasty, which see.

MAAD.

The son of Adnan, king of the Hedjaz.   In his childhood, during the invasion of Arabia by Nebuchadnezzar, he remained hidden in the town of Haran in Yemen, but when he became a man he returned to his people, and marrying Maana, the daughter of Jorham, son of Djahla, re-established his kingdom.   He and his father must not be confounded with the Adnan and Maad, the progenitors of Mahomet.

MAA-ANTEF-EF.

One of the seven mystical spirits who are mentioned in the XVIIth chapter of the Ritual of the Dead.   *See* Ket-ket.

MAANA.

The daughter of Jorham, son of Djahla.   She married Maad, king of the Hedjaz, and assisted him to re-establish his kingdom.

MAA-NA-HESE-MAN.

The chief of the boatmen of an unknown Egyptian king, probably of the XIXth dynasty.

MAANAI.

The mother of Unnefer, a grand priest of Osiris in the reign of Rameses II. of the XIXth dynasty.

MAANI.

An Egyptian lady, the wife of Mai, chief priest of Osiris, and mother of Unnefer and the lady Ta-i-af, which see.

MACEDO.

An Egyptian deity. He was represented like the god Anubis, as a man with a jackal's head, and wearing the skin of a wolf. (Wilkinson.) He was a form of Anubis Ap-heru. *See* Ap-heru.

MACHANATH. "The Camp."

A Tyrian settlement in the Island of Sicily, called by the Greeks Pan-ormus, and by the moderns Palermo.

MACHOSCOLERUS.

The name of an Assyrian king in the Greek lists, possibly the same as Nebuchadnezzar.

MACORABA.

The ancient name of the city of Mecca, in Arabia.

MACROCEPHALIC. "Long-headed."

A term used by modern anthropologists to describe a species of skull in which the length exceeds the breadth. *See* Brachycephalic.

MACRU.

In Chaldean astronomy the name of the planet Mercury in the month of Ab.

MADA. "The Country."

The Accadian name of the district of Media.

MADAHIR.

A city to the East of Assyria, which was conquered by Dayan-assur, the Tartan of Shalmaneser II.

MADAKTU.

A capital city of Kudurnankhundi the Elamite, and which he abandoned in alarm at the approach of the army of Sennacherib.

MADSENEN.

A queen of Egypt in the Ethiopic period, or the XXVth dynasty. She was the wife of King Aspalut.

MADYAS.

The leader of the Scythians who invaded Media and Assyria in the reign of Bel-zikir-iskun, king of Assyria.

MAFKA.

The Egyptian name of the turquoise stone.

Magalani.

An Arabian kingdom rendered tributary by Esarhaddon.

Maganki.

The Accadian name of the city or land of Muzur or Egypt.

Maganna.

A city or kingdom conquered by Sargina I. and his son Naramsin. It has not yet been identified.

Maganna.

The most ancient Assyrian Cuneiform name of the kingdom of Egypt.

Maget.

A mystical demon in the Ritual of the Dead.

Magi.

A great caste among the Medes. *See* Magus.

Magru-sha-addari.

An intercalary month which was interpolated after Addaru every fourth year by the Assyrian astronomers.

Magru-sha-ululi.

An intercalary month, interpolated after Elul every eighth year by the Assyrian astronomers.

Magupaiti. "Chief of the Magi."

The Median term for a high-priest. It is rendered Mobed in the Behistun Inscription of Darius Hystaspes.

Magus.

In Phenician mythology a son ot the deity Agrotus and the brother of Amynus, the teacher of agriculture. *See* Amynus.

Magus. "The Great Ones."

The first caste of the ancient Medes; the Magi of the Greek historians.

Maha-deswara.

A Badaga idol. A form of Siva.

Mahallibausu.

A Phenician city conquered by Sennacherib on his first invasion of Palestine. It was the Hosah of Hebrew history.

Maha-negs.

The Egyptian little cubit, equal to five palms.

Mahar-gargar.

An Assyrian measure of length. The walls of Babylon were declared by Nabukuduruzur to extend to 4,000 *Mahagargar*, a distance which is supposed to equate exactly with the 480 stadia of Herodotus.

MAHA-SUTEN.

The royal Egyptian cubit, equal to seven palms, or 20·728 inches.

MAHA-UR.

The Egyptian great cubit, equal to six palms.

MAHINDO.

The brother of the Hindu emperor Asoka, who sent him, together with his sister Sangamitta, to convert the Ceylonese to the Buddhist faith, in which mission he was eminently successful. *See* Asoka.

MAHRAH.

A petty Arabian kingdom, which first became independent during the misgovernment of Yashdjob, king of Yemen.

MAHTE.

Among the Lithuanians the goddess of the procreative power of the earth. The Demeter of the Greeks.

MAHU.

A private Egyptian name, which occurs in the time of the XVIIIth dynasty.

MAHUT.

A kind of Egyptian hound used in the XIth dynasty. *See* Bahaka.

MAI.

The chief priest of the deity Osiris. He was a member of the great Egyptian family of Un-nefer. His wife was named Maani, and his son Un-nefer, which see.

MAI.

The son of Ua. He was the scribe of the army of an Egyptian king of the XVIIIth dynasty.

MAIN.

A Himyaritic capital city in South-western Arabia.

MAINYU.

In Zendic mythology a name of the Supreme Being.

MAI-PARI-NEFER.

A priest of Apis in the reign of Se-ra-nefer-tai, of the XVIIIth dynasty.

MAIRSURU.

The capital city of the kingdom of Harru, East of Assyria. It was conquered by Dayan-assur, the Tartan of Shalmaneser II.

MA-KA-RA.

The second title of Queen Hatasu, which see.

MAKARGINA.

A kind of Egyptian corslet or breastplate, which was sometimes wrought in gold and inlaid with lapis lazuli.

MAKARU.

An Assyrian measure of capacity, at present not exactly identified.

MAKATALA.

The Egyptian name of the Syrian city Migdol of Hebrew history.

MAKATARU.

A fortified city where Rameses III. counted the heads of the dead after his wars in Palestine. It was the Migdol of Rameses, of Hebrew history.

MAKDABI.

A city to the East of Assyria which was conquered by Dayan-assur the Tartan of Shalmaneser II.

MAKET-ATEN.

A daughter of Amenhotep IV. of the XVIIIth dynasty.

MAKHEN.

The mystical name of the boat of the souls of the dead in the Egyptian Ritual.

MAKKAN.

The Assyrian name of the kingdom of Lower Egypt.

MAKRU.

The astronomical name of the deity Marduk as the planet Mercury in the month of Ab.

MAKS.

An Egyptian town which was sacred to the deity Horus. Its site is unknown.

MAKT.

An uncertain Egyptian deity.

MALAMIR.

A place in Media where Sutur-Cit, king of Amardi, executed an inscription in honour of the gods Dipti and Turutur. It is now called Kul Faraum.

MALATYA.

Another name of the kingdom of Milid, near Armenia.

MALAVISKH.

A richly-dressed Etruscan goddess, with diadem, necklace, and jewels. She was represented as seated on a throne, and served by three female divinities, one of them being Munthukh, while Turan stands by.

MALEK-TAUS.

A deity adored by the Yezedees, in the Lebanon range. He was represented either as a cock, or a man with a cock's head.

MALICHAS.

A king of the Nabatheans, who is mentioned in the Periplus of Hanno.

MALICU.

The Assyrian title used to denote a petty chief, literally "A Kinglet."

MALIK. "King."

A son of Kahlan, king of Sabæa, in South-western Arabia. He wrested the province of Oman from his brother Wathil, king of Sabæa, and maintained it as a separate kingdom.

MALOULI.

An Egyptian deity of the later period. He was represented as wearing the warlike crown crested with the *Atef*. He was worshipped in Nubia.

MA-MAI.

A "Divine Father," or priest of Amen Ra and the goddess Maut. Period unknown.

MA-MA-MI-AMEN.

A surname of Rameses IV. of the XXth dynasty.

MAMAMIS.

A king of the country of the Luksai, who paid tribute to Samas Rimmon, king of Assyria.

MAMI. "The Waters."

The Accadian word from which the name of the Greco-Babylonian deity Moumis was derived.

MANAFF.

An ancient Arabian divinity. He was possibly a form of the sun.

MANAGINA.

An Assyrian measure of weight, equal to sixty shekels or *Ig*, equal to 1lb. 4oz. 8dwt.

MANDAUCES.

A king of the Medes, the successor of Arbaces. He reigned fifty years. (Ctesias.)

MANDONOPHIS.

The Greek form of the royal name Mentuhotep, which see.

MANDOTHPH.

A petty prince under the Persian rule in Egypt who revolted against Darius, and made himself king of Egypt for a short time.

MA-NEFER.

The son of Se-khem-ka, an Egyptian officer of the Vth dynasty.

MA-NEFER.

An Egyptian functionary in the court of King Assa-Tatkera, the last king but one of the Vth dynasty.

MANEH.

An Assyrian measure of weight, composed of two *Managineh*, equal to 2lbs. 8oz. 16dwt.

MANET-ANKH.

The wife of Harbenen, and mother of Ra-kherpa, a priest of Osiris in the XIIth dynasty.

MANETHO.

An Egyptian high-priest of Heliopolis in the reign of Ptolemy Philadelphus, about B.C. 290, by whose desire he compiled a History of Egypt, the materials for which he asserted he had obtained from inscriptions preserved in the temple of Thoth, or Hermes Trismegistus. His chronology, which has been handed down in a condensed condition by Africanus, and afterwards still further reduced by Syncellus and Eusebius, gives a period of 53,535 years for the duration up to that date of the Egyptian empire. The arrangement of the dynasties of Manetho is very uncertain, and though monumental records attest the general truth of his statements, the synchronization of them is one of the most difficult problems in Archaic chronology. *See* Table of Dynasties in the Appendix.

MANFALUT.

The modern name for the city and nome in Upper Egypt which was called by the Greeks Lycopolis-parva. It is famous for its mummy pits.

MANI.

In Scandinavian mythology the name of the moon deity.

MANIYAHE.

The king of the Dahe, one of the Persian tribes. He attempted to resist Sennacherib in his strong city Ukku, but was compelled to abandon the defence upon the approach of the Assyrians. The Dahe are supposed to have been the Dinaites of Hebrew writers.

MANNU-KI-ASSUR.

Governor of Gozan, in the reign of Vulnirari III. He was eponym of the year B.C. 794, the chief event in which was an expedition to Media.

MANNU-KI-ASSUR-LIHA.

The governor of Bile in the reign of Sargon I. He was eponym of the year B.C 709, the chief event in which was an expedition to Chaldea.

MANNUKIBABIL.

The governor of Dakkuri. He joined the revolt of Saulmugina, but was defeated and severely punished by Assurbanipal.

MANNU-KI-VUL.

The governor of Sallat in the reign of Shalmaneser III. He was eponym of the year B.C. 773, the chief event in which was an expedition to Damascus.

MANNUS.

In Teutonic mythology the son of the giant Tuisco, and the father of Istio, Ingnio, and Hermino, from whom the German races were descended.

MANSAKA.

A king of Magalani in Arabia, who paid tribute to Esarhaddon, by whom he was afterwards put to death.

MANSAKIR.

A king of Marabanu in Arabia. He was conquered by Esarhaddon.

MAN-TEF-EF.

The mystical name of one of the planks of the boat of souls in the XCIXth chapter of the Ritual of the Dead.

MANTU-MI-ANKHU.

The Assyrian form of the Egyptian royal name Mentu-em-ankh, which see.

MANU.

A name of the Supreme Being in the Vedic literature of Hindustan.

MANU.

A mythical personage in Vedic mythology to whom the Deluge was foretold by a fish, who further directed him to build an ark, and thus escape the flood. He did so, and on performing a sacrifice to the deity he had a daughter named Ida or Ila, by whom he became the father of mankind.

MANU.

The Egyptian name of the West, which was represented as a basin or deep valley in which the setting sun rested.

MARABANU.

A small kingdom in Arabia which was conquered for the first time by the Assyrians under Esarhaddon.

MARAD.

The Assyrian name of a city which was called by the Accadians Amardaki. Its site is unknown.

MARAIU.

One of five chiefs who incited the Libyans, to their great loss, to revo t against Rameses HI.

MARAM.

An unidentified Syrian town which was taken by Rameses II. after the battte of Kadesh.

MARAPHIANS.

The second of the ten great tribes of Persia. They were all warriors by profession.

MARASARA. *Or* MAURSAR.

A king of the Hittites. He was the son of Sapalala, and one of their most powerful leaders. Taking advantage of the discontent of the Canaanites with the Egyptian rule, he extended the power of the Hittite confederacy, which caused the invasion of Syria by Rameses I. to suppress it. His son Khitasira, or Khitasa, made peace with Rameses II. of the XIXth dynasty.

MARBUDA. "Long Road."

In Chaldean astronomy an unidentified fixed star.

MARDIANS.

The eighth of the ten great tribes of Persia. They were a nomadic shepherd caste.

MARDONIUS.

A Persian officer, the father of Gobryas, an officer and friend of Darius Hystaspes.

MARDUK.

Whose name is written Amarud or Silikmuludug, or phonetically Mar-duk, and is the Hebrew מארדך, was the son of Hea and Dav-kina, and the father of Nebo or Nabu, and the presiding deity of Eridu. The philosopher Damascius says that from Aus and Dauce came Belus the demiurgus, from whence it follows that Dauce is clearly Davkina. Marduk appears to partake of two natures : one as the servant of Anu and Elu or Bel, and also of his father Hea, in which he appears to resemble the Classic Mercury (Hermes) ; another attribute of his which would connect him with this deity was that of the guide of the souls of the deceased in Hades. In an Assyrian hymn he is spoken of as " He who raises the dead to life," and in cases of magic spells on a man, it is Marduk who, with the aid of his father Hea, delivers them. In his character of the warrior he resembles the Classic Zeus, in the " War of the Gods," especially where he fights against the evil and rebellious spirits as his Classic proto-type did against the Titans. It is Marduk also who in the creation legends plays the part of the archangel Michael, and fights against Tiamtu and her allies, being armed by Anu in the presence of the other gods, with a *saparra* or sword (comp. sabre) and a bow. Astronomically he is identified with the star Dil-gan or Mercury.

In the later Babylonian empire Marduk became the chief object of worship in his famous temple of Bit-saggal at Babylon. From the great importance of his worship in their times the Greek authors identified him with Zeus, and made him the head of the Babylonian pantheon. Marduk's consort was Zirat-banit, who may be identified with the Succoth-banit of the Bible. (Boscawen.)

MAREOTIS.

A nome of Lower Egypt on the lake of the same name. Its chief cities were Apis or Tapososiris, Marœa, and Phamothis.

MARGIANA.

The Greek name of the Iranian district of Muru, which see.

MARHASIKI.

The Accadian name of a town, the site of which is unknown.

MARHUNT.

An unidentified Egyptian city, which was vainly held by the rebel chiefs against Piankhi Mer-amen of the XXIInd dynasty.

MARIB.

A Himyaritic capital city, which was founded by the pre-Kahtanide Arabs. It was famous for a great dyke, the execution of which marked an era in Arabic history.

MARIHA.

A king of Damascus, and successor to Benhadad III. He, upon being threatened with an invasion by Vul-nirari III., at once tendered his submission and paid a heavy tribute; which example was followed by all the confederate states of Syria.

MARILSHI.

An Hindu deity, emanating from Brahma, and having the power of creation. *See* Angiras.

MARIS-HALNA.   "The Boy of Halna."

A boy who, on an Etruscan mirror, sits on the thigh of Lenith, the Etruscan spirit of "life." Probably he was the genius of beauty.

MARIS-HUSRNANA.   "The Boy of Husrnana."

A boy who, on an Etruscan mirror from Vulci, stands over a water-jug by the side of Menerva.

MARIS-ISMINTHIANS.   "The Boy of Isminthians."

A boy who, on an Etruscan mirror, sits on the thigh of Hermes.

MARIS-TURAN.   "The Boy of Venus."

The Etruscan Cupid. He was the Eros of the Greeks.

MARKATA.

A mystical title of Amen Ra, applied to him in the CLXVIth chapter of the Ritual of the Dead.

MARMAIU.

A king of the Libyans. He was the son of King Batta and Queen Deid, or Dido. He was lost in the battle fought against Menepthah II., by whom his people were with great loss defeated.

MARŒA.

The chief town of the Mareotic nome of Lower Egypt. It was also called Palæ-marea.

MARO-IUA-AMEN.

The chief and scribe of Kush, an officer in the court of King Aspalut of the XXVth dynasty.

MARQASI.

The capital city of Mutallu, king of Gaugama. After the captivity of Mutallu by Sargon II. the city was placed under the rule of an Assyrian governor.

MARRUAI.

A country rendered tributary by Samas-Rimmon, king of Assyria.

MARTHAD.

The brother of Abd-shems-aslam, which see.

MARTIUS.

The son of Sisicres. He incited the people of Susiana to revolt against Darius Hystaspes, himself claiming to be one of the old royal family named Omanes. He was slain by the Susians, when they found out that he was an impostor and that Darius was marching to attack them.

MARUBISTI.

The capital city of the kingdom of Illipa, in Elam, where Nipa, the rival king in opposition to his brother Ispabara, was defeated by Sargon I.

MARUDUK-BALAD-SU-IQBI. " Marduk proclaims his Life."

A king of Babylonia, who was completely routed and his kingdom plundered by an invasion of the Assyrians, under Samsi-Vul or Samas Rimmon III., king of Assyria, about B.C. 810.

MARUDUK-BAL-IDINNA I. " Marduk a Son has given."

An early Babylonian king, the son of Iribamaruduk. He built a temple to the goddess Nin-dimirri, probably one of the names of the goddess Nana, as her temple was called Bit-anna.

MARUDUK-BEL-USATE.

The foster-brother of Maruduk-zikur-izkir, king of Babylonia, against whom he rebelled, but who defeated and slew him by the help of Shalmaneser II., king of Assyria.

MARUDUK-BEL-UZUR.

The governor of Amida, in the first year of Shalmaneser IV. He was eponym of the year B.C. 726, in which year there "was peace in the land."

MARUDUK-MU-DAMIK. " Marduk the Prosperer."

The king of the country of Zimri, South-east of Assyria. He fled from the army of Shalmaneser II., who carried the spoil of his city to Assyria, and raised to the Zimrite throne Yanzu, the son of Haban.

MARUDUK-NADIN-AHI. " Marduk has given a Brother."

A king of Babylon. He twice made war with Assyria, defeating Tiglath-Pileser I., and carrying off into Babylon the statues of the deities Vul and Sala, where they remained till the capture of Babylon by Sennacherib, 418 years later.

MARUDUK-SADUA.

The governor of Sallat in the reign of Vul-nirari III. He was eponym of the year B.C. 796, the chief event in which was an expedition to Deri.

MARUDUK-SALIM-ANNI. " Marduk to me is Peace."

The chief of the palace of Assur-nirari II. He was eponym of the year B.C. 751, in which year there was peace in the land.

MARUDUK-SALIM-ANNI.

The Rabbitur of Assyria under Shalmaneser III.

MARUDUK-SAPIK-ZIRRAT.

A king of Babylon, about B.C. 1100. He preserved amicable relationship with Assur-bel-kala, king of Assyria.

MARUDUK-SAR-UZUR.

An Assyrian officer, to whom Tammaritu, king of Elam, submitted himself after his defeat by the Assyrian army.

MARUDUK-SAR-UZUR.

An Assyrian governor, in the reign of Vul-nirari III., the name of whose district is lost. He was eponym of the year B.C. 785, the chief events in which were an expedition to Hupuskia, and " the great god to Deri went."

MARUDUK-TAR. " Marduk the Judge."

The governor of Amidi, in the reign of Vul-nirari III., and eponym of the year B.C. 800, the chief event in which was an expedition to Media.

MARUDUK-UTU-LANI. " Marduk exalts me."

The Rabbitur of Shalmaneser III., and eponym of the year B.C. 779, the chief event in which was an expedition to Ararat.

MARUDUK-ZIKIR-IBNI. " Marduk, Maker of Renown."

The general of Urtaki, king of Elam. He persuaded his master to declare war against Assurbanipal, king of Assyria ; a war which was attended with fatal results to the Elamites.

MARUDUK-ZIKUR-IZKUR. " Marduk proclaims Renown."

A king of Babylon ; the son of Nabu-bal-idinna, whom he succeeded. His foster-brother, Maruduk-bel-usate, revolted against him, and took the city of Akkad ; but the king of Babylon defeated and killed the enemy by the aid of Shalmaneser I., king of Assyria.

MARUSU.

A tribe in Mesopotamia which was conquered by Tiglath Pileser II.

MARUTS.

In Vedic mythology the winds adored as deities. They are supposed to have been the origin of the Tritopatores of ancient Greek religion.

MARWA.

A hill near Mecca, where originally a sacred stone or Bætylia was adored by the ancient Arabians. It was displaced, and the idol Mazel, a figure representing a woman, erected there in its stead about the third century A.D. *See* Safa.

MARYAB.

An early capital city of the Himyarites in South-western Arabia.

MARYATALE.

In Hindu mythology the headless goddess of the Pariah caste ; she is said to have been the wife of a man named Shamadagani, by whose order his sons beheaded her.

MASA-HA-ROTA.

A son of Herhor-si-amen, of the XXIst dynasty.

MASA-KA-HAROTA.

A son of Herhor-si-amen, of the XXIst dynasty.

MASEMITAKI.

An Accadian city the site of which is not known.

MASEPAALKI.

An Accadian city the site of which is not known.

MASESARKI.

An Accadian city the site of which is not known.

MASHAKEN.

One of the five confederate chiefs who incited the Libyans to revolt against Rameses III.

MASHASHAR.

The son of Kapur, king of the Mashuasha. His father was killed and himself taken captive by Rameses III. in the war between the Egyptians and the Libyans.

MASHUASHA.

A people probably of Libyan origin, who on the Hieroglyphic inscriptions are classed with the Tamahu. They formed part of a coalition of the peoples of the Mediterranean, who invaded Egypt in the time of Menepthah, and afterwards again also in the reigns of Rameses II. and III. of the XIXth dynasty. This latter monarch completely subdued them, and they were then incorporated into the Egyptian army as an auxiliary body. They have been identified by Brugsch with the Maxues of Herodotus.

MASKIM. "Layer of Ambushes."

In Accadian mythology the name of a class of wicked spirits which afflicted mankind. They were called by the Assyrians Rabiz.

MASKU.

An Assyrian superficial measure, containing 60 square *sosses*, or 21,600 yards English.

MASPIANS.

The third of the ten great tribes of Persia. They were a warrior caste.

MASSA.

In Arabian history an Ishmaelite settlement mentioned by the Hebrew writers; probably Meshalik.

MASSUI.

A prince of Kush, in the reign of Rameses II. of the XIXth dynasty.

MASSUT.

An Elamite city (called Massut the Lower), which was destroyed by Sennacherib.

MASTARNA. Etruscan, MACSTRNA.

According to Etruscan tradition, the companion of Cœles Vibenna, who accompanied him to Rome, and there exchanged his name to Servius Tullius, and succeeded Tarquinius Priscus as king.

MATA. "Land *or* Country."

The Turanian word from which the name of the province of Media was derived.

MATABINTAIN.

A Himyaritic goddess, the chief deity of the capital city of Harâm.

MATAMIN.

The Egyptian name of an uncertain Egyptian city.

MATANBAAL.

A king of Arvad, or Aradus. He was a tributary of Esarhaddon.

MATAR.

In Arabian history an Amalekite tribe which settled in the district of Yathrib.

MATARUH. *Or* MATAREAH.

The modern name of the city and nome of Hak, in Lower Egypt.

MATEN.

The Egyptian name for Asia Minor, when it was rendered tributary by Thothmes III.

MATER-TURRITA. "Mother of Towers."

An ancient title of the goddess Rhea-Kybele.

MATHAN.

A king of Tyre; the son and successor of Baal-eazar II. He was rendered tributary to Assyria by Shalmaneser IV.(?) and during his reign the Tyrian settlements of Melos, Thera, and Rhodes were conquered by the Dorians. Mathan, on dying, left his crown to his son and daughter jointly, Pümeliun and Elissa, which see. That act led to the foundation of Carthage and the ultimate decadence of Tyre.

MATHAN-BAAL. *Or* MATINUBAHAL.

Another form of the name of Matan-bahil, king of Arvad, or Aradus.

MATIHIL.

The son of Agus, a Syrian prince, who was defeated by Tiglath Pileser II.

MATINUBAHAL.

King of Arvad. One of the confederacy of Syrian kings who were defeated at the battle of Qarqar by Shalmaneser II.

MATGENUS.

Another form of the Tyrian royal name Metinna, or Metinti, which see.

MATOI.

The name by which foreign auxiliary troops were called by the Egyptians under the Middle Empire.

MAT-QIU.

A people in the mountains of Mesopotamia who were subdued by Assur-risilim, king of Assyria.

MAT-SIRAUSAI.

A country which was rendered tributary by Samas-Rimmon, king of Assyria.

MATSURAMA.

The half-brother of Khitasira, king of the Hittites, who was killed by the Egyptians at the battle of Kadesh under Rameses II.

MATTI.

The king of Atuna. He was a tributary of Sargon I. ; and continuing faithful to that monarch during the revolt of the Armenian princes, was by him placed upon the throne of Sinuhta, in place of Kakki, the rebel king of that country, whom he had taken captive.

MATUZZA.

The father of Sasi, king of Patina. *See* Sasi.

MAURSAR.

A king of the Khitæ, or Hittites. He was the son of Sapalala, and the father of Khitasira, both of whom were defeated by, and made treaties of peace with, the Egyptians. No particulars are known of his reign.

MAUSHID.

The present name of the great seaport of ancient Arabia, which is called Muza.

MAUT. *Or* MUT.

A chief Egyptian goddess, the wife of Amen Ra, and the second member of the great Theban triad. She was considered as the mother goddess *par excellence*, or the great receptive female principle ; and she was generally represented as seated upon a throne, wearing either the Pschent, or sacred double crown, or else the body and plumes of a vulture as her headdress. She was dressed in a long robe, often richly ornamented, and she held in her right hand the usual Crux-ansata, and in her left the papyrus staff of the goddesses. Her chief titles were, " The Mother," " The Lady of Heaven," and " The Regent of all the Gods." The vulture was both her symbol and her sacred animal. Her analogues were in some of her attributes the Hera and Kybele and Thermuthis of the Greeks, and possibly the Bonadea of the Romans.

MAUTENARA.

A king of the Hittites. He was the son of Marasara, and was chiefly in wars with the kings of Egypt. He was succeeded by his brother Khitasira, who made peace with Rameses II.

MAUT-MAI.

An Egyptian lady, the wife of Hek-nofre, and the mother of Amen-her-atf, which see.

MAUT-NEFER. "The Good Maut."

An Egyptian lady, the wife or daughter of Se-maut, a priest of the XVIIIth dynasty.

MAUTNUR.

A king of the Khitæ, or Hittites, who was conquered by Seti I. of the XIXth dynasty, by whom he was restored to his dominions, upon signing a treaty more advantageous to himself and his people than to the Egyptians.

MAUTSE.

A priest of the god Horus, in the XVIIIth dynasty.

MAYCAR.

Among the ancient Arabs a gambling game, whereby lots were drawn for the limbs of a dismembered camel, and bets were made on the result of the lots.

MAZAIOU. *Or* MADJAIOU.

The Mazaiou were, in the time of the XIIth dynasty, a nation with whom the armies of the Egyptians had to contend ; but afterwards they became associated with them, and became incorporated into their service, in nearly the same manner as the Hebrews were at a later period. The Mazaiou do not appear on the inscriptions among the number of the regular troops, or among the auxiliaries employed in the military expeditions ; they corresponded exactly to the Phylakitai, whom Letronne regarded as a species of police, distributed over different nomes, and having the charge of certain specified towns. The chief of the Phylakitai of Thebes occupied a high position in society. (Chabas.)

MAZDEISM.

The general name of the Zendic religion of Dualism, or universal knowledge, containing the good law or Zend Avesta, said to have been compiled by Zarathustra.

MAZEL.

An idol in the form of a woman, which was erected on the hill Marwa, near Mecca, about the third century A.D., in place of a stone which had been formerly worshipped there. *See* Bætylia.

MAZIRAVUS.

A district bordering upon Assyria rendered tributary by Samsi-Vul or Samas-Rimmon III.

MAZZAROTH. "The Watch."

A constellation mentioned in the Book of Job. It may be considered to mean any constellation which indicated the three watches of the Babylonians by their successively rising over the meridian. (Fox Talbot.)

MEAN.

An Etruscan female spirit, with coronet, earrings, and wings, who seems to have borne the same office as Lasa. Sometimes she has two palm-branches in her hands, she is sometimes represented as crowning Herakles.

MECHIR.

The sixth month of the Egyptian sacred year. It began about the 17th of December.

MEDINET-ABU.

The present name of the ruins of the temples of Thothmes II. and Rameses III. at the base of the Theban mountains, on the left bank of the Nile.

MEDJMAA.

An Arabian town in the Northern Neged. It was the Mishma of Hebrew writers.

MEGABIGNES.

A Persian officer, the father of Hydarnes, an officer and friend of Darius Hystaspes.

MEGIDDO.

A town in Palestine where Thothmes III. of the XVIIIth dynasty defeated the combined armies of the Syrians, taking captive 340 prisoners, 2,132 horses, and 924 war chariots. The city was afterwards blockaded and reduced to submission by famine, and rendered tributary to Egypt. It was subsequently re-built by Solomon, and again conquered by Shishak of the XXIInd dynasty.

MEHERBAAL.

King of Tyre. He succeeded Baal-ator, who was dethroned, and himself, a prince of the ancient royal house, released from captivity in Babylon, and made king by Nabonidus, king of Chaldea. He reigned four years, and was succeeded by his brother, Hiram III.

MEHHUR.

A mystical divinity, " The Flood." (?) He is mentioned in the LXXIst chapter of the Ritual of the Dead.

MEHI.

An Egyptian lion-headed goddess ; one of the forms of Pasht, or Sekhet.

MEHT-EM-I-SEKHET.

The wife of Psametik I. of the XXVIth dynasty.

MEHT-NASKHTI.

An auditor of justice in the royal throne room of an unnamed king.

MEINES.

A prince of Kush, in the reign of Amenhotep III. of the XVIIIth dynasty.

MEIRE.

A priest of Netpe. Period uncertain. He was called also a "Guardian of the White Hall," probably the city of Memphis.

MEIRI.

A priest of the temple of Pthah, at Memphis. Period uncertain.

MELEKITHIAN.

A king of Kition and Idalion, in the Island of Cyprus.

MELEK-KIRYATH. *Or* MELKARTH. "King of the City.

A Phenician title of the deity Baal, as titular lord of Tyre. *See* Baal.

MEMNON.

The name given by the Greeks to a colossal statue of Amenhotep III., one of two which was set up by that king in the Nubian desert. Having been many times restored, it was at last thrown down by an earthquake, in the reign of Tiberius Cæsar, B.C. 27, and after it was rebuilt, was found to possess the strange property of uttering a musical sound upon the first light of day falling upon its face. The Greeks, according to their mythology, explained this as an adoration by Memnon to his mother Aurora; but the wonder was probably the result of art. The legs are covered with Greek inscriptions recording the visits of kings and philosophers to hear the sacred music. This statue and its companion are now popularly called by the Arabs Shamy and Damy.

MEMPHIS.

The Greek form of writing the name Mennefer, "Good Port." A town at the base of the Delta, now called Menf and Mitraheneh, the seat of empire of the IIIrd, IVth, Vth, VIIth, and VIIIth Egyptian dynasties, and perhaps the oldest capital of Lower Egypt. Of the former greatness of this city there are now no remains except funereal ones; the whole district is a vast necropolis, extending from the pyramids of Gizeh to those of Sakkara. The deities chiefly adored in the city were Pthah and his son Imhotep, and with these two gods was conjoined the goddess Sekhet to complete the triad, Sekhet being called in that capacity the "Chief Friend of Pthah." Near to Memphis was the temple of the Serapeum, or the subterranean tombs of the Apis bulls. The ancient name of the city, Mennefer, "The Good Port," occurs in the inscriptions, and it was probably on account of its proximity to the water that Thothmes I., Rameses I., and Menepthah II., had palaces there; but of those buildings not even the indications remain.

MEMPHITE NOME.

The Greek name for the city and nome in Lower Egypt which was called by the Egyptians Seb-thet.

MEMRA.   "The Word."

The name employed in the Targum of Onkelos, and all later Hebrew books, for the expression of the name of the Deity in all his relations to man.

MEMRUMUS.

In Phenician mythology a giant descended from Capius.   He with his brother inhabited Tyre.   *See* Usous.

MEMRUN.

The Etruscan form of the name of a mythological personage who was analogous to the Memnon of the Greeks.

MEN.

A peculiar form of wide-mouthed jar, used by the Egyptians for offering food to the gods.

MEN.

Another name of the great Egyptian deity Amen Ra, which see.

MEN.

A royal Egyptian scribe.   The period when he lived is uncertain.

MEN.

A city and nome in Lower Egypt, sacred to the ram deity Ban-ded, Ba-en-tattu, or Mendes.   It was the Mendesian nome of the Greeks.

MENA.

A name by which the Hykshos kings were called by the Egyptians.

MENAHEM.   In Assyrian, MINIHIM.

King of Israel.   He slew the usurper Shallum, and seized the throne of Samaria, where he reigned ten years.   His first act was to capture Tiphsah (Thapsacus?).   In B.C. 743 and B.C. 738 he paid tribute to Tiglath Pileser II., the Assyrian king (called Pul in the Old Testament). He was succeeded by his son Pekahiah.

MENA-NU-SAT.   "Shepherds of the East."

A nomadic people of Arabia who were subdued by king Senefru of the Vth dynasty.

MENAT-KHUFU.

A province in Eastern Egypt which was governed by the semi-royal family of Khnum-hotep in the XIIth dynasty.

MENCHERES I.

According to the Greek lists the successor of Sensuphis, king of Memphis; possibly the Menkera of the IVth dynasty.

MENCHERES II.

The Greek form of the name of King Menkauhor of the Vth dynasty, which see.

MENDES.

A town in the Delta, Lower Egypt, now called Ashmoun, the seat of empire of the XXIXth Egyptian dynasty. It was raised to the dignity of a kingdom under the name of Bendidi during the Assyrian Icosarchy. It was held by the Calasirian class of warriors. Here also was fought the battle of Mendes between Nekhtarhebi of the XXXth dynasty, and Artaxerxes II., his suzerain, king of Persia, whom he utterly defeated, and together with his army, expelled from the Delta. It was sacred to the worship of the ram Mendes.

MENDESIUS.

A nome of Lower Egypt, East of the Phatnitic branch of the Nile. Its chief cities were Thmuis and Mendes.

MENELAITES.

A nome in Lower Egypt, West of the Phatnitic branch of the Nile. Its chief city was Anthylla. The nome was named after Menelaus, a brother of Ptolemy Soter.

MENENBA.

An overseer of the temple of Amen Ra at Thebes. Period uncertain.

MENEPTHAH I. " Beloved by Pthah."

The second title of Seti I. of the XIXth dynasty, the founder of the Semitic race of the Ramesside dynasty. *See* Seti I.

MENEPTHAH II.

A king of the XIXth dynasty, and the son and successor of Rameses II. He was originally appointed governor of Memphis by his father, and to that city he removed the seat of empire, probably in order to keep in subjection the people of the Delta, who were being continually harassed by the Canaanites and Libyans. He also raised the worship of Pthah, the local deity of Memphis, to greater honour than that of Amun. At Paari in Libya, he fought against the Libyans and Greeks who, assisted by the Mashuash, had invaded Egypt, and defeated them with a loss on the side of the enemies of 12,535 people and 9,376 prisoners. After this he returned to Egypt with great spoil, and carried on the important works begun by his father. Towards the close of his reign a second foreign invasion is said to have occurred, an event which has been confounded with the exodus of Hebrew history, and of which no complete particulars remain. Menepthah II. married a queen named Hesi-nefer-et, by whom he had a son Seti II. or Menepthah III., who succeeded him on the throne. He reigned thirty years.

MENEPTHAH III.

The son of Menepthah II. and Queen Hesi-nefer-et. He was properly called Seti Menepthah II., and it is uncertain whether he immediately succeeded his father, or whether another short reign intervened between them. According to some historians he was taken for safety to Ethiopia, during the second Semitic invasion of Egypt under Osarsiph(?). He at first recognised the rule of the usurper Sipthah, or the pseudo-Menepthah II., and received from him the title of Viceroy of Ethiopia, but after a lapse of thirteen years (Manetho) he caused himself to be proclaimed king. and entering Thebes in triumph deposed both Sipthah and his co-adjutor Amenmeses. He reigned for many years, but except a small temple at Thebes, has left no memorials deserving notice. On a tablet at Abusimbel he is called a conqueror, but details of his conquests are wanting. It is even uncertain whether Amenmeses and Tauser or Sipthah did not again succeed him on the throne. It is however certain that he left no issue, and that with him terminated the XIXth dynasty.

MENERUVA.

An Etruscan form of the name of the Latin goddess Minerva. *See* Menerva.

MENERVA. *Or* MENRVA, *or* MENERUVA, *or* MENARVA.

The Latin Minerva, a deity borrowed by the Etruscans. The word is derived from the root *man*, " to think," whence come in Latin *mens*, " mind," *memor*, " mindful," and *moneo*, " to advise."

MENES. " The Stable," *or* " Firm."

The first king of Egypt, founder of the Egyptian empire and of the city of Memphis. He was a great law-giver, embanked the river Nile, and excavated a canal. He fought against the Libyans, and was devoured by a crocodile while bathing in the Nile.

MENES. *Or* MENA.

A name which was also borne by a Coptic Christian long after the downfall of the Egyptian empire.

MENF.

The modern name for the Egyptian city and nome of Memphis, which see.

MENHIT.

An early Egyptian royal name.

MENKAUHOR.

A king of the Vth dynasty. He made an expedition to the copper mines at Mount Sinai, reigned eight years, and was buried in a pyramid the site of which is not known. He was the Mencheres II. of the Greeks.

MENKERA.

A king of Egypt of the IVth dynasty. He built the third pyramid, restored the worship of the gods which had been neglected, and greatly increased the adoration of Osiris. He reigned sixty-three years, and was the Mycerinus of the Greeks. His sarcophagus and a portion of his mummy is in the British Museum.

MENKHEPER.

A high-priest of the god Mentu. Period uncertain.

MEN-KHEPER-RA.

A king of the XXIst dynasty, the successor of Pisem I. He was succeeded by Petu-ankhi I.

MEN-KHEPER-RA.

The royal surname of Thothmes III., king of the XVIIIth dynasty.

MEN-KHET-U.

An Egyptian lady, the mother of Merri, the superintendent of public works and canals in the reign of Osirtesen I. of the XIIth dynasty.

MEN-KHET-U.

An Egyptian lady, the wife of the captain Mentun-sasu in the reign of Amenemha I. of the XIIth dynasty.

MEN-NA.

The charioteer of Rameses II., whose bravery enabled his royal master almost single-handed to escape from an ambuscade into which his impetuosity had led him at the battle of Kadesh.

MEN-NEFER.   " The Good Port."

The ancient name of the city of Memphis.

MEN-NEFER.

The name given to the pyramid in which Pepi-Merira, an Egyptian king of the VIth dynasty, was interred.

MEN-NEFER-EN-KABI.

A kind of bracelets which were worn by the ancient Egyptians.

MEN-NEFER-ENTUT.

Another kind of bracelets worn by the ancient Egyptians.

MEN-NEFER-HET.

An early unarranged Egyptian king.

MEN-NU.

An Egyptian officer, the son of the captain Mentun-sasu and the lady Men-khetu, in the court of Amenemha I. of the XIIth dynasty.

MENOUTHES.

The Greek name of the Egyptian city Mer-neter, which see.

MENSA.   " City of Pots" (Vases).

An early Egyptian town sacred to Athor.   Site unknown.

MENSH.

The name of the Egyptian mercantile boat, or one-sailed galley.

MENSHECH.

The modern name of the Greco-Egyptian town of Ptolemais in the Thebaid.

Menskhera.

An early unarranged Egyptian king. *See* Menkera.

Ment-em-saf.

An Egyptian king of the VIth dynasty, and the brother of Queen Neit-aker. He reigned only one year, being assassinated in a revolution. He was the Menthesuphis of the Greeks.

Menthesuphis.

According to the Greek lists he was the successor of Phiops, king of Memphis. This is the Greek form of the Egyptian royal name Ment-em-saf, which see.

Mentu.

A first priest of Amen Khem. The time when he lived is uncertain.

Mentu.

An Egyptian warlike deity, a form of the god Ra. He was worshipped at Hermonthis and the Thebaid generally. He was represented with the head of a hawk, surmounted by the solar disk with two upright feathers, and holding the sword called a *Khopesh* in his hand. He is the form of Amen, of whom, in the poem of Pent-aur, Rameses II. implored, and was believed to have received help, when he fought against the Hittites at the battle of Kadesh.

Mentu-em-ankh. "Mentu the Living."

King of Thebes, one of the twenty kings of Egypt under the Assyrian Icosarchy.

Mentu-hotep I. "Peace of Mentu."

The second king of the XIth dynasty of Egypt. He succeeded Antef I. He was the Mandonophis of the Greeks.

Mentu-hotep II.

The fourth king of the XIth dynasty. He succeeded Antef-Aa II., and is said to have conquered thirteen nations. He dwelt chiefly at Coptos, where he built a temple to Ammon and Khnum.

Mentu-hotep III.

The sixth king of the XIth Egyptian dynasty. He appears to have been the first king to whom while living the title of "His Holiness" was applied. He reigned forty-three years.

Mentu-hotep.

The father of Sebekhotep II. of the XIIIth dynasty, but he was not himself a king of Egypt.

Mentu-hotep.

The son of Ankh-karo-amat, the daughter of Takelot II. of the XXIInd dynasty.

MENTU-HOTEP.

A grandson of King Sebekhotep II. of the XIIIth dynasty.

MENTU-HOTEP.

An Egyptian officer of the XIIth dynasty, the son of Mentuhotep, a royal officer, and his wife Ai. He was the General in Chief of the royal army, and as such accompanied the king in all his expeditions. He was also called a " Royal Parent," and a prophet of Ma.

MENTU-HOTEP.

An Egyptian, the son of Iri-sen-aker and his wife Hapu, by whom he was named after the name of the reigning sovereign of the XIth dynasty.

MENTUN-SASU.

An Egyptian captain and *Sutenrekh*, in the reign of Amenemha I. of the XIIth dynasty. He had a wife named Men-khetu, and a son Mennu.

MENTU-RA.

A priest of Amen Ra, under the reign of Osorkon I. of the XXIInd dynasty. He was also surnamed Neb-neteru.

MER.

The water-coast or canal boundary of an Egyptian nome.

MERA.

A mystical divinity who is mentioned in the CXLth chapter of the Ritual of the Dead.

MERA.   *Or* MERI-RA.

The surname of the Egyptian king Pepi of the VIth dynasty, which see.

MERA-HBA-SAHU.   " Lower World Mummy."

The name of the fourth of the seven mystical cows or Hathors of Egyptian mythology, who are mentioned in the CXLIXth chapter of the Ritual of the Dead.

MER-AMEN.   " He who loves Amen Ra."

The royal surname of Aahmes I. of the XVIIIth dynasty.

MER-AMEN.

The surname of Piankhi II., an Egyptian king of the XXIInd dynasty. *See* Piankhi.

MER-AMEN-SE-AMEN.

Another name of the Egyptian king of the XXIst dynasty who was called Smendes by the Greeks.

MER-ANKHES.

The daughter of an unidentified early Egyptian king.

MER-BA.

The sixth king of Egypt, of whom no events are recorded. He reigned twenty years. He was called by the Greek writers Miebies.

MERED. "Rebel."

A Hebrew prince, who is said to have taken to wife Bithiah, the daughter of Pharaoh, a circumstance not yet discovered in the Egyptian inscriptions.

MEREN-HOR.

An early Egyptian king, who is named on the Tablet of Abydos.

MERE-PHRE.

An overseer of the gatekeepers of the temple of Amen Ra. Period uncertain. His name is also written Meri-ra.

MERE-SU-RA.

A royal scribe, the father of the scribe Heti, and grandfather of Eopeii, the royal scribe of the palace of Memphis.

MERET-PA.

The mother of the royal scribe Sa-pthah, which see.

MER-HAB.

A high functionary of the IVth dynasty, the father of Nesemab, which see.

MER-HET.

The son of an early Egyptian king.

MERHET-NETS.

The grandson of Tetet, an early Egyptian king of the Ist dynasty.

MERHU.

An Egyptian prince, the son of Pthah-neferka and his sister Ahura. According to the romance of Setnau he was drowned in the river Nile as a punishment for his father's sacrilege. *See* Pthah-neferka *and* Setnau.

MERI.

An Egyptian lady, the sister of the priest and doctor Rekh-mara, of the XVIIIth dynasty.

MERI.

A grand priest of Osiris, in the reign of Rameses II. *See* Unnefer.

MERI. "The Lake."

The Egyptian name given to the great reservoir of Amenemha III., which the Greeks pronounced Mœris and converted into the name of a king.

MERI.

An Egyptian official of the Vth dynasty. He was chief of the writers of the Royal Register, chief of the sacred scribes, chief of the House of War, chief of the House of the Princess, priest of the goddess Rannu, and priest of the god Horus. This accumulation of offices was common at all times in Egyptian history.

MERI-AMEN. "Beloved of Amen."

The sacerdotal title of the Egyptian king Rameses II., which see.

MERI-AMEN-RAMESES.

The name of a well dug by order of Rameses II. for the use of the Egyptian miners at the gold mines of Akaitau or Kuban.

MERI-AN.

A royal personage of the XVIIIth or XIXth dynasty. He was royal secretary, royal writer, and master of the Royal House, either at the same time or successively. He had a sister a priestess, named Anai.

MERI-BAST.

The father of a high-priest of Amen Ra, in the reign of Rameses IX. of the XXIst dynasty.

MERI-EM-A.

An Egyptian king of the Vth dynasty. He was the son and successor of Pepi Merira.

MERI-EN-SEKAR.

An Egyptian goddess, generally represented as an uræus serpent. She was more frequently called Rannu, the goddess of harvest.

MERI-RA.

An Egyptian captain of the XVIIIth dynasty. His father's name was Atef-neb-ma, and that of his mother Hapiu.

MERI-RA. "He who loves Ra."

The surname of Thothmes III. of the XVIIIth dynasty.

MERI-S-ANKH.

A queen of Egypt, priestess of Thoth, and wife of Shafra, a king of the IVth dynasty.

MERISMOI.

The trades taxes of the Greco-Egyptian Empire under the Ptolemaic dynasties. They were collected three times a year.

MERI-S-TE-KHU. "That which loves Joy."

The mother of Ameni a great officer of state in the reigns of Amenemha I. and II. of the XIIth dynasty.

MERIT.

The wife of Antef, an Egyptian officer of the XIIth dynasty.

MERI-TUM.

The seventh son of Rameses III., who is said by some authorities to have succeeded Rameses VIII.

MERIUI.

A royal scribe of the XVIIIth dynasty. His father, Uetu, was the chief of the Keneb, an uncertain Egyptian priestly class.

MER-KA-NESHU. *Or* ANKH-HOR.

One of the thirteen petty kings of Egypt, who rebelled against, and were subdued by, Piankhi the Ethiopian, of the XXIInd dynasty.

MER-MER-TI.

According to M. Brugsch the Egyptian name of the country of Marmorica, in Lower Libya.

MER-MES. *Or* MERI-MES.

A prince of Ethiopia. The period when he lived is uncertain.

MER-NEB-PTHAH.

An unknown Egyptian king. He was the father of Pthah-nefer-ka and Ahura, in the ancient Egyptian romance called the Story of Setnau.

MER-NETER. "Divine Mer."

An Egyptian city, the Menouthes of the Greek writers. It was also called Pe-neter.

MERODACH.

A Babylonian deity. *See* Marduk *and* Silik-mulukhi *or* Silik-muludug.

MERODACH-BALADAN. *Or* MARUDUK-BAL-IDDINA.

He was son of Yagina (Ptolemy's Yugæus), and king of the Caldai (Chaldeans), a tribe settled on the shores of the Persian Gulf. Tiglath-Pileser II. received tribute from him at Sapiya, in B.C. 731. In B.C. 721, he conquered Babylon, and made himself king of Babylonia; the Chaldeans henceforth becoming part of the Babylonian population. In B.C. 711 he sent an embassy to Hezekiah to ask for alliance, and in B.C. 710 was dethroned by Sargon. On Sargon's death he returned to Babylon, but was defeated at Kis, by Sennacherib, and driven to his ancestral kingdom in the marshes. Thence he was expelled by Sennacherib, in B.C. 700, and fled to Nagitu-Racci, at the mouth of the Eulæus, his younger son, Nahid-Merodach, being made king of the sea-coast. He died before the destruction of Nagitu by the Assyrians, in B.C. 697. Two kings of the same name have been assumed, but the Cuneiform inscriptions know only of the son of Yagina. He was the Mardokempadus of Ptolemy. (Sayce.)

MERODACH-BALADAN.

The form of the Babylonian royal name Maruduk-bal-iddina in Hebrew history.

MERODACH-BAL-UZUR.

The governor of the city of Amida, in the reign of Shalmaneser VI.

MERODAK-MU-BASA.

An early Chaldean astronomer, some observations by whom have been preserved in the Cuneiform inscriptions. He was the father of Nebozucipunu, who was also an astronomer.

MERRI.

An Egyptian superintendent of canals and public works, in the reign of Osirtesen I. of the XIIth dynasty. He was the son of Menkhetu, and had a son named Antef.

MER-SEN-AKI.

The chief commander of the troops in the nome of Kahesbu. He revolted against Piankhi Meramen, together with other chiefs of Lower Egypt, but he was compelled to yield obedience.

MERTE. *Or* MILT.

An uncertain Egyptian goddess, who was generally represented as wearing a tuft of lotus or papyrus flowers upon her head.

MER-TETES.

The granddaughter of Tetet, an early Egyptian king of the Ist dynasty.

MER-TETES.

The wife of Saf-hotep-heta, the son of King Tetet. She was also called Hap-tek.

MERT-HAPI.

The sister of Nectanebos I. or II. of the XXXth dynasty.

MERT-KHA-RA.

A son of Rameses II. of the XIXth dynasty.

MERT-U.

An Egyptian officer of the Ancient Empire, between the VIth and XIIth dynasties. His wife's name was the same as his own, which was another instance of masculine names as applied to women in ancient Egypt.

MERT-U.

The wife of the preceding officer of the same name.

MERU.

.In Hindu mythology a mountain in the North-west of Thibet. It was supposed to be the pillar which unites the earth and heaven, and also the abode of the gods.

MES.

An early Egyptian astronomer, some observations by whom have been preserved.

MESHA.

A king of Moab. He was the son of Chemosh-Gad, and successfully resisted the invasion of the land of Moab by Jehoram king of Israel and Jehoshaphat king of Judah. He was a great builder and restorer, and rebuilt many towns which had fallen into decay. The famous Moabite Stone was erected by him as a thank-offering to Chemosh.

MESHALIK.

A district in Arabia, the Massa of Hebrew writers.

MESHIA.

In Zendic mythology the name of the first man created by Ahuramazda. Contrary to the express direction of Ahuramazda, he was seduced by Ahriman into believing creation to have been the work of that demon ; and when his heart was thus inclined towards him, he was persuaded to eat some evil fruit, and thus became one of the Darvands, and lost Paradise.

MESHIANA.

In Zendic mythology the name of the first woman, who shared in all the advantages, and fell into all the sins, of her husband.

MESISIMARDOCH.

A rebel king of Babylon who usurped the throne after the death of Assurnadin, and during the exile of Merodach-baladin. He seems to have reigned but for a short time.

MESKA.

A region of the Ker-neter which is mentioned in the XCIXth chapter of the Ritual of the Dead.

MESKEN.

According to the Egyptian Ritual of the Dead a place of new birth, situated in one of the islands of the celestial Nile.

MESOCHRIS.

According to the Greek lists a king of the IIIrd Egyptian dynasty. He reigned seventeen years.

MESORE.

The twelfth month of the Egyptian year. It began about 15th June.

Mes-sit.

A granddaughter of Tetet, an early Egyptian king of the Ist dynasty.

Mesta.

A feminine divinity or spirit who is mentioned in the CXXXVIth chapter of the Ritual of the Dead.

Mestem.

The Egyptian name of kohl or stibium, a preparation of antimony which was used for darkening the eyelashes both of men and women.

Mesu.   "Son."

A common Egyptian name in the XIXth and XXth dynasties.

Metelis.

The chief city of the Metelite nome.

Metelites.

A nome of Lower Egypt, West of the Phatnitic branch of the Nile. Its chief city was Metelis.

Meten-hont.

The mother of Namurot or Nimrod, a prince of the blood royal of the XXIInd dynasty.

Metenna.

A king of Tyre who paid tribute to Tiglath Pileser I., king of Assyria. He was the successor of Lulya.

Met-hont-mimut.

The chief of the palace of Amen in the reign of Sheshonk I.

Methusuphis.

According to the Greek lists the successor of Phiops, king of Memphis. He has not yet been certainly identified.

Metinti.

A king of Ascalon who was defeated by Tiglath Pileser I.

Met-naschti-s-mouth.

An Egyptian lady attached to the worship of Amen Ra.   Her statue is in the Leyden Museum.   Period uncertain.

Met-su-khons.

An Egyptian gentleman, whose statue is in the Leyden Museum.

Meturnat.

A town in Babylonia near the river Turnat. It was conquered by Shalmaneser II., king of Assyria, when he marched to the relief of Maruduk-zikur-izkur, king of Babylonia.

MI-AMEN.

A son of Rameses II. of the XIXth dynasty.

MI-AMEN.

The surname of Rameses XII. of the XXth dynasty.

MIANE.

An Egyptian (?) lady, the wife of Ua, the scribe of the cavalry of an unnamed king of the XVIIIth dynasty.

MI-ATUM-U.

A son of Rameses II. of the XIXth dynasty.

MIBAHU.

The son of an Egyptian king, but of what king it is not known.

MIBAMPES.   " Lover of Iron."

According to some Egyptologists the seventh king of the Ist Egyptian dynasty. (Basil H. Cooper.)

MICATH-EL-MAKT.   "Shameful Marriages."

In pre-koranic history the Arabian name for the unions of step-mothers and step-sons, an ancient custom which was abolished by Mahomet.

MICHÆL.

In Cabalistic astronomy the angel of the planet Mercury.

MICROCEPHALIC.   " Small Headed."

A term used by modern anthropologists to describe a species of skull which is generally smaller than the proportion ordinarily found to prevail in a race or tribe.

MIDAS.

An early Phrygian king, whose tomb exists in the valley of Sangarius. He must not be confounded with the mythical Midas of Classic history.

MIDGARD.

In Scandinavian mythology the name of the great evil serpent inhabiting the ocean which surrounds the mundane ash tree Yggdrasil.

MIEBIES.

The Greek form of the name Merba, which see.

MI-EN-PTHAH.   " Loved of Pthah."

A son of Rameses II. of the XIXth dynasty.

MIGDIARA.

The father of Khirtsina, king of the Nahri. *See* Khirtsina.

MIKDIARA.

The father of an Elamite or Armenian king named Sarzina, which see.

MILDIS.

A mountain district in Mesopotamia which was conquered by Tiglath Pileser I.

MIL-HEKAL.

The controller of the palace of the kings of Assyria.

MILID.

A kingdom near Armenia which paid tribute to Tiglath Pileser II.

MILIK.   " King."

The minister of state in the palace of the kings of Assyria.

MILIK-HARBAT.

An early Babylonian name rendered also Nis-Belu, " Man of Bel."

MILI-SIHU.

An early Babylonian king, the successor of Nazirudas, of whom nothing else is known.

MILKIASAPA.

A king of Gebal.   He was a tributary of Esarhaddon.

MILLID.

A district to the North-west of Assyria, conquered by Shalmaneser II.

MILT.

See the goddess Merte.

MILUKHA.

The Accadian name of the land of Kusu or Ethiopia.

MIMANSA.

An ancient Hindu treatise on divine wisdom and on religious ceremonies.   It is one of the greater Shastras.

MIMIR.

In Scandinavian mythology the name of the great giant, the keeper of the fountain of wisdom beneath the mundane ash tree Yggdrasil, which see.

MIN.

An Egyptian deity who was worshipped in the town and nome of Hor-ti and Se-khem.   He was a form of the ithyphallic deity Amen Khem.

MINASE.

The Assyrian form of the Hebrew royal name Manasseh.

MINIEH.

The modern name of the city and nome in Upper Egypt which was called by the Greeks Hermopolis the Lower.

MINIHIM.

A king of Samaria. He paid tribute to Tiglath Pileser II. after the defeat by that king of the Syrian confederation. He was the Menahem of Hebrew history.

MINUA.

The son of Ispuni, king of Ararat or Armenia. He increased the extent of his kingdom by making inroads into Syria, Media, and Minni, and was succeeded by his son Argistis.

MI-RA.

A son of Rameses II. of the XIXth dynasty.

MI-RA.

Another son, so named, of Rameses II.

MISA-NANA-KAL-AMMI.

An early Chaldean king and priest. His capital city was Ridu. No particulars of his reign are known.

MISAPHRIS.

According to the Greek lists the name of an Egyptian king of the XVIIIth dynasty. He is not certainly identified.

MISHMA.

An Arabic town mentioned by Hebrew writers. *See* Medjmaa.

MISIANDA.

A district of Minni which unsuccessfully revolted against Sargon II.

MISOR. "The Egyptian."

In Phenician mythology a descendant of the mythical semi-deities Amynus and Magus, which see.

MISPHRAGMUTHOSIS.

As recorded by the Greek writers, the name of one of the XVIIIth dynasty kings. He is not certainly identified with any known king of Egypt.

MISTA.

In Scandinavian mythology one of the two Walküres of Odin. *See* Nista *and* Walküres.

MISTHOTAI.

The publicans to whom the Ptolemaic kings of Egypt farmed out the collection of the trades taxes. They were replaced by the Epiteretai.

MITA.

The king of Muska, a kingdom on the Black Sea. He several times revolted against the Assyrians, and slew the king of Que, adding his provinces to his own ; but he was at last defeated by the new governor, whom Sargon II. sent to control the state of Que, and his kingdom was then added to Assyria.

MIT-AMEN.

A daughter of Rameses II. of the XIXth dynasty.

MIT-ATEN.

A daughter of Amenhotep IV. of the XVIIIth dynasty.

MIT-ATEN.

The wife Ra-saa-k̇a-kheper-u, a king of the XVIIIth dynasty.

MITATTI.

The king of Zikarti in Armenia. He urged the people of Minni to rebel against Sargon I., king of Assyria, who quickly reduced them to obedience and carried the inhabitants of the towns of Suandahal and Zurzukka into slavery.

MITHRA.

In Zendic mythology a son of Ahuramazda, and consubstantial with him. He was the great mediator between the gods and men. He was also the guardian of men during life, and their judge after death. (Lenormant.) *See* Mithra-Daradj.

MITHRA-DARADJ.　"The Evil Mithra."

In Zendic mythology a powerful and wicked spirit created by Ahrimanes, in antagonism to the Mithra, son of Ahuramazda, and being in all respects his counterpart in an evil sense. (Lenormant.)

MITUNA.

A city near Damascus conquered by Tiglath Pileser II. on his way to assist Ahaz, king of Judah.

MITUNU.

The governor of Isana in the reign of Sennacherib. He was the eponym of the year B.C. 700, the chief event in which was an expedition to Babylon.

MLAKUKH.

An Etruscan love-goddess, who was represented as violated by Herakles.

MNA.

A species of jewelled or embroidered collar among the Egyptians ; it differed from the *Uskh* in being concentric, and not like the other, a half hoop only.

Mnestasa.

The wife of Evagreton, the Cretan, which see.

Mnevis.

The sacred bull of Heliopolis. It was black in colour, and was regarded as an incarnation of the god Ra. On a medal of the Heliopolite nome Mnevis is represented as wearing the solar disk, surmounted by the two feathers of Amen Ra ; but in a bronze statuette in the possession of M. Selim of Paris, he is adored simply with the disk and uræus.

Mobed.

The Persian word for a high-priest. *See* Magupaiti.

Modgudhr.

In Scandinavian mythology a virgin goddess who guarded the bridge over the river Giöll, which formed the boundary of hell.

Modiniel.

In Cabalistic mythology the spirit of the planet Mars.

Mœotes.

A mud fish which was worshipped at the Egyptian town of Abu or Elephantine.

Mœtis.

The Greek form of the name of the lake Meri, which see.

Mohar.

The title of an Egyptian superintendent or military officer.

Moloch-ram.

Another form of the name of that king of Edom who was contemporary with the invasion of Edom by Sennacherib. He was also called Airammu, which see.

Momemphis.

A town in the Hermopolite nome in Lower Egypt. It was famous for the battle fought there by Psametik, king of Egypt of the XXVIth dynasty, aided by the Lydians lent by Gyges, king of Lydia, and the Assyrian army headed by the tributary kings of the Icosarchy.

Monat.

An Arabian goddess, possibly a form of the moon. She was called by the Egyptians the Lady of Arabia, and was worshipped at Codayd, between Mecca and Yathrib, where she was represented as a shapeless stone.

Mons-troicus.

A town in the Aphroditopolite nome, anciently called Toura, which see.

MONT-EM-HA.

The fourth priest or prophet of Amen Ra, the son of Nes-pthah and the lady Nes-khons, which see.   Period uncertain.

MONT-EM-HA.

A priest of Amen Ra, the father of the priestess Isi-em-kheb, which see.

MONTH.   Or MENTU.

An Egyptian deity represented as a hawk-headed man.   He was an incarnation of the sun Ra in his attribute of death giver (by coup de soleil).   He was also an avenging deity.   He was worshipped at the town of Tsam.

MOSTAREBA.

An Ishmaelite Arabian tribe, originally of little importance, but which afterwards absorbed the other rival and larger tribes.   *See* Motareba.

MOSYLON.

An ancient sea-port of Arabia, the mart for goods coming from Africa. It is now called Ras Abourgabeh.

MOT.   "Βώθ."

In Greco-Chaldaic mythology the primitive substance that was the mother of all the gods.

MOTAREBA.

An early Arabian Joktanite tribe.   They are not to be confounded with the Mostareba, who were a later race.

MOTYA.   "The Muddy."

A Tyrian settlement on the West coast of the Isle of Sicily.

MOUMIS.

In Greco-Babylonian mythology the intelligent world, the first born son of Apason and of Tauthe, the mother of the gods.   Moumis was derived from the Accadian word Mami, "The Waters."

MOUTH-EN-AP.

A priestess of the god Amen Ra of Thebes.   Period uncertain.

MU-BAL-LIDAT-SERUA.

The daughter of Assur-ubalid, king of Assyria, and the mother of Kara-hardas, king of Babylonia, who was slain by the Kassi.

MUDAD.

According to Arabic historians the chief of a Jorhamite tribe, whose daughter Rala or Sayyida married Ishmael, the son of Abraham.   *See* Samayda.

MUECPHORITES.

A nome in Lower Egypt, East of the Phatnitic branch of the Nile. The name of its chief town is not known.

MUGALLI.

A king of Tubal in Asia Minor. He sent a present and tribute of horses to Assurbanipal, king of Assyria, and also one of his daughters for the harem of that monarch.

MUGHEIR.

The modern name of the ancient Chaldean city Ur or Calneh.

MUI-EN-HIKU. "The Lion of Kings."

A royal surname of Amenhotep III. of the XVIIIth dynasty. *See* the following name.

MUI-EN-HIKU.

The flabellum bearer of Amenhotep III. of the XVIIIth dynasty. He had a son named Nohem-maschuf, which see.

MULAGUNNUNA.

An early Chaldean king, possibly belonging to the IInd dynasty of Berosus.

MULGE.

In Accadian mythology a form of the god Bel as "The Lord of the Underworld."

MULILKI.

The Accadian name of the city of Nipur.

MULIS-ASSUR.

The chief of the commanders of the army under Samas-Rimmon or Samsi-Vul III. He subdued 500 cities and ravaged the country of the Sunbai.

MULLIAS.

An Assyrian city called Abnunaki by the Accadians.

MUMMIES. MOUM, "Wax."

One of the most remarkable classes of Egyptian antiquities is the mummies, or dead bodies prepared by salt, bitumen, cedar oil, and other substances, so as to resist decay and the ravages of time. The reason of the process is unknown, but is supposed to have been either sanitary, or to enable the soul, after it had passed through its transformations for 3000 or 10,000 years, to return to the body. Immediately after death the corpses of men were delivered to the eviscerators, or *parachistæ*, or preparers, *taricheutæ*, and removed to their establishments; a line was drawn on the right side, which was opened by an Ethiopian stone-knife, the viscera removed, and were either placed in four Canopic jars dedicated to the genii of the dead, packed in separate bags and laid with the mummy, or else were thrown into the river. The brain was extracted by a curved bronze instrument, and the body then treated according to the practice of the period, or the wealth of the family. The corpses of females were mummied at their homes. In the days of Herodotus, three modes were employed. The first, or most expensive, cost a talent, about 244*l.*; in which, after the preliminary operations, the body was bathed in palm wine, filled with cassia and other drugs, then plunged in natron for seventy days, and finally wrapped in linen bandages and a cartonage. The second process cost 20 *minæ*, or about 81*l*. In it the brain was removed, the viscera injected with cedar oil, and the body was steeped in natron for seventy days. An examination of different mummies shows, however, that there was a great difference in the mode of preparation. The brain, when extracted, left the skull hollow, and sometimes the nostrils were plugged with pledgets ; the eyes were occasionally removed, and their places supplied by others of ivory and obsidian ; the hair was often removed, and made into an oval packet, covered with linen and bitumen. The flank incision varied in length, and was covered by a tin plate, on which a symbolic eye was engraved. The viscera were separately embalmed, and placed in Canopic jars laid outside or in the bellies of the mummies. Silver gloves or stalls were placed on the fingers to prevent the tearing off the nails, or else they were secured with thread. The bodies were laid straight, the hands at the sides, on the breast or groin, so as to be symmetrical for bandaging. When finally prepared, the mummies were wrapped in linen bandages, principally strips of three or four inches wide, several yards in length, laid on wet, and kept level by pledgets. Remnants of old linen were extensively used for the purpose. As many as 700 yards are said to have been employed for one mummy. The bandages are generally coarsest near the body, and finer outside. Some mummies have an outer linen shroud dyed red by the *carthamus tinctorius*, and over that a network of porcelain bugles, amidst which figures of sepulchral deities and other emblems are introduced. On a few mummies of the earlier dynasties and of the age of the Ptolemies, portions of the Ritual of the Dead were written on the outer bandages after they had been laid on. Other mummies have leather straps crossing the shoulders and breast, and stamped at the ends with the names and figures of· kings of the XXth and following dynasties, standing in adoration to Osiris. A very common mode of ornamentation was the cartonage, composed of twenty or forty layers of linen tightly pressed and glued together like pasteboard, and covered with a thin layer of stucco. This was modelled in shape of the figure of the dead, with a pedestal. It was laced up or closed behind, and appropriately painted with colours in tempera, with figures of deities and inscriptions. When bandaged, the mummies were generally deposited in coffins and sarcophagi ; the coffins were of wood, chiefly of cedar and sycamore ; and these again were either plain with inscriptions cut upon them, or else covered with a layer of stucco, painted like the cartonages, in tempera. Sometimes there were three or more coffins fitting in one another, like a nest of boxes. The bodies of kings and persons of high rank or wealth were deposited in massive sarcophagi, or outer stone coffins of granite, basalt, alabaster, breccia, and other materials. These sarcophagi were either rectangular with a cover, or else in the shape of the mummied body. Some were plain, but many more were covered with scenes and inscriptions in relief or intaglio, chiefly extracts from the

Ritual and other religious works. Considerable variety prevails in the range of subjects selected for the ornamentation of the coffins and sarcophagi, due to the caprices or different tastes of the relatives of the deceased. The art was practised from B.C. 2000 to A.D. 700, and it has been calculated that about 420,000,000 bodies may have been thus pre-prepared. The principal cemeteries were the Gournah quarter of Thebes, Abydos, and the plains of Sakkara. The mummies of the period of the first six dynasties found at Sakkara are enclosed in wooden coffins with human faces, placed in a rectangular sarcophagus, and have only been slightly preserved, dropping to pieces on exposure to the air, or preserving a faint odour of bitumen. At Thebes, under the XIth dynasty, bitumen and other drugs were used for the preparation of mummies, which are, however, yellow, and falling to pieces; they were deposited either in cases in shape of a mummy, hollowed out of the trunk of a tree, or in rectangular chests. The mummies of the XIIth and XIVth dynasties generally found at Thebes, are black, with flexible and dried skin, and were placed in inferior coffins of the same kind. Under the XVIIth dynasty the coffins renew the style of the XIth, and some are yellow from head to foot. From the XVIIIth to the XXIst dynasty at Memphis the mummies are black, and so dried that they break at the least touch: they were placed in granite sarcophagi more or less massive. At Thebes the mummies are exquisitely made; the bodies yellow, rather shining, and very flexible; deposited in wooden coffins, generally sycamore, with tenons of *sunt* or acacia wood. Sometimes as many as three are used, one within the other. After the XXIst dynasty the mummies at Thebes continue to show the perfection of the art; are enveloped in cartonages, and placed in wooden coffins, rather plain, with inscriptions or else with a white ground and scenes traced on them. The mummies of the cemeteries of Memphis of this period are poor and few, but become better under the XXVIth dynasty, and are often placed in sarcophagi of granite, basalt, and other stone. Under the Ptolemies, the art of mummification declined. Inferior ones at Thebes were often buried in the soil; the jaws were tied up, and plates of gold placed on the tongue; portions of the skin were gilded, and the bodies either black or of an ashen grey colour. At Memphis the use of stone sarcophagi still continued, and a new kind of wooden coffin was introduced, the bottom of which was a flat board, into which fitted a vaulted cover, with pillars at the four ends, fitted by four tenons. Under the Romans, after the first century A.D., the mummies and coffins rapidly decline. The bodies are black, heavy, and the bandages adhere so to the liquid bitumen in which they were boiled, that they cannot be detached without an instrument, and the Hieroglyphs and pictures are coarse daubs or illegible scrawls. The outer wrappers and bandages are decorated in another style, and encaustic portrait pictures are placed over the head, and the influence of a foreign art, itself in a state of decline, is everywhere visible. The bodies were often secured by cords with leaden or wax seals, to protect the arrangements and amulets from plunder or violation; and, as at an early period, memoranda, in an encaustic ink, of the name, age, or time when the deceased lived are found on the bandages. (Birch's *Guide to the British Museum, Egyptian Gallery.*)

MUNAMMIH.

The father of Nebosarziltimu, a great author and astronomical compiler in the reign of Sargon I.

MUND KARNIKU KOOND.

A sacred fountain in Benares, which the god Vishnu produced with his discus, and then filled with sweat from his own body.

MUNGA. " Of Bricks."

The Accadian name of the month Sivan, which see.

MUNIN. " Memory."

In Scandinavian mythology one of the two ravens which sat upon the shoulders of the great divinity Odin, and brought intelligence to him. *See* Hugin.

MUNIRSUARTA.

A king of the Araziasai, who together with 1070 of his soldiers was slain by Samas-Rimmon III., king of Assyria, who destroyed his cities, and carried his wife and family into captivity.

MUN-KHET-ISI.

An Egyptian lady, the mother of the royal scribe Pet-amen, which see.

MUNTHUKH. *Or* MUNTHKH.

An Etruscan guardian spirit who seems to have watched over the health. She sometimes had a dove on the right arm. Corssen compares her with the Greek Graces. She was winged, wore a necklace, and had a box of cosmetics and pencil in her hands.

MUNTU-HIK-HOPSEF.

A son of Rameses II. of the XIXth dynasty.

MUNTU-HIK-HOP-SEF. *Or* MENTU-HIK-HOP-SEF.

A son of Rameses III. of the XXth dynasty.

MUNTU-HOTEP.

The consort of Antefaa II. of the XIth dynasty.

MUPALLIDAT-SERUA. " She that is quickened by Serua."

An early Babylonian princess. *See* Mu-bal-lidat-serua.

MURADDAS.

A city in South-eastern Assyria, which was conquered by Tiglath Pileser I.

MURDUS.

The true name of the Kassite deity Kharbat. He was identified by the Assyrians with the Bel of the Babylonians.

MUR-KAU.

An Egyptian officer in the XIIth dynasty. His wife's name was Uaemma. Nothing else is known respecting him.

MUR-MAZ-A.

An Assyrian pilot in the reign of Sennacherib.

MURU.

In Zendic mythology the third dwelling-place of the Iranians, or their second residence after leaving Aryanem-Vaedjo. It was the Margiana of the Greeks.

MURU.

A city in Syria, which was conquered by Shalmaneser II., who afterwards erected a palace there.

MUS.

In Chaldean astronomy a name of the planet Mercury, as one of the twelve stars of the West.

MU-SAL-LIM-MARUDUK.

A Chaldean prince, the son of Ukani, who paid tribute to Shalmaneser I., king of Assyria.

MU-SAL-LIM-NINIP.

The governor of Bile, in the reign of Vul-nirari III. and Assurdan III. He was eponym of the years B.C. 793 and 766, in both of which years took place expeditions to Media.

MU-SIG-SAR.

The governor of Kirruri, in the reign of Samsi-Vul IV., and eponym of the year B.C. 814, the chief event in which was an expedition to Ahsana.

MUSKI.

A Hittite tribe, which overran Assyria during the weak state of the empire under Bel-kudur-uzur and Assur-dan. They were defeated, and their king Kiliteru slain, by Tiglath Pileser I.

MUSON.

A chief town in the Cynopolite nome of the Heptanomos.

MUSTARILU.

In Chaldean astronomy a name of the planet Jupiter.

MUSTELIL. "The Brilliant."

In Chaldean astronomy the name of the planet Venus.

Musuri.

A king of Moab. He was rendered tributary to Assyria by Esar-haddon.

Mut.

See Maut, the Egyptian mother goddess.

Mutaggil . . . .

The Rabsaki of Vul-nirari III., and eponym of the year B.C. 799, the chief event in which was an expedition to Lulimu.

Mutaggil-Assur.   "Trusting in Assur."

The governor of Gozan, in the reign of Sargon II. He was eponym of the year B.C. 706.

Mutaggil-Nebo.   "Trusting in Nebo."

An early king of Assyria. He was the son of Assurdan I., and rebuilt the royal palace of Nineveh. Nothing else is known respecting him.

Mutaggil-Nusku.

See Mutaggil-nebo.

Mutallu.

The son of Tarhulara, king of Gaugama. He murdered his father, who was a faithful ally of the Assyrians, and then ascended the throne, and began a revolt against Sargon II. The king of Assyria soon, however, invaded Gaugama, and conquering Mutallu, sent him and his family into captivity, and placed an Assyrian governor over the capital city Marqasi.

Mutariz-Assur.

The Rabsaki of Samsi-Vul III., who invaded and conquered for his master the whole of the districts of Nahiri and 500 towns in the neighbourhood of Lake Van, bringing back with him much spoil, tribute, and many chariot horses.

Mut-hat-ankhes.

The second wife of Osorkon II. of the XXIInd dynasty.

Muthon I. and II.

Kings of Tyre, of whom nothing except their names is known. Muthon is another form of the Tyrian royal name Mathan.

Muthon III.(?)

The son of Abdelim. Together with his brother Gerashtoreth, he was elected co-king or suffete of Tyre, upon the death or deposition of Habbar, the high-priest of Melkarth. He and his brother reigned for six years, after which a sole royalty was established by Baalator.

Muthon IV.

The son and successor of Hiram III., king of Tyre. He was reigning about the time of the expedition of Xerxes against Greece.

Muthum.

A chief town of the Antæopolite nome in the Thebaid of Upper Egypt.

Mut-iritis. *Or* Maut-iritis.

A daughter of Pianki, an obscure king of the XXIVth dynasty.

Mut-snat-em.

A lady of royal birth at the close of the XVIIIth dynasty, who married Horus Haremhebi, and ruled both in consort with him and also in her personal right. She is supposed to have survived her husband. Her birth and pedigree are at present unknown.

Muza.

A great sea-port of ancient Arabia whence Indian goods were imported to Syria and Egypt. It is now called Maushid.

Muzazina.

A chief of the city of Bunasi in the land of Nizir or Armenia. He was conquered by Assurnazirpal.

Muzazir.

A district to the South of Armenia, conquered, together with fifty of its chief towns, by Shalmaneser II.

Muzazir.

The great sacred city of Ararat, containing the temples of the national deities Haldi and Bagmasti, which were plundered and burnt by Sargon II., king of Assyria. On hearing the news of that calamity the brave king Urza of Armenia lost hope, and committed suicide.

Muzri.

An Egyptian colony settled in the valley of the Euphrates. They were defeated and subdued by Shalmaneser I., king of Assyria.

Muzur.

A district to the extreme North of Assyria, now called Jebel Maklub. It was conquered by Tiglath Pileser I.

Muzur.

The Semitic name of the land of Egypt, called by the Accadians Maganki.

Myas-hormos.

An Egyptian port on the Troglodytic coast of the Red Sea.

Mycephoris.

According to Herodotus a nome in Egypt held by the Calasirian class of warriors.

Mycerinus.

The Greek form of the royal name Men-ker-a, which see.

Mygale.

The shrew mouse which was sacred to the goddess Sekhet, and was worshipped at the city of Bubastis.

N.

NA. "The Sky."

Another form of the name of the Assyrian deity Anu, which see.

NA.

A mystical title of Amen Ra, which occurs in the CLXVIth chapter of the Ritual of the Dead.

NAA.

The mother of Smen, a great Egyptian captain in the reign of Thothmes IV. of the XVIIIth dynasty.

NAAL.

A mountain district between Assyria and Armenia. It was conquered by Tiglath Pileser II., who built there a garrison city called Assur-basa.

NAARATH.

The name of two Canaanitish cities : one in Palestine in the tribe of Ephraim, and the other a Tyrian settlement on the West coast of Sardinia, now called Nora.

NA-AU. "Air."

A mystical divinity who is mentioned in the CXLth chapter of the Ritual of the Dead.

NABATU.

A tribe in Mesopotamia which was conquered by Tiglath Pileser II.

NABIRTU.

A deity of the Susians, of whom nothing is known.

NABLA.

Another name of the Egyptian guitar. *See* Nefer.

NABO-BAL-ATIR-RIB.

A Chaldean chief, the father of Nabonahid, the last king of Babylon before its conquest by the Medes and Persians.

NABONAHID. "Nebo is Majestic."

The son of a Chaldean chief named Nabo-bal-atir-rib. He was raised to the throne of Babylon by an insurrection of the great lords against Bellabarisruk, the infant son of Nergalsarussur. He did little but repair a few temples of the deities whose worship he declared himself to have neglected, and had throughout his reign to contend with the encroachments of the Persians. Towards the close of his reign he made his son Bel-sarra-uzur joint king of Babylonia, and left him to sustain the defence of Babylon against Cyrus, king of Persia. After the fall of the city he tendered his submission to the victor, by whom he was sent into exile into Carmania, where he died in obscurity after a troubled reign of seventeen years, and with him perished the second empire of Babylonia. He was the Labynetus of the Greek historians. (Lenormant.)

NABONASSAR.

The Greek form of the Babylonian royal name Nabu-nazir, which see.

NABONIDUS.

Another form of the Chaldean royal name Nabonahid, which see.

NABU. " Proclaimer."

In Chaldean astronomy the name both of the planets Venus and Mercury as morning stars.

NABU. Or NABO.

Another form of the name of the Assyrian deity Nebo, which see.

NABUA.

An early Chaldean astronomer, some observations by whom have been preserved.

NABU-AHI-ERIS.

A prefect of Samalla. He was the eponym of the year B.C. 681, in which Sennacherib was assassinated by his sons.

NABU-BA-BA-DUKIN.

The Tukulu of Assyria under Shalmaneser III.

NABU-BAL-IDINNA.

A king of Babylonia who assisted Sadudu, king of Suhi, to fight against Assur-na-zir-pal, king of Assyria. His endeavours were unsuccessful, and the Suhites being defeated he had to make peace with the Assyrians.

NABU-BEL-SHUM.

Another form of the Chaldean royal name Nebo-bel-zikri.

NABU-BEL-UZUR.

The governor of Arbaha in the last year of the reign of Assur-Nirari II. He was eponym of the year B.C. 745, the chief events in which were the accession to the throne of Tiglath Pileser II., and a march to the borders of the river.

NABU-BEL-UZUR. " Nebo, protect the Lord."

The governor of Sihima in the reign of Tiglath Pileser II. He was eponym of the year B.C. 732, the chief event in which was an expedition to Damascus. He may have been the same as the preceding.

NABU-DAMIQ.

An officer and ambassador of Tiumman, king of Elam. *See* Umbadasa.

NABU-DAN-ANNI.

The Tartan of the first years of the reign of Tiglath Pileser II. He was eponym of the year B.C. 742; the chief events in which were the conquest of Arpad, and the overthrow of Damascus.

NABU-DAN-NIN-ANNI.

The Tartan under Tiglath Pileser I., king of Assyria.

NABU-DEN-IPUS.

The governor of Nineveh under the reign of Sargon II. He was eponym of the year B.C. 704, the chief events in which were an expedition to Babylon, and the construction of the palace of the city of Kalzi.

NABU-DIM-TIR.

A relative of Merodach Baladan, the deposed king of Babylon. He attempted to raise a revolt in Babylonia, aided secretly by Urtaki, king of Elam. The Chaldean chiefs refused, however, to revolt from their lord Nahid-maruduk, who was their ruler and a tributary of Assurbanipal.

NABU-EDIR-ANNI.

The Rabbitur of Tiglath Pileser II. He was eponym of the year B.C. 740, the chief event in which was an expedition to Arpad.

NABU-EKHI-ERBA.

An early Chaldean astronomer, some observations by whom have been preserved.

NABU-ESDU-UKIN.

The Tukulu of Shalmaneser III. He was eponym of the year B.C. 777, the chief event in which was an expedition to Ituha.

NABU-IKBI.

An early Chaldean astronomer, some astrological tablets by whom are preserved.

NABU-KIN-UZUR.

The governor of Nineveh in the reign of Assurdan III. He was eponym of the year B.C. 761, the chief event in which was the commencement of a revolt in the city of Arbaha.

NABU-KUDUR-UZUR OR NEBUCHADNEZZAR I.

An early king of Babylonia. He invaded Assyria three times, in the last utterly defeating the king, Assur-risilim.

NABU-KUDUR-UZUR.

See Naditabirus.

25*

NABU-KUDUR-YUT-SUR.

An early Chaldean astronomer of Elamite origin. He recorded the phases of Jupiter.

NABU-KUDU-ZUR.

The son of Nabonahid, the last king of Babylon. Under this name a Chaldean, one Nidintabel, usurped the throne of Chaldea for a short time on the death of Cambyses.

NABU-KULLANI.

An early Chaldean astronomer ; a tablet of observations by whom has been preserved.

NABU-LIHA.

The governor of Arbela in the reign of Sargon II. He was eponym of the year B.C. 702, the chief event in which was an expedition to Kassi and Ellipi.

NABU-MU-SET-SI.

An early Chaldean astronomer. Some records on the planet Jupiter by him are in the British Museum.

NABU-NAZIR.

One of the later kings of Babylonia. He was conquered and his kingdom ravaged by Tiglath Pileser II., king of Assyria. He was succeeded by Nabu-sabri, the last king but one of Babylonia before its annexation to Assyria.

NABU-PAK-ID-ILANI.

An Assyrian officer who was placed as Satrap on the throne of Babylon by Sargon I., after his conquest of Merodach Baladin I.

NABU-PAL-UZUR.

A great Assyrian general who defeated the revolted Babylonians for his master Bel-zikir-iskun, by whom he was made vice-king of Babylon. On the accession of Assur-ebil-ili to the throne of Assyria, he and his son Nabu-kudur-uzur conspired with Necho, king of Egypt, and made war with the king of Assyria, whom he defeated in his own capital city of Nineveh, and thus terminated the Assyrian empire. Shortly afterwards he quarrelled with Pharaoh Necho, and sent his son against him, who completely routed the Egyptians. He was succeeded by his son Nabu-kudur-uzur, the Nebuchadnezzar of Hebrew history. Nabu-pal-uzur married the Saite princess Neitaker, and was the Nabopalassar of the Greek writers. (Lenormant.)

NABU-SALIM.

The son of Balasu, a Chaldean who was raised to the kingship of the Dakkusi by Esarhaddon, after the death of Samas-ibni, which see.

NABU-SAR-UZUR.

The governor of Kurban in the reign of Vul-nirari or Rimmon-nirari III. He was eponym of the year B.C. 784, the chief event in which was an expedition to Hupuskia.

NABU-SHA-PIK-ZIR.

See Nabu-zikir-iskun, king of Babylon.

NABU-TARIZ.

An Assyrian officer in the reign of Shalmaneser IV., whose titles are lost. He was eponym of the year B.C. 721, the chief event in which was a war with Babylon and Elam.

NABU-U-SABSI.

A Chaldean chief, the son or descendant of Silani. He ruled at Sarrapanu, and upon Tiglath Pileser I. proclaiming himself king of Babylon, of Sumir, and of Accad, he rose in rebellion against him, whereupon the king of Assyria besieged him, and taking his capital city, impaled him alive upon its walls.

NABU-ZAKIR-ERES.

The Assyrian governor of a Babylonian province. Together with Urtaki, king of Elam, and Belbasa, king of Gambuli, he revolted against Assurbanipal, king of Assyria, who defeated him and his allies.

NABU-ZAR-ADAN.

The general of the Chaldean army of Nabukuduruzur the Great. He entered Jerusalem after the fall of the Hebrew kingdom, and destroying the temple and all the principal buildings of the city, carried the people into captivity to various cities of the Assyro-Chaldean empire.

NABU-ZIKIR-ISKUN.

A king of Babylonia who reigned about B.C. 1050. He was conquered by the king of Assyria, but afterwards concluding a treaty of peace with him, married the daughter of his conqueror, and was restored to his kingdom.

NABU-ZIR-NAPIS-TI-ESIR.

A son of Merodach-Baladan, king of Babylon. On the death of Sennacherib he proclaimed himself king, and went to attack the city of Ur, which was held by a prince named Ningal-idina. Him he defeated, and added his principality to his own. As soon, however, as Esarhaddon ascended the throne of Assyria, he sent an army under some trusted generals against Babylon, and Nabu-zir-napis-ti-esir, with his brother Nahid-maruduk, fled for shelter to the king of Edom, Ummanaldas, who not only refused him an asylum, but put him to death. Nahid-maruduk escaped, and was pardoned by Esarhaddon.

NACKA.

The name of one of the books of the original Zendavesta, of which there were said to have been twenty-one prior to the period of Sassanidæ. There is now only one left, the Vidæ-vadata or Vendidad, which see.

NADAN.

The governor of Pekod. He joined the revolt of Saulmugina against Assurbanipal, and was defeated and severely punished by the victor.

NADITABIRUS.

A Babylonian chief, who called himself Nabu-kudur-uzur, the son of Nabonidus. He revolted against Darius Hystaspes, by whom he was twice encountered and defeated, once on the Tigris, and once on the Euphrates. Darius then entered Babylon in triumph and slew Naditabirus.

NADITU.

An Elamite city which was destroyed by Sennacherib.

NAEIA.

An overseer of the bulls of Pthah. His funereal statue is in the Leyden Museum. Period uncertain.

NAFI.

A priest of Amen Ra in the XIXth dynasty.

NAGIEL.

In Cabalistic mythology the intelligence of the sun.

NAGITU.

An Elamite city on the Persian gulf, where Merodach-Baladan sought to establish a Babylonian colony after his expulsion from Chaldea by Sennacherib. *See* Merodach-Baladan.

NAGLFARI.

In Scandinavian mythology the first husband of the goddess Nott, who bare to him the deity Udr.

NAHAB.

A mystical viper in the first abode of Osiris, who is mentioned in the CLth chapter of the Ritual of the Dead.

NAHAI.   " Sycamore Land."

An Egyptian adjective signifying the land of Egypt.

NAHAM-S-RATA.

A priestess of Amen Ra. The period in which she lived is uncertain.

NAHAM-UA.   *Or* NEHEMCOU.

A name of the goddess Hathor, under which she was adored in her emblem of a fish.

NAHARAINA.

The Egyptian name for the whole district of Mesopotamia.

NAHAR-HAMMURABI.   " Canal of Hammurabi."

See Hammurabi.

NAHARMALCHA.   "River of the King."

The Chaldean name of the great canal of Hammurabi when it was re-opened and enlarged by Nabu-kudur-uzur, the Nebuchadnezzar of Hebrew writers.

NAHI.

A prince who was appointed by Thothmes III., of the XVIIIth dynasty, to the viceroyalty of Ethiopia.

NAHID-MARUDUK.

The son of Merodach-Baladan, king of Babylon. On the death of Sennacherib he and his brother both revolted from the power of Assyria, but after a little while his brother Nabu-zir-napis-ti-eser was defeated by Esarhaddon, and put to death by the king of Elam, whereupon Nahid-maruduk, who had fled into Elam, recrossed the frontier, and placed himself at the mercy of Esarhaddon, who pardoned him and restored to him his brother's dominions.

NAHR-EL-KELB.   "Dog River."

The modern name of the wady near Beirout, called by the Assyrians Bahlirasi, where Esarhaddon and Rameses II. both set up rock-cut stèle recounting their Syrian victories.

NAHRESI.

See Khnum-hotep, an Egyptian governor in the time of the VIth dynasty.

NAHSI.

A tribe of Negroes in Ethiopia, from whom king Pepi-Merira of the VIth dynasty formed an army. This is the first mention of the Negroes in Egyptian history, but they were afterwards conquered repeatedly by the later Pharaohs.

NAHSI.

The Egyptian name of the Negroland generally.

NAI-F-AA-RUT.

A king of Egypt under the XXIXth or Mendesian dynasty. He restored several temples and aided the Lacedemonians in their wars against their mutual enemies the Persians. He reigned seven years, and was the Nepherites of the Greeks.

NAILA.

An ancient Arabian goddess. She was possibly a form of the moon.

NAIRI.

A wild district near the Upper Euphrates, which was conquered by Tiglath Pileser I., and was repeatedly subdued by the Assyrian monarchs.

Najaran.

A Himyaritic city in South-western Arabia.

Nakarah.

A deity of the Himyarites, who was worshipped at the city of Maîn.

Nakh-ke.

A king of Khininsi or Herakleopolis. One of the petty kings of Egypt under the Assyrian Icosarchy.

Nakhla.

An ancient Arabian town near Mecca. It was sacred to the worship of the deity Alozza.

Nakht. "Strength."

An Egyptian officer, whose period is uncertain. He was the son of a functionary named also like himself, Nakht.

Nakht.

An Egyptian lady, the wife of Uah and the mother of Senbu a priest of Osiris. *See* Senbu.

Nakht-ankh. "Life and Strength."

An Egyptian gentleman, the son of Khair. His wife's name was Anneke. His period and acts are uncertain.

Nakhti-kharu-anshini.

The Assyrian form of the Egyptian royal name Nekht-har-en-shen, which see.

Nalakhu.

One of the twenty petty kingdoms of Lower Egypt which were established by the Assyrians under Esarhaddon.

Namar-bili. "The Illumination of Bel."

The name of the great astrological cyclopædia of the Chaldeans, which was compiled for Sargon, or Sargina, of Agane. Of this work considerable portions remain in the Collection in the British Museum.

Namerta.

The brother of Uah, an Egyptian gentleman, which see.

Namms.

The Egyptian name of the double flute.

Namms.

The peculiar striped or plaited shawl worn by the Egyptians on the head, and generally gathered up into a queue behind. It was used from the earliest to the latest times.

NAMRUT. *Or* NIMROD.

A petty king of Egypt in the XXIInd dynasty. He reigned over Hermopolis, but rebelled against Piankhi of Ethiopia, who besieged and took his capital city after a three days' siege, and compelled him to pay tribute and do homage. He married a queen named Nestennest, whom together with his other wives he sent to make peace with Piankhi.

NAMRUT.

A son of Uaserken II. and father of Takarut II., of the XXIIIrd dynasty, who on the death of Sheshanka II. became king of Egypt. Nothing else is known of him.

NAMTAR. *Literally* " The Fixer of Destiny."

In Accadian mythology " The Plague Demon," which was adopted into the Assyrian mythology.

NAMUROT. *Or* NAMROT.

The son of a late Egyptian king, but of what king it is not known.

NAMUROT.

The son of Takelot I. of the XXIInd dynasty.

NAMUROT.

The grandfather of Sheshonk or Sheshanka I. of the XXIIIrd dynasty.

NAMUROT.

A son of Osorkon II. of the XXIIIrd dynasty ; probably the same as Namrot the father of Takarut II.

NANDA.

In Hindu mythology a shepherd who was the reputed father of the god Vishnu when he was born under the form of the baby Khrishna, which see.

NANE.

An Armenian warlike deity, adopted from the Adar-Samdan of the Assyrians.

NA-NEFRU-SEKHET.

A priestess of the goddess Neith, the wife of Pef-aa-neit, which see.

NANI.

The wife of Nemur, an Egyptian governor and *Smer* in the XIIth dynasty.

NANIKIRI.

A country rendered tributary by Samas-Rimmon III.,(?)king of Assyria.

NANJUNDA.

A Hindu idol, one of the numerous forms of Siva.

NANNA.

In Scandinavian mythology the wife of Baldur the beautiful, and the mother of Forseti.

NANNACHUS.

An early king, in whose reign the Phrygians believed the Deluge to have taken place.

NAOPHOROI.   " Shrine Bearers."

A class of Egyptian priests whose duty it was to carry the sacred shrines of the different deities to whose worship they were devoted, and to hold them on their knees exposed to the adoration of the people.

NAOUSCHERI.

The grandfather of the Egyptian lady Siotio, which see.   (Leemans.)

NAPATA.

The capital of Nubia and of the kingdom of Egypt during the XXVIth dynasty.   It is now called Gebel Barkal.   It was famous for its great temple of Amen Ra, which was often enriched by the kings of the Ethiopian dynasty, especially Nastosen, Horsiatef, and Piankhi-Meramen.

NAPHARILI.

The governor of Kirruri, in the reign of Tiglath Pileser II.   He was eponym of the year B.C. 729, in which year " the king took the hands of Bel," i.e., held a religious festival.

NAPHTUHIM.

In Hebrew history a son of Mizraim, who is supposed to have given his name to the people of Memphis.

NAPIATU.

A small kingdom in Arabia, which was conquered for the first time by the Assyrians under Esarhaddon.

NAPSA.

A deity of the Susians of whom nothing is known.

NAPSHU.

An Elamite deity of whom nothing is known, possibly the same as the preceding.

NA-PTHAH.   "Part of Pthah."

The sacerdotal name of the race and people of Memphis.   They are supposed to have been the Naphtuhim of Genesis.

NAPULU.

An Assyrian city which revolted to Assurdan, and was reconquered by Samas-Rimmon or Samsi-Vul IV.

NARA.   " Spirit."

In Vedic mythology a name of the Supreme Being.

NARADA.

In Hindu mythology a deity who was invested by Brahma with the power of creation.   *See* Angiras.

NARADAS.

In Hindu mythology the divine messenger of Indra.

NARAMSIN.   " He who exalts Sin," (the Moon God).

An early monarch of Babylonia ;   the son and successor of Sargon I. He completed his father's conquest, and invaded the kingdom of Maganna, which has been conjectured to have been Egypt, as it was known to the Babylonians by that name.

NA-SA-KABU.

A mystical title of Amen Ra, which is mentioned in the CLXVIth chapter of the Ritual of the Dead.

NA-SA-NEB-USA-KEN-EN.

The superintendent of the Great Hall, a functionary in the court of King Aspalut of the XXVth dynasty.

NASATYAS.

In Zendic mythology the fourth of the Darvands, which see.

NASCHT-AMEN.   " Strength of Amen."

An Egyptian royal scribe whose monument is in the Leyden Museum. Period uncertain.

NASCH-TI.

A prophet of Haroeri, of Amen Ra, and a sacrificiant of their respective temples.   He was the father of the priest Pef-nifi-neith, which see.

NASCH-TI-NEBEF.

Another form of the Egyptian royal name Nekh-ta-nebi, which see.

NASCHT-MES.   *Or* NEKHTMES.   " Born of Strength."

An Egyptian sacred chorister.   Her statue is in the Leyden Museum. Period uncertain.

NASR.   " Eagle."

A Sabæan deity ; the analogue of the Chaldean eagle-headed divinity Nisroch-Samdan.   (Lenormant.)

NASR.   " Eagle." (?)

A Himyaritic deity, probably the Nisroch of the Chaldeans, said to have been the chief god of the Himyarites.

NASTOSENEN.

A king of Egypt in the Ethiopian period, or the XXVth dynasty He conquered the Negro tribes, and made large presents to the temple of Amen at Napata. His surname was Ra-ka-ankh.

NASTRAND.

In Scandinavian mythology the name of the dreadful hall in hell, the roof of which was formed of serpents vomiting venom, through which the wicked had to wade. All its gates opened Northward.

NATHAN.   " The Given."

A king of Nabathea. He remained faithful to Assurbanipal, king of Assyria, during the outbreak of the great Syro-Arabian revolt, but joined in the second revolt, under Vaiteh II., and was completely defeated.

NATHO.

According to Herodotus a nome in Egypt held by the Hermotybian class of warriors. It was more anciently called Athu by the Egyptians.

NATHUM.

An Etruscan Fury. She was analogous to the Greek Até, with tusk-like fangs, and a serpent in the hand. She was represented as urging Urusthe (Orestes) to slay Kluthumustha (Klytemnestra).

NATKU.

One of the twenty petty kingdoms of Egypt established by the Assyrians under Esarhaddon, after the defeat of Tirhakah of the XXIInd dynasty.

NAU.

The Egyptian goddess of the hour impersonified. She was represented as a woman with a star upon her head.

NAUCRATIS.

In the Ptolemaic period a chief city in the Saitic nome of Lower Egypt, West of the Nile. It contained the docks for foreign shipping.

NAZANA.

The Egyptian name of an unidentified Syrian city.

NAZARATUS.

A Babylonian priest, by whom, according to the Greek authors, Pythagoras was instructed into divine mysteries.

NAZI-BIRA.

A city or district of which Taggil-ana-bil was prefect, under Tiglath Pileser I. and Sargon II.

Nazi-bugas.

An obscure man whom a revolt of the Kassi against their lord Kara-hardas raised to the Babylonian throne about B.C. 1400. He was attacked and defeated by the king of Assyria, who was a relative of the dethroned monarch.

Naziru.

A tribe in Mesopotamia which was conquered by Tiglath Pileser II.

Nazi-rudas.

An early king of Babylonia. He succeeded Ulamburyas, which is all that is at present known about him.

Neb-amen. "Lord of Amen Ra," or "Amen is Lord."

A flabellum-bearer of one of the kings of the XVIIIth dynasty.

Neb-amen.

An Egyptian judge. His period is uncertain.

Neb-ankh. "Lord of Life."

A sacred scribe and prophet of Horus. He was the son of Psametik, who was also a sacred scribe in the Ptolemaic period.

Neb-ankh.

The grandson of a king (?) Nefer-hotep, of the XIIIth dynasty.

Neb-anu.

An uncertain Egyptian goddess, of the Ptolemaic period.

Neb-e-chot.

According to some Egyptologists another form of the Egyptian royal name Taf-nekht.

Neb-em-akhut.

The son of Shafra, king of Egypt, and his queen Meri-s-ankh of the IVth dynasty. He acted as sacred scribe and privy counsellor to his father.

Neb-em-chut-et.

The son of an early Egyptian king.

Neb-en-khata.

A son of Rameses II. of the XIXth dynasty.

Neb-en-toneb.

A son of Rameses II. of the XIXth dynasty.

Neb-en-toti.

A daughter of Rameses II. of the XIXth dynasty.

NEB-ER-ZER. "The Lord Intact."

A title of the deity Osiris, in opposition to the epithet Sepi, "Dismembered," the name under which he was venerated after his being torn in pieces by his brother Set.

NEB-IU.

An unidentified Egyptian fortress. It was situated probably near Memphis.

NEB-KA. Or SEKER-NEFER-KE.

The first king of the IIIrd Memphite dynasty of Egypt. In his reign the Libyans revolted, but being terrified by a lunar eclipse, submitted themselves to his arms. He reigned twenty-eight years, and was the Necherophes of the Greeks.

NEB-NEFER. "The Justified Lord," or "Lord of Justification."

An early Egyptian astronomer; some observations by whom have been preserved.

NEB-NEN-BUTA.

The fourth prophet of Amen Ra, in the reign of King Aspalut of the XXVIth dynasty.

NEB-NETER-U. "The Divine Lords."

An Egyptian priest in the XIXth or XXth dynasties. Like many other similar functionaries, he was at the same time priest and *Sam* of Pthah in Memphis, and chief of the priests of the temple of Amen Ra at Ement or Hermonthis.

NEB-NETER-U.

The surname of Mentu-ra, a priest of Amen Ra, in the reign of Osorkon I. of the XXIInd dynasty.

NEB-NOFRE. "The Good Lords."

A son of Amen-em-ap, a priest of the XVIIIth dynasty, which see.

NEBO. NABU or NEBU. "The God Nebo."

A common element in the names of the Babylonian kings. It may be written either way indifferently.

NEBO. In Assyrian, NABIU and NABU, "The Proclaimer," or "Prophet."

A great Babylonian deity of the second order, although he practically became a god of the greatest rank. He was represented as a king crowned with the triple-horned cap and holding a sceptre or staff. This deity was called also "The Eastern Sun in the height of Heaven," and has been identified with the Mithras of Persian mythology. Nebo was called Pa, the god of "the stylus," and Ac or Gar, "The Maker," in Accadian; and one of his early Assyrian titles was Nuscu, which afterwards became differentiated into a separate deity. Nebo was the god of literature and science, and the library of Assur-bani-pal was placed under the protection of himself and his wife Tasmit. Nebo and

Tasmit are said to have instructed the king like a father and mother, and the invention of the Cuneiform system of writing was ascribed to them. Nebo was also called "The Overseer of the Multitudes of Heaven and Earth," and special worship was paid him by Nebuchadnezzar. His cult had originally spread from Borsippa. In Assyria he had a temple at Calah, and another in conjunction with Merodach at Nineveh. His symbol was the number ten.

NEBO-ATSIB.

An Assyrian officer in the court of Esarhaddon. He was called " The Holder of the Two Sceptres " of that monarch.

NEBO-BEL-UZUR.

The governor of the town of Sihime, in the reign of Tiglath Pileser II.

NEBO-BEL-ZIKRI.

The grandson of Merodach-Baladan, and chief of a tribe on the Persian Gulf; he assisted Saulmugina in his revolt from Assur-bani-pal. When the revolt was crushed, Nebo-bel-zikri fled to Inda-bigas, king of Elam. The latter was murdered by the usurper, Umman-aldas, from whom Assur-bani-pal demanded the surrender of Nebo-bel-zikri. Nebo-bel-zikri thereupon slew himself, and his corpse was sent to Nineveh.

NEBO-CAR-ZIL-TUM-U.

The author of the great astronomical work called the Namar Bili, compiled by the order of Sargon I., king of Agane. He was the son of a man named Munammih, and was a native of Lasanan, " The Great Country."

NEBO-DUR-SANIN.

An Assyrian officer who was called "The Partitioner of the Enemy." He lived in the reign of Sennacherib, king of Assyria.

NEB-OO.

An uncertain Egyptian goddess. She was probably a form of one of the greater divinities.

NEBO-PAL-ASSAR.

The Greek form of the Chaldean royal name Nabu-pal-uzur, which see.

NEBO-RAHIM-BALADHI.

The keeper of the crown in the reign of Esarhaddon, B.C. 667.

NEBO-SUM-IDDIN.

An Assyrian officer, the son of Nebo-rahim-baladhi, the keeper of the crown in the reign of Esarhaddon.

NEBO-SUM-IDDIN.

An early Chaldean astronomer, some observations by whom have been preserved on the tablets in the British Museum.

Nebo-sur-zidi.

The principal librarian of Assurbanipal, king of Assyria.

Nebo-zucipunu.

An Assyrian or Chaldean astronomer. He was the son of the astronomer Merodak-mu-basa.

Neb-pu.

The father of Ra-s-hotep-ab-ankh-netem and Ra-s-hotep-ab, which see.

Nebs.

The Egyptian name of the date fruit.

Neb-se-mennu.

An early Egyptian astronomer, some observations by whom have been preserved.

Neb-seni.

An Egyptian functionary, whose funereal papyrus is in the British Museum.

Neb-tef-au.

The chief of the boatmen, and bearer of the royal parasol of either Amenhotep III. or IV. of the XVIIIth dynasty.

Nebt-hotep. "Peace of Nebt."

An uncertain Egyptian goddess of the latest period.

Nebt-nehi.

An uncertain Egyptian goddess of the latest period.

Neb-uau.

A royal treasurer, the father of Userhat, a high-priest of Amen Ra. *See* Userhat.

Nebuchadnezzar I. *Or* Nebuchadrezzar. *Or* Nabu-kudur-uzur.

(Incorrectly written Nebuchadnezzar; in Assyrian, Nabiu-cudurri-yutsur, "Nebo creates Submission," or "Nebo defend the Landmark.") An early king of Babylon who reigned about B.C. 1150. He twice invaded Assyria in the reign of Assur-risilim, by whom he was defeated, his plunder recovered, and his standard captured. Nothing else is known respecting him.

Nebuchadrezzar II., or The Great.

Nebuchadrezzar was the son of Nabopolassar, who associated him in the government of Babylonia two years before his death. In B.C. 605 Nebuchadrezzar defeated Pharaoh Necho at Carchemish, and overthrew the Egyptian empire in Asia. He was summoned home immediately afterwards by his father's death. Nebuchadrezzar reigned alone from 604 until his death in 561, when he was succeeded by his son Evil-

Merodach. He had married Amuhia or Amytis, the daughter of the Median king during Nabopolassar's lifetime, but since Herodotus ascribes his buildings at Babylon to a queen Nitokris, it has been supposed that Amuhia died before her husband, and that he then married an Egyptian princess called Nitokris. It was for Amuhia that the hanging gardens were constructed. In 597 Nebuchadnezzar commenced the siege of Tyre, which was concluded in 585. Jerusalem had already been destroyed, its king Zedekiah carried to Babylon, and Palestine thoroughly subdued in 587. He is supposed to have afterwards invaded Egypt, and ravaged the Northern part of the country, and Susiania must have been conquered about the same time. The Cuneiform inscriptions show him to have been a pious monarch and a great builder. He completed the two walls of Babylon begun by his father, built a palace for himself in fifteen days, lined the Euphrates with brick, constructed reservoirs and canals, and erected numberless temples. Many other temples, like that of Borsippa, were restored, Babylon was enlarged and beautified, and gold and other costly materials brought from all parts of the world to adorn his buildings. Of his temporary insanity no mention has yet been found on the Babylonian monuments, the reference which was by M. Oppert at one time supposed to refer to the event, having been since read more satisfactorily in another manner by its discoverer. (Sayce.)

NEBUCHADREZZAR II.

Two impostors arose in Babylonia at the beginning of the reign of Darius Hystaspes, who each claimed to be Nebuchadrezzar II., the son of Nabonidus, the last king of Babylon. The first of these was a Babylonian named Nadinta-Bel, the son of Œnares, who was defeated on the banks of the Tigris, and again at Zarana, and finally captured and put to death at Babylon. The second was an Armenian called Aracus, the son of Handita, who had settled in Dobana, a district of Babylonia. Intaphres, the general of Darius, however, took Babylon and seized Aracus, who was brought to Darius and executed. (Sayce.)

NEB-UER.

The son of Nianni, a commander in the army of Seti I. of the XIXth dynasty.

NEB-UKI.

A high-priest of Amen Ra, in the reign of King Aspalut of the XXVth dynasty.

NECHEPSO. *Or* NECHEPSUS.

An Egyptian king of the XXVth dynasty. His name is only found on the Greek lists, and it is doubtful what monarch is intended by it. He was said to have been a priest, and to have written a treatise on astronomy.

NECHEROPHES.

The Greek form of the name Neb-ka, which see.

Necho I.

The chief of the petty kings of Egypt under the Icosarchy. He was ruler of Memphis or Sais, and was a tributary of the Assyrians, who at last raised him to the viceroyalty of Egypt as a means of subduing Tirhakah, king of Ethiopia, who was continually instigating the natives to revolt. He governed at Sais for some years, and was succeeded by his son Psametik, or Psammetichus.

Necho II.

A king of Egypt in the XXVIth dynasty. He was the son of Psametik I., and the princess Shap-en-ap. His first work was the continuation of the war with Palestine which had been begun by his father. On his progress he was stopped at Megiddo by Josiah, king of Judah, whom he defeated and slew, and setting up his son Jehoahaz in his stead, imposed a heavy tribute on the land; but he was himself met at Carchemish by Nebuchadnezzar, king of Babylon, at that time the master of Assyria, by whom he was utterly routed, and driven back into Egypt with the loss of all his Asiatic possessions. He was the last king of Egypt who came into conflict with the Jews. Confining his attention to Egypt for the rest of his reign, he attempted to dig a canal from the Mediterranean to the Red Sea, a work in which 120,000 labourers perished. He further reopened the old canal from the Nile to the Red Sea, and gave great impetus to commerce, and attention to maritime affairs generally. The circumnavigation of Africa was first accomplished in his reign, which lasted sixteen years, when he was succeeded by his son Psametik II. The monuments of the reign of Necho II. are remarkable for an affectation of naturalism in the delineation of the human figure, and for a want of accuracy in the Hieroglyphic texts.

Nechtanebos I.

A king of Egypt of the XXXth dynasty. He was contemporary with Artaxerxes II., against whom he unsuccessfully revolted. *See also* Nekhtarhebi I.

Nechtanebos II.

A son and successor of the preceding. He revolted against Artaxerxes III., and was the last king of the XXXth dynasty.

Nechtarhebi.

A great officer in the reign of Nekhtarhebi I., sometimes supposed to have been that monarch himself prior to his accession to the throne. He was the son of the lady Taf-nekh-ta, and held a variety of important offices, being apparently at one and the same time "Chief of the Palace," "Chief of the North and South," "First Officer of the King," "Chief of all the Higher Dignitaries," "Chief of the Army," "Chief of the College of Sacred Writers," and *Khenmes* or "Father with the King." He lived in the time of the first Saitic or XXIVth dynasty.

Nechtu. *Or* Nekhtu.

An early Egyptian astronomer, some observations by whom have been preserved.

NECTANEBO.

The Greek form of the Egyptian royal name Nekhtarhebi, which see.

NEFER. " Good."

The Egyptian guitar. It had from two to four strings, and was sometimes called *Nabla*. It was used as the Hieroglyphic character for the adjective " good."

NEFER.

An Egyptian *Sutenrekh* or royal father, and " Chief of the Place of Light,(?)" " Chief of the Commissariat of the Young Soldiers," and " Chief of the great House of Provisions " of an unnamed Egyptian monarch.

NEFERA.

An Egyptian sculptor, the father of Abet, a sculptor likewise, in the XIIth dynasty.

NEFER-AMEN. " The Good Amen."

The proto-prophet of the god Month or Mentu. Period uncertain.

NEFER-BAI. " The Good Soul."

An Egyptian scribe of the white house (Memphis). Dynasty uncertain, but of the Second Empire.

NEFER-HEB-EF.

An Egyptian functionary of the XVIIIth dynasty. He married the lady Ta-ei. His surname was Uah-er-meri, which see.

NEFER-HEB-EF.

An Egyptian priest of King Amenhotep II. under his form as a deity. Period uncertain.

NEFER-HOR-HEMT-OO-UEN-RA.

A royal priest, " Spondist of Pthah," " Chief of the Scribes of Pthah," and " Priest of the goddess Arsinoe Philadelphus at Memphis." His father was named Irehemho, and his mother Haankh.

NEFER-HOTEP I., II., III., IV., ETC.

The name of many Egyptian kings of the XIIIth dynasty, who ruled over the whole of Egypt, and were succeeded alternately by other kings named Sebekhotep. There are no materials yet existing for a history of their reigns.

NEFER-HOTEP. " Good Peace."

A fourth priest of Amen Ra. Period uncertain.

NEFER-HOTEP.

A governor of the town of Apu or Panopolis. The period when he lived is unknown.

NEFER-KA-RA.

A king of Egypt of the Vth dynasty. He reigned twenty years, and like most of the kings of that dynasty was buried in a pyramid. He was the Nephercheres of the Greeks.

NEFER-KA-RA.

The seventh king of the IInd Thinite dynasty of Egypt. The Nile is said to have flowed with milk and honey during his reign, which lasted forty-eight years. Called by the Greeks Nephercheres.

NEFER-KA-RA-SOTEP-EN-RA.

A title of Rameses IX. of the XXIst dynasty.

NEFER-KA-SOKER.

The eighth king of the IInd Thinite dynasty of Egypt. He was stated to have been ten feet high (five cubits), and twenty-eight inches (three palms) broad. He reigned forty-eight years, and was the Sesochris of the Greeks.

NEFER-NAI.

An Egyptian chief of the archers, probably of the period of the XVIIIth dynasty.

NEFER-NEFER-KHEPER-RA-KA.

The prenomen of Osirtesen I. of the XIIth dynasty.

NEFER-PU.

The husband of the lady Ketet, and father of the lady Hathorsetmonth, in the Greco-Egyptian period.

NEFER-RA.   " The Good Ra."

An Egyptian queen of the XVIIIth dynasty.

NEFER-REMPE.   " The Good Year." (?)

A royal scribe, whose funereal statue is in the Leyden Museum. His period is uncertain.

NEFER-SHU-U.   "The Good Shu."

A city in Egypt sacred to the goddess Sekhet as Shu.   Site unknown.

NEFER-T.

An Egyptian princess of the IIIrd dynasty. She was a sister of the prince Ra-hotep.

NEFER-TITAI.

The Egyptian name of the queen of Amenhotep IV., or Khuenaten of the XVIIIth dynasty.   *See* Amenhotep *and* Taia.

NEFER-U-PTHAH.   " The Good Pthah."

A priestess of the goddess Hathor in the period of the XVIIIth or XIXth dynasty.

NEFER-U-SEBEK. " The Good Sebek."

An Egyptian lady, the mother of the great commander Horus, which see.

NEGATIVE CONFESSION.

The name given by Egyptologists to a declaration which is contained in the CXXVth chapter of the Ritual of the Dead, which the soul of the deceased is supposed after death to make in the presence of Osiris, declaring that he has not committed certain great crimes, forty-two in number ; after having made this confession he was declared to be justified, and was conducted by Thoth, Horus, Isis, and the deities into the Elysium or Ker-neter.

NEHA-CHENT.

A city and nome in Upper Egypt called by the Greeks Arsinöe the Upper. It was sacred to the worship of the deity Sebek.

NEHA-PEHU.

A city and nome in Upper Egypt, called by the Greeks Arsinöe the Lower. It was sacred to the deity Hathor.

NEHAR.

An Asiatic people who paid tribute to Rameses XII.

NEHA-RA.

An Egyptian prince, governor in the reign of Amenemha II. He was the father of Khnum-hotep, governor of Menat-Khufu. He claimed to have been descended from the god Khnum.

NEHIMEOU.

An Egyptian goddess who was represented as wearing a temple upon her head. Her attributes are uncertain ; she may have been a form of the goddess Hathor.

NEHRAHRUTA.

One of the two favourite horses of Rameses II. They stood unaffrighted while the king was surrounded by the Hittites at the battle of Kadesh, and by so doing enabled him, with the help of his squire Menna, to defend himself successfully, till his soldiers came and rescued him. In gratitude for this wise instinct of the animals, the king vowed "to let them eat corn before Ra daily," *i.e.* consecrate them to the temple of that divinity upon his safe return to Egypt.

NEIRIOUI.

An Egyptian lady, the mother of Pet-osiris, a priest of Pthah in the XXVIth dynasty.

NEIT-AKER. "Victorious Neith."

An Egyptian queen of the VIth dynasty, sister to Mentemsaf, whom she succeeded after his murder in a revolution. She reigned well for twelve years, and was famous for her wisdom and beauty according to the Classic authors. She avenged the death of her brother by inviting the conspirators to a banquet and then drowning them ; but she was obliged afterwards to commit suicide to save herself from the popular indignation which the act caused, after which she was buried in the Pyramid of Menkara. She was one of the queens who were called Nitocris by the Greeks.

NEIT-AKER.

An Egyptian princess of the royal House of Sais. She was the wife of Nabupaluzur or Nebopalassar, the first king of Babylon after the fall of the Assyrian empire, and by her energy and taste she considerably beautified and strengthened the capital city of Babylon. She was the Nitocris of the Greeks. (Lenormant.) *See also* the preceding queen Neitaker, *and* Nebuchadrezzar.

NEIT-AKER.

An Ethiopian princess, the daughter of Queen Shap-en-ap, and granddaughter of Queen Amen-iritis. Her nephew Psametik I., king of Egypt in the XXVIth dynasty, married her in order to establish a claim to the crown of Ethiopia.

NEIT-AKER.

A princess of Egypt and chorister of Amen Ra. She was the daughter of Psametik and Maut-iritis.

NEIT-AKER.

An Egyptian lady, the mother of Houteoiri, a royal scribe, which see. (Leemans.)

NEITH.

Among the Egyptians the goddess of the lower heavens. She often interchanged offices with her sister Nephthys, and like her was represented as furnished with wings. Her emblem was either the flat disk representing the heavens, or a weaver's shuttle, as the inventress and deity of weaving. She was equated with the goddess Minerva by the Greeks. Neith was often represented with a bow and arrows ; this or the weaver's shuttle was generally figured as a part of her headdress. As a nature goddess she personified the celestial space, and played in the town of Sais a part similar to that of the goddess Hathor. She was called like her " The Generating Cow," or " The Mother of the Sun." On the Canopic vases Neith was described as the protectress of the viscera which they contained, and on certain mystical stèle she was represented as suckling two crocodiles, an allusion to the myth of Horus, who was also related to her as " Son of the Sun." *See* Horus, Cippi of.

NEITHOKER.

Another form of the Egyptian royal name Neit-aker, which see.

NEITH-SI.

A surname of Aahmes, a king of the XXVIth dynasty.

NEKHESIA.

A Greco-Egyptian port on the Red Sea.

NEKHT. "Strength."

A great Egyptian officer, the commandant of Lower Egypt in the reign of Osirtesen I. of the XIIth dynasty.

NEKHTARHEBI I. *Or* NECTARHEBI, *or* NEKHTENHEBEF, *or* NEKH-TA-NEBI.

The first king of the XXXth Egyptian or Sebennytic dynasty. He fought against the Persians under Artaxerxes II., and taking advantage of a dissension which arose in the invading army between its two commanders, he succeeded in defeating the Persians at the battle of Mendes, and drove them from the Delta. He was a great promoter of the arts, and restored many of the buildings and temples of the older dynasties. He reigned nineteen years, and was succeeded by his son Teos. He was the Nectanebo of the Greeks.

NEKHTARHEBI II.

The last of the native princes of Egypt. He was summoned from Phenicia to ascend the throne on the revolt of the people against Teos, who overtaxed them. He met with a rival in the person of an unnamed prince of Mendes, who was defeated by the energy of the great captain, Agesilaos. After a little while the Persians, under Ochœs, again entered Egypt, and Nekhtarhebi, unable to sustain a siege at Memphis, fled into Ethiopia with all his treasures, after a reign of nineteen years. Thus ended the XXXth dynasty, and even the vassal kingdom of Egypt, after its destruction as an independent empire under Cambyses.

NEKHT-HAR-EN-SHEN.

King of Pisab-ti-nuti, one of the twenty petty Egyptian kings established by the Assyrians, who called him Nakhti-kharu-anshini.

NEKHT-HOR-NASH-ENTOU.

An Egyptian town which was mentioned as possessed by the rebels against Piankhi-meramen of the XXIInd dynasty, who subjugated it.

NEKHT-KHEM. "Khem in Strength," *or* "Khem the Victor."

The first prophet of the god Khem, in the reign of an unnamed king of the XIXth dynasty.

NEKHT-KHEM.

An auditor of the court of justice, under Amen-hotep III. of the XVIIIth dynasty.

NEKHT-KHEM.

An Egyptian priest of the ancient faith of the king Ai, of the XVIIIth dynasty, who was by his successors treated as a heretic and an usurper.

NEKHT-MUTF.

An Egyptian priest. Period unknown.

NEKHT-SET.

Another form of the Egyptian royal name Seti-nekht, the father of Rameses III. of the XIXth dynasty. *See* Seti-nekht.

NEKHT-U.

A prince of Kush, in the reign of Rameses II. of the XIXth dynasty.

NEM.

An Egyptian lady, the sister of two private individuals, named Antef and Ameni, probably of the XIIth dynasty.

NEM-ANKH-ANEMS. "Imparting Life to her Skin."

The name of the seventh and last of the mystical cows or Hathors of Egyptian mythology.

NEM-MESTU.

The name of the royal ensign of Osirtesen I. of the XIIth dynasty. It was also a proper name.

NEM-UR.

An Egyptian officer, who was a *Smer*, and governor of a town in the XIIth dynasty. His wife's name was Nani.

NENA.

The consort of Sebekhotep II. of the XIIIth dynasty.

NEN-SALA.

A queen-consort of Egypt, in the Ethiopic period or the XXVIth dynasty.

NEOCAISAROS.

The monumental name of the infant son of Julius Cæsar and Queen Cleopatra. *See* Cæsarion.

NEPHELCHERES.

According to the Greek lists a king of Tanis. He has not yet been certainly identified.

NEPHERCHERES.

The Greek form of the name Nefer-ka-ra, which see.

NEPHERITES.

The Greek form of the Egyptian royal name Nai-f-aa-rut, which see.

NEPHTHYS.

The sister of Isis, and the goddess of the lower firmament. Her emblem was a dish or basin. Her office was, together with Isis, to introduce and perfect the souls of the deceased in the Judgment Hall of Osiris. She was the special deity of the town of Tsebets, or Aphroditopolis. According to the tradition of the Greeks this goddess was also the wife of Set, and on the death of Osiris, she as the guardian of the mummy protected his remains. Hence she was always represented as standing at the foot of the sarcophagi, while Isis stood at the head. Often also she was figured shielding the mummy with her wings, or as weeping over the deceased kneeling on her knees with her face shielded in her hands.

NEP-RA.

An Egyptian deity, a form of the god Ra as the god of corn.

NERGAL.

An Assyrian deity, the god of war. He was represented as a man having the legs of a cock, and holding a sword in his hand. His titles were "The Great Hero," "King of Fight," "Master of Battles," "Champion of the Gods," and "God of the Chase."

NERGAL-EDIR.

An early Chaldean astronomer, some observations by whom have been preserved in the Cuneiform tablets.

NERGAL-NAZIR.

The governor of Nisibin, in the reign of Assurnirari II. He was eponym of the year B.C. 746, the chief event in which was a revolt in the city of Calah.

NERGAL-SAR-USSUR. *Or* NERGAL-SHAREZER. "Nergal protects the King."

The son of the archmagi Bellabarisruk. He was the son-in-law of Nabu-kudur-uzur, and murdered that monarch's son and successor, Evil Merodach, and ascended his throne. He built a palace outside the royal city of Babylon, and dedicated in it great silver statues of the deity Bel. He attempted to dispute the sovereignty of Media with Cyrus, king of Persia, by whom he was slain in battle, after a short reign of four years. He was succeeded by his son, an infant, named it is conjectured Bellabarisruk. He was the Neriglissar of the Greeks. (Lenormant.)

NERGAL-UBALID.

The governor of Ahisuhina, in the reign of Tiglath Pileser II. He was eponym of the year B.C. 731, the chief event in which was an expedition to Sapiya.

NERI.

In Scandinavian mythology a giant who was the son of Loki and the father of the deity Nott.

NERIBUKI.

The Accadian name of a city or district the site of which is not known.

NERIGLISSAR.

The Greek form of the Chaldean royal name Nergal-sar-ussur, which see.

NERTHUS.

In Scandinavian mythology the goddess of the earth.

NES-A.

A royal lady of the IIIrd or IVth Egyptian dynasty.

NES-A-HOR. "Follower of Horus."

An Egyptian functionary, the son of Aufrer or Hophra. He was commandant of the regions of the South, and bore the surname of Psametik-Munkh, or Psammetichus, the Beneficent.

NES-ANHUR. "Follower of Anhur."

A high-priest of Amen Ra, in the reign of King Aspalut of the XXVth dynasty.

NES-EM-AB OR -AP. "Follower in the Ap."

A chief officer of an unnamed monarch of the IVth dynasty.

NES-KHONS. "Follower of Khons."

An Egyptian lady, the wife of a priest named Nespthah. Period uncertain.

NES-MAUT. "Follower of Maut."

An Egyptian lady, mother of the priest Auf-aad, and wife of the priest Scheds-nefer.

NES-MAUT.

The scribe of the temple of Amen Ra at Napata, in the reign of King Aspalut of the XXVth dynasty.

NES-PA-KHUEN-NU.

A priest of Apis, the son of Nesunnefer. He lived during the time of Darius Hystaspes.

NES-PTHAH. "Follower of Pthah."

A priest of Apis, in the reign of King Sheshank IV.

NES-PTHAH.

An Egyptian magician and priest, who is mentioned as the author of Pthah-nefer-ka's misfortunes in the ancient Egyptian romance, the Story of Setnau.

NESTANA.

An unidentified lake in Syria, where Thothmes III. fought a small battle, and took 490 prisoners.

NES-TAUTA-KHUT.

The wife of Prince Sheshonk the son of Osorkon I. of the XXIInd dynasty.

NES-TEN-NES-T.

An Egyptian queen of the XXIIIrd dynasty, the wife of King Namrut of Heliopolis, who sent her, together with the rest of his wives, to make peace with Piankhi of Ethiopia, his suzerain, against whom he had rebelled.

NESU.

The general of the foot soldiers in the army of Ummanigas, king of Elam, against Assurbanipal, king of Assyria.

NES-UNNEFER. "Follower of the Good being" (Osiris).
The father of Nes-pa-khuen-nu, which see.

NETEM-MENNEFER. "The Delight of Memphis."
An Egyptian lady, the wife of Pa-karkar, the feather-bearer of a king of the XXVIth dynasty.

NETER-AAT. "The Great Gods." (?)
An Egyptian town, called by the Greeks Menouthis; sacred to Isis and Osiris.

NETER-TEB.
One of the Egyptian cities which was held by the rebel chief Ankhhor, against Piankhi-mer-amen.

NETHUNS.
The Etruscan Neptune. He was represented as wearing a laurel crown, and carrying a trident. The name and deity were perhaps borrowed by the Etruscan from the Italians.

NETOS.
A sacred bull which was worshipped at Heliopolis as an incarnation of Amen Ra.

NEUT.
A nome of Lower Egypt, East of the Phatnitic branch of the Nile. Its chief town was Panephysis.

NEZEMAB.
A high functionary, the overseer of the palace in the IVth dynasty. He was the son of a similar officer named Merab.

NIA.
The Assyrian form of the name of the Egyptian capital city Thebes, which see.

NIANAI.
A commander-in-chief of the armies of Seti I. of the XIXth dynasty. His wife's name was Hentnofre, and that of his son Nebuer.

NIBARTI-ASSUR.
A strong fortress built by Assurnazirpal, king of Assyria, on the right bank of the river Euphrates.

NIBAT-ANU.
In Chaldean astronomy the name of the planet Mars, as one of the twelve stars of the West.

NIBAT-ANU. "Sanctuary of Anu." (?)
In Chaldean astronomy the usual name of the planet Mars.

NIBAT-ILAI.
The governor of Rezeph, and eponym of the year B.C. 818; Tartan of Vul-nirari III., and then eponym of the year B.C. 809.

NIBE.

The nephew of Dalta, king of Ilipa. He disputed the succession to the throne with his brother Ispabara, and called in the Elamites under Sutruk-Nanhundi to help him, but in vain, as Sargon I. defeated them both and placed Ispabara on the throne.

NIBIRU.

The astronomical name of the deity Marduk as the planet Mercury in the month of Tisri.

NIBISE.   " Armaments."

A phrase which continually occurs in the Assyrian inscriptions, " His *nibise* I took," that is, his armaments or artillery.

NICIUM.

A chief town in the Prosopite nome of Lower Egypt.

NIDINTABEL.

An impostor, who after the fall of Babylon claimed to have been Nabu-kudur-uzur, the son of Nabonahid, and for a short time usurped the Chaldean throne.   He was slain by the Persians under Darius Hystaspes.

NIFFER.

The modern name of the Chaldean city Nipur, the capital of the Accadians.

NII.

A country, supposed to be India, where Thothmes III. hunted 120 elephants.

NIKHARU.

The king of Gahupani, an unidentified country in Arabia.   He was conquered and put to death by Esarhaddon.

NIKU.

The Assyrian form of the Egyptian royal name Necho, which see.

NILO-POLIS.   " City of the Nile."

A Greco-Egyptian town, probably anciently called Hap.   It was situated on an island in the Herakleopolite nome of the Heptanomos. *See* Hap *or* Pehap.

NILQURADE.

A tribe in Mesopotamia which was conquered by Tiglath Pileser II.

NIMIT-MARUDUK.

The name of a wall which was built around his capital city by Vul-pal-idinna, king of Babylonia.

NIMROD.

The Assyrian name which the Egyptians changed into Namrut when it was borne by the princes of the XXIInd dynasty.

NIMROD.

According to Gen. x. 8-10, Nimrod was the son of Cush, and a mighty hunter, the beginning of whose kingdom "was Babel and Erech, and Accad and Calneh, in the land of Shinar." Shinar is Sumir or Sungir (North-western Chaldea), and Cush is probably to be identified with the Cassi or Cossæans of Susiania. Nimrod has been identified with Merodach, whose Accadian name was Amar-ud, and who was also the patron of Babylon, and a divine hunter, as well as with Izdubar, the hero of the great Babylonian epic, who seems to have come from the town of Marad, and was reputed "a mighty hunter." Izdubar was the Greek Herakles, and his twelve adventures answer to the twelve labours of Herakles. As both Merodach and Izdubar were solar heroes, the identification of Nimrod with both can be well maintained.

NIMRUD.

The modern name of the Assyrian city Calah.

NIN-AKHA-GUDDU.

In Accadian mythology the name of a goddess whose attributes are not well known.

NIN-BUBU. "Lord *or* God, of Sailors."

A title applied to the Assyrian deity Nin or Nindar.

NIN-DAR.

In Accadian mythology the name of the god Adar of the Assyrians, the god of the planet Saturn.

NINEVEH.

The capital city of the Assyrian empire, which according to the Hebrew writers was founded by Asshur, the descendant of Nimrod, B.C. 2245. With the exception of a few scattered notices in the book of Genesis, we know nothing of the kings who succeeded Nimrod, or of the early times of Assyria. The names only of a few almost mythical kings have been preserved in the Cuneiform tablets. The earliest historical record of Nineveh in the Hieroglyphic writings shows it to have been one of the chief cities of the confederacy of the Upper Rotennu, and as such it was the centre of a great battle, in the sixth year of his reign, between Thothmes III. of the XVIIIth dynasty, and the Syrian states. The Egyptian monarch gaining the day, imposed tribute upon the city, and placed Egyptian governors over the annexed provinces. Nineveh was again plundered in the thirty-third(?) year of the reign of Thothmes, and a few years later by Amenhotep II. Gradually the Assyrians became more and more powerful, till in the reign of Seti I. of the XIXth dynasty the Ninevites refused to pay their stipulated tribute, whereupon the Egyptian king invaded Mesopotamia, and reduced the city to obedience. Rameses II. and III., Menepthah III., and even the later Ramesside Pharaohs, all kept up the titular lordship over Nineveh, but receiving less tribute in each reign. The last of the Egyptian monarchs to form an alliance with the people of Nineveh was Harhor, who chiefly rose to the throne in the XXIInd dynasty by the help of the Assyrian princes. The people alike of Nineveh and Babylon were generally in opposition to each other, although frequently united for a time under one sceptre. The chief temples were erected by Vulnirari III. ; Sargon, Sennacherib, and Esarhaddon, all enlarged the city, and adorned it with beautiful palaces. Sennacherib indeed rebuilt the city after its first destruction by the Medians and Babylonians B.C. 789, in the reign of Asshur-likkish. Assurbanipal on his invasion of Egypt, and conquest of Thebes, brought two large obelisks to Nineveh to adorn his palace there, and his son Assur-edil-ilani fortified and improved the walls of the city. The great wealth of the Assyrian capital, and the increasing power of the revived empire of Babylonia, hastened its ruin, and the city was finally destroyed by Nabopalassar and Cyaxares B.C. 606. The circumstance of both these sieges and conquests having been carried on by the Medes and Babylonians, has caused many writers to confuse the two events into one narrative, disregarding the authenticity of the first catastrophe, and indeed the point is one which is still unsettled. The devastation of Nineveh was so complete that in the days of Alexander the Great it had ceased to become even a town. The Romans when they annexed Mesopotamia, partially rebuilt the city under the name of Ninus, but this new town was destroyed by the Sassanians, from which time every recollection of its site passed from the pages of history. In the Middle Ages the Arabs built the town of Mosul upon some of the mounds of debris which covered the ruins of the Assyrian capital, and it has only been within the last thirty-five years that its site has been rediscovered and its ruins disinterred, chiefly by Mr. A. H. Layard, and in 1848 and still more recently by George Smith in his excavations in Assyria in 1873-4. *See also* Assurbanipal, Sammuramat, Sennacherib, *and* Koyunjik.

NIN-GAL-IDINA.

A king of Ur. He was conquered by Nabu-zir-napisti-esir, who had claimed the throne of Babylon, but who was soon defeated by Esarhaddon. Nothing else is known respecting him.

NIN-GELAL.

In Accadian mythology the name of the goddess Belit.

NINHARRISSI. "Lady of the Mountains."

A title of the Assyrian goddess Ishtar.

NINII.

The Egyptian name by which the city of Nineveh is mentioned among the capitals conquered by Thothmes III.

NINIP.

A Babylonian warlike deity, and a son of the divinity Bel. He was also called Bar. His analogue was the Ares of the Greeks.

NINIPALESAR.

An early king of Assyria. He ascended the throne after the defeat and death of his father,(?) Bel-kudur-uzur, by the Babylonians, with whom he had continually to struggle for the crown. He was succeeded by his son Assurdan I.

NINIPALIKPANI.

The governor of Sihime in the reign of Sargon II., and eponym of the year B.C. 711, the chief event in which was an expedition to Ashdod.

NINIPIDIN.

The governor of Kurban in the reign of Assurdan. He was eponym of the year B.C. 757, in which year there "was peace in the land."

NINIP-ILAI.

The governor of Ahizuhina in the reign of Vulnirari III., and eponym of the year B.C. 802, the chief event in which was an expedition to Hupuskia.

NINIP-ILAI.

The governor of Nisibin in the reigns of Tiglath Pileser II. and Shalmaneser IV. He was eponym of the years B.C. 736, in which took place an expedition to the foot of Mount Naal; and 722, the chief events in which were the accession of Sargon, and the siege of Samaria.

NINIP-KIN-UZUR.

The governor of Nineveh in the reign of Vulnirari III. He was eponym of the year B.C. 790, the chief event in which was an expedition to Media.

NINIP-MUKIN-NISI.

The governor of Kirruri in the reign of Assurdan III. He was eponym of the year B.C. 765, the chief events in which were a pestilence, and an expedition to Hadrach.

NINIP-NAZUR.

The governor of Mazamua in the reign of Vulnirari III. He was eponym of the year B.C. 783, the chief event in which was an expedition to Ituha.

NINIP-SEZI-BANI.

The governor of Rimusi in the last year of the reign of Assurdan III. He was eponym of the year B.C. 754, the chief events in which were an expedition to Arpad, and the return from the city of Assur.

NINIP-TUGULTU-ASSUR.

Another name for the early Assyrian king called Assur-zikur-esir, which see.

NINIP-UZUR.

The governor of Sallat in the reign of Samsi-Vul or Samas Rimmon IV., and eponym of the year B.C. 813, the chief event in which was an expedition to Chaldea.

NINIT-GAL.   " Lord of the Strong Hand."

A title of the deity Hea, which see.

NIN-KAT-TIN-BARZIL.   " Lord of the Coat of Iron."

An Assyrian title of the god Ninip.

NIN-KI-GAL.   " Lady of the Great Earth."

The queen of Hades, the sister of Ishtar, and the wife of Hea in his character as deity of the earth.   She was supposed to have been both a sister and also another form of the goddess Davcina, and she was possibly also the goddess Mot, which see.

NIN-KUMMU.   " Lady of the Palace."

The name of an Assyrian lady or female functionary.

NIN-MAKH.   " The Mighty Lady."

In Chaldean astronomy one of the twelve stars of the West.

NIN-MARKI.

A Chaldean goddess, to whom Dungi, king of Ur, erected a temple called Bitgilsa.

NIN-MUK.

In Accadian mythology the wife of the god Turtak, the deity of the river Tigris.   *See* Turtak.   (Lenormant.)

NINNI.

A mountain district North of Assyria which was conquered by Shalmaneser II.

NIN-RIDU.

An early Chaldean deity which was worshipped by the first Chaldean kings in their capital city Ridu.

NIN-SI.

In Chaldean astronomy an unidentified planet or fixed star, possibly Venus.

NIN-UKI.

The Accadian name of the capital city Ninua, or Nineveh, now called Koyunjik.

NINUS.

The form in which the name of the city of Nineveh is preserved by Moses of Khorene.

NIORDHR.

In Scandinavian mythology the god or ruler of the winds and sea.

NIPUR.

The later name of the capital city of the Southern Chaldeans called Accad ; it was named also " The City of the Lord of the World."

NIRBA.

In Assyrian mythology the god of harvests. He was called Serakh by the Accadians in their magical incantations.

NIRGAL-LI.

The Assyrian name of the winged human-headed lions which, together with the Alapi, were used to guard the entrances of the royal palaces.

NIRI.

A people who were conquered by Budil, a very early king of Assyria.

NIRI-SAMAS.

The governor of Isania, in the reign of Vul-nirari or Rimmon-nirari III. He was eponym of the year B.C. 791, the chief event in which was an expedition to Ituha.

NIRI-SAR.

A prefect of the city of Sirgardi. He revolted against Sargon II., who captured him and added his district to the Persian provinces of Assyria.

NIRU. "Yoke."

In Chaldean astronomy an unidentified fixed star.

NIRUKTA.

An ancient Hindu etymological treatise, dealing chiefly with the difficult words and phrases of the sacred Vedas.

NIRVANA.

That condition of unconscious absorption into deity, to attain which is the highest ambition of every Buddhist. It is not annihilation, but is the absolute and the infinite. (Oriental Congress, 1874.)

NISAN-NU.

The first month of the Assyrians, dedicated to the deities Anu and Bel, answering roughly to our March. Its Accadian name was Sara-ziggar, "The Sacrifice of Righteousness."

NISAYA.

In Zendic mythology the fourth resting-place of the Iranians after their exile from Aryanem-Vaedjo, which see. It was the Nisæa of the Greeks.

NIS-BELU. "Man of Bel."

An early Babylonian proper name.

NISHEM.

Another name for the Egyptian goddess Seben, which see.

NIS-INKI.

The Accadian name of the city of Karrak.

NISINNA.   *Or* KARRAK.

A city in Babylonia, the capital of Gamil-ninip, an early Chaldean king. Its site is not known.

NISROCH.

Another name of the Assyrian deity who was more properly called Shalman. He was " The King of Fluids, " He who Presides over Destinies," and the protector of marriages. He was one of the eight greater gods, and was represented as a human figure, having an eagle's head, and being furnished with large wings. In his hands he generally held a basket of offerings and a pine cone. The true position of Nisroch is not at present fully ascertained, some Assyriologists refusing to believe in him as a separate deity, while others regard him as a form of the Chaldean Oannes. (Lenormant.)

NISTA.

In Scandinavian mythology one of the two Walküres or Fates who supplied the god Odin with mead in Asgard, the City of the Gods.

NISURA.

A city in Assyria which revolted to Assurdan, and was conquered for Shalmaneser II. by his son, Samas-Rimmon IV.

NITAKRET-MIMUT.

The regent of the kingdom in the reign of Psametik I. of the XXVIth dynasty.

NITAKRET-SERET-EN-PI-MUNTU.

A royal lady, in the reign of Psametik II. of the XXVIth dynasty.

NITETIS.

An Egyptian princess, the daughter-in-law of Uahprahet, of the Saite dynasty. Aahmes II., king of Egypt, sent her in the place of his own daughter as a wife to Cambyses, king of Persia, a fraud which led to the Persian conquest of Egypt.

NITHINE.

A chief city in the Hermopolite nome of Lower Egypt.

NITK-HOTEP-IRI-BENT.

The wife of Necht-anebos, or Nekhtarhebef, a king of the XXXth dynasty.

NITK-HOTEP-IRI-BENT.

The mother of Nechtanebos, a king of the XXXth dynasty.

NITOCRIS.

The Greek form of the royal name Neit-aker, which see.

NITRITES.

A nome of Lower Egypt, West of the Nile. It was situated on the Natron lakes, and its chief city was called Scetis.

NITUKKI.

The Accadian name of the Assyrian city Asmun, on the Persian Gulf.

NIVIT-BEL.

The name of the second of the great walls of Babylon built by Nabukuduruzur (Nebuchadrezzar) the Great.

NIVIT-MARDUK. "The Dwelling of Merodach."

A Babylonian name applied to the city Nipur, which see.

NIZIR.

A mountain district in Armenia, where, according to the Chaldean legend of the Deluge, the ark of the patriarch Adra-hasis stopped.

NOFRE. *Or* NEFER. "Good."

An Egyptian sacerdotal functionary, the superintendent of the stores of wine of the West and North. Period uncertain.

NOFRE-ARI.

The surname of the lady Tai-af, of the House of Unnefer, which see.

NOFRE-ARI.

A priestess of Amen Ra, and the wife of Har-a the royal secretary of Seti-Menepthah I. of the XIXth dynasty.

NOFRE-ATEN-NOFRE-TITI.

A wife of Amenhotep IV. of the XVIIIth dynasty.

NOFREATEN-TASERAT.

A daughter of Amenhotep IV. of the XVIIIth dynasty.

NOFRE-ATEN-TUNEN-ET.

A queen of Egypt of the XIIth dynasty, the mother of Sesertesen or Osirtesen I.

NOFRE-ATEN-TUNEN-ET.

The mother of Sesertesen II. or Osirtesen II. of the XIIth dynasty.

NOFRE-HOTEP. "Good Peace."

The master of the table of Rameses II. His father's name was Ra-ai, and that of his wife Takha.

NOFER-HOTEP. "Good Peace."

A spondist of Amen Ra. The period when he lived is uncertain.

NOFRE-HOTEP-ES.

The son of an early Egyptian king.

NOFRE-IT.

The father of an Egyptian gentleman named Senbetef, who probably lived in the XIIth or XIIIth dynasty.

NOFRE-KA-ANNU.

An early Egyptian king, who is named on the Tablet of Abydos.

NOFRE-KA-PEPI-SENEB.

An early Egyptian king, named on the Tablet of Abydos.

NOFRE-KA-RA.

An early Egyptian king, named on the Tablet of Abydos.

NOERE-KA-RA-KHEN-TU.

An early Egyptian king, named on the Tablet of Abydos.

NOFRE-KA-RA-NEBI.

An early Egyptian king, named on the Tablet of Abydos.

NOFRE-KA-RA-RE-RE-LE.

An early Egyptian king, named on the Tablet of Abydos.

NOFRE-KA-U.

Another name, or surname, of Thothmes II. of the XVIIIth dynasty, which see.

NOFRE-KHEPER-U.   " The Good Creator."

A surname of Thothmes III., which see.

NOFRE-MAT.

The son of Nofret-kau, the daughter of King Snefru of the IIIrd dynasty.

NOFRE-RA.

A daughter of Amenhotep IV. of the XVIIIth dynasty.

NOFRE-RENPE.   *Or* NEFER-RENPE.   " The Good Renpe."

An Egyptian priest, a singer in the temple of Amen Ra. He had a sister who bore the Semitic name of Sera. He lived in the time of the XVIIIth dynasty.

NOFRE-RENPE.

The keeper of the treasure of an unnamed king of Egypt. He was succeeded in his office by his son Roma.

NOFRE-T-ARI.

A daughter of Rameses II. of the XIXth dynasty.

NOFRE-T-ARI.

A princess of Ethiopia, who, by becoming the wife of Aahmes, king of Egypt, terminated a war between the two counties and practically added Nubia to Egypt. She acted as regent after the death of Aahmes during the earlier part of the reign of her son, Amenhotep I.

NOFRE-T-ARI-MITEN-MUT.

A wife of Rameses II. of the XIXth dynasty.

NOFRE-TITI.

A queen of Egypt, the first wife of Amenhotep IV. of the XVIIIth dynasty. *See* Nofre-aten-nofre-titi..

NOFRE-T-KAU.

The daughter of King Snefru, of the IIIrd dynasty.

NOFRE-TUM-IRI-HOTEP.

The father of At-ha-ankht-senbt, a priest of Apis.

NOGUEL.

In Cabalistic mythology the spirit of the planet Venus.

NOHEM-MASCHUF. " He who saves his Soldiers."

An Egyptian officer, the son of Mui-en-hiku, in the reign of Amenhotep III.

NOHEM-S.

An Egyptian lady, whose mummy is in the Leyden Museum.

NOMAN.

A king of Sabæa. He succeeded to the throne of his father Yafar after the temporary reign of the usurper Dhu-riash. Nothing else is known respecting him.

NOMARCH. " Chief of a Nome."

The Greek name for the local governor or viceroy of an Egyptian nome.

NOME. In Egyptian, HESEP.

A province or district in Egypt, having its own local deity, temple, capital city, and governor. There were twenty-two of these provinces in Upper, and the same number in Lower Egypt, during the empire of the Pharaohs. Every nome had also its own *Pehu* or frontier town, its *Mer* or lake, and its *Uu*, which see.

NOPH.

The Hebrew name of an Egyptian city, held by some Egyptologists to have been Memphis, near the Delta, and by others Napata, the capital of Ethiopia.

NORDRI. " North."

In Scandinavian mythology one of the four horns which support the vault of heaven." *See* Austri.

NORNES.

In Scandinavian mythology the name of the deities of Fate, who were also called Walküres, which see.

NORTIA.

According to Livy and Martial the Etruscan goddess of Fortune. A Latin inscription calls Nursia "a *lar*" of Volsinii.

NORWI.

Another form of the name of the mythical giant Neri, which see.

NOTT.   " Night."

In Scandinavian mythology the daughter of the giant Neri, the son of Loki. She had three husbands : to her first, Naglfari, she bore Udr ; to her second, Onar, she bore a daughter Iord, " the earth ;" and by her third she had Dag, or " the day." She rode on a mythical horse called Hrimfaxi, the foam from whose lips formed the dew.

NTAHRU.

Another form of the name of the Egyptian town Denderah or Tentyra, which see.

NTARIUSHA.

The Egyptian form of the Persian royal name Darius.

NU.

The name of the great primordial water in the Ist chapter of the Ritual of the Dead.

NU-AMEN.   " The Way of Amen."

The Egyptian phrase for an upright walk. The exact rendering is "the water of Amen," the water or Nile being the " highway" of Egypt. (Goodwin.)

NU-ANTEF.

The form in which the Egyptian royal name Antef or Entef is written by some Egyptologists.

NUB.   " Gold."

A priestess of " Amen Ra, king of the gods." Uncertain period.

NUB.   " Gold."

An Egyptian goddess. She was a form of Hathor as a funereal deity.

NUBAIT.

An uncertain Egyptian goddess.

NUB-EM-HET.

The daughter of an Egyptian king, but of what king it is not known.

NUB-EM-TEKH.

An unknown Egyptian princess, probably of the XIXth dynasty.

NUB-EM-USEKH.   " Gold of the Hall of Assembly." (?)

An Egyptian lady, the wife of Piaa, a functionary of the XVIIIth dynasty.

NUBEN-AMEN-HA (Masc.).   NUBEN-AMEN-MA (Fem.).

Common Egyptian names in the XVIIIth dynasty.

NUB-HOTEP. "Peace of Nub."

The son of an early Egyptian king.

NUB-HOTEP.

The wife of Neb-em-khutet, the son of Tetet, an early Egyptian king.

NUB-KHAS.

The consort of Antef III. of the XIth dynasty.

NUB-KHAS.

The wife of King Sebek-em-saf of the XVIIIth dynasty.

NUB-NA.

An Egyptian lady of rank. The wife of the councillor Ra-n-senb of the XIIth dynasty. She was a Bektenhak, which see.

NUB-NOFRE. "Good Nub," *or* "Good as Gold." (?)

The daughter of Uetu, the chief of the Keneb in the XVIIIth dynasty.

NUB-NOFRE.

An Egyptian lady, the wife of Amenmes, and the mother of Amen-hotep, who was surnamed Hui.

NUB-SAS.

An Egyptian queen of the XIth dynasty, the consort of Antef III.

NUBUKHA.

The consort of Sebekhotep V. of the XIIIth dynasty.

NUHA.

Another name of the Assyrian goddess Nukimmut, which see.

NUHEM.

A deity worshipped at Nishem in Upper Egypt.

NUHER.

A mystical region of Amenti, which is often mentioned in the Ritual of the Dead.

NUKIMMUT.

An Assyrian goddess. She was the mother of the gods Ninip and Nebo.

NUMIA. "Is wanting," *i.e.* recedes.

In Chaldean astronomy a name of the planet Mars.

NUMKI.

The Accadian name for the district of Elamu, now called Khuzistan.

NUN.

This deity was properly the personification of the primordial water of chaos, out of which all life, even that of the gods, and all material things proceeded. On the sarcophagus of Seti I., in the Soane Museum, he is represented as holding up the boat of Kheper Ra and the goddess Isis. Considered as the consort of Isis, the goddess of the heavens. Nun was also the father of Horus Ra ; while on the papyri the deity is often spoken of as the creator of vegetation, and of all things sustainable by water. His name has been supposed to be derived from the Coptic *noun* "the abyss," and it is generally written with three *n's* or water bottles, having the vault of heaven as a determinative, and three signs expressing either water, or the letter *n*, as the plural of majesty.

NU-NEKHT-IK-NU-EN-NEB-BEK-I.

An Egyptian scribe. His period and works are uncertain.

NUN-NU.

An Egyptian gentleman in the latter years of the XVIIIth dynasty. His mother's name was Atef, and his daughter's Hat-schep-u.

NUNU.

An uncertain deity who was worshipped in Upper Egypt in later times.

NURAY.

Another form of the Arabian royal name Hazael, father of Vaiteh, which see.

NURVAL.

An early Babylonian king. He reigned at Larsa, where he built the temples of Bit-rubmah, Bit-minuni, and Bit-galzib, to the deities Ur and Ningal.

NUSHIM.

An early Egyptian goddess, who was worshipped in the city of Ankaf.

NUSTHIEH.

A mystical dragon, who was represented on an Etruscan mirror as devouring a man armed with a sword.

NUT.

A name of the firmament adored as a goddess in the Egyptian Ritual of the Dead. Like Hathor and Neith this goddess personified the celestial space, but more especially the vault of heaven, under the form of a woman bending down and touching the earth with her hands. She was also called the mother of the gods, and of the stars also, being often represented as having them in her womb, or giving birth to them. She was also often sculptured or painted on the underside of the lids of the sarcophagi, as protecting the mummy of the deceased. On the sarcophagus of A-ero-ai in the Amhurst (formerly Lee) Collection, she is represented as a woman, blue in flesh, extended over a man, also blue in colour, who is rising up towards her, while his body falls to the ground, the body being painted red or flesh colour. In the LIXth chapter of the Ritual of the Dead, her office was to sustain the soul of the deceased by pouring out the water of life, the goddess herself standing in the boughs of the sacred sycamore tree. Nut must not be confounded with the deity Nun, the personification of the primordial waters of chaos, or with the goddesses Hathor, Neith, or Nephthys, although she fulfilled very much the same offices, and was also represented occasionally like them as cow-headed.

NUTERHEK.

The surname of Amenhotep II. of the XVIIIth dynasty.

NUTERHEK.

The original surname of Amenhotep IV. of the XVIIIth dynasty. *See* Khu-en-aten.

NUT-MI-AMEN.

Another form of the Egyptian royal name Amen-meri-nut, which see.

NYAYA.

An ancient Hindu sacred treatise upon ethics and morality. One of the greater Shastras.

O.

OANNES.

An Assyrian deity, half man and half fish, who according to the Greek mythologists, floated on the waters of chaos. He was called the " Lord of the Lower World," and " Lord of Darkness," and was probably analogous to the Dagon of the Phenicians.

OASES.

Certain depressions in the deserts to the West of Egypt, which were famous for their fertility and temples. Hibe was the capital of the great Oasis ; the other three were the Western Oasis, eighty miles from Hibe ; the little Oasis, and the Oasis of Amun, 320 miles from Memphis, and 160 from Parœtonium.

OBAL.

The Hebrew name of the Arabic district called Jobal.

OBELISK.   *Or* TEK-KEN, in Egyptian.

The obelisk proper, as distinguished from the Hindu *Lat*, or Classic column, or Phenician pillar, is a monolithic quadrangular prism, with sloping sides and right angled, and diminishing gradually to the summit, where it is suddenly terminated by a small trapezium. No real obelisk has an entasis or swelling in the sides, or is terminated by a conical cap, although obelisks are frequently so represented in inaccurate drawings. The apex of an Egyptian obelisk is also sometimes plain, and sometimes inscribed ; when the latter it is generally with a representation of the king by whom it was erected, making offerings to a deity, or receiving gifts from him. The inscriptions on the sides are almost always a laudatory series of titles with little historical information, and very often the centre line, as at Karnak, was the work of one monarch, and the outer columns that of another. Obelisks were further generally set up in pairs at the entrances of the outer and inner pylons of the temples, and they were, there is reason to believe, in the case of those of Hatasu of the XVIIIth dynasty, capped with pyramids of gold or gilded bronze. The monuments of the Fayum and Axum in Abyssinia, are not properly obelisks, but rather military stèle ; and the so-called obelisks of the Phenician deities were generally cylindrical stones, symbolical of the deities Asher and Asherah. According to Bonomi there are about forty-two known obelisks of Egyptian origin, either in Egypt, Rome, Paris, or London. There were probably as many more, which have since been broken up for building materials, besides one which is known to exist under the walls of a palace at Rome, and two which were carried off from Thebes by Assurbanipal, and taken to Nineveh, where they have not been discovered. The famous column called Pompey's pillar, erected by Diocletian, stands upon a fragment of an ancient obelisk, and tradition asserts that there are many similar fragments of greater or less antiquity under the ruins of the older houses of Alexandria. The following list of the dimensions of the principal obelisks was drawn up in 1840 by Bonomi. Those marked * are only approximate measures, the bases of the monuments being hidden :—

Obelisk of	Lateran (Thothmes III.)	105 ft.	0 in.*	Rome.
,,	Karnak (Thothmes I.)	93 ft.	6 in.	Karnak.
,,	Piazza San Pietro	83 ft.	2 in.	Rome.
.,	Piazza del Popolo (Seti I.)	87 ft.	5 in.	Rome.
,,	Luxor (Rameses II.)	85 ft.	0 in.*	Luxor.
,,	Paris (Rameses II.)	76 ft.	6 in.	Paris.
,,	Piazza Citorio (Psametik I.)	71 ft.	5 in.	Rome.
,,	Karnak (Thothmes III. and Hatasu)	70 ft.	0 in.*	Karnak.
,,	Alexandria (Thothmes III.)	69 ft.	1 in.	Alexandria.
,,	Matarieh (Osirtesen I.)	67 ft.	4 in.	Matarieh.
,,	Arles	56 ft.	9 in.	Arles.
,,	Al-Meidan (Thothmes III.)	50 ft.	0 in.*	Constantinople.
,,	Piazza Navona (Domitian)	54 ft.	3 in.	Rome.
,,	Maria Maggiore	48 ft.	5 in.	Rome.
,,	Piazza Quirinale	47 ft.	6 in.	Rome.
,,	Trinita del Monte (Seti I.)	43 ft.	6 in.	Rome.
,,	Constantinople	35 ft.	0 in.	Constantinople.
,,	Philæ	30 ft.	0 in.*	Philæ.
,,	Monte Pincio (Hadrian)	30 ft.	0 in.	Rome.
,,	Corfe Castle (Alexander I.)	22 ft.	0 in.	Corfe.
,,	Piazza Rotunda (Rameses II. ?)	19 ft.	9 in.	Rome.
,,	Al Karnak (Thothmes III.)	19 ft.	0 in.*	Karnak.
,,	Piazza Minerva	17 ft.	0 in.	Rome.
,,	Villa Mattei	8 ft.	3 in.*	Rome.
,,	Alnwick (Amenhotep II.)	6 ft.	0 in.	Alnwick.
,,	(2) British Museum (Amyrtæus)	8 ft.	1 in.	London.
,,	Museo Florentino	7 ft.	0 in.	Florence.
,,	Ditto	5 ft.	10 in.	Florence.
,,	(2) Benevento	9 ft. (?) in.		Benevento.
,,	Soughton Hall	(?)		

Besides these there are many prostrate obelisks as follows :—Nine at Tanis ; two at Karnak ; one at Alexandria, given to the English government at the capitulation of Alexandria, but never removed, and suffering much damage from neglect.

Od.

In Accadian mythology the name of the Assyrian deity Shamas, the sun, as " The King of Justice." *See* Shamas *or* Samas.

Odin.

In Northern mythology a great deity and the son of Borr. He and his brethren slew the frost giant Ymir. He was the Scandinavian god of war.

ODULAM.

The Egyptian name of an uncertain Syrian town, Adullam.(?)

ŒAEI.

An Egyptian lady, the wife of Ra-amen, the spondist of Pthah, which see. (Leemans.)

ŒR.

An Egyptian, the father of the lady Ten-chei-hat, and husband of Isi-oer, a priestess of Amen Ra.

ŒRI.

An Egyptian doctor in the Vth dynasty. Nothing else is known respecting him.

ŒR-NEKHT-U.

Another name of the great Egyptian fortress called Tatehu, which see.

ŒSAR.

See Asera, an Etruscan deity.

ŒTO-SYRUS.   " The Sun."

According to Herodotus the name of a Scythian deity answering to the Apollo of the Greeks.

OIMENEPTHAH I.

The name given by Mr. Sharpe to Seti-Menepthah I. of the XIXth dynasty, which see.

OITOSYRUS.   " The Sun."

The Sanskrit name of the Scythian deity Œto-syrus, which see.

OLLER.

Another form of the name of the Scandinavian deity Uller, which see.

OMAN.

The modern name of the country in Southern Arabia, which was called Raamah by the Hebrew writers.

OMANES.

The name of one of the ancient kings of Susiana. It was the name assumed by the rebel Martius when he revolted against Darius Hystaspes.

OMBITES.

The last nome in the Thebaid of Upper Egypt. It took the place of the ancient nome of Tokens, and its capital city was Ombos.

OMBOS.   *Or* KOUM-OMBOS.

The chief city in the Ombite nome of the Thebaid in Upper Egypt. It contained a grand double temple to the two forms of Horus. Hor-sebek and Har-uer.

OMBTE.

Another name of the deity Set or Sutekh. He was represented as a man with the head of a peculiarly long snouted animal, having square erect ears, by some confounded with the ass, and by others with the Fennek, a species of Abyssinian dog. (Wilkinson.)

OMPHIS.

According to Herodotus a nome in Egypt held by the Calasirian class of warriors.

OMRI.   In Assyrian, KHUMRI.

A king of Israel. He founded the IIIrd Israelitish dynasty after defeating Zimri, who had murdered Elah, and compelling him to burn himself in the palace of Tirzah. He also defeated Tibni, another competitor for the crown, and reigned six years in Tirzah. He then made Samaria the capital of the kingdom, and reigned there another six years. He allied himself with the Phenicians, and married his son Ahab to the daughter of the Sidonian king Ethbaal. Samaria is sometimes called Bit-khumri or Bit-khumriya, " The House of Omri," in the Assyrian inscriptions.

ONAERGES.

A king of Limenium in the Island of Kypros. *See* Unasagos, which is probably the same name.

ONAR.

In Scandinavian mythology the second husband of the goddess Nott, by whom he had a daughter Iörd, or the earth. He was also called Anar.

ONNOS.

The Greek form of the royal name Unas, which see.

ONOURIS.

Another name of the Egyptian deity Anhur, which see.

OOHHOTEP.

See Aahotep, a queen of the XIIth dynasty.

OOHMES.

The form adopted by some Egyptologists for the royal name Aahmes. The same rule applies to the use of the initial Oo throughout in lieu of Aa.

OOHMES.   *Or* AAHMES.

An Egyptian priest and officer, whose monument is in the Leyden Museum.   Period uncertain.

OPADARMES.

The father of Atrines, the rebel king of Susiana. *See* Atrines.

Ops.

In Roman mythology an ancient name of the deity of the earth.

Orchamus.

The Greek form of an early Chaldean king, who was at one time supposed to have been the same as Urukh, but he was more probably the Urhamsi of the Izdubar legends.

Orchoe.

The Greek name of the ancient Chaldean city of Erech.

Ormazd.

The form in which the name of the great deity of good Ahura-mazda is written on the Behistun inscription of Darius Hystaspes.

Ortospana.

A great city on the Southern road from Babylon to India.

Oshe.   *Or* Ushe.

An Egyptian officer, whose monument is in the Leyden Museum.

Osirei-menepthah.

The name given by some Egyptologists to Seti-Menepthah I.

Osir-hapi.

The soul of the deceased animal deity Apis assimilated into the nature and deity of Osiris, a very late Egyptian mythos, from whence in Ptolemaic times the god Serapis was educed.

Osiris.   *Or* Asi.

The deity Ra in his attribute of judge of the deceased, the Rho-t-amenti. He was one of the principal as well as the oldest of the Egyptian deities, and the deceased when justified was by some mysterious inspiration believed to partake of his divine nature, and was henceforth called the Osirian.   On the monuments and in the statuettes Osiris was represented as a man clothed in a very light robe, which descends to his feet, and in which his arms up to the hands are covered.   On his head was the *Atef* crown, peculiar to himself, and in his hands he held the cucufa staff, the flabellum, the pedum or crook, and the crux ansata.   The head of the divinity was covered with a closely fitting skull cap, and he wore his beard long and closely plaited into the form of the letter J.   This shape of beard was characteristic of Osiris alone, and of the statues of kings and defunct persons who were assimilated to him.   In the genealogy of the gods Osiris was the brother of Typhon, and of Isis and Nephthys, and the father of the deity Horus by his sister wife Isis.   He was considered to have reigned as one of the divine kings in Egypt in the prehistoric period, and to have been dethroned and slain by Typhon, who cut him to pieces, scattering portions of his body throughout the country. Ultimately, however, his son Horus Teti ("The Conqueror"), aided by his mother Isis, raised an army, and defeating Typhon, dismembered him in the like manner as Osiris was mutilated. In the mean time the goddesses Isis and Nephthys had gone over the land seeking the remains of the god, and raising a temple tomb over every portion of his body wherever it was found ; the chief members and consequently the principal tombs of Osiris being at This or Abydos, and on the Island of Philæ. As the deity Ra in the lower world Osiris was regarded as the judge of the dead, or the Rho-t-amenti, in the hall of the two truths, where were the openings respectively of heaven (Aalu), hell (Karr), and purgatory (Ker-neter), and where a court composed of forty-two assessors adjudicated with him on the life and actions of the deceased. As the author of all life, animal and vegetable, Osiris was also regarded as the god of agriculture, probably on account also of the resurrection being pictorially represented by the growth of a plant. The offices and characteristics of Osiris were many, and were very complicated, as is the case with the characteristics of all the Egyptian deities. His worship dated back to the earliest times of the empire, and continued almost without interruption till the Roman conquest, when the cultus of Osiris-Apis, or the god Serapis, was introduced. He had a variety of names, many of them mystical, and to which Herodotus refers when he declares that the name of the deity was not to be uttered. The chief titles of Osiris were Unnefer, "The Good Being," *par excellence;* Neb-er-jer, " The Lord over All ;" Neb-ua, " The One ;" Rho-t-amenti, " Judge in Amenti," etc. *See also* Horus, Isis, Nephthys.

OSIRIS-AAH.   " Osiris the Moon."

A very rare form of the deity Osiris. It is an instance of the interfusion of characters and attributes of the Egyptian divinities.

OSIRIS-PETHEMPAMENTES.

A title given to Osiris as the Egyptian Pluto. (Wilkinson.)

OSIRTESEN I.

The second king of the XIIth dynasty, and the son of Amenemha I. He conquered a great part of the land of Kush or Ethiopia proper, and erected fortresses to repel the incursions of the Negroes into Egypt. A great inundation of the Nile, followed by a famine, took place in his reign, the terrors of which were alleviated by the wisdom of his chief officer Ameni. After reigning thirty-eight years he associated Amenemha II. with himself, and then reigned jointly four years longer. The name Osirtesen is also written Sesertesen, and Usertesen by the Continental Egyptologists. Osirtesen I. was the original founder of the temple of Karnak, and the obelisk bearing his name at Heliopolis is the only monument of the Ancient Empire which remains in situ.

OSIRTESEN II.

A king of the XIIth dynasty, of whose reign nothing has been recorded.

OSIRTESEN III.

A king of the XIIth dynasty. He carried on wars against the Negroes whom he forbad to enter Egypt except as traders. He reigned thirty-eight years, and was subsequently deified by Thothmes III. of the XVIIIth dynasty. His divine or sacerdotal name was Ra-sha-ken.

OSIRTESEN.

An Egyptian official, the son of Hathorse, chief of the country, etc., in the reign of Amenemha II. of the XIIth dynasty.

OSIRTESEN.

A private Egyptian, the son of Tata and the lady Hathorse. He lived probably in the XIIth dynasty.

OSIRTESEN.

A "Friend of the King," " Keeper of the Treasure," and "High Officer of the Court" of an unnamed monarch of the XIIth dynasty.

OSIRTESEN.

An Egyptian officer in the XIIth dynasty. He was named after a king of that name. His wife's name was Ta-hut-senu, and he had a large family, most of whose names are lost.

OSIRTESEN.

An Egyptian officer, the son of Antef-aker and the lady Hotep. His wife's name was Setap. His period is unknown.

OSIRTESEN.

An Egyptian official, the son of the lady Hotep, and father of two sons who were named Khati and Hotepui respectively. His period and position are unknown, except that they were anterior to the XVIIIth dynasty.

OSIRTESEN.

An Egyptian gentleman of importance, although not a state officer, in the reign of Osirtesen II. of the XIIth dynasty.

OSIRTESEN-ANKH.   "The Living Osirtesen."

The son of a priest named Shotephet, who probably lived in the time of the XIIth dynasty.

OSIRTESEN-PEPA.

The son of the lady Ankh-atefs. He was a *Toparch* or governor of a town under one of the kings of the XIIth dynasty.

OSOCES.

A Persian officer, and the father of Ardomanes, an officer and friend of Darius Hystaspes.

OSOCHOR.

According to the Greek lists a king of Tanis. He has not yet been certainly identified.

OSORHE.

Another son of the Egyptian Pneihor.

Osorkon I.

A king of the XXIInd dynasty, of whom little is known.

Osorkon II.

A king of the XXIInd dynasty, of whom little is known.

Osorkon III.

The second king of the XXIIIrd dynasty. He succeeded Pettubast, and was himself succeeded by King Psimut.

Osorkon. *Or* Osorchen.

The Greek form of the Egyptian royal name Uaserken, which see.

Osorkon.

The son of Prince Sheshonk, son of Osorkon I. of the XXIInd dynasty.

Osorkon.

The son of Takelot II. of the XXIInd dynasty.

Osorsen.

An early unarranged Egyptian king. (Leemans.)

Ostara.

Among the Germans the goddess of the dawn. Her analogue was the Ushas of Vedic mythology.

Ostracena.

An Egyptian city on the Arabian frontier, near to Palestine.

Osymundyas.

According to the Greek historians the name of an Egyptian king of the XIXth dynasty, of whom many wonderful things are related. He has been identified with Seti-Menepthah I.

Othoes.

According to the Greek lists, the successor of Thampsis, king of Memphis. He has not yet been certainly identified.

Othoes.

The Greek form of the royal name Teta, or Ati, which see.

Otiara.

A district of Armenia, where the army of Dadarses the rebel for a fifth time was defeated by Vomises, the general of Darius Hystaspes. *See* Atchidu.

Otiartes.

Possibly a Greek form of the Chaldean name Ubaru-tutu, which see.

OTIARTES of Larsam.

According to Berosus the ninth antediluvian king of Babylon.

OTOUG.   *Or* OUTOUG.

In Accadian mythology a class of wicked spirits which afflict mankind.

OUAHABRA.   *Or* HOPHRA.

The surname of Psametik I., which see.

OUAPHRES.   *Or* OUBHARA, *or* HOPHRA.

An early unarranged monarch of the Ancient Empire.

OUAPHRES.

A devotee of Apis, in the XXVth dynasty.   He was the son of Hap-mu.

OUDYANA.   " The Garden."

In Hindu mythology a district near Cashmere, by some writers considered to have been the site of the Garden of Eden.

OUEI.

An Egyptian lady, the sister of the scribe Thoth who was an overseer of the bulls of Amen Ra.

OULTARA-KOUROU.

In Hindu mythology the name of the Garden of Paradise.

OUM-EL-AWAMID.

The modern name of the Phenician town Caicna, which see.

OUNEPHES.

The fourth king of Egypt.   He built for his tomb the pyramid of Sekkarah, the oldest Egyptian monument extant.   During his reign Egypt was visited by a famine.   He reigned twenty-three years.

OUNNEFER.   *Or* UNNEFER.   " *The* Good Being."

In Egyptian mythology a title applied to Osiris, and by incarnation to the soul of the deceased as an Osirian.

OUNNEFER.

The chancellor of King Ouaphres, an early Egyptian monarch.

OUONSOU.

A priest of Anubis and scribe of the South country.   His monument is in the Leyden Museum, and the period when he lived is uncertain ; it may have been the XVIth dynasty.

OUS.

A Phenician city near the town of Melkarth, of which it was a dependency.   It was the Alexandroschœne of the Greeks.

Ousor.

The Egyptian name of an uncertain Syrian mountain.

Outhor.

An Egyptian gentleman, the father of the functionary Hor-irem and the husband of the lady Tahart.

Ouza.   *Or* Uza.

The Egyptian name of the symbolical eye of Horus.   It is supposed originally to have had an astronomical import.

Ouzahor.   " Eye of Horus."

A priest of Apis, in the XXIVth dynasty.

Ouzahor.

The father of Doun-se-pa-nefer, which see.

Ouzahor.

A priest of Apis, of the XXVIth dynasty.

Owl-headed Minerva.

The idea of this goddess is due to the imaginative enthusiasm of Dr. Schliemann, who believed that he saw an Owl-headed Athena in the rude attempts at the imitation of the human face on vases and other objects discovered by him at Hissarlik.   The faces of certain images of Apollo found on the coasts of Asia Minor, and now in the British Museum, are ruder than those of the Hissarlik antiquities. Similar faces are also found on the Etruscan black-ware from Chiusi, where the spout of the vase serves for a nose ; and it is probable that the ornamentation originated in two eyes being set on each side of a vessel's spout, or mouth, to ward off the evil eye.   Two large eyes are sometimes introduced on Greek vases in the midst of a group of figures. (Sayce.)   *See also* Uza.

Oxyrynchus.

The Greek name for the city and nome in Upper Egypt which was called by the Egyptians Seb.   It was sacred to the goddess Hathor.

Ozier.

The Arabic form which sometimes represents the Hebrew name Ezra.

P.

PA-AMEN. " Town of Amen."

An Egyptian town, now called Sebua, which Rameses II. founded, and where he built a temple to Amen-Rameses, one of his protecting deities.

PA-ANEBU. " Town of Anubis."

An unidentified Egyptian city which was held by the rebel chiefs against Piankhi-Meramen, and which was one of the last to submit to him.

PA-ANKH. " The Living."(?)

An official title of the Egyptian kings, to swear by which, unless in the case of a state functionary, was a great crime.

PA-ANMU.

An Egyptian, the father of the priest Pse-pthah, which is all that is known concerning him.

PA-ASCH.

A priest of the goddess Bast, in the reign of Bakenranf, of the XXIVth dynasty.

PA-BARIS. " Town of the Boat."

An Egyptian town where the Greeks were arrested on their invasion into Egypt, in the reign of Menepthah II.

PABAS.

An Egyptian chief, governing the cities Kher and Pehap. He was one of the rebels who unsuccessfully revolted against Piankhi-Meramen.

PA-BE-KHEN-NU.

A mystical name of Amen Ra, in the CLXVIth chapter of the Ritual of the Dead.

PACHNAMUNIS.

The chief town in the Lower Sebennytic nome of Lower Egypt.

PACIS. *From* PA-KA, " Bull Town."

A sacred bull worshipped at Hermonthis during the Greek period as an incarnation of the compound deity Amen-Horus.

PADI. *Or* PADIAH.

The king of Migron. He was a faithful tributary to Sennacherib, and was driven from his throne by a revolution of his subjects, who sent him a prisoner to Hezekiah, king of Judah, at that time the head of a rebellion against Assyria. This led to Sennacherib's invasion of Judea, when he first captured Migron and crucified the leading rebels, and then, entering Jerusalem, brought Padi out and restored him to his throne, apparently in the absence of Hezekiah, whom he soon blockaded in Jerusalem and compelled to submit, and to send an embassy with a servile message and abundant treasure, including thirty talents of gold and 400 of silver.

PA-DU-AMEN-NES-TA-UI.

The third priest of Amen-Ra-Schep-Maut, and the father of Bentedhor and Her-khe-ba, both priests of Amen. The *d* in these names would be better rendered by the letter *t*.

PA-DU-BAST.

A devotee of Apis in the thirty-third year of Darius. He was the son of Pef-a-bast.

PA-DU-EN-RA.

The father of Ankh-hor, the priest of Apis. Period uncertain.

PA-DU-ISI.

A singer and harpist in the temple of Pthah-Sokari-Osiris.

PA-DU-NEIT.

The son of Pa-du-pthah, priest of Apis.

PADUNEITH.

The high-priest of Pthah, in the reign of Amasis II. and his son Psametik.

PA-DU-NUB.

The signet-bearer of King Aspalut, of the XXVth dynasty.

PA-DU-PTHAH.

A priest of Apis. Period unknown.

PA-DU-PTHAH.

The son of Pa-du-bast, priest of Apis. *See* Pa-du-bast.

PA-DUS.

An Egyptian official, son of the governor Horirem and father of the priest Horirem, which see.

PA-DU-UZA-HOR.

The father of Par-du-bast, a priest of Apis, in the XXIVth dynasty.

PAHAS-BEL.

The governor of Amida, in the reign of Sargon II. He was the eponym of the year B.C. 705.

PAHATES.

A stout kind of mastiff which was used for hunting by the ancient Egyptians ; called also *kamu*, "black."

PAHE.

An Elamite officer, who claimed the crown of Elam against the usurper Ummanaldas. He submitted to Assurbanipal after the sack of Shashan and was carried captive to Nineveh.

PA-HEB.

An Egyptian devotee whose name is only known from an inscription on an Apis tablet in the Museum of the Louvre.

PAH-NASI.

The chief of the boatmen of an unnamed Egyptian king, probably of the XIXth dynasty. He was a *Seka* of the king, which see.

PAH-OS.

A prophet of Amen Ra. Period uncertain.

PAH-UER-NEFER. "That which arrives at Perfection."

An Egyptian officer, the chief of the granaries and of the royal cattle of a king of the Vth dynasty.

PA-ILAK.

The Egyptian name of the island on the Nile which was called by the Greeks Philæ.

PAI-NETEM.

A king of the XXIst dynasty, the grandson of Har-hor, the usurper. He married a lady of the deposed royal House of Rameses, the princess Ra-ke-maa, and thus consolidated his right to the throne. He paid tribute to Tiglath-Pileser I., king of Assyria. Nothing certain is known as to the length of his reign, or the events which took place in it.

PAKA. "Town of the Bull" (Apis).

An early Egyptian name for the town of Athribis.

PA-KA-IKNA.

The Egyptian name of an unidentified Syrian city.

PA-KAMSI.

A royal scribe in the reign of Rameses II. of the XIXth dynasty.

PA-KAR. "Battle City."

An Egyptian town of early origin (VIth dynasty). The site of this city is the Egyptian Babylon of Hebrew writers.

PA-KAR-KAR.

A feather-bearer of a king of the Saitic period, *i.e.* the XXIVth or XXVIth dynasty.

PAKHATEM-GARU.

The full name of the Egyptain town Garu, founded by Rameses II. *See* Garu, *or* Rameses.

PA-KHNUTI.

One of the twenty petty kingdoms of Egypt under the Assyrian Icosarchy.

PAKHRAT-HAR-AA-USKH.

An incense-bearer of the temple of the god Khons at Thebes. His sarcophagus and mummy are in the British Museum.

PAKHRUA.

The father of Ankhkheperra, priest of Apis.

PAKHUNA-NIAPI. *Or* IPHKHARDESU.

The Assyrian name for the Egyptian king He-pthah-esis, which see.

PAKHUR-NINIP.

The king of Pakhnuti, one of the twenty petty kingdoms of Egypt under the Assyrian Icosarchy.

PAKI.

The Accadian name of several cities or districts, the sites of which are not known.

PAKU.

In Accadian mythology the name of the Assyrian deity Nebo, which see.

PAKU-RU. *Or* PAQURU.

. The king of Pisabtu. One of the first petty kings of the Assyrian-Egyptian Icosarchy.

PALÆMAREA.

Another name of the town of Marea, in Lower Egypt.

PALAUL.

An ascetic, who lives upon milk and dwells in the holy mountains of the Todas. *See* Kavilaul.

PALDARA.

In Chaldean astronomy an unidentified fixed star.

PALIYA.

The governor of Mazamua, in the reign of Assurdan III. He was eponym of the year B.C. 768.

Paliya.

The son of Nabu-sapau and grandson of Merodach-baladan. He was taken captive by Assurbanipal, king of Assyria, against whom he rebelled, and was then disjointed alive as a spectacle in the court of his captor.

Pallakists.

In Egyptian mythology certain ladies who were attached to the temple of Amen Ra and the greater male deities as a kind of superior servant. They were called the "concubines of the god," and the office was frequently held by the inferior wives of the kings of Egypt. The title does not necessarily imply any impurity in the Pallakists, who may rather be regarded as ladies of the harem of the monarch in his divine capacity, in contradistinction to those belonging to him as personal friends.

Pa-mai.

An Egyptian king of the XXIInd dynasty. He succeeded She-shanka III. He reigned more than twenty years, which is all that is recorded of him. He was succeeded by Sheshanka IV., the last king of the dynasty.

Pa-mau.

An Egyptian priest of the goddess Mehi. He was one of a family which had held the like office for five generations.

Pam-panis.

A town in the desert belonging to the Tentyrite nome, in the Thebaid of Upper Egypt.

Pamu. "The Lion."

The chief commander of the mercenaries, and one of the rebel chiefs who was defeated by Piankhi-Meramen of the XXIInd dynasty.

Pamurkau.

The son of an officer in the reign of Queen Aahmes Nofre-tari, named Iou-ernuf, which see.

Pa-naham.   "Town of the Saviour." (?)

An Egyptian city of early origin. Its site is unknown.

Panammu.

The king of Samhala, a Syrian state which was conquered by Tiglath-Pileser II.

Pan-assur-lamur.

An Assyrian officer, who was governor of Arbela in the reigns of Shal-maneser III. and Assurdan III. He was eponym of the years B.C. 776, in which year took place an expedition to Ararat, and 759, the chief events in which were a revolt in the city of Gozan, and a pestilence.

PANDOSIRIS.

A Kypriote deity, whose name occurs on an inscription in the Cesnola Collection.

PA-NEB-AP-UKA. "House of the Lord of Chieftains."

An Egyptian city in the twenty-second nome of Lower Egypt.

PA-NEBT-MA.

An early Egyptian astronomer, some observations by whom have been preserved.

PA-NEHES.

A royal scribe of the period of the XIXth dynasty.

PA-NEPHYSIS.

The chief town of the Grecian nome of Lower Egypt.

PANINTIMRI.

A deity of the Susians of whom nothing is known.

PANKHI.

An obscure Ethiopian king of the XXIVth dynasty.

PAN-OPOLIS. "City of Pan."

The Greek name for the Egyptian city called Chemmis by the natives, and Khimuni by the Assyrians, by whom it was raised to the rank of a petty kingdom under the Icosarchy.

PANORMUS.

The ancient Greek name of a Tyrian settlement in Sicily, called by the Phenicians Machanath, which see. It is now called Palermo.

PANTABIBLOS.

A city in Chaldea where, according to Berosus, a great library was founded. It is supposed to have been Uru or Larra, which see.

PANTHIALEANS.

According to Herodotus the fourth of the ten great tribes of the Persians. They were agriculturists.

PANTINA.

An Egyptian official, the son of Aker and his wife Ana. He had the overseership of the (royal) scribes of the South, which constituted him an administrator also. His period is unknown, except that it was between the XIIth and XVIIIth dynasties.

PAOPHI.

The second month of the Egyptian sacred year. It began about August 19.

PAOUT.

The Egyptian name of a group of nine deities, male and female. There were several of these Paouts, in each of which Thoth was the chief deity.

PA-PA.

A city which revolted against Sargon II., who reduced it, and sent the inhabitants into slavery to Damascus.

PAPÆUS. "Ancestor."

According to Herodotus the name of a Scythian deity answering to the Zeus of the Greeks.

PAPI. *Or* PEPI.

The father of Pthah-hotep, an early Egyptian sculptor of the Ancient Empire.

PAPI.

An Egyptian priest, probably of Osiris. He was the son of Henne. Nothing is known respecting him, except that he lived between the XIIth and XVIIIth dynasties.

PAPIEUS.

The Kypriote form of the name of the town of Paphos in the Isle of Cyprus.

PAPREMIS.

According to Herodotus a nome in Lower Egypt which was held by the Hermotybian class of warriors.

PAPSILAK.

In Chaldean astronomy one of the seven stars of the week.

PAP-SUCUL.

An Assyrian deity of whom little is known. The month Dharbitu was sacred to him.

PA-PTHAH. "Town of Pthah."

A town in Egypt founded by Rameses II., who built there a temple to Pthah-Rameses, his special protecting divinity. It is now called Gerf Hussein.

PAPYRI.

The papyrus or Egyptian paper, made of thin slices of the reed *Cyperus papyrus*, called by the Egyptians *gama*, and by the Greeks *Byblos*, was the precursor of modern paper. On it were written rituals, prayers, public documents, histories, poems, and all literary and other works. The width of the papyrus sheets so prepared was generally 15 inches, but their length sometimes though rarely extends to 150 feet. The papyri, both before use and afterwards, were rolled up into cylindrical volumes, and when opened for the purpose of reading, were unrolled from the ends. The rolls of papyri were placed in rectangular wooden boxes close to the scribe or readers. Those found in the tombs were differently placed, according to their nature ; papyri relating to private life, history, or literature were placed in jars of terra cotta, or else in the coffins of the deceased, or deposited near them in a wooden box. The Rituals of the Dead, generally distinguished by their vignettes, were either placed rolled up within the bandages of the dead, at some part of the body, as on the chest, in the hand, or at the feet, or else stretched over the mummy. Besides these methods, they were occasionally placed in wooden figures of the god Osiris, standing on a pedestal, either in the hollowed body of the god, or else in a place in the pedestal covered by a small slip, the whole so carefully stuccoed and painted over as not to give any indication of the papyrus within. These figures were always coloured black, the colour of the coffins of the XVIIIth dynasty, but they appear from their style to have been made at a later period. (Birch.)

PAQAHA.

The Assyrian form of the Hebrew royal name Pekah, which see.

PAQAR-HU-BUNU.

A mountain city near the Euphrates, which was conquered by Shalmaneser II.

PA-RA. "Town of Ra."

An Egyptian town now called Der, founded by Rameses II., and where he built a temple to Ra as one of his protecting deities.

PAR-AB-HOR.

A priest of Apis. He was the son of Pse-isi.

PARACHISTÆ.

A class of Egyptian undertakers, whose office it was to eviscerate the body previous to its embalmment. *See* Mummies.

PARAITAKA. "Nomads."

According to Herodotus the name of the last and lowest of the six great castes of the Medes. They were the Paretaceni of the Greek historians.

PA-RAMESSU. "Town of Rameses."

An Egyptian city now called Ipsambul, founded by Rameses II., where he erected a temple to himself in the character of a deity.

PA-RAMESSU.

A strong fortress built by Rameses II. of the XIXth dynasty, in the erection of which some writers believe the Israelites to have been employed. Here the king of Egypt, and Khitasira, king of the Hittites, concluded a defensive and extraditionary treaty of peace, after the battle of Kadesh, which was won by Rameses II.

PA-RA-NEFER.

The surname of Khonsu, a fan-bearer of Amen Ra.

PARAZA.

The son of Gagi, chief of the Medes of Saki. His provinces were despoiled by Assurbanipal, king of Assyria.

PARCÆ.

The "Fatal Sisters" of Greek mythology. They were derived from the Egyptian Hathors.

PAR-DU-BAST.

A priest of Apis. He was the son of Pa-du-uza-hor in the XXIVth dynasty.

PARDUKKA.

A petty kingdom in Media, one of the tributaries of Esarhaddon. It must not to be confounded with Partakka, which was a neighbouring Median state.

PAREMBOLE.

The Greek name of a chief town in the Dodecaschœnon of Nubia. It is now called Dabood.

PARETACENI.

The Greek form of the name of the Median caste Paraitaka, which see.

PARGA.

A mountain in Persia, where Veisdates, the rebel king, was defeated for a second and last time by Artabardes, the general of Darius Hystaspes.

PARNUSUR.

An Assyrian city which revolted to Assurdan, and was re-conquered by Samas Rimmon.

PARŒTONIUM.

The Greek name of a Libyan city on the West of the lake Mareotis.

PARS.

The Egyptian name of the land of Persia.

PARSANI.

A district bordering on Assyria, which was rendered tributary by Samsi-Vul or Samas Rimmon III.

PARSANIYAI.

A city near Media which was rendered tributary by Samas Rimmon, king of Assyria.

PARSAUVARDA.   "The Persian Fortress."

A great city in Persia, from whence the principal tribe of the country was named. It was the Pasargadæ of the Greek historians. The inhabitants were the original aristocracy.

PARSHA.

An Egyptian town sacred to the deity Bast. Site unknown.

PARSURA.

An erroneous rendering of the name of the Etruscan goddess Tarsura, which see.

PARTAKKA.

A petty kingdom in Media. It was one of the tributaries of Esarhaddon.

PARTHIVI-MUTAR. " Earth Mother."

The Vedic name of the creative power of the Supreme Being in a receptive and feminine form. From hence was derived the Demeter of the Greeks.

PARTICERA.

A deity of the Susians, of whom nothing is known.

PARU. " The Lion."

A mystical epithet which is applied to one of the greater divinities in the CLXIIIrd chapter of the Ritual of the Dead.

PARU.

The lord or chief of Hilmu. He was one of the chiefs who, with Ummanigas, king of Elam, and Saulmugina, king of Babylon, conspired against Assurbanipal.

PARU.

One of the two sons of Ummanaldas, king of Elam, who fled for refuge into Assyria with the sons of Urtaki. *See* Ummanigas.

PA-RU-HAKA.

A mystical title of Ra, the creator, in the CLXVth (supplemental) chapter of the Ritual of the Dead.

PARUSHTA. " The Mystic Lion."

The name of a mystical divinity in the CLXVth chapter of the Ritual of the Dead.

PARUSTA.

The king of Kimaru in the country of Cimarusai, who paid tribute to Samas Rimmon or Samsi-Vul III., king of Assyria.

PA-SANKH-URU.

The king of Natku, one of the first petty kings of Egypt under the Icosarchy.

PASARGADÆ.

The Greek form of the name of the great Persian city Parsauvarda, which see. It is now famous for the ruins of the palace, and the tomb of Cyrus.

PASARGADIANS.

The first of the ten great tribes of ancient Persia.

Pa-schep.

A priest of Horus in the XXVIth dynasty. His father was the priest Pef-aa-neit, and his mother was Na-nefru-sekhet, a priestess of Neith.

Pa-se-en-pthah.

A priest of Apis. He was the son of Ankh-sam-taui, in the period of the XXIInd dynasty.

Pa-sen-en-khons.

The father of the priest Khasu-en-amen, which see.

Pashakasa.

A mythical name of one of the greater divinities in the CLXVth (a supplemental) chapter of the Ritual of the Dead.

Pashet.

An Egyptian judicial officer. His period is uncertain.

Pashons.   *Or* Pachons.

The ninth month of the Egyptian sacred year. It began about the 17th of March.

Pasht.

The name given by the Greeks to the Egyptian goddess Sekhet, which see.

Pasht.

An Egyptian lady, the wife of Psamektia, prefect of the archers, and mother of the lady Ta-sen-kno.

Pasicrates.

A king of Soli in the Island of Kypros, possibly an error of the Greek scribe for Stasicrates, which see.

Pasicyprus.

A king of Soli and the friend of Solon. *See* Stasicrates, who was probably the same person. He was also called Kypranor.

Pasiuenkha.

The Greek form of an Egyptian royal name in the lists of the XXIst dynasty. It is supposed to have been the same as Pai-netem, which see.

Paslikira.

An Elamite deity of whom nothing is known.

Pastophoroi.

A class of Egyptian priests who carried the shrines of the divinities on their heads, or knelt with them on their knees, for the adoration of the faithful.

PASUPTI.

An Egyptian deity, represented as a hawk, wearing two upright feathers, and having a pyramid before him. He was another form of Horus of the East.

PAT.

A species of Egyptian sceptre used by the chiefs and heads of families.

PATAIKOS.

The name given by the Greeks to the pigmy god Pthah-Sokari-Osiris of Lower Egypt.

PATANUT.

A city and nome in Lower Egypt, sacred to the goddess Buto. It was the Phthenotes of the Greeks.

PATARBEMIS.

An Egyptian officer in the court of Uahprahet, king of Egypt, who sent him to quell an insurrection which had broken out among his soldiers, who had crowned Amasis king. He was unsuccessful in his attempt, and on returning to his master had his ears and nose cut off as being a traitor. This cruel treatment of his emissary caused the revolt against Uahprahet to become general, and Amasis ascended the throne. The fate of Patarbemis is not known.

PAT-EN-ANKH-NEB-KA-NOFRE.

An unidentified Egyptian royal name.

PATES.   "Place or Town of Flint" (Flint Weapons).

An early Egyptian town, site unknown. The name is interesting archæologically, as flint weapons were used up to a late period. (Chabas.)

PATESI.   "Viceroy."

The Assyrian name for the early governors of Chaldea.

PAT-HOR-SAM-TA-TUI.

An Egyptian chief who unsuccessfully revolted against Piankhi-Meramen, by whom he was subdued.

PATHRUSIM.

According to Hebrew tradition the name of the people of Southern Egypt. They were called by the Egyptians Ptores.

PATIKANIK.

The name of a canal from the river Zab to the city of Calah, which was dug by the orders of Assur-nazir-pal.

PATINA.

A tribe inhabiting the Northern part of the river Orontes, in Syria. The people paid tribute to Assur-nazir-pal.

PATNAM.

In Hindu mythology one of the four sacred streams which form the Ganges.

PATUBISTI.

The Assyrian form of the Egyptian royal name Petubastes, which see.

PATUSARRA.

A district in Media which was conquered by Esarhaddon, and its two kings, Sidirparna and Eparna, brought captive to Nineveh.

PA-UER.

A prince of Kush, in the reign of Rameses II. of the XIXth dynasty.

P-AUF-NEIT.

A priest of Apis in the reign of Darius.

PAURUMARKA. "The Destroyer."

In Zendic mythology the name of the evil deity Agramainyus in his attribute as a destructive agency.

PAUSIRIS.

A petty vassal king of Egypt under Artaxerxes, king of Persia. He succeeded Amyrtaios, who was driven into exile by the Persians after an unsuccessful revolt.

PAWANA.

In Hindu mythology the god of the winds.

PAYNI.

The tenth month of the Egyptian sacred year. It began about the 16th of April.

PAZITU.

A city of the Dunaites of Lower Chaldea. It was conquered by Tiglath Pileser II.

PE.

An unidentified city in the Lower Egyptian nome of Patanut. The name was a common one.

PE-ANKH-EM-TANEN.

An Egyptian gentleman in the XIXth dynasty. He was the son of the lady Hotep-beset.

PE-BA-NEB-TATTU. "Temple of the Ram Lord of Tattu."

The sacred name of the city of Mendes, which see.

PEDUIL.

Another form of the Ammonite royal name Buduil, which see.

Pef-aa-bast.

An Egyptian petty king of the XXIInd dynasty who, together with many others, revolted against Piankhi, king of Egypt and Ethiopia, who subdued him and accepted his submission, but refused to accept his wives and horses which the Egyptian offered as a present.

Pef-aa-bast.

The father of Patubast or Padubast, a worshipper of Apis in the thirty-third year of Darius.

Pef-aa-khons.

The auditor of the palace of a king of the XXIst dynasty. His sarcophagus and mummy are in the British Museum.

Pef-aa-khonsu.

An Egyptian devotee of Apis in the XXVIth dynasty.

Pef-aa-neit.

A priest of Amen Ra in the XXVIth dynasty.

Pef-aa-neit.

An Egyptian functionary, the son of the prince or prophet Sebek-se. He was " Chief of the Treasuries of the King," " Chief of the Great Palace," and governor of the district of Abydos. He greatly improved the district by introducing a series of watercourses, and establishing orchards and vineyards, in the latter of which he made the captives taken in war to act as gardeners. He caused the royal palace to be considerably embellished, and made some costly presents, especially of a sacred boat, to the temple of Osiris. He lived at the close of the XXVIth dynasty, or about the sixth century B.C.

Pef-nifi-neith.

A prophet of the goddess Neith, and grandfather of the following.

Pef-nifi-neith.

A chief of the sacrificants of the temples of Neith, Amen, etc. His mother was named Mert-neith, and his father Naschti or Nekht. His sarcophagus and mummy are in the Leyden Museum.

Pe-hap.

An Egyptian city, probably the Nilopolis of Greek writers. It was vainly held by the rebel chief Pa-bas against Piankhi-Meramen.

Pe-hebi.

One of the towns of Lower Egypt. It was held by Ankh-hor, the rebel chief, against Piankhi-Meramen.

Pe-he-mato.

A part of the necropolis of the city of Coptos.

Pe-hon-neter.

A *Sam* and " Chief of the Works of Pthah" in the period of the XIXth dynasty.

Pehu.

The Egyptian general name of the frontier town of each of the twenty-two nomes into which the kingdom was divided.

Peisdadien.

A name given by the Persian historians to a primæval dynasty of kings, " Men of the Ancient Law," who lived on pure *homa* (water of life), and who preserved their sanctity.

Pekah. Assyrian, Pakakhu.

A king of Israel. He was son of Remaliah, probably from the land of Gilead, and murdered Pekahiah, king of Samaria, whose throne he usurped. He allied himself with Rezon of Damascus, and Metinti of Ascalon, and carried on a successful war with Judah. Judah and its king Ahaz were only saved from destruction by the intervention of Tiglath Pileser of Assyria, who besieged and destroyed Damascus, deposed Metinti, made Samaria tributary, and attached to Assyria the Northern part of the kingdom of Israel, and the whole country to the East of the Jordan. This was B.C. 732. In the Assyrian inscriptions Tiglath Pileser claims to have dethroned Pekah, and to have made Hoshea king in his place.

Pekalel.

An unidentified Egyptian town, the ruler of which was one of the rebels defeated by Piankhi-Meramen.

Pekhi.

A king of the XXIInd dynasty, the successor of Sheshonk III. He was succeeded by Sheshonk IV., the last king of that dynasty.

Pekhrari.

An Egyptian officer who was called the " Chief of the Shepherds." His period is uncertain.

Pelkha.

A royal lady, the sister or mother of King Nastosenen of the XXVth dynasty.

Pelusium.

A great Egyptian city on the Pelusiac branch of the Nile.

Peme.

An Egyptian city in the Memphite nome of the Heptanomos.

Pe-meht-khonsu.

A son of Her-hor-si-amun of the XXIst dynasty.

Pen-ame

An Egyptian priest, the door-keeper of the temple of Ra. His sarcophagus and mummy are in the British Museum.

Pen-amen.

The father of an Egyptian officer named Pnaaku, which see.

Pen-amen.

A high-priest of Amen, whose coffin is in the British Museum.

Pen-amen.

An early Egyptian astronomer, some observations by whom have been preserved.

Pen-ba-kak-amen.

An officer of state who conspired with his chief Penhuiban against Rameses III., for which he was executed.

Pen-en-aau.

An Egyptian gentleman whose statue is in the Leyden Museum.

Pen-eoou.

An Egyptian scribe whose monument is in the Leyden Museum. Period uncertain.

Pen-haka-haka-har.

The name of a mystical cow, who is adored in the last chapter, the CLXIIIrd, of the Ritual of the Dead.

Pen-huiban.

A great officer of the court of Rameses III. who, led by the women of the Harem, instigated a conspiracy against that king, for which he and his colleagues were executed, and their less guilty accomplices mutilated.

Pen-ina-fu-aa.

An unidentified Egyptian district or city, situated probably near Memphis.

Pen-nekheb.

The surname of Aahmes, the general of Amenhotep I. and Thothmes I. and II. of the XVIIIth dynasty.

Pen-nu.

The prince of Kush in the reign of Rameses VI. of the XXth dynasty.

Pen-nub.

An early Egyptian astronomer, some observations by whom are preserved.

Pen-piei.

A priest of the temple of Amen Ra at Thebes, in the reign of Amenhotep I. of the XVIIIth dynasty. His father was named Sa-amen.

Pen-ses-khemet.

The father of Asch-sep-sen, which see.

Pentaschœnum.

In the Greek period an Egyptian city situated on the Arabian frontier between Pelusium and Palestine.

Pent-aur.

An Egyptian poet attached to the court of Rameses II., whose wars and exploits, especially those against the Khitæ, he related in a long and beautiful poem, many copies of which, more or less complete, exist on the temple inscriptions and Egyptian papyri.

Pent-aur.

One of the officers of the court of Rameses III., who with Penhuiban and others conspired against his sovereign. He was a member of the royal family, but in what relationship is not known.

Pent-aur.

A commander of the mercenaries. He together with other chiefs revolted against Piankhi-Meramen of the XXIInd dynasty, by whom he was reduced to obedience.

Pent-bek-hen.

A commander of the mercenaries, and a prophet of the god Horus. He, together with other chiefs, revolted unsuccessfully against Piankhi-Meramen.

Pent-ehi.

The father of Zet-isi-auf-ankh, a priest of Apis.

Pent-eni.

A priest of the deity Anhur at Abydos. His father's name was Tatai, and that of his mother Apu.

Pent-uau.

A principal officer in the court of a king of the XVIIIth dynasty. He was the son of Teti, who filled the same office before him.

Pe-nub.   " City of Gold."

An Egyptian city near Sais, now called by the Arabs Badnub.

Pen-ures-nes.

The mother of an Egyptian prince named Namurot, but in what reign it is not known.

PE-PAK. "City of Flax." (?)

An unidentified Egyptian city on the banks of the Nile, near to which the army of the rebel chiefs was defeated by Piankhi-Meramen, king of Egypt.

PEPI.

A shorter form of the name Pepi-merira.

PEPI-MERIRA.

An Egyptian king of the VIth dynasty. He is said to have reigned 100 years. He conquered the Mentu, the Asiatic enemies of Egypt, and the Herusha or Arabs of the desert, and for this purpose raised an army of Negroes. He carried on several other wars, and married a queen named Rameri-Ankhas. He was buried in the pyramid called Mennefer, and was the Phiops of the Greeks.

PE-RA-SECHEM-KHEPER.

An ancient Egyptian city. Its site is unknown.

PER-KHEM.

Another name of the town in Upper Egypt called by the Greeks Panopolis.

PERSEPOLIS. (Now CHEL MINAR.)

The chief town of ancient Persia. It was made the capital city of Darius Hystaspes and his successors. Persepolis was situated at the junction of the Araxes and Medus. Extensive ruins of its great buildings still remain, with Cuneiform inscriptions commemorating the kings by whom they were erected. Persepolis fell into decay after the conquest of Alexander.

PER-TOT-KAI. "Let Violence kill."

One of the names of an heretical sect in Upper Egypt during the XXVIth dynasty. *See* Tumpesi.

PER-UI.

The name of an unidentified king of Ethiopia.

PE-SAHI.

A prophet of Amen-Ra. His triple sarcophagus and mummy are in the Leyden Museum; and his father's name was Dsja-khons. Period uncertain.

PE-SCHALI-EN-KHONS.

An Egyptian functionary, the father of Pet-isis. His wife was named Ten-pepiou.

PESLA.

A chief town in the Antæopolite nome in the Thebaid East of the Nile.

PET-AMEN.

An Egyptian royal scribe and priest of the goddess Hathor, in the XXVIth dynasty. He was the son of the lady Mun-khet-isi.

Pet-amen.

A high-priest of Amen-Ra, in the reign of King Aspalut of the XXVIth dynasty.

Pet-amen.

The consort of Tekh-bes, a royal lady of the line of Nechtanebos of the XXXth dynasty.

Pet-amen.

A wife of Panki, an obscure king of the XXIVth dynasty.

Pet-amen-neb-katta.

A priest of the living Cynocephali of the god Khons at Thebes, in the XXVIth dynasty.

Pet-amen-neb-katta.

An Egyptian chancellor, councillor, and fourth priest of Amen Ra. Period uncertain.

Pet-amen-neb-nes-ataui.

An Egyptian official, the son of the lady Tat-maut-as-ankh. He was the premier *Heb*, and sacred scribe, and his wife's name was Ta-schep-en-maut, a lady attached to the temple of Amen Ra. His name was written by the Greeks Petemnestheus.

Pet-ament.

The gatekeeper of the Golden Hall of Amen-Ra. He was the son of Sa-pi-hor, a gatekeeper of the same temple. His double sarcophagus and mummy are in the Leyden Museum.

Pet-ebar.

The founder of the family of Titia, the chief of the scribes of Amen-Ra, in the reign of Thothmes III. of the XVIIIth dynasty.

Pet-e-hake.

An Egyptian priest of the XXVIth dynasty, the father of the priest Taho.

Pet-e-harpocrates.

Another form of the Egyptian name Peti-har-pe-khruti, which see.

Pet-e-khons.

The father of Psametik, a priest of Amen Ra. *See* Psametik.

Pet-emenophis.   *Or* Pet-amen-hotep.

An Egyptian functionary of the XXVIth dynasty, in whose tomb at El Asaseef an important copy of the LXIVth chapter of the Ritual of the Dead was found.

Petemet.

An Egyptian gentleman, the father of the lady Hathor-het-aei, which see.

PETEMNESTHEUS.

The Greek form of the Egyptian name Pet-amen-neb-nes-ataui, which see.

PET-EN-SENAS. "That which is Sea."

An Egyptian deity; probably a form of the deity Senem, of Syene. The name is of the Ptolemaic period.

PE-TEP-MUNKH.

The father of Taho, a priest of Imhotep, in the XXVIth dynasty.

PET-HAR-PE-KHROT.

An Egyptian functionary of the Middle Empire.

PET-HISET.

A son of Takelot II. of the XXIInd dynasty.

PETI-HAR-PE-KHRUTI.

An Egyptian priest who was "Director of the Royal Boatmen," "Royal Scribe of the South," "Scribe of the Sacred Territory of Abydos," "Scribe Administrator," "Treasure Keeper of the Second Sacerdotal Tribe," "Fourth Prophet of Amen at Userhat," "Fourth Prophet of Osiris at Uupeka," and also a "Prophet of the Deity Mehut at Abydos." His mother's name was Kharat-ankh or Kharatannekha, and that of his wife Ise-ta-ari. His eldest son was called Imhotep, and his granddaughter Hor-uta. The period when he lived is uncertain, but it was not in the true Pharaonic times.

PETISIS.

The grandson of Osorkon II. by his mother, who was a daughter of Takelot. He was a chief of the Mashouasha, a *Sam*, and chief overseer of the works of Pthah. He was the grandfather of the following.

PETISIS.

One of the thirteen petty kings of Egypt, who rebelled against, and were subdued by, Piankhi-Meramen, of the XXIInd dynasty.

PET-ISIS.

An Egyptian priest, the son of Pe-schali-en-khons and the lady Tenpepiou. His triple sarcophagus and mummy are in the Leyden Museum. Period uncertain.

PET-NETER. "Divine City."

Another name of the Egyptian city generally called Mer-neter, which see.

PET-NIT.

A prince of the blood royal of the XXIVth dynasty, the son of the princess Tantebast, which see.

PET-OSIRIS.

A chief wardrobe-keeper to an unnamed Egyptian king. Period uncertain.

PET-OSIRIS.

A priest and auditor of the temple of Pthah, in the XXVth dynasty. He was the son of the lady Neirioui, and he had a brother named Pthah-hotep. His sarcophagus is in the Leyden Museum.

PETSIBAST.   *Or* PATUBAST.

The first king of the XXIIIrd dynasty.   He was succeeded by Osorkon III.

PET-TI.

Another name of the nomadic Egyptian people who were called Anti.

PETU-ANKHI I.

A king of the XXIst dynasty. He succeeded Men-kheper-ra, and was himself succeeded by Pisem II.

PETUBAST.

A priest of the deities Pthah and Bast in the Ptolemaic period.

PETUBASTES.

The king of Zanu, one of the petty kings of Egypt under the Assyrian Icosarchy.

PETUBASTES.

The name of a petty king of Egypt at the time of the first Olympiad, or B.C. 776. He is not yet certainly identified. He may have been the preceding.

PETUBASTES.

The first king of the XXIIIrd dynasty.   *See* Petsibast.

PHACUSA.

The chief town of the Arabic nome of Lower Egypt.

PHAMENOTH.

The seventh month of the Egyptian sacred year. It began about the 16th of January.

PHAMOTHIS.

A chief town in the Mareotic nome of Lower Egypt.

PHANEH-BAAL.   "Face of Baal."

A Phenician town which was called by the Greeks Theon Prosopon, a name of the same meaning. It was one of the great triple confederation with the towns of Calamus and Gigastus. Its site is now covered by the town of Tripoli.

PHANES.

A Greco-Egyptian officer in the court of Psametik II., to whom he was commander of the Greek body guard. He revolted to Cambyses at the period of the Persian invasion of Egypt, to the success of which his advice and treason mainly contributed.

PHARAOH. *Also* PHRA *and* PHRE.

The Hebraised form of Pir-aa, the official title of the Egyptian monarchs. It has been variously rendered " Great Gate," analogous to the " Sublime Porte " of the Turkish empire, and, Pi Ra, " The Sun," but this latter explanation is now given up. In ordinary language the Egyptian kings were referred to by their prenomens, and not by their surnames or order of succession, as in Western countries.

PHARBŒITES.

A nome in Lower Egypt, East of the Phatnitic branch of the Nile. Its chief town was Pharbuthus. It was held by the Calasirian class of soldiers.

PHARBUTHUS.

The chief town of the Pharbœitic nome of Lower Egypt.

PHARMUTHI.

The eighth month of the Egyptian sacred year. It began about the 15th of February.

PHATHYRITES.

The Greek name for the city and nome in Upper Egypt which was called by the Egyptians Seshesh.

PHELES.

One of the many usurpers who occupied the throne of Tyre after the murder of Abdashtoreth, the last of the house of Hiram.

PHILÆ.

An island in the Nile near Nubia, anciently called Pa-ilak. The reputed tomb of Osiris, and a place of such sanctity that the Egyptians are said to have sworn " By him who sleeps at Philæ," *i.e.* Osiris. It is famous for the ruins of its great temples, chiefly of the Greek and even Roman period, but there are some of the time of Nectanebo.

PHILINOS.

The father of Pyrrha, the athlophoros of the goddess Berenice Euergetes under Ptolemy V.

PHILITIS.

An Egyptian architect, who is traditionally said to have designed the great pyramid.

PHILOTERA.

An Egyptian town on the Red Sea, seventy-five miles from Coptos. It was also called Ænum.

PHILOTERA-HER-SANKH.

A priestess of the god Pthah-Sokari-Osiris, and princess of the house of Ptolemy. She was the daughter of the prophet Ra-nofre-ab.

PHIOPS. *Or* PHIUS.

According to the Greek lists a king of Memphis, the predecessor of Methu-suphis. He has been supposed to have been the same with Pepi-Merira, which see.

PHLOX. "Flame."

In Phenician mythology one of the sons of Genus, the discoverer of fire, and one of the fathers of the giants. *See* Pur *and* Phōs.

PHŒNIX.

The Greek name of the mystical bird Bennu, the lapwing, or the soul of Osiris. It was the emblem alike of the soul and of the great solar astronomical cycle of 1461 (1265?) years, the recurrence of which formed a national epoch called the return of the Phœnix.

PHŌS. "Light."

In Phenician mythology the son of Genus. He and his brethren discovered the art of making fire, and were the parents of the giants. *See* Phlox.

PHRAHIUNAMIF.

A son of Rameses II. of the XIXth dynasty.

PHRAORTES.

A Median chief who revolted against Darius Hystaspes by himself claiming to have been Xathritas of the race of Cyaxares. He prevailed upon the Medians to make him king, but he was defeated by Hydarnes, the general of Darius, and then raising another army was again defeated by Dadarses, whom he in turn blockaded till the arrival of the Persian general Vomises, who took Phraortes prisoner, and then cutting off his nose, ears, and lips, sent him to Darius, who chained him to the door of the royal palace at Ecbatana.

PHRAORTES.

The son of Diaku, king of the Medes. He still further enlarged and consolidated the kingdom made by his father, and conquered the Persian tribes who dwelt to the South of Media. He combined with the disaffected tribes of Babylon to resist the power of the Assyrians, but he was defeated and slain at the battle of Rhages. His son Vakistar, the Cyaxares of the Greeks, succeeded him, and delivered his country from the power of the Assyrians. (Lenormant.)

PHRESEUTAS.

The son of Aristagoron the Cypriote.

PHTHEMPHUTHUS.

A Greek nome of Lower Egypt, West of the Phatnitic branch of the Nile. Its chief town was named Tava.

PHTHENOTES.

A Greek nome of Lower Egypt, West of the Phatnitic branch of the Nile, anciently called the city and nome of Patanut. Its chief town was Butos.

PHTHONTIS.

A Greco-Egyptian town in the desert belonging to the Apollinopolite nome of the Thebaid in Upper Egypt.

PHUT.

An uncertain Egyptian goddess. (Wilkinson.)

PHYLACE.

A chief town in the Hermopolite nome of the Heptanomos. It was the seat of the transit duties under the Ptolemaic dynasty.

PIAA.

An Egyptian functionary of the XVIIIth dynasty. He married the lady Nub-em-usekh, which is all that is known concerning him.

PIAI.

An Egyptian functionary of the XVIIIth dynasty. He was the " Bearer of the books of the king in the chair of justice," in other words, a clerk of the legislature. He had a son named Apui or Amen-em-ab.

PIAI.

The father of the royal scribe Amen-em-ap, which see.

PIAI.

A keeper of the gates of the palace of an unnamed king of the XIXth dynasty.

PIANKHI.   *Surnamed* MERAMEN.

A king of Ethiopia, who held Egypt under his control at the close of the XXIInd dynasty, at which time the kingdom was divided into thirteen petty principalities. In the twenty-first year of his reign Tafnekht, king of Menouthes, and commander of the troops, incited the whole of the confederate princes to revolt, which they did, entrenching themselves under the charge of Prince Namrut in the city of Hermopolis. This city Piankhi reduced by a sharp blockade, and then advanced to Memphis, which still held out. After a savage siege Piankhi reduced the capital, and then received tribute and honour from the priests and the rebels. Tafnekht escaped to Cyprus, whence he sent his submission to the king. After this Piankhi was allowed to enter the most sacred shrines of the deities Ra and Tum, and returned to Thebes with great power and glory. He was remarkable for his great veneration of the deity Amen, and for his clemency to the conquered. The length of his reign and the time of his death are unrecorded. The stele recording the victories of Piankhi is one of the longest historical documents of ancient Egypt.

PIANKHI II.

A king of Ethiopia. He succeeded Amen-meri-nut, and married the princess Amen-iritis, the sister of Shabaka, who had been regent of Egypt under the reigns of his predecessors. He was completely subordinate to her, and was succeeded by his son-in-law, Psametik I.

PIANKHI III. *Surnamed* RA-USER-MA.

A king of the XXIInd dynasty who is only known from his statuette in the Museum of the Louvre, in which he is called a " Son of Bast" and an *Erpa*, or hereditary prince, apparently by virtue of his marriage with a princess of the Bubastite dynasty.

PIANKHI.

The high-priest of Amen Ra in the reign of Her-hor-si-amun in the XXIst dynasty.

PIANKHI.

A son of Her-hor-si-amun, of the XXIst dynasty.

PIB-AMEN. *Or* PEB-AMEN.

A functionary in the temple of Amen Ra. His father's name was Dsja-ta-baf-ankh, and his mummy is in the Leyden Museum.

PIEA.

An overseer of the White House or Hall of some deity. His statue is in the Leyden Museum. Period uncertain.

PIE-AEI.

A priest of the god Ra. Uncertain period; possibly the XVIIIth dynasty. (Leemans.)

PIEN-NUN-ENPE.

A prophet of the deity Month, the husband of the priestess Teti-hor-noub, which see.

PIHIRIM.

The king of Cilicia, in the time of Shalmaneser II., king of Assyria.

PI-HOR.

A priest of the temple of Amen Ra. He was the son of Isi-tefnaschti. His double sarcophagus and mummy are in the Leyden Museum.

PILASTYA.

An Hindu deity, who was invested by Brahma with the power of creation. *See* Angiras.

PINEPTI.

One of the false mouths of the river Nile.

PINETSEM. *Or* PINEZEM.

Another form of the Egyptian royal name Painetem, which see.

PIOUER.

A royal scribe attached to the temple of Amen. Period uncertain.

PIPUI.

A sister of the priest Pthah-em-hebi. She was a priestess of the goddess Hathor, but the period of her existence is not known.

PIRISATI.

King of the city of Huras in Girubbunda. He was taken captive, together with all his army and family, by Samas-Rimmon, king of Assyria, who then slew his chief men and burned his city to the ground.

PISABTINUTI. *Or* PISABTU.

One of the twenty petty kingdoms of Egypt under the Assyrian Icosarchy.

PIS-AEI.

A chorister of Amen Ra. He was the son of a man named Pet-mouthf. His sarcophagus and mummy are in the Leyden Museum. Period uncertain.

PIS-ANHOR.

An Egyptian, the father of the lady Taskhtali, which see.

PIS-AROER.

A spondist of Amen Ra. He married the lady Tali or Tari, who was a priestess of the same divinity.

PISEM I.

A king of the XXIst dynasty, of whom little is known. He was succeeded by Menkheper.

PISEM II.

A king of the XXIst dynasty. He succeeded Petu-ankhi I., and was himself succeeded by Hor-petu-ankhi II.

PISIRIS.

A king of Carchemish who paid tribute to Tiglath-Pileser I.

PISON.

In Hebrew tradition a river of Paradise, which is now considered by Aryan scholars to have been the Upper Indus.

PITHOTHAPREHUHU.

An unidentified Egyptian city held by the rebel chief Semsem, which see.

PITRU.

A city in Mesopotamia, which was conquered by Assur-nazirpal, who impaled alive 700 of the brave garrison upon its walls.

PIZATTIKHURUNPI.

One of the twenty petty Egyptian kingdoms which were established by the Assyrians under Esarhaddon.

PLINTHINE.

A Libyan city, situated on the West of the lake Mareotis.

PNAAKU.

An Egyptian officer, the flabellum-bearer to Aahmes I. of the XVIIIth dynasty.   His surname was Mer-amen.

PNEBTO.

An uncertain Egyptian deity, perhaps a form of Harpakrut, which his statues much resembled.   (Wilkinson.)

PNEI-HOR.

An Egyptian priest, the father of the priest He-hor-rei, which see.

PNOFREHI.

A son of Her-hor-si-amun, of the XXIst dynasty.

POARMA.

A captain of Piankhi-Meramen, king of Egypt, who sent him to subdue the insurrection of the princes Taf-nekht and Nimrod.

POTHOS.

In Phenician mythology an elementary deity, the union of the wind and of chaos.   He was also a Gnostic deity or essence.

POTI-AMEN-NESA-TATUI.

The chief of the sacred rites under Piankhi-Meramen, who sent him, together with the captain or marshal Poarma, to receive the allegiance of the rebel chiefs after their defeat.

POU-ISIS.

An Egyptian officer, the son of Har-si-esi and the lady Taterkat.   A portion of his sarcophagus is in the Leyden Museum.

POUNT.

The Egyptian name for Arabia Barbarica, which was first invaded and conquered by Hatasu, the great queen of the XVIIIth dynasty. It was supposed to be under the special care of Hathor, the goddess of beauty.

POUREM.

A priest of Horus, in the XXIVth or XXVth dynasty.

PRA-EN-AMEN . . . .

A son of Her-hor-si-amun of the XXIst dynasty. This name is incomplete.

PRAGAPATI.   "Lord of the World."

A Vedic title of the Supreme Being as the creator.   *See also* Ivashtri *and* Dhatar.

PRAHIUNAMIF.

A son of Rameses III. of the XXth dynasty.

PRAMZIMAS.

In Lithuanian mythology a great deity who observing that the world was full of wickedness sent the two giants, Wandu and Wejas (water and wind), to destroy it. This mission the giants carried out so unfeelingly that the deity relenting, and seeing a few men alive on the top of a mountain, let fall a nutshell to protect them, which the giants feared to disturb. The men who were thus rescued afterwards repeopled the earth.

PRAYAS.   *Or* VADJA.

In Vedic mythology the name of an offering of *soma* juice when consumed by fire.

PRAYASITTA.

In Hindu mythology a special sacrificial rite of atonement for sins committed.

PREALE.

A nude, effeminate youth, with long hair, sword and buskins, who was represented on an Etruscan mirror as sitting opposite the armed Lalan.

PROMACHUS.   "Front of Battle."

An ancient title of the goddess Athene, or Minerva.

PROPHTHASIA.

A great city on the road from Babylon to India.

PROSOPITIS.

An island and nome in Lower Egypt at the head of the Delta, which was held by the Hermotybian class of warriors. Its chief towns were Papremis and Nicium.

PROTOGONOS.

In Phenician mythology the son of the primæval deities Colpas and Baau (wind and night), and the brother of Æon, the first mortal man.

PROXTERES.

The receivers of the inland taxes of Egypt. They were appointed by the Ptolemaic kings, and were probably Greeks. Their clerks however, were Egyptians.

PSA-BEN-HOR.

The father of Ahmes, a chief of the soldiers in the time of Darius Hystaspes.

PSAMEKTIA.

The prefect or overseer of the bowmen of an Egyptian king of an uncertain period. He married the lady Pasht, by whom he had a daughter named Ta-sen-kno.

PSAMETIK I.

The son of Necho I., and petty king of Sais. He, incited it is supposed by the Egyptian priests, took measures to consult an oracle to induce the other kings of the Dodecarchy to acknowledge him as king. This they refusing to do he had to fly into exile, but after a few years returned with a large body of Greek mercenaries, chiefly Lydians, sent by king Gyges, he invaded the Delta, encountered the Assyrian troops at Momemphis or Menouf, defeated and drove them permanently out of Egypt, thus terminating at once the Assyrian suzerainty and the duration of the Egyptian Dodecarchy. In return he settled his allies the Greeks in various cities of the Delta, and permitted them to be governed by their own laws, an action which caused 200,000 of his Egyptian subjects to quit Egypt, and seek a new country in Ethiopia. He married the princess Shepenaput, the daughter of Piankhi II., and rebuilt most of the temples of Egypt, and especially enlarged the temple of Pthah at Memphis, and the Serapeum. He then attempted to conquer Syria, but was detained at the siege of Ashdod twenty-nine years. Psametik was the first monarch who made the study of Greek imperative in Egypt. The last revision and collation of the great Ritual of the Dead took place in his reign. He reigned more than fifty-two years, and was succeeded by his son Necho II.

PSAMETIK II.

The son of Psametik I. He claimed the throne of Ethiopia in addition to that of Egypt, and to establish a right to his desire married his aunt, the princess Neit-aker, daughter of Queen Shapenap, and granddaughter of Queen Amen-irit-is. He reigned six years, during which he conquered Ethiopia. He was the Psammis of the Greeks. He was succeeded by his son Uahprahet, the Hophra of Hebrew history.

PSAMETIK III.

The son and successor of Aahmes or Amasis II. He ascended the throne at the advent of the Persian invasion, which he was powerless to avert. At the very first battle the Greeks were led into Egypt by Phanes, the commander of his own Greek body guard, who had revolted to Cambyses. In the engagement the Persian king placed in front of his army all the animals which were held sacred by the Egyptians, who were thus afraid to discharge their arrows, lest they conducted themselves impiously. The result was an easy victory of the Persians, who then besieged Memphis, the capital, where they put to death the son of Psametik and 2000 of the principal Egyptians. The life of the king of

Egypt was spared for a short time, but being accused of taking part in a conspiracy against Cambyses, he was put to death by being compelled to drink bull's blood. With Psametik III. ended the XXVIth dynasty and the Archaic history of Egypt. He reigned only six months, and was the Psammenitus of the Greeks.

PSAMETIK.

A prophet of Pthah, of Nofre-atum, and of the gods of the white temple (Memphis). He was the son of the lady Ankh-hi.

PSAMETIK.

A prophet and "Overseer of the Mountains of Ra." He was the son of a functionary of the palace of the same god, who bore the name of Sheshonk.

PSAMETIK.

A sacred scribe, the father of Neb-ankh, which see.

PSAMETIK.

A priest or prophet of Amen Ra. His father's name was Pe-te-khons, and the period when he lived is uncertain.

PSAMETIK.

A prince of the blood royal of Panki, an obscure king of the XXIVth dynasty.

PSAMETIK.

A son of Aahmes, a king of the XXVIth (?) dynasty.

PSAMETIK.

A royal chancellor in the XXVIth dynasty. He was the son of Zet-pthah-auf-ankh and the lady Ise-kheb-au.

PSAMETIK-KHU.

A royal steward in the reign of Psametik I.

PSAMETIK-MUNKH. "Psammetichus the Beneficent."

The surname of the Egyptian governor Nes-ahor, which see.

PSAMMENITUS.

The Greek form of the Egyptian royal name Psametik, more especially of Psametik III., the last of the Egyptian kings.

PSAMMETICHUS.

Another Greek form of the Egyptian royal name Psametik, which see.

PSAMMIS.

A name given by the Greeks to several Egyptian kings, but chiefly those of the Saite dynasty.

PSAR.

The "Scribe of the Palace" of Rameses II. of the XIXth dynasty.

PSAR.

The "Chief of the Country" and priest of the temple of Neith in the XIXth or XXth dynasty. His mother was a priestess of Amen Ra named Ra-mai, and his father Neb-neteru was a *Sam* of the temple of Pthah.

PSCHENT.   *Or* SCHENT.

The crown of the united kingdom of Upper and Lower Egypt. It was formed by the union in one headdress of the linen Shaa, and the golden Teshr, the distinctive crowns of the two separate kingdoms.

PSE-ISI.

The father of Pa-ab-hor, priest of Apis.

PSELCIS.

A chief town in the Dodecaschœnon, a Greco-Egyptian district of Nubia. It is now called Dakke.

PSELK.

The Egyptian name of the town called Pselcis by the Greeks.

PSE-NIO.

An Egyptian gentleman, the son of the lady Bab-mouth. His sarcophagus and mummy are in the Leyden Museum.

PSE-NIRINA.

A boatman in the temple of Amen Ra in the XIXth dynasty.

PSE-NUTER.

The father of Ankh-hapi, a priest of Apis. Period uncertain.

PSE-PTHAH.

An Egyptian priest, the son of Pa-anmu. He is only known from a dedication on an Apis tablet in the Museum of the Louvre.

PSE-SEKHET.

A devotee of Apis in the XXVIth dynasty.

PSI-MUT.   *Or* PSE-MAUT.

The last king of the XXIIIrd dynasty. He succeeded Osorkon III.

PSI-NACHES.

The name of an Egyptian monarch of Tanis, of the XXIst dynasty. He is only found in the lists of Manetho, and has not yet been certainly identified.

PSONKHENS.

A son of Aahmes of the XXVIth dynasty.

PSUSENNES.

According to the Greek lists a king of Tanis. He has not yet been certainly identified.

PTAH-ASES.

An Egyptian officer, probably of the IVth dynasty. He was " Chief of the Royal Works," " Great Chief of the Works," and " Premier Chief-priest of Memphis."

PTAH-KA. " Bull of Pthah."

An ancient name of the capital city Memphis, in Lower Egypt.

PTEI.

A grand priest of Amen Ra. Dynasty uncertain, but of the Second Empire.

PTEROPHOROI. " Feather-Bearers."

In Egyptian history certain officers, who were so called from the feathers which they wore in their headdress as a mark of their rank, in the court of the kings of Egypt. They carried the great feather fans beside the royal throne, when the king was borne in procession in the sacred palanquin, or gestatorial chair.

PTHAH.

The chief deity of Lower Egypt. According to the XVIIth chapter of the Ritual of the Dead, Pthah was one of the primordial deities who were created by Ra, and he was a symbolic personification of the elements of creation and of embryonic life. He was, accordingly, generally represented as a deformed or new-born child, having a very flat head, projecting forehead, thick lips, prominent abdomen, and distorted legs. On his head was generally figured a scarabæus. He holds two serpents against his chest and treads like Horus upon two crocodiles ; sometimes also a hawk rests upon each shoulder. In this form and with these attitudes Pthah was called Pthah-Sokari-Osiris, from whence was derived the Pataikos of the Greek authors. This was the representation of the god as he was adored at Memphis. Another form of Pthah, that in which he was venerated in Upper Egypt, represented the god as an upright mummy, standing upon a pedestal, and wearing a closely fitting cap ; his neck was adorned with a large and beautiful collar, having a counterpoise at the back : his hands, which alone were free, held the *tat*, or emblem of stability, the *cucufa* staff, and the crux ansata. In this form he was analogous to the deity Khonsu, the peculiar deity of the kings of Upper Egypt. In the Hieroglyphic texts Pthah was called " The Father of Beginnings," " The Creator of the Eggs of the Sun and Moon," and in common with many other divinities, " The Lord of Life." (Pierret.)

PTHAH-ASES.

The son of the great Egyptian officer Ha-ka, of the Vth dynasty.

PTHAH-EM-HE-BAI.

An overseer or keeper of the bulls of Pthah. His statue is in the Leyden Museum.

PTHAH-EM-HEBI.

An Egyptian priest. The period when he lived and the deity to whom he was priest are unknown. He had a daughter named Bek-pthah.

Pthah-hat-ankhef.

The son of Prince Namurot, and the grandson of Osorkon II., of the XXIInd dynasty.

Pthah-hotep. "Peace of Pthah."

An early Egyptian sculptor, probably of the XIIth dynasty. His father's name was Papi.

Pthah-hotep. *Or* Phthaophis.

An Egyptian writer of proverbs; the son of Assa Tat-keres, king of Egypt. He declares himself to have attained the age of 110 years, and his writings are characterised by strong good sense and filial piety, rather than by any depth of religious expression. He is sometimes called Pthah-heft and Aphobis.

Pthah-hotep.

An Egyptian officer, whose monument is in the Leyden Museum. Period uncertain.

Pthah-mai.

The *Sam* and priest of Pthah, in the XVIIIth dynasty.

Pthah-mai.

A great Egyptian officer of the XIXth dynasty, of whom, however, little is known except the names of the members of his family.

Pthah-mai.

A poet and member of the royal family, in the reign of Rameses II. of the XIXth dynasty.

Pthah-mei-t.

An Egyptian lady, the mother of the priest Fai-iten-hemh-bai, which see.

Pthah-meri.

The son of the royal scribe Pueri, of the XVIIIth dynasty.

Pthah-mes. "Born of Pthah."

An overseer of the palace of Pthah and a royal scribe. Period uncertain.

Pthah-mes.

A chief overseer of the House of Pthah. His monument is in the Leyden Museum. Period uncertain.

Pthah-mes.

A priest and spondist of the temple of Pthah-sokari, in the reign of Rameses III. He had a son named Si-uskh, who was a priest of Pthah likewise.

PTHAH-NEFER. "Good Pthah."

An auditor of the temple of Pthah in the period of the Second Empire.

PTHAH-NEFER-KA. " The Good Bull of Pthah."(?)

An Egyptian prince, in the ancient romance of the Story of Setnau. He was the son of Mer-neb-pthah, an unidentified king of Egypt. He married his sister Ahura, by whom he had a son named Merhu.

PTHAH-NES-ANB-EF.

A name of the deity Pthah, under which he had a special temple at the city of Memphis.

PTHAH-SE.

The daughter of Ameni, the chief of the embalmers of an unnamed king of the XVIIIth dynasty.

PTHAH-SOKARI-OSIRIS.

A form of the demiurgic deity Pthah peculiar to Memphis, in Lower Egypt, in which he was represented as a deformed hydrocephalous dwarf.

PTHAH-UR.

An augur in the temple of Pthah. His precise date is uncertain.

PTOLEMAIS.

In the Greco-Egyptian period the chief city of the Thinite nome in the Thebaid. It is now called Menshech.

PTOLEMY (I.) SOTER. " The Saviour."

The son of Lagus, a somatophylax in the army of Philip of Macedon and of Arsinöe his cousin.(?) He was one of the chief generals and advisers of Alexander the Great, whose natural brother he was generally thought to have been, and to whom he was heir presumptive. On the death of Alexander he voted for a division of his empire among his officers, but being overruled in this, he accepted the government of Egypt under Philip Arridæus. He put to death Cleomenes, the receiver-general of taxes, who had been made sub-governor of Egypt, and then annexed the kingdom of Cyrene, which was at that time torn to pieces by an internal faction, to his own, in B.C. 321. He gave a magnificent funeral to the body of Alexander, and then met the army of Perdiccas, the governor of Philip Arridœus and Alexander Aegus in battle, when he became master of the field. The next year he conquered Libya and Phenicia, and received the general, or rather king, Seleucus of the East in Egypt after his expulsion by Antigonus, B.C. 315, taking up arms in his defence. Ptolemy Soter then conquered Cyprus, and defeated Demetrius Poliorcetes at Gaza, and recovering Babylon for Seleucus, conquered Judea, and transplanted many of the Jews to Alexandria and Cyrene, where he afforded them special privileges. After that he resigned Phenicia to Antigonus, with whom, however, he soon was at war again, and a second time overran Palestine and Phenicia, in B.C. 302. Finally he defeated Antigonus at the battle of Ipsus, and then settled himself to adorn and strengthen his dominions, B.C. 300. He erected at Alexandria the museum, the serapeum or temple of Serapis, and began the famous national library. He ordered the architect Sostratus to build the pharos, or lighthouse, and encouraged the fugitive Jewish high-priest, Hezekias, to complete the canon of the Old Testament, B.C. 298. A few years afterwards he associated his son Ptolemy Philadelphus in the empire with him, B.C. 285, and died two years following. *See* Alexandria.

PTOLEMY (II.) PHILADELPHUS. "Brother Loving."

The son of Ptolemy Soter by his queen Berenice. He was born B.C. 311, and became co-regent with his father B.C. 285, Ptolemy Soter himself taking the title of viceroy to his son. He began his reign by a magnificent triumphal procession, followed by public games and shows. His first troubles were a revolt in Cyrene, instigated by his half-sister Berenice. This he soon quelled, and then, to secure his possession of Egypt, put to death his half-brothers by Eurydice, the first wife of his father, and sent a friendly embassy to Rome to congratulate the Senate upon its victory over Pyrrhus, thus commencing the intercourse between Egypt and the West which was ultimately to prove the ruin of his kingdom. Being anxious to increase the Alexandrian library, founded by his father, he forbade the exportation of papyrus, chiefly to defeat the attempts of Philoterus, king of Pergamus, to found a rival institution. This led to the more general use of leather for a writing material, in the form now called parchment, from Pergamena, where it was produced. Ptolemy Philadelphus also invited to Alexandria the leading scientific men of the day, including Demetrius Phalereus, once archon of Athens, who became his librarian; Zenodotus, Euclid, Ctesibus the mathematician, Theocritus and Callimachus the poets, Hegesius and Aristippus the philosophers, Philostephanus the naturalist, Aratus, Aristarchus, Timocharis, and Claudius Ptolemy the geographer, besides many other writers of less note. The priests of Egypt having made his mother, Berenice, a goddess, he held another series of festivals, and made further rich endowments in her name to the temples. The chief temple of Philæ was begun in his reign, and he also completed many other of the restored shrines of the older divinities. The so-called Septuagint Version of the Old Testament was carried on by the orders of Ptolemy Philadelphus, who still further enlarged the privileges of the Jews and Greeks, and considerably increased the mercantile importance of Egypt. He re-erected an obelisk of Nectanebo on the tomb of his sister Arsinöe at Alexandria, and died B.C. 247, after a splendid reign of thirty-seven years. In the reign of Ptolemy Philadelphus the historian Manetho, by the order of the king, compiled his lists of the Egyptian Dynasties.

PTOLEMY (III.) EUERGETES.

The son of Ptolemy Philadelphus. He succeeded to the throne of Egypt B.C. 247, and commenced his reign by making war with Antigonus and his son Seleucus, king of Syria, to avenge the murder of his sister Berenice, who, together with her son, had been put to death by Seleucus. Asia Minor and Syria at once submitted to Ptolemy, B.C. 245, and he extended his conquests in the East as far as Media, Babylon, and Bactria, regaining there many trophies and prizes which the Persians had previously carried away. He was recalled to Egypt by internal differences which had broken out during his absence, but on his way home stopped at Jerusalem, and presented offerings at the temple there. Having quelled the disturbances in Egypt, Ptolemy was desirous of emulating the actions of the Ramesside kings, and for that purpose marched an army into Ethiopia, which he subjugated, and set up a monument of his victories in the shape of a great marble chair with a Greek inscription at Adule, a port of the Red Sea. He enlarged and repaired the great temple of Karnak, began that of Esneh, and added to the temple of Amen at the oasis of Hibe. He further erected a temple to Osiris at Canopus, in the name of himself and his wife and sister Berenice. He strove in all things to be an Egyptian rather than a Greek monarch, and took the surname of Meri-en-pthah, " Beloved of Pthah," similar to the custom of the Pharaohs of the older dynasties. He continued the patronage of literature and art which distinguished his predecessors, and died leaving Egypt in a prosperous condition, B.C. 222, after a reign of twenty-three years. He was succeeded by his son, Ptolemy Philopater.

PTOLEMY (IV.) PHILOPATER.   " Father Loving."

The son of Ptolemy Euergetes, whom he succeeded, B.C. 222, and owing to the wisdom of his predecessors, found himself at the head of the greatest naval power in the world, and an empire extending from Ethiopia to Upper Syria, and including Cyrene, the cities of the coast of Asia Minor, and Ænos and Maronea in Thrace. By the advice of his chief minister, Sosibius, he commenced his reign by putting to death his mother Berenice, and his brother Magus, and then soon gave himself up to pleasures and excesses. The kingdom falling into decay, Philopater was roused into action by Antiochus the Great, who had obtained Seleucia by the treachery of the Egyptian garrison, and had become master of Syria and Palestine before Ptolemy was able to bring his army into the field. In the battles which ensued between the two monarchs, the king of Egypt was defeated at many places and finally at Raphia, B.C. 217, and thus lost the whole of his Asiatic dominions. He still continued, however, to follow the dictates of an imperious voluptuousness, and marked his want of policy by a specious attention to literature and art, more especially the arts of music and poetry. He died, worn out with disease, in the seventeenth year of his reign, B.C. 205, leaving the empire of the Ptolemies weakened by misrule and over taxation, and attacked both by the Syrians and Easterns.

PTOLEMY (V.) EPIPHANES.

The son of Ptolemy Philopater, whom he succeeded when only five years of age, B.C. 205. His accession to the throne was followed by a fearful riot in Alexandria, which resulted in the death of Agathocles, the prime minister, and Agathoclea the mistress, of the late king, together with all their adherents. Taking advantage of his youth, and the troubled condition of Egypt, Antiochus, king of Syria, and Philip V., king of Macedon, endeavoured to dismember the empire of Egypt ; but the Egyptian ministers applied to the Roman Senate for aid, and by their assistance the enemies were repulsed, B.C. 202, and Marcus Lepidus sent as governor to Egypt over King Ptolemy. In B.C. 198, however, Antiochus conquered Cœle-Syria, and Palestine, and by the advice of the Roman Senate Ptolemy was declared of age, and crowned at Memphis, B.C. 197, soon after which the famous decree, now known by the name of the Rosetta Stone, was set up in his honour by the Egyptian clergy. Peace was then concluded between the kings of Syria and Egypt, and Ptolemy married Cleopatra, the daughter of Antiochus, receiving Palestine and Cœle-Syria as her dowry. He assisted the Romans still in their war with his father-in-law, and entered into the Achæan League, B.C. 187. Finding the colonies of Egypt nearly all fallen off, except Cyprus and Cyrene, he planned an attack upon Cœle-Syria, which was only nominally in his power ; but having no resources wherewith to pay his army, and his friends being apprehensive that he would make a levy upon them, he was assassinated by poison, B.C. 181. His name merely occurs on a few temples in Egypt, and he does not appear to have executed any great work, or to have restored, or even repaired, any of the national edifices. *See* Rosetta Stone.

Ptolemy (VI.) Philometer. "Mother Loving."

The son of Ptolemy Epipanes. He was born B.C. 187, and succeeded his father when six years old, reigning jointly with his mother Cleopatra. The Syrian dominions of his empire were wrested from him on the death of the queen by Antiochus Epiphanes, upon whom his ministers declared war, but they were defeated together with the Egyptian army near lake Serbonis, B.C. 173. The king of Syria then marched to Memphis, which he took B.C. 171, and capturing Ptolemy VI., declared himself his guardian. Upon that Ptolemy Physcon proclaimed himself king of Egypt under the name of Euergetes II., and sent to Rome for assistance. In the mean time Philometer married his sister Cleopatra, and agreed to reign jointly with his brother. Alexandria being still besieged by Antiochus in B.C. 170, the Romans deputed the ambassador Popilias to cause the siege to be raised, and to that the king of Syria consented, but not until he had carried off nearly all the wealth of the country. Peace between the two brothers was only restored for a time, for again war broke out, and the Romans interposing a second and a third time gave Egypt to Philometer, and Cyrene, Lybia, and Cyprus to Physcon. This settlement was also unsatisfactory, and ultimately Ptolemy VI. defeated and conquered his brother, and then forgave and restored him to his dominions B.C. 154. The subsequent history of Ptolemy was one of continual altercations. He gave his daughter Cleopatra to the impostor Alexandra Bala, and endeavouring to support Demetrius Nicator, as king of Syria, was slain in battle at Antioch, B.C. 146, having reigned forty-one years, and was succeeded by his brother Ptolemy Physcon. The temple of Edfu may have been rebuilt by this monarch, but it is uncertain, as the royal cartouch is left blank.

Ptolemy (VII.) Physcon. "Big Bellied."

A second son of Ptolemy Epiphanes. Although subordinate to his brother, he claimed to have been always the rightful king of Egypt, and hence on the death of Philometer he called the first year of his sole reign the twenty-fifth, having reigned before six years jointly with Ptolemy VI., and eighteen by himself as king of Cyrene. Immediately upon his accession he was crowned with great state at Memphis, and to flatter the people of Memphis named his son Memphites after the name of that city. He was very cruel and capricious, and soon after his coronation put away his wife and married her youngest daughter, his niece Cleopatra Cocce, an act for which he was universally detested. The Roman Senate sent Scipio Africanus to congratulate him, and he was received with high honours by the Egyptian king. He was still more unpopular than ever after the return of Scipio, and at last the people of Alexandria rose in revolt against him, and expelled him from the throne, setting up instead his divorced queen Cleopatra. Upon that Physcon, who had already put to death her son by Philometer, now slew his own son by the queen, the prince Memphites, and sent the head, hands, and feet, in a box as a birthday present to her. A fierce revolt followed, and Ptolemy was deposed; the kingdom of Egypt being thus lost to him, he claimed the throne of Syria against Demetrius, and the people of Alexandria then being afraid of Egypt being annexed to Syria dethroned Cleopatra, who had gone thither for help, and received Ptolemy Physcon back again as joint sovereign with her B.C. 125. Physcon maintained a troubled empire for a few years longer, and died B.C. 117, having reigned in all fifty-four years, with the least credit of any of the Ptolemies who had preceded him. He left the kingdom of Egypt to his second wife Cleopatra Cocce, and that of Cyrene to his illegitimate son Ptolemy Apion, who bequeathed it to the Romans. The chief Archaic interest of the reign of Ptolemy Physcon consists in the great temple erected by the Jewish high-priest Onias at Tel el Yahoudeh, " Mound of the Jews," being built under his care and patronage, and as the temple itself was supposed to have been 'a copy in plan of that of Jerusalem, and its ruins have now been discovered. Its ruins are of high value as settling several disputed questions on Jewish art.

PTOLEMY VIII. SOTER II. *or* LATHYRUS, " Vetch."

The son of Ptolemy Physcon, whom he succeeded B.C. 117. He reigned at first jointly with his mother Cleopatra Cocce who induced him to divorce his sister Cleopatra, and to marry his other sister Selene, hoping thereby to cause internal dissentions in Egypt, and to place her younger son Ptolemy Alexander on the throne. Soon after this Ptolemy Lathyrus was compelled to admit Alexander to a share in the crown, and therefore made him king of Cyprus. Ptolemy Apion, his half brother, then seized the throne of Cyrene, and the kingdom of Egypt was broken up by a number of contending armies and fraternal enemies. Lathyrus assisted Antiochus Cyzicenus to contest the dominion of Syria, insti- gated thereto by his wife Cleopatra, the divorced queen of Ptolemy himself, and his mother Cleopatra Cocce assisting Antiochus Gryphus, and placing her own army under the command of two Jews, Chelcias and Ananias, led to an outbreak in Alexandria, wherein Lathyrus was deposed, his second wife Selene and her two children taken from him, and himself driven into exile into Cyprus, B.C. 107. Ptolemy Alexander was next recalled to govern Egypt, but soon quarrelling with his mother he put her to death. For this crime another outbreak of the people drove Alexander into exile, and restored Ptolemy again, B.C. 89; he reigned but a short time afterwards, dying in the next year. The famous temple of Contra Latopolis was erected in this reign. He conquered

the city of Thebes, which had revolted from his authority, and in so
doing destroyed more of the ancient temples than had hitherto been
done by the Assyrians or the Persians.   Lathyrus was so named from a
wart like a vetch seed upon his face.

Ptolemy (IX.) Alexander.

A younger son of Ptolemy Physcon by Queen Cleopatra Cocce.   He
was a mere tool in the hands of his intriguing mother, who forced him
to contest the crown of Egypt with his brother Ptolemy Lathyrus, and
afterwards to rule jointly with herself and him.   In B.C. 107 an outbreak
of the people of Alexandria against Lathyrus recalled him from his own
petty kingdom of Cyprus to the sole empire of Egypt.   His throne being
still claimed by his mother he then had her put to death.   This bar-
barism led to a renewed revolt, and Alexander was driven out of Egypt
into Myra, a city of Lycia.   In attempting, however, to cross into
Cyprus, he was overtaken by the Egyptian fleet under Chabrias, and
slain in battle.   By some writers Ptolemy Alexander is reckoned the
ninth of the Ptolemies, and by others he is not included in the separate
lists.   He married for his second wife Cleopatra Berenice, the daughter
of his brother Lathyrus.   The name of his first wife, by whom he had a
son called Ptolemy Alexander also, is not known.

Ptolemy (X.) Alexander II.

The son of Ptolemy Alexander.   On the expulsion of his father from
the throne of Egypt, B.C. 89, Ptolemy with his grandmother Cleopatra
took refuge in the Island of Cos, and on the death of Ptolemy Lathyrus
claimed the crown against his step-mother Cleopatra Berenice.   By the
assistance of Sylla and the Roman people, whom he promised to make
heirs of his kingdom, Alexander II. was sent from Rome to reign jointly
with his step-mother and to marry her, which he did, and the same day
put her to death, thus leaving himself without a rival.   The natural
consequence of the act was, however, a revolution in Alexandria, headed
by his own guards, who dragged the king from his palace to the
gymnasium, where they put him to death, B.C. 80, after a troubled reign
of nine years.

Ptolemy XI.   Neus Dionysus or Auletes, " The Piper."

An illegitimate son of Ptolemy Lathyrus.   On the assassination of
Ptolemy Alexander II., the people having no nearer of kin to the
deceased sovereign raised him to the throne, but from the first day of his
reign he gave himself up to pleasures and debauchery, valuing more his
skill in flute playing (hence his surname) than in kingcraft, and therefore
the Romans refused to acknowledge him, but at the same time left him
alone.   The first twenty-four years of the reign of Auletes are not
recorded in history ; after some time however, Ptolemy his brother, who
was king of Cyprus, was dispossessed of his kingdom by the Romans,
whereupon the Egyptians urged Auletes to take up his cause.   Being
however too weak to do so with any probability of success, he refused,
and was driven by his subjects into exile, B.C. 58.   He next went to
Rome for help, and the Senate restored him to the crown again in B.C. 56,
five years after which he died, leaving the Roman influence paramount
in Egypt.   In his reign were begun the great temples of Denderah and
Esneh in Upper Egypt.

PTOLEMY XII.

The eldest son of Ptolemy Auletes, whom he succeeded B.C. 51. By the will of his father he married his elder sister Cleopatra VI., the most famous or infamous of her race, and began to rule under the direction of Pompey, the dictator. The power of Pompey had however fallen when Auletes died, and so Photinus the Eunuch, the governor of Egypt, induced the young king to reign alone, and to dispossess his sister wife. On this Cleopatra fled into Syria, and raising an army, came back to Egypt and regained her share of the throne, B.C. 49. About this time, Pompey flying to Egypt for protection, was put to death by Ptolemy and his advisers, and the dictator Julius Cæsar was welcomed to settle the kingdom between the brother and sister, whose armies were preparing for a decisive battle. The Romans were unable to reconcile the competitors, and in the war which ensued, the fleet, the museums, and the library were destroyed. Cleopatra in the mean time had won over Cæsar to her side, and in another naval engagement, in which the fleet of Cæsar was strengthened by the army of Mithridates, king of Pergamus, Ptolemy was drowned, and first Arsinöe, then Cleopatra, and finally Cleopatra and her infant son Cæsarion, were declared sovereigns of Egypt, B.C. 47.

PTOLEMY XIII.

A younger son of Ptolemy Auletes. On the death of his brother Ptolemy, B.C. 47, he was declared joint sovereign of Egypt with his brother's wife Cleopatra, he being then eleven years old. He was a mere instrument in the hands of Cæsar and Cleopatra, whom he, as was the custom of the Ptolemaic kings, also married. He visited Rome and was well received there, but on his reaching the age of fifteen, at which period he could have claimed to be of age, he was poisoned by his sister wife, B.C. 44.

PTOLEMY (XVI.) CÆSARION.

The infant son of Cleopatra VI. and Julius Cæsar. *See* Cæsarion. He was made joint king with his mother, but was put to death by Marc Antony, who made his own son by Cleopatra king instead. He is called by some writers Ptolemy XVI., and he was the last of his race. To make up the number of sixteen Ptolemies, Ptolemy Memphites, and Ptolemy Apion, would have to be included in the lists, but the enumeration of the kings of the house of the Lagidæ differs in almost every author. The names here given, and most of the facts, are those of Mr. Sharpe.

PTOLEMY.

A Greco-Egyptian priest or officer, the father of Eirene, the priestess of the goddess Arsinöe Philopater under Ptolemy V.

P-TO-RES.

The Egyptian name for the people of Upper Egypt. They were the Pathrusim of the book of Genesis.

PUAIMA.

The Assyrian form of the Egyptian royal name Puma, which see.

PUDIL.

An early king of Assyria, who flourished about B.C. 1350. He was the father of Vulnirari I.

PUER.

A prince of Kush during the reign of Atef-nuter-ai of the XVIIIth dynasty.

PUERI.

A royal scribe in the time of the XVIIIth dynasty. He had a son named Pthàh-meri.

PUJA.

In Hindu mythology any act of ceremonial worship having various names according to the deities adored ; as, Durga-puja, Linga-puja.

PUKHUNINIAPI.

The king of Khatkhiribi, the Athribis of the Greeks. He was one of the first petty kings of Egypt under the Assyrian Icosarchy.

PULAHA. *Or* PALAHA.

A Hindu deity who was invested by Brahma with the power of creation. *See* Angiras.

PULTIPHAGI. "Eaters of Pulse."

An epithet applied by the Classical writers to the Phenicians from their consumption of pease.

PULUSATA.

The name by which the Pelasgians were known to the Egyptians in the time of Rameses III.

PUMA.

The king of Bendidi, the Mendes of the Greeks. He was one of the first of the twenty petty kings of Egypt under the Assyrian Icosarchy.

PÜMELIUN.

A king of Tyre, the son and successor of Mathan. He was declared by his father's will co-monarch with his sister Elissa ; but the people, desirous of changing the form of government, raised a democratic opposition and declared Pümeliun the sovereign. On this Elissa married Zicharbaal, the high-priest of Melkarth, but he was assassinated by the king, whereupon she, with 300 of the nobility, revolted, and being unsuccessful, quitted Tyre. Pümeliun after that reigned forty years, and had to pay tribute to Binlikkish or Vul-nirari, king of Assyria, who had conquered all Phenicia. He reigned forty-seven years in all, and was the Pygmalion of Classic history and mythology.

PUNNU.

A prince royal of Ethiopia, who presented offerings to Rameses VI. of the XXth dynasty.

PUQUDU.

A people of Mesopotamia who were conquered by Tiglath Pileser II.

PUR.   " Fire."

In Phenician mythology the son of Genus, and one of the discoverers of the art of creating fire.

PURANAS.

In Hindu mythology the name of a series of poetical histories of the principal divinities, of which the Vishnu Purana, concerning the birth and actions of the deity Krishna, is best known.   The treatises are of late authorship.

PURIKH.

A subordinate Etruscan goddess, who was represented as wearing a Phrygian cap.

PURULUZ.

A district near the Upper Euphrates which was usurped by the Hittites till they were defeated by Tiglath Pileser I.

PURUSATA.

The Egyptian name of the land of Philistia.

PURUSHA.   " The Supreme Spirit."

The Vedic title of the Supreme Being as the spirit of life.

PUZUS.

The king of Aphrodisia in the Island of Kypros.   He was one of the tributaries of Esarhaddon.

PYGMALION.

The Greek form of the Tyrian royal name Pümeliun, which see.

PYRAMID, THE GREAT.   In Egyptian, MER, or AB-MER.

The name applied to the huge sepulchral monument of King Cheops, or Khufo, of the IVth dynasty.   It is situated on an artificially levelled plateau of limestone rock to the West of the city of Memphis, in Lower Egypt, and almost at the apex of the triangle formed by the Delta of the Nile, at a place now known by the name of Geezeh, or Ghizeh.   It is surrounded by a number of smaller pyramids and tombs, apparently belonging to the families of the nobles of the court of the king by whose order it was erected.   It is externally constructed of Nummulitic limestone, but the interior works, the corridors. and the chambers, are lined with granite.   It contains several vaults and air-passages, and a large funereal chamber, which was once protected by a stone portcullis.   In this chamber the body of the founder was interred in a massive sarcophagus, now much mutilated, and about which many unsupported theories have been advanced.   There are no inscriptions or decorations used in any part of the massive structure ; but on recently opening one of the upper chambers the name of Khufu was found rudely painted upon one of the walls in red ochre, thus confirming the concurrent statements of Greek and Egyptian tradition as to the date of its erection.   The external slope of the outer angles is about 51° 50′, and the area covered by its base is one-seventh larger than the entire width of Lincoln's Inn Fields, when measured from the walls of the houses.   (Bonomi.)

The corner-stones are polished and fitted with singular accuracy, but there is no such exact parallelism as to the lines of the bases or the length of their sides. "The total structure is formed of more than 200 steps, or layers of enormous blocks. When entire, it was 480 feet high, nearly double the elevation of the towers of the cathedral of Notre Dame, at Paris; its base measured 756 feet (French), and it was composed of the truly astonishing mass of more than 10,000,000 of cubic yards of stone, material sufficient to build a wall six feet high, a foot thick, and nearly 3000 miles long. To relieve the enormous weight that the chamber intended for the royal sarcophagus had to support, open spaces have been left in the mass of the monument above it, forming five small chambers. A second sepulchral chamber is situated almost exactly below the first, and a third at a great depth below, excavated in the rock, and forming no part of the building. The orientation of this gigantic monument is perfect, its four sides exactly facing the four cardinal points." (Lenormant.) "The principle upon which this and the other pyramids were constructed appears to have been the following :—Very early in the life of the king the surface of the lime-stone rock was levelled for the base, a shaft more or less inclined was sunk leading to a rectangular sepulchral chamber in the rock itself. The distance from the entrance of the shaft or gallery to the chamber was calculated at the distance the square base of the pyramid would cover, so as to exceed and not be overlapped by it. Should the king die during the year the work was finished at once, but should he live on another year a second layer of masonry was placed on the substructure of the same square shape as the base, but smaller, with the sides parallel to those of the base. The process went on year after year, each layer being smaller than the previous one. When the king died the work was at once stopped, and the casing or outer surface of the pyramid finished. This was effected by filling up the masonry with smaller stones of a rectangular form, so that the pyramid still presented a step-shaped appearance. The casing of each triangular face was then smoothed from the top or apex, the masons standing on the steps and hewing away the edges of each row of stones as they descended to the base. When finished the faces were perfectly smooth, and the top inaccessible. Each of the casing stones capped the other so as to leave no vertical joint. The principle of the pyramid combined the power of increase in size without alteration in form, and its sloping side carried off the occasional rainfall without allowing the water to penetrate the building. Simple in shape, it was eternal in duration, and exhibited a perfect mathematical knowledge of the square and the triangle." (Birch.)

PYRRHA.

An Egyptian lady, the daughter of Philinos. She was an athlophoros of the goddess Berenice Euergetes under Ptolemy V.

PYTHAGORAS.

The king of Kidrusi in the Island of Kypros. He was one of the tributaries of Esarhaddon, about B.C. 684.

PYTHAGORAS.

A king or chief magistrate either of Kition or Idalion, in the Island of Kypros, about the fourth century B.C.

Q.

QABIHA.

A tribe in Mesopotamia which was conquered by Tiglath Pileser II. Many of these names are also written with a guttural *Kh* instead of a *Q*.

QAGABU.

The "Scribe of the Royal Treasury," and a poet in the reign of Amenemha I. of the XIIth dynasty.

QAH-AUF-AA.

A devotee of Apis in the thirty-fourth year of Darius Hystaspes.

QANA.

A mountain district on the borders of Media and Susiana, which was conquered by Sennacherib.

QARQAR.   *Or* KAR-KAR.

The Assyrian name of the city of Aroer in Palestine.

QATIZILLI.

A king of Kummuha, or Commagene, who submitted to Assurnazirpal.

QAVUS-GABRI.

A king of Edom.   He was one of the tributaries of Esarhaddon.

QAVUS-MALKA.

A king of Edom, who paid tribute to Tiglath Pileser II. after the fall of Damascus.

QEBEH.

The Egyptian name of a city at the cataracts of the Nile, near Elephanta, where there was a famous temple of the god Khnum-Ra.

QELHATAT.

A queen of Nubia, the sister or wife of Nuat-amen or Nud-mi-amen, an Ethiopian king of the XXVth dynasty.

QINNIPUR.

A city in Babylonia, which was conquered by Tiglath Pileser II. and added to the kingdom of Assyria.

QIRBUTU.

A city in Babylonia which was conquered by Tiglath Pileser II. and added to the kingdom of Assyria.

QODESH.

The Egyptian name of an unidentified Syrian city, perhaps Kadesh.(?)

QOOS.

The modern name of the Greco-Egyptian city called Apollinopolis, which see.

QUA.

A mountain district on the borders of Media and Susiana. It was conquered both by Tiglath Pileser II. and Sennacherib.

QUAZI.

A city or district of which Ganrubai was prefect under Sennacherib.

QUE. *Or* KUE.

A district in Syria, which was conquered by Shalmaneser IV., after several previous invasions.

QUMANI.

A people North of Assyria, who, coming to the relief of the people of Muzur, when attacked by the Assyrians, were, together with their allies, defeated and subjugated by Tiglath Pileser I.

QURAZITU.

A city or district in Nabathea, where the armies of Vaiteh II. were completely defeated by Assurbanipal.

QURDI-ASSUR.

The governor of Ahizuhina, in the reign of Assurdan III. He was eponym of the year B.C. 767, in which year there was an expedition to Gannanati.

QUTI.

A people conquered by Budil, a very early king of Assyria. They were called also the Goim.

R.

RA. " To Make, to Dispose."

In Egyptian mythology the deity of the mid-day sun, of which the other deities were more or less manifestations. Ra was adored all over Egypt, but chiefly at Heliopolis as the most striking manifestation of the Supreme Being, and the organiser of the world, of which the material fabric had been made by Pthah. He was represented as a man with the head of a sparrow hawk, and holding the usual *cucufa* staff and cross of life. Although a benevolent deity, in anger at the sins of men, he once, assisted by Tefnut, destroyed the entire human race, which he afterwards revived afresh out of the blood of the slain, at the intercession of Nu and the other deities. The name Ra is also written with the article, Phre. *See also* Horus.

RA.

A royal scribe, and superintendent of the granaries of the North and South. Period uncertain.

RA.

A scribe of the offerings of an unknown deity. The period when he lived is uncertain, but his monument is in the Leyden Museum.

RAA.

An Egyptian lady, one of the family of the priest Amen-em-ap, of the XVIIIth dynasty. *See* An.

RAA.

An Egyptian lady, of the family of the treasurer Iuiu, of the XVIIIth dynasty.

RA-AAH-MIN-AA.

An early unarranged Egyptian king. Leyden Collection.

RA-AA-KHEPER.

The prenomen of Amenhotep II. of the XVIIIth dynasty.

RA-AA-KHEPER-KA-SEN-BU.

The first prophet or priest of the temple of Thothmes I., adored as a deity. *See* Thothmes I.

RAAMAH.

A country in Southern Arabia, now called Oman.

RA-AMEN.

A spondist of the god Pthah, whose statue is in the Leyden Museum. His wife was named Ocaei. Period uncertain.

RA-AMEN-EM-HA.

The prenomen of King Amenemha I. (?) of the XIIIth dynasty.

RA-AMEN-MEI-NITO.

An early unarranged Egyptian king. (Leemans.)

RA-AMEN-MERN-BA.

The prenomen of Menepthah I. of the XIXth dynasty.

RA-AMEN-MESES-AT-NUTER-HIQ-AN.

The prenomen of Rameses VII., the son of Rameses III. of the XIXth dynasty.

RA-AMEN-MESES-NUTER-HIQ-AN.

The prenomen of Rameses VI. of the XXth dynasty.

RA-AMEN-SOTEP-EN-MER.

The prenomen of Philip Arridæus, as king of Egypt under the Grecian rule.

RA-AMEN-SOTEP-EN-MER.

The prenomen of Ptolemy Soter I.

RA-AMEN-SU-MESES.

The prenomen of Rameses X. of the XXth dynasty.

RA-AMEN-TUT-ANKH-HIQ-AN-RES.

The prenomen of Tut-ankh-amen, a king of the XVIIIth dynasty.

RA-APEPI.

Another form of the royal name Pepi or Apepi, which see.

RA-BAKA.

The surname of Nut-mi-amen, a king of Nubia, in the XXVth dynasty.

RABAYA.

An Elamite city, which was destroyed by Sennacherib.

RABBITURI. "The Chieftainess."

The feminine of Rabbu, "Great."

RABBU. "The Mighty."

The astronomical name of the deity Marduk as the planet Mercury, in the month Marchesvan.

RABEKUKI.

The Accadian name of the city Rapiqu, which see.

RAB-IZ.

The Assyrian name of the class of evil spirits, or demons, which were called by the Accadians Maskim.

RAB-SAKI. "Chief Saki."

The superior officer in the Assyrian army, next to the Tartan or commander-in-chief, and having control over the Saki or captains. This is the same name as the Rabshakeh of Hebrew history.

RAB-SARIS.

The title of the chief of the eunuchs in the court of the kings of Assyria.

RAB-SHAKEH.

A chief officer in the Assyrian army. *See* Rabsaki.

RAB-SUNA.

The general of the troops of the army of Khitasira, the king of the Hittites, who was killed in the battle of Kadesh, won by Rameses II.

RABTU.

An Assyrian measure of length, equal to one cubit of twenty inches. It was called also Suklu and Ammat.

RACHA.

A city in Persia, where Veisdates the rebel king was defeated for a first time by Artabardes, the general of Darius Hystaspes.

RADHA.

In Hindu mythology the first wife of the god Khrishna. She was afterwards adored as the goddess of love.

RA-EAI.

An Egyptian gentleman, whose statue is in the Leyden Museum.

RA-EN-HET.

A prenomen of Aahmes or Amasis II. of the XXVIth dynasty.

RA-EN-KA.

An early Egyptian king who is named on the Tablet of Abydos.

RA-EN-KA-NEB.

An early unarranged Egyptian king. His name occurs on a scarabeus in the Leyden Museum.

RA-EN-KAU.

The grandson of Tetet, an early Egyptian king.

RA-EN-KAU.

The son of another early Egyptian king.

RA-EN-MA.

A *Sutenrekh* and prophet of Hathor, in the reign of Amenemha III. of the XIIth dynasty.

RA-EN-NITO-IRI-EN-TME.

An early unarranged Egyptian king.

RA-EN-SESUR.

The prenomen of the fourth king of the Vth Egyptian dynasty.

RA-EN-TME.

A prenomen of Amenemha III. of the XIIth dynasty.

RA-EN-USER. *Surnamed* AN.

A king of Egypt of the Vth dynasty. He reigned fourty-four years, continued the works at the copper mines of Sinai, and was buried in the middle pyramid of Abuseir. He was the Rathoures of the Greeks.

RA-ER.

The father of Uermu, the "Guardian of the Magazines" of an unnamed king, probably Seti I. of the XIXth dynasty.

RAGHA.

In Zendic mythology the eleventh resting-place of the Iranians after their exile from Aryanem Vaedjo, which see. It was the Rhages of the Greeks, now called Rey, near Teheran.

RAGIBA.

A deity of the Susians, of whom nothing is known.

RA-HA-HET.

The husband of the lady Ta-kel-heb, and father of Saho, the priest of Amen at Thebes.

RAHIQU.

A tribe in Mesopotamia, which was conquered by Tiglath Pileser II.

RAHMAN. "The Merciful."

A Himyaritic deity. He was a form of the god Il, which see.

RA-HOTEP. "Peace of Ra."

An Egyptian prince of the IIIrd dynasty.

RA-HOTEP.

A king of the XIIIth dynasty. He succeeded Sebak-em, and was himself succeeded by a king named Ai.

RA-I.

An Egyptian lady of the family of Uermu, the guardian of the magazines of a king of the XIXth dynasty.

RAIDAN. *Or* DHU-RAIDAN.

A royal fortress of the kingdom of Sabæa near Zafar. It was always held by the eldest son of the reigning monarch. It was the capital of the Sabæan kingdom of South-western Arabia.

RAIDISADI.

A general of Ahsera, king of Minni, who vainly resisted the army of Assurbanipal as it advanced to the conquest of the country. He was slain in battle by the king of Assyria.

RAJAH. " King."

A royal title, very anciently in use among the Hindus, some of whose sovereigns bore the title of Rajaraja, " King of Kings," and Maharajah, " Great King."

RA-KA-ANKH. " The Living Bull of Ra."

The prenomen of King Nastosenen of the XXVth dynasty.

RA-KA-MAT.

A royal lady, a wife of Osorkon I. of the XXIInd dynasty.

RA-KA-MAT.

The daughter of Petuankhi II., the last king of the XXIInd dynasty.

RA-KA-MAT.

The daughter of Pisem I., a king of the XXIst dynasty.

RA-KATI.

The Egyptian name of the town in the Delta, which was called Rhacotis by the Greeks, and now Alexandria.

RA-KA-TME.

Another form of the royal name of a queen named Amense of the XVIIIth dynasty.

RA-KHA-KA.

The prenomen of Osirtesen III. of the XIIth dynasty, which see.

RA-KHA-KA-U-SENB.

An officer of state, the son of Thoth-hotep in the reign of Osirtesen III. of the XIIth dynasty. His name is curious as being in part exactly the same as the sacerdotal surname of Osirtesen himself.

RA-KHEM-SMEN-TOTI.

An early Egyptian king who lived before the period of the Vth dynasty.

RA-KHEPERA. " Ra the Creator."

A son of Thothmes IV. of the XVIIIth dynasty.

RA-KHEPER-KA.

A priest of Osiris in the XIIth dynasty. He was the son of Har-benen and the lady Ma-net-ankh.

RA-KHEPERU-ARI-MAT. " Sun of both Worlds making Justice."

The prenomen of Horus " The Restorer" of the XVIIIth dynasty.

RA-KHEPERU-NEB.

The prenomen of Tut-ankh-amen, a king of the XVIIIth dynasty.

RA-KHER-PA-PUH-ERMA.

The prenomen of Antef III. of the XIth dynasty, which see.

RAK-HOR.

An Egyptian royal officer, who was also keeper of the place of the lion of Pthah. His funereal statue is in the Leyden Museum. Period uncertain.

RAKSHAS.

In Hindu mythology a species of monstrous evil beings, analogous to the Typhonic monsters of the Egyptians.

RALA.

According to Arabic historians the daughter of Mudad, chief of the Jorhamites. She was one of the wives of the patriarch Ishmael. She was also called Sayyida.

RA-M-AA-UR-NEFRU.   " Gift of the Great Sun of Justice."

The daughter of Khitasira, king of the Hittites. She married Rameses II., by whom her father and his people were conquered. Her Syrian name has not yet been discovered.

RAMATEA.

The king of Urakazaparna, a petty Median state. He was conquered by Esarhaddon, king of Assyria.

RA-MA-UER-NEFRU.

A daughter of Rameses II. of the XIXth dynasty.

RA-MEI.

An early unarranged Egyptian king. His name occurs on a scarabeus in the Leyden Museum.

RA-MEI-AMEN.

An early unarranged Egyptian king. His name occurs on a scarabeus in the Leyden Museum.

RA-MEI-NI-OURO.

An early unarranged Egyptian king. His name occurs on a scarabeus in the Leyden Museum.

RA-MEI-PASHT.   *Or* RA-MEI-SEKHET.

An early unarranged Egyptian king. His name occurs on a scarabeus in the Leyden Museum.

RAMEN.   " Ether."

An Assyrian deity. He was called also " The Meridian Sun in Elam."

Ra-men-ankh.

An early unarranged Egyptian king. His name occurs on a scarabeus in the Leyden Museum.

Ra-men-ka.

An early unarranged Egyptian king. His name occurs on a scarabeus in the Leyden Museum.

Ra-men-kheper.   " The Sun establishes his Form."

The prenomen of Thothmes III. of the XVIIIth dynasty.

Ra-men-kheper.

The last monarch of the sacerdotal line of Har-hor of the XXIst dynasty, of whom no particulars are known, save that he married the princess Hesi-em-kheb of the royal house of Seti I. of the XIXth dynasty.

Ra-men-tau-neb.

The prenomen of an Egyptian king, but of whom it is not known.

Ra-men-tme.

Another form of the royal name of Menepthah I., which see.

Ra-men-to-ka.

An early unarranged Egyptian king. It occurs in the Leyden Collection.

Ra-mere-nefer.

An early unarranged Egyptian king.

Ra-meri-ankh-nas.

The queen of King Pepi-Merira of the VIth dynasty.

Ra-mes.   " Son of Ra."

An Egyptian officer who flourished in the early part of the XVIIIth dynasty. His son's name was Aa-bau.

Ra-mes.

A royal scribe and chief of the servants of the king. His monument is in the Leyden Museum. Period uncertain.

Ra-mes.

A son or brother of the preceding. He was a " Scribe of the Tribunal of Justice."

Ra-mes.

An herald and ambassador of Khitasira, king of the Hittites, who sent him with a treaty of peace to Rameses II. after the battle of Kadesh. See Tatisbu.

Ra-mes.

A son of King Aahmes I. of the XVIIth or XVIIIth dynasty.

Ra-meses I. " Son of Ra."

The first king of the XIXth dynasty. He was probably related by marriage to the family of his predecessor Haremhebi, but his pedigree and connection are not known. In the second year of his reign he associated his son Seti I. with himself, and made him marry the princess Touaa, a direct descendant of Amenhotep IV. From his features he was evidently of Semitic origin, and possibly was even descended from some of the Hykshos chiefs who still remained in Egypt after the bulk of their nation was expelled. Warlike as were all the kings of his race he fought against the Hittites, and claimed to have been the first of the Pharaohs who had pursued that nation into the valley of the Orontes. He concluded a treaty of peace with their king Separuru or Sap-or. and he returned to Egypt with a large number of prisoners, or rather slaves, whom he employed in the erection of temples to the deities Khem and Amen Horus. Rameses I. died after a short reign, and was succeeded by his son, or as some texts call him, his son-in-law Seti I., the Sesostris of the Greeks. The name Rameses should be pronounced Ra-meses, not as is commonly done Ram-eses, as if it were a compound of the name of the Hindu deity Ram.

Ra-meses II. *Surnamed* Meriamen, " Beloved of Amen."

The son of Seti I., with whom he was associated on the throne of Egypt when only ten years old, becoming sole king at the age of eighteen or twenty. He was as great a warrior as his father, and even a still greater builder of temples and palaces, chiefly of the temples of Ipsambul, the Ramesseium, Memphis, Karnak, Luxor, Abydos, and Tanis. He also constructed a great colossus representing himself at Memphis. On these monuments his name is found written in thirty different ways. His first wars were against the Ethiopians, whom he completely overcame ; but his chief wars were against the Khitæ, where by his extreme hardihood he nearly lost his life in an ambush set by his foes, from which he was only delivered by his own bravery and that of his armour-bearer Menna. Ultimately Rameses concluded a treaty of peace with Khitasira, the king of the Hittites, and took his daughter to wife, giving her the Egyptian name of Ra-m-aa-ur-nefru. He invaded Palestine and took the fortress of Shaluma or Shalem, the Jerusalem of Hebrew history ; and besides many other fortresses he built those of Pakhalem and Raameses, supposed to have been the Pithom and Rameses of the Bible, in which case he must have been the Pharaoh of the Exodus. Rameses II. also continued a wall which was begun by his father Seti, from Pelusium to Heliopolis, as a defence to the kingdom against the Asiatics. He married many times, and one of his daughters named Bantanath, became a queen, but of what country it is not known. He was generally accompanied in battle by his favourite lion and dog. He reigned alone for sixty-seven years, and was buried, not as was usual among the kings of Egypt, but in one of the chambers of the Serapeum or burial place of the bull Apis at Memphis. He was succeeded by Menepthah II., his thirteenth son, all his younger sons having died before him. One of his surnames, Setesura, was the origin of the royal name Sesostris of the Greeks. He is doubtfully said to have had 166 children, 59 of them being sons, and by one Egyptologist, to have married his own daughter, the Queen Bantanath.

RA-MESES III. *Surnamed* HEK-AN, *and* PA-ASER-MA-AMEN-MERI.

The first monarch of the XXth dynasty, and the son and successor of Prince Seti-Nekht. He was like Rameses I. of Semitic birth, and he came to the throne at a very early age, as perhaps the richest of all the kings of Egypt. On his accession he re-organized the kingdom, which had been disarranged by the revolution of Arsu the Syrian, who had overthrown the worship of the divinities and reduced them to the rank of men, and established the castles, officers, and chiefs anew. He held a large army of mercenary soldiers, many of them coming from Grecian colonies. The Mashuasha having settled in the Delta, he fought against and expelled them. He then, accompanied by the council of thirty, crossed into Asia, and defeated the Hittites, the Syrians, and the Pelasgians, who all attacked him at one and the same time in different quarters. He subdued them with a great slaughter, and on finding himself opposed in the forests of Ephraim by a large number of lions which the Syrians had driven there to check the advance of his army, slew the animals at a general hunt, and then extended his conquests to Lebanon. The Philistines were in turn conquered, and he took the whole nation prisoners, deporting the people to various cities where the Egyptian garrisons could keep them in check. He then fought against the combined European nations, the Sardinians, the Thracians, and the Etruscans, and was victorious in all his undertakings. Returning to Egypt he built the palace temple of Medinet Habu to record his victories, and constructed a great reservoir in Eastern Egypt. The greatest donations which were ever made to the temples of Karnak were those of Rameses II., the list of which fills one of the longest papyri (the Harris) in existence. A fleet of ships was also kept by him for the purposes of trade, new mines were opened, and the land of Egypt systematically cultivated, and the people fed by the crown, from which it has been thought that Rameses had made himself sole proprietor of the country. Despite his great talents he was addicted to sensual indulgencies, which exposed him to the ridicule of his subjects, and led to a conspiracy against him among the chief officers of the palace and the women of the harem. Evil was hoped to have been wrought to the king by the use of magical charms and figures of wax. The conspirators were twice tried, and the first time the judges having dealt leniently with them the king ordered the judges themselves to be beheaded. The second trial was more to the sovereign's wish, most of the traitors suffering death, and the others being mutilated. The reign of this king is the first to which a date can certainly be assigned, as from an astronomical calendar in the palace of Medinet Habu, the heliacal rising of the star Sothis, or the great Sothic cycle, is marked as an event in the twelfth year of his reign. As this cycle is known to have occurred B.C. 1300, Rameses must have come to the throne in B.C. 1311. He reigned thirty-one years, and was the Rhampsinitus of the Greeks. The tomb of Rameses III. is one of the most magnificent in the valley of the tombs of the kings, and the representations are of considerable interest.   Its entrance is open to the sky, and at the end of the passage the ceiling is supported by four pillars with capitals formed by the heads of bulls, the horns curved inwards, as in the headdress of the king.   The scenes in it represent Isis and Nephthys kneeling before the god Chnoumis and the scarabeus.   On the right wall of the first corridor is Ma, the goddess of truth, winged, kneeling, on the emblem " Lord," or " Dominion," facing the entrance, repeated again on the left wall.   These goddesses, respectively the lotus and papyrus emblems, have the Upper and the Lower country.   On the right wall of the first corridor is the figure of Rameses III. adoring the solar disk and the sun disk on a hill, between a crocodile and a serpent, both referring to the sun's path.   The other scenes chiefly relate to the usual passage of the sun in the lower heaven during the night, and through the regions of the Karneter, or Hades.   The tomb is particularly distinguished by eight small halls pierced laterally in the walls of the first and second corridors.   In these are representations not of a mythical nature, but of objects of civil and political life, as the work of the kitchen, the rich and sumptuous furniture of the palace, the weapons and military standards of the army, the war galleys and transports of the fleet, and twelve representations of the Nile, or Hapi, and Egypt.   It is the fifth tomb of the valley, and a papyrus with the plan and description is said to have been found by Champollion in the Museum of Turin   It had clearly been accessible, and apparently rifled at an early period, for the Hieratic inscriptions on its walls record the names of different scribes who had visited it in Pharaonic times, as Greek inscriptions do the Greek and Roman travellers who penetrated during the period of the Roman empire.   The mummy of Rameses had been destroyed, and his tomb in recent times rifled of its contents ; sepulchral figures of the king, there once deposited, being found in the museums of Europe.   (Birch.)

RA-MESES IV.

The son of Rameses III.   He ascended the throne when quite young, and the highest date known of his reign is that of his eighteenth year. Except that he obtained tribute from the Assyrians, Rameses IV. apparently did nothing worth recording.   He died childless.

RA-MESES V.

An usurper who is supposed to have succeeded to the throne by a revolution consequent on the previous monarch having left no heirs. Except a tablet recording some local benefits bestowed by him on the town of Silsilis, no particulars are known of his reign.   The tomb of Rameses V. is remarkable for the long series of sculptures or painting adorning a succession of halls or galleries, excavated in the side of the mountain, and forming the approach of the Sarcophagus Hall.   The wells are adorned with mythological and astronomical scenes, representing the sun's course, and the rewards or punishments to be awarded to a soul in a future life.   The Sarcophagus Hall, described in great detail in the letters of Champollion, shows us the course of the sun, and the walls are covered with thousands of Hieroglyphics.   Among the sixteen tombs of the valley of Biban-el-Moluk, a part only have their decorations completed throughout their whole extent, and these belong to princes who had a long reign; for the construction of the royal sepulchre was begun at the commencement of the reign, and, more or less, was accomplished according to the length of time that the king occupied the throne. When once the corpse was deposited in the sepulchre, the door was closed, to be re-opened no more." (Lenormant.)

RA-MESES VI.

The successor of Rameses V. and the son of Rameses III. He maintained the sway of the empire over the Southern provinces, and received tribute from Punnu, prince or viceroy of Ethiopia. Nothing else is recorded of his reign. His tomb is remarkable for its astronomical inscriptions.

RA-MESES VII.

The successor of Rameses VI. and a son of Rameses III. His name only occurs on some unimportant monuments.

RA-MESES VIII.

The successor and brother of Rameses VII. Nothing of importance is known of either of these monarchs.

RA-MESES IX. *Surnamed* KHAEM-MI-AMEN.

The successor, whether immediately or not is uncertain, of Rameses VIII. During his reign the tombs of ten great kings and queens of the earlier dynasties were opened by robbers and plundered. The accused were at first acquitted, but were afterwards retried, condemned to be bastinadoed, and put to death. Towards the close of his reign, Rameses IX. associated his son Rameses X. with himself on the throne.

RA-MESES X.

The son of Rameses IX., with whom for a short time he reigned jointly. Nothing is known of his works or reign.

RA-MESES XI.

The successor of Rameses X. Nothing but his name is known. During the reigns of all these later Ramesside kings the real power was lodged in the hands of the high-priest of Amen, who with his colleagues appears to have reduced the monarchs to little better than a nominal possession of the throne, and in the end to have usurped the government.

RA-MESES XII.

The successor of Rameses XI. He still maintained the sovereignty of Egypt over Assyria, though in a merely nominal form. He married the daughter of the prince of Bakhtan, in Mesopotamia, and changed her name into that of Raneferu, "Most Beautiful Sun." At the request of his father-in-law he sent the sacred ark of the deity Khons, of Thebes, to Bakhtan, in order to relieve Bent-aresh, the sister of his queen, who was possessed by a demon, which Tet-em-hebi the royal secretary had been unable to subdue. The mission of the god Khons was successful, and for a while the ark remained at Bakhtan. After a residence there for more than three years, the priest returned with a large number of valuable offerings, in the thirty-third year of the reign of Rameses, who, it is supposed, died not long afterwards. He was succeeded by Rameses XIII., the last of the great family of Ramesside kings.

RA-MESES XIII. *Surnamed* KHAEM-MI-AMEN-NUTER-NIK-TEN.

The successor of Rameses XII. No particulars of his reign are known, and at its close the high-priest of Amon, Har-Hor, whose predecessors had long commanded the troops and worn the uræus badge of royalty, assumed the throne. *See* Har-Hor.

RA-MESES.

A royal scribe and chancellor, in the reign of Tirhakah. He was the son of the lady Zesmehentperu.

RA-MESES.

A son of Rameses I. of the XIXth dynasty. He probably died before his father.

RA-MESES.

The names of three successive sons of Rameses III. of the XXth dynasty.

RA-MESES-KHAEM.

A son of Rameses III. His name only occurs on the royal lists.

RAMESES-MI-AMEN.

Another son of Rameses III.

RA-MESES-MI-ATUMU.

A third son of Rameses III.

RA-MESES-MI-EN-RA.

One of the fifty-nine sons of Rameses II. of the XIXth dynasty.

RA-MESES-NEKHT. "Rameses in Victory."

The high-priest of Amen Ra, in the reign of Rameses IX. of the XXth dynasty.

RA-MESES-SET-HIK-HOPSEF.

A son of Rameses III.

RA-MES-MI-AMEN.

One of the last kings of the XXth dynasty.

RA-MES-SU.

The true Hieroglyphic form of the Egyptian royal name generally written Ra-meses, which see.

RA-NA-NITO.

A prenomen of Amen-hotep II. of the XVIIIth dynasty.

RA-NEB-KRU.

The prenomen of Mentu-hotep II. of the XIth dynasty.

RA-NEB-NEM.

An Egyptian king, or perhaps the prenomen of an Egyptian king of the XIth dynasty, of whom little is known.

RA-NEB-NITO.

A name given by some Egyptologists to Amen-tu-ankh, whom they consider to have been the brother of Amenhotep III. of the XVIIIth dynasty.

RA-NEB-PEH.

The prenomen of Aahmes I., which see.

RA-NEF-ANKH.

An Egyptian lady, the mother of En-antef, the overseer of the altar of Osiris, in the reign of Amenemha II. of the XIIth dynasty.

RA-NEFER.

An early unarranged Egyptian king, whose name occurs on a scarabeus in the Leyden Museum.

RA-NEFER-AB.

An Egyptian priest of the Alexandrian epoch, the father of the priestess and princess Philoterahersankh, which see.

RA-NEFER-KA-SOTEP-EN-RA.

The sacerdotal title or prenomen of Rameses IX.

RA-NEFER-NITO.

An early unarranged Egyptian king, whose name occurs on a scarabeus in the Leyden Museum.

RA-NEFER-U. " Most Beautiful Sun."

The daughter of a prince of Bakhtan, probably Bagistan, in Mesopotamia. She married Rameses XII., the last king but one of the XXth dynasty.

RA-NEFRU.

A daughter of Thothmes III. of the XVIIIth dynasty.

RANNO. RANEN, " To Suckle."

In Egyptian mythology the serpent goddess of corn and of harvest. She was generally represented as a goddess with the head of an uræus serpent, or the crown of Hathor. It was her province, together with the god Shai or Shu, to give new life to the deceased in Hades.

RA-NOUB-HOTEP.

An early unarranged Egyptian king.

RANPU.

According to Wilkinson the Egyptian goddess of war. She was generally represented as a woman in male costume, holding a sword and shield. *See also* Anta *or* Anaitis.

Ra-ns-neb.

The name of an Egyptian archer, probably of some renown, of the family of Ressenba. His period is unknown, except that it was between the XIIth and XVIIIth dynasties.

Ra-nub-kheper.

The prenomen of Antef IV. of the XIth dynasty.

Raphæl.

In Cabalistic astronomy the angel of the sun.

Raphia.

A town on the borders of Syria and Egypt, where Sargon II., king of Assyria, defeated the combined armies of Sibahe or Shabaka, king of Egypt, and Hanun, king of Gaza, whom he carried off into Assyria. It was continually the scene of military conflicts between the Egyptians and the Asiatics.

Ra-pioses.

According to the Greek lists the name of an Egyptian king of the XIXth dynasty. He is not certainly identified.

Rapiqi.   *Or* Rabilu.

A Babylonian town which was conquered by Tugulti-palesar, or Tiglath Pileser II., king of Assyria.

Ra-saa-ka-nekht-kheperu.   '

The prenomen of a king of Egypt in the XVIIIth dynasty. He was one of the contending successors of Amenhotep IV., whose daughter Aten-merit he married.

Ras-abourgabeh.

The modern name of the Arabian sea-port Mosylon, which see.

Ra-s-ankh.

A priest of Horus about the time of the IIIrd or IVth dynasty.

Ra-s-an-kh-ka.

An Egyptian monarch of the XIth dynasty, of whom little or nothing is known.

Ra-sebek-nefru.   *Or* Neferu.

The eighth king of the XIIth Egyptian dynasty.

Ra-senb.

An Egyptian officer of state, one of the council of ten in the XIIth dynasty. His wife was the lady Nub-na, one of the dames of the royal palace. This name is sometimes written Ra-n-senb.

Ra-senb.

An Egyptian gentleman, the son of Tuba, which is all that is known respecting him.

Rasenna.

According to Dionysius of Halicarnassus, the native and proper name of the Etruscans. *Rasne,* which occurs in the inscription of the Cippus Perusinus and elsewhere, has been identified with Rasenna, but, as it would seem, incorrectly.

Ra-sha-a-kheper-s-nab. *Surnamed* Ankh.

A schoolmaster of Heliopolis. Period uncertain. An inscribed board with rhetorical instructions used in his school is in the British Museum.

Ra-sha-ankh.

An early unarranged Egyptian king, perhaps one of the Sebek-hoteps.

Ra-sha-ken.

The sacerdotal or divine name of Osirtesen III., an Egyptian king of the XIIth dynasty. He is supposed by some to have been the Asychis of the Greeks.

Ra-sha-keu-asychis.

Another name of the Egyptian king Osirtesen I.

Ra-s-hotep-ab.

A priest of Pthah, the son of the following.

Ra-s-hotep-ab-ankh-netem.

A priest of Pthah, the son of Neb-pu, and a *Sam* of the XIIth dynasty. He was the father of the foregoing.

Ra-s-hotep-ab-senb.

A sacred scribe, the son of Senb, the *Kherheb* or funereal priest of Horus Khem or the Generator. His name is the same as that of the prenomen of Amenemha I. of the XIIth dynasty, in whose reign he may therefore have been born.

Ra-s-hotep-ab-senb.

The prenomen of Amenemha I. of the XIIth dynasty.

Ra-s-hotep-het.

Another form of the prenomen of King Amenemha I. of the XIIth dynasty.

Ra-s-khem-ka.

The son of an early Egyptian king.

Ra-s-khem-ka.

A grandson of Tetet, an early Egyptian king.

Ra-skh-het-sotep-en-amen.

A prenomen of Amyrtæus, a prefect king of Egypt under the Persian rule.

Rass.

A province in Yemen which was inhabited by the Hadura. *See* Shoaib *and* Hadura.

Rassu.

An Elamite city which was destroyed by Sennacherib.

Rassuah.

An Assyrian pilot in the reign of Sennacherib.

Ratams.

A mystical deity mentioned in the XLth chapter of the Ritual of the Dead.

Ra-theris.

According to the Greek lists the successor of Mencheres, king of Memphis. He has not yet been certainly identified.

Ra-thos. *Or* Ra-thoth.

According to the Greek lists the name of an Egyptian king of the XVIIIth dynasty. He is not certainly identified.

Ra-thoures.

The Greek form of the royal name Ra-en-user, which see.

Ra-tmeto.

An early unarranged Egyptian king. Leyden Collection.

Ra-to.

Another form of the name of the Egyptian goddess Ratta or Ritho, which see.

Ra-to-ker.

A prefect of the palace of an Egyptian king of the XXVIth dynasty. His father was named Fai-horouser, and his mother Sotemeit.

Ra-to-men.

An early unarranged Egyptian king. Leyden Collection.

Ra-to-neb.

An early unarranged Egyptian king. Leyden Collection.

Ra-tser-kheper-u-sotep-en-ra.

The sacred title of Horus Haremhebi, king of Egypt of the XVIIIth dynasty.

Ratta. *Or* Ritho.

An Egyptian goddess, the wife of the god Mentu. She was adorned with the disk and horns of Hathor, and was particularly invoked at the accouchement of royalty. Her analogue was the Lucina of the Romans.

RA-UA-HAB.

Another form of the surname Ouahbra, or Hophra, of Psametik I.

RA-USER - MA-SOTEP - EN - RA-MI-AMUN-RA-MES-SU.   " Sun Strong in Truth, Approved of the Sun, Loved of Amen, Born of the Sun."

The full name and prenomen of Rameses II.

RAYAM.

An unidentified Himyaritic deity, which according to Mahometan authors was worshipped at Sana.

RAZANU.

The king of Damascus. After the defeat of the Syrian kings by Tiglath Pileser II. at the battle of Kummuha, he paid tribute to the Assyrians. He was the Rezon of Hebrew history.

REBU.   Or LEBU.

The name of a mystical divinity who is adored in the LXXXVth chapter of the Ritual of the Dead.

REFAH.

A small stream which was called the " River of Egypt," it being the boundary line between that kingdom and Palestine.

REHOBOTHAIR.

The name by which the city of Assur is mentioned in early Hebrew history.

REHU.

Certain mystical deities who are mentioned in the XVIIth chapter of the Ritual of the Dead. They are the gods Horus and Set, or good and evil personified. They, or rather he, is represented as a man with a double head, one that of a hawk (Horus), and the other that of a long snouted animal with erect ears (Set). Rehu is represented among other mystical deities on the sarcophagus of Seti I. in the Soane Museum.

REKH.

The Egyptian name of the plover.

REKHET.

Another name of the town of Thmuis. It was sacred to the goddess Sekhet.

REKH-GET-AMEN.

The name of the doctors of magic who were much consulted in the temples of Egypt. They are supposed to have been the Chartummin of Hebrew history.

REKH-KHET.

The college of sacred scribes attached to the temples of the different deities of Egypt.

REKH-KHET-SA. "Knowing the Things of Books."

An Egyptian title, probably meaning a sacred physician.

REKH-MARA.

An Egyptian doctor, and prophet or priest of the goddess Ma, and chief of the district where he resided. He lived in the time of the XVIIIth dynasty.

REKH-MARA.

An Egyptian officer, whose tomb at Gournah is one of the most magnificent in the district. He must not be confounded with the preceding.

REKH-MARA.

An officer of high rank in the court of Thothmes III. of the XVIIIth dynasty. From the inscriptions on his funereal monument much of our knowledge of the events of the long reign of that king is derived.

REMEN.

The Egyptian name of the pomegranate fruit. Compare Rimmon of the Hebrews.

REMEN-AA.

The Egyptian large span, equal to fourteen digits.

REMENEN.

The Egyptian name for the Armenians who were conquered by Seti I. of the XIXth dynasty.

REMEN-NEGS.

The Egyptian small span, equal to three palms, equal to 8·583 inches.

REM-REM. "Weeping."

A mystical region of the Egyptian Kerneter, which is mentioned in the LXXVth chapter of the Ritual of the Dead.

RENEN. _Or_ RANNO.

In Egyptian mythology the goddess of harvest. She is specially mentioned in the CLXth chapter of the Ritual of the Dead.

RENPA. _Or_ RENPIT.

An Egyptian deification of the year. She was generally represented as a woman holding a stripped palm branch, the emblem of a calendar of days, in her hand.

RENPE-NOFRE. "The Good Renpe," _or_ "Good Year."

An Egyptian lady, the mother of the priest Taho in the XXVIth dynasty.

REPA. _Or_ ERPA.

The official title of the heir apparent of the king of Egypt, who was generally also prince royal of Ethiopia after the time of Thothmes II.

Rere.

An Egyptian officer in the court of Seti I. of the XIXth dynasty. He was the son of Bek-aa and the lady Hent-anu, and he held the offices of "Royal Scribe," "Superintendent of the Royal Palace," "Chief of the Cavalry," and "Favourite of the King."

Reseph-Mikal. "The Thunderbolt."

The fire deity of the Phenicians. On a bilingual inscription, Cypriote and Phenician, his name is translated by that of Apollo. He was chiefly adored in the Island of Kypros. His feminine form was the goddess Anath or Anaites of the Egyptians, the Reshpu of the Canaanites and Phenicians.

Reshpu.

A Semitic goddess. She was the feminine form of the Reseph-Mikal of the Phenician inscriptions. Her worship was introduced into Egypt by Seti I. after his return from his Syrian conquests.

Reskhual.

In Etruscan mythology one of the divinities attendant upon Malaviskh.

Res-sen-ba.

An Egyptian gentleman, of whom nothing is known except that one of his family was a chief archer named Ra-n-senb.

Rezon.

A king of Damascus. He was the son of Eliadad, a skilful Syrian general who rescued the city from the hands of the Jews. He was able successfully to repulse the endeavours of Solomon to obtain the Syrian crown, and he was succeeded by his son Tabrimmon. Rezon is the Hebrew form of the Syrian royal name Razanu.

Rhacotis.

The ancient name of the Egyptian town which is now called Alexandria.

Rhages.

The ancient capital of the kingdom of Media, where Phraortes, king of Media, was defeated and slain in battle by Bel-zikir-iskun, king of Assyria.

Rhampsinitus.

The name by which Rameses III. of the XIXth dynasty is mentioned by the Greek writers.

Rhamschosi.

An Egyptian gentleman whose statue is in the Leyden Museum.

Rhinocolura.

An Egyptian city on the Arabian frontier near to Palestine.

RHODODACTYLOS. "Rosy Fingered."

In Grecian mythology a poetical epithet applied to the goddess Aurora.

RHOT-A-MENTI.

A title of the deity Osiris as judge of the souls of the dead in the lower world or Amenti. From this epithet the Greeks derived the name of their semi-deity Rhadamanthus.

RI.

An Assyrian or Babylonian goddess, after whom Hammurabi, king of Babylonia, named his citadel.

RIBU.

An Assyrian measure of length. It was composed of twelve *kassi*.

RIE-AEI.

A grand priest of Pthah. Dynasty uncertain, but of the Second Empire.

RIEI.

An overseer of the Royal House. Dynasty uncertain, but of the Second Empire.

RI-IS-VUL.

An early Babylonian monarch. He was the last king of Apirak. Nothing else is known respecting him.

RIM-AGU.

An early Babylonian king, the seat of whose government has not yet been discovered.

RI-MARDUK.

The name of a citadel which was erected at Babylon by Hammurabi, who named it after his two protecting deities.

RIMES.

An overseer of the bulls of Amen. Period uncertain.

RIMMON-ICAB-BID. "Rimmon is Terrible."

In Chaldean astronomy an unidentified fixed star.

RIMMON-NIRARI.

The son of Pudil, king of Assyria. *See* Vul-nirari I.

RIMSIN.

The last king of Larsa, in Babylonia. He conquered the city of Karrak, and annexed the kingdom to his own, an event of sufficient consequence to have been used as an era by the Babylonians. After that event he ruled over both North and South Babylonia till he was conquered by Hammurabi. He made a channel from the river Tigris to the sea.

RINDR.

In Scandinavian mythology a wife of the god Odin, by whom he had Wali, the avenger of the death of Baldur.

RINGS.

The Egyptians used finger and signet rings on the fingers, and even thumbs, of both hands, and often many in number. The oldest signet rings were made with solid or revolving bezels, often of rectangular shape, and with the name of the monarch inscribed upon them. Some of solid gold, others with glass or cylindrical bezels of hard stone. Besides rings with swivel setting, the Egyptians also had others of gold, silver, bronze, carnelian, or jasper, made of a solid piece of metal, with an oval bezel engraved in intaglio with the name of a deity, king, or person. There were also finger rings of coloured porcelain with a bezel, and inscriptions, some of which bear the names of kings of the XVIIIth and XIXth dynasties; but they seem too fragile for ordinary use, and were probably only employed for funereal purposes. (Birch.)

RIS-RIS-ATI. "Chief of the Beginning."

In Chaldean astronomy a name of the planet Mercury.

RITHO.

The wife of the deity Mentu, or Month, who was the sun deified as a death giver. Her Egyptian name was Ra-Taoui. (Wilkinson.)

RITUAL OF THE DEAD.

The name given by Egyptologists to the oldest sacred book of the Egyptian theology. Portions of this work date from the time of King Gaga-makheru, a monarch of the IIIrd dynasty, the text itself being in many places accompanied by a gloss, which was added at a later period, to render it intelligible. The deities principally mentioned in it are Osiris, Anubis, Horus, and Tum; Amen Ra as a distinct divinity being only indirectly referred to. Although the mystical work is now treated as one book it is really made up of a collection of not less than eighteen separate treatises, including three supplemental chapters and two Litanies, which seem to have been added at the time of the New Empire. Selections of chapters and illustrations from the Ritual abound on the walls of many of the tombs of the XVIIth and XIXth dynasties, and notably on that of Seti-Menepthah I., in the Biban el Moluk. Other chapters were used as mystical formulæ to avert diseases, others as a part of the religious worship of the Egyptians, and a few obscure passages as secret mysteries, the meaning of which is now lost. Many hundreds of papyri have been found in the mummy-cases, which contain different portions of the Ritual with their accompanying vignette and rubric, but a complete recension and comparison of all the existing texts has not at present been effected. The text of the Ritual underwent no less than three different revisions, namely in the Ancient Empire, in the period of the XIXth dynasty, and in the reign of the Saite kings. This last was the edition which is most commonly met with, but there appears to have been an attempt at a partial re-edition in the Ptolemaic period. The chief divisions or books of which the Ritual of the Dead is composed are as follows :—

CHAPS.

1. The Manifestation to Light. (First Book) . . i.—xvi.
2. The Egyptian Faith . . . . . . xvii.—xx.
3. The Reconstruction of the Deceased . . . xxi.—xxvi.
4. The Preservation of the Body in Hades . . xxvii.—xlii.
5. The Protection in Hades . . . . . . xliii.—li.
6. The Celestial Diet . . . . . . lii., liii.
7. The Manifestation to Light. (Second Book) . . liv.—lxxv.
8. The Metamorphoses . . . . . . lxxvi.—xc.
9. The Protection of the Soul; or Forms for Various Occasions . . . . xci.—cxvi.
10. The Going into and out of Hades . . . cxvii.—cxxiv.
11. The Hall of the Two Truths . . . . . cxxv.
12. The Gods of the Orbit . . . . . . cxxvi.—cxxix.
13. The Passage to the Sun, or Adorations to the Sun. cxxx.—cxl.
14. The Festival (Litany) of the Names of the Gods cxli.—cxliii.
15. The House of Osiris; or, The Chapter of Making the Amulets . . . . cxliv.—clxi.
16. The Orientation . . . . clxii., clxiii.
17. The Three Supplemental Chapters . . . . clxiv.—clxvi.
18. The Assistances of Horus . . . . . i., ii.

From these it will be seen the arrangement of the chapters is inconsecutive as far as their subjects are concerned; and there is every reason to believe that the order in which they now occur, especially in the English translation, is somewhat arbitrary. The Ritual is rarely found written in Hieratic, and still more rarely in Demotic. The finest examples are those in the Museums of the Louvre and Turin.

Roads, Egyptian.

From the earliest periods of their history, the Egyptian monarchs were solicitous to establish a quick intercourse between all parts of their dominions, by the formation of a series of national roads, which were generally of good width, tolerably direct course, and which were defended at intervals along their route by fortresses and caravansaries. The traces of many of these roads still remain, and the directions of nearly all of them are known from the great military survey which, after the fall of the Egyptian empire, was made by the order of the emperor Antoninus, and which is called the Antonine Itinerary. From this survey it appears that at that time " the chief roads in Egypt were six in number. One was from Contra Pselcis, in Nubia, along the East bank of the Nile, to Babylon, opposite Memphis, and there turning Eastwards through Heliopolis and the district of the Jews to Clismon, where Trajan's canal entered the Red Sea. A second, from Memphis to Pelusium, made use of this for about thirty miles, joining it at Babylon, and leaving it at Scenæ Veteranorum. By these two roads a traveller could go from Pelusium to the head of the Red Sea; but there was (thirdly) a shorter road through the desert, which joined the first at Serapion, about fifty miles from Clismon, instead of Scenæ Veteranorum, and which was therefore above a hundred miles shorter. A fourth road was along the West bank of the Nile, from Hiera Sycaminon, in Nubia, to Alexandria, leaving the river at Andropolis, about sixty miles from the latter city. A fifth was from Palestine to Alexandria, running along the coast of the Mediterranean from Raphia to Pelusium, and thence, leaving the coast, to avoid the flat country, which was under water during the inundations ; it joined the last at Andropolis. The sixth and last chief road was from Coptos, on the Nile, to Berenice, on the Red Sea, between which towns there were ten stations, about twenty-five miles apart, where the traveller might rest with his camels each day, after travelling from the previous station by night to avoid the heat. These six were probably the only roads which were under the care of the Roman prefect. (Sharpe.)

Rodha.

An Arabian deity who was worshipped in the Neged. His character and attributes are not known.

Roi.

The high-priest of Amen in the reign of Seti-Menepthah II.

Rokah.

An Egyptian sacred festival which was held in the sixth month.

Roma.

The keeper or guardian of the treasure of an unnamed Egyptian king. He was the son of Nofre-renpe, who had held the like office before him.

Roma.

A priest of Pthah. Period uncertain.

Roma.

A high-priest of Amen in the reign of Seti-Menepthah II.

Romis.

Another form of the Kypriote royal name Karmes, which see.

Rosetta Stone.

This famous tablet is thus described by Dr. Birch, in his Appendix to Wilkinson's *Egyptians:*—" In 1792, M. Boussard discovered, near Rosetta, a large stone, of black granite, commonly known as the Rosetta Stone or Inscription. This appears, from late researches of Mr. Harris, to have originally been placed in a temple of Tum, or Tomes, " The Setting Sun," erected to that god by the Pharaoh Necho. It was originally presented to the French Institute of Cairo ; but subsequently, at the capitulation of Alexandria, it was surrendered to General Hutchinson, and presented by King George III. to the British Museum. It contained a trigrammatical inscription ; one in Hieroglyphs, a second in the Demotic or vernacular, a third in Greek. From this last it appeared that it was a solemn decree of the united priesthood in Synod at the temple of

Pthah at Memphis, in honour of Ptolemy V., who had conferred upon them certain benefits, in gratitude for which they had ordered it to be erected in every temple of the first, second, and third rank throughout the country, in the three forms of writing. About half of the Hieroglyphical part had been destroyed, but enough remained for decipherment. The mode of deciphering the Demotic was as follows:—First, it was perceived that the words Alexander and Alexandria in the fourth and seventeenth lines of the Greek inscriptions corresponded with two other groups in the second and tenth lines of the Demotic inscription. A group of characters which occurred in almost every line was supposed to be the word "and." A group of characters repeated twenty-nine or thirty times in the Enchorial inscription could only correspond to the word "king" in the Greek, which, with its compounds, is repeated about thirty-seven times. Another group of characters, recurring fourteen times in the Enchorial, corresponded to the word "Ptolemy," which occurs eleven times in the Greek, and generally in passages in the same relative position." "The text of the tablet itself is a decree by the priests of Pthah in Memphis, in honour of King Ptolemy's accession, who is there styled "King of Upper and Lower Egypt, Son of the Gods, Philopateres, approved by Pthah, to whom Ra has given victory, a Living Image of Amun, Son of Ra, Ptolemy Immortal, Beloved by Pthah, God Epiphanes, Most Gracious." In the date of the decree 18th Mechir, B.C. 196, we are told the names of the priests of Alexander, one of the gods Soteres, of the gods Adelphi, of the gods Euergetae, of the gods Philopateres, of the god Epiphanes himself, of Berenice Euergetes, of Arsinöe Philadelphus, and of Arsinöe Philopater. The preamble mentions with gratitude the services of the king, or rather of the wise minister Aristomanes; and the enactment orders that the statue of the king shall be worshipped in every temple of Egypt, and be carried out in the processions with those of the gods of the country; and lastly, that the decree shall be carved at the foot of every statue of the king, in sacred, in common, and in Greek writing." (Sharpe.)

Rotennu.   "Men of the Mist."

The Egyptian name of the Syrians of Mesopotamia who were repeatedly conquered by the Egyptian kings of the XVIIIth, XIXth, and later dynasties, but who always recovered their independence after the death of the conqueror. They were the first inhabitants of Nineveh and Babylon. The Hieroglyphic inscriptions distinguish between the upper and lower Rotennu.

Ru.

An Egyptian measure of length, a fraction of a digit.

Rua.

A state functionary of the princess Amen-iritis and the prince Schap-en-ap of the XXVIth dynasty.

Ruau.

A country to the South of Egypt, probably a part of Ethiopia, whence the early Egyptian kings imported granite for their sarcophagi and pyramids.

RUBA.

A mystical lake in the Egyptian Ker-neter. It is mentioned in the CVIIth chapter of the Ritual of the Dead.

RUBA-TA.

The name of a mystical cow who is adored in the CLXIIIrd chapter of the Ritual of the Dead.

RUBATI.

An Assyrian or Chaldean goddess. She was called " The Lady of the Gods."

RUB-BU.

A tribe in Mesopotamia which was conquered by Tiglath Pileser II.

RUBI.

A mystical person who supplies the deities with incense in Hades. He is mentioned in the CIVth chapter of the Ritual of the Dead.

RUBU.

A tribe of the Arabs, two men of whom pretended to betray the Khitæ and their allies to Rameses II., with whom they were at war. Their treachery was, however, detected by the king, who bastinadoed them, and extorted from them the true position of his enemies, whom he completely subdued.

RUBU.

In Egyptian mythology the mystical lake of primordial matter in the Elysian valley of Aahlu.

RUBU.

The Egyptian name for the Libyans who were defeated by Menepthah II.

RUBUHA.

A tribe in Mesopotamia which was conquered by Tiglath Pileser II.

RUCUBI.   "The Chariot."

In Chaldean astronomy the name of an unidentified star.

RUDRAS.

In Hindu mythology eleven deities subordinate to the great deity Indra.

RU-EN-KAU.

An early Egyptian town, the site of which is unknown.

RUHA.

A tribe in Mesopotamia which was conquered by Tiglath Pileser II.

RUHAK.

A mystical snake seven cubits long, inhabiting the seventh abode of Hades, mentioned in the CLth chapter of the Ritual of the Dead.

RUMENEN.

The Egyptian name of Mount Hermon in Palestine.

RUMMU-LUSU.

A tribe in Mesopotamia which was conquered by Tiglath Pileser II.

RUNGASWAMY.

A Badaga idol consisting simply of a sacred stone, or Bætylia.

RURE.

A district North of Assyria which was conquered by Shalmaneser IV.

RUSA.

The king of Armenia. After the battle of Shushan, when the Elamites were defeated, he sent ambassadors with tribute to Assurbanipal, who accepted the homage, and had the Elamite prisoners tortured for their entertainment.

RUSTA. "Gate of the Passage."

In Egyptian mythology the name of the entrance to the tomb, and by analogy also, of the region or Hall of the Two Truths, the judgment place of Osiris. *See* Rhotamenti.

RUSTAM.

A great Iranian hero, to whom many mythical acts, and the deliverance of the Iranians from the Turanians is ascribed.

RUT. *Or* LUT, "The Men."

The name of the aboriginal race of Egypt, supposed to be the same with the Ludim of Genesis.

RUTA.

A mystical title of Amen Ra in the CLXVIth chapter of the Ritual of the Dead.

RUT-AMEN.

A king of Egypt of the XXVth dynasty, and the successor of Tirhakah I. He was the son of Shabaka, and revolted against Assurbanipal, king of Assyria, whose vassal he was, and with the assistance of the king of Tyre, he defeated the Assyrians at Memphis. This brought the king of Assyria to the rescue, who first blockading Tyre led his army through Samaria into Egypt, and gave battle to and defeated Rut-amen at Memphis, which city he pillaged and destroyed. Rut-amen fled to a city named by the Assyrians Kip-kipi, and died after a reign of twelve years. He was called Urdamani by the Assyrians.

RUTA-SA-SHA-KA.

A mystical title of Amen Ra in the CLXVIth chapter of the Ritual of the Dead.

RUTUPIS.

See Faün.

RUTUR.   " Giver of Rest."

In Chaldean astronomy an unidentified fixed star.

S.

SA.

The ancient Egyptian name of the town of Sais or Elephantine.

SA.

An Egyptian prefix, signifying " South" or " South Land."

SA-AMEN.

An Egyptian priest, the father of the priest or scribe Pen-piei, which see.

SA-ASSUR-GUBBU.

The governor of Tushan in the reign of Sargon I. He was eponym of the year B.C. 707, in which year took place a festival of the gods of Dur-Sargon.

SAB.

A high-priest of Amen Ra in the reign of King Aspalut of the XXVth dynasty.

SABA.

An early name of the Arabian district of Sheba.

SABA.

A Himyaritic kingdom in South-western Arabia, the capital of which was at first Zhafar, and subsequently Marib.

SABACON.

The Greek form of the Egyptian royal name Shabaka, which see.

SABÆANS.

Two races mentioned by Hebrew writers, which are often confounded. The Cushite Sabæans are however written with the letter *Sin*, and the Joktanite with a *Samech*.

SABAHU.

The eleventh month of the Assyrian year. It was sacred to the god Rimmon or Vul, the air god, and was called by the Accadians Asaan, " Abundance of Rain." It answered roughly to our January.

SABATA.

A Libyan tribe in the time of Rameses III., by whom they were subjugated.

SABATHIEL.

In Cabalistic mythology the spirit of the planet Saturn.

SABATOK.

The second and last king of the XXVth dynasty. He is not to be confounded with Sabak, or Sebek-em-hof, the first king of the dynasty who was the Sabakoph of the Greeks.

SABBATHA.

A Himyaritic city mentioned in the Periplus of Hanno, supposed to have been Shabwat, which see.

SABO-EN-EA.

Another form of the Egyptian name Si-en-ea, which see.

SABOTA.

The name given by Pliny to the city of Shabwat, the capital of the ancient kingdom of Hadramaut.

SABTECHAH.

The name of the earliest Sabæans of the coast of Africa. They were called Sahaba by the ancient Egyptians.

SABU.

A peculiar sacerdotal dress which was worn by the Egyptian priests.

SABWAH.

A Himyaritic city in South-western Arabia.

SACEES.

The name of a great summer festival among the Chaldeans, when a slave was selected for five days to wear the ensigns of royalty, and the others were served by their masters. The festival took place in the month Nisan, and was called Cakmuku by the Babylonians.

SAC-SAC.

A king of Sabæa. He succeeded his father Shammir, and for a short time recovered the principality of Oman. He was succeeded by his son Yafar.

SAD.

An Amalekite tribe which settled in the district of Yathrib in Arabia.

SADA.

A name of the mystical screech owl of Arabian mythology, generally called Hama, which see.

SADALAM.

In Hindu mythology one of the four sacred streams which form the Ganges. *See* Alaguni.

SADAM-BAAL.

A form of the deity Baal as adored by the Phenicians in the Isle of Gozo.

SADASSON.

In Hindu mythology one of the four heavenly streams which form the Ganges. *See* Alaguni.

SADASTARA.

A king of Kypros (Cyprus) who reigned about the fourth century B.C.

SADIKAN.

A town on the banks of the Khabour. It was conquered by Assur-nazirpal.

SADI-MA-TATI. "Mountain of the World."

The name of the great temple of the deity Assur in the city of Assur. It was the centre of Assyrian worship.

SADI-TERU.

The king of the city of Urrahinas in Mesopotamia. He was conquered by, and together with his people rendered tributary to, the Assyrians under Tiglath Pileser I.

SADUDU.

The king of the Suhites. Assisted by Nabu-bal-idinna, king of Babylon, he revolted against Assur-nazir-pal, king of Assyria, by whom he was utterly defeated.

SA-EI-NUB-EU.

A priest of Amen Ra, and the father of the priestess Teti-hor-noub, which see. (Leemans.)

SAFA.

A hill near Mecca where a sacred stone or Bætylia was worshipped by the ancient Arabians. It was displaced by the idol Asafai, a figure in the form of a man about A.D. 300. *See* Marwa.

SAF-HOTEP-HETA.

A son of Tetet, an early Egyptian king.

SAGA. *Or* SAGAMA.

A people in the mountains of Mesopotamia who were subdued by Assur-ris-ilim, king of Assyria.

SAGARDIA.

A great city in the kingdom of Parthia, which was often in revolt against the kings of Assyria.

SAGARTIANS.

The tenth and last of the great tribes of Persia. They were a nomadic or shepherd caste.

SAGA-SALTIYAS.

An early king of Babylonia. He rebuilt the temples of Shamas and Anunit at Sippara.

SAGBA.

The Accadian name of the talisman which was called by the Assyrians Mamit.

SAH.

The sixth division of Upper Egypt. It was rendered famous by the wise government of the general Ameni during the XIIth dynasty. It was called by the Greeks Hermopolis the Lower. Sacred to the worship of the deity Horus.

SAH. "Mummy."

In Egyptian mythology one of the five component principles of the human body. *See* Akh, Kha-ba, *etc.*

SAHABA.

A people on the coast of Africa. They were the first of the Sabæan tribes, and the Sabtechah of Hebrew writers.

SAHARRI.

A town in South Palestine, which was conquered by Vaiteh I. on his invasion of Palestine against Assurbanipal.

SAHO.

A prophet of Thebes, the son of Ra-hahet and the lady Ta-ket-heb. His period is uncertain. His name is also written Dsjaho by some Egyptologists.

SA-HOR-SET.

An Egyptian lady, the daughter of the lady Tarot-en-pasht.

SAHOU.

The Egyptian name of the constellation which was called by the Greeks Orion.

SAHURA.

A king of the Vth dynasty. He reigned thirteen years, and he was buried in a pyramid called the Sha-ba, or pyramid of the rising soul. He was the Sephres of the Greeks.

SAI-MEHIT.

A city and nome in Lower Egypt called by the Greeks Sais the Lower. Like Sai-res it was sacred to the worship of the goddess Neith. *See* Alexandria.

SAI-RES.

A city and nome in Lower Egypt which was called by the Greeks the Upper Saite. Sacred to the worship of the goddess Neith.

Sais.

A town in the Delta now called Sa-el-Hagar. It was held by the Hermotybian class of warriors, and was the seat of empire of the XXIVth, XXVIth, and XXVIIIth Egyptian dynasties.

Saites.

The Greek form of the royal name Seti-pet-i-nubti, which see.

Sakanaka.

The mystical name of a great fire which is mentioned in the CLXVth chapter of the Ritual of the Dead.

Sakasutu.　"Eldest-born of the Sun God."

In Chaldean astronomy a name of the planet Saturn.

Sakbita.

The royal city of Haniziruka, king of the Medes. It was conquered by Samsi-Vul III.

Sa-khons.

An Egyptian lady, the wife of Ankh-pis-khe, and mother of the priest Ei-amen-nef-neb-oui, which see.

Sa-khonsu.

A priestess of Amen Ra of Thebes. Period uncertain.

Saki.

The name of an officer or chief in the Assyrian army; the commander-in-chief being called Tartan and his inferior officer Rabsaki.

Sakkarah, Tablet of.

A famous historical inscription or chronological list of the kings of Egypt. It was found in the tomb of a priest named Tu-nari, who lived during the reign of Rameses II., and who is represented on the monument as entering after death into the society of the great and good kings of Egypt, the names of fifty-eight of whom are given, including especially those monarchs whose memory was most revered at Memphis. The selection is similar to that of the Tablet of Abydos. There are, nevertheless, some interesting differences. Once or twice a king whose name is omitted in one list is registered in the other; and even sometimes of two princes whose reigns were incontestably simultaneous, one figures at Sakkarah and the other at Abydos. This, the third of the incised monumental calendars of Egypt, is preserved in the Museum of Boulaq. (Mariette.)

Sakuka.

A Sacan officer, who revolted against Darius Hystaspes, by whom he was defeated and slain.

Sak-visa.　Or Sak-misa.

In Chaldean astronomy the name of the planet Mercury, in the month Elul.

SAKYAMUNI. *Or* SADDARTHA.

A great Hindu reformer, who originated the system of the Buddhistic religion, about B.C. 600. (Sayce.)

SALA.

An Assyrian deity worshipped at Ekali, whose statue was carried off by Maruduk-nadinahi, king of Babylon, about B.C. 1125.

SALA-MAN-U.

A king of Moab, who paid tribute to Tiglath-Pileser II. after the fall of Damascus. His name was the same as that written by the Hebrews Solomon.

SALANT-MOUTH.

An Egyptian lady, the wife of Thoth-hotep and the mother of the lady Tates, which see. (Leemans.)

SALATIS.

According to the Greek lists an early Egyptian king of Bubastis. He has not yet been certainly identified.

SALE-BON-ISI.

An Egyptian functionary, but of what office and of what period is uncertain. (Leemans.)

SALEH.

In Arabic history a prophet who entreated the Thamudites to renounce idolatry, and as a sign of his miraculous mission made a camel with its colt to come out of the solid rock. The Thamudites continuing incredulous, to please them a man named Codar el Ahmar slew the sacred beast, whereupon Saleh announced the destruction of the tribe, which took place three days afterwards, when a thunderbolt fell from heaven and consumed them all.

SALHIN.

A royal fortress of the kingdom of Sabæa, near Mareb.

SALIMAN-UZUR.

The Assyrian form of the royal name generally written in Hebrew history Shalmaneser.

SALKARGA.

In Chaldean astronomy an unidentified fixed star.

SALLAD. (?)

An Assyrian city, which revolted to Assurdan, and was reconquered by Samas-Rimmon IV.

SALMAN-HAMAN-ILIN.

A king of the Sadikannai, or Sadikan, who paid tribute to Assurnazir-pal.

SALMAT.

An Assyrian city which supported Assur-dain-pal in his revolt against his father, Samsi-Vul or Samas-Rimmon IV.

SALUDARI.   *Or* SARLUDARI.

A king of Ascalon, who was placed upon the throne by Sennacherib, who carried away captive the reigning king Zedek, which see.

SAMAH.   " The Elevated."

A Himyaritic deity, a form of the god Il.

SAMAHALI-YANAF I.

A king of the Himyarites, about the first century A.D.   He was succeeded by Yathaamir-Watr.

SAMAHALI-YANAF II.

A king of the Himyarites, about the first century A.D.   He was succeeded by Yathaamir-Bayyin II.

SAMAHALI-YANAF III.

A king of the Himyarites, about the close of the first century A.D. He was succeeded by Yadail-Dhâli.

SAMALA.

A district in Mesopotamia which was conquered by Shalmaneser II. *See* Hani.

SAMALLA.

A town near Damascus which was conquered by Tiglath-Pileser II. on his march to assist Ahaz, king of Judah, against Rezon, king of Damascus.

SAMASA.

A king who paid tribute to Samsi-Vul or Samas-Rimmon III. His district was probably near Armenia.

SAMAS-BEL-UZUR.

The governor of Ahizuhina, in the reign of Sargon II. He was eponym of the year B.C. 710, in which year the conquest of Babylon took place.

SAMAS-IBNI.

A king of the Dakkuri, a desert tribe on the West of Babylon. He taking advantage of the weak state of the Assyrian empire on the death of Sennacherib, pillaged the borders of the country of Babylon ; but he was defeated by Esarhaddon, who burned him alive, and made one Nabu-salim, son of Balasu, king over the Dakkuri.

SAMAS-ITTA-LIK-SUM.

The Tukulu under Assur-nirari I.(?), king of Assyria.

SAMAS-KUMUA.

The governor of Arbaha in the reign of Samsi-Vul or Samas-Rimmon IV., and eponym of the year B.C. 812, the chief event in which year was an expedition to Babylon.

SAMAS-MUKIN-DURUK.

The Tukulu of Assur-nirari II. and eponym of the year B.C. 749, in which year took place an expedition to Zimri.

SAMAS-UPAH-HAR. *Or* SAMAS-UPACH-CHIR.

The governor of Kirruri or Yelruri, in the reign of Sargon II. He was eponym of the year B.C. 708, in which year chiefs were sent to the land of Kummuha.

SAMAYDA.

The chief of a tribe of Katoora Arabs, who were friendly with Ishmael. He and Mudad were attacked by the Amalika, who were driven back by a miraculous flock of ants. He was ultimately killed in a quarrel with the Ishmaelites. *See* Mudad.

SAMDAN.

An Assyrian deity, the god of strength. His analogue was the Herakles of the Greeks.

SAMDAN-MALIK. " Samdan is King."

The younger son of Shalmaneser IV. He reigned for three years under the regency of Sargon II., the Tartan of his father's army, who then deposed him and usurped the throne.

SAMGUNU.

The brother of Dunanu, king of Gambuli. He was taken captive by Assurbanipal, against whom he had rebelled, and was led in triumph into Nineveh with the head of his ally Tamritu prince of Elam, hung round his neck, after which he was flayed alive.

SAMHALA.

A state in Northern Syria which was conquered by Tiglath Pileser II.

SAMHANA.

An Elamite city on the borders of Babylonia, which was conquered by Sargon II. in his wars with Sutruk-nan-kundi, king of Elam.

SAMHUT.

A city and nome in Lower Egypt which was sacred to the worship of the god Samta. Its site is not at present known, but it was held by the rebel chief Ankh-hor against Piankhi-Meramen of the XXVIth dynasty.

SAMMURAMAT.

A princess of Babylonia, the wife of Vulnirari or Rimmon-Nirari III., king of Assyria. She greatly fortified and improved the city of Babylon, and was the true Semiramis of Classic history. Her name only occurs on a statue of Nebo in the British Museum.

SAMNEH.   *Or* SEMNEH.

A town and fortress which was erected by the Egyptian kings of the XIIth dynasty to repress the Cushites of Ethiopia. It was for some time the Southern boundary of the kingdom of Egypt.

SAMOULSAMOUKEN.

Another form of the name of the rebel king of Babylon, Saul-mugina, which see.

SA-MOUTH.

An Egyptian lady, the wife of Hor, and mother of Ankh-hor, the prophet of the god Month.

SAMSI.

A queen of the Arabs. She at first promised allegiance to Tiglath Pileser II., but afterwards revolted, upon which she was driven from her throne, and an Assyrian governor appointed over the kingdom. After a while she was captured and restored to the crown, but under the control of an Assyrian officer.

SAMSI-IL.

The Tartan of Shalmaneser III., Assurdan III., and Assur-nirari II., and thrice eponym, namely in the year B.C. 780, the chief event in which was an expedition to Ararat; 770, the chief event in which was an expedition to Surat; and 752, when there was peace in the land.

SAMSI-LUNA.

An early king of Babylonia. He erected many temples to the deities of Babylonia, especially Marduk and Shamas, of whom he made several images or cherubim overlaid with gold. He excavated a canal called Samsi-iluna-nagab-nushi, and he also dug a canal or moat around the city of Sargon. He was further a great builder and restorer at Babylon and Larsa.

SAMSI-ILUNA-NAGAB-NUSHI.

The name of a great canal which was excavated at the city of Sargon by Samsiluna, an early Chaldean king.

SAMSI-VUL I.   *Or* SAMAS-RIMMON.

The son of Ismi-Dagan, king of Assyria. He reigned about B.C. 1800 to 1820, and built temples at Assur to the deities Anu and Vul. These were restored seven hundred years later by Tiglath Pileser I.

SAMSI-VUL II.

An early king of Assyria, B.C. 1800. He was the son of Igur-kap-kapu, but nothing is known concerning him except that he founded the great national temple of Assur.

SAMSI-VUL III.

An early king of Assyria, about B.C. 1080 to 1060. He was the son of Tiglath Pileser I., and the brother and successor of Assur-bel-kala, king of Assyria. He restored the temple of the goddess of Nineveh, and nothing else is known respecting him. After his reign for a century and a half the power of the Assyrian empire was very small, and the very names of its sovereigns are lost.

SAMSI-VUL IV.

The younger son of Shalmaneser II., king of Assyria. He ascended the throne B.C. 825. His first work on ascending the throne was to consolidate the empire which had been weakened by the revolt of his elder brother Assurdainpal. After this he commenced a series of wars to reduce the provinces of the empire to submission, in most of which he was successful. He then conquered Media, and after a few years invaded Babylonia, defeating the king Maruduk-balad-su-ikbi, and compelling him to sign a treaty ceding large border provinces to Assyria. After this he returned to Nineveh, where he erected an obelisk to the deity Ishtar, and another to the god Nebo in the city of Calah. He does not appear to have erected any great works, but to have been solely a warrior. He died after a reign of thirteen years, and left his throne to his son Vulnirari III., at that time a mere boy.

SAM-TA.

An Egyptian deity who was worshipped in the city and nome of Samhut, which was named after him.

SAM-TATI.

A late Egyptian deity who was adored at Ahehu.

SAM-TATI-TAF-NEKHT.

A high Egyptian officer in the Persian period. He was " President," " Keeper of the Signet," " Companion of the Javelin," " Prophet of Har." " Lord of Hebnu," " Prophet of the Gods of Sah," " Prophet of Samtati of Ahehu," " Spiritual Superior of the Un," and " Chief of all the Priests of Sekhet." His mother's name was Ankh-ta. He fought against the Greeks, and was sent on a private mission alone to Sutensenen and executed his commission in safety.

SAN.

An unidentified Assyrian deity.

SANA.

A Himyaritic capital city in South-western Arabia, from whence many bronze inscriptions have been recovered.

SANA-KHA.

An Assyrian city which revolted to Assurdan, and was reconquered by Samas-Rimmon. Its name was at one time translated Arapkha, but it is believed erroneously.

SANA-PANU.

The capital of Babylonia under Nabu-u-sabsi. It was destroyed by Tiglath Pileser II.

SANA-SU. *Or* SANISU.

The king of Kipa-bara-taka, a district bordering upon Assyria, which was rendered tributary by Samsi-Vul IV.

SANBATHA.

A Himyaritic city mentioned by Ptolemy. It is supposed to have been Shabwat, which see.

SANDARRI.

A king of Sisir and Kundi. He combined with Abdi-milkutti, king of Zidon, to resist the power of Assyria, but he was defeated, and together with his ally beheaded by Esarhaddon after the fall of Zidon.

SANDASARMI.

A king of Cilicia. He paid tribute to Assurbanipal, king of Assyria, and sent his daughter also to the harem of that monarch.

SANDRACOTTUS.

The Greek form of the Hindu royal name Chandragupta, which see.

SANGAMITTA.

The sister of the emperor Asoka, and one of the first Buddhist missionaries to Ceylon. *See* Asoka *and* Mahindo.

SANGARA.

The king of Carchemish. He was one of the kings of the Hittites who submitted and paid tribute to Assurnazirpal. His name is also written Sangala ; and in most of these names, both Assyrian and Egyptian, the *l* and the *r* are used indifferently. Except in those cases where the Semitic name has come down to us in a Greek form, the exact phonology cannot be ascertained.

S-ANKH. ANKH, " Life." (?)

An early Egyptian city. Site unknown.

S-ANKHUA.

The son of an Egyptian king, but of what king it is not known.

SANYASI.

A kind of Hindu or Toda hermit.

SAP.

An unknown Egyptian deity. He was the tutelary god of the Oxyrynchite nome. *See also* the following.

SAP.

A mystical deity who is mentioned in the XVIIth chapter of the Ritual of the Dead.

SAPA-DI-BAHAL.

One of the ten competitors for the crown of Arvad after the death o King Yakinlu.

SA-PAKHI.

The high-priest of Amen Ra in the reign of King Aspalut of the XXVth dynasty.

SAPALALA.

The king of the Hittites, the father of Marasara, and grandfather of Khitasira, which see.

SA-PAR.

A Theban judge. Period uncertain.

SAPAR.

Another form of the Hittite royal name Separuru, which see.

SAPE.

A royal city in Babylonia, where Kinziru, the last king of the country, was utterly defeated by Tiglath-Pileser, king of Assyria.

SAPIBEL.

A chief town of the Gambuli, which was originally fortified by Esarhaddon. It was destroyed by Assurbanipal as a punishment for the continual revolts of the inhabitants against the Assyrians.

SA-PI-HOR.

A "Gatekeeper of the Temple of Amen Ra," and father of the high-doorkeeper Pet-ament, which see.

SA-PI-NEB.

A priest of Khons and "Keeper of the Vestments" in the temple of that deity. Period uncertain.

SA-PI-NITO.

An Egyptian gentleman, whose statue is in the Leyden Museum.

SAPT.

A foreign goddess who was adopted into their mythology by the Egyptians.

SA-PTHAH.

A royal scribe who had judicial charge of the district of Sais. He was the son of the lady Meret-pa. Period unknown.

SAPULULMI.

A king of Patina, who vainly attempted, in conjunction with the other kings of Mesopotamia, to resist the armies of Shalmaneser II., B.C. 859.

Sar.

In Chaldean astronomy one of the twelve stars of the West.

Sar. "King," *or* "Lord."

The Chaldean title of their early monarchs. *See also* Patesi.

Saradavas.

A city in South-east Assyria which was conquered by Tiglath-Pileser I.

Sarapou.

A very late Greco-Egyptian, or rather Romano-Egyptian male proper name.

Sarapous.

An Egyptian lady, the wife of Heraclius Soter and mother of the lady Tphous, A.D. 127.

Sarasu.

A city of the Hittites, which was sacred to its own local form of the god Sutekh.

Sarasvati.

In Hindu mythology the goddess of speech, by which the divine will was revealed to man. She was the Sackti of the deity Brahma.

Sarati.

A son of Gagi, chief of the Medes of Saki. His provinces were despoiled by Assurbanipal, king of Assyria.

Saravas.

A Mesopotamian people who were conquered by Tiglath-Pileser I.

Sara-ziggar. "The Sacrifice of Righteousness" *or* "of Bel."

The Accadian name of the month Nisannu, which see.

Sardanapalus I.

A name at one period applied by early Assyriologists to Assur-nazir-pal, which see.

Sardanapalus II.

A name applied by the Greek writers to both Assurbanipal, the son of Esarhaddon, and to his own son Assur-ebil-ili, who burnt himself to death in the palace at the fall of Nineveh.

Sardanapalus III.

The name given by some Assyriologists to the king who is generally called Assur-acus, which see.

SARDURI.

The king of Ararat, or Armenia. He headed the combination of the Syrian states against Tiglath-Pileser II., by whom he was utterly defeated under the walls of Kummuha, and compelled to make his escape by night, leaving his entire army of 72,950 soldiers and all his baggage in the hands of the victor.

SA-RENEN.

The " Gardener of the House of Perfumes," in the XVIIIth or XIXth dynasty. He was the son of a man named Apap or Apepi.

SARGON I. *Or* SARGINA.

An early, almost mythical Babylonian king, about the sixteenth century B.C. He was a bastard, born at the city of Azupirani, and was exposed by his mother, probably at the command of his uncle, in a basket on the river Euphrates. Here he was found by a husbandman named Akki, who took care of him and taught him agriculture. After some years Sargina became the head of a race of wild or dark people, probably outlaws, by the help of whom he seized the throne of Babylonia, and founded the city of Dur-Sargina. He built a great temple at Agane, and a palace named Ekiam-izillik, which he established as the capital of his empire, and where he founded a library, for which the great astronomical cyclopædia, the Namar-bili, was compiled. He fought with great success against the Elamites and Syrians. After that he was besieged in his own capital by the Kassi, or men of all countries, whom he ultimately defeated. The events of the rest of his reign are unknown. He was succeeded by his son Naramsin.

SARGON II.,

Who claimed descent from Bel-bani, an ancient king of Assyria, and took the name of the old Babylonian hero king, was an officer who usurped the throne of Assyria on the death of Shalmaneser, B.C. 722. His first campaign was against Khumba-nigas, of Elam. In B.C. 721-20 he captured Samaria, carrying away 27,200 of its inhabitants. Ilu-bihdi of Hamath, who had organised a confederacy against him, was defeated and flayed alive in B.C. 720, Hamath colonised by 4300 Assyrians, and Khanun of Gaza and Sibahe of Egypt defeated at Raphia. The Minnians were overthrown in B.C. 719; and the allied armies of Pisiris of Carchemish and Mita (Midas) of the Moschi in B.C. 717; Carchemish, with all its treasures, falling into Sargon's hands. The Armenians, Moschi, and Minnians, were defeated in B.C. 716, and the capital of the latter destroyed; and in B.C. 715 the whole country of the Minni was overrun by Sargon, while an expedition was also sent into Arabia. In B.C. 714 the Minni were completely subdued, Ursa of Armenia forced to escape to the mountains, and Muzazir (Southern Armenia) ravaged. Media submitted in B.C. 713, and Ambaris of Tubal (the Tibareni) was conquered. In B.C. 711, Sargon overran Palestine, breaking up the confederacy of Egypt, Moab, Edom, Judah, and the Philistines, and destroying Ashdod (see Isa. xx. 1). In B.C. 710, Merodach-Baladan, and his ally Sutruk-nan-khundi of Elam, were defeated, and Babylon taken; Sargon henceforth assuming the title of " King of Babylonia." Merodach-Baladan was pursued to the shores of the Persian Gulf in B.C. 709, and there captured. Seven of the kings of Cyprus sent tribute in B.C. 708, and Sargon set up a stele in the island. The kingdom of Comagene was also reduced. Dur-Sargina (Khorsabad) was finished about this time, and another war with Elam broke out. Sargon was murdered on the 12th day of the month Ab (July), B.C. 705, and was succeeded by his son, Sennacherib.

SAR-ILI. "King of the Gods."

A Babylonian deity, to whom Urukh, king of Babylonia, erected a temple at Zirgulla.

SAR-IQBI.

An Assyrian city, conquered by the king of Minni, who was soon afterwards defeated by Assurbanipal.

SARKIMUNA.

An unidentified Babylonian deity.

SAR-KUDIRI.

An Elamite city which was destroyed by Sennacherib.

SAR-PAT-IBEL.

The governor of Nisibni, in the reign of Samsi-Vul IV., and eponym of the year B.C. 816, the chief event in which was an expedition to Zarati.

SAR-RAP-ANU.

A capital city in Babylonia, where Nabu-u-sabsi, the last king, was conquered by Tiglath-Pileser I. and crucified upon its walls.

SAR-RAT. "Queen."

The Assyrian feminine of the title Sar, "King."

SAR-RU. "The King."

The astronomical name of the deity Marduk as the planet Mercury in the month Tebet.

SARRU-ETIQ-DAIRI.

The king of Tanis, one of the petty Egyptian kings under the Icosarchy established by Esarhaddon.

SAR-TUDA.

A Babylonian deity, to whom a temple was erected by Sin-gasit, king of Urukh.

SARUC. *Or* SARAC, *or* SARACUS.

According to the Greek historians the last king of Assyria. He was also called Assuracus. *See* Assur-ebil-ili.

SAR-UEMUR-ANNI.

The governor of Lullume, in the reign of Sargon II. He was eponym of the year B.C. 712, the chief event in which was an expedition to Milid.

SARUKA.

The king of the Sacæ on the borders of the Jaxartes. He revolted against Darius Hystaspes, but without effect, as that monarch having pacified the rest of his kingdom marched against Saruka and took him prisoner. His fate is not known.

SARUM.

A mountain people on the borders of Media and Susiana, who were conquered by Sennacherib.

SARZINA.

The king of a district near Lake Van. He was the son of Mikdiara, and his kingdom, together with 300 of its villages, was invaded and plundered by Mutariz-assur, the Rabsaki of Samsi-Vul or Samas-Rimmon III.

SASI.

The son of Matuzza, king of Patina. He was raised to the throne after the death of the usurper Surrila by Shalmaneser II., who imposed on him a heavy tribute.

SASI.

In Chaldean astronomy the name of an unidentified star.

SASINGU.

The Assyrian form of the Egyptian royal name Sheshanka or Shishak, which see.

SASU-KHONS-PA-SET.

A priestess of Amen, the daughter of Sasur-amen, a prophet of Amen also. Period uncertain.

SASUR-AMEN.

A prophet of Amen, the father of the lady Sasu-khons-pa-set, a priestess of Amen.

SA-TAT-NEB-ENITO.

A priestess of Amen. The period when she lived is uncertain.

SATAU.

Another form of the name of the romantic hero Anepou or Anep, of the ancient Story of the Two Brothers.

SAT-BU.

An Egyptian lady, the wife of Hor-im-hotep, and the mother of Ankh-hapi, a priest of Pthah and Snefru at Memphis.

SATEMI.

An Egyptian deity. He was the god of hearing. (Wilkinson.)

SATI.

In Egyptian mythology the goddess of the sunbeam, and the consort of Khnum. She was represented wearing the white crown and lunar horns. (Wilkinson.)

SATI.

A mystical snake seventy cubits long, inhabiting the fourth abode. He is mentioned in the CLth chapter of the Ritual of the Dead.

SATIRIAI.

A king of a country of the Nahri, who paid tribute to Samas-Rimmon III.(?), king of Assyria.

SAULMUGINA.

The brother of Assurbanipal, king of Assyria, by whom he was made king of Babylon. Tired of his subjection to his suzerain, he combined with Nebo-bel-zikri, the grandson of Merodach-Baladan, Ummanigas, or Khum-ba-nigas, and afterwards Tammaritu, kings of Elam, to declare war with Assyria. For a time he had partial success, but soon Assurbanipal sent a still larger force against him, and his allies falling off, he in desperation set fire to his own palace at Babylon, and perished in its ruins. NOTE.—The fate of Saulmugina is a contested point with Assyriologists, Lenormant holding that he was pardoned at the intercession of his sister Seruya-edirat ; Fox Talbot that he was devoured by lions or cast into a furnace ; and Smith, whose views as those of the latest writers, are given above.

SAURVA.

In Zendic mythology the third of the Darvands, the representative and opposite of the Siva of the Vedas. *See* Darvands.

SAVITRI. " The Progenitor."

A Vedic title of the Supreme Being as the common ancestor.

SAWAHA.

An ancient Arabian goddess who was possibly a form of the moon.

SAXNOT.

Another form of the name of the Scandinavian deity Tyr, which see.

SAYYIDA. "Lady."

In Arabic history another name of Rala, the wife of Ishmael. *See* Rala.

SBA. "A Star, a Gateway."

The name which is applied in the Ritual of the Dead to the mystical pylons of the Ker-neter, which see.

SBANTARAD.

An Armenian warlike deity who was adopted from the Merodach of the Chaldeans.

SCARABEUS.

The Ateuchis sacer or sacred beetle of Egypt. It was the emblem of the great deity Kheper Ra in his character of producer and sustainer of life. The sacred scarab is more extensively found than any other divine emblem in Egypt, and in the form of an amulet or ornament was imported into Syria and Phenicia.

SCAVISTIKA.

An early Buddhistic symbol, a combination of the Greek fret or clawed cross. It was originally a monogram of the word happiness, a meaning which it still bears in Japan.

SCEMIOPHRIS.

According to the Greek lists the name of an Egyptian queen of the XIIth dynasty. She has not yet been certainly identified.

SCENÆ-MANDRARUM.

In Ptolemaic times a chief town in the Aphroditopolite nome of the Heptanomos.

SCHA-EA.

An overseer of the choristers of Amen Ra. Period uncertain. (Leemans.)

SCHÆDIA.

In the Ptolemaic period a great dock city in the Hermopolite nome of Lower Egypt.

SCHA-EM-TENU.

The " Overseer of the Sculptors of the Temple" of Amen Ra. The time when he lived is uncertain, except that it was in the Second or Middle Empire.

SCHA-REI.

The wife of Amen-nekht, an officer of justice in the XVIIIth dynasty.

SCHEDS-NEFER.

An Egyptian priest of Apis in the XXVIth dynasty.

SCHENT.

An obscure Egyptian goddess, who was called the lady of heaven. She was one of the many forms of the goddesses Isis or Nut.

SCHEP-MAUT.

The wife of Pa-du-amen-nes-ta-ui, the third priest of Amen-Ra-Schep-Maut, which see.

SCHESCHANQ.

The French form of the Egyptian royal name now generally read Shishank, which see.

Se-anhur.

According to some writers the more correct form of reading the Egyptian name Anhur-se.

Seb.   " Time."

In Egyptian mythology the deity Seb was regarded as a kind of cosmical deity, and as such the oldest of and the father of the gods.   In other words, he represented the earth, as his consort the goddess Nut did the heavens.   Seb was rarely figured, but when he was referred to it was as the " Great Cackler " or goose which laid the cosmic egg ; hence the goose was both the symbol of his person and the Hieroglyphic of his name.   Sometimes Seb was represented on the papyri as a human figure, sitting or lying on the ground, with vegetation either proceding from or covering his body, while his consort Nut is bending like an arch over him.   Occasionally, also, Seb was called the " Lord of Aliments," and was figured ithyphallically.   Like Osiris and Horus he was said to have reigned for a mystical period upon earth, and to have been one of the first of the gods that did so : hence he was also often called on the monuments, " The Father of the Gods."

Seb.

The son of Hui, the " Auditor of the Palace of Justice" in the reign of an unnamed king of the XVIIIth dynasty.

Seb.

A city and nome in Upper Egypt which was called Oxyrynchus by the Greeks.   It was sacred to the deity Anubis.

Seba.

The Egyptian name of the single flute.

Se-bast.

The second wife of Aahmes, of the XXVIth dynasty.

Sebek.

One of the solar deities of the Egyptians.   He was represented as a man with the head of a crocodile, surmounted by the solar disk and ram's horns of Amen Ra.   He was regarded also as the son of Osiris, and therefore assimilated to Horus in his character of Teti, " The Avenger."   The date of the cultus of Sebek goes back to a remote period in Egyptian history, and his chief temple was at Ombos.   It would seem, from the accounts of Herodotus, that his worship, in which the crocodile was sacred, was chiefly local and led to severe conflicts with the men of Tentyra, by whom that animal was always destroyed. Statues of this divinity are rarely found, and his chief influence appears to have been under the XIIIth dynasty.

Sebek-ari.

The nephew of the councillor Sebek-hotep, and the son of the lady Sennu.   Period uncertain.

Sebekem.

A king of the XIIIth dynasty, the successor of Sebekhotep V. He was succeeded by Ra-hotep.

Sebek-em-isis. (?)

The daughter of the lady Sotemheit, which see.

Sebek-em-of.

An uncertain king, possibly of the XXVth dynasty. (Leemans.)

Sebek-em-saf.

A king of the XIIIth dynasty.

Sebek-hotep I.   "Peace of Sebek."

A king of Egypt of the XIIIth dynasty, of whom nothing is as yet known. (Brugsch.)

Sebek-hotep II.

Another king of the XIIIth dynasty, who is also unrecorded in history. (Brugsch.)

Sebek-hotep III.

A king of the XIIIth dynasty, of whom also nothing is known. (Brugsch.)

Sebek-hotep IV.

A king of the XIIIth dynasty. He succeeded Sebekhotep III. He recorded the annual risings of the Nile at Samneh, from the first to the fourth year of his reign. His successor was Sebekhotep V., who was also called Sebekem. (Brugsch.)

Sebek-hotep V.

A king of the XIIIth dynasty. He succeeded Sebekhotep IV., and was succeeded by Sebekem. This dynasty consisted of kings who seem to have been named Sebek-hotep and Mentu-hotep alternately. (Brugsch.)

Sebek-hotep.

A son of King Nefer-hotep, of the XIIIth dynasty.

Sebek-hotep.

A grandson of King Sebek-hotep II. of the XIIIth dynasty.

Sebek-hotep.

The first *Heb* of an unnamed divinity, in the time of the XIIth or XIIIth dynasty.

Sebek-hotep.

An Egyptian officer. He was a member of the royal council of thirty, which was a kind of Egyptian parliament, as the members were elected by certain villages who possessed that privilege. His period is uncertain, possibly of the XIIIth dynasty.

SEBEK-NEKHT. "Strength of Sebek."

An Egyptian official, of the family of Senbu, priest of Osiris, which see.

SEBEK-TETU.

A " Chief of the Sacred Scribes," in the reign, probably, of one of the Sebek-hoteps.

SEBEN.

An Egyptian goddess who was worshipped at Syene and Eilethya. She represented the upper country, and was sometimes called Nishem.

SEBENNYTUS.

A nome in the Delta of Lower Egypt, which according to Herodotus was held by the Calasirian class of warriors.

SEBENNYTUS.

A town in the Delta, now called Semenood, the seat of empire of the XXXth, the last but one of the Egyptian dynasties.

SEBERCHERES.

According to the Greek lists the successor of Bicheres, king of Memphis. He has not yet been certainly identified.

SEBICHOS.

Another form of the name of King Shabatuk, of the XXVth dynasty.

SEB-TET.

An uncertain Egyptian goddess.

SEBT-HET.

A city and nome in Lower Egypt which was called by the Greeks the Memphite. It was sacred to the worship of the god Pthah-Sokari-Osiris.

SEBT-IHUT. "City of White Walls."

The Egyptian name of the Acropolis of Memphis.

SECHEM.

A city and nome in Upper Egypt which was called by the Greeks Panopolis. It was sacred to the worship of the deity Min.

SEDD-MARIB.

The present name of the ruins of the dyke of Marib, which was constructed by Lokman, the Adite. *See* Lokman.

SEDIR. " Dark (Month) of Sowing."

The Accadian name of the intercalary month Arakh-makru, which see.

SEDURI.

The king of Ararat or Armenia. A great and wise monarch, during the reign of Shalmaneser II. He introduced the art of Cuneiform writing into Armenia, together with other arts, and considerably improved the condition of the country. Resisting the encroachments of the Assyrians, he was attacked by Dayan-assur, the Tartan of Shalmaneser, and totally defeated by him near the river Arzania. **Seduri** died shortly afterwards and was succeeded by his son Ispuni.

SEEZTUI.

A priest of King Psametik I. or II.

SEFKH. " Capturer."

A mystical divinity, who is mentioned in the LXIVth chapter of the Ritual of the Dead.

SEFKHABU. " Seven Rayed."

A mystical goddess, who is mentioned in the LVIIth chapter of the Ritual of the Dead.

SEFT.

A city and nome in Upper Egypt, which was called by the Greeks Heracleopolis. Its special deity is not at present known.

SEGAR.

The Egyptian name for the Syrian city Zoar, of Hebrew history.

SE-ISI.

A royal scribe and superintendent of the granaries of a king of the XIXth dynasty.

SEKA.

An Egyptian official title, applied to functionaries of the royal court. Its meaning is not known.

SEKEN-EN-RA. *Or* RASEKENEN.

The sacerdotal name of Tiakken, king of Thebes. *See* Apophis *and* Tiakken.

SEKER-NEFER-KE.

Another form of the name Neb-ka, which see.

SEKETT.

The name of the sacred ark of the Egyptian gods. It was generally made of wood, richly inlaid and painted, and constructed in the form of an Egyptian doorway, with an uræus cornice above. These arks held the sacred figures of the gods, and they were covered over with a fine gauze curtain or canopy. The Seketts were placed in the centre of the sacred boats, called *Ua*, and they were generally carried with great pomp on the shoulders of the priests. Sometimes kneeling statuettes of

Isis and Nephthys were placed beside the ark as protecting it, with other sacred symbols also. A smaller species of shrine was made in the shape of a rectangular box with a flat lid, upon which were placed either a statue of the deity or models of sacred trees. These were borne in procession by means of two long staves which passed through rings, affixed to the side, in a manner precisely similar to the ark of the covenant of Hebrew writers.

SE-KHEM-KA.

Another form of the Egyptian royal name Skhem-ka, which see.

SE-KHER-TA.

A high Egyptian officer, a " Functionary of the Interior," in the reign of an unnamed king of the XIIth dynasty. His wife's name was Ankhes. His own name can also be read Kher-ta-se.

SEKHET.

An Egyptian priestess of Amen Ra, the sister of the great officer Rere, of the XIXth dynasty.

SEKHET.

This goddess, whose name was formerly written Pasht, was the daughter of Ra, and the consort of the god Pthah, whence one of her chief titles was derived, "The First Friend of Pthah." She was represented as a lion-headed woman, having upon her head the lunar horns and solar disk, and holding in her hands either the crux ansata, and the papyrus staff of the goddesses, or else a kind of shield or ægis, and a basket. She was a destroying deity, and seemed to symbolise the deathly power of the sun's rays. She had also as an infernal deity the care of the Egyptian hell, and the direction of the torture of the souls immured therein. Sekhet had a variety of offices and attributes, and bore different names in them all. As the goddess of Northern Egypt she was Ouati ; as the consort of the god Shu, and his associate in the destruction of mankind at the command of Ra, she was named Tefnut ; as the creatress of the Asiatic or yellow race, a race despised by the Egyptians and regarded as impure, she was called Pasht (?) and in her more favourable aspect, as the protectress of mankind, she was called Beset, from whence was derived the Bubastis of the Greek writers. In this last characteristic she was figured as holding a sistrum or a vase for libation, and the cat was especially sacred to her. The Greeks equated her with Diana, and possibly Latona. Seti I. built a temple for her adoration at Speos Artemidos, after his return from his Syrian victories.

SEKHET-HOTEP-ET.

An Egyptian lady, the mother of Iusenb, which see.

SEKHMAKH.

The queen of Nastosenen, a king of the XXVth dynasty.

SEKISIT.   " Sowing of Seed."

The Accadian name of the twelfth month Addaru, which see.

SELAH.   " Stone" or " Stony."

The capital city of the Nabatheans.   It was often attacked, and was completely destroyed by Nebuchadnezzar, but was afterwards restored under the reigns of the Persian kings Cyrus and Darius.

SELINON.

A chief town of the Panopolite nome of the Thebaid in Upper Egypt.

SELK.

An Egyptian goddess, an unidentified form of the goddess Isis.   She was also one of the protecting goddesses of the human body, and as such her name was placed on the vase of Kabhsenuf.   Selk was generally represented as a woman with a scorpion upon her head, that insect being her emblem.

SE-MAUT.

The son of Toti, a flabellum-bearer of the XVIIIth dynasty.

SE-MAUT.

A noble priest in the reign of Thothmes III.   See Maut-nefer.

SEMEMPSES.

According to the Greek lists the seventh king of Egypt, in whose time a dreadful plague prevailed.   He reigned eighteen years.

SEMER.

An Egyptian hierarchical title, of which the precise significance is unknown.   See Smer.

SEMET.

The wife of King Her-hor-si-amen of the XXIst dynasty.

SEMIRAMIS.

The Greek form of the Assyrian royal name Sammuramat, which see.

SEMIT.

An Egyptian prefix signifying West.   It was sometimes represented as a goddess.

SEM-SEM.

The rebel commander of the troops in Pi-thoth-apre-hu-hu.   He submitted and made offerings to Piankhi-Meramen of the XXIInd dynasty.

SEMT-MUT.

Another form of the name of Muts-netem, a queen of Egypt in the reign of Har-em-hebi of the XVIIIth dynasty.

SEMT-MUT.

A daughter of Rameses II. of the XIXth dynasty.

34*

SEMUT.

The father of Amen-uahsu, an Egyptian sacerdotal officer of the XVIIIth dynasty.

SEN.

The Egyptian name of the town which was called Latopolis by the Greeks.

SEN.

An Egyptian priest in the time of the Vth dynasty.

SENB.

The son of Senbesen. He was *Heb*, or rather *Kherheb*, in the temple of Horus Khem. He may have lived in the time of Amenemha I., of the XIIth dynasty, as one of his sons was named Ra-s-hotep-ab-senb, which was the prenomen of that monarch.

SENB.

An Egyptian lady in the time of Amenemha III. of the XIIth dynasty.

SENB.

A peculiar bandlet which was worn on the arms of the Egyptian priests. It somewhat resembled the maniple of the mediæval priests.

SENB.

The favourite dog of Abet, an Egyptian sculptor of the XIIth dynasty. His name is an illustration of the inappropriate use of official titles among the ancient Egyptians.

SENB-EB.

An Egyptian gentleman, the son of Hathor. Period uncertain. His parent's name is curious as showing that the names of the Egyptian deities were also given to private individuals without any alteration, contrary to the usage of Semitic nations. *See also* Ra *and* Horus, as other examples of this custom.

SENB-ESEN.

The father of the *Kherheb* Senb, which see.

SENB-ETEF.

A private individual who lived probably about the time of the XIIIth dynasty. His father's (or perhaps mother's) name was Nofreit.

SENB-U.

The son of Uah and the lady Nakht. He was a priest of Osiris, and his period is uncertain, except that it was prior to the XVIIIth dynasty.

SENDAD.

An Arabian town near the Euphrates, which was sacred to the worship of the god Dhu-l-Calat.

SENEBSIMA.

The sister of an Egyptian king, but of what king it is not known.

SENEM.

The Egyptian name of the town now called Begbe.

SENEN.   " City of Registers."

An Egyptian town of early date.   Site unknown.

SENES.

An Egyptian title, the meaning of which is not known.   *See* Amen-aa.

SEN-HAKAR-U-KANA.

A mystical abode of the body of the deceased.   It is mentioned in the supplemental, or CLIVth chapter, of the Ritual of the Dead.

SENI.

The king of Dayani, one of the tribes of the Nairi who submitted to Tiglath Pileser I., who spared his life and restored him to his dominions. *See* Nairi.

SENKEREH.   *Or* SINGURA.

The modern name of the Chaldean city Larsa.   It was the Ellasar, " City of Assur," of Hebrew history.

SENKEREH.

The ancient name of a Chaldean city, whose king or chief brought tribute of lapis lazuli to Thothmes III., together with the head of a ram in gold, weighing fifteen Egyptian ounces, equal to 2100 grains troy.

SEN-MA.

The father of the state priest Hor of the XIIth dynasty, which see.

SEN-MES.

A scribe and treasurer of Amen Ra.   He was the father of the scribe Heb-i, which see.

SENNA.

An Egyptian architect, who was the father of Amenhotep, an architect likewise.   Period uncertain.

SENNACHERIB.   SIN-AKHI-ERBA, " Sin has multiplied her Brothers."

A younger son of Sargon. He succeeded his father, B.C. 705, and defeated an insurrection in Babylonia, headed by Merodach-Baladan, shortly after; upon which Bel-ibni was made king of Babylonia. After the conquest of the Kassi and of Ellipi (Ispahan), Sennacherib invaded Palestine, B.C. 701, captured Zidon and other Phenician cities, took Askelon and its king Zidka, obliged the revolters in Ekron to receive back their king Padiah (who had been kept a prisoner in Jerusalem by Hezekiah), defeated the Egyptian and Ethiopian forces at Eltakeh, and overran Judæa, taking forty-six fortified cities, and large quantities of cattle and treasure, and carrying 200,150 persons into captivity. Hezekiah sent thirty talents of gold and 800 talents of silver, besides other treasures, in the hope of making peace ; Sennacherib, however, gave portions of the Judæan territory to the Philistine princes, and sent a force to besiege Jerusalem. This having been destroyed (2 Kings xix. 35), Sennacherib returned to Nineveh, and in the following year (B.C. 700), drove Merodach-Baladan out of Babylonia to Nagitu, at the mouth of the Eulæus, overthrew Suzub, who had revolted in Southern Babylonia, and made his own eldest son, Assur-nadin-suma, king of Babylon. The tribes in the North, from Lake Van to Cilicia, were next reduced, and in B.C. 697 Sennacherib had a fleet built and manned by Phenicians, in the Persian Gulf, with which he destroyed Nagitu. A revolt had meanwhile broken out in Babylonia, under Suzub, but it was soon repressed, and Erech sacked. About B.C. 695, Sennacherib finished his great palace at Nineveh, and two or three years later overthrew the combined forces of Suzub and Ummanminan of Elam, in a decisive and bloody battle at Khalule. In B.C. 691 Babylon was besieged and razed to the ground. In December, B.C. 681, Sennacherib was murdered by his two eldest sons, Adrammelech and Nergal-sharezer.

SENNOFRE. *Or* SEN-NEFER, " Making Good."

A title of Osiris as the creator of good desires.

SENNOFRE.

The father of Bek-en-amen, a royal scribe of the XVIIIth dynasty.

SEN-NU.

An Egyptian officer, of the XVIIIth dynasty. He was " Lieutenant of the King," " Scribe of the Young Soldiers," and " Royal Scribe." He had a son named Amen-se.

SEN-NU.

An Egyptian lady, the mother of Sebek-ari, and the sister of Sebekhotep, who was a member of the royal council of thirty in the XIIIth dynasty.

SENOUPHIS.

According to the Greek lists the successor of Suphis, king of Memphis. He has not yet been certainly identified.

SENSAOS.

A Greco-Egyptian lady, whose name was also Hathor-set-dsjatho. She was the daughter of Cleopatra surnamed Candace and Soter the grandson of Cornelius. She died in the twelfth year of Trajan, aged sixteen. Her sarcophagus and mummy are in the Leyden Museum.

SENT.

An Egyptian gentleman, who was the father of Hor, which see.

SENT.

An Egyptian lady, the sister of Antef and Ameni, and the daughter of Antefaker, all private personages. She lived probably in the XIIth dynasty.

SENT.

Among the ancient Egyptians the name of a kind of game of draughts. It was played by two persons, each having five conical men called *Abu*, which were arranged on a board, having thirty squares in three rows of ten each. The game dated from the Vth dynasty, and is mentioned in the ancient romance of Setnau. It was the game which according to the Greek writers Rhampsinitus played with Persephone in Hades. *See* Rameses III.

SENT. *Or* SETHENES.

The fifth king of the IInd or Thinite dynasty of Egypt. He introduced the doctrine of the personal adoration of the king, and reigned forty-one years.

SENT-EN-ANTEF.

The father of En-antef, and grandfather of En-antef, an " Overseer of the Altar," in the reign of Amen-em-ha II.

SENT-UR.

A high sacerdotal title which was peculiar to the Theban priests of Amen.

SEPA.

An Egyptian functionary of the IInd dynasty.

SEPA.

A prince and *Sutenrekh* of the IIIrd or IVth dynasty. *See* Sutenrekh.

SEPA-RU-RU.

A king of the Khitæ, or Hittites, who was conquered by Rameses I., with whom he concluded a treaty of peace. His name is written by some Egyptologists Sapar and Seplul.

SEPHERES. *Or* SEPHRES.

The Grecian form of the royal name Sahura, which see.

SEPHORIS.

The Grecian form of the Egyptian royal name Snefru, which see.

SEPI. " Dismembered."

A title of the deity Osiris, under which he was venerated during his dismemberment by the evil deity Set.

SEPLUL.

Another form of the Hittite royal name Sepa-ru-ru, which see.

SEPT-ACHEM.

An Egyptian deity, who was chiefly worshipped in the city and nome of Sept-hor, which was named after him.

SE-PTHAH.

A priest of Apis, in the thirty-fourth year of Darius Hystaspes. He was the son of Har-em-khu, and the grandson of Nes-pthah, which see.

SEPT-HOR.

A city and nome in Lower Egypt which was sacred to the worship of the god Sept-achem.

SEPUNTEPET.

A daughter of Pankhi, an obscure king of the XXIVth dynasty.

SEPUNTEPUT.

A royal pallacist in the reign of Psametik I., of the XXVIth dynasty.

SERA.

An Egyptian lady, who was the sister of the priest Nofre-renpe, which see.

SERAA.

A Phenician city, to the South of Tyre. It was perhaps the Sana of Classic writers.

SERACH.

Another form of the Ethiopian royal name Zerah, by which title King Azech-Amen is supposed to be mentioned in Hebrew history.

SERAKH.

The Accadian name of the Assyrian deity Nirba, the god of harvests.

SE-RA-NEFER-TAI.

An obscure king of the XVIIIth dynasty. He was perhaps the Rathothis of the Greeks.

SERAPEUM.

The great temple at Memphis where the sacred bull Apis was buried in a very large sarcophagus surrounded with funereal tablets of the various priests who died during his Apis-ship. From these tablets, several hundred of which were lately discovered by Mariette Bey, some important chronological data have been obtained.

SERAPIS.

An Egypto-Grecian deity who was made out of the deified dead Apis when assimilated to Osiris as Osir-Api. This worship suddenly arose into importance in the time of the Ptolemies and has no analogue in Archaic mythology.

SERBES.   *Or* TSESHORTSA.

The second king of the IIIrd dynasty of Egypt. He was the author of many medical books, and practised cutting for the stone. At a later period he was deified under the name of the god Aiemapt or Imouthes, or Imhotep, the son of Pthah. He was the Tosorthrus of the Greeks.

SER-HAT.

An Egyptian lady. She was the sister of the royal scribe User-hat, which see.

SERIS.

A city on the river Tigris, where Kiliteru, king of the Hittites, fled for refuge after the battle of Kummuha. The city was stormed by Tiglath-Pileser I., and the Hittites and their king defeated and slain.

SERK.

Another form of the name of the scorpion goddess Selk, the Selcis of the Greek writers.

SERUYA.

An Assyrian goddess. She was the wife of the deity Assur.

SERUYA-EDIRAT.

The sister of Assurbanipal and Saulmugina the rebel vice-king of Babylon. She is said by some writers to have caused the life of Saulmugina to be spared after his defeat by the king of Assyria, his brother and lord. *See* Assurbanipal *and* Saul-mugina.

SE-SEN-NU.

The Egyptian name of the town which was called by the Greeks Hermopolis, which see.

SE-SHESH.

A city and nome in Upper Egypt, called by the Greeks Phathyrite. It was sacred to the worship of the goddess Hathor.

SESOCHRIS.

The Greek form of the name Nefer-ka-sokar, which see.

SESONCHOSES.

According to the Greek lists the name of an Egyptian king of the XIIth dynasty. He has not yet been certainly identified.

SESOSTRIS.

A mythical Egyptian prince, whose history was compiled by the Greek historians out of the lives and actions of Seti I. and Rameses II. and III. of the XIXth dynasty, with the addition of many romantic adventures derived from the knowledge and traditions of the writers several centuries later. *See* Seti I. *and* Rameses II. *and* III.

SESSRUMMIR.

In Scandinavian mythology the name of the palace of the goddess Freyia, in the sacred city of Asgard, which see.

SESTSU-EM-PAIF-NAKHT-U-USER-MA-RA. "Rameses II. in his Victories."

The name of a great fortress which was erected in Palestine by Rameses II. after his conquest of that country,

Sesu.

A Mesopotamian people who were conquered by Tiglath-Pileser I.

Sesupti.

An Egyptian functionary, who was called an "Officer of the Interior," in the reign of Osirtesen I. of the XIIth dynasty.

Sesur-hat.

A wife of Amenhotep II. of the XVIIIth dynasty.

Sesur-sati.

The prince royal of Ethiopia, in the reign of Amenhotep II.

Set. *Or* Sutekh.

An ass-headed deity, the national god of the Semitic Hykshos, who on their invasion of Egypt in the interval between the XIIIth and XVIIIth dynasties, forced his sole worship upon the Egyptians. Set was already one of the cosmical deities of the country ; but after the expulsion of the Hykshos his worship was annulled, his statues defaced, and his name everywhere erased. He was represented as an ass-headed man, holding the usual crux ansata or staff of life and the *cucufa* staff of divine power. The Egyptians were accustomed to regard Set as a personification of the evil principle. "The worship of this god passed through two historical phases. At one time he was held in honour and accounted as qne of the greater gods of Abydos. He appears to have had a position analogous to that of the Theban deity Mentu, in which he was the adversary of the serpent Apophis, the symbol of wickedness and darkness. Some time later on, in consequence of political changes, the worship of Set was abolished, and his statues destroyed. It is difficult to state at what period Set was introduced into the Osirian mythos as a personification of evil, and thus became identified with Typhon as the murderer of Osiris. The contests of Horus, the avenger of his father Osiris, are related at considerable detail in the inscriptions of the temple of Edfu which have been published by M. Ed. Naville in *Textes relatifs au Mythe d'Horus*, 1870. The treatise (by Plutarch) *De Iside et Osiride* makes Nephthys the companion of Set, and she is represented united with him in a group in the Museum of the Louvre, in the Hall of the Gods. The animal symbolical of Set was a carnivorous quadruped, at one time confounded with the ass-god of Josephus and Apion, having a long curved snout and upright square topped ears, which characters are often exaggerated to distinguish him from the jackal of Anubis." (Pierret.) After the second restoration of the old mythology in the period of the XIXth dynasty, Set was identified with the Hykshos Sutekh, who was properly an Asiatic divinity, and whose worship was maintained even by Seti I. and Rameses II. Both gods, however, were treated as impious, and their worship as heretical, and it is at the present time impossible to distinguish exactly between them, owing to the complete destruction by the Egyptians of all those parts of the monuments whereon their names occur.

SET-AKORF.

An Egyptian lady, the mother of Fai-hor-ou-oer, and grandmother of Ra-t-oker, the prefect of the palace of a king of the XXVIth dynasty.

SET-AMEN.

The wife of Antef, an Egyptian officer of the XIIth dynasty.

SET-AMEN.

A daughter of Antef, an Egyptian officer of the XIIth dynasty.

SET-AP.

An Egyptian lady, the daughter of Hapiu and the wife of Osirtesen; a private person, probably of the XIIth dynasty.

SET-AUAN.

A prince of Kush, in the reign of Rameses II. of the XIXth dynasty.

SET-EM-ASH.

The servant and *Pandar* of Prince Setnau-chaem-uset, in the Egyptian Romance of Setnau.

SET-EN-ET.

The grandson of Tetet, an early Egyptian king.

SET-EN-ISI.

An Egyptian princess, the daughter of Ti-osiris.   Period uncertain.

SETETA.

The daughter of Tetet, an early Egyptian king.

SET-HATHOR.

A second wife of Antef, an Egyptian officer of the XIIth dynasty.

SETHENES.

An early king of Egypt.   *See* Sent.

SET-HIK-HOPSEF-MI-AMUN.

The surname of Rameses VIII. of the XXth dynasty.

SETHLANS.

The Etruscan fire-god, or Vulcan.

SETHOS.

An obscure king of the XXIVth dynasty.   His position and the length of his reign are uncertain.

SETHROITES.

A nome of Lower Egypt, East of the Phatnitic branch of the Nile. Its position is uncertain, but its chief towns were Sethrum and Heracleopolis Parva.   According to M. De Rouge this nome formed a portion of that of Khent-abet.

SETHRUM.

A chief town in the Sethroic nome of Egypt.

SETI I.   *Or* SETI MENEPTHAH, *Surnamed* MERENPTHAH, "The Living like Set."

A famous king of the XIXth dynasty, the adopted son or son-in-law and the successor of Rameses I. He seems to have been a soldier of fortune, of Hykshos extraction, who by marriage with the heiress to the crown established himself on the throne. On his accession he re-introduced the worship of Sutekh, which was still further strengthened by his son Rameses II., who founded a temple to that deity at Tanis. Seti was a great warrior, and in the first year of his reign drove back the Shashu, who had attacked the city of Zal, near Heliopolis. Having thrust the Arabs into the desert, he in the next year crossed over to Palestine, where all the Canaanitish princes paid him tribute and homage. Gathering his army together, he then entered the valley of the Orontes, where he defeated the Khitæ, and captured their capital city Kadesh, and made peace with Mautnur, the king of the Khitæ, whom as a tributary he restored to his dominions. After this the king of Egypt turned back to conquer the Rotennu, on this side the Euphrates, they having discontinued the tribute imposed on them by the Thothmes kings of the XVIIIth dynasty. The nations of the Arameans were easily subdued, but those beyond the Euphrates gave more trouble to the Egyptian conqueror ; some great battles, however, brought about the complete subjection of Mesopotamia, Assyria, and Chaldea. Seti admitted to an interview the chiefs of Babylon, Nineveh, and Singar, and a last campaign in the mountains of Armenia re-established the supremacy of Pharaoh in that country also. On returning to Egypt, Seti sent a series of slave-hunting expeditions into Ethiopia, and completely conquered the more barbarous Negroid races to the South of Egypt. On the North-west frontier the victorious monarch then repulsed the incursions of the Libyans, and in turn successfully invaded their kingdom. Finally, he reconstructed the Egyptian fleet on the Red Sea, and re-asserted the power of the Pharaohs on the shores of Arabia Felix. The Mediterranean conquests of Thothmes III., Seti was, however, unable to regain, owing to the rapid growth of the Pelasgic and Phenician colonies, which had settled themselves in all the islands of the inland sea. It was not only as a warrior that Seti was a great monarch : in his internal policy he was also distinguished. He commenced the large canal from the Nile to the Red Sea, a work which was completed by his son Rameses II., who has usurped the credit of it. He caused an artesian well to be sunk at the mines of Kuban, and he built several important fortresses along the frontiers of his kingdom. The palace at Kurnah was founded by Seti as a country residence, and the stupendous temples of Karnak and of Osiris at Abydos were designed and begun by him. His tomb in the Valley of the Kings at the Biban el Moluk is one of the grandest and deepest in existence, extending as it does for upwards of three hundred yards into the solid rock, and having many splendidly adorned chambers leading from it, in one of which nearly 1000 votive *Shabti* figures of the monarch were discovered when the tomb was opened by Belzoni, its discoverer, on the 19th October, 1817. His alabaster sarcophagus, now in the Soane Museum, is unique for beauty of workmanship, the value of its material, and the extent of the text, chiefly selections from the Ritual of the Dead, which is incised upon it. Most of the national works of Seti were, however, finished by Rameses II., who, by inserting his own name on the sculptures, has obtained the credit of them all. Seti was one of the several great kings of the XIXth dynasty out of whom the Greek authors manufactured the fabulous Sesostris. He was probably, also, the Osymandyas of history, and according to the lists of Manetho reigned for fifty years. His name is written Osirei-Menepthah by Champollion, Oimenepthah by Sharpe, Asi-menepthah by some Egyptologists, and Psammis and Sethos by others. In his cartouches the first letters of his name, which began with the figure of the god Set, have been carefully chiselled out ; and in the Flaminian Obelisk at Rome, which was originally a work of his reign also, the figure of the god Ra inserted instead. This mutilation of the names of Set and Amen took place several times in the history of Egypt. *See* Rameses II. *and* Amenhotep IV.

SETI II. *Surnamed* MENEPTHAH.

The son of Menepthah I. and his queen Hesi-nefer-et. He had to contend for some years with the usurper Sipthah or Merenpthah II., with whom for a while he shared the kingdom under the title of " Viceroy of the Southern Kingdom." He reigned for many years, but particulars of his government are wanting, although it appears to have been a prosperous one. He left no issue, and with him ended the XIXth dynasty, after it had lasted 174 years. After his death his name was effaced from the monuments, as was also that of his predecessors Seti I. and Rameses I., on account of the figure of the god Set occurring in them, for which the figure of the god Osiris was substituted, the adoration of Set being again hateful to the Egyptians. *See also* Set *and* Apepi.

SETI.

A prince of Kush during the reign of the usurper Sipthah, of the XIXth dynasty.

SETI.

A son of Rameses II. of the XIXth dynasty.

SETI-NEKHT.   " Set in his Strength."

An Egyptian prince, and the founder of the XXth Egyptian dynasty. He arose into importance during the revolution caused by the invasion of Arsu, the Syrian, which led to the destruction of the established religion for the third time (*See* Apepi *and* Taia), and caused the different great lords of the provinces to arrogate the crown to themselves in their own districts, after the death of Merenpthah I. These Syrians and their leader, Arsu, the Osarsiph of Josephus, Seti-Nekht expelled, and gradually subdued or pacified the revolted chiefs of Egypt, whereupon the priests appear to have placed him on the throne as the restorer of order and religion. Having effected this great result he died after a short reign, and left the throne to his son and associate Rameses III.

SETI-PETI-NUBTI.

The first king of the Hykshos, under whom they invaded Egypt, and introduced the absolute worship of the god Set as Sutekh. He built the strong city of Ha-ur or Avaris, which he made the capital of his empire.

SET-KHERTA.

The sister of Sekherta, an Egyptian functionary of the XIIth dynasty.

SET-KHONSU.

A sister of Sekherta, an Egyptian functionary of the XIIth dynasty.

SET-MENA.

The father of Antef, an officer of the XIIth dynasty.

SETNAU-CHAEM-USET.

The son of a king named Usermat, who is by some Egyptologists supposed to have been Rameses II. He is the hero of the Egyptian romance entitled "The Story of Setnau," in which he figures with little credit.

SE-UATI.

An Egyptian official in the court of Osirtesen I. and III. and Amenemha III. of the XIIth dynasty. His father's name was Khatiur.

SEVEKCHUS.

Another form of the Egyptian royal name Sebeka, or Shabaka, which see.

SFENTK-HAK.

The grandson of Tetet, an early Egyptian king.

SHAA.

The linen cap or crown of Upper Egypt, which when the two kingdoms were united, was generally worn inside the Teshr or golden crown, and thus the two together formed the Pschent.

SHAA-EM-UAS. *Or* KHŒM-UAS.

A son of Rameses II., king of Egypt. He fought beside his father in his wars against the Negroes, and was outlived by him.

SHAARILOBUR.

The star Sirius adored as a divinity by the people of Sabæa.

SHAA-TA-EM-UA. "Crowned by Truth."

The name of the royal boat of Thothmes III.

SHA-BA. "Rising Soul."

The name of the pyramid in which Sahura, a king of Egypt of the Vth dynasty, was interred.

Shabaka I.

The first king of the XXVth dynasty. He was the son of Kashta, and the brother of Amen-iritis, and was born at Akesh in Ethiopia. Having raised a mingled army of Negroes and Ethiopians, he invaded and conquered Egypt from Nubia to the Mediterranean, taking Bak-en-ran-f prisoner, and burning him to death. Palestine being at that time invaded by the Assyrians, Shabaka marched to the relief of Hoshea, king of Israel, but arrived too late to save Samaria from capture by Shalmaneser VI. He, however, made some conquests in Palestine, for on his return to Egypt he recorded the land of Syria as one of his tributary states. Shortly afterwards Sargon, king of Assyria, inflicted a crushing defeat upon him at Raphia, and then reconquered Syria and part of Egypt. Nothing else is known of the life and reign of Shabaka, except that on his death he was succeeded by his son(?) Shabaka II. According to some writers he was the So of Hebrew history, and the Sabacon of the Greeks. *See* Sibahe.

Shabaka II. *Or* Shabatuk.

The successor of Shabaka I. He marched to the assistance of Khanunu, king of Gaza, whose country was invaded by the Assyrians. He was however defeated at another battle of Raphia, and retreated into Egypt. The Assyrians did not recognise him as a legitimate king of Egypt, but he figures on a bas-relief at Karnak as a royal worshipper of Amen Ra. He was the Sebichos of the Greeks.

Shabti.

The name given by Egyptologists to the small inscribed Osiride figures wrought in wood, glazed steatite or terra cotta, which were generally buried in great quantities in the tombs of the XIXth dynasty, and which according to the VIth chapter of the Ritual of the Dead, were supposed to possess some mystical power of assisting the deceased, whose name they bore, in his labours in the Aahlu.

Shabwat.

The capital city of the Himyaritic kingdom of Hadramaut, now called Sabota. *See* Sanbatha *and* Sabbatha.

Shadu-nakhunda.

Another form of the Elamite royal name Sutruk-nakhunta.

Sha-en-sen-sen. "The Book of the Respirations."

The name of an Egyptian mystical book concerning the metempsychosis of the souls of the justified after death. It has been translated both by M. Brugsch, and De Horrack, in the *Records of the Past*, Vol. IV.

Shafra.

An Egyptian king of the IVth dynasty. He was the builder of the second pyramid, which he called the "Greatest of the Pyramids." He married Meri-s-ankh, the priestess of Thoth, and was the Chafren of the Greeks.

SHAGARAKTIYASH.

An early Chaldean king who is said by Berosus to have built the great temple at Sippara. He was succeeded by his son Naram-sin. *See* Sargon.

SHAHAR.

A town in Upper Egypt sacred to Seb. Site unknown.

SHAI.

A Libyan tribe who were subjugated by Rameses III.

SHAKA.

The Egyptian name of an earring. These were wrought in gold, porcelain, and various other materials. The earlier examples were in the form of an engraved button or stud, which was passed through a hole cut in the lobe of the ear. In the middle and later dynasties they were simply circular gold wires, often of large size. Afterwards jewels and pendants were added, and towards the period of the Greco-Egyptian empire small figures of deities and animals, in the style of Etruscan workmanship were introduced.

SHAKALUSHA.

The name by which the Sicilians were known to the Egyptians. They, together with their allies, combined against Menepthah II., by whom they were defeated.

SHAK-AMEN.

The name of a mystical divinity who is mentioned in the supplemental or CLXIVth chapter of the Ritual of the Dead.

SHAKANA.

An Egyptian canal at the North of the pool of Har.

SHAKANASA.

The mystical name of one of the greater divinities in the supplemental or CLXIVth chapter of the Ritual of the Dead.

SHALMAN.

Another name of the Assyrian eagle-headed deity Nisroch. His title was " The King of Fluids." He presided over the destinies of mankind, and was the protector of marriages. (Lenormant.) He was originally a Himyaritic deity.

SHALMAN.

The brother of Assur-ebil-ili, the last king of Assyria. He was slain in the siege of Nineveh by the Medes and Persians under Nabu-kudur-uzur.

SHALMANESER I. *Or* SHALMANUASHIR. " Shalman protects."

An early king of Assyria. The son of Vulnirari or Rimmon-Nirari I., whom he succeeded about B.C. 1300, and whose conquests he continued. He defeated the Muzri or Egyptians who had settled in Asia, and settled an Assyrian colony at the head waters of the Tigris. The fame of Shalmaneser rests now more on his buildings than his conquests. At Assur, the old capital, he enlarged the palace, and restored the great temple called "The Mountain of the World." He however gave a severe blow to the importance of the city by founding a palace at Nineveh, and making that city a royal residence, and further also by building a new town about eighteen miles South of Nineveh, which was called Calah. Shalmaneser besides this restored the temple of Ishtar at Nineveh, and dedicated some votive dishes to the goddess. He died after a reign of about thirty years, and was succeeded by his son Tugulti-Ninip. (Smith.)

SHALMANESER (II.)

According to Lenormant the successor of Belkatirassu or Belitarus, B.C. 1070, in which case he would correspond to the Samsi-Vul III. or Samas-Rimmon III. of Smith and Sayce.

SHALMANESER II.

The son of Assurnazirpal, whom he succeeded about B.C. 860. He was a great warrior, and the first of the Assyrian kings who came into contact with the Jews. His first care on ascending the throne was to reduce all the tributary states of Assyria to subordination, in which he was ably assisted by his Tartan Dayan-assur. He then repeatedly crossed the Euphrates, and dispersed the great confederation of the Syrian kings, who had combined against him under Hazael of Damascus and Ahab of Israel. These he defeated in two separate engagements, but with a severe loss to the Assyrian army. He again passed through the North of Palestine to the Mediterranean, taking tribute of the Phenicians and Hittites ; afterwards he subdued the kings of Ararat and Hupuskia. The latter years of his life were embittered by the attempts of his eldest son, Assurdainpal, to usurp the throne. Shalmaneser II. was also great as a statesman, he died after a reign of thirty-one years, and was succeeded by his son, Samsi-Vul IV., B.C. 825. "Shalmaneser II. was a great builder, like several other of the Assyrian kings. During his first twelve years he resided at the city of Nineveh, and there he made additions to the palace, which had been rebuilt by his father, and adorned the temple of Ishtar, the goddess of the city. Somewhere about his thirteenth year he changed his capital, and went to reside at Calah, where he ruled for the rest of his life. At this place he built a new palace South of the one raised by his father, and completed the the building of the city and raising of the walls. At the Northern corner of the palace platform at Calah, near the temples, he built an enormous tower or *Ziggurat* one hundred and sixty-seven feet in length and breadth, faced with stone to the height of twenty feet, and still standing one hundred and forty feet high. At the city of Assur, the old capital of the country, the wall having become ruinous, Shalmaneser restored it and greatly strengthened it, which he records on a statue of black stone, which he raised in the city." (Smith.) The chief interest in the reign of Shalmaneser II. centres in the great black obelisk now in the British Museum, upon which he records his conquests in Syria, Damascus, the Hauran, and the land of Bashan, and describes Jehu the king of Israel, as Yehu the son of Omri, as paying him tribute of gold, silver, buckets of gold, cups and bottles of gold, lead, and rods of ornamental wood for maces and articles of furniture, some of which are represented on the monument itself. Shalmaneser II. of Smith is the Shalmaneser IV. of Lenormant. NOTE.—The succession of these monarchs is at present hopelessly confused, the French and English Assyriologists differing widely in their identification. There is, therefore, no other course to be adopted than to insert the names upon the authorities of the authors cited.

SHALMANESER (III.)

The successor of Assur-nadin-akhi, king of Assyria. Nothing is known respecting him. He was succeeded by Assur-edil-ilani. (Lenormant.) This king would be therefore Assur-nirari I. of Smith and Sayce, B.C. 1500.

SHALMANESER III.

The son and successor of Vulnirari III. about B.C. 783. No memorial of Shalmaneser has come down to us, and the Assyrian Canon history is at present the only source of our knowledge of his reign. On his accession, B.C. 783, he went to Babylon, to the region of Ituah, on the Euphrates. B.C. 782, he attacked again the same region. B.C. 781, Shalmaneser made war with the Armenians, called the kingdom of Ararat. Seduri, king of Ararat, during the reign of Shalmaneser II., had introduced Cuneiform writing and various arts into Armenia ; and since his time the Armenian monarchy had rapidly risen under his son Ispuni, his grandson Minua, and Argisti, the son of Minua. These monarchs had increased the extent of their dominions, making conquests in Syria, Minni, Harhar, Media, and had even made raids into the Assyrian territory, thereby calling for their effectual repression. The war now carried on by Shalmaneser against the Armenians appears to have been an obstinate one, and lasted from B.C. 781 through B.C. 780 and 779, closing in the year B.C. 778. Then after a short expedition against Ituha, B.C. 777, Shalmaneser again fought with the king of Armenia, B.C. 776. An interval of a year once more followed, Shalmaneser going to Syria B.C. 775, when again war broke out with Armenia, in conjunction this time with Zimri, B.C. 774. About this time Shalmaneser died, when he was succeeded by Assurdan III. Six years out of his short reign of ten years had been spent in war with these growing Northern powers, and at his death the Armenians recommenced their inroads upon Assyria. (Smith.) Few, if any, monuments have yet been found which were executed in the reign of this monarch.

SHALMANESER IV.

The successor of Tiglath-Pileser II., about B.C. 727. His relationship to the previous monarch, if any, is unknown, and he probably obtained the crown by the sword. He had scarcely ascended the throne when he was called to quell a revolt in Palestine, and quickly following the subjugation of that first war, came a second one, the insurgents being encouraged by Sibahe, king of Egypt. He, however, with some difficulty obtained the mastery, and forced the kings of Tyre and Sidon to pay tribute. They in their turn destroyed his navy of sixty vessels, and compelled him to prolong the siege both of Tyre and Samaria, which he carried on at the same time. After a five years reign an insurrection took place in Assyria, headed it is probable by his chief officer Sargon, and Shalmaneser IV. was dethroned and the crown placed on the head of Sargon II., while the Syrian and Phenician sieges were still going on, about B.C. 722. The annals of the reign of Shalmaneser IV. have not been found, and there are but few memorials of his reign with the exception of private and especially trade documents. Besides his Syrian wars only a single other expedition of his, viz. one against Deri, in Babylonia, is known. He was devoted to the worship of Nerza or Nergal, the god of war, and dedicated some fine ivory furniture to the temple of that deity at Tarbizi, North of Nineveh. That as a king of Assyria he favoured commerce is attested by the fact that most of the Assyrian standard weights in the British Museum date from his reign. This monarch is the Shalmaneser VI. of Lenormant, and the IVth of Smith.

SHALMANESER (V.)

According to Lenormant one of the successors of Binlikkish (Vulnirari) III. He reigned from B.C. 828 to 818. He made an expedition to Damascus, and no less than six successive campaigns into the revolted provinces of Assyria.

SHALMAN-HU-ASIR.

The Assyrian form of the royal name which is more generally written Shalmaneser. The Shalman of Hebrew history.

SHALMAN-HU-ASAR-ILANI.

The chief of the town of Sadikan on the river Khabour. He paid tribute to Assurnazirpal, king of Assyria, and his seal in the British Museum is perhaps the most beautiful in the collection.

SHALUMA. Or SALEM.

The Egyptian name of the city of Jerusalem, which was captured by Rameses II. after the battle of Kadesh, in which he utterly defeated the Hittites and their Syrian allies.

SHAMADAGINI.

In Hindu mythology the reputed husband of the Pariah goddess Maryatali, whose sons he commanded to behead her.

SHAMAS. Or SHEMS. "The Sun."

A Himyaritic deity, the same as the Shamas of the Chaldeans and the Shemesh of Hebrew history.

SHAMASH-BEL. "Servant of Bel."

A mythical Chaldean king of the Ist dynasty. His name is only found on the lists of Berosus, by whom he is called Chosmasbelus.

SHAMIRAMIGUERD. "The City of Semiramis."

The Armenian name of the great fortifications near Lake Van, which were attributed to Sammuramat, the Semiramis of the Greeks.

SHAMMIR.

The king of Sabæa, in Arabia. He succeeded his father, Alamluk, and founded the town of Zafar in Yemen, but nothing else is known respecting him.

SHAMSH-IBIN.

Another form of the Assyrian royal name Samsi-Vul, which see.

SHAMUL-SHA-MUGIN.

Another form of the Assyrian royal name Saul-mugina, which see.

SHAMY AND DAMY.

The modern name given by the Arabs to the two colossal statues of Amenhotep III. and his queen, which now exist in a very ruined condition in the Nubian Desert. *See also* Memnon.

SHAP.

The Egyptian palm, equal to four digits.

SHAPU-ARKA.

A mystical name of the deceased when hidden in the pupil of the eye of Osiris, as described in the CLXIVth (supplemental) chapter of the Ritual of the Dead.

SHAPU-ARKAT.

The name of the litui of the left mystical eye of Osiris in the CLXIVth chapter of the Ritual of the Dead.

SHARESER.

A son of Sennacherib. He was one of the murderers of his father, and is not mentioned by name in the Assyrian inscriptions. *See* Assurmulik.

SHARHABIL.

A king of Saba, who is sometimes called Kharabail.

SHARU.

In Egyptian mythology the mystical "Lake of Sacred Principles" in the valley of Elysium.

SHARUHANA.

A town in Southern Palestine which was besieged by King Aahmes of the XVIIIth dynasty for six years, as a stronghold of the Hykshos. He ultimately conquered and garrisoned it. It was the Sharuen of Hebrew history.

SHARU-SHARU.

Another name of the mystical pupil of the right eye of Osiris, wherein the deceased is said to be hidden in the supplemental or CLXIVth chapter of the Ritual of the Dead.

SHARU-SHARU-KHET.

Another name of the curved line or litui of the right mystical eye of Osiris in the CLXIVth or supplementary chapter of the Ritual of the Dead.

SHARU-SHA-TA-KATA.

A mystical title of Amen Ra in the CLXVIth chapter of the Ritual of the Dead.

SHARUTANA.

The name by which the Sardinians were known to the Egyptians. They served as mercenaries in the army of Rameses II. in his Syrian wars, but combined with the Libyans against his son Menepthah, by whom they were defeated.

SHARYUKIN.

A mystical king of the ancient city of Agani in Chaldea, who was regarded as a legendary hero and demigod. *See* Sargon I.

SHASTRAS.

The general name applied to their sacred books by the Hindu theologians and philosophers, of which the four Vedas are the chief.

SHASU. *Or* SHASHOUS.

The Egyptian name of the Bedouin tribes inhabiting the North-eastern frontier of the Delta. They were partly subdued by Aahmes, king of the XVIIIth dynasty, but always continued to be a source of annoyance to the Egyptians.

SHAT.

A mystical reptile, one of the enemies of the soul of the deceased. He is mentioned in the XLIst chapter of the Ritual of the Dead.

SHAUF-SA-KARTA.

An Egyptian scribe who wrote upon the advantages of the profession of a scribe and on the cultivation of letters. He lived in the period of the XIXth dynasty.

SHEBA.

The ancient name of the Adite capital Marib. *See* Abd-shems.

SHEBA.

The surname of Abd-shems, king of Yemen, which see.

SHEBETUN.

A place in Syria, site unknown, where Rameses II. was encamped when the Arabs treacherously endeavoured to betray him into an ambush before the battle of Kadesh.

SHED.

The principal deity of the Northern Hittites.

SHEDAD.

In Arabian history the son of the patriarch Ad. He conquered all Arabia and Irak, and built a splendid palace or paradise which he called Irem, but he was miraculously slain on account of his impiety. He and all his family were giants.

SHEDATH.

The feminine form of the Hittite deity Shed.

SHEDID.

In Arabian history the son of Ad. He reigned over the Adites, and was succeeded by his brother Shedad.

SHEMESH. *Or* SHAMASH, *or* SAMAS.

In Babylonian mythology the son of Ningal, and the god of the sun. He was called the " Judge of Heaven and Earth," " Director of All," and " Lord of the Cities of Larsa and Sippara." His consort and sister was the goddess Ishtar, the daughter of Sin, who must not be confounded with Ishtar, the daughter of Anu. His analogue was the Shemesh or Shems of the Syrian religions.

SHEMS.

A solar deity of the Sabæans, the analogue of the Chaldean divinity Shamash.

SHEMS.

A Himyaritic goddess, the feminine form of the deity Shemesh.

SHEMSH-IBIN I., II.,` ETC.

Another rendering of the name Samsi-Vul, which see.

SHEN. *Or* SUNT.

The Egyptian name of the acacia tree, the wood of which was much used for ordinary carpentry, its bark for tanning, and its resinous gum for the preparation of varnishes and cements.

SHEN-PE-UTS-NETER. " Turn of Heaven, Conductor of the Gods."

The second of the mystical cows or Hathors of Egyptian mythology.

SHEN-SHEN.

The Egyptian mystical name of the sacred Heron, into which among other animals the souls of the justified deceased were transformed.

SHENTI.

The Egyptian name of the sin of simple cursing or of incantation.

SHENTI.

The short loin cloth worn by the Egyptians alike by princes and peasants. It seems to have been made of the same materials as the Namms, which see.

SHENUT.

A town in the first Northern nome of Lower Egypt. It was sacred to the deity Sekar.

SHEPEN-APUT. *Or* SHAP-EN-AP.

The daughter of Piankhi II. of the XXIInd dynasty. She married Psametik I., king at first of Sais, and afterwards of all Egypt, and thus consolidated her husband's right to the throne.

SHEPEN-HESI.

An Egyptian lady, the sister of Nekhtmutf, which see.

SHEPES-KAF.

The chief priest of the temple of Khufu in the period of the Ancient Empire.

SHEP-SHET.

An Egyptian lady of the XXVIth dynasty, whose mummy and coffin are in the British Museum.

SHES.

An Egyptian amulet in the form of a peculiar kind of tie. It was usually carved in cornelian.

SHESHA.

In Hindu mythology the great seven-headed serpent which floats upon the cosmical ocean, and upon whose folds the throne of Brahma is situated.

SHESHANKA I. *Or* SHISHAK, *or* SHESHONK.

The son of Nimrod or Namurot, a great officer in the court of one of the last kings of the house of Her-hor, and of a princess of the blood royal. He was adopted by his grandfather, and at first governed Egypt as regent, but afterwards ascended the throne and founded the XXIInd dynasty. He supported Jeroboam in his revolt against Rehoboam, king of Judah, and gave him one of his daughters in marriage. By the influence of Egypt Jeroboam was made king of Israel, and shortly afterwards Sheshanka invaded Judah in three directions, pillaged and partly destroyed Jerusalem, and subdued 133 cities in Palestine. He transferred the seat of empire from Thebes to Bubastis, and reigned twenty-one years, leaving the crown of Egypt to his son Uaserken or Osorkon I.

SHESHANKA II.

The son of Uaserken II., king of Egypt of the XXIInd dynasty. He is only known from the monuments.

SHESHANKA III.

An Egyptian king of the XXIInd dynasty. He succeeded Takelot II., and reigned fifty-one years, but no particulars of his long reign are known. He was succeeded by his son (?) Pamai or Pekhi.

SHESHANKA IV.

The successor of Pamai. He reigned thirty-six years, but nothing is known of the events which took place in them. With him closed the XXIInd dynasty, after which the Ethiopians again overran Egypt.

SHESHANKA.

One of the petty kings of Egypt under the Assyrian Icosarchy. His capital was the town called by the Assyrians Busiru.

SHESHANKA.

The son of Osorkon I. of the XXIInd dynasty.

SHESHANKA.

The son of Osorkon II. of the XXIInd dynasty.

SHESHANKA.

A prince of the blood royal of the house of Piankhi, of the XXIInd dynasty, the son of Prince Petnit, which see.

SHESHANKA.

The father of Namurot, a prince of the blood royal of Sheshanka I. of the XXIst dynasty.

SHESHANKA.

An Egyptian priest and officer of the temple of Ra of the Delta. He was the father of Psametik, a prophet of Pthah.

SHES-HOTEP.

A city and nome in Upper Egypt which was called by the Greeks Anteopolis. It was sacred to the worship of the deity Khnum.

SHILAGARA.

An Elamite deity, of whom nothing is known.

SHIMGAM.

Another Elamite deity, of whom nothing is knowr

SHISHAK.

In Hebrew history the name by which Sheshanka, or Scheschang, the first king of the XXIInd dynasty is mentioned.

SHIWARATI.

A great festival held in India, in the month of March, in honour of the god Siva.

SHOAIB.

In pre-Koranic history an Arabian prophet, the son of Dhumahdam. He was slain by the people of Hadura, who were idolaters, to whom he had been sent to preach for their conversion. The tribe were afterwards destroyed from heaven in retribution for their crimes.

SHODB.

The modern name of the Greco-Egyptian town of Hypsele in the Thebaid.

SHOEM-UAS. *Or* KHAEMUAS.

A son of Rameses II. He was appointed governor of Memphis by his father. No particulars are preserved of his life, save that he died before Rameses II.

SHOPHETIM.

In the time of the Hebrew commonwealth the name of elders or judges. *See also* Suffetes.

SHORIN.

An Egyptian amulet, in the form of a lotus flower. It was often wrought in gold, inlaid with lapis lazuli or enamels.

S-HOTEP-EN-RA.

A son of Rameses II. of the XIXth dynasty.

S-HOTEP-HET.

An Egyptian gentleman, who lived probably in the XIIth dynasty. One of his sons was named Osirtesen-ankh, after the reigning monarch of that name.

SHTAM.

An Egyptian amulet in the form of a ring, cartouch, or signet. It was an emblem of the solar orbit.

SHU. "Light."

In Egyptian mythology the deity of light. He was sometimes called Sos. *See also—*

SHU.

One of the mystical deities of the Ritual of the Dead. He was one of the children of Ra, and the consort of Tefnut, which see.

SHUDAMI.

An Elamite deity, of whom nothing is known.

SHUI.

An Egyptian architect, whose funereal stele, with that of his companion Har, is in the British Museum.

SHUI.

An Egyptian generic name denoting weeds or water-flowers.

SHUITES.

A Mesopotamian people, who paid tribute to Assurnazirpal, king of Assyria.

SHUMUD.

An Elamite deity, of whom nothing is known. These Elamitic deities are simply enumeratéd in the Assyrian annals as having been carried off by Assurbanipal, about B.C. 660.

SHUSHAN.

An Elamite capital city, on the river Ula, where Assurbanipal defeated the army of Tiumman, king of Elam, B.C. 645.

SI-AMEN.

A son of King Amenhotep I. of the XVIIIth dynasty.

SIANNU.

A city on the sea-coast of Palestine, which was conquered by Tiglath Pileser II.

SIAYUT.

The modern name of the city of Lycopolis of the Greek historians. It was raised to the rank of a petty Egyptian kingdom under Esarhaddon.

SIBAHE.

A petty Egyptian monarch, who is mentioned in the Assyrian inscriptions, and was at one time erroneously supposed to have been the same as Sabako. He assisted the Tyrians in their revolt against Shalmaneser IV., king of Assyria, and is now generally accepted as having been the So of Hebrew history.

SIBAHI.

The once supposed Assyrian form of the Egyptian royal name Shabatuk. *See* above.

SIBANIBA.

An eponym city of Assyria. It supported Assurdainpal in his revolt against his father, Shalmaneser II.

SI-BAST.

The surname of Osorkon II. of the XXIInd dynasty.

SIBIT-TI-BAHALI.

A Syrian prince, and king of Gubal. He was conquered by Tiglath Pileser II. after the battle of Kummuha.

SIBKHINIS.

An Assyrian city, which revolted to Assurdan, and was reconquered by Samas-Rimmon or Samsi-Vul IV.

SIBRI.

A king of Babylonia, whose date is uncertain. He is only known from an inscription of Assurnazirpal.

SICTACHOTES.

A fortress in Nisæa, a district of Media, where Gomates the rebel was slain by Darius Hystaspes.

SIDIRPARNA.

A Median chief or king of the country of Patisarra. His district was annexed and himself brought captive to Nineveh by Esarhaddon, king of Assyria.

SIDU-ERIS.

The governor of Rezeph in the reign of Shalmaneser III. He was eponym of the year 775, the chief event in which was an expedition to Erini.

SIDU-ERIS.

The governor of Rezeph in the reign of Vulnirari III., and eponym of the year B.C. 804, the chief event in which was an expedition to Bahili. He was probably the same as the preceding.

SI-EN-EA.

A priestess of Amen Ra. Her name can also be read Sabo-en-ea. Her funereal statue is in the Leyden Museum.

SIGE.

In Greco-Babylonian mythology the primitive substance of the universe, from which the gods were created. The name of Sige is derived from the Accadian Zicu or Ziggara, "The Heaven."

SIGILA.

A Mesopotamian prince who was brought captive to Tiglath Pileser II.

SI-HATHOR.

A son of a King Nefer-hotep of the XIIIth dynasty.

SIHIME.

An Assyrian town. Its place is not known.

SIHR.

The art of magic as practised among the ancient Arabians.

SIHUA.

A town of Minni or Ararat, which was destroyed by Assurbanipal after the defeat of Ahsera.

SIKSHA.

An ancient Hindu treatise dealing chiefly with the true pronunciation of the words in the sacred Vedas.

SILAGARA.

A deity of the Susians, of whom nothing is known.

SILANI.

The father of Nabu-u-sabsi, the last, or last but one, of the independent kings of Babylonia of the old dynasty.

SILE.

In the Greek period a chief city of Lower Egypt. It was situated East of the Delta.

SILFRINTOPPR. " Silver Tress."

In Scandinavian mythology the name of one of the horses of the gods.

SILIBTA. *Or* SILIPTU.

An Elamite city which was destroyed by Sennacherib.

SILIK-MU-LU-KHI. *Or* SILIK-MU-LU-DUG.

The Accadian name of the deity Marduk or Amarud.

SILPA-VEDA.

An ancient commentary on the Hindu Atharva-veda, dealing chiefly with the science of mechanics. It is sometimes called the Sthapatya-veda.

SILSI.

A prophet priest of the temple of Pthah in the time of the Second Empire.

SILSILIS.

A town on the Upper Nile, on the rocks near which are the remains of a temple which was erected by Horus of the XVIIIth dynasty. It is now called Gebel, " Rock."

SILTHAN.

A title applied by the Assyrians to Sibahe, king of Egypt, whom they regarded as not entitled to the usual style of Pharaoh. It is the origin of the modern name Sultan. (Lenormant.)

SIMBURU.

An Elamite chief who deserted the cause of Tiumman, king of Elam, just before the battle of Shushan.

SIMDAN. " The Powerful."

A Himyaritic deity, a form of the god Il.

SIMISI.

A mountain district North of Assyria, which was conquered by Shalmaneser II.

SIM-MA-SIHU.

An early king of Babylonia, of whom nothing is known, save that he certainly reigned more than twelve years, as that date occurs on a sale tablet bearing his name.

SI-MOUTH.

A priest of Osiris, whose monument is in the Leyden Museum. His wife was named Tohem-sou-eits. The period when he lived is uncertain.

SIMTI-SIL-HAK.

An early Babylonian king of Elamitic origin. He was the father of Kudur-mabuk. Nothing else is known respecting him.

SIMU.

An Assyrian city which revolted to Assurdan, and was reconquered by Samas-Rimmon or Samsi-Vul IV.

SI-MUNTU. *Or* SA-MENTU.

A son of Rameses II. of the XIXth dynasty.

SIMYÁRA.

A Syrian town which was conquered by Thothmes III.

SIN.

The Moon-god. He was the father of the younger Ishtar. He was the favourite deity of the Cushite kings of the early Babylonians, and the principal object of worship in the city of Ur. In the later periods of Assyrian mythology he became a divinity of only secondary importance. His titles were " Lord of Crowns," " Maker of Brightness," and " Lord of the City of Ur."

SIN.

A Sabæan deity. The analogue of the Chaldean divinity of the same name.

SIN-AHI-IRI-BA.

An early king of Assyria, of whom next to nothing is known.

SIN-BALADAN.

An early Babylonian monarch who ruled at Ur.

SI-NEN-UER.

A mythical or divine prehistoric king of Egypt.

SINER.

In Scandinavian mythology the name of one of the horses of the gods.

SIN-GASIT.

An early Babylonian king who reigned at Urukh. He was the son of Queen Belatsunat. He built there a temple of the goddess Anunit, and a palace for himself.

SINGURIAI.

A country which was rendered tributary by Samas-Rimmon II. or III., king of Assyria.

Sin-idinna.

An early Babylonian king. He reigned at Larsa, where he dug a river or canal called Kibigana for the improvement of the country, and erected several temples to the gods Samas and Ur, that of the former containing a golden throne. The use of dated sale and loan tablets commences from his reign.

Sin-inun.

An early Babylonian monarch who reigned at Ur.

Sin-mat-ikali.

The executioner, or one of the executioners, of the palace of Esarhaddon.

Sinna.

The most ancient capital of the Sinites of Phenicia. It was afterwards deserted for Gebal, which see.

Sin-sada.

Another form of the Assyrian royal name Sin-gasit, which see.

Sin-said. "Sin is his Lord."

A very early Babylonian king; possibly the same as Abel-sin or Iribasin. He ruled at Erech, where he executed many important works.

Sin-salim-anni.

The governor of Rezeph, in the reign of Assur-nirari II. He was eponym of the year B.C. 747, in which year there was "peace in the land."

Sin-taggil.

The Tukulu of Tiglath Pileser II. He was eponym of the year B.C. 739, in which year took place an expedition to Ulluba, and the city of Birtu was built.

Sinukta.

A district in Asia Minor, which was conquered by Sargon II.

Siofn.

In Scandinavian mythology the goddess of affection, tenderness, and sympathy.

Siotio.

An Egyptian lady, the granddaughter of Naouscheri. Her sarcophagus is in the Leyden Museum.

Siout.   Or Siayut.

The modern name for the city and nome in Upper Egypt which was called by the Greeks Lycopolis Magna, which see.

Sioutmoutf.

Another form of the name of the god Taut-mutf, one of the four genii of Amenti.

SIPHINIS.

An Assyrian city which supported Assurdan in his revolt against his father, Shalmaneser II.

SIPNA.

An Etruscan female divinity, who was an attendant of Alpanu, and was represented carrying a mirror in her hand.

SIPPARA.

A Chaldean city, the Heliopolis of the Greeks, now called Sufeira.

SIPTHAH.   *Or* MER-EN-PTHAH II.

An usurping king of Egypt, in the XIXth dynasty. He was probably the son of Amenmes, a prince of the royal family of Rameses II. He ascended the throne in a period of popular confusion, and for a time reigned jointly with Seti II., the legitimate heir of the previous monarch, Merenpthah I. He afterwards married a daughter of Merenpthah, the princess Tauser, and admitted her to the sovereignty, through the influence of Bai the chancellor, whose power was acknowledged over the country. The length of his reign is not known ; and after his death he was treated as an usurper, and his tomb opened, and its sculptures defaced, and appropriated to himself by his successor, Seti-nekht. Sipthah was called also Menepthah or Mer-en-pthah II., and must not be confounded with his predecessor, Seti Menepthah II.

SIRASMI.

A king of the Babarurai, who paid tribute to Samas-Rimmon or Samsi-Vul III., king of Assyria.

SIRASU.

A king of the Singuriai, who paid tribute to Samas-Rimmon or Samsi-Vul, king of Assyria.

SIRIUS.

The common name of the dog-star. One of the chief objects of Egyptian astrology. It was called also Sothis, which see.

SI-SEBEK.

A priest of Pthah. The period when he lived is unknown.

SISHESH.

The Egyptian name of the sistrum, or shaking-rod, used chiefly in the worship of Isis and Hathor.

SISICRES.

The father of the rebel Martius, who claimed to have been Omanes, king of Susiana. *See* Martius.

SISIT.

The rendering which was at one time adopted of the Cuneiform characters of the Chaldean name Adra-hasis, which see.

SISTRUM.

A peculiar instrument in the shape of a loop crossed with loose bars ; it was almost always made of brass, and had generally the figure of a cat on the top and the head of the goddess Hathor on the handle. It was chiefly used by the priestesses of Isis, and was shaken in token of joy. At Egyptian funerals it was customary to deposit little terra cotta sistrums, which were broken in testimony of affliction.

SISUTHRUS. *Or* XISUTHRUS.

In Grecian mythology the hero of the Flood. His name has been supposed to have been Accadian, and to have meant Susru, " The Founder." (Sayce.)

SIT-AAH.

An unidentified Egyptian name of a royal lady.

SIT-AMEN.

A daughter of Amenhotep III. of the XVIIIth dynasty.

SITAMRAT.

A mountainous country on the West of the Upper Euphrates, where Ahuni, king of Lahlahte, was finally conquered by Shalmaneser II., after a series of conflicts extending over four years.

SITIRIBEU.

A royal lady or consort in the reign of Aahmes I. of the XVIIIth dynasty.

SITIUKI.

The Accadian name for a city or district, whose site is not known.

SIT-KA-MAS.

A royal pallacist in the reign of Amenhotep I. of the XVIIIth dynasty.

SITON. " Bread Corn."

A name which was given by the Greco-Phenician historians to the deity Dagon or Dakan, as the discoverer of the art of making bread.

SITRA.

A wife of one of the last kings of the XXth dynasty.

SITRA.

The mother of one of the last kings of the XXth dynasty.

SITRAPHERNES.

The Persian form of the royal name which was written by the Assyrians Sidirpana, which see.

SITRATACHMES.

A Median officer, who revolted against Darius Hystaspes, claiming himself to have been one of the blood royal of Cyaxares. He was defeated and taken prisoner by Camaspates, the general of Darius, who cut off his nose, lips, and ears, and then sent him to his master, who chained him to the door of his palace. *See also* Phraortes.

SIVA.

In Hindu mythology a form of the abstract Deity Brahma as the destroyer and reproducer of life. He forms the third in the great Hindu triad, and his representations are horribly obscene.

SIVANU. *Or* SIVAN.

The third month of the Assyrians. Its Accadian name was Munga, "Of Bricks," or Kas, "The Twins." It was sacred to the Moon-god Sin, and answered roughly to our May.

SIZANA.

A Syrian kingdom, which was one of the great Palestinian confederacy against Shalmaneser II.

SKEJDBRIMER.

In Scandinavian mythology the name of one of the horses of the gods.

SKHAI.

An Egyptian name for a clerk or scribe. *See* An.

S-KHEM-KA.

An early Egyptian nobleman, who was "Chief of the Writers of the Fields" of King Suten-rekh-ata of the Vth dynasty. He was called also Se-khemka.

SKINFAXI.

In Scandinavian mythology the horse of the goddess Dag or Day, whose mane lit up the heavens and the earth.

SKÖLL.

In Scandinavian mythology the name of the wolf which caused eclipses by pursuing and temporarily catching the sun. He was the son of the giantess Jarnwidr.

SKULD.

In Scandinavian mythology the last of the three deities of fate or Nornes. *See* Urd.

SLEIPNUR.

In Scandinavian mythology the name of the horse of Wodin. It had eight legs, four of which rested alternately to allow of its continuing in constant action.

SLEPARIS.

An Etruscan female divinity, who on a mirror in the Vatican was represented as being clothed in a mantle and listening to Faün.

SLIDHR.

In Scandinavian mythology one of the thirty-two filthy streams of Hell.

SMA.   "Smiter."

A mystical pool near the celestial Nile, which is figured in the vignette to the CXth chapter of the Ritual of the Dead.

SMA-EM-NEKHT-EF.

The name of the favourite lion of Rameses II. The animal appears to have attended his master in his battles, and to have accompanied him in his state processions.

SMELIEL.

In Cabalistic mythology the spirit of the sun.

SMEN.

An Egyptian captain in the Syrian wars of Thothmes IV. He was also the bearer of the royal parasol. His mother's name was Naa, and that of his wife Nes-ra.

SMEN.

A town in the Memphite nome which was sacred to the god Sebek.

SMENDES.

According to the Greek lists a king of Tanis of the XXIst dynasty. He has not yet been certainly identified, unless he be the Sementu-Meramen, whose name occurs on a brazen sphynx in the Louvre Collection.

SMENTO.

A son of Anhur-mes, a priest of the deity Anhur in the XVIIIth dynasty. His wife's name was En-nub.

SMERDIS I.

A king of Persia who was set up by the Magi on the death of Cambyses, B.C. 521. He was assassinated after a brief reign of seven months.

SMERDIS II.   (The Second False One.)

One of the many impostors who, claiming descent from Cyrus, raised a revolt against Darius Hystaspes. *See* Vahyazdata.

SMER.   *Sometimes written* SMER-UA.

An honorific Egyptian title. The sense is unknown, but it is generally rendered "High Courtier" or "Friend of the Prince." It was used chiefly in the Saite period. *See also* Suten-rekh.

Smot.

An uncertain Egyptian deity who was represented as a king wearing the solar disk upon the lunar horns.   (Wilkinson.)

S-nefer-ka.

An early Egyptian king who is named on the Tablet of Abydos.

S-nefru.

The last or last king but one, of the IIIrd Egyptian dynasty.   He conquered the nomadic tribes of the Anu of Arabia Petrea, and discovered the turquoise mines in the Peninsula of Mount Sinai.   He reigned thirty years, and was the Sephoris of the Greeks.

S-nekht-en-amen.

A son of Rameses II. of the XIXth dynasty.

Snenath.

An Etruscan guardian spirit, who, according to Taylor, presides over the health.

Snotra.

In Scandinavian mythology the goddess of cleanliness.

So.

The name by which Shabaka or Sibahe, king of Egypt, is mentioned in Hebrew history.

Socris.

A Persian officer, the father of Otanes, an officer and friend of Darius Hystaspes.

Sofh.

The Egyptian goddess of writing.   She was generally represented as wearing an expanded Doum palm leaf on her head beneath two inverted cow horns.   She was chiefly adored at Memphis in the IVth dynasty.

Sohail.

The star Canopus adored as a divinity by the people of Sabæa.

Sokari.

A deity of Lower Egypt.   He was a compound form of the god Pthah of Memphis.   *See* Pthah-Sokari-Osiris *and* Tanen, *or* Tanentu.

Sokari.

Among the ancient Egyptians the festival of the fifteenth day of the month.

Sol.

The Scandinavian name of the sun, which was believed to have been a feminine deity.

SOMA.

In Hindu mythology an intoxicating liquor, the fermented juice of the stem and leaves of the *Asclepias acida*. It was indispensable in Vedic sacrifices, and was ultimately elevated to the rank of a deity as a form of the god Agni.

SON.

The prince royal of Ethiopia under Thothmes II. of the XVIIIth dynasty.

SONI-VAPHRA.

The name given by some Egyptologists to the queen of Amasis II., the daughter of Psametik II.

SOPHIEL.

In Cabalistic mythology the intelligence of the planet Jupiter.

SORIS.

The Grecian name of an Egyptian king of Memphis, who is supposed by some authors to have been Snefru or Senefru.

SOS.

Another form of the name of Shu, the Egyptian deity of solar light.

SOSARMON.

A king of the Medes. He succeeded Mandauces, and reigned thirty years. (Ctesias.)

SOSCHE.

The surname of a scribe of Amen Ra, named Tahut-nefer, which see.

SOSS.

An Assyrian measure of length, composed of sixty *Ribu*, which see.

SOTB.

The modern name of the city and nome in Upper Egypt, called by the Greeks Hypselos.

SOTEMEIT.

An Egyptian lady, the wife of Fai-hor-ouser, and mother of Ratoker, a prefect of the palace in the period of the XXVIth dynasty.

SOTEMHEIT.

The mother of Sobek-em-isis, a royal lady of the XIIIth dynasty.

SOTEP-ET-EN-RA.

A daughter of Amenhotep IV. of the XVIIIth dynasty.

SOTER. " Saviour."

An archon of Thebes in the time of the Emperor Trajan, A.D. 98. His sarcophagus is in the British Museum. His wife was named Cleopatra; she was the daughter of Ammonius.

SOTER.

The son of Cornelius, the husband of the lady Cleopatra Candace, and the father of the lady Sensaos.

SOTHIC CYCLE.

" The beginning of the reign of Antoninus Pius, or A.D. 138, was remarkable as being the end of the Sothic period of 1460 years. The moveable new year's day of the calendar had come round to the place in the natural year from which it first began to move. In the reign of Menophres (Thothmes III. ?) B.C. 1321, it had come round to the day when the dog-star, Sothis, rose heliacally. If the years had been counted from the beginning of this great year, there could have been no doubt when it came to an end, as from the want of a leap year the new year's day must have been always moving one day in four years ; but no satisfactory reckoning of the years had been kept, and as the end of the period was only known from observation, there was some little doubt about the exact year. Indeed, among the Greek astronomers Dosistheus said the dog-star rises heliacally twenty-three days after Midsummer, Meton twenty-eight days, and Euctemon thirty-one days ; thus they left a doubt of thirty-two years as to when the period should end, but the statesmen placed it in the first year of the reign of Antoninus Pius. This end of the Sothic period was called the return of the Phœnix, and had been looked forward to by the Egyptians for many years, and is well marked on the coins of this reign, which for the first eight years teem with astronomy. This would correspond with the year of Rome 800, but in A.U.C. 1100, or A.D. 347, the Emperor Constantius marked on his coins the return of the Phœnix for that year also." (Sharpe.) The Sothic and Phœnix Cycles are now hopelessly confounded, although originally distinct. According to some authors the Phœnix was a smaller and a totally different stellar cycle.

SOTHIS. *Or* SEPET, " Triangle."

The Grecian name of the dog-star Sirius, which was consecrated to the goddess Isis. " The heliacal rising of this star marked the commencement of the Egyptian civil year, and in their astronomy Sothis was regarded as the queen of thirty-six constellations, which presided successively over the thirty-six decades of the year. The Sothic Cycle was one of the most important eras in Egyptian chronology, and its recurrence has been recorded in several temples. A portion of that of Denderah was consecrated to celebrating the rising of this star, which was also worshipped at Assuan at the temple of Isis Sothis, from which the first meridian was taken. The heliacal rising of Sothis is recorded in the temple of Medinet Habu as taking place in the twelfth year of Rameses III., thus giving by astronomical calculation the year 1311 for that monarch's accession, the first really fixed point in Egyptian history." (Pierret.) That Sothis is the dog-star is proved by the Canopus inscription, but it was known to be so long before. " My own impression is that the Egyptians confounded the dog-star with the planets, Sothis being in the astronomical ceilings and other places represented in a boat like the planets. The double character of Sothis has probably induced certain authors to regard her as the planet Venus. What the

Bennu or phœnix was appears uncertain. It is seen in the zodiacal ceilings." (Birch.) *See* Isis, Bennu, *and* Phœnix.

SOUBAN.

An uncertain Egyptian goddess, the representative of the South land or Ethiopia. The reading of her name is doubtful. She was generally represented under the form of the vulture.

SOUNIRO.

An overseer of the archers of an unnamed Egyptian king. His statue is in the Leyden Museum. Period uncertain.

SOUPHIS.

According to the Greek lists a king of the IIIrd Egyptian dynasty. He reigned sixteen years.

SPENTA-ARMAITI. "Holy Earth."

In Zendic mythology the fourth of the heavenly Amshaspands, which see.

SPENTA-MAGNIUS. "The Holy Spirit."

The Zendic name of the Spirit of Ahuramazda, by whose agency the world was created. It was also called his son.

SPEOS-ARTEMIDOS.

The ancient name of the town now called Beni-Hassan, where many of the great officers of the earlier Egyptian dynasties were buried, and where a temple was erected to the goddess Sekhet by Seti I.

SPHYNX.

A large statue of a seated human-headed lion, 140 feet long and proportionately high, wrought out of the solid rock, in front of the Pyramid of Cheops in Egypt, to which it was long anterior. Originally it was surmounted by a crown, which was formed of a separate block of stone. This statue was intended to represent the king under the form of the Egyptian deity Ra Harmachis. Long avenues of sphynxes, both human and ram-headed, formed the entrances to some of the chief of the Theban temples at Karnak and Luxor. The Egyptian name of this singular creature was Sesheps.

SPONDISTS.

In Egyptian mythology certain ladies who were attached to the temples of the Egyptian deities, and chiefly of that of Amen Ra. They took rank below that of the priestesses proper.

SPOT.

An uncertain Egyptian deity, who was represented as a king, wearing the solar disk only. (Wilkinson.)

SPURKALIA.

The annual festival of the Scandinavian goddess Spurke, which see.

SPURKE.

In Scandinavian mythology the goddess of the month of February, in whose honour was held an annual festival called Spurkalia, analogous to the Februalia of the Romans.

SSA.

The modern name of the city and nome in Lower Egypt which was called by the Egyptians Sai-res.

STASANOR.

A prince of Soli. He followed Alexander the Great into Asia, and was a son or brother of the king Stasicrates, or Pasicrates.

STASIAGORAS.

A king either of Kition or Idalion, in the Island of Kypros (Cyprus), about the fourth century B.C. No particulars are known concerning him.

STASIAS.

A king of Soli, in the Island of Kypros. He was the father of Stasicrates, who also succeeded him on the throne.

STASICRATES.

The king of Soli, and son of Stasias. He was probably the same as Pasicrates, king of Soli, who took part in the festivities of Alexander the Great after his return from Egypt.

STASIOIKOS.

A king of the town of Marium, in the Island of Kypros (Cyprus). He was the last king of the place, and was conquered by Ptolemy Soter.

STAU.

A prince of Kush, in the reign of Rameses II. of the XIXth dynasty.

STELE, SEPULCHRAL.

" The sepulchral stele were generally placed at the bottom of the principal chamber of the tombs of the old dynasties. They are square, and often of colossal proportions, with large Hieroglyphs, sometimes in bas-relief, and spaced out. The representations are the façade of a building or tomb. At the time of the VIth dynasty they still have a degree of Archaism. From the earliest period till the XIIth dynasty these tablets are dedicated to Anup or Anubis, not Osiris, whose name is rarely found. Anubis is invoked as the god who presided over the funereal chapel and the embalming of the dead. The formula of dedication is short and elliptical, the usual expression "to give" is omitted, as also that of the gift ; the name of Osiris is not found before that of the deceased, or the expression "justified" after the name. In the formula at this time a kind of abridgment of the calendar is often introduced, as a mention of the festivals of the beginning of the year, the new year, Thoth, that of the greater and lesser heat, the monthly and half-monthly. The numerous titles of the offices held by the deceased are given in detail. The tablets continued rude until the time of the XIth dynasty, when the mention of the festival of the heliacal rising of Sothis or the dog-star is added to that of the festival already mentioned. Under the XIIth dynasty the tablets change in shape and texts ; most of them being rounded at the top and forming the *hutu* of the texts. The upper part of the tablet has often the winged disk, the *Hut* or *Teb-hut*. The dates of the years of the monarchs under whom the deceased was buried appear. The scenes represented are the acts of sepulchral homage or ancestral worship made by the children or other relatives of the dead to himself and his wife, the tables before them being loaded with offerings, amongst which appear the head and haunch of a calf, and other joints of the same animal, ducks, or geese, circular and oval loaves or cakes of bread, gourds, onions, and papyrus or lotus flowers, while jars of wine or beer of conical shape are seen placed under the tables. The name of the god Anubis, which is so prominent in the tablets of Memphis, either disappears or becomes secondary to that of Osiris, and the dedication often contains the names of other deities, as the frog-headed goddess Haka, the ram-headed god Khnum, and others ; but no god is represented on the tablets. The texts themselves also differ, as in addition to the expressions of the IVth dynasty, the verb " to give," omitted at that time, as also the subject of the gift, is introduced into the text, the deceased is called "justified," but the name of Osiris does not precede his. His merits are often told in a verbose style, to which is sometimes added the public works in which he was engaged. The contents of these texts often contain curious historical and other information, throwing much light on the mythology and ethics of the Egyptians. Under the XVIIIth dynasty the tablets changed again, and the scenes of ancestral or sepulchral worship became subordinate. The principal scene of the tablet, placed at the upper part, represents the deceased, sometimes attended by his wife, sister, son, or other member of the family, standing or kneeling in adoration to the solar boat, or deities, or Osiris, accompanied by Isis, Nephthys, Anubis, Horus, and other deities who presided over embalming and the future state, before whom is placed a table or altar of offerings. A second division generally has the scenes of family worship, while in the accompanying text the adorations to the deities occupy the most important portion ; and the merits of the deceased, or allusions to his public works, are only slightly mentioned. At the time of the XIXth dynasty the name of Osiris appears first placed before the name of the deceased, which the title of "justified," or *makheru*, always follows. These tablets were in general use during the XVIIIth and XIXth dynasties, but became rarer under the XXth, and exceedingly rare at the period of the XXVIth dynasty, and disappear after that time, at which they are much rarer than during the preceding periods. They reappear, however, again under the Ptolemies, and besides the usual formula of dedication, often contain interesting notices relative to the functions and offices discharged by the deceased, and family details. They are at this period often accompanied by inscriptions in the cursive handwriting, the so-called Demotic, or Enchorial. Under the Romans the art and inscriptions of the tablets change. The subjects are in bas-relief, and the deities represented in the hybrid types prevalent at the epoch. The inscriptions are in Greek, and follow the usual formulas used at that period, the older dedications to the gods being omitted, only the name of the deceased and date of his death being retained, a valedictory address being substituted. The Coptic sepulchral tablets made after the introduction of Christianity into Egypt and at a late period, and those in Cufic, the tombstones of the Mohammedan conquerors of Egypt, follow also the forms of their respective nationalities, all trace of the old representations and formulas having been obliterated or superseded." (Birch's *Guide to the British Museum, Vestibule.*)

STEPHINATES.

An Egyptian king of the XXVth dynasty. His name is only found in the Greek lists.

STHAPATYA-VEDA.

Another name of the Hindu treatise on mechanics, more generally called the Silpa-veda, which see.

STRUCHATES.

The Greek form of the name of the Median caste Tchatrauvat, which see.

SUA.

Another form of the Egyptian royal name Shabaka, which see.

SUA.

A king of the Nanikirians,(?) who paid tribute to Samas-Rimmon or Samsi-Vul III., king of Assyria.

SUANDAHAL.

One of the principal cities of Minni. The inhabitants urged their king Iranzu to revolt against Sargon II., who soon conquered them, and carried off the inhabitants into slavery.

SUBARTI.

A district in Mesopotamia which was subject to the Assyrians, who were there conquered by the Hittites, who were themselves again subjugated by Tiglath Pileser I., who restored the bounds of the Assyrian dominions, and expelled and subdued the Hittites.

SUBARTI.

An early Babylonian(?) town, which was destroyed by Sargina or Sargon I.

SUBURGILLU.

A city which was conquered for Tiglath Pileser II. by the governor of Nahiri, in Assyria.

SUCCOTH-BENOTH.

The name by which the Assyrian goddess Zirrat Banit is mentioned in Hebrew history.

SUDRAS.

The lowest actual caste in the Hindu system. They were said to have been created from the soles of the feet of Brahma.

SUDRI. "South."

In Scandinavian mythology one of the four horns which support the vault of heaven. *See* Austri.

SUDUNU.

A deity of the Susians, of whom nothing is known.

SUFEIRA.

The modern name of the ancient Chaldean city Sippara.

SUFFETES.

Among the Ethiopians and the Hebrews the name of the chief officer, who has been called generally "Judge." His duties partook of those of a magistrate and priest, and he was elected for life.

SUGHDHA. "Sogdiana."

In Zendic mythology the first resting-place of the Iranians after their departure from Aryanem Vaedjo, or the plateau of Pamir.

SUGI.

A district North of Assyria, which was conquered by Tiglath Pileser I.

SUGI.

In Chaldean astronomy one of the seven stars of the week.

SUGI.

In Chaldean astronomy also one of the twelve stars of the West. (Sayce.)

SUHI.

A kingdom in Chaldea, which was conquered by Assurnazirpal, king of Assyria.

SUKHATARA.

The true name of the Arabian island called by the moderns Socotra.

SUKLU.

An Assyrian measure of length, sixty of which made one *suklu rabtu*, or cubit, equal to twenty inches.

SUKUL-NA. "Seizer of Seed."

The Accadian name of the month Duzu, which see.

SUKULU-RABU. "Great Attendant."

An Assyrian chief officer of state in personal attendance on the king.

SULPA-UDDU. "The Messenger of the Rising Sun."

The name of the deity Marduk as the planet Mercury in the month Nisan.

SULUM.   "Rest."

The name of the Assyrian Sabbaths, which were held on the seventh, fourteenth, twenty-first, and twenty-eighth days of the moon's age. They were regulated by restrictions similar to those among the Hebrews.

SULUMAL.

The king of Milid, one of the Northern states of Syria. He and other princes combined against Tiglath Pileser II., who utterly defeated them.

SUMA.

A king of the country of the Cinucai or Kinuka, who paid tribute to Samas-Rimmon or Samsi-Vul III., king of Assyria.

SUMAI.

An early Chaldean astronomer, some observations by whom are preserved in the Cuneiform inscriptions.

SUMIRIANS.

The ethnological name for the peoples inhabiting the countries North of Chaldea.

SUMUDU.

A deity of the Susians, of whom nothing is known.

SUNA.

A town on the banks of the Khabour which was conquered by Assur-nazir-pal.

SUNBA.

A district near Lake Van which was plundered by Mutariz-assur, or Mulis-assur, the Rabsaki of Samsi-Vul or Samas-Rimmon III. This war was the second which took place in the reign of Samsi-Vul, and it is one of the first instances of a chief officer being allowed to represent the monarch, and his campaign being registered in the royal name.

SUNGUR-SARA.

A deity of the Susians of whom nothing is known.

SUPARRUN.

A people in the mountains of Mesopotamia who were subdued by Assur-ris-ilim, king of Assyria.

SUPHIS.   *Or* SOUPHIS.

According to the Greek lists the successor of Soris, king of Memphis. He has not yet been certainly identified.

SUPOT.

The son of Sheshanka I. of the XXIInd dynasty.

SUPTI.

A form of the god Horus, represented as a mummied hawk, as adored in Arabia and the twentiéth or Arabian nome of Lower Egypt. His title was " Lord of the East."

SURAPPI.

A small river of Babylonia, from which the ancient city of Surippak was named.

SURDIRA.

A small kingdom East of Assyria, which was conquered by Dayan-assur, the Tartan of Shalmaneser II.

SURGARDI.

A district near Persia, which was conquered by Sargon II., and added to the kingdom of Assyria.

SURHET-HET-U.

A granddaughter of King Sebekhotep II. of the XIIIth dynasty.

SURHET-HET-U.

The mother of King Sebekhotep II. of the XIIIth dynasty.

SURHET-HET-U-FENT.

A daughter of King Sebekhotep II. of the XIIIth dynasty.

SURIA.

A people in the mountains of Mesopotamia who were subdued by Assur-ris-ilim, king of Assyria.

SURIPPAK.

The birthplace of Adrahasis, the Chaldean hero of the Deluge. The town has been identified with the Larsa of the Assyrians.

SURRILA.

An usurper whom the people of Patina on the Orontes raised to the throne after they had deposed and slain their king Laburna. Dayan-assur, the Tartan of Shalmaneser II., invaded Patina to avenge the death of Luburna, and Surrila committed suicide to save himself from a worse death. He was succeeded by Sasi, the son of Matuzza, who paid a heavy tribute to Shalmaneser II., who set him upon the throne.

SURU.

The capital city of the kingdom of Suhi, which was conquered by the Assyrians about B.C. 880.

SURYA.

The Vedic title of the Supreme deity as symbolised by his attribute the sun. The Helios of the Greeks, and Shemesh and Shamsu of the Hebrews and Assyrians.

Susiana.

The Greek name of the province called Khapisti by the Chaldeans.

Susinak.

A divinity of the Susians which was not allowed to be seen. Its statue was carried off by Assurbanipal, king of Assyria.

Sut.

The name of the guardian of the first of the seven halls of Osiris.

Sutekh.

The local deity of the Hykshos. He is generally accepted as having been another form of the name of the Semitic deity Set, which see.

Sutekh of Khirabu.

A local name of the Hittite deity Sutekh, adored at that town as a separate divinity. *See* Ishtar.

Sutekh of Khisasap.

A local name of the Hittite deity Sutekh, adored at that town as a separate divinity. *See* Ishtar.

Sutekh of Pairaka.

A local name of the Hittite deity Sutekh, adored at that town as a separate divinity. *See* Ishtar.

Sutekh of Sarapaina.

A local name of the Hittite deity Sutekh, adored at that town as a separate divinity. *See* Ishtar.

Sutekh of Sarasu.

A local name of the Hittite deity Sutekh, adored at that town as a separate divinity. *See* Ishtar.

Sutekh of Taaranta.

A local name of the Hittite deity Sutekh, adored at that town as a separate divinity. *See* Ishtar.

Sutenha.   " Royal House."

An unidentified Egyptian city.

Suten-hem-he.

A great chief in the court of Osirtasen I. of the XIIth dynasty.

Suten-hi.

The father of Nechtanebos of the XXXth dynasty.

Suten-khen.

A name of the district of Bubastis which occurs in the Egyptian Ritual of the Dead.

SUTEN-KHEN.

An early Egyptian name of the town called by the Greeks Herakleopolis, which see.

SUTEN-KHENN.

One of the mystical countries in the Egyptian Ritual. It was the place of the god Shu.

SUTEN-RA-ANKH.

An early unarranged Egyptian king, whose name occurs on a scarabeus in the Leyden Museum.

SUTEN-REKH.

An Egyptian title variously rendered "Grandson of the King," "Father of the King," and "Personal Friend of the King," which last is now the generally accepted rendering.

SUTEN-REKH-ATA.

An early Egyptian king of the Vth dynasty.

SUTENS . . . .

A granddaughter of Tetet, an early Egyptian king. This name is imperfect.

SUTI.

A people who were conquered by Budil, a very early king of Assyria.

SUTRUK-NANKHUNDI.

A famous king of Elam. He was the son of Khalludus I. and king of Elam. He assisted Merodach-Baladan against Sargon, but was defeated and driven to the mountains, B.C. 710. In B.C. 707, he was again defeated at Marubisti, by the seven generals of Sargon and their ally, Ispabara of Ellipi; but he afterwards took his revenge upon Assyria. He is called Sutruk-Nakhkunte on the Susian bricks.

SUTUR-CIT.

An early king of Amardia. He was the son of Khanni-Cit, and executed an inscription at Malamir in honour of the deities Dipti and Turutur.

SUVAN.

An Egyptian goddess worshipped at Ten. She was probably the same as Souban, which see.

SUZUB.

The son of Gahul, a chief of the Kaldai, who, after the emigration of Merodach-Baladan to Nagitu, raised revolt in Southern Babylonia, but was routed by Sennacherib, at Bit-Tutu, in B.C. 700. In B.C. 697, with the help of the Elamites, he proclaimed himself king of Babylon, but was again defeated and sent bound to Nineveh, Erech being sacked.

Suzub soon escaped, and about B.C. 692 was assisted by the Elamites to enter Babylon and re-ascend the throne. He purchased the aid of Umman-minaro of Elam, with the treasures of the temples of Bel, Nebo, and Nergal; but the confederates were totally routed in the great battle of Khalule, and in the following year Babylon was taken by storm and razed. Suzub died soon afterwards, through a fall from his horse.

SWASUDHR.

In Scandinavian mythology the name of the father of the summer.

SYENE.

The Greek name of the town now called Essouan, the extreme frontier town on the South of Egypt towards Ethiopia, whence the red granite used in the temples of Karnak was obtained.

SYLOSON.

A king of Samos. *See* Æaces.

SYN.

In Scandinavian mythology the goddess who guarded the thresholds of houses from evil persons.

SYNODONTIS-SCHAL.

A fresh-water fish which was worshipped by the Egyptians as the emblem of the goddess Nahemua, or Hathor.

T.

TA.

An amulet in the shape of the tie of a girdle. It was directed by the CLVIth chapter of the Ritual to be made of red jasper, and placed on the neck of the mummy. It was supposed to have the virtue of enrolling the dead amongst the servants of Osiris, by placing him under the protection of Isis, enabling him to pass the gates of Hades, and receive the food of the Aahlu or Elysium. The Tat or Nilometer was sometimes substituted instead of this amulet.

TA.

An unidentified stellar deity of the ancient Nabatheans.

TA.

The Egyptian name of a tie or ribbon which was sometimes offered to the gods. *See also* Ta, the amulet.

TAA.

A daughter of King Thothmes IV. of the XVIIIth dynasty.

TA-AMENT.

The wife of Uermu, the guardian of the magazines. *See* Uermu.

TA-APENHA.

An Egyptian lady, who was the wife of Psabenhor and the mother of Ahmes, chief of the soldiers under Darius, king of Persia and Egypt.

TA-APEP.

An Egyptian lady. Period unknown. The name occurs in the Leyden Collection.

TA-ARANTA.

A town of the Hittites, which was sacred to its local form of the deity Sutekh.

TAAU.

An Egyptian name of the town of Tyre.

TAAUT.

A Phenician divinity, to whom according to the Greeks was ascribed the sacred books of the law. He was the analogue of the Egyptian deity Thoth.

TAAUTH. " The Great Lady."

In Phenician mythology the feminine form or "reflection" of the Assyrian deity Ao. *See* Bilit-Taauth.

TA-BA-RET.

The wife of Hor, the scribe of the army of Amenhotep III., and the keeper of the house of Queen Taia.

TA-BAT.

A singer in the temple of Amen Ra, whose votive statuette is in the Louvre Museum.

TA-BE.

A governor of Ethiopia, or Kush, in the XIIIth dynasty.

TABEAL.

The father of Ashariah, the usurper claimant to the throne of Judah. *See* Ashariah.

TABITI. " Fire."

According to Herodotus the name of a Scythian goddess, answering to the Vesta of the Greeks.

TABLETS, PECTORAL.

Among the decorations of the mummies are frequently found many small pectorals of soft stone, having the figure of a Bennu or heron, the soul as the bird of Osiris, engraved like a mould upon them. These objects, which were at one time supposed to have been matrices for casting from, were certainly used in a religious sense, although we are not at present in a position to ascertain what. The Bennu, or the phœnix of the Greeks, rising from its ashes, was an emblem of the reproduction and regeneration of the soul ; and the tablet would seem to insure that the mummy upon which it was laid should arise to a new birth, and be destined to renew again its former existence. The same idea is also frequently expressed under another form on the sarcophagi, namely, Isis and her sister Nephthys impressing a seal upon the ground. (Birch.)

TAB-NITH.

King of Sidon and son of Eshmonazer I., and father of Eshmonazer II. Nothing else is known concerning him.

TAB-RIMMON.

The son of Rezon, king of Damascus. He raised the state from that of a petty kingdom to one of importance in Syria, and was succeeded by his son Benhadad I., the Benhadad of Hebrew history.

TABU.

The son of an Egyptian king, but of what king it is not known.

TA-BU-BU.

An Egyptian priestess of the goddess Bast, at Memphis. She is the courtesan and evil heroine in the ancient Egyptian romance of Setnau.

TABU-SAR-ASSUR.

The great Tukulu under Tiglath Pileser I. and Sargon II., kings of Assyria.

TABUYA.

A young Assyrian woman in the harem of Esarhaddon, whom the king of Assyria placed on the throne of Addumu, in Arabia, after he had deposed the queen of that country.

TABU-ZILLI-ZARA.

The prefect of Assur, under Tiglath Pileser I. and Sargon II.

TACHUS.

The Greek name of a king of Egypt, about the XXXth dynasty. By some conjectured to have been Nectanebo.

TA-EI.

An Egyptian lady, the wife of Nefer-heb-ef, which see.

TA-EI-OUIH-RA.

A priestess of Amen Ra. She was the daughter of Khons-mes, a male spondist of Amen, and the lady Tent-amen, who was also a priestess of the same divinity.

TA-EN-HANNU.

A peculiar form of ornamental bread used by the ancient Egyptians. It was moulded in the form of a phallus, and was sometimes offered to the gods.

TAF-NEKHT.

A priest of Osiris, in the thirty-fourth year of Darius Hystaspes.

TAF-NEKHT.

A petty Egyptian prince of the XXIInd dynasty. He incited the other chiefs of Egypt to rebel against Piankhi, king of Ethiopia, who then governed the land as suzerain. The revolution was rapidly quelled by Piankhi, and Tafnekht fled to the Isle of Cyprus, from whence he sent his submission to the conqueror.

TAF-NEKHT.

A petty Egyptian king of Sais. He is said to have been remarkable for his wisdom. He was succeeded by his son, Bak-en-ran-f, the only king of the XXIVth dynasty. He was the Tnephactes of the Greeks.

TAF-NEKHT.

The king of Bunu. He was one of the twenty petty kings of Egypt established by the Assyrians, by whom he was called Tap-nakh-ti.

TAF-NEKHTA.

An Egyptian lady, the mother of the great officer Nechtarhebi, which see.

TAGAB-LISHUR.

An Elamite city, called the city of the Nakindati. It was destroyed by Sennacherib.

TAGES.

According to Classical authors, the son of Genius and the grandson of Jupiter, who taught the Etruscans the science of augury and divination. He was discovered by a Tuscan ploughman in the form of a clod of earth. His name is not found in the inscriptions ; but he is represented on two gems as a boy, half ploughed up from the earth, teaching the Etruscan priests.

TAGGIL-ANA-BEL.

The governor of Nisibin in the reign of Sargon II. He was eponym of the year B.C. 715, in which expeditions to Minni, Asia Minor, and Arabia took place.

TA-HA.

The Egyptian name of a town in Palestine, near the Amorite country, where Rameses III. assembled his army prior to his great war against the Syrians, the Philistines, and the Greeks, who were simultaneously allied against him.

TA-HAI.

The Egyptian name of the town of Gaha.

TA-HAI.

A people inhabiting Northern Palestine, who were famous for their inlaid and enamelled metal work. They were rendered tributary to Egypt by Thothmes III.

TA-HAI.

The Egyptian name for the country of Northern Phenicia, which was conquered by Thothmes III.

TAHARKA. *Or* TAHRAKA, *or* TIRHAKA.

A king of Egypt of the XXVth dynasty. He succeeded Shabaka I., whose sister he married, and at the request of Hezekiah, king of Judah, invaded Palestine to repulse Sennacherib, king of Assyria. The news of his arrival caused that monarch to withdraw from Judea, whereupon a few years later Taharka incited Bahal, king of Tyre, also to revolt against Esarhaddon, the son and successor of Sennacherib, B.C. 672. The two kings were, however, defeated by the Assyrians, and in the twenty-third year of the reign of Taharka, Esarhaddon invaded and conquered all Egypt, parcelling the country out into an Icosarchy of twenty kings, and annexing it to Assyria. On Esarhaddon falling ill the king of Egypt again raised an army, and re-conquered Upper and

Lower Egypt as far as Memphis. A second time he was defeated by Assurbanipal, who now reigned as joint king with his father Esarhaddon. On the Assyrians quitting the kingdom, the Egyptians for a third time rose in insurrection under Taharka, but he was at last finally subdued by Assurbanipal selecting one of the minor kings of Egypt, Necho of Memphis, to govern the country as his viceroy. Upon the approach of Necho with the Assyrian army, Taharka retired to Napata, the capital of Nubia, where he died after a reign of twenty-six years, leaving the throne of Ethiopia to Rut-amen the son of Shabaka. Taharka repaired several temples, and built the colonnade which precedes the Hypostyle Hall of Columns at Karnak.

TA-HEMI.

A daughter of Rameses-Miamun of the XXth dynasty.

TA-HEN-KHAU. "Splendour of Diadems."

The surname of Horus I. of the XVIIIth dynasty.

TAHENNU.

The Egyptian name for the white people of the coast of the Mediterranean on the West of Egypt. They were subdued by Seti I.

TAHO.

A royal scribe and priest of Imhotep in the XXVIth dynasty. His father was named Pe-tep-munkh, and his mother Renpe-nofre. The name Taho is the same as the Teos or Tachos of the Greeks.

TAHO.

A priest and prophet of the deities Pthah and Amen Ra of Memphis, in the XXVIth dynasty. His father was named Pe-te-ha-ke, and his mother Ta-sche-ra-he.

TAHORT.

An Egyptian lady, the wife of Out-hor, and the mother of Horirem, which see.

TAH-RUMA.

The Egyptian name of the capital city of Rome.

TAHU.

The incense bearer of a king in the XVIIIth dynasty.

TAHUT-AA. "The Great Thoth."

An Egyptian official superintendent of the royal works, and a member of the royal council of ten. Period unknown.

TAHUTIA.

The true form of the name of the deity Thoth, which see

TAHUT-NEFER. "Good Thoth."

A scribe of the temple of Amen Ra in the XVIIIth dynasty. He married a lady named Benemba, and was surnamed Sosche.

TAHUT-NEFER.

An Egyptian officer, " The Chief of the House" of a princess of the XXIVth dynasty, but of what princess it is not known.

TAHUT-SEN-U.

An Egyptian lady, the wife of an officer named Osirtesen of the XIIth dynasty.

TAI.

An Egyptian lady, the mother of the treasurer Iuiu, which see.

TAIA. *Or* TAII.

A noble lady of an unknown Japhetic tribe, the daughter of a chief named Iuaa, and his wife Tuaa. She became the wife of Amenhotep III., king of Egypt, and the regent of the kingdom during the reign of her son Amenhotep IV. Taia exercised a powerful influence over both her husband and son, and forcibly introduced the worship of the solar disk under the name of Aten Ra in place of the deities of the national poly-theistic religion, changing the capital city from Thebes to Tel el Amarna, the better to effect her purpose. This led to a revolution, which probably cost the lives of both her son and herself, as is implied in the complete destruction of all her temples, and the erasure of her name from the monuments of Egypt. *See* Amenhotep III. *and* IV., *and* Khuenaten.

TAIA.

The daughter of Ua, the scribe of the cavalry of an Egyptian king of the XVIIIth dynasty.

TAIA.

A pallacist of Isis, and the wife of Un-nefer, high-priest of Osiris in the reign of Rameses II.

TAI-AF.

An Egyptian lady of the great house of Un-nefer, which see. She was also surnamed Nofre-ari.

TAINI.

A city in Egypt which was raised to the rank of a kingdom by the Assyrians under Esarhaddon.

TAIRIN.

The sister of Amenhotep I. of the XVIIth dynasty.

TAITI. *Or* DIDI.

One of five chiefs who incited the Libyans to revolt against Rameses III., who utterly defeated them.

TAIUTIT.

Another form of the name of the Egyptian boundary town Ti-ta-ta, which see.

TA-KA.

A priestess of Amen, and the mother of the royal butler Aia, which see.

TAKA.

The Egyptian name of a tree, which is supposed by some Egyptologists to have been the Yew (*Taxus*).

TA-KANS.   *Or* TO-KENS.

An Egyptian name of the kingdom of Nubia.

TAKA-RA-AR.

The Egyptian name of an uncertain Syrian city.

TAKARUT I.   *Or* TAKELOT.

A king of Egypt of the XXIInd dynasty.   He succeeded Uaserken or Osorkon I.   Nothing is recorded of his reign.   He was the Take-lothes of the Greeks, and was probably named after Tuklat (Tiglath Pileser), king of Assyria.

TAKARUT II.

A king of Egypt in the XXIInd dynasty.   He was the son of Prince Namrut, and married a lady named Karu-ma-ma.   He reigned more than fifteen years.

TAKELOTHES.   *Or* TAKELUT.

The Greek form of the Egyptian royal name Takarut, which see.

TA-KHA.

The wife of Nefer-hotep, the master of the table of Rameses II. of the XIXth dynasty.

TA-KHA.

An Egyptian lady, the daughter of Uetu, chief of the Keneb, and his wife Apu.

TA-KHA.

An Egyptian pallacist of the period of the XVIIIth or XIXth dynasty. Her mother's name was Uer-na-ra.

TA-KHARA.

A priestess of Osiris of the Hades in the XXVIth dynasty.   Her mother's name was Ariuru.

TA-KHAT.

An Egyptian lady, the sister of the treasurer Iuiu of the XVIIIth dynasty.

TA-KHAT.

The daughter of Ankh-karo-amat, the daughter of Takelot II. of the XXIInd dynasty.

TA-KHAT.

The mother of Amen-meses or Amen-messu, a king of Egypt in the XIXth dynasty. *See* Sipthah.

TA-KHA-UAT.

The queen of Psametik I., king of Egypt, and mother of Psametik II., by whom he was succeeded.

TA-KHEBA.

A place probably in Arabia, wheret Una, the general of King Pepi-Merira, gave battle to and defeated the Herusha.

TA-KHIS.

The Egyptian name of an uncertain Syrian country, probably a shorter form of the following.

TA-KHISA.

A town in Mesopotamia where Amenhotep II. killed seven Syrian kings with his own hands, and afterwards mutilated their bodies.

TA-KHOT.

The wife of Necho I.(?) of the XXVIth dynasty.

TA-KHROT-IKA.

A royal lady or consort in the reign of Aahmes I. of the XVIIIth dynasty.

TA-KI-UATA.

An Egyptian lady, the daughter of the lady Kha-ta. Nothing is known of her except the existence of her votive statuette in the Louvre Museum.

TAK-SHARU.

A mystical title of Amen Ra in the CLXVIth chapter of the Ritual of the Dead.

TALAB.

A Himyaritic deity who was worshipped at Hamdan, if the bronze tablets recording the name are authentic.

TALENT.

An Assyrian measure of weight composed of 30 manehs, equal to 82 lbs. As a money value the worth of the talent differed with the counties. *See* Appendices.

TALI.

A priest of Amen Ra, and wife of Psar-oer, a spondist and priest of the same divinity.

TALMIS.

A chief town in the Dodecaschœnon, a Greco-Egyptian district of Nubia. It is now called Kalabshe.

TAMAHU.

An African people, neighbours, or perhaps a branch of the Tahennu or Libyans who were conquered by Seti I. They were possibly the Troglodytes of Classic history. The name was also a generic one as applied to the nations North of Egypt.

TA-MENAT-KHONSU.

The wife of Osorkon I. of the XXIInd dynasty.

TAMISSUS.

A petty kingdom in the Island of Kypros (Cyprus), which paid tribute to Esarhaddon and Assurbanipal.

TAMMARITU.

One of the three sons of Urtaki, king of Elam, who after their father's death fled for refuge to Assurbanipal, king of Assyria, and took service in his army. He was afterwards king of Hidalu, and when his uncle Ummanigas revolted against Assurbanipal, he slew him, thinking also to be made thereby king of Elam, but he was himself murdered by one of his own servants, named Indabigas, who was then proclaimed king at Shushan.

TAMMUZ.

A Syrian deity who was the husband of the goddess Ishtar, the analogue of the Adonis of the Greeks. *See* Duzi, Tamzi, *and* Ishtar.

TAMNA.

The capital city of the district of Gobal, in Arabia, which contained, it was said, sixty-five temples. Gobal is supposed to have been the Obal of Hebrew writers. The district was the Gebanitæ of Pliny.

TAMNA.

A city in Palestine which was conquered by Sennacherib after his defeat of the Egyptian army at Abtaqu. It was the Timnah of Hebrew writers.

TAMRITU.

The son of Tiumman, king of Elam. He fought with his father in the great battle of Shushan against Assurbanipal, and was slain together with him, while endeavouring to protect his father when he was wounded and thrown out of his chariot.

TAMUN.

Another form of the name of the Egyptian goddess Amunta, which see.

TAMZI.   "The Sun of Life."

An Assyrian or Babylonian deity, the husband of the goddess Allat, or Ishtar.

TAN.

In Egyptian mythology the mystical region called the "Land of Millions of Years."

TANAI.

See Danai.

TANAKUN.

A city in the district of Hamanu, which was conquered, together with its king Tulka, by Shalmaneser II.

TA-NARO.

An Egyptian lady, the daughter of Amenemap, a priest of Amen Ra. *See* Amen-em-ap.

TA-NA-SA-TA-NASA.

A mystical title of Amen Ra, in the CLXVIth chapter of the Ritual of the Dead.

TANAU.

The name by which the Daunians were known to the Egyptians in the time of Rameses III.

TANDAI.

The chief of the city of Karbat, in the district of Halehazta. He defied the power of Assurbanipal, king of Assyria, and ravaged his tributaries' states. He was soon conquered by the Assyrians, and carried off captive into Nineveh.

TANEN-TU.

An Egyptian goddess who was worshipped at the town of Ter, near Hermonthis. She was a form of the goddess Hathor.

TA-NETER. "Holy Land," or "Land of the Gods."

The Egyptian name for the country of Palestine.

TA-NETER.

The Egyptian name for Pount or Arabia Felix, which was first invaded by Queen Hatasu, of the XVIIIth dynasty.

TANIS.

A town in Lower Egypt, now called San, the seat of empire of the XVth, XVIth and XVIIth (Shepherd), and XXIst and XXIIIrd (revived) Egyptian dynasties. The ruins of this important city have only lately been discovered by Mariette Bey. The most interesting of the remains are those of the Hykshos period, which show these invaders to have been an educated race, and far from the barbaric destroyers that they have been hitherto represented. The style of art of the sphynxes and statues discovered at San is strongly Semitic, and less conventional than that of the native Egyptians; the features of the kings, evidently

portraits, are characteristically cut and indicate an Asiatic type.   Tanis
was for many centuries the capital of the Lower Empire; its chief deity
was Sutekh, who was afterwards assimilated with the god Set.   On the
expulsion of the Hykshos, in the commencement of the XVIIIth
dynasty, the city was overthrown and abandoned as impure; but at the
commencement of the following dynasty Rameses II., who with his
father, Seti Menepthah, was also a Set worshipper, rebuilt the capital,
and restored the temples and obelisks, dedicating them again to Sutekh,
with whom he associated, however, as joint deities the Egyptian gods, Ra,
Tum, and Horus.   In the period of the XXIst dynasty Tanis was again
the capital of the empire, and it continued one of the chief cities of
government till the rise of the XXVIth .dynasty, when the seat of
empire was removed to Sais.   After that time the prosperity of Tanis
declined, but its local advantages still maintained it in some degree of
importance, and the Ptolemaic sovereigns repaired some of the religious
edifices.   The glory and wealth of the capital had, however, departed,
and the last blow to its decaying power was given to it, as well as to
many of the other cities of the empire, by the decree of Theodosius
which established the Christian religion, to the exclusion of all other
creeds, and enforced the destruction of the pagan temples, A.D. 379.
(Mariette.)

TANIS.

According to Herodotus a nome in Lower Egypt held by the Calasirian
class of warriors.

TAN-TE-BAST.

An Egyptian princess, the daughter of Prince Psametik, of the
XXIVth dynasty.

TA-PERA.

An Egyptian lady, the mother of the great officer Ahmes-senet-uahbra,
which see.

TA-PHIS.

A chief town in the Dodecaschœnon, in Nubia, which see.

TAP-NAKHTI.

The Assyrian form of the Egyptian royal name Tafnekht, which see.

TAP-OSIRIS.

In the Ptolemaic period the chief town of the first nome of Lower
Egypt.

TAP-TU.

A mystical country which is mentioned in the XLth chapter of the
Ritual of the Dead.

TAPURA.

The Egyptian name for an Amorite city in Syria, which was captured
by Rameses II. It is supposed to have been the Dabir of Hebrew
history.

Tarakennas.

The general of the cavalry of Khitasira, king of the Hittites. He was killed, together with many other chief officers, at the battle of Kadesh.

Taraui.

An Ethiopian people, who were conquered by Rameses III.

Tarba.

A city in Persia, in the district of Yutiya. It was the birthplace of Veisdates, the rebel king of Persia, which see.

Tarbizi.

A city to the North of Nineveh, where Shalmaneser IV. erected a fine temple and dedicated some rich ivory furniture to Nergal, the god of war. A second temple to the same deity was also erected there by Assurbanipal.

Tarchnas.

The Etruscan name of a noble house, from whence the Tarquinii of mythical Roman history were descended.

Tarechites.

An Asiatic people who are supposed by some Assyriologists to have been the descendants of the patriarchs Heber and Terah.

Tar-hu-nazi.

The king of Millid. He revolted against Sargon II., and conquered the district of Kummani. He was then attacked and defeated by the king of Assyria, who destroyed the city of Millid. Tarhunazi managed to escape to the fortress of Tulgarimmi, where he was at last captured with his family and placed in irons, ultimately being sent into slavery to Assyria, together with 5,000 of his subjects.

Taric. "Darkness."

In Zendic mythology the fifth of the evil Darvands, which see.

Taricheutæ.

A class of Egyptian undertakers, who prepared the bodies of the deceased for the embalmers after the evisceration by the Parachistæ, which see.

Tar-ili-su. "Son of his God."

A common Assyrian phrase, which was used in the sense of "pious," or "accepted of the gods." (Fox Talbot.)

Tariush. *Or* Ntariush.

The Egyptian form of the Persian royal name Darius, which see.

Tar-khulara. *Or* Tarhulara.

The king of the Syrian province Gaugama, or Gaugulama, who assisted Sarduri, king of Armenia, and was defeated with him by Tiglath-Pileser, in Commagene, B.C. 743. Tarkhulara remained a faithful tributary, attending Tiglath-Pileser's court at Damascus, in B.C. 732, until he was murdered by his son, Mutallu.

TA-ROTEN-SEKHET. *Or* TA-ROTEN-PASHT.

An Egyptian lady, the mother of the lady Sa-horset. Period uncertain.

TA-ROTEN-SEKHET.

An Egyptian lady, who with her husband Pamau belonged to a family which had been priests and priestesses of the goddess Mehi for five generations.

TAR-QU.

The Assyrian form of the Egyptian royal name Tirhakah.

TAR-SU.

The Etruscan name of the Gorgon Medusa slain by Perseus. Gorgons and Gorgon-heads are plentiful in Etruscan art.

TAR-SURA. *Wrongly read* PARSURA.

An Etruscan nereid, who was the attendant of Thetis.

TAR-TAKHI.

In Chaldean astronomy the name of an unidentified star.

TAR-U.

Another form of the name of the Egyptian city Garu, which see.

TAR-ZI.

A city in Northern Syria which was conquered by Shalmaneser II., who placed upon the throne Kirri, the brother of Kati, king of Que.

TAR-ZI-HU.

The king of Maziravus, a district bordering upon Assyria. He was rendered tributary by Samsi-Vul or Samas-Rimmon III.

TA-SCHEP-EN-MAUT.

An Egyptian lady, attached to the temple of Amen Ra, of which she was spondist. She was the wife of the sacred scribe Pet-amen-neb-nes-ataui, which see.

TA-SCHE-RA-HE.

An Egyptian lady, who was the wife of the priest Pet-e-hake and the mother of the priest of Pthah Taho, in the XXVIth dynasty.

TA-SE-EN-HES.

A devotee of Apis, about the close of the reign of Darius Hystaspes.

TA-SEN-KNO.

An Egyptian lady, who was the daughter of Psametkia, overseer of the archers, and the lady Pasht. A portion of his sarcophagus is in the Leyden Museum.

TA-SER. "Hill."

One of the mystical abodes in the Ritual of the Dead.

TA-SE-SERT.

The wife of the usurper Sipthah, king of Egypt, in the XIXth dynasty.

TA-SET-TA.

A pallacist and assistant to the palace of the god Ra. She was the daughter of Isi-oer, probably of the period of the XVIIIth dynasty.

TASHTER.

In Zendic mythology the creator spirit. To punish the sins of man after the fall from Paradise, together with the wickedness of the Khar-festers, he and the Yzeds caused a deluge to arise which drowned them all.

TA-SI-TEN-HISET.

The daughter of Aahmes II., of the XXVIth dynasty.

TASKHTALI.

An Egyptian lady, the daughter of Pisanhor. Her double sarcophagus and mummy are in the Leyden Museum.

TASM.

An early Arabian race, of Aramæan or Semitic origin; one of the minor populations of the Peninsular.

TASMIT. *Misread* URMIT, "She that Hears."

In Assyrian mythology Tasmit was the wife of Nebo, and inspired the gift of readily hearing and understanding the utterances of her consort. Assurbanipal asserts that Nebo and Tasmit had "made broad his ears and enlightened his eyes," so that he ordered all the characters of the syllabaries and the ancient writings of Accad to be explained and written down. (Sayce.)

TAS-NEKHT.

Another form of the Egyptian name Taf-nekht, which see.

TASPU.

The daughter of Hor-mi-nuter, a wife of Takelot I., the third king of the XXIInd dynasty.

TASRITU.

The seventh month of the Assyrians. It was sacred to Samas, the Sun-god, and was called by the Accadians Tulcu, "The Holy Altar." It answered roughly to our October.

TASSI-GURU-BAR.

An early king of Babylonia, of whom nothing is known, except that he was of the house of Suqamuna, and was the father of the conqueror Agu-kak-rimi.

TAT.   *Or* DAD.

An Egyptian deity, the spiritualised emblem of stability, generally represented by the peculiar stand with four shelves, often called a Nilometer, but which is now known to have been an altar. In the temples it was used as a pedestal to the statues of the gods. As the special emblem of the god Pthah it was always suspended round the neck of that divinity and of his favourite animals, and it was also a part of the figure of Osiris-Tat, as " The Resident in Amenti."

TATA.

An Egyptian royal scribe and chief of the palace, probably of the XXVth dynasty.

TATA.

An Egyptian gentleman, the father of Osirtesen, a private individual, probably of the XIIth dynasty.

TATAI.

A king of the country of Ginginai, who paid tribute to Samsi-Vul or Samas-Rimmon III., king of Assyria.

TAT-AKAT.

An Egyptian lady, the wife of Har-si-esi, and the mother of Pou-isis, which see.

TAT-ARA.

An Egyptian lady of the family of the Captain Hui of the XIXth dynasty.

TAT-ASU.

The name of the pyramid in which King Teta, the Othoes of the Greeks, was buried, and where he was afterwards worshipped as a god.

TAT-EHU.

A strong fortress held by the rebel chiefs against Piankhi, king of Egypt, whose army destroyed it, and took its garrison prisoners. It was also called Oer-nekhtu.

TATES.

An Egyptian lady the daughter of Thoth-hotep and the lady Salant-mouth. Her mummy and sarcophagus are in the Leyden Museum.

TATHRA.

An Egyptian functionary in the time of the XIXth dynasty, whose tomb is in the Louvre Museum.

TATI-NAS-KA-NOFRE.

The son of King Imhotep of the IIIrd (VIth) dynasty.

TATISBU.

The herald of Khitasira, king of the Hittites. He was employed, together with the herald Rames, by his master, to convey the treaty of peace to Rameses II., an office which he successfully performed.

TAT-KERA.

See Assa-Tatkeres.

TAT-KERA-MA.

An early Egyptian king who is named on the Tablet of Abydos.

TAT-MAUT-A-S-ANKH.

An Egyptian lady attached to the temple of Amen Ra. She was the mother of Pet-amen-neb-nes-ataui, which see.

TA-UAU.

An Egyptian lady of high, probably of royal rank, in the XVIIIth dynasty. One of her sons was named Ahmes, and another Bak.

TAU CROSS.

The mediæval name of the St. Anthony's cross, which with a handle for suspension, was used alike by the Egyptians and the Christians in Egypt. *See* Crux Ansata.

TA-UER.

An Egyptian lady, the sister of Khetef, the "Captain of the Boatmen" of Rameses II.

TAUR.

An Egyptian infernal goddess. *See* Thoeris.

TAURLAI.

A country which was rendered tributary by Samas-Rimmon III., king of Assyria.

TA-USER.

An Egyptian princess, the daughter of Merenpthah I. of the XIXth dynasty, who with her husband Sipthah usurped the throne of Egypt to the exclusion of the rights of her brother Seti II.

TAUT-MUT-F.

The Painter, one of the four genii of the dead. He was represented as a vase with a jackal's head as a lid. Upon the vase was often inscribed a prayer to the goddess Neith.

TAUT-MUT-F.

One of the seven great spirits of the Ritual of the Dead.

TAUT-MUT-F.

The mystical name of one of the planks of the boat of souls in the XCIXth chapter of the Ritual of the Dead.

TAU-UER.

The father of Ameni, a great officer of state in the reigns of Amenemha I. and II. of the XIIth dynasty.

TAVA.

In the Greco-Roman period the chief town of the Phthemphuthic nome of Lower Egypt.

TAVTHE.

In Greco-Babylonian mythology the daughter of Sige, or the primœval matter, the sister and wife of Apason, and the mother of the gods, and of Moumis, the intelligent world. Tavthe was derived from the Accadian Tihamtu, "The Sea."

TAWAF.

In ancient Arabian mythology certain circuits or runnings round the sacred stones in the temples, which had to be repeated seven times while certain invocations were uttered. The custom was also a Hindu one.

TAWATANA.

An unidentified country of the Hittites.

TAYF.

A town near Mecca, which was anciently sacred to the worship of the goddess Allat.

TAYMI.

In ancient Nabathean mythology the local deity of the town of Taym in Arabia Deserta.

TAZANA.

A city on the Euphrates where Naditabirus, the Babylonian rebel, was encountered and slain by Darius Hystaspes.

TCHATRAUVAT.   " Dwellers in Tents."

The fourth great caste of the Medes. It was the Struchates of the Greek historians.

TEARA-SAMAS.

A town in Babylonia. *See* Ka-ra-samas.

TEARASAMAS.

The name of the great wall which was erected by Hammurabi, king of Babylon, to restrain the inundations of the Euphrates.

TEB.

The Egyptian name of the fig.

TEB.

The Egyptian digit, four of which equalled one palm.

TEB.

The Egyptian name of small coffers for domestic use, which were made of various materials, as wood, reeds, palm fibres, papyrus, and ivory ; the more costly were either gaily painted with colours or else inlaid with ivory, porcelain, and other substances. They were used for holding the objects of civil life, and they are to be distinguished from others which were employed in the sepulchral rites for the purpose of holding funereal objects. With the *Teb* were frequently buried many spoons or little boxes employed in the toilet, often in the form of animals and fruits, and combining a kind of bowl or spoon of elliptical shape. The materials which these objects held were probably cosmetics, and one in the British Museum has still remaining in it two little cakes of white wax. Sometimes these boxes contained flour, but in general they were empty. The Egyptian *Teb* had no locks, and could only be secured by tying a piece of cord from a stud on the cover to another stud on the body of the box. (Birch.)

TEBALA.

A Sabæan city famous for its great temple of the deity Dhu-kholosa, to whose shrine there were annual pilgrimages, a custom which was abolished by Mahomet.

TEBI.

The *tebi*, or Egyptian bricks, made in a mould, of sun-dried clay mixed with straw, pounded pottery, and other materials, were extensively used for construction in ancient Egypt. At the earliest period the use of kiln-baked bricks was unknown, but some objects of this class occur at the time of the XIIth and following dynasties, of baked red terra cotta, of conical, or square shape, the use of which is not decidedly known. The bricks of unbaked clay vary in dimensions from 1 ft. 8 in. to 1 ft. 3 in. long, and are in thickness from 8½ in. to 4½ in., and weigh about 16 lbs. The largest are those of the earliest dynasties before the VIth, and they become of smaller dimensions under the XVIIIth and following dynasties. At the earlier period rude marks, spirals, curves, or devices, made by pressing the finger or fingers of the hand into the moist clay, were impressed on the bricks, but at the time of the XVIIIth dynasty stamps were introduced of an oval or square shape, having in relief the prenomen, or name of the monarch, or the names and titles of the persons for whose buildings or constructions they were made. The stamps on the bricks commence under the XVIIIth, and continue till the XXIInd dynasty. These bricks were extensively used for the construction of pyramids, palaces, walls, private houses, fortresses, and other constructions, the absence of rain making them sufficiently hard to withstand the climate. Representations of the manufacture of bricks by foreign captives, or prisoners of war, corresponding with the account of the bondage of the Israelites, and the labours imposed on them, are seen in the tombs of the XVIIIth dynasty. (Birch.)

TEBU.

The name of a mystical divinity who is mentioned in the LXXXVth chapter of the Ritual of the Dead.

Tef-amen.

A son of Herhor-si-amun of the XXIst dynasty.

Tefnut.

In Egyptian mythology a goddess analogous to the Daphne of the Greeks. She was the associate of Shu, and was a daughter of the sun.

Teh-neh.

The modern name of the Greco-Egyptian town Acoris in the Heptanomos.

Teiharset.

A lady of the family of Ra-toker, a "Prefect of the Palace" in the XXVIth dynasty.

Tekem.

A mystical divinity who is represented as adored by the deceased in the LXXIInd chapter of the Ritual of the Dead.

Tekh-bes.

The daughter of Mert-hapi, the sister of Nechtanebos, a king of the XXXth dynasty.

Tela.

A Mesopotamian city which was conquered by Assurnazirpal, who erected a tower of alternate layers of brick and of living captives, whom he thus slowly starved to death, and burned the remainder of the boys and girls alive.

Tel-abni.   "Mound of Stones."

An Assyrian city which revolted to Assurdan, and was reconquered by Samas-Rimmon III. It was again subdued by Assurbanipal.

Telal.   "Warrior."

In Accadian mythology the name of a class of mysterious evil spirits, who afflicted mankind. They were called by the Assyrians Gallu.

Tel-assar.

A mountain district South-east of Assyria. It was subjugated by Esarhaddon.

Tel-aswad.

The modern name of the Babylonian city Akkerkuf.

Tel-basta.

The modern name of the city and nome of Habu in Lower Egypt. The Bubastis of the Greeks.

Tel-el-amarna.

The modern name of Alabastron, the new capital of Egypt under the reign of Amenhotep IV. and the Disk worshippers. Upon his decease the city was destroyed, and the inscribed stones of its temples having been first carefully defaced, were used to enlarge those of Karnak at Thebes in the time of the XIXth dynasty.

TEL-EL-YAHOUDEH. "Hill of the Jews."

The modern name of the city of Onion, where Onias, the exiled high-priest of Jerusalem erected a second temple for the use of the Jews in the reign of Ptolemy Physcon.

TELLUS-MATER. "Earth Mother."

Among the ancient Romans the goddess of the reproductive powers of the earth. She was called also Ops.

TEMA.

An Ishmaelite town or settlement mentioned by Hebrew writers. It is the modern Teyma.

TEMENOS.

The sacred grove of olive or cypress trees which surrounded the earlier altars of the Greeks and Phenicians.

TEMSU.

The Egyptian word for a crocodile. Hence the name of Lake Timsah in the Isthmus, which abounded with crocodiles.

TEN.

An Egyptian measure of weight, equal to 1 lb., equal to 1400 grains troy.

TEN.

The Egyptian name for the city and nome of Latopolis, now called Esneh, sacred to the goddess Suvan.

TENA.

An early Egyptian name of the town of This.

TENA.

An Egyptian lady of rank in the XIIth dynasty. Her stele is remarkable as indicating her to have been very wealthy, and to have lived unmarried.

TENA.

An island people in the Mediterranean who were conquered by Thothmes III. They were probably the same as the Danai or Daunians.

TEN-AMEN.

An incense-bearer of Amen Ra, whose mummy is in the British Museum.

TEN-EM-HAA-PTHAH.

A " Chief of the Singers of Pthah," in the XXVIth dynasty.

TENI.

A prince of Kush in the reign of Rameses I.

Teniluki.

An Accadian city, the site of which is not known.

Ten-kheiat.

An Egyptian lady, the daughter of Oer and Isi-oer, a priestess of Amen Ra.

Ten-kheta.

An Egyptian queen, the wife of Amasis II.

Ten-pe-piou.

An Egyptian lady, the wife of the functionary Pe-schali-en-khons, and mother of the priest Pet-isis, which see.

Tent-amen.

A priestess of Amen Ra. She was the wife of Khons-mes, a " Keeper of the White Hall of the Deity," and of Ta-eiouih-ra, a priestess of Amen.

Tent-es-peh.

The wife of Prince Namurot, the son of Osorkon II. of the XXIInd dynasty.

Tent-es-peh.

A grandmother (?) of Sheshanka I. of the XXIInd dynasty.

Tent-es-peh.

The wife of Pthah-hat-ankhef, the grandson of Osorkon II. of the XXIInd dynasty.

Tent-kheta.

The first wife of Aahmes II. of the XXVIth dynasty.

Tent-kheta.

The wife of Panki, the last king of the XXIVth dynasty.

Tent-sos-ra.

A priestess of Amen Ra. Period uncertain.

Tentyra.

The Greek name for the city and nome in Upper Egypt, called by the Egyptians Emsah. *See* Denderah.

Tentyris.

In Egyptian mythology the city of Tentyra personified as a goddess.

Teos. *Or* Tachos.

The second king of Egypt in the XXXth dynasty, and the son and successor of Nekhtarhebi. He held the throne for two years chiefly by the help of Agesilaos, the Greek. He much oppressed the Egyptians by his taxations, and they calling in Nekhtenebef, the last of the native princes, drove him from the throne after a short reign of two years. He was the Geos of the Greeks.

Tep.

A city in the Lower Egyptian nome of Patanut.

Tept.

A mystical region of the Egyptian Kerneter. It is mentioned in the LXXVth chapter of the Ritual of the Dead.

Ter.

An Egyptian city near to Hermonthis. It was sacred to the goddess Tanentu.

Terah.

A Hebrew patriarch, the grandfather of Abraham. *See* Tarechites.

Teren-ra.

An obscure Egyptian monarch, of the XIIIth or XIVth dynasty.

Tes-amen.

An Egyptian lady, the mother of Hem-bai, a scribe and priest of Amen.

Tes-amen.

A private Egyptian gentleman. His father's name was Kebu, and his daughter's Ama, which is all that is known respecting him.

Tes-bast-peru.

The second wife of Takelot II. of the XXIInd dynasty.

Tes-batat.

The consort of Mert-hapi, the sister of Nechtanebos I. or II.

Tes-hor.

The Egyptian name of Apollinopolis, in Upper Egypt. It was sacred to the deity Horus as Har--hut.

Teshr.   "Red."

The Egyptian name for the desert or desert lands generally.

Teshr.

The peculiar high gold crown of Lower Egypt, which, when the two kingdoms were united, was generally worn by the sovereign together with the Shaa. *See* Pschent.

Tes-kartes.

An Egyptian proper name, which was the Tisicrates of the Greeks.

Teta.

Another form of the name of King Ati, which see.

Teta.

The second king of the Ist dynasty.

Teta.

An unplaced king of the VIth dynasty.

Tet-anhur.

An Egyptian lady who was an assistant in the temple of the god Anhur.

Tet-em-hebi.

The secretary of King Rameses XII., who was sent by his master to cure a princess of Bakhtan, but unsuccessfully, as he found that her malady was beyond his skill, she being possessed by a demon. *See* Bentaresh *and* Rameses XII.

Tet-en-hor.

The father of Anima, a priest of Anhur. *See* Anima.

Tet-hapi.

A mystical divinity, who is mentioned in the LXIInd chapter of the Ritual of the Dead.

Teti.

An Egyptian official in the XVIIIth dynasty, the father of Pent-uau, who succeeded him in his office.

Teti.

An Egyptian lady, the wife of Sebek-nekht, which see.

Teti.

An Egyptian priest, the son of Antef, a great Egyptian governor of the nome of Abydos, in the XIIth dynasty. *See* Antef.

Teti-hor-noub.

A choristress of Amen Ra, the daughter of Sa-ei-nub-eu the priest of Amen, and the wife of Pi-en-nun-en-pe the prophet of the goddess Month. Her double sarcophagus and mummy are in the Leyden Museum.

Teti-ma-nefer.

An Egyptian lady, the wife of Empe-ankh, and the mother of Harsaf, a spondist of Thoth.

Tet-pthah-af-ankh.

A son of Takelot II. of the XXIInd dynasty.

Teubani.

The king of the Shuites, a Mesopotamian people, who paid tribute to Assurnazirpal.

Teukros.

A king of Paphos, in the Island of Kypros (Cyprus), who reigned about the fourth century B.C.

TEUMMAN.

The son of Khumba-nigas or Humbanigas(?). He succeeded his brother Urtaki, as king of Elam, cir. B.C. 660. His nephews, fearing that he intended to murder them, fled to Assur-bani-pal for protection. Teumman sent two officers to demand their surrender. This was refused, the officers were imprisoned, and war broke out. Teumman met the Assyrian forces at Duran, on the frontier, but retired before them to Shushan, where he was totally routed owing to the defections of his princes, and severely wounded. His son, Tamritu, defended him till both were slain, when their heads were sent to Nineveh, cir. B.C. 655.

TEYMA.

An Arabian town near Djebel Shammar. It was the Tema of Hebrew writers.

TEZCALLICOPA.

In Mechoacanese mythology the name of the Great Spirit.

TEZPI.

The name given by the Mechoacanese to a mythical patriarch, who, together with his wife and family, escaped the Deluge by building an ark.

THABASIUM.

In the Greek period a chief city on the Crocodile Lakes of Lower Egypt.

THALANA.

An Etruscan female divinity, who was represented as holding a fruit. She was the attendant of Thanr.

THALES.

A Greek astronomer, who foretold an eclipse which took place during a battle between Cyaxares and the Ionians. It constitutes a datum in history, and the following years are given for its occurrence: Volney, B.C. 625; Clinton, B.C. 603; Bosanquet, B.C. 585; Larcher, 597; Clemens Alexandrinus, B.C. 579.

THALNA.

An Etruscan goddess of beauty, who was represented with a coronet, earrings, necklace, and tunic, a fillet or twig in her hand, and a green branch before her face. Perhaps she personified the Spring. On a mirror from Vulci, Thalna appears as a male god, half nude, with a coronet and staff. *See* Thalana.

THAMIMASADAS.

According to Herodotus the name of a Scythian deity, answering to the Poseidon of the Greeks.

THAMPSIS.

According to the Greek lists the successor of Sebercheres, king of Memphis. He has not yet been certainly identified.

THAMUDITES.

In prekoranic history an early Arabian race of Hamitic origin. Their successors were considered as impious and idolaters.

THANA.

The Etruscan Juno. Her name enters into the composition of the name Thankvilus or Tanaquil.

THANNYROS.

The king of Libya, under the Persian rule. He was placed on the throne by Artaxerxes I., after the defeat and impalement as a rebel of his predecessor, Inarus. (Sharpe.)

THANR.

An Etruscan goddess, the attendant of Akhuvitr. She was represented with a dove on the finger of the right hand. *See* Alpanu.

THANR.

An Etruscan goddess, with wings, diadem, tunic, and necklace, who aided women in childbirth ; she was probably the same as Thanr, the attendant of Akhuvitr.

THARGAL.

The Septuagint form of the Susianian royal name Tidal, or more properly Turgal, which see.

THEANDRIOS.

The Greek form of the name of an unidentified Nabathean deity.

THEBAID.

The Grecian name of the kingdom of Upper Egypt, the centre of the civilization of the Revived Empire.

THEBE.

In Egyptian mythology the city of Thebes, sometimes personified as a goddess.

THEBES.

A great city in Upper Egypt, the capital of the united kingdom of Upper and Lower Egypt. It was the seat of empire of the XIth, XIIth, XIIIth (ancient), and XVIIIth, XIXth, and XXth (or new) Egyptian dynasties. Thebes was anciently called Ous in Egyptian, and Ta-pe in Coptic, and was divided into several districts. Its chief deities were Amen Ra, Maut, and Khonsu. It was plundered and partly ruined by the Assyrians under Assurbanipal in the seventh century B.C., who removed two obelisks from a temple there to Nineveh, but the chief overthrow of the great buildings appears to have been due to an earthquake in the time of the first emperors of Rome. It was one of the grandest cities in ancient history, and was the Hecatompylos of Homer. The site is now called Medinet Abu. *See* Luxor *and* Karnak, *and* Appendices, Egyptian Triads.

THEBES.

According to Herodotus a nome in Upper Egypt, held by the Calasirian class of warriors.

THEIR.

Another form of the Arabian name Tehar.

THEORUS, GAIUS.

A famous pantomimic actor, in the reign of Augustus Cæsar.

THEOS. "God."

The Sole and Eternal Entity; variously, and always imperfectly defined; and variously, universally, and always inadequately worshipped. The sum and substance of all religious systems.

THERMUTHIS.

The Greek form of the divine name Maut, the great mother goddess of the Egyptians.

THERMUTHIS.

An unidentified Egyptian princess, to whom some writers have attributed the adoption of Moses, the lawgiver of the Hebrews.

THESAN.

The Etruscan goddess of the dawn. She was sometimes represented as embracing Tinthun (Tithonus), and sometimes as in company with Memrun (Memnon).

THIMONEPSI.

In the Greek period the chief town in the Aphroditopolite nome.

THIS. Or TENI.

A town in Lower Egypt now called Harabat-el-Madfouneh, from whence the two first, or Tanite, Egyptian dynasties took their rise.

THIUS.

The old Gothic word for the Supreme Being.

THMEI.

The Egyptian goddess of justice. She was generally represented as a sitting figure, holding erect the crux ansata, and wearing a single ostrich feather, the emblem of truth, on her head. She was the Themis of the Greeks, and perhaps the Thummim of the Hebrews.

THMUIS. THMEI, "Goddess of Truth."

According to Herodotus a nome in Egypt which was held by the Calasirian class of soldiers.

THOERIS. Or TA-UR. Or TA-OUERT. "The Great."

An avenging deity of the Egyptians, and a feminine form of Typhon. She was generally represented as a hippopotamus, standing erect and holding a knife in her hands. She lived by devouring the wicked in Hades, and was the companion to Set. In Egyptian astronomy she was the constellation Ursa Major of the Greeks and Romans.

Thomum.

In the Greek period a chief town in the Panopolite nome of the Thebaid.

Thonosconcoleros.

In the Greek lists the name of an Assyrian or Chaldean king ; possibly the same as Nebuchadnezzar.

Thor.

In Scandinavian mythology the son of the deity Iord. He was the great ruler of the elements of nature, and the protector of all the arts of life. He fought against the great frost giants, and was the god of fire, of agriculture, and of the domestic hearth. He was represented as a red-haired and red-bearded man, holding a ponderous hammer.

Thoth.   *Or* Tahutia, *or* Touth.

The Egyptian deity of written learning, the author of the mystical Book of Life, and of the mystical treatises on medicine and sacred literature, which were afterwards called by the Greeks the Hermetic books, and himself, as the author of them, Hermes Trismagistus, and in his character of introducer of the souls in Hades, Hermes Psychopompos. This deity had, like many of the other Egyptian gods, a variety of names, and a variety of occupations, which led to his identification with many of the chief divinities, by virtue of a parity of offices. He was called on a statue in the Leyden Museum, " He who is the Good Saviour," and on some of the funereal papyri he takes the place of Anubis, or even Horus, with respect to the soul of the deceased. " He was the faithful councillor of Osiris ; he aided Horus in his pious combats which he undertook on behalf of his father with the evil being Set. Like Horus, to him was attributed the special honour of having justified his father Osiris against his enemies, and by similitude the soul of the deceased, as an hypostasis of Osiris likewise. In the Hall of the Two Truths it was the duty of Thoth to weigh the soul of the deceased, and to read from his tablets a record of his actions in the past life. Thoth was also the god of writing, and the founder of all the sciences. He brought to the gods a translation of all the sacred books, and he was called the " Scribe of the Gods," and the " Lord of the Divine Words " (in this attribute he was represented on the funereal papyri and in the Ritual of the Dead as furnishing the deceased with the book of mystical instructions, armed with which he would be able to repel all the assaults of his spiritual foes in the underworld, and to force an entrance into Amenti itself by pronouncing the secret names of the great gods). In another form the god Thoth was identified with the moon, in which case he was represented with the head of an ibis, surmounted by the horns and lunar disk ; but oftentimes he was figured with a human head, having that of the ibis as a *coiffure* and wearing the *Atef* crown (and still more rarely as a double-headed Ibis, as regarding the past and the future of human life at one time). As Thoth-Aah, or Thoth the Moon, he was generally entirely naked, and in the figure of an infant with thin bowed thighs, possibly to indicate the moon in its first quarter. At other times he was represented as an adult man, bearded and wearing the short loin cloth, or *Shenti*, of the Egyptians; sometimes he carried in his hand the eye of Horus, the symbol of the full moon, and, in common with all the other divinities, the *Cucufa* or *Uas* sceptre and crux ansata. In his latter characteristics Thoth was regarded as one and the same with Khonsu of Thebes. The Cynocephalus ape was also sacred to the god Thoth and hieroglyphically figured for him." (De Rougé.)

THOTH.

Among the ancient Egyptians the sacred festival of the first day of the month.

THOTH.

An Egyptian royal scribe, and overseer of the district of foreigners. Period uncertain.

THOTH. *Or* TAHUTIA.

An Egyptian officer in the reign of Rameses III., who treacherously delivered up to his master a fortress of the Emu, into which he had obtained access by stratagem.

THOTH.

The first month of the Egyptian sacred year, began about 20th July.

THOT-HARTAIS.

An Egyptian lady in the XIXth dynasty, the mother of the lady Hotepbeset, and the grandmother of Pe-ankh-em-tanen.

THOTH-HOTEP. "Peace of Thoth."

A state official at the close of the IInd Thinite dynasty.

THOTH-HOTEP.

The husband of the lady Salant-mouth, and father of the lady Tates, which see.

THOTH-MES I. "Son of Thoth." *Surnamed* RA-AA-KHEPER-KA.

An Egyptian king of the XVIIIth dynasty. He followed up the conquests of his father Aahmes I. in Ethiopia, defeated the Canaanites of Palestine, and crossing the Euphrates conquered the Rotennu at the battle of Circesium, the Carchemish of Hebrew history. He then fought against and subdued the Assyrians near Nineveh, being the first Egyptian monarch who led an army into Asia, and returning to Egypt introduced studs of chariot horses. Thothmes commenced the great temples of Karnak in Upper Egypt, and completely incorporated the Ethiopians with his kingdom, making his son "Prince Royal of Ethiopia." He reigned twenty-one, or according to Manetho thirteen years, and was worshipped as a deity after his decease. He was the Thothmoses of the Greeks.

THOTH-MES II. *Surnamed* RA-AA-KHEPER-EN.

The son and successor of Thothmes I. He appears to have been a a weak monarch, and to have been under the regency of his sister

Hatasu, whom according to some accounts he married. He reigned but a few years, during which however he repressed a revolt in Ethiopia. On his return he was apparently dethroned by a revolution, of which no records remain. He was nominally succeeded by his brother Thothmes III., but practically by Hatasu, who reigned alone.

THOTHMES III. *Surnamed* MENKHEPERA *and* RA-MEN-KHEPERA-USER-MAT, "Holder of the Plains of the Sati."

The second son of Thothmes I., and the greatest king of the XVIIIth dynasty. His empire extended over the countries now called Abyssinia, Soudan, Nubia, Syria, Mesopotamia, Arabia, Kurdistan, and Armenia. The earlier years of his reign were passed under the regency of his sister Hatasu, whom he probably drove into retirement, as after her death he effaced all the inscriptions bearing her name upon the monuments of Egypt. He opened a road for the commerce of Egypt to Central Asia by defeating the allied Syrian kings at the battle of Megiddo. He made no less than six expeditions into Syria, subjugating the Rotennu and the Assyrians. He built a fleet of ships on the Euphrates, and conquered the Isles of Cyprus and Crete in the Archipelago, reducing the Phenicians and Pelasgic races. Botanical and Zoological gardens were first planted by him, and the practice of making slave hunting expeditions into the South dates from his time. Nearly all of the great temples of Upper Egypt were either founded or enlarged during his reign. He finally extended his conquests to the very borders of Egypt, and died in his sixtieth year after having held the throne of Egypt for fifty-four years. The chief buildings erected or begun by Thothmes III. were the temple of Ra at Amada, the temple of Osirtesen III. (as a god) at Semneh, other smaller temples at Mount Doshe, at the Isle of Sai, at Korte, Ombos, Pselcis, and Talmis, all in Ethiopia. In Egypt proper he built a magnificent palace temple at Gourneh, which was afterwards finished by Seti I. He also erected temples at Esneh, Hermonthis, and above all Thebes at Karnak. Monuments recording the reign of Thothmes have been found even on the borders of Algeria, and in the Island of Kypros, and the chief fictile and artistic remains of the Egyptian empire date either from his reign or that of the Ramesside kings.

THOTHMES IV. *Surnamed* KHA-KHAU-RA-MEN-KHEPERU.

The successor of Amenhotep II. Few annals of his reign remain, but he was able to hold the empire of his father together. He ascribed his elevation to the throne chiefly to the favour of the god Ra, symbolised by the great sphynx, in front of which he built a small temple between its paws. He conquered or re-subdued some Negro tribes to the South of Egypt, and greatly improved the cities of Heliopolis and Memphis. Thothmes IV. died after a short reign of nine years, when he was succeeded by Amenhotep III.

THOTH-MES.

An Egyptian officer who was "Spondist of Amen Ra," "Overseer of the Palace," "Overseer of the Bulls of Amen," and "Keeper of the Golden Crowns" of the same god. He probably lived in the time of the XVIIIth dynasty.

THOTH-MES.

A subordinate prince in the reign of Amenhotep II.

THOTH-MES.

A prince of the blood royal in the reign of Amenhotep II.

THOTH-MES.

A prince of Kush in the reign of Amenhotep III. of the XVIIIth dynasty.

THOTH-MES.

A son of Thothmes IV. of the XVIIIth dynasty.

THOTH-MES.

A prophet of an unnamed divinity. He married the lady Barchas, by whom he had a son, the prophet Eintosch. Ptolemaic period.

THOTH-MES.

The mother of the Egyptian officer named Pnaaku, which see. The name is an example of the use of masculine names applied to females in ancient Egypt.

THOTH-MES.

A son of Rameses II. of the XIXth dynasty.

THOTH-MES, TABLET OF.

A famous mural inscription containing a chronological selection of sixty-one of the kings of Egypt, the ancestors of Thothmes III. of the XVIIIth dynasty, to whom he was represented as making the usual offerings. As it was designed more as an architectural feature in a chamber in the palace of Karnak, than as a historical record, its value is not so great as that of the two tablets of Abydos, and the correct succession of the royal names is obviously disregarded. It is, however, an important document serving to complete the materials for the early history of Egypt. The inscription, which is also sometimes called the Tablet of Karnak, is now in the Museum of the Louvre. (Mariette.)

THOTHMOSES.

The Greek form of the Egyptian royal name Thothmes, which see.

THRAETAONA.

The true form of the name of the Persian mythical sovereign Feridun, which see.

THUORIS.

According to the Greek lists the name of an Egyptian king of the XXth dynasty. He is not yet certainly identified.

THURO. " The Law."

A Phenician deity representing the law personified as a divine being. His wife was the goddess Khusareth or Harmony.

Thynis.

The Greek name for the Egyptian city Taini, which see.

Ti.

The wife of the royal secretary Ai, in the court of the heretic King Atef-nuter-Ai of the XVIIIth dynasty.

Ti.

The wife of King Atef-nuter-Ai of the XVIIIth dynasty.

Tiah-hor.

An Egyptian lady, the mother of a priest named Hor-naskht.

Tiakken. *Or* Sekenen-ra.

One of the vassal kings of Thebes during the usurpation of the Hykshos conquest.   His refusal to worship the Asiatic god Set provoked a war which led to the expulsion of the Hykshos.

Tiamat.

In Accadian mythology the goddess who presided over the creation. She was a form, or rather another name, of the goddess Tihamtu, " The Sea." *See* Tihamtu.

Tibilti.   " Stream of Fertility."

An ancient name of the river Tigris.

Tidu.

An Assyrian city which revolted to Assurdan, and was reconquered by Samas-Rimmon III.

Ti-ei.

A chief of the pure house (temple) of an unnamed deity.   Period of the Second Empire.

. Ti-ei-mest-nibs.

A priestess or " Divine Spouse" of Amen Ra.   Her statue is in the Leyden Museum.   Period uncertain.

Ti-em-ua.

The mystical name of one of the planks of the boat of souls in the XCIXth chapter of the Ritual of the Dead.

Tiggaba.   " Lofty Head."

An Assyrian city, probably Arbela, so named from its great acropolis.

Tigga-baki.

The Accadian name of a city or district called by the Assyrians Kute, and at present Ibrahim.

Tiglath.   *Or* Tuklat.

The Assyrian name which the Egyptians changed into Takarut or Takelot, when it was borne by the kings of the XXIInd dynasty.

TIGLATH PILESER I. *Or* TUKLAT-PAL-ASSUR I.

One of the most famous of the older Assyrian monarchs. He was the son and successor of Assur-ris-ilim, about B.C. 1120. He began his reign by resubduing the tribes around Assyria which had revolted from their allegiance, after which he conquered the Muski, a people of Hittite origin, who had invaded the region of the Upper Euphrates, and ravaged the land. These nations with their kings were defeated by the king of Assyria, who marched into Kummuha, re-annexed the country, and subdued all the petty kingdoms on the borders of the Tigris. Seris, with its monarch Kiliteru, was plundered and burnt, as were also Urrahinas, which with its king Saditeru, submitted and escaped complete destruction. The states of Subari, Alzi, and Puruluz, were next reduced, and this was followed by a desperate attempt of the Hittites to again repulse the Assyrians, but on the approach of the king their army of 4000 men surrendered at discretion, and 120 chariots were delivered up to Tiglath Pileser, who a second time plundered Kummuha. The four following years of his reign were simply a series of victories over the Adavas of the mountains, the people of the plain country by the Lower Zab, and the districts of the Northern Sugi, Kirhi, Luhi, Arirgi, Alamun, and Elani. From these countries the Assyrian conqueror carried off as trophies twenty-five images of their respective gods, which he placed in the temples of Beltis, Anu, Vul, and Ishtar. Nairi and sixteen districts North of the Upper Euphrates were then annexed. The Nairi gathered an army headed by sixty local kings, but all were defeated by Tiglath Pileser, who imposed on the confederation a tribute of 1200 horses and 2000 oxen. In his later years Karchemish, Northern Syria, and part of Babylonia, then ruled by Maruduk-nadin-ahi, were invaded, as also the Nairi for a third time. Tiglath Pileser was passionately fond of hunting. He chased wild bulls on the Lebanon, he slaughtered 120 lions, besides numerous other wild animals. At his capital city Assur he established a park or plaisaunce for battues of wild animals. The local princes paid him tribute of bulls and beasts, and the king of Egypt sent him a present of a crocodile. In his domestic or official capacity the king was a great builder and restorer of the various national temples and public works, and on his death " Tiglath Pileser I. left Assyria the foremost monarchy of the world, his empire extending from below the Lower Zab to Lake Van and the Upper Euphrates (Karasu), and from the mountains East of Assyria to Pethor in Syria, including all the region of the Khabour, while his conquests and expeditions extended on every side outside this line, on the West to the Mediterranean, and on the South to Babylon." (Smith.) Tiglath Pileser I. reigned in all about twenty years, and he was succeeded by his son Assur-bel-kala, of whom little is known, and under whose feeble reign, and that of his brother Samsi-Vul III., nearly all the conquests of the great king were lost.

TIGLATH PILESER II.

According to the inscriptions this monarch was not related to the royal family, but was an usurper who fought his way to the throne of Assyria, B.C. 745, during the revolts which followed the death of Assur-nirari II. As soon as he had firmly established himself he made a war against the princes of Armenia, who incited by Sarduri of Ararat, disputed the power of Assyria. These rebels he utterly defeated at the battle of Kummuha (Commagene), and again crossed the Euphrates and conquered the city of Arpad, which required a year's warfare to subdue it. He then divided the conquered country of Hamath among his generals, and in a few years afterwards had again to fight against the armies of Sarduri and his allies. These he again defeated, and ravaged their country. Scarcely was that war terminated when his aid was implored by Ahaz, king of Judah, against Rezon of Damascus. Advancing therefore to his aid Tiglath Pileser conquered the whole of Syria, and delivering Ahaz compelled him to pay tribute. About that time he obtained possession of Damascus, and held there a grand court, where nearly the whole of the princes of Syria and Mesopotamia paid him homage and brought offerings. He then returned to Nineveh, and declared himself king of Babylon, of Sumir, and of Accad, a proclamation which stirred up a fresh revolt which was headed by the chief of the city of Silani, Nabuusabsi. Him he defeated and crucified on the walls of his city. After this he returned in peace to Babylon, and held a great festival to the deity Bel. Scarcely had that finished when another revolt arose, of which no particulars remain. Tiglath Pileser was for a fourth time victorious, and shortly afterwards died, leaving the throne of the united empire to his successor Shalmaneser IV. His empire extended from Persia to Egypt, and from the Persian Gulf to Armenia, respectively 1200 by 800 miles.

Tigra.

A fortress in Armenia where the army of Dadarses the rebel was defeated by Darius Hystaspes for the second time. *See* Zoza.

Tigulti-ninip I. *Or* Tuklat Samdan I.

A king of Assyria who conquered all Babylonia, and then reigned over the two kingdoms, B.C. 1271 to 1240.

Tigulti-ninip II.

The son and successor of Vulnirari, ascended the throne B.C. 891, and died after a short reign of six years. He warred in the North in the district of Nairi, and set up a commemorative tablet near the sources of the Tigris. At his death in B.C. 985 his empire extended from below the Lower Zab across to the Khabour, then North to the region of Diarbekr, along the South of Lake Van to the mountains East of Assyria. (Smith.)

Tihamtu. *Or* Tiamat, "The Deep."

The Assyrian goddess Tihamtu represented the principle of chaos, and was given the form of "The Dragon of the Sea," or "The Seven-headed Serpent." She was the Ταυθέ of Endemus (Damasc. *De Princ.*, ed. Kopp. p. 324), and in the legend of the creation she is "The Begetter" of the universe. Bel-Merodach fought against her and her allies in heaven, and drove her back to primæval darkness. This war forms the subject of a grand myth, at the bottom of which lay a representation of the defeat and repulse of the storm-cloud and the powers of the night by the Sun-god Merodach, a subject often represented on the walls of the Assyrian temples.

Tihrak.

Another form of the Egyptian royal name Taharkah, which see.

Tii.

Another form, adopted by some Egyptologists, of the name of Queen Taia, of the XVIIIth dynasty.

Tii-mer-ast.

The wife of Seti-nekht, king of Egypt, and mother of Rameses III. of the XIXth dynasty.

Tikar.

An Egyptian lady, wife of Djobbons, and mother of Ankh-s-nef, which see.

Tilkumbi.

An Elamite city, destroyed by Sennacherib.

Tilukhuri.

An Elamite city, destroyed by Sennacherib.

Timin.

The name of the inscribed cylinder of burnt brick, which was generally placed by the Assyrians under the foundations of their public buildings. Four were always used, one at each corner of the edifice, and their preservation was the subject of terrible curses and formulæ.

Timur.

A Syrian city, which was conquered by Shalmaneser II.

Tina. *Or* Tinia.

The Etruscan Jupiter, who wields the thunderbolt.

Ti-nefer-hotep.

A priestess of Amen Ra at Thebes. She married Horh-bai, a priest of the same deity, by whom she had a son, Hor-sonf, who was a priest of Amen likewise.

Tinthun.

The Etruscan form of the name of a deity analogous to the Tithonus of the Greeks. *See* Thesan.

Ti-osiris.

An Egyptian royal lady, the mother of the princess Seten-isi, which see.

Tipanu.

An Etruscan female divinity, who carried a mirror in her hand, and was an attendant of Alpanu.

39

TIPHANATI.

An Etruscan goddess. This name is read by Corssen as the name of a goddess who, on an Etruscan mirror, stands by Atunis (Adonis). It would, therefore, be a title of Turan. Mr. Taylor believes it represents the Latin *diva Anaitis*.

TI-POUEI.

An Egyptian lady, the sister of the priest Fai-iten-hemh-bai, which see.

TIR-ANNA.   "Life of Heaven."

In Chaldean astronomy an unidentified fixed star.

TIR-IEL.

In Cabalistic mythology the Intelligence of the planet Mercury.

TIR-UTUR.

An early Amardian or Cassite deity. His attributes and offices are not known.

TISKHU.

In Accadian mythology the name of the Assyrian goddess Ishtar. She was called the "Mistress of Armies." *See* Ishtar.

TISU-EM-AB.

The "Superintendent of the Royal Grooms," in the reign of an unnamed king of the XIXth or XXth dynasties.

TITAMASCA.

A king of the Samasai, a mountain district in Armenia, who paid tribute of horses to Samas-Rimmon or Samsi-Vul III., king of Assyria.

TITATA.

A fortress near to Memphis, the boundary between the kingdoms of Upper and Lower Egypt. Its name was also written Taiutet.

TITI.

The name of the mother of one of the last of the Ramesside kings of the XXth dynasty, who is called by some writers Rames-Miamun.

TITI.

The name of the wife of the preceding monarch.

TITI.

The name of the sister of the preceding monarch.

TITI.

The name of the daughter of the preceding monarch.

TITIA.

The chief of the scribes of Amen Ra, in the reigns of Aahmes and Thothmes III. of the XVIIIth dynasty. His wife's name was Aui.

TITIU.

An Egyptian governor of a district, the name of which is destroyed, in the XVIIIth dynasty. His wife's name was Hats-cheps or Hat-a-su.

TIUMAUTEF.

Another form of the name of the infernal deity Tautmutf, which see.

TIZKARUIQBI.

The governor of Nineveh, in the reign of Shalmaneser IV. He was eponym of the year B.C. 725, in which year took place an expedition to a country the name of which is lost.

TLAS.

Another name for Utnas, an early king of Egypt.

TMEMEI.

A sacred scribe. Period uncertain.

TNA. "Basket."

An Egyptian measure of capacity. Quantity unknown.

TNEPHACHTHES.

The Greek form of the Egyptian royal name Tafnekht, which see.

TO.

An auditor of the temple of Memphis in the period of the Second Empire.

TOBBA-SHARAHBIL.

A king of Saba, the successor of Dhamarali-Bayyin, of whom little or nothing is known.

TO-HEM-SUEITS.

An Egyptian lady, the wife of Simouth, the priest of Osiris.

TO-IA.

An Egyptian officer, the "Chief of the Great Grooms of the King," but of what king is unknown.

TO-MERI.

An Egyptian lady, the wife of the priest Anhur-mes, which see.

TON-EN-AMEN.

The third prophet of Amen Ra, in the reign of King Aspalut, of the XXVth dynasty.

TOPARCHS.

In the Ptolemaic period certain petty magistrates, subordinate to the nomarchs or governors of nomes, who governed the smaller divisions or counties of the province.

TORNADOTUS.

The name given to the Chaldean river Dhurnat by the Greek writers.

TOSERTOSIS.

According to the Greek writers a king of the IIIrd Egyptian dynasty. He reigned nineteen years.

TOSES.

An uncertain Egyptian goddess.

TOSH.

The peculiar tall military cap of state worn by the Egyptian kings. It was made of embroidered linen, and was fastened to a framework of metal for the security of the wearer.

TOSORTHRUS.

The Greek form of the name Tseshortsa, or Serbes, which see.

TOTA.

According to the lists a king of the IIIrd dynasty. He reigned seven years, and was known to the Greek historians as Tureis.

TOTHI.   Or THOTH.(?)

The high-priest of Amen Ra, in the reign of Aahmes I.

TOTI.

The flabellum-bearer of one of the kings of the XVIIIth dynasty, an assistant or successor to Neb-amen, which see.

TOTOUON.

An uncertain Egyptian deity.

TOUNI.

Another name of the city of Thinis, in the nome of Abydos, where the god Anhur and the goddess Tafne were worshipped.

TOURA.

A town on the West of the Nile, in Middle Egypt, from whence the stone for the great pyramid was obtained. The town was afterwards called by the Greeks Mons Troicus.

TOU-TOU-EA.

An Egyptian lady, the mother of Amenhotep, a priest of the temples of Pthah and Sekhet, at Memphis.

TPHOUS.

An Egyptian lady, the daughter of Heraclius Soter and Sarapous. She died A.D. 127-8. Her mummy and coffin are in the British Museum.

TRIACONTERIDES.

The sacred thirty years' festival, or Panegyry of the Egyptians.

TRIAD.

A form of Egyptian mythology, in which the powers of the Supreme Being as the producer, the producing, and the produced, were symbolized by deities who were respectively father, mother, and child of each other. Every Egyptian town had its local triad, but the most famous was the great Theban Triad of Amen Ra, Maut, and Khonsu. Sometimes the king himself as a god made the third member of the triad. These combinations of divine properties must not be confounded with the dogma of a trinity, either of creator, preserver, and destroyer as in Hindu mythology, or of Creator, Redeemer, and Sanctifier of the Christian faith, their anomalies being greater than their analogies. *See* Appendix, Egyptian Triads.

TRIAPOLIS.   " Three Cities."

An ancient union of three Phenician cities, Phaneh-Baal, Calamus, and Gigastus. It is now known by the name of Tripoli.

TRIMURTI.

In Hindu mythology the name of the great mystical triad of the primary deities, Brahma, Vishnu, and Siva, more especially applied to the great three-headed bust of Brahma in the cave of Elephanta.

TRITON.   " Lake, *or* Water."

The name of the sacred lake of the Libyans.

TRITOPATORES.

In Grecian mythology certain ancient divinities who were analogous to the Maruts of the Vedas.

TRUIALS.

The Etruscan name of the people who were called by the Greeks the Trojans.

TRUTVEKIE.

According to Deecke, a subordinate Etruscan deity ; but the word is more probably no proper name, but is to be compared (as by Taylor) with the *trutnut* of the bilingual inscription of Pisaurum, where *netsvis trutnut* is translated " haruspex."

TSAFENTO.   " Sustainer of the World."

A title given by the Egyptians to Kames, king of Thebes, and which has been compared with the Zaphnath Paaneah of the patriarch Joseph.

TSAHI.

The Egyptian name for the valley between the Lebanon mountains called in Classical history Cœle, or Hollow Syria.

TSAM.

The Egyptian name for the city and nome in Upper Egypt which was called by the Greeks Diospolis. It was sacred to the deity Month or Mentu.

Tsebets.

A city and nome in Upper Egypt, which was also called by the Greeks Aphroditopolis. It was sacred to the worship of the goddess Nephthys and the deity Harsiesis.

Tsekkariu.

The name by which the Teucrians were known to the Egyptians in the time of Rameses III.

Tser.

The Egyptian foot, equal to four palms, equal to 81·844 inches.

Tsets.   Or Tsebets.

The Egyptian name for the city and nome in Upper Egypt, called Aphroditopolis by the Greeks.

Tsezphath.   Or Zephath.

The name of a town on the Northern frontier of Judah where King Asa utterly defeated Azech-Amen, the Ethiopian.

Tsibarai.

A city or district of Girubbunda conquered by Samas-Rimmon or Samsi-Vul III., king of Assyria, who placed there a statue of himself, inscribed with an account of his conquest of that country.

Tsidphoth.

The Egyptian name of an uncertain Syrian town.

Tsilar.

A country which was subjugated by Samas-Rimmon III., king of Assyria.

Tsillu-assur.

An Egyptian astronomer in the court of Sennacherib, king of Assyria.

Tsiskha.

The king of Siayut, the Lycopolis of the Greeks. He was one of the twenty petty kings of Egypt under the Assyrian Icosarchy.

Tsont-nofre.

An Egyptian goddess, a form of the goddess Isis.

Tu.   Or Tutu.

According to the Izdubar legends the Babylonian god of death. *See also* Ubara-tutu.

Tu.

A mystical region of the Egyptian Kerneter. It is mentioned in the LXXVth chapter of the Ritual of the Dead.

TUAA.

An early Egyptian city in the Oxyrhynchite nome, where the goddess Apitus(?) was worshipped.

TUAA.

A Japhetic chieftainess, the wife of Iuaa, and the mother of Taia, queen consort of Amenhotep III. in the XVIIIth dynasty.

TUAA.

A wife of Rameses I. of the XVIIIth dynasty. She was the mother of Rameses II.

TUAU.

A priest of the temple of Anhur, and the father of the priest Penteni.

TUBA.

The father of Ra-senb, which see.

TU-BAHAL.

An Assyrian or Syrian officer whom Sennacherib placed on the throne of Zidon after his conquest of that city on his first invasion of Palestine.

TUBAKKHI.

The Egyptian name of an unidentified Syrian city.

TUBAL.

A district in Asia Minor which was famous for its mineral wealth. It was governed by twenty-four petty kings, and paid tribute to Shalmaneser II.

TUBUSI.

A prince of the land of Nahiri. *See* Labturi.

TU-EN-HOR.

The son of an early Egyptian king.

TUF.

A city and town in Upper Egypt called by the Greeks the Hypselite nome. Sacred to the worship of the deity Anubis.

TUGULTI-NINIP I.

An early king of Assyria. He ascended the throne B.C. 1271, and was the son of Shalmaneser I. He still further extended the limits of the Assyrian empire, and lived chiefly at Nineveh, where he enlarged the temple of Ishtar. He reigned forty years, and was succeeded by Belkuduruzzur.

TUGULTI-NINIP II.

The son and successor of Vulnirari II., king of Assyria. He ascended the throne B.C. 891, and re-conquered the district of Nairi. During a reign of six years he considerably enlarged the empire. He set up a commemorative tablet near the source of the Euphrates recording his victories. Tugulti-ninip died B.C. 885, and was succeeded by his son Assurnazirpal.

TUGULTI-PAL-ESIR.

The more correct form of the name of the Assyrian king who is usually called Tiglath Pileser I.

TUHAMMI.

The king of Istunda, one of the many Syrian states tributary to Tiglath Pileser II.

TUHANA.

A small Syrian state which paid tribute to Tiglath Pileser II.

TUISCO.

In Teutonic mythology a giant deity, analogous to the frost giant Ymir of the Eddas.

TUKHULKHA.

An Etruscan demon, or Fury. She was represented with woman's body, wings, bird's beak, snakes for hair, and a serpent in her hand.

TUKLAT-SAMDAN I. AND II.

Another form of the Assyrian royal name Tugulti-ninip, which see.

TUKULLU.

The Assyrian title of a privy councillor.

TUKULTI-PAL-ZARA.

Another rendering of the Assyrian royal name Tiglath Pileser I.

TUL-BURSIP.

A city on the East of the Euphrates where Ahuni was defeated by Shalmaneser II., who changed the name of the city to Kar-Shalmaneser.

TUL-CU. "The Holy Altar."

The Accadian name of the month Tasritu, which see.

TUL-GARIMMI.

A strong fortress in Kummani where Tarhunazi, king of Milid, attempting to defy Sargon II., was by him captured and sent into captivity.

TUL-KA.

The king of Tanakun, a petty district in Syria which was conquered by Shalmaneser II.

TUL-SA-ABIL-AHI.

A city near to the river Belichus, which was conquered by Shalmaneser II., the inhabitants having murdered the king who had attempted to resist him.

TUM.

Another form of the name of the deity Atum, which see.

TUMENTU-AF-ANKH.

An Egyptian priest of the deity Mentu Ra. His period is uncertain, but his name occurs on a stele in the Leyden Museum.

TUMMITES.

A daughter of Rameses II. of the XIXth dynasty.

TUMPESI. "Do not Cook." *And* PER-TOT-KHAI. "Let Violence Kill."

Among the Egyptians the names of a heretical sect, in the time of the XXVIth dynasty. Nothing is known respecting them, except that they ate raw meat, and that they were officially excommunicated by the priests of Thebes. They are mentioned in the Stele of the Excommunication.

TUMURRA.

A mountain people on the borders of Media and Susiana, who were conquered by Sennacherib.

TUNA.

A small Syrian state, which paid tribute to Tiglath Pileser II.

TUNA-PUTA.

A Syrian country which was ravaged by the armies of Thothmes III. of the XVIIIth dynasty.

TUNAR-I.

An Egyptian priest, of the time of Rameses II., in whose tomb was found the historical Tablet of Sakkarah.

TUNEP.

The king of the country of Tuna-puta. He was taken prisoner, and his country plundered by Thothmes III. of the XVIIIth dynasty.

TUPHIUM.

In the Ptolemaic period a chief city in the Thebaic nome of Upper Egypt.

TUPURKI.

The Accadian name of a city or district the site of which is not known.

TURAH.

In the "Eleventh Abode" of the Ritual of the Dead a synonym of the mystical name Bah, which see.

TURAN.

The Etruscan Venus. Besides the female Turan, there was also a male Turan, who appears on a mirror as a youthful god, in company with a warrior named Avun.

TUREIS.

The Greek form of the name Tota, which see.

TURES.

A daughter of King Amenhotep I. of the XVIIIth dynasty.

TURGAL.   " Great Chief."

The Assyrian form of the name of the Susianian king, who was called in Hebrew history " Tidal King of Nations." The Thargal of the Septuagint.

TURMAS.

The Egyptian name of the town of Talmis in Nubia.

TURMS.   *Or* TURM.

The Etruscan Hermes, who presided over boundaries and conducted the dead to Hades.   In the latter capacity he is called Turms Aitas, the " Turms of Hades."

TURMUKAS.

In Etruscan mythology one of the messengers of Hades.   Compare Turms.

TURO.

A son of Amen-em-ap, a priest of Amen Ra, in the XVIIIth dynasty.

TURSHA.

The name by which the Turseni or Etruscans were known to the Egyptians.   They invaded Egypt, and were defeated by Menepthah II.

TURTAK.

In Accadian mythology the deity who specially presided over the river Tigris.   His wife was called Ninmuk.   He was the Tartak of the Hebrew writers.   (Lenormant.)   This deity is now called Ztak or Ittak.

TURUKI.

A Chaldean people who were conquered by Budil, a very early king of Assyria.

TURUSPA.

The capital city of Sarduri, king of Ararat.   It is now called Van.

TUSHAN.

A city in Mesopotamia which was conquered, rebuilt, and converted into a military station by Assurnazirpal, and which was governed by Dur-assur, in the reign of Tiglath Pileser II.

TUSKHA.

A city or district of which Sa-assur-gubbu was the prefect or governor under Sargon II.

TUSNA.

The Etruscan name of the " Swan " of Venus and Leda.

TUTAMU.

The king of Unqi, who revolted against Tiglath Pileser II., by whom he and his great men were captured and his capital city Kunali destroyed. The city was afterwards rebuilt as an Assyrian garrison town.

TUT-ANKH-AMEN.

A king of Egypt, of the XVIIIth dynasty. He was one of the last kings of that dynasty, and did not probably reign long. He, however, received a costly tribute from Hui, the former viceroy of Ethiopia under Amenhotep III., and he received tribute also from the Rotennu.

TUT-HATHOR-HON-TOTTI.

The daughter of Pisem II. of the XXIst dynasty.

TUTU.

An Egyptian official, in the reign of Men-ka-hor, of the IVth dynasty. His tomb was destroyed to furnish materials for the Hall of Rameses IV. of the XXth dynasty at the tombs of the Apises.

TUTU.

The name of an Egyptian lady, the wife of a gentleman named Asennu, in the XVIIIth dynasty.

TUTU-AMEN.

A priest or scribe of Amen Ra. The exact time when he lived is unknown.

TUTU-TEN-APET.

The daughter of Rameses-Miamun, of the XXth dynasty.

TUTU-TEN-APET.

The wife of Rameses-Miamun, of the XXth dynasty.

TUTZIS.

In the Ptolemaic period a chief town in the Dodecaschœnon, in Nubia.

TYBI.

The fifth month of the Egyptian sacred year, began about 17th November. In was the first month of the four winter months.

TYPHON.

The name given by the Greeks to the evil deity Set, the brother of Osiris. The Egyptian form of the name was Teb-ha.

Tyr.

In Scandinavian mythology the god of battles and of bravery, whose symbol was a sword.

Tyre.   In Phenician, Tsur.   "The Rock."

One of the chief of the Phenician cities. It was built on a rocky island half a mile from the shore of Phenicia, and joined by a mole in later times to Palætyrus, or Old Tyre, on the mainland. It was less ancient than Sidon, but yet must have been founded earlier than B.C. 2000, as the great temple of Baal Melkarth was erected 2300 years before the time of Herodotus. Hiram, the son of Abibal, who died at the age of fifty-three, after a reign of thirty-four years, was the friend of David and Solomon, and furnished the latter with the materials for the temple at Jerusalem. His successors were Baleazur, Abdastartus, Astartus, Astarmius, and Phelles; then came Ithobal, Badezon, Matgenus, and Pygmalion, whose sister, Elisa or Dido, founded Carthage. Hiram, king of Tyre, sent tribute to Tiglath-Pileser in B.C. 740. He was succeeded by Metenna, or Matgenus, who was obliged to pay 150 talents of gold (£400,000) to Assyria. In B.C. 724 the king, Elulæus, was besieged by Shalmaneser, whose fleet, however, was defeated by the Phenicians. Elulæus was again assailed by Sennacherib in B.C. 702, and fled to Cyprus, and his successor, Bahal, sent tribute to Esar-haddon in B.C. 678. Shortly afterwards he revolted in concert with Tirhakah the Ethiopian, and Tyre was besieged by the Assyrians. It submitted to Assurbanipal after a long siege, Yahimelek, the eldest son of Bahal, arranging the conditions of peace. The conquest of Tyre brought the commerce of the world into the hands of the Assyrians. The city was besieged by Nebuchadnezzar, though apparently without success. Baal, the successor of Ithobal II. proved such a tyrant, that in B.C. 562 he was deposed, and a series of annual Suffetes or judges appointed. Royalty was restored in the person of Balaton, in B.C. 556, who was followed by Merbal, Irom, Marten, Strabo, and Azelime, in whose reign Tyre was taken and burnt by Alexander the Great, B.C. 332. (Sayce.)

Tyrrhenus.

A mythical Lydian hero.   *See* Lydus.

Tzitzi.

In the Ptolemaic period a chief town in the Dodecashœnon, a Greco-Egyptian district of Nubia.

U.

Ua.

An Egyptian officer, the scribe of the cavalry of an unnamed king of the XVIIIth dynasty. He had two sons Teti and Mai, and a daughter Taia.

Ua.

The Egyptian name of the sacred boat in which the ark of the gods was placed to be carried on the shoulders of the priests.

Uabbaiathos.

The Grecian form of the name of an unidentified Nabathean deity.

Uab-tot.

An Egyptian official who was called " The Lover of the King," or *Suten-rekh*, but of what king and of what dynasty is unknown.

Uaem-kau.

The father of the Egyptian officer Amen-i-senb of the XIIth dynasty, which see.

Uaem-ma.

An Egyptian lady, the wife of an officer named Murkau of the XIIth dynasty.

Uagi.

The Egyptian name of a Syrian desert which was crossed by Seti I. on his way to conquer the Rotennu.

Uah.

The father of Senbu, an Egyptian priest of Osiris, whose period is uncertain.

Uah.

An Egyptian gentleman, of the period of the XIXth dynasty.

Uah-abra.   *Or* Hophra.

A governor of the South country, and superintendent of the royal dwellings in that district in the XXVIth dynasty.

Uah-er-meri.   " Increase of Love."

The surname of an Egyptian named Neferhebef, which see.

Uah-mani-amen.

The second prophet of Amen Ra in the reign of King Aspalut of the XXVth dynasty.

Uah-prahet. "The Sun enlarges his Heart."

A king of Egypt of the XXVIth dynasty, and the son of Psametik II. He was successful in some wars which he undertook against the people of Cyprus and Phenicia, and induced the Jews under King Zedekiah to revolt from the Assyrians. The result was unfortunate for both parties, as the Babylonians destroyed Jerusalem, and then invaded the Eastern provinces of the Delta. At that time Uahprahet was attacking the Greek settlement of Cyrene with the help of Adiacras, king of the Libyans. His army being defeated, he returned to Egypt only to find his Greek subjects discontented at the threatened approach of the Babylonians. To appease them he sent a favourite officer named Aahmes or Amasis, but him they immediately proclaimed king in despite of his master, who raised an army against Amasis, who defeated him in a battle near Momemphis, but placed him in honourable confinement in the royal palace at Sais. Before long, however, the Egyptians and Greeks clamouring for his death, he was strangled in prison after a reign of nineteen years, and was succeeded by the usurper Amasis. Uah-prahet was the Hophra of the Hebrew writers.

Uah-prahet.

A prince of the blood royal of Panki, an obscure king of the XXIVth dynasty.

Uak.

An Egyptian sacred feast.

Ua-khons.

An Egyptian gentleman in the XIXth dynasty. His wife's name was Aahartais, and that of his son Nesa-khons.

Uapat.

One of the thirteen petty kings of Egypt who rebelled against, and were subdued by King Piankhi, the Ethiopian, of the XXIInd dynasty.

Uarseken.

A great officer in the court of Ramen-kheper, the last king of the XXIInd dynasty. He married the daughter of his sovereign, and his son Sheshanka was adopted by Ramen-kheper, and afterwards ascended the throne of Egypt. Uarseken was of Libyan or Semitic parentage, and all his family had Chaldean names.

Uart.

An Egyptian lady of the family of the captain Hui of the XIXth dynasty.

Uaruu.

The Egyptian title of any very high military and civil officer in the realm. It is sometimes translated "Prince."

Uaserken.

See Osorkon I.

UASHASHA.

A maritime people of Europe who were completely subdued and scattered by Rameses III.   They were the Osci of the Greeks.

UAT.   *Or* BUTO, " The Lake."

In Egyptian mythology the female principle of water personified as a goddess.   The Latona of the Greeks.

UAT.

Another name of the Egyptian goddess Buto, or Bubastis, which see.

UATA-HOR.

A royal scribe in one of the later Egyptian dynasties.

UATHA.   " Lengthy Reeds."

A mystical lake near the celestial Nile, which was figured in the vignette to the CXth chapter of the Ritual of the Dead.

UATI.

The name of one of the royal crowns of Egypt.

UATIT.

A name of the Egyptian goddess Bast.   *See* Sekhet.

UAT-UR.

The *Pehu* of the first North-eastern nome of Egypt.

UAT-UR.

The Egyptian name of the Red Sea.

UAU.

An Egyptian title now generally rendered " Captain."

UAU-AT.

A people of Ethiopia nearest to Southern Egypt, who were rendered tributary by Thothmes III.

UAZUZ.

The Egyptian name of the Mediterranean Sea.

UBARATUTU.   " Worshipper of (the god) Tutu."

The father of Adrahasis, the hero of the Chaldean legend of the Deluge.   This name in another form Ardu-tutu may have given rise to the Ardates of the Greeks.

UBRUHUNDA.

A people in the mountains of Mesopotamia who were subdued by Assurrisilim, king of Assyria.

UBUDU.

A tribe in Mesopotamia who were conquered by Tiglath Pileser II.

UBULU.

A tribe in Mesopotamia conquered by Tiglath Pileser II., probably another reading of the name of the preceding.

UBUMMI.

An Assyrian district which was invaded by the rebel Tartan, Iludaria, who was slain while attacking one of its cities named Kullimir.

UCCUMU.

One of the dogs of Marduk. He was called a god by the Assyrians.

UDA.

A city and district in Mesopotamia, which was conquered, together with its chief, Labturi, by Assurnazirpal.

UDAKI.

The king of Minni. Upon Dayan-assur, the Tartan of Shalmaneser II., entering his dominions, he abandoned his capital city, Zirtu, and the whole of his country was pillaged by the Assyrians.

UD-IS.

A district of Minni, which unsuccessfully revolted against Sargon II.

UD-KI.

The Accadian name of several cities or districts whose sites are not known.

UD-KIP-NUNU-LAKI.

The Accadian name of the Babylonian city called Old Sippar, in contradistinction to Sippara, the modern Sura. *See* Sippara.

UD-LABKI.

An Accadian city which was called by the Assyrians Larsa.

UD-NUNKI.

An Accadian city, site unknown.

UDR.

In Scandinavian mythology the son of Naglfari and the goddess Nott. *See* Audr.

UDURAN.

A deity of the Susians, of whom nothing is known.

UER-MU.

The guardian of the magazines of an unnamed king, probably Seti I. His wife's name was Ta-ament, his father's Ra-er, and his mother's Uer-naro.

UER-NARO.

The wife of Ra-er, and mother of Uer-mu, the royal guardian of the magazines.

UER-NARO.

A priestess of Amen Ra, and wife of the captain Aai, of the XIXth dynasty.

UER-NARO.

An Egyptian lady, mother of the priestess Ta-kha, of the XVIIIth or XIXth dynasty.

UER-NARO.

A daughter of Rameses II. of the XIXth dynasty.

UERTHEKU.

An Egyptian goddess who was represented as a serpent.

UETU.

The chief of the Keneb in the reign of an unnamed king of the XVIIIth dynasty. His wife's name was Apu, his son's was Meriui, and his daughters' Ta-kha and Nub-nofre.

UEZ.

An Egyptian amulet, in the form of a papyrus column. It was generally wrought in green feldspar, and bore the meaning of prosperity especially in a mystical sense.

UGA. "The Eye."

A mystical divinity who is mentioned in the CXLth chapter of the Ritual of the Dead.

UHKI.

The Accadian name of the city or tribe of Ruha.

UHYAMA.

A fortress in Armenia, where the army of Dadarses the rebel was defeated by Darius Hystaspes for a third time. *See* Zoza *and* Tigra.

UKA.

An annual festival of the deity Thoth.

UKANI.

The father of the prince Mu-sal-lim-Maruduk, which see.

UKHAUAHA. "Meadow."

A mystical being, who is mentioned in the CXth chapter of the Ritual of the Dead.

UKHSYAD-EREMA. "The Increasing Light."

One of the three prophets descended from Zarathustra, by whom the evil principle, Agramainyus, was to be ultimately destroyed.

UKHSYAD-ERETA. "The Increasing Truth."

One of the three spirits, or prophets, by whom Agramainyus was to be destroyed.

40

Ukhulaga.

Another form of the Chaldean name of the star Urakhga.

Ukku.

The chief city of Maniyahe, king of Dahi. It was completely demolished by Sennacherib.

Ukni.

A small river in Babylonia.

Ukni.

The name of a precious stone in use among the Assyrians, by some thought to have been the onyx.

Ulamburyas.

An early king of Babylonia. He succeeded Sim-ma-sihu, but he has left no monuments, and nothing else is known respecting him.

Ulam-khala.

An early Babylonian proper name, meaning Lidan-Gula, "Offspring of Gula."

Ulba-sur-ki-dina.

Another form of the name of the successor of Nergal-sar-usser. *See* Bella-baris-ruk.

Ul-khum-khum. "The Sultry."

In Chaldean astronomy one of the seven names of the planet Mars.

Uller.

In Scandinavian mythology the god of winter.

Ullu-sunu.

The son of Iranzi, king of Minni, and brother of the assassinated King Aza. He was placed upon the throne of Minni by Sargon II. after that monarch had put down the Armenian rebellion, and had caused its chief, Bagdatti, to be flayed alive. He afterwards himself revolted against his benefactor, who when he had put down this second rebellion forgave him, and restored him to his throne as a tributary. After this he revolted a second time, and he was a second time taken prisoner, but compelled to forfeit his throne, and to go into slavery into Hamath.

Ul-man-ma-cacab-akhu. "The Luminary Reigning over the Star of the Hyena."

In Chaldean astronomy one of the seven names of the planet Mars.

Ul-maski.

An Accadian city, the site of which is not known.

Ul-nacaru. "The Hostile."

In Chaldean astronomy one of the seven names of the planet Mars.

UL-TSARRU.   "The Enemy."

In Chaldean astronomy one of the seven names of the planet Mars.

ULULU.

The sixth month of the Assyrian year.   It was sacred to the goddess Ishtar, and it was called by the Accadians Ki-gingir-na, "The Errand of Ishtar."   It answered roughly to our August.

UL-ZIBU.   "Of the Wolf."

In Chaldean astronomy one of the seven names of the planet Mars.

UMBA-DASA.

An officer of Teumman, king of Elam, who sent him, together with Nabudamiq, to demand the return of his nephews, who had taken refuge with Assurbanipal, king of Assyria.   The Elamite war resulted from that mission.   He killed himself when a prisoner in Nineveh, at seeing the head of his master brought in triumph before Assurbanipal. His companion Nabudamiq at the same time committed suicide also.

UMBA-GNA.

An Elamite officer who on the death of Indabigas, king of Elam, contested the crown with Umman-aldas, the usurper, a contest in which he was unsuccessful.

UMBA-KIDINNA.

An Elamite chief who deserted the cause of Teumman, king of Elam, and proffered his submission to Assurbanipal.

UMMAN-ALDAS.

The son of Attamitu, an Elamite officer.   He revolted against his master Indabigas, king of Elam, and killed him and all his family, and then became king.   Ummanigas, who was made king by Assurbanipal, joined battle with Ummanaldus, and was defeated by him.   About that time his ally, Nabu-bel-zikri, fled to him for refuge, but killed himself, fearful that he would be delivered up to make peace with the king of Assyria.   Ummanaldas sent his head to Nineveh, and soon after war broke out in favour of Tammaritu, the former monarch.   The war was carried on with great severity on both sides, but in the end the usurper was entirely defeated, and his capital and kingdom ravaged.

UMMAN-APPA.

One of the three sons of Urtaki, king of Elam, who after their father's death fled for refuge into Assyria.

UMMAN-IGAS.

One of the three sons of Urtaki, king of Elam, who on the accession of their uncle Teumman, fled for shelter to Assurbanipal, king of Assyria, who received them favourably, and made them officers in his army. Ultimately Ummanigas was made king of Elam.   He then joined the revolt of Saul-mugina, king of Babylon, against Assurbanipal, and being again defeated was slain by his nephew Tammaritu.

40*

UMMAN-MIMAN.

King of Elam, brother and successor of Kudurnankundi. He commenced his wars with Sennacherib by combining with Suzub and Nebo-zikir-iskun, king of Babylon, against Assyria. The allied armies took up their position at the town of Halule on the Euphrates, and there waited. Owing to the treason of an Elamite chief, Humba-undasha, the fatal battle soon took place, and the king of Elam had to fly for his life, and his entire army was dispersed and slaughtered.

UMMIAH-ZIRITI.

An early Babylonian king of the Kassite dynasty. Nothing is known respecting him, except that he was succeeded by his son Agu-ragas.

UN.

The Egyptian name for the city and nome in Upper Egypt, called by the Greeks Hermopolis Magna. Sacred to the deity Thoth.

UN.

Another form of the name of the city of An, which see.

UNA.

A great general and officer under King Pepi-Merira of the VIth dynasty. He was sent to fetch the sarcophagus designed for the tomb of his master from Ethiopia, and afterwards fought many battles against the Aamu and the Herusha (*see* these names), whom he conquered, and was allowed as a mark of honour ever afterwards to wear his sandals in the presence of the king.

UN-AMEN.

The king of Nalakhu, one of the petty kings of Egypt under the Assyrian Icosarchy.

UN-AMUNU.

The Assyrian form of the Egyptian royal name Un-amen, which see.

UNAS.

The last Egyptian king of the Vth dynasty. He reigned thirty-three years, and built the town of Unas in Middle Egypt, and was buried in an enormous tomb at Sakkarah. His reign was used as a chronological period by the Egyptians. He was the Onnos of the Greeks.

UNASAGOS.

The king of Lidini in the Island of Kypros. He was one of the tributaries of Esarhaddon.

UNBU.   " Flower."

A mystical title of the soul of the deceased in the LXXIst chapter of the Ritual of the Dead.

UNDASI.

The son of Teumman, king of Elam.   He conspired with Saulmugina, king of Babylon, against his brother Assurbanipal, king of Assyria, but was defeated together with him.

UNI.

An Etruscan goddess, who was represented as assisting at the birth of Athena from the head of Zeus.   Elsewhere she is conjoined with Menerva, Tinia, Letham, and Laran ; or is figured as present at the chaining of Here by Hephæstus.

UN-NEFER.   Or OUNNEFRE, " The Good Being."

A funereal title of Osiris.

UN-NEFER.

A great Egyptian priest of the XVIIIth dynasty.   His sarcophagus is in the Leyden Museum.

UN-NEFER.

The son of Iuiu, high-priest of Osiris, whom he succeeded in his office.   He was the grandson of the preceding Unnefer.

UN-NEFER.

A grand priest of Osiris in the reign of Rameses II.   His father's name was Meri, and he also was a chief priest of the same deity.   His mother's name was Maanai, and that of his wife Taia.   She was attached to the worship of Isis.

UN-NEFER.

A high-priest of Osiris in the XIXth dynasty.   He was one of a noble Egyptian family having that surname.

UN-NEFER.

The shrine keeper of the deity Amen Ra, at Napata, in the reign of King Aspalut, of the XXVth dynasty.

UNQI.

A petty kingdom in Northern Syria, which was conquered by Tiglath Pileser II.

UNSU.

A royal steward of Amenhotep III. of the XVIIIth dynasty.

UPANGAS.

The name of four treatises or commentaries on the Hindu Vedas, which are called the Puranas, the Nyaya, the Mimansa, and the Dharma Shastra respectively.

UPAS.

The son of Kipsi, a Median prince, who vainly attempted to oppose Tiglath Pileser II. on his invasion of Media.

UPA-VEDAS.

The collective name of four commentaries on the Hindu Vedas, called respectively the Ayus, the Gandharva, the Danu, and the Silpa or Sthapatya Vedas, which see.

UPERI.

The king of Dilmun, on the Persian Gulf. He was one of the tributaries of Sargon II.

UPPIS.

The king of Partakka, a district in Media. He was attacked by, and paid tribute to, Esarhaddon, king of Assyria.

UPRI.

Another form of the name of the petty Kypriote kingdom of Aphrodisia, which see.

UR. "The City."

The name of the ancient capital of Chaldea, Calneh. It was the "Ur of the Chaldees" of Hebrew history.

UR.

The ancient name of the Babylonian capital city of Erech, which see.

UR. ———

An Assyrian or Chaldean deity, who was called also "The God of the Foundation." He was the local deity of Erech.

URÆUS.

The sacred cobra (*haje*) serpent of the Egyptians, under which form all the goddesses were represented, and which was also used on the royal headdress as a symbol of the king as a divine personage, and as the principle of immortality. It was the Basilisk of the Greeks.

URAK-AZA-PARNA.

A petty Median kingdom, which was one of the tributaries of Esarhaddon.

URAKH-GA.

In Chaldean astronomy an unidentified star.

URAKH-GA.

An Assyrian bird, mentioned in the Izdubar legends. It is not yet certainly known what species it represents.

URAKH-GABBU.

In Chaldean astronomy an unidentified fixed star.

URAK-KA.

A city in Assyria, which supported Assurdainpal in his revolt against his father, Shalmaneser II.

URAS.

A town in the region of Girubbunda. It was assaulted by Samsi-Vul III., who captured there its king, Pirasati, and slew 6,000 of his soldiers.

URAU.

An Egyptian amulet, in the shape of a vulture. It was usually made of some valuable and hard dark stone.

URD. "Past."

In Scandinavian mythology one of the three Nornes or Fates. They were born prior to the gods, and on their birth the Golden Age passed away. *See* Nornes.

URDAMANI.

The Assyrian form of the Egyptian royal name Rut-amen, which see.

URGAL.

Another form of the name of the early Chaldean king Ilgi, who reigned at Ur.

URGUNDUB.

The capital city of the Iranian district of Khnenta, which see.

URHAMMU. "Light of the Sun."

An early Chaldean monarch, the first whose name has come down to us on the Cuneiform inscriptions. He was the seventh king of his dynasty, and built temples to the goddess Bilit-Taauth at Ur, a great pyramid to the Moon-god Sin, and several temples to the sun at Sippara and Larsam. He was succeeded by his son, Ilgi.

URHAMSI.

The boatman and friend of Izdubar, whom he conducted to the patriarch Adrahasis, and with whom, on his return to Chaldea, he helped to erect a monument of the Deluge in the city of Erech.

URIMMI.

The king of Husinna, one of the many petty Syrian states paying tribute to Tiglath Pileser II.

URIYAKKI.

The king of Que, a Syrian kingdom which was subjugated by Tiglath Pileser II.

UR-LABKI.

The Accadian name of the city Uru.

UR-MERITS-TESHR-SHEN. "The greatly Beloved, Red-haired."

In Egyptian mythology the name of the fifth of the seven mystical cows or Hathors.

URMITU.

An Assyrian goddess, the consort of Nebo. Her name is now generally written Tasmit. She and her husband, as the deities of writing and learning, were supposed to have charge of the education of the kings of Assyria. Her worship was introduced into Babylonia by Hammurabi.

UROTAL.

The Greek form of the name of the Arabian solar deity Urtaal. His analogue was the Shamsu of the Babylonians.

URPALLA.

The king of Tuhana, a small Syrian state, which paid tribute to Tiglath Pileser III.

URRAHINAS.

A city in Mesopotamia which was conquered by Tiglath Pileser I., to whom their king, Saditeru, consented to pay a heavy tribute.

URS.

An Egyptian amulet, in the shape of a wooden head-rest. It was usually made of dark stone or black slate.

URSA.

The king of Ararat or Armenia, whose reign is placed between Minuas and Argistis by M. Lenormant. He fomented revolts against Sargon, in B.C. 719; and in B.C. 716 joined Mita (Midas), of the Moschians, the Tiberani, and ·the Minnians, in a war against Assyria, but without success. In B.C. 715, in return for twenty-two cities, he aided the Minnians in a revolt; but the latter were overrun and conquered by Sargon, who in B.C. 714 defeated Ursa, captured 260 of the royal tribe, and wasted the country. Muzazir, in Southern Armenia, was stormed, and the gods Khaldi and Bagmastu carried away. Ursa, who had fled to the mountain, hearing of the loss of his god, Khaldi, committed suicide. (Sayce.)

URSA-KI-INGI-KI-URKI.

An Accadian generic geographical title, meaning "Cities of Sumir and Accad," *i.e.*, of both races of Mesopotamia and Chaldea.

URSHU.

The superintendent of the watermen or boatmen of Amen Ra. His wife's name was Hant. Period uncertain.

URSI.

A king of the country of Ginkhukhtai, who paid tribute to Samas-Rimmon or Samsi-Vul III., king of Assyria.

URTAAL.   "The Supreme Light."

The true name of the Arabian deity called by the Greeks Urotal. *See* Urotal.

URTAKI.

A king of Elam. He and his brother Teumman murdered their brother Ummanaldas, king of Elam, because he refused to break treaty with the Assyrians. Urtaki then tried to stir up sedition among the Chaldeans, in favour of a chief named Nabu-dimtu, but in that he was unsuccessful. A famine shortly afterwards broke out, when the Elamites emigrated to Assyria for food, and were generously received by Assurbanipal. In spite of that kindness, at the instigation of his general, Maruduk-zakir-ibni, he invaded Babylonia, in concert with Belbasa, king of the Gambuli ; but he was utterly defeated by the king of Assyria, and returning into Elam, cut his throat in despair. He was succeeded by his brother, Teumman, who continued the war with Assyria.

URTAKI.

A relative and officer of Teumman, king of Elam, whom he assisted in his battle with Assurbanipal. Being mortally wounded, and seeing that the day was lost, he called to an Assyrian soldier to cut off his head and take it to his master, which was done. Teumman and his son were also slain.

URTSA.

A king of Armenia. He succeeded his father Baruir, and combined with the Medes against the Asssyrians. He was the Hartchea of Moses of Khorene.

URU-CI.   " The City of the Land."

The Accadian full name of the city Ur, Urukh, or Erech, which see.

URUKH.

An early king of Babylonia, reigning at Ur. He was a great builder, erecting temples to the moon, to Beltis, and to the sun. He surrounded the city of Ur with a wall, and was succeeded by his son Dungi. Urukh has been compared with the Arioch of Hebrew history.

URU-MELEK.

The king of Gebal. He was one of the tributaries of Sennacherib.

URU-SU.

A Mesopotamian people who were conquered by Tiglath Pileser I.

URVA.

In Zendic mythology the seventh resting-place of the Iranians after their exile from Aryanem Vaedjo, which see. It is supposed to have been the country now called Cabul.

URZA.

A harder form of the name of Ursa, king of Ararat, or Armenia, which see.

URZA-HA.

Another form of the Armenian royal name Urza or Ursa.

URZANA.

The king of the sacred city of Muzazir, in Ararat. On the approach of Sargon II., king of Assyria, after the defeat of the Armenian revolt, he abandoned his city, and fled to the mountains, leaving his army, wife, children, and the temple treasures to the mercy of the conqueror, who took them all captive into Assyria, and destroyed the town, which he afterwards annexed to his empire.

USAAU.

The name of the third of the seven halls of Osiris in the Ritual of the Dead.

USANATA.

A small Syrian state, one of the confederacy which was defeated by Shalmaneser II., against whom they rebelled.

USAPHAIDOS. *Or* OUSAPHAIS.

The Greek form of the name Hespu, which see.

USER. " Power."

A mystical pool near the celestial Nile, which is figured in the vignette to the CXth chapter of the Ritual of the Dead.

USER-CHES.

The Greek form of the royal name User-kaf, which see.

USER-HAT.

An unidentified Egyptian town sacred to the worship of Amen Ra.

USER-HAT.

A priest of Amen Ra, the son of the scribe and treasurer Neb-uau. The period when he lived is unknown.

USER-KAF.

The first king of the Vth dynasty. He reigned twenty-eight years, and was the Userches of the Greeks.

USER-KERA.

A competitor for the throne of Egypt in the time of Ati, a king of the VIth dynasty.

USER-MAT.

An unknown Egyptian king, the father of Prince Setnau Chaem-u-set in the Egyptian romance called " The Story of Setnau." He has been conjectured to have been Rameses II.

USER-SON.

An Egyptian monarch of the XIth dynasty. He is not placed in the regnal lists.

USER-T.   " Sustenance."

A mystical being who is adored in the CXth chapter of the Ritual of the Dead.

USHAS.

In Vedic mythology the goddess of the dawn. The analogue of the Eos of the Greeks, and the Ostara of the Germans.

USHITTI.

The king of Tuna, a state in Syria. He paid tribute to Tiglath Pileser II.

USIL.

The Etruscan Apollo. He was represented on a mirror from Vulci as carrying a bow. He wore laced sandals, and was crowned with the rays of the sun.

USIRTASEN.

Another form of the royal name Osirtesen, which see.

USOUS.

In Phenician mythology one of the early giants. He was the inventor of the art of making clothes from the skins of animals, and also of navigation by swimming upon the water on a bough of a tree which he broke off during a storm.

USPINA.

A district near Media, containing more than 200 cities. It was ravaged and the people taken into captivity by Mulisassur, or Multariz-assur, the commander in chief of Samas-Rimmon.

USSUR.

Another form of the name of the Assyrian deity Adar. *See also* Bar *and* Ninip.

USTASA.

A district bordering upon Assyria, which was rendered tributary by Samsi-Vul III. *See also—*

USTASSAI.

A country near Media rendered tributary by Samas-Rimmon or Samsi-Vul III., king of Assyria.

USU.

A city near Tyre which was subjugated and plundered by Assur-banipal. It was also called Hosah.

USUR-HA.

A royal scribe in the time of the XVIIIth dynasty. He had two sisters named respectively Khat and Ser-hat.

USUR-T-KAU.   " The Most Powerful of Beings."

A title of Hat-a-su, a queen of the XVIIIth dynasty.   This epithet was said to have been given to her by the deity Thoth himself, after whom her brothers Thothmes II. and III. were named.   *See* Hat-a-su.

USURU-SWAMY.   " Lord of Life."

The name given by the Todas to the Christian Deity.

UT.

The Egyptian name of the town called by the Greeks Lycopolis, which see.

UTA.

In Egyptian mythology the left symbolical eye, an emblem of the moon.   All good beings were created from the eye of Ra, and all evil things from the eye of Typhon.

UTA.

The amulet in the form of the right eye of Osiris, called *uta*, was extensively used by the Egyptians both as the pendant or ornament of a necklace during life, or else as a sepulchral amulet. It represented the eye of a cow, especially that of the cow form of the goddess Hathor, who was supposed to be the mother of the sun.   The right eye was supposed to symbolise the sun, the left the moon.   It was also called the eye of the god Har or Horus, probably in allusion to that which he snatched from Set or Typhon, swallowed and gave the sun.   Another of its names was the eye of the god Shu, a solar deity, and as such it preserved the body from decay.   (Birch.)

UTA.   " Pectoral Tablets."

These objects, which were called also *uta*, were suspended as a pendant on the neck or throat of the mummy.   They are principally in the shape of a pylon or other small building, and are made of basalt, steatite, or porcelain.   Their subject is generally the boat of the sun holding the scarabeus or *kheper*, placed vertically, supposed to signify the mystical regeneration of the dead.   This scarabeus has frequently the XXXth or the latter part of the LXIVth chapter of the Ritual of the Dead upon it, and probably was used instead of the sepulchral scarabei when they were not employed.   The goddesses Isis and Nephthys are represented standing at the sides of the boat, saluting it in the same manner as they do Osiris.   The jackals of Anubis, symbolic eyes, and other subjects, are occasionally introduced upon them.   (Birch.)

UTA.

The gold pectoral plate of the ancient Egyptians.   That worn by officers had often the royal cartouche upon it, that of the judges the figure of the goddess Tmai, or " Truth," and that of the priests the figure of the jackal of Anubis, the god of the dead.

UTA-HAR-PEN-RES.

An Egyptian priest and high admiral of Egypt under Cambyses, who bestowed peculiar honours upon him, and allowed him to use a royal prenomen. He restored peace to the country under Darius after the revolt of the Magi.

UTA-HOR.   " Eye of Horus."

The chief of the palace of Heliopolis in the XXIVth or XXVth dynasty.

UTENSU.

The name of a mystical box mentioned in the CLIVth chapter of the Ritual of the Dead.

UTET.   " Green."

A mystical being who is mentioned in the CXth chapter of the Ritual of the Dead.

UTNAS.   *Or* TLAS.

The fourth king of the second Thinite dynasty of Egypt. He reigned seventeen years.

UTTE-DUM-MARI.

In Chaldean astronomy the name of an unidentified star.

UTU.

An Egyptian amulet in the shape of a sceptre. It was usually made of feldspar.

UTU-ALTAR.

In Chaldean astronomy an unidentified star.

UTU-CAGABA.   " Light of the White Face."

In Chaldean astronomy one of the seven stars of the week.

UTUG.

In Accadian mythology the name of a specific class of evil spirits or demons which afflict mankind with diseases.

UTULTAR.   " The Light of the Heavenly Spark."

In Chaldean astronomy the name of the deity Marduk as the planet Mercury, in the month of Iyyar.

UUHETU.

The mother of Sebek-hotep II. of the XIIIth dynasty.

UUHETU.   *Surnamed* FENT.

A princess of Egypt, the daughter of Sebek-hotep II. and his wife Anna, of the XIIIth dynasty.

Uupeka.

An unidentified Egyptian town, which was sacred to the worship of the deity Osiris.

Uwaja.

The ancient Persian name of the kingdom of Elam.

Uwakhshatarah.

A king of the Medes, who is mentioned in the Behistun inscriptions of Darius, and is by some writers believed to have been Cyaxares.

Uxians.

An Aryan people inhabiting Susiana.

Uz.

A district in Arabia, probably the same which was known to the Assyrians as Hazu, which see.

Uzal.

A province of Yemen, in South-western Arabia, where is now situated the town of Sana.

Uza-rans.

An Egyptian lady, the wife(?) of Psen-maut.

Uze.

A town in South-eastern Assyria which was conquered by Assur-nazir-pal.

Uznu.

A city in Palestine, on the sea-coast, which was conquered by Tiglath-Pileser II.

Uzziah.   *Called also* Azariah.   In Assyrian, Azriyahu.

A king of Judah, and the son of Amaziah, whom he succeeded about the eighth century B.C.   He reigned prosperously fifty-two years, dying finally of leprosy.   Uzziah conquered Elath, on the Red Sea, and subdued the Philistines and some of the tribes in Arabia Petræa.   He formed an alliance with Hamath, but the Hamathites were defeated by Tiglath Pileser II., and their land parcelled out among the Assyrian generals.

V.

VA-ANNA.

The Turanian name of the early Chaldean king Bel-samu.

VACH.   "The Word."

A Vedic title of the goddess Sarasvati, as the instrument of visible speech to man.

VADJA.

In Vedic literature another name for a liquid burnt-offering.

VADRA-KALI.

In Hindu mythology the daughter of the god Siva, who overcame the giant Darida when he fought against her father.

VAEKERETA.

In Zendic mythology the sixth resting-place of the Iranians after their exile from Aryanem Vaedjo, which see. It was the birthplace of their great hero Rustem.

VAHAKN.

An Armenian warlike deity. He was adopted from the Chaldean god Nergal, or Ninip.

VAHAKU.

The son of Tigranes, king of Armenia. He was a faithful ally of Darius Hystaspes, whereupon his subjects wished to drive him from the throne. In the end the insurgents were defeated, and Vahaku firmly established in his kingdom by the king of Persia.

VAHYAZDATA.

A Persian chief who claimed to have been Smerdis, the son of Cyrus. He raised a revolt against Darius Hystaspes, but in vain, for he was defeated by the Persian general Artavardes, and sent a prisoner to Darius, who mutilated and crucified him.

VAISYVAS.

The merchant caste of the Hindus, said to have been created from the thighs of Brahma.

VAITEH I.

The king of the Arabs and son of Khazael, who had sent tribute to Esar-haddon. He succeeded his father, and was confirmed on the throne by Esarhaddon, king of Assyria, to whom he had sent his submission. The other Arabian chiefs conspired against him, and set up an usurper named Wabu as an opponent. Upon that Vaiteh implored the help of the Assyrians, who defeated the insurgents, and carried Wabu captive to Nineveh. Despite these services Vaiteh joined the revolt of Saul-mugina against Assur-bani-pal, together with his queen, Adiya, and Ammuladi, king of Kedar. Half of his forces he despatched to Saul-mugina, under Abiyateh and Aimu, the sons of Tehar; with the other half he overran Edom, Ammon, Hauran, Moab, and Zobah. Here he was defeated, and fled to Nathan, of Nabathea, who gave him up to Assur-bani-pal. The Arabs then elected his nephew Vaiteh II., king in his place.

Vaiteh II.

The son of Bir-Dadda, and nephew of Vaiteh I., whom the Arabs elected king in the place of his uncle, Vaiteh I. Abiyateh, who had been sent to help Saul-mugina, after a vain attempt to cut his way through the Assyrian camp round Babylon, surrendered, and offered to take service under Assur-bani-pal. The latter proclaimed him king of Arabia ; and he agreed with Vaiteh II. to share the government together. He induced Nathan, king of Nabathea, also to join the insurrection, but directly the war began in earnest they were compelled to retreat; the Arabians wanted water, and could not readily engage but in a succession of small battles. The Assyrians therefore drove them through the desert to Khadatta, Laribda, and Aialla, 600 or 700 miles from Nineveh. The Nabatheans were defeated fifty miles from Aialla, and Vaiteh forty miles beyond. After returning to Damascus, the Assyrian army again marched into Arabia, defeating and capturing Abiyateh and his brother Aimu, who were sent to Nineveh and flayed alive.

Valli.

The son of Ahsera, king of Minni. On the murder of his father and family by his indignant subjects, he ascended the throne and made peace with Assyria, sending his eldest son, Erisinni, with an embassy to Nineveh for that purpose. Assurbanipal, who had already subjugated nearly the whole of Minni, accepted his submission, demanding the daughter of Valli for his harem, and an annual tribute of thirty horses, which conditions were at once granted.

Val-saggatu.   "Temple of the Lofty Head."

Another form of the name of the temple at Babylon, which was also called Bit-saggatu.

Val-zida.

The Chaldean name of the great temple of Bel at Babylon. *See also* Bit-zida.

Vaman.

In Hindu mythology the third incarnation of the god Vishnu, in the form of a dwarf.

VANTH.

The Etruscan angel of death, who was generally represented as a maiden, with cap and wings, and a huge key. She urged Akhle (Akhilles) to slay the Truials (or Trojans), and on the sarcophagus of Chiusi the goddess is depicted opening the doors of the tomb.

VARENA.

In Zendic mythology the thirteenth resting-place of the Iranians after their exile from Aryanem Vaedjo, which see. It was the district now called Demavend. After that they entered Irania, or Persia proper.

VARSARMI.

The king of Tubal, a small Syrian state, which paid tribute to Tiglath Pileser II. *See* Hulli.

VARSHALY.

Among the Todas the title of the village priest.

VARU-DASA-RABBI.

In Hindu mythology the goddess of the earth.

VARUNA.

The Vedic name of the Supreme Being as the Deity of the visible heaven, from whence originated the Ouranos of the Greeks. His attributes were often confused with those of Indra and the other deities.

VAS.

A Nabathean desert which was crossed by the army of Assurbanipal in the war with Vaiteh II. and Abiyateh.

VAS.

A town in Nabathea, which was the birthplace of Aikamaru, the murderer of the Nabatheans, in the reign of Assurbanipal.

VASES.

The Egyptians used different kinds of stone for making bowls, jugs, and other vases, which were destined to hold the liquids and other substances offered to the gods, or were otherwise employed for religious or private purposes. The principal materials used for this purpose were granite, basalts, serpentine, and alabaster, or arragonite, which was a kind of stalagmite, of great beauty of a creamy-white colour, and more extensively employed than any other material, especially for vases of the toilet. The kind in use at the earliest period of the Vth and VIth dynasties was plain, and of one uniform layer ; but about the XXVth dynasty a zoned arragonite of yellow colour, and many layers, came into use. The principal shapes of the vases were a hemispherical vase, with wide open mouth, for holding wine ; cylindrical vases with wide rims for holding unguents or oils ; an elongated vase with pointed foot, also for holding unguents or perfumes; a vase with cylindrical body, large flat lips, and mouth, often employed for holding cosmetics; and vases in shape of the wine-jugs, the Greek *olpe* or the *oinochoe*, the two-handled *amphora*, and drop-shaped *alabastros*, circular and oval basins and vases of irregular shapes. On many of these alabaster vases the name of the monarch in whose reign they were made, of the person in whose tomb they were deposited, and even the amount of their capacity, or their dedication for sepulchral use was incised in Hieroglyphs. The alabaster vases appear to have been highly prized. They had covers of the same material, and were used only for domestic purposes by the upper classes. So much were they esteemed, that they were exported from Egypt, and the names of Persian monarchs (notably Xerxes) have been found in Hieroglyphs and Cuneiform characters upon them, while vases apparently of Egyptian material, if not of Egyptian fabric, have been discovered in the early tombs of Asia Minor, Greece, and the isles of the Archipelago. Besides alabaster and stone, the Egyptians used a kind of porcelain or fayence composed of a white sand, slightly fused, glazed by lead, silica, or soda, and covered with a coloured gauze or enamel for vases : they also employed a whitish steatite for the same purpose, which, when carved of the required shape, was covered with a frit or glaze, and then sent to the furnace and fused. Porcelain vases were principally of a blue or green colour, and made chiefly in the shape of basins or bowls, or tall cups on a stand or stem ; the whole in shape of the flower of a water-plant. Some were employed for perfumes or unguents, and had a flat, slightly convex body, and a small neck, like the flower of the papyrus, often supported at the sides by two sitting apes. Others were cylindrical, resembling unguent-vases. The bowls and basins were frequently ornamented with figures of persons, animals, water-plants, and other subjects. Small vases in the shape of animals for the toilet were made also of porcelain, traced in a dark outline. Some of these objects were inlaid, or glazed in various colours ; and yellow, violet, white, and other colours, are found to have been so employed. The use of porcelain was certainly as old as the XVIIIth dynasty, when the blue colour came into use ; but at the period of the XXVIth dynasty a pale apple-green coloured ware came into use, and continued till the time of the Greek and Roman rule, when jugs in the shape of the *oinochoe*, or wine-bottle, ornamented with figures in relief, were fabricated, and bore incised inscriptions with the name of the reigning monarch. It was not uncommon, as appears from the fragments discovered at the Sarabut el Khadem, near Mount Sinai, to place the name of the ruling monarch on the porcelain vases which were used in the palaces or temples. Like the alabaster vases, those of porcelain were exported, and are found in the same distant localities, whither they had been carried by trade or other intercourse. They are found in the tombs with other sepulchral furniture. The beautiful blue colour of the vitrified ware is due to the use of copper. The vases of stone and porcelain had often disk-shaped or convex covers fitting into the mouth. (Birch.)

Vasus.

In Hindu mythology certain deities created by Indra out of the elements of nature. Of these there were eight.

VE.

In Scandinavian mythology the son of Borr, and brother of Odin and Vili, which names see.

VE-ADAR.

The intercalary month of the Jewish year, which answered to the Assyrian Arakh-makru.

VEDA.

The great collection of sacred books of the Hindus, the date of the compilation of which is unknown, but the hymns in which were probably written about B.C. 1500. It consists chiefly of four chief sections called respectively the Rig-veda, the Yajur-veda, the Sama-veda, and the Atharva-veda.

VEDI.

In Vedic mythology the holy place immediately round an altar.

VEISDATES.

A Persian chief of the city of Tarba, who claiming to have been Bardes, the son of Cyrus, incited the Persians to rebel against Darius Hystaspes, and for a time became king of Persia. Darius sent against him his general Artabardes, who defeated him first at the city of Racha, and afterwards at the mountain of Parga, whither Veisdates had fled. He was then sent prisoner to Darius, by whom he was impaled at the town of Chadidia, together with his principal officials.

VEISPARES.

The father of Intaphernes, the chief officer of Darius Hystaspes.

VENDIDAD-SADE.

The Persian name of the Vidæ-vadata, which see.

VETAS.

A fortress city, the stronghold of Lalla of Millid. It was conquered by Shalmaneser II., king of Assyria.

VETOS. *Or* VETCIFEU, " Soaker."

An epithet applied to the god Bacchus on a Cypriote inscription in the Cesnola Collection.

VIBANUS.

The satrap of Arachotia under Darius Hystaspes. He was invited to rebel by Veisdates, the rebel king of Persia, and upon his refusing to do so was attacked by Veisdates. Darius, however, sent an army to his relief, and Vibanus defeated the rebel army at the fort of Capiscane, and also a second time at Gadytia, and following the rebel leader to the town of Arshadu slew him there.

VIDÆ-VADATA.

In Zendic mythology the book of the law against demons. It is the only one of the original sacred books of Zarathustra which has been preserved to us entire. It is now generally called by the Persians the Vendidad.

VILA.

A district bordering on Assyria which was rendered tributary by Samsi-Vul or Samas-Rimmon III.

VILI.

In Scandinavian mythology the son of Borr, and the grandson of Bure, the first man. He was one of the three murderers of the frost giant Ymir.

VIRABHATTARAYA.

A granite figure from Mysore. It was worshipped as a deity by the Badagas.

VIRACOCHO.

According to Peruvian tradition a primæval king in whose reign the Deluge took place.

VISHNU.

In Hindu mythology the third member of the Trimurti, and preserver of the world. He had undergone ten Avatars or incarnations, viz., a bird, tortoise, wild boar, andro-lion, the deity Khrishna, etc.

VISPERED.

In Zendic mythology one of the collections of fragments of the lost books of Zarathustra which go to make up the Vendidad-sade.

VISTASPA, the Great.

A famous king of Bactria, the son of Auravadaspu of the Keanian dynasty. He was converted from Paganism into the religion of Dualism by Zarathustra, and introduced the Zendic faith into the whole of his dominions.

VITRA.

In Vedic mythology darkness represented as a deity, and the antagonist of Indra as the personified light.

VIVANA.

The satrap of Arachosia in the reign of Darius Hystaspes. He was at first defeated by the rebels whom Vahyazdata, the Mede, had urged to rebel, but being reinforced with a larger army sent by Darius, he completely put down the rebellion. He was called Hyana by the Greek historians.

VOHU-MANO.   " The Good Spirit."

In Zendic mythology the first of the heavenly Amshaspands, which see.

Volla.

Another form of the name of the Scandinavian goddess Fulla, which see.

Volta.

According to Pliny the name of an Etruscan monster, who depopulated the district of Volsinii.

Vomises.

A Persian officer sent by Darius Hystaspes to the relief of his general Dadarses, who having been sent to reconquer Media was by them blockaded under the rebel Phraortes, whom Vomises took prisoner, and so ended the war.

Vul.

The Assyrian god of the atmosphere. His name is now more generally written Rimmon.

Vul-bel-ukin.

The governor in the reign of Assurnirari II. and Tiglath Pileser II. He was eponym of the year B.C. 738, the chief event in which was the capture of the city of Kullani (Calno), and 748, in which took place an expedition to Zimri.

Vul-bel-ukin.

Another and more correct rendering of the Assyrian name Vul-bel-uzur.

Vul-musam-mir.

The governor of Kalzi in the reign of Vulnirari III. He was eponym of the year B.C. 789, the chief event in which was an expedition to Media.

Vul-nirari I.

An early and powerful king of Assyria about B.C. 1330. He defeated the Babylonians and conquered the Rapiqu and Shuites, and considerably enlarged the extent of the Assyrian dominions. He was succeeded by his son Shalmaneser I., B.C. 1300. He was also called Benlikkish.

Vul-nirari II.

The son and successor of Assurdan II., king of Assyria. He reigned about B.C. 913 to 891, and was a great warrior, and restored the power of the Assyrian empire, which he left in an improved condition to his son Tugulti-ninip II. The Assyrian eponym canon commences from his reign.

Vul-nirari III.

The son of Samsi-Vul III., king of Assyria. He ascended the throne when a mere boy, about B.C. 812, but he was able by means of his generals not only to continue, but to extend the conquests of his father. In twenty-five successive expeditions he subdued all the sea-coast of Palestine, and conquered Mariha, king of Damascus, with the other Syrian states. Vulnirari invaded Syria as far as the tribe of Manasseh, but does not appear to have actually come into conflict with the Jews. About the middle of his reign he invaded Babylonia, and his last expeditions were against the Medes and the surrounding countries of Hupuskia and Kibiki. He married the princess Sammuramat, who is by some believed to have been the Semiramis of the Greeks. He built several great palaces at Nineveh and Calah, and died after a reign of twenty-nine years, leaving the throne to his son Shalmaneser III. B.C. 783.

VUL-PAL-IDINNA.

An early king of Babylonia. Little or nothing is known concerning him, except the erection of a wall of defence around Babylon. He appears to have been engaged in war with Ninipalassur, king of Assyria.

VUL-U-BALLAD.

The governor of Rimuri in the reign of Vulnirari III. He was eponym of the year B.C. 786, the chief event in which was an expedition to Kiski.

Vyakarana.

An ancient Hindu grammatical treatise dealing chiefly with the language of the sacred Vedas.

W.

WABU.

An Arabian usurper, whom the discontented chiefs of the Hedjaz placed on the throne in opposition to Vaiteh I., their king. He was defeated and carried captive to Assyria by Esarhaddon, who confirmed Vaiteh on his throne.

WADD.

One of the principal deities of the Himyarites of South-western Arabia.

WAD-EL-BENAT.

In prekoranic history the name of a custom among the ancient Arabs whereby they were allowed to bury alive such female children as the parents were unwilling to maintain.

WADGELMIR.

In Scandinavian mythology one of the thirty-two (or thirty-seven) muddy streams of hell.

WADY-TUMILAT.

The modern name of the city and nome of Chun-abt in Lower Egypt. It was the Hero-opolis of the Greeks.

WAHABA-IL-YAHAT.

An early Himyaritic monarch, whose date and place of government are not known.

WALASKIALF.

In Scandinavian mythology the name of the palace of Odin in the sacred city of Asgard, which see.

WALHALLA.

In Scandinavian mythology the name of the great palace in the sacred city of Asgard, which was the home of heroes who had bravely died in battle. It had 541 gates, and was entirely built of gold to an altitude exceeding the powers of sight.

WALI.

Another form of the name of the Scandinavian deity Ali, which see.

WALKURES.

In Scandinavian mythology certain deities who selected the souls of the slain heroes in battle, and conducted them to the Walhalla of Asgard. They were the deities of fate, sometimes called Nornes, which see.

WANDU.   'Water."

In Lithuanian mythology one of the two great giants by whom the world was all but destroyed.   *See* Wejas.

WANES.

In Scandinavian mythology a group of deities of the lowest rank, of whose special office little is known.

WARA.

In Scandinavian mythology the goddess of social contracts.

WARKA.

The modern name of the ruins of the ancient Chaldean city Erech, which see.

WASISHKA.

A Hindu deity who was invested by Brahma with the power of creation. *See* Angiras.

WATHIL.

The son of Himyar, and king of Sabæa.   He was succeeded by Alamluk.

WATR.   "Eminent."

An order of military nobility in the Sabæan kingdom of Yemen in South-western Arabia.

WATR-IL-DHARAH.

An early Himyaritic sovereign ruling at Haram.   He was the son of Yadhar Malik.

WEJAS.   "Wind."

In Lithuanian mythology one of the two great giants by whom the world was nearly destroyed.   *See* Pramzimas.

WERDANDI.   "Present."

In Scandinavian mythology one of the three deities of fate.   *See* Urd.

WESTRI.   "West."

In Scandinavian mythology one of the four horns which support the vault of heaven.

WIDAR.

In Scandinavian mythology the deity of silence.

WIDFINUR.

In Scandinavian mythology the father of the two children in the moon, Bil and Hiuki, whose presence causes the spots on the moon's face.

WINDSWALR.

In Scandinavian mythology the name of the father of the winter considered as a personification.

WINGOLF.

In Scandinavian mythology the region appointed to the goddesses in the sacred city of Asgard, which see.

WODIN.

The principal deity of the old German nations, to whom, as the god of battles, the captives taken in war were sacrificed. He was the analogue of the great Scandinavian god Odin, which see.

WUOTAN.

In old German mythology another form of the name of the principal Scandinavian divinity Wodin, or Odin, which see.

X.

XATHRITES.

An Assyrian leader, whose proper name was Phraortes. He incited the Assyrians to rebel against Darius Hystaspes, but unsuccessfully, as he was defeated and slain by Vomises, the general of Darius, at the town of Achitu.

XERXES.   " Warrior."

A king of Persia, and the second son of Darius Hystaspes, whom he succeeded, B.C. 485. The principal event of his life, viz., his invasion of Greece, belongs to the annals of Classic history : but his name, written Khshairsha, occurs on the monuments of Egypt, that country being then a Persian province. Disregarding the policy of his father, Xerxes treated the Egyptians with great severity, and with equal rigour he governed the conquered empire of Babylonia, delivering up the city of Babylon to a complete pillage, and carrying off to Persia the golden statue of Nebo and the treasures of the temple tomb of Bel Merodach. The name of Xerxes has also been found written in Cuneiform, Babylonian, Persian, and Median characters, and in Hieroglyphics on an Egyptian alabaster vase, recently discovered in the ruins of the mausoleum at Halicarnassus. After an inglorious reign of twenty years, Xerxes was assassinated by Artabanus, B.C. 465.

XESBET-MA.

The Egyptian name of the blue stone, generally known as lapis lazuli, which was much used for amulets, statues, and decorations, especially in the later dynasties.

XISUTHRUS.

According to Berosus the tenth and last of the antediluvian kings of Babylon. The dynasty of which he was chief is said to have reigned for 432,000 years.

XISUTHRUS.

According to Greek tradition the hero of the Flood. *See* Adra-hasis *and* Sisit.

XOCHIQUETZAL.

In Mexican mythology the wife of the patriarch Coxcox. She together with her husband survived the great Deluge, and re-established the human race.

XOIS.

A town in the Delta anciently called Aaskh, but now Sakha. It was the seat of empire of the XIVth Egyptian dynasty.

XONSU. *Or* KHONSU.

An Egyptian queen or queen consort of the XIth dynasty. Perhaps another wife of Antef III.

XULLI.

A king of Tubal who paid tribute to the Assyrians. He was succeeded by his son Ambaris, who was carried off to Nineveh, by Sargon II., king of Assyria.

Y.

YABRUD.

A town in Southern Palestine, which was conquered by Vaiteh I., king of Arabia, on his invasion of Palestine against Assurbanipal.

YADAIL-BAYYIN.

A king of the Himyarites, about the first century A.D. He was succeeded by Yakrab-Malik-Watr.

YADAIL-DHALI.

A king of the Himyarites, about A.D. 120. With him closed the reign of the kings at Marib, and the removal of the capital to Sana commenced ; from that period the Himyaritic empire declined.

YADAIL-DHARAH I.

A king of the Himyarites, about the first century A.D. He was succeeded by Samahali-Yanaf III.

YADAIL-WATR.

A king of the Himyarites, in the first century B.C. He was succeeded by Samahali-Dharah.

YADHAR-MALIK.

A Himyaritic sovereign, ruling at Harâm, of whom nothing is known.

YAFAR.

The king of Sabæa, and the son and successor of Sacsac. He lost the principality of Oman, which his father had regained, and his whole reign was spent in repressing revolutions. His son Noman, a posthumous child, ultimately succeeded him.

YAGHUTH. " Fire."

A local Sabæan divinity, who was worshipped at Djorash by the Benu-Madhidj. He was probably a form of the sun.

YAH-LU.

One of the forms in which the Arabian royal name Vaiteh was written by the Assyrians.

YAH-TA.

Another Assyrian form of the Arabian royal name Vaiteh.

YAHU-A.

The Assyrian form of the royal name Jehu, which see.

YAHU-BIDI.

A king of Hamath, who was conquered by Sargon II.

YAHU-HAZI. *Or* HAZI-YAHU.

The Assyrian name of that king of Judah who was called by the Hebrews Ahaz. He applied for help to Tiglath Pileser II., king of Assyria, against the kings of Israel and Damascus. The king of Assyria delivered him from those foes, but rendered his kingdom tributary to himself.

YAHVE. *Or* YAH.

The Assyrian form of writing the name of the Jehovah of the Jews, whom they regarded as a local deity.

YAHVEH.

The form of the name of the Jewish Deity, Jehovah, as it is written on the Moabite stone.

YAKINLU.

A king of the Island of Arvad, in the Mediterranean Sea. He paid tribute to Assurbanipal, king of Assyria, to whose harem he sent his daughter as a gift. On his death the throne was contested by his ten sons, and Azi-bahal was accepted as the heir by Esarhaddon, to whose decision the brothers had referred.

YAKRAB-MALIK-WATR.

A king of the Himyarites, about the first century A.D. He was succeeded by Yathamir-Bayyin.

YALA.

The son of Hasan, king of Yathrib, in Arabia. He succeeded his father on the throne, but he had to pay a heavy tribute to Esarhaddon, king of Assyria, for the right of succession.

YALMAN.

A district or city in Babylonia, which was conquered by Samsi-Vul or Samas-Rimmon III., king of Assyria.

YAMA.

In Hindu mythology the god of hell and also the deity of justice. *Cf.* Rhot-a-menti *and* Osiris.

YAMAN.

An usurper, whom the people of Ashdod raised to the throne, in opposition to their own king Akhimit, who was placed over them by Sargon II. That act of insubordination led to the great siege of Ashdod by the Assyrians. *See* Akhimit.

YAMIN.

A king of Ascalon, who was deposed by Sargon II., who set up Zedek in his stead as a tributary.

YAMUT-BUL.

An ancient name for the kingdom of Elam, when it was under the rule of Kudur-Mabuk and his successors.

YAN-BO.

A seaport of the Jorhamite Arabs, in the Hedjaz.

YAN-ZU.

The king of the land of Nahiri, in Hupuskia. He was a faithful tributary of Sargon II.

YANZU.

The son of Haban. He was placed on the throne of Zimri by Shalmaneser II., after the flight of its king, Maruduk-mudamik. He afterwards revolted against the king of Assyria, by whom he was overthrown.

YAOUAH.

Among the Dyaks of Barneo said to be the name for the Supreme Being. (Cameron.)

YAPAA. *Or* YAPAH.

A queen of Dihutani, or Dihtan, in Arabia, who was conquered and put to death by Esarhaddon.

YAPPU.

A Phenician city which was conquered by Sennacherib. It was the Joppa of Hebrew and Mediæval writers.

YARKI.

A Nabathean town which was conquered by Assurbanipal, in the second Arabian war.

YARUB.

In prekoranic history the son of Kahtan, and king of the Joktanidæ. He invaded the kingdom of Yemen, and overthrew the dynasty of Lokman, driving the Adites to take shelter in the mountains of Hadramaut. He was succeeded by his son, Yashdjob.

YASHDJOB.

The son of Yarub, the great king of the Joktanite race of Yemen. He soon lost the power obtained by his father, and the provinces of Mahrah and Hadramaut made themselves independent.

YASNA.

One of the collections of fragments of the lost book of Zarathustra, which go to make up the Vendidad-sade.

YATA-AMIR.

A king of Sabæa, in South-western Arabia. He was one of the early successors of Himyar, and paid tribute to Sargon II.

YATAL-BAYYIN.

A petty king of Saba, after the fall of the Himyaritic empire. *See* Faram-Yanhab.

YATHA. " Saviour God."

A Himyaritic deity, to whom, in conjunction with the other local gods, a temple was erected in Abyan by Abd-shems-Aslam and his brother Marthad. He was the special guardian of the town of Aden, and his analogue was the Chaldean divinity Salman.

YATHA-AMIR-WATR.

A king of the Himyarites about the first century A.D. He was succeeded (?) by Halak-amir.

YATH-AMIR-BAYYIN I.

A king of the Himyarites about the first century A.D. He was succeeded by Karibail-bayyin.

YATH-AMIR-BAYYIN II.

A king of the Himyarites about the first century A.D. He was succeeded by Yadail-dharah.

YATHRIB.

A district in Arabia which was early settled by the people of the Djasim, a collection of Amalekite tribes. It was afterwards conquered by Esarhaddon, who imposed a heavy tribute on its king Yala. It is now called Medineh.

YATSU-BIGALLA. " Men of Great Stature."

A tribe of the Kassi, or the mountain people North of Elam, conquered by Sennacherib in his first campaign, who deported them to the cities of Kar-thisbe and Beth-kubitti.

YATU.

An unknown region which was conquered by Shalmaneser II., king of Assyria.

YAUBID.

The form in which the French Assyriologists translate the Hamathite royal name Ilubihid, which see.

YAU-HAZI.

Another form of the name by which Ahaz, king of Judah, was known to the Assyrians.

Yauk.

A local Sabæan deity who was worshipped by the Benu-murad and the tribe of Khaywan. He was possibly a form of the sun.

Yautah.

A different transcription of the Arabian names Yahlu and Vaiteh.

Yav.

An Assyrian deity who was called "The Inundator." He was another form of Vul, the god of the atmosphere. (This should be Rimmon. The Assyrian is *Ra-ma-nu ra-kha-tsu*, "Rimmon the Inundator." Sayce.)

Yavan. *Or* Yaman.

An usurper whom the people of Ashdod raised to the throne in the room of Akhimit, the nominee of the Assyrians. Yavan entered into alliance with Hezekiah of Judah, as well as with Moab and Edom, and sent for aid against Assyria to the king of Egypt. The confederacy, however, was broken up by Sargon, B.C. 711, Ashdod was taken, and Yavan fled to Ethiopia, but the Ethiopian king delivered him in chains to Sargon.

Yavana.

In the Sanscrit inscriptions the name of a country and people to the West of Kandahar, which may have been either Arabia, Persia, Media, or Assyria, most probably the last. In later times the name was used to embrace the area of all those countries, and there is no evidence to show that it was at any one time the exclusive name of the Greeks. (Mitra.)

Yavana. "Young Ones."

The original Aryan root from whence the ethnical names Jaones, Javan, Jaunas, were derived. (M. Müller.)

Yazatas.

In Zendic mythology certain heavenly spirits lower than the Amshaspands, and whose special care was the preservation of local parts of the universe. *See* Amshaspands.

Yazbuk.

A country between the Orontes and the sea, which was conquered together with its king Burante by Shalmaneser II.

Year, Assyrian.

The Assyrian year consisted of twelve lunar months, each month commencing on the evening when the new moon was first observed, or in case the moon was not observed the new month started thirty days after the last month. The months were thus all either of twenty-nine or thirty days, and these two numbers generally, but not always, alternated. The year commenced at the vernal equinox, the new moon next before the equinox marking the commencement of the new year, the equinox thus falling some time during the first month Nisan. As twelve lunar months make about 354 days, or eleven days less than the solar year of 365 days, therefore, in order to keep their year in its proper position in regard to the seasons, the Assyrians adopted an occasional thirteenth month, to be intercalated whenever the twelfth month ended more than thirty days before the equinox. Since the Assyrians had official astronomers, who observed the heavens and regulated the calendar, they could not be far out in their calculations, probably one or two days would be the limit of error. On the average in the Assyrian calendar the year would begin about fourteen days before the vernal equinox, and the night of the fifteenth day of the tenth month would thus be about the longest night. Among the Assyrians the first twenty-eight days of every month were divided into four weeks of seven days each, the seventh, fourteenth, twenty-first, and twenty-eighth days respectively, being Sabbaths, and there was a general prohibition of work on those days. Besides the ordinary Ve-adar, or intercalary thirteenth month, the Assyrians had two other intercalary months, one a second Nisan, and the other a second Elul. When all three intercalary months were used the year would have fifteen months, and judging from the fact that an intercalation of three months is required in every eight years, it appears probable that these two extra months were connected with a cycle of eight years, seven years in succession being normal, that is having twelve months each, while the eighth year had fifteen. Only in early Babylonian dated tablets however has there been found any notice of this fifteen months year, and it may be doubted if it was ever used in Assyria. (Smith, *Assyrian Canon.*)

YEAR, EGYPTIAN.

The Egyptian year, like that of most of the ancient nations, was a lunar one, with a movable New-year's day. The months were divided into three decades, of which the first day was a festival in honour of the dead. The civil year began in the month of Thoth. *See* Appendix, Egyptian Calendar, *and* Sothic Cycle, Canopus, Decree of, *etc.*

YEAREA-SWAMY.

A Badaga deity who was originally a refractory chief in Coimbatoor.

YEDIH.

A petty kingdom in Arabia which was rendered tributary to Assyria by Esarhaddon.

YELRURI.

A district of which Samas-upach-chir was prefect under Sargon II.

YEMEN.

A province in Arabia peopled by the descendants of Ad and his sons Shedid and Shedad, which see.

YERIM.

The modern name of the site of the famous gardens of Irem in Yemen, which see.

42

YESHT-SADE.

A collection of fragments of Zoroastrian literature. A kind of appendix to the Vendidad-sade, which it resembles.

YGGDRASIL.

In Scandinavian mythology the name of the sacred ash tree, whose leaves canopied the heavens, whose stem went into Hel, while beneath its roots were three fountains, one of them belonging to the giant Mimir, being that of wisdom, while around and in the ocean beneath was coiled the serpent Midgard.

YIMA-KHACTA.

The real name of the Aryan mythical hero Djemshid, which see.

YMIR.

In Scandinavian mythology the great frost giant, who was slain by Odin, Vili, and Ve, the three sons of Borr, the son of the first man. Out of the body of Ymir the earth was constructed, and in the blood which issued from his veins all of the race of giants were drowned except one, Begelmir, who escaped the sanguous deluge in a ship, and together with his wife repeopled the earth.

YONI.

In Hindu mythology an oviform or boat-shaped emblem, the symbol of the receptive or maternal power of nature. *See* Lingam.

YSODHA.

In Hindu mythology the mother of Khrishna, or the god Vishnu in a human form. *See* Vishnu *and* Khrishna.

YUTIYA.

A district in Persia in which was situated the city of Tarba, the birth-place of the rebel king Veisdates, which see.

YWAITE.

Another form of the Arabian royal name Vaiteh, which see.

YZEDS.

The Persian name of the inferior deities which were called by the Zends Yazatas, which see.

Z.

ZAB.

An Assyrian river running into the Euphrates, having in the time of the early kings of Assyria many important towns upon its banks. Assurnazirpal excavated a canal from the city of Calah to its shores, a work which necessitated one of the first tunnels on record.

ZAB.

An Assyrian ·town which revolted to Assurdainpal, and was re-conquered by Samas-Rimmon or Samsi-Vul IV. about B.C. 825. *See also—*

ZABA.

A city in Babylonia which was plundered by Assurdan, king of Assyria, about the twelfth century B.C.

ZAB-ANU.

A king of the country of the Zuzarurai, who paid tribute to Samas-Rimmon or Samsi-Vul III.

ZABAR.

The Assyrian name of copper or bronze.

ZAB-DANU.

The brother of Naɒu-bal-idinna, king of Babylon, who unsuccessfully sent him with an army of 3000 men to assist the revolt of King Sabadu of Sùhi against the Assyrians, by whom he was defeated.

ZABEL.

A king of the country of the Dimamai who paid tribute to Samas-Rimmon III., king of Assyria.

ZABIBE.

The queen of the Arabs. She was conquered by and paid tribute to Tiglath Pileser II.

ZABNUTI.

One of the twenty petty kingdoms of Egypt under the Assyrian Icosarchy.

ZABU.

An early Chaldean monarch ruling at Sippara, where he built temples in honour of the goddess Anunit, and of Shamas, the sun, which temples were restored many centuries afterwards by Nabonidus.

ZAB-VUL.

A chief of the district of Dagara in the South-east of Assyria. He revolted with some success against Assurnazirpal, king of Assyria, who ultimately defeated his army and annexed his kingdom after some years resistance. The fate of Zabvul is not known.

ZACYNTHUS.

The ancient name of the Island of Zante in the Grecian Archipelago.

ZADAKIEL.

In Cabalistic mythology the spirit of the planet Jupiter.

ZADDI.

A Chaldean city which is mentioned in the inscription of Samsi-Vul or Samas-Rimmon III., king of Assyria.

ZADKHIAU.

An Egyptian chief, who unsuccessfully revolted against Piankhi-Meramen of the XXIInd dynasty. He was Lord of Khent-nofre. His name is of Semitic origin, and is the same as the Zedekiah of Hebrew writers.

ZADKIEL.

The governor of Tushan, in the reign of Assurdan III. He was eponym of the year B.C. 764, in which year there was "peace in the land."

ZAFAR.

A town in Yemen, which was founded by Shemmir, king of Sabæa. This town is not to be confounded with that of Zafar in Mahrah.

ZAFAR.

A famous capital city in Mahrah in South-western Arabia.

ZAGROS.

A mountain district on the frontiers of Elam. It was subdued by Assurbanipal, king of Assyria.

ZAIDU. "The Hunter."

An early Chaldean king. He was the son of Izdubar, and succeeded his father to the throne of Babylonia. *See also* Duzi *and* Tamzi.

ZAK-DINU-ISHA. "Has not an Equal."

The name of the great palace of Sennacherib, on the river Tigris.

ZAL.

The Egyptian name of the chief town of the fourteenth nome of Lower Egypt, or the Heliopolis of the Greeks. It was attacked by the Shashu, who were repulsed and driven back into the desert by Seti I. of the XIXth dynasty.

ZALISHA-TAR-BIT.

An Elamite city which was destroyed by Sennacherib.

ZALMOXIS.

According to Herodotus the great deity of the Getæ; the same god was sometimes called Gebeleïzis. The Getæ are said to have offered human sacrifice to him every five years.

ZAMAMA-ZIKUR-IDINNA.

An early king of Babylonia about B.C. 1200, in whose time the country was invaded and plundered by Assurdan, king of Assyria.

ZAMANA.

A Babylonian deity to whom Hammurabi, king of Babylonia, erected at the city of Kis, now called Hymir, a *Ziggurrat* or tower, called "The Tower of the Country."

ZANASARNA.

The king of Pardukka. He was attacked by, and rendered tribute to, Esarhaddon, king of Assyria.

ZANU.

The Assyrian name of one of the twenty petty kingdoms established in Egypt by Esarhaddon.

ZAPHNATH-PAANEAH.

An Egyptian title given to the patriarch Joseph by the Egyptian king under whom he was viceroy. The name has been interpreted Tsafento, "Sustainer of Many," Zepnat-Pœnich, "Joseph the Phenician," and "Revealer of Secrets."

ZAPKIEL.

In Cabalistic astronomy the angel of the planet Saturn.

ZARATHUSTRA.   "Splendour of Gold."

In Zendic mythology the almost mythical sage who was the author of the books of the Zend-avesta. His name was written by the Greeks Zoroaster.

ZARATU.

A city in Babylonia which was invaded and conquered by Samsi-Vul or Samas-Rimmon III., king of Assyria.

ZAREPHATH.

The Hebrew name of the city of Zariptu, which see.

ZARIC.   "Poison."

In Zendic mythology the sixth and last of the evil Darvands, which see.

ZARILAB.

A city in Babylonia, where Hammurabi built a temple to the goddess Nana.

ZARIPTU.

A Phenician city which was conquered by Sennacherib on his first invasion of Palestine. It was the Zarephath of Hebrew history.

ZARISU.

A king of the city of Khundurai, or Parsaniyai, who paid tribute to Samas-Rimmon III. or IV., king of Assyria.

ZARVAN-AKAR-ANA.   "Time without Limits."

According to the Parsees the name of a deity or abstract principle which existed even before the eternal birth of Ahuramazda and Agramainyas.

ZAZA.   *Or* ZAZAI.

The archon of the city of Arpad, and eponym of the year B.C. 692, in the reign of Sennacherib, king of Assyria.

ZAZAZ.

The governor of Billati. He was one of the chiefs who conspired with Saul-mugina against his brother, Assurbanipal.

ZEDEK.

A king of Ascalon. He was placed upon the throne by his suzerain, Sargon II., who deposed his predecessors Metinti and Yamin to make way for him. Revolting from his allegiance he was carried off captive into Assyria by Sennacherib.

ZEET.

According to the Greek lists a king of Tanis. He has not yet been certainly identified, unless the name is another form of the name of the Egyptian or Ethiopian monarch Zerah, which see.

ZEMARITES.

A Phenician people, whose town was on the Nahr el Kelb in Northern Syria. They did not, however, join the Phenician confederation against the Assyrians and Egyptians, but allied themselves with the Arameans of the Orontes valley.

ZEMZEM.

The sacred well of Mecca, which is said to have arisen from the earth at the striking of the ground by the foot of the dying Ishmael.

ZENDAVESTA.   "Text and Comment."

The name of all that remains of the lost Nackas, or books of the Parsee or Zendic religion. *See also* Vidæ-vadata,

ZEPHATH.

A town in Palestine, where Azech-amen the invader was defeated by King Asa. *See* Tsezphath.

ZERAH.

According to some Egyptologists the name by which Azech-amen, king of Ethiopia, is mentioned in Hebrew history.

ZERGHUL.

The modern name of the ancient Babylonian capital Zir-gulla.

ZERVAN.

According to the Grecian mythologists one of the three sons of Xisuthrus. He made war upon his brothers, Titan and Japhetos, in order that his own children might reign over the world ; but his sister Astlik made peace between them. He has been compared with the patriarch Shem of Hebrew history.

ZES-MEHENT-PER-U.

An Egyptian lady, the mother of Rameses, the royal chancellor of Taharkah.

ZET.

The last king of the XXIIIrd dynasty. At present his name is only found on the lists of Manetho. *See* Zeet.

ZET-AUF-ANKH.

The son of Hotep-pthah, and a priest of Apis in the XXIInd dynasty.

ZET-AUF-PTHAH.

A priest of Apis, and the son of Hotep-pthah. Period uncertain.

ZET-AUN-PTHAH-MER-ATEF-S.

A priest of Apis, in the time of Amasis II.

ZET-ISI-AUF-ANKH.

A priest of Apis. He was the son of Pentkhi. His period is uncertain.

ZET-PTHAH-AUF-ANKH.

A chorister in the temple of Pthah in the XXVIth dynasty. He was the father of Psametik, a royal chancellor.

ZEUS-ATROTIUS.

According to a Greco-Phenician writer a name given to the deity Dagon after his discovery of the plough.

ZEUS-BELUS.

A late Phenician name of the deity Bel, as identified with the Zeus of the Greeks.

ZEUS-CLARIOS.

In the district of Arcadia a local name of the deity Zeus.

ZEUS-ITHOMATES.

The name under which Zeus was the national deity of Messenia.

ZEUS-LYCÆOS.

In ancient Arcadia another local name of the deity Zeus.

ZHAFAR.

The earliest capital of the Himyaritic kingdom of Saba, in South-western Arabia.

ZI.

In the Izdubar Legends a kind of spiritual essence or fetish residing in every organic thing, each created object having its special Zi, of which the Supreme Being was a more exalted genus. Zi was also by parity of reasoning regarded as the soul of man, and even man himself.

ZIANU.

The Assyrian form of the name of the Egyptian city Tanis, or Zoan, under the Icosarchy established by Esarhaddon.

ZIB-ANNA.   *Or* ZIB-ANITU.

In Chaldean astronomy a name of the planet Saturn.

ZIBARA.

A city which was conquered by Samsi-Vul or Samas-Rimmon III., who set up there his own statue to record his victory over the inhabitants.

ZICHÆUS.   *Or* SICHÆUS.

The Romanized form of the Tyrian name Zicharbaal, which see.

ZICHAR-BAAL.

The high-priest of Melkarth.   He married Elissa, the sister of Pümeliun, king of Tyre, by whom he was put to death as a dangerous rival.   He was the Sichæus of Virgil, and the Acerbas of traditional history.   *See* Elissa *and* Pümeliun.

ZICU.   " The Heaven."

The Accadian word from which the name of the Greco-Babylonian god or primæval substance Sige was derived.

ZID-QA.   *Or* ZEDEK.

A king of Ascalon.   He refused to submit to Sennacherib upon his invasion of Palestine, who defeated him, sending his wife, his sons, and daughters, into captivity, and placing Sar-lu-dari, the son of Rukibti, on the throne, about B.C. 703.

ZID-UNNU-RABI.   " Great Zidon."

The Assyrian name of the Phenician city of Zidon, which was conquered by Sennacherib in his first invasion of Palestine.

ZIGGURRAT.

A temple tower surmounted by a fire-altar. These towers were much in use among the Babylonians. *See* Zamana.

ZIKAR-SIN. "Servant of Sin."

Another form of the Babylonian royal name Ardu-sin, which see.

ZIKARTI.

A petty kingdom in Media. It was the Sagartia of Classical history. *See* Mitatti.

ZILLI-BEL.

The king of Gaza. He was one of the tributaries of Sennacherib, king of Assyria, by whom was assigned to him one-fourth of the towns taken by the Assyrians from the West of Palestine.

ZILLI-BEL.

The Rabbitur of Vul-nirari III., and eponym of the year B.C. 807, the chief event in which was an expedition to Minni.

ZILLI-ISTAR.

The governor of Arbela in the reign of Vul-nirari III. He was eponym of the year B.C. 788, in which year was held a great festival at the termination of the sacred cycle.

ZIMRI.

A country to the South-east of Assyria. It was ravaged by Shalmaneser II., who driving off its king Maruduk-mud-amik, placed on the throne in his stead Yanzu, the son of Haban.

ZINENI.

The confidential servant of Teumman, the Elamite, who was sent with the consent of his brother Urtaki, king of Elam, to stir up a revolt in Babylonia. His mission was without success, and an open war soon broke out between Elam and Assyria, when Zineni deserted the cause of Teumman, just before the fatal battle of Shushan. *See* Urtaki.

ZIO.

A deity of the Suevians, answering it is supposed to the sword-bearing god Tyr of the Scandinavians.

ZIRA-BANI.

An Assyrian officer in the reign of Sargon II., whose titles are lost. He was the eponym of the year B.C. 718, the chief event in which was an expedition to Sinukta.

ZIR-GULLA.

An ancient Chaldean city, once the seat of empire. It is now called Zerghul.

ZIR-LABKI.

The Accadian name of the city Zarilab.

ZIRNA.

An Etruscan winged goddess, who was represented as sitting at the side of Turan and Adonis, with a pencil and box of cosmetics. A half-moon hangs from her necklace.

ZIRRATBANIT.

An Assyrian and Babylonian goddess, the consort of the god Marduk. A temple was erected at Babylon to her by Hammurabi. Her worship was carried into Samaria by the Babylonians after the fall of the kingdom of Israel. She was the Succoth-Benoth of Hebrew history.

ZIRTU.

The capital city of the kingdom of Minni, or Armenia. It was abandoned to the Assyrians by its king Udaki, and the district was soon after annexed by Shalmaneser II.

ZIU.

Another form of the name of the Scandinavian deity Tyr, which see.

ZOAN.

The Biblical name of the capital city of Tanis, or San, in Lower Egypt. *See* Tanis.

ZODIAC.

Many of the Egyptian temples have astronomical representations; and notably those of Esneh, Contra Latopolis, and Denderah, were famous for their zodiacal ceilings. According to the positions of the stars on their monuments the records of the Egyptian empire were traceable to a very remote, if not indeed a fabulous antiquity. A more careful criticism of the constellations depicted, and of the archæology of the temples in which they are contained has proved that all these representations are of the Ptolemaic and even the Roman period, and are consequently from a historical point of view wholly unauthentic. The Zodiac of Denderah has been removed to Paris, where it forms the chief ornament of the Museum of the Louvre. Those still remaining in Egypt have suffered much deterioration, and will probably in no great length of time absolutely disappear.

ZOHAK.

In Arabic history a mythical conqueror and demon who carried two great serpents coiled on his shoulders, which were fed with the brains of young men. Having long corrupted and destroyed the people of Ispahan, he was slain by the people in an insurrection headed by one Caveh, a blacksmith, whose two sons had been slain to feed the snakes of Zohak. The people then placed on the throne of Persia, Feridun, the grandson of Djemshid, which see.

ZOPHASEMIN. "Overseers of the Heavens."

In Phenician mythology certain insensible creatures in the form of eggs, from which at the beginning intelligent beings were created.

ZOROASTER.

A Persian philosopher who was reputed by the Greeks to have written the books of the Magi during the reign of Darius, and who has been confounded with the great religious writer of the Zends. *See* Zarathustra.

ZOZA.

A village in Armenia where the army of Dadarses the rebel was defeated by Darius Hystaspes for the first time.

ZU.

In the Izdubar Legends a mystical deity who appears to have been a kind of Babylonian Prometheus. He stole the tablets of destiny and other secrets of the gods, for which Bel ordered Rimmon to slay him. Zu, however, fled to desert places, and Rimmon was unable to effect his purpose. Nebo who was sent next failed equally. After this Zu seems to have been changed into a bird, called by the Assyrians "The Divine Zu Bird," and by the Accadians "The Divine Bird of the Tempest." It was a species of vulture, and an emblem of the storm-cloud, of which the god Zu was originally an impersonation. It is possible that he is to be identified with the god Zi (in Assyrian, Nisu or "Man,"), who seems to be regarded as the first human being in the tablets which describe the fall.

ZUAB.

In early Chaldean mythology the generic name of the ocean, and more especially that which was supposed to encircle the world. (Maspero.)

ZUHAL.

The planet Saturn adored as a deity by the ancient Arabians.

ZUKKA.

A city near to Armenia which allied with Urza, king of Armenia, against Sargon II., who conquered it and sent the inhabitants into slavery into Palestine and Phenicia.

ZUL-KARNAIM. "The Two Horned."

An oriental title which was given to Alexander the Great in allusion to his descent from Jupiter Ammon ; an allusion also perhaps glanced at by the Hebrew writers.

ZUR-SIN.

An early Babylonian king ruling at Ur. He was deified after death.

ZURZUKKA.

A city of Minni, which with its neighbour city Suandahal, revolted against Sargon II., who soon besieged it and took the inhabitants for slaves. *See* Iranzi.

Zuzarunai.

A country which was rendered tributary to Assyria by Samas-Rimmon III., king of Assyria.

Zuzim.

In Hebrew history the fourth of the five great divisions of the Rephaim. They were said to have resided in the district of Ham, but their precise position is not yet ascertained. They belonged to the great ethnical body which was called by the ancient Egyptians Sati, and have been supposed to have had a Semitic origin.

APPENDICES.

No. 1.

ROUGH OUTLINE

OF

BABYLONIAN CHRONOLOGY.

From SMITH's *Chaldean Genesis.*

B.C. ANTE 2000   Epoch of independent kingdoms in Babylonia. Accad the metropolis.

,,   2000   Era of Urukh, king of Ur.   Rise of Sumir. Ur the metropolis.

,,   1850   Era of Ismi-dagan, king of Karrak. Karrak the metropolis.

,,   1700   Rise of Larsa as metropolis.

,,   1600   Era of Sargon, king of Accad.   Revival of the power of Accad.

,,   1550   Era of Hammurabi, king of Babylon.   Babylon the metropolis.

No. 2.

LIST OF CONTEMPORANEOUS

ASSYRIAN AND CHALDEAN KINGS.

Contributed by W. St. Chad Boscawen.

In the sixteenth century B.C. Hammu-rabi conquered Kurdur-mabug and founded the Kassite line. It was about this period that the formation of the Assyrian empire began, but no definite synchronism can be arrived at until the fifteenth century. For the compilation of this list I have used the following lists of kings, viz. :

(1) Lists in Smith's *Assyrian Discoveries.*

(2) " Early History of Babylonia," by same author in *Records of the Past*, Vol. III. ; and

(3) Synchronous History, *W. A. I.*, II., 65, III., 43, and un-published fragments.

(4) List in Paper of Mr. G. Smith's on the Assyrian original "Canon of Berosus," *Trans. Soc. Bib. Arch.*, Vol. III., Part ii.

CHALDEA.		ASSYRIA.	
B.C.			B.C.
1450	Kari-indas	Assur-bil-nisi-su	
1430	Burna-buryas II.	Buzur-assur	
1410	Kara-hardas (murdered)	Assur-ubalid	
1400	Nazi-bugas (usurper)	,,	
1380	Kuri-galzu II.[1]	Bel-nirari	
1350	Mili-sihu II.[1]	Pudil	
		Vul-nirari I.	1330-1300
1325	Marduk-baladan I.[1]	Shalmaneser I.	1300-1271
1300	Nazi-muru-das II.	Tugulti-ninip	1271
	Assyrian Dynasty.		
	Tugulti-ninip	Bel-chadressar	1240
1230	Vul-bi	Ninip-palesar	
1200	Qamama-zakir-idin	Assur-dayan	
		Mutagil-nuscu	1170-1150

Found on a stone brought by Mr. Smith from Babylonia.

	CHALDEA.	ASSYRIA.	
B.C.			B.C.
1150	Nabu-chad-nezzar I.	Assur-risilim	1150
	Kara-buryas		
1100	Marduk-nadin-ahi	Tiglath-Pileser I.	1120
	Marduk-sapik-zirrat	Assur-bil-kala	1080
1080	. . . . sadua		

After this there is a great break, and it is impossible to arrange the monarchs in any contemporaneous order until the reign of Tugulti-ninip II.

Samas-sihu, 17 years	Samsi-vul III.
Hea-mukin-ziru (usurper)	Assur-rab-amar
Kassu-nadin-ahu, 6 years	Assur-dan II.
Ulbar-zirki-idinna, 15 years	Vul-nirari II.
Nabu(?)chadnezzar II. 2 yrs.	Tugulti-ninip II.
. . . saga-muna, 3 months	
(An Elamite king reigns 3 years)	
Vul-pal-idina [1]	
Nabu-zakir-iskum.	(A war with Assyria, but no contemporaneous records of it.)
Isba-marduk	
Marduk-baladan II.	
Vul-zakir-iskun	

885	Sibur	Assur-nazir-pal
	Nabu-bal-idinna	Shalmanesar II.
	Marduk-zakir-izkur	,,
	Marduk - bel - usate revolts against him.	Assur-dain-pal (rebel)
	Chaldea partly under Assyrian rule(?) and native princes.	Samsi-vul IV.
		Vul-nirari III.
	,,	Shalmanesar III.
	,,	Assur-dan III.
	,,	Assur-nariri
747	Nabu-nazir (Nabonnassar)	Tiglath-Pileser II.
732	Kin-ziru	,,
		Shalmanesar IV.
722	Marduk-baladan III.	Sargon
	Sargon	
705	Marduk-baladan III. (restored)	Sennacherib
703	Bel-ibni	,,

722	Marduk-baladan III.	Sargon	721

[1] These monarchs are from the list in *Trans. Soc. Bib. Arch.*, Vol. III., Part ii. "The supposed Assyrian original of Canon of Berosus."

CHALDEA.	ASSYRIA.

<table>
<tr><td>B.C.</td><td></td><td></td><td>B.C.</td></tr>
<tr><td>700</td><td>Assur-nadin-sum[1]</td><td>Sennacherib</td><td></td></tr>
<tr><td>693</td><td>Suzub</td><td>Esarhaddon</td><td></td></tr>
<tr><td>689</td><td>Esarhaddon</td><td></td><td></td></tr>
<tr><td></td><td></td><td>Assur-bani-pal</td><td>668</td></tr>
<tr><td>668</td><td>Saul-mugina</td><td></td><td></td></tr>
<tr><td>648</td><td>Assur-bani-pal</td><td>Bel-zikir-iskun</td><td></td></tr>
<tr><td></td><td></td><td>Assur-ebni-ili (?) } (?)
Assaracus</td><td></td></tr>
<tr><td>626</td><td>Nabu-pal-assar</td><td>Fall of the Assyrian Empire.</td><td></td></tr>
<tr><td>605</td><td>Nabu-chadnezzar III.</td><td></td><td></td></tr>
<tr><td>562</td><td>Evil-marduk</td><td></td><td></td></tr>
<tr><td>556</td><td>Nergal-sar-uzur
Ulbar-zurki-iddina</td><td></td><td></td></tr>
<tr><td>536</td><td>Nabu-naid (Nabonidus)
associated with</td><td></td><td></td></tr>
<tr><td>536</td><td>Bel-sar-ussur (in whose reign</td><td></td><td></td></tr>
<tr><td>536</td><td>Babylon was taken by Cyrus).</td><td></td><td></td></tr>
</table>

Fall of the Babylonian Empire.

[1] Son of Sennacherib. See Taylor Cylinder, Col. iii., line 63.

No. 3.

BABYLONIAN COSMOGONY.

From SMITH's *Chaldean Genesis.*

Tautu (*the Sea*)　　　　Absu (*the Deep*)

Mummu (*Chaos*)

Lahma (*Force*, mas.)　　　Lahama (*Force*, fem.)

Kisar (*Lower expanse*)　　Sar (*Upper expanse*)

Anu (*Heaven*)　　Anatu (*Earth*)　　Elu　　Beltis

Vul (*Atmosphere*)　Belkan (*Fire god*)　Hea—Davkine　Ishtar (*the Elder*)

Merodach—Ziratbanit

Nebo—Tasmit

Elu—Beltis

Sin　　　Ningal　　　Ninip

Samas　　　　　Ishtar (*the Younger*)

43

No. 4.

LIST OF THE SUCCESSION

OF

THE ASSYRIAN KINGS,

WITH THEIR APPROXIMATE DATES.

From SMITH'S *History of Assyria.*

Ismi-dagan	B.C.	1850-1820
Samsi-Vul I. (or Samas-Rimmon)	,,	1820-1800
Igur-kap-kapu ⎫ Samsi-Vul II. ⎭	About ,,	1800
Ilu-ba ⎫ Iritak ⎭	About ,,	1750
Bel-kap-kapu	About ,,	1700
Adasi ⎫ Bel-bani ⎭	About ,,	1650
Assur-zakir-esir ⎫ Ninip-tugul-assuri ⎭	About ,,	1600
Iriba-vul ⎫ Assur-nadin-ahi ⎭	About ,,	1550
Assur-nirari I. ⎫ Nabu-dan ⎭	About ,,	1500
Assur-bel-nisisu	,,	1450-1420
Buzur-assur	,,	1420-1400
Assur-ubalid	,,	1400-1370
Bel-nirari	,,	1370-1350
Budil (or Pudil)	,,	1350-1330
Vul-nirari I.	,,	1330-1300
Shalmaneser I.	,,	1300-1271
Tugulti-ninip I.	,,	1271-1240
Bel-kudur-uzur	,,	1240-1220
Ninip-pal-esar	,,	1220-1200
Assur-dan I.	,,	1200-1170
Mutaggil-nusku	,,	1170-1150
Assur-risilim	,,	1150-1120

Tiglath-Pileser I.	B.C.	1120-1100
Assur-bel-kala	,,	1100-1080
Samsi-Vul III.	,,	1080-1060
Assur-rab-amar ⎫ or ⎬	About ,,	1050
Assur-rabbur ⎭		
Assur-nimati	About ,,	1000
Assur-dan II.	,,	930-913
Vul-nirari II.	,,	913-891
Tugulti-ninip II.	,,	891-885
Assur-nazir-pal	,,	885-860
Shalmaneser II.	,,	860-825
Assur-dain-pal (rebel king)	,,	827
Samsi-Vul IV.	,,	825-812
Vul-nirari III.	,,	812-783
Shalmaneser III.	,,	783-773
Assur-dan III.	,,	773-755
Assur-nirari II.	,,	755-745
Tiglath-Pileser II.	,,	745-727
Shalmaneser IV.	,,	727-722
Sargon	,,	722-705
Sennacherib	,,	705-681
Esarhaddon	,,	681-668
Assur-bani-pal	,,	668-626
Bel-zakir-iskum	,,	626-620
Assur-ebil-ili (Assuracus?)	,,	620-607

Fall of the Assyrian Empire.

No. 5.

THE EARLY KINGS OF DAMASCUS.

From Smith's *Eponym Canon.*

	B.C.	CONTEMPORARY WITH OR REFERRED TO IN
Rezin I. . . .	990 to 970	Solomon; 1 Kings xi. 23-25; called Hezion; 1 Kings xv. 18.
Tab-rimmon . .	970 to 950	Jeroboam; 1 Kings xv. 18.
Ben-hadad I. . .	950 to 930	Baasha; 1 Kings xv. 18-20.
(King, name unknown)	930 to 910	Omri; 1 Kings xx. 34.
Ben-hadad II. . .	910 to 886	Ahab; 1 Kings xx.
Hazael I. . . .	886 to 857	Jehu; 2 Kings viii. 9.
Ben-hadad III. . .	857 to 844	Jehoahaz; 2 Kings xiii. 3. Inscriptions of Shalmaneser.
Hazael II. . . .	844 to 830	Jehoahaz and Joash; 2 Kings xii. 17; xiii. 22.
Ben-hadad IV. . .	830 to 800	Joash and Jeroboam; 2 Kings xiii. 24.
Mariha . . .	800 to 770	Jeroboam. Inscription of Vul-nirari III.
Hadara (?) . . .	770 to 750	Menahem. Inscription of Tiglath Pileser.
Rezin II. . . .	750 to 732	Pekah; 2 Kings xv. 37. Inscriptions of Tiglath Pileser II.

No. 6.

LIST OF THE

KINGS OF ISRAEL,

MENTIONED IN THE CUNEIFORM INSCRIPTIONS.

From SMITH'S *History of Assyria.*

Humri (or Khumri)	Omri
Ahabbu	Ahab
Yahua	Jehu
Minihimmu	Menahem
Paqaha	Pekah
Husia	Hosea

LIST OF THE

KINGS OF JUDAH,

MENTIONED IN THE CUNEIFORM INSCRIPTIONS.

Azri-yahu	Azariah
Yahu-hazi	Ahaz
Haza-qi-yahu	Hezekiah
Minase	Manasseh

No. 7.

THE ASSYRIAN CALENDAR.

———

THE Babylonian Year was divided into 12 months of 30 days each, with an intercalary month every 6 years. The night had originally been divided into 3 watches, but afterwards the more accurate division into hours came into use, the day and the night severally containing 6 *casbu* (or *asli* as the Assyrians called them). According to the lunar division, the 7th, 14th, 19th, 21st, and 28th, were days of "rest," on which certain works were forbidden;

ASSYRIAN NAME.	JEWISH (Aramaic) NAME.	ENGLISH MONTH (roughly).
1. Ni'sannu	Ni'san	March
2. Airu	Iyyar	April
3. 'Sivanu *or* Tsivan	Sivan	May
4. Duzu	Tammuz	June
5. Abu	Ab	July
6. Ululu	Elul	August
7. Tasritu	Tisri	September
8. Arakh-samna ("the 8th month.")	Marchesvan	October
9. Cisilivu *or* Cuzallu	Chisleu	November
10. Dharbitu	Tebet	December
11. Sabahu	Sebat	January
12. Addaru	Adar	February
Arakh-makru ("the incidental month.")	Ve-Adar	✱

and the two lunations were divided each into three periods of 5 days, the 19th ending the first period of the 2nd lunation. Each month was under the protection of some deity, and its Accadian name answers to the corresponding sign of the Zodiac. The Assyrians seem to have once possessed a calendar of their own, in which the months had native names, like the old Jewish Calendar with its Bul, Ethanim, etc. Thus the third month was called "The Royal," and another month *mukhur ili*, "The Gift of the Gods." But along with the Jews they afterwards adopted the Aramaic Calendar, which was based upon that of the Accadians; indeed, the names of the months in this Calendar, wherever they are explicable, seem to be derived from the Accadian titles of the months and Zodiacal signs. This Aramaic-Accadian Calendar began with Nisan.

ACCADIAN NAME.	ZODIACAL SIGN.	DEITY TO WHOM THE MONTH WAS DEDICATED.
Sara zig-gar ("the sacrifice of righteousness," or "of Bel.")	Aries (the most usual object of sacrifice.)	Anu and Bel
Khar sidi ("the propitious bull.")	Taurus	Hea
Mun-ga ("of bricks,") & *Kas* ("the twins.")	Gemini	Sin (the moon-god.)
Su kul-na ("seizer of seed.")	Cancer	Adar
Ab ab-gar ("fire that makes fire.")	Leo	"The Queen of the spear" (Allat)
Ki Gingir-na ("the errand of Istar.")	Virgo	Istar
Tul-cu ("the holy altar.")	Libra	Samas (the sun-god.)
Apin am-a ("the bull-like founder." ?)	Scorpio	Merodach
Gan ganna ("the very cloudy.")	Sagittarius	Nergal
Abba uddu ("the father of light." ?)	Capricornus	Papsucul
As a-an ("abundance of rain.")	Aquarius	Rimmon (the air-god.)
Se ki-sil ("sowing of seed.")	Pisces	"The 7 Great Gods"
Se dir ("dark [month] of sowing.")	*	Assur

No. 8.

TITLES

OF THE

TWELVE GREATER DEITIES.

From SMITH'S *Chaldean Genesis.*

ANU.   King of Angels and Spirits, Lord of the city of Erech.

BEL.   Lord of the World, Father of the Gods, Creator, Lord of the city of Nipur.

HEA.   Maker of Fate, Lord of the Deep, God of Wisdom and Knowledge, Lord of the city of Eridu.

SIN.   Lord of Crowns, Maker of Brightness, Lord of the city of Ur.

MERODACH.   Just Prince of the Gods, Lord of Birth, Lord of the city of Babylon.

VUL.   The strong God, Lord of Canals, Lord of the Atmosphere, Lord of the city of Muru.

SHAMAS.   Judge of Heaven and Earth, Director of all, Lord of the cities of Larsa and Sippara.

NINIP.   Warrior of the Warriors of the Gods, Destroyer of the Wicked, Lord of the city of Nipur.

NERGAL.   Giant King of War, Lord of the city of Cutha.

NUSKU.   Holder of the Golden Sceptre, the Lofty God.

BELAT.   Wife of Bel, Mother of the Great Gods, Lady of the city of Nipur.

ISHTAR.   Eldest of Heaven and Earth, raising the face of warriors.

No. 9.

TABLES OF

ASSYRIAN WEIGHTS AND MEASURES.

COMPILED BY

R E V. A. H. S A Y C E, M.A.

MEASURES OF LENGTH:—

60 ubani = 1 suklu, rabtu or ammat ("cubit" = 20 inches)

6 ammat = 1 kanu ("cane" = 10 ft.)

12 kani = 1 ribu or gar

60 ribi = 1 soss

30 sosses = 1 kasbu or aslu ("a day's journey," about 7 miles)

For field measures the square of 60 yards was the unit, and the *soss* was called *ammat-gagar*, containing 360 yards. Sixty of these made one *masku* of 21,600 yards.

WEIGHTS AND MONEYS:—

8 ig or "royal shekels" = 1 shekel (5 dts., 4 fifteenths.)

60 shekels = 1 mana-gina (1 lb., 4 oz., 8 dts.)

2 mana-gina ("standard manehs") = 1 maneh (2 lbs., 8 oz., 16 dts.)

30 manehs = 1 talent (82 lbs.)

The talent was according to the standard either of Assyria ("the royal talent" or "the talent of the country") or of Carchemish. The contract-tablets variously give 1 talent of silver as equivalent to 5 manehs of gold, 5 manehs of silver to 2 manehs of gold, 10 manehs of silver to 1 maneh of gold, etc.

MEASURES OF CAPACITY :—

Land and grain were alike measured by the *log* (*lagitu*) which contained respectively 10, 9, and 8 subdivisions called *baru*, *aru*, and *arrat*. Grain was also measured by the *makaru;* and we find 100 *makarrat* of barley in a contract-tablet. The *arrat* was divided into the "*baru*" or "half of wood" and the "baru of stone."

The tonnage of ships was reckoned by the *gurru;* thus we have ships of 15 and 60 *gurri*.

No. 10.

PHENICIAN DIADS

(OR DIVINE COUPLES)

From LENORMANT's *Ancient History*.

SIDON—Baal Sidon and Ashtaroth.

GEBAL—Thammuz and Baalath.

CARTHAGE—Baal Hamon and Tanith.

N. PALESTINE—Shed and Shedath.

DAMASCUS—Hadad and Atargath.

CYPRUS—Reshep and Anath.

These Deities were chiefly solar and lunar symbolisms.

No. II.

THE SUCCESSION

OF

THE EGYPTIAN DYNASTIES,

WITH THEIR APPROXIMATE DATES.

From LENORMANT's *Manual of Ancient History.*

	Site.	Modern Name.	Duration.	B.C.
I.	This	Harabat-el-Madfouneh	253	5004
II.	,,	,, ,,	302	4751
III.	Memphis	Mit-Rahineh	214	4449
IV.	,,	,,	284	4235
V.	,,	,,	248	3951
VI.	Elephantine	Essouan	203	3703
VII.	Memphis	Mit-Rahineh	70	3500
VIII.	,,	,,	142	3500
IX.	Herakleopolis	Ahnas-el-Medineh	109	3358
X.	,,	,, ,,	185	3249
XI.	Thebes	Medinet-Abu	} 213	3064
XII.	,,	,,		
XIII.	,,	,,	453	2851
XIV.	Xois	Sakha	184	2398
XV.	Shepherd	San (Tanis)	} 511	2214
XVI.	,,	,,		
XVII.	,,	,,		

	Site.	Modern Name.	Duration.	B.C.
XVIII.	Thebes .	. Medinet-Abu .	. 241 .	1703
XIX.	„ . .	„ .	. 174 .	1462
XX.	„ . .	„ .	. 178 .	1288
XXI.	Tanis .	. San (Tanis) . .	. 130 .	1110
XXII.	Bubastis .	. Tel Basta . .	. 170 .	980
XXIII.	Tanis .	. San (Tanis) . .	. 89 .	810
XXIV.	Sais (1) .	. Sa-el-Hagar . .	. 6 .	721
XXV.	Ethiopian	. Napata (Gebel Barkal) .	50 .	715
XXVI.	Sais (2) .	. Sa-el-Hagar . .	. 138 .	665
XXVII.	Persians .	. Persepolis . .	. 121 .	527
XXVIII.	Sais (3) .	. Sa-el-Hagar . .	. 7 .	406
XXIX.	Mendes .	. Ashmoun . .	. 21 .	399
XXX.	Sebennytus	. Simenood . .	. 38 .	378
XXXI.	Persians .	. Persepolis, (Takt-i-Jemshid) 8	.	340

No. 12.

SUCCESSION OF THE MONARCHS

OF THE

XVIIIth, XIXth, and XXth DYNASTIES.

From MASPERO'S *Histoire Ancienne des Peuples de l'Orient. Deuxième Edition.*

XVIIIth DYNASTY.

1 AAHMES I., surnamed Ra-neb-peh-ti.
2 AMENHOTEP I., surnamed Ra-sar-ka.
3 THOTHMES I., surnamed Ra-aa-kheper-ka.
4 THOTHMES II., surnamed Ra-aa-kheper-en.
5 HATA-SU (Amen-Knoumt), surnamed Ra-ma-ka.
6 THOTHMES III., surnamed Ra-men-kheper.
7 AMENHOTEP II., surnamed Ra-aa-kheperu.
8 THOTHMES IV., surnamed Kha-khau, Ra-men-kheperu.
9 AMENHOTEP III., surnamed Ra-ma-neb.
10 AMENHOTEP IV., surnamed Ra-aa-neferu-khu-en-aten.
11 AI (Nuter-atef), surnamed Hik-nuter-uas, Ra-kheper-kheperu-ar-ma.
12 TUT-ANKH-AMEN, surnamed Hik-on-res, Ra-kheperu-neb.
13 RA-SA-AKA-KHEPERU, surnamed Ra-ankh-kheperu.

(Names wanting.)

HAREMHEBI (Horus), surnamed Ra-t-seser-kheperu-sotep-en-Ra.

XIXth DYNASTY.

1 RAMESES I., surnamed Ra-men-peh-ti.
2 SETI I., MENEPTHAH, surnamed Ra-ma-men.
3 RAMESES II., MIAMEN I., surnamed Ra-user-ma-sotep-en-Ra.
4 MENEPTHAH I., surnamed Hotep-hi-ma, Ban-Ra-mei-amen.
5 AMEN-MESES, surnamed Hik-on, Ra-men-kha-sotep-en-Ra.
6 MENEPTHAH II. (Sipthah), surnamed Khu-en-Ra-sotep-en-Ra.
7 SETI II., MENEPTHAH, surnamed Ra-user-kheperu-mei-amen.

(ARISU?).

XXth DYNASTY.

1 SETI-NEKHT, surnamed Meri-ra-mei-amen, Ra-user-khau-mei-amen.

2 RAMESES III., surnamed Hik-nuter-on, Ra-user-ma-mei-amen.

3 RAMESES IV., surnamed Hik-ma, Mei-amen, Ra-user-ma-sotep-en-amen.

4 RAMESES V., surnamed Amen-hi-khopesh-ef-mei-amen, Ra-user-ma-s-kheper-en-Ra.

5 RAMESES VI., surnamed Amen-hi-khopesh-ef-nuter-hik-on, Ra-neb-ma-mei-amen.

6 RAMESES VII., surnamed At-amen-nuter-hik-on, Ra-user-ma-mei-amen-sotep-en-Ra.

7 RAMESES VIII., surnamed Set-hi-khopesh-ef-mei-amen, Ra-user-ma-khu-en-amen.

8 MEI-AMEN, surnamed Meritum . . . . (rest of the surname wanting).

9 RAMESES IX., surnamed Sipthah-sek-han, Ra-mei-amen.

10 RAMESES X., MEI-AMEN I., surnamed Nefer-kau, Ra-sotep-en-Ra.

11 RAMESES XI., MEI-AMEN II., surnamed Ra-user-ma-sotep-en-Ra.

12 RAMESES XII., surnamed Kham-uas-nuter-hik-on-mei-amen, Ra-men-ma-sotep-en-pthah.

13 RAMESES XIII., MEI-AMEN III., surnamed Amen-hi-khopesh-ef, Ra-kheper-ma-sotep-en-Ra.

14 (HER-HOR-SI-AMEN, surnamed Nuter-hon-tep-en-amen.)

15 RAMESES XIV. (?)

16 RAMESES XV. (?)

17 RAMESES XVI.

NOTE.—The above list which has only just been issued, and which embodies the results of the researches of the continental Egyptologist, sufficiently attests the impossibility of at present fixing any synchronistic argument on the contemporaneous history of the Egyptian kings.

No. 13.

THE FAMILY OF THE LAGIDÆ.

From SHARPE'S *Chronology of Ancient Egypt.*

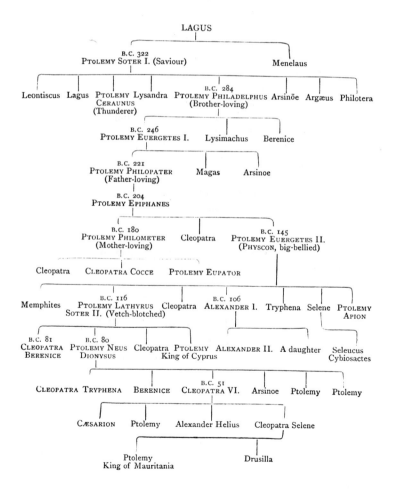

LAGUS

B.C. 322
PTOLEMY SOTER I. (Saviour)   Menelaus

Leontiscus   Lagus   PTOLEMY   Lysandra   B.C. 284   PTOLEMY PHILADELPHUS   Arsinöe   Argæus   Philotera
CERAUNUS (Thunderer)   (Brother-loving)

B.C. 246
PTOLEMY EUERGETES I.   Lysimachus   Berenice

B.C. 221
PTOLEMY PHILOPATER   Magas   Arsinoe
(Father-loving)

B.C. 204
PTOLEMY EPIPHANES

B.C. 180
PTOLEMY PHILOMETER   Cleopatra   B.C. 145   PTOLEMY EUERGETES II.
(Mother-loving)   (PHYSCON, big-bellied)

Cleopatra   CLEOPATRA COCCE   PTOLEMY EUPATOR

Memphites   B.C. 116   PTOLEMY LATHYRUS   Cleopatra   B.C. 106   ALEXANDER I.   Tryphena   Selene   PTOLEMY
SOTER II. (Vetch-blotched)   APION

B.C. 81   B.C. 80
CLEOPATRA   PTOLEMY NEUS   Cleopatra   PTOLEMY ALEXANDER II.   A daughter   Seleucus
BERENICE   DIONYSUS   King of Cyprus   Cybiosactes

B.C. 51
CLEOPATRA TRYPHENA   BERENICE   CLEOPATRA VI.   Arsinoe   Ptolemy   Ptolemy

CÆSARION   Ptolemy   Alexander Helius   Cleopatra Selene

Ptolemy   Drusilla
King of Mauritania

No. 14.

THE EGYPTIAN TRIADS.

Chiefly from WILKINSON's *Ancient Egyptians.*

ABYDOS AND PHILÆ—Isis, Horus, and Osiris.
CHEMMIS—Khem, Thriphis . . . . . (name lost).
DABOD—Malooli, Seb, Nut.
EDFOU—Hor-Hat, Athor, Hors-enet-to.
ELEPHANTINE—Kneph, Anouke, Sate.
ESNEH—Kneph, Neboo, Hake.
HERMONTHIS—Mandoo, Reto, Horpe-Re.
KALABSHE—Horus, Isis, Malooli.
LAPIDIS—Thoth, Nehemeou, Aroeris.
MEMPHIS—Pthah, Pasht, Imhotep.
      ,,   Pthah, Merenpthah, Nefer-Atum.
OMBOS I.—Sebek, Athor, Khonso.
   ,, II.—Aroeris, Isont-Nope, Nebto.
SILSILIS—Ra, Pthah, Hapimou.
THEBES—Amen-Ra, Maut, Khonso.
   ,,   II.—Amun-Khem, Tamunta, Harka.
   ,, III.—Katesh, Anta, Reschep.

PSEUDO TRIADS.

ABUSAID—Rameses II., Ra, Rameses, Atmoo.
HERMONTHIS—Julius Cæsar, Cleopatra, Neocæsar.
SILSILIS—Rameses II., Osiris, Rameses, Isis.
THEBES—Rameses III., Osiris, Rameses III., Pthah.

EGYPTO-GNOSTIC TRIADS.

Kosmos, Theos, Pothos.
Knumis, Nabis, Biennous.
Bait, Athor, Akori.
Serapis, Knumis, Osiris.
Serapis-Knumis, Sate, Anucis.
Bythos, Ennoia, Pneuma.

PHENICIAN.

Baal, Ashtaroth, Asherah.

No. 15.

EGYPTIAN CALENDAR.

CIVIL YEAR.	SACRED YEAR begins	ALEXANDRIAN [1] begins
Thoth	July 20	August 29
Paophi	August 19	September 28
Athyr	September 18	October 28
Choiak	October 18	November 27
Tybi	November 17	December 27
Mechir	December 17	January 26
Phamenoth	January 16	February 25
Pharmuthi	February 15	March 27
Pashons	March 17	April 26
Payni	April 16	May 26
Epiphi	May 16	June 25
Mesore	June 15	July 25 [2]

[1] The Alexandrian Year was introduced in the reign of Augustus, B.C. 25.

[2] Epagomenæ, 24th to 28th August.

No. 16.

EGYPTIAN MEASURES AND WEIGHTS.

1 *Suten maha*	Royal cubit	=	7 palms.
1 *Maha ur*	great cubit	=	6 palms.
1 *Maha negs*	little cubit	=	5 palms.
1 *Tser*	foot	=	4 palms.
1 *Remen aa*	large span	=	14 digits.
1 *Remen negs*	small span	=	3 palms.
1 *Khep*		=	5 digits.
1 *Shap*	palm	=	4 digits.
4 *Teb*	digits	=	1 palm.
½-¹/₁₆ *Ru*	fractions	=	1 digit.

These, according to Sir Henry James, are as follows :—

					INCHES
1 Royal cubit	=	7 palms	=		20.728.
1 palm	=	4 digits	=		2.961.
1 digit			=		.743.
1 span	=	3 palms	=		8.583.
1 foot	=	4 palms	=		11.844.
1 common cubit	=	6 palms	=		18.240.
1 palm	=	4 digits	=		3.040.
1 digit			=		0.760.
1 span	=	3 palms	=		9.120.
1 foot	=	4 palms	=		12.160.

					TROY GRAINS
1 *Ten*,	pound	=	10 *kat*	=	1400
1 *Kat*,[1]	didrachm or ounce			=	140
1 *Hon* (*hin*)				=	75 pints.

MEASURES OF WHICH THE EXACT EQUIVALENTS ARE NOT KNOWN.

Tna, basket. | *Hetp*, bushel. | *Khersh*, truss.

---

[1] The *half, quarter, two-thirds, one-sixth,* and *one-sixteenth,* of a *kat* are found.

No. 17.

TABLES

OF

HEBREW AND CHALDEAN MEASURES.

From CONDER's *Ancient Metrology, Trans. Soc. Bib. Arch.*, Vol. IV. i.

LONG MEASURE.

2 Barley Corns	Digit . . .	⅔ Inches
8 ,, ,,	Palm . . .	2⅔ ,,
40 ,, ,,	Artificers' Cubit .	13⅓ ,,
48 ,, ,,	Land Cubit .	16 ,,
52 ,, ,,	Sacred Cubit .	17⅓ ,,

SQUARE MEASURE.

104·15 Cubits	Rebah . .	20·5 Sq. Yds.
416·6 ,,	Cabus . .	2·67 Poles
2,500 ,,	Satum . .	16·32 ,,
7,500 ,,	Zemeed . .	·306 Acre
75,000 ,,	Kor . . .	3·06 ,,

CUBIC MEASURE.

24 Cubic Inches	Log . . .	·675 Pint
96 ,, ,,	Cabus . .	.675 Quart
288 ,: ,,	Hin . . .	1·0128 Gallon
576 ,: ,,	Satum . .	2·0385 ,,
1,728 ,, ,,	Ephah . .	6·2355 ,,
172·8 ,, ,,	Omer . . .	2·494 Quart
17,280 ,, ,,	Kor . . .	·993 Quarter

SHEKEL SYSTEM.—SILVER.

WEIGHT.			
40 Troy Grains	Octave		
53⅓ ,, ,,	Garmes		
80 ,, ,,	Zuza		
120 ,, ,,	Half Righia		
160 ,, ,,	Beka . . .	Half Ducat
240 ,, ,,	Righia		
320 ,, ,,	Shekel . .	Ducat (Neapolitan)

SELA SYSTEM.—SILVER.

WEIGHT.			
48 Troy Grains	Octave		
64 ,, ,,	Garmes		
96 ,, ,,	Dinar		
144 ,, ,,	Half Righia		
192 ,, ,,	Thebah . .	Six-Carlino Piece
288 ,, ,,	Righia		
384 ,, ,,	Sela . . .	Piastre (Neapolitan)

SELA SYSTEM.—COPPER.

WEIGHT.	
About 20 Troy Grains . .	Prutha
,, 53⅓ ,, ,, . .	Shemun
,, 106⅔ ,, ,, . .	Hanitz
,, 213⅓ ,, ,, . .	Hadres
,, 40 ,, ,, . .	Kontrinek
,, 80 ,, ,, . .	Musmes
,, 160 ,, ,, . .	Assarion
,, 320 ,, ,, . .	Pondion
,, 640 ,, ,, . .	Asper

No. 18.

SUGGESTIONS

FOR A

SYSTEMATIC STUDY OF EGYPTIAN HISTORY.

GYPT is perhaps the only country of which an historical account cannot be compiled from the resources of an ordinary library and a retentive memory. It is certainly the only kingdom whose annals have for four thousand years been only tentatively written, and upon the subject of which the ingenious conjectures of classic and modern authors have been of almost equal value and nearly equally misleading. Even now, when the records of Egypt have been discovered and the legends of its contemporary monuments translated, it must still be said that many of the facts commemorated on them are self-contradictory, and that the evidence they afford must be used with great discretion. It is for these reasons, that while on the one hand there have been lately published very many popular treatises on Egypt, from Osburn's *Monumental History* to Keary's *History of Egypt for the Young*, yet there is not one of them which can be regarded as an authority ; and the chief in number, from Long's *History of Egypt* to Ingraham's romance *The Pillar of Fire*, are more than useless from their being vitiated by one of two errors, and often by both, viz., the support of a preconceived idea, or false inferences from mistranslated texts. A scientific history of the country, except what is contained in Bunsen's crudely philosophical *Egypt's place in the History of the World*, does not exist in English. The continental scholars have in Germany Histories by MM. Brugsch-Bey (*Histoire d'Egypte*) and Lepsius (*Königsbuch der Egypter*), and in France, by MM. Mariette-Bey, Maspero, and Lenormant ; of these works English translations only exist of Lenormant's and Mariette-Bey's (*in press*), and there is a valuable but too condensed *History of Egypt from the Monuments* by Dr. Birch. These are the only reliable authorities. It would therefore be better for one who really desires to study out for himself the Archaic History of Egypt, to read systematically at the same time several of these histories qualifying the statements of one author by those of another, comparing both with the facts of a third, and taking as his basis different chapters from their respective treatises for different periods in Egyptian chronology, according as the researches of a particular student have been devoted to that special epoch more than another. Fortunately for the scholar the chief *work-books* required are neither numerous or expensive, and a few hour's examination of the costlier authorities which contain large illustrations, can be readily obtained at most of the national libraries. These reference books are principally Denon's *Description de l'Egypte*, valuable only for its accurately measured drawings of temples no longer extant; Rosellini's *Monumenti dell'Egitto*, especially the section *Monumenti Civili;* Lepsius' *Denkmäler aus Aegypten*, especially section *Aelteste Reiche;* Mariette-Bey's *Fouilles d'Abydos* and *Tentyra;* De Rougé's *Album Photographique;* Leeman's *Monumens du Musee de Leide;* Birch's *Rhind Papyrus* and *Great Harris Papyrus;* Lepsius' *Todtenbuch;* Prisse's *L'Art Egyptien;* Burton's *Excerpta. Hieroglyphica;* and Devéria's *Papyrus de Nebqed.*

The first point to be considered by a student is the position of Egypt to the surrounding nations, the origin of its races and the nature of its country; these will be found related in an admirably succinct manner in Lenormant's *Manual of the Ancient History of the East*, Vol. I., Cap. iii., Sec. 4, to Cap. iv., Sec. 5, and Maspero's *Histoire Ancienne des peuples de l'Orient*, Liv. I., Caps. 1 et 2; while the geography of the special district will be best found in Murray's *Handbook to Egypt*, Lepsius' *Letters from Egypt and Nubia*, and Wilkinson's *Geography of Thebes* and *Ancient Egyptians*, Vol. I. Subsequent reference should be made to the *Ægyptus Antiqua, Karte von Unter-Ægypten* and *Geographie des Alten Ægyptens* of Brugsch-Bey, the great map in Denon's *Egypt, Cartes Geographiques*, "*Etat Moderne*," and the sheets of the survey now in progress under the auspices of H. H. the Khedive.

The geography ascertained the student will have, with constant references for Egyptian words and rites to Piérret's *Dictionnaire*.

d'Archéologie Egyptienne, to enter at once upon his task, and the events of the earliest six dynasties will have first to be considered. This section of Egyptian history is best contained in Mariette-Bey's *Aperçu sur l'Histoire d'Egypte*, Birch's *Egypt*, Cap. i., and especially, if it can be obtained, E. De Rougé's *Histoire les six premieres Dynastes*. The the book of Lenormant, Cap. i. to Sec. 5 can also be read with profit if it is read with care, and especially Chabas' learned treatise *Etudes sur l'Antiquité Historique;* after this it would be expedient for the student, if he is able, to visit the Egyptian Vestibule of the British Museum, and to *avoid seeing anything else which belongs to a later period of history*, and as a companion for this purpose he will find Birch's *Guide to the Egyptian Vestibule* invaluable. He should then step into the Reading Room and look over the plates of the first volumes of Lepsius' *Denkmaler*, and of Vyse's *Pyramids of Gizeh*, and then dismiss the subject of pyramidology from his mind at once and for ever, or it will else prove an insufferable and inconvinceable bug-bear to him throughout all his future studies.

For the next period, or that extending from the VIth to the XIIth dynasty, Birch's *Egypt* is by far the most reliable general guide, Maspero's *Histoire*, Caps. ii. and iii., come next in order, and lastly Lenormant's *History*, Book II., Cap. ii. Here it would be well to read over those texts belonging to this period in *Records of the Past*, such as the *Inscription of Una* and the *Instructions of Amenemhat*, in Vol. II., and the *Story of Saneha* in Vol. VI. Owing to the changes undergone by the religious system of the Egyptians at various times, it would only lead to confusion if texts of a later age were consulted at the same time. Points of interest are best noted down in an *Index Rerum*, and kept for consideration when the course of reading has been terminated.

Having closed the study of the annals of the Ancient Empire, and before proceeding to work upon the better known portions of Egyptian history, it would be proper for the student here to peruse, with much deliberation, the singularly Egyptian history of Joseph, as given in Genesis, Caps. xxxvii. to l., and he will have again to read this beautiful episode when he parts from the period, XIXth dynasty, and when he will do well to compare it with the analogous *Story of the Two Brothers* in *Records of the Past*, Vol. II., and of *Setnau* in Vol. IV. Referring again to continental authorities the following works may be now read, Champollion Figeac's *Le Panthéon Egyptien*, and the figures contained therein, compared with those of the same deities in Wilkinson's *Materia Hieroglyphica*, Barry de Merval's *Etudes sur l'Architecture Egyptienne*, and De Rouge's *Monnaies des Nomes*; this latter book, together with Harris's *Standards of the Nomes*, will have again to be examined at the close of the history of the XXth dynasty.

From the XIIIth to the XVIIth dynasties, overlapping the fall of the Ancient Empire and the terrible rule of the Hykshos, perhaps the best source of general information is Maspero, Livre II., Cap. iv.; Birch's *History*, has little or nothing on the subject; Lenormant, Cap. ii., Secs. 3, 4, has hardly more information; Brugsch-Bey's great History is somewhat better, but at present there is only a German edition, the English translation by Danby Seymour not having yet appeared. Treatises on the Hykshos there are in abundance in the Transactions of the archæological and literary societies, the best is Chabas' *Les Pastures en Egypte*, but they are all hypothetical, the only texts relating to the period in question are *Sallier Papyrus I.* in *Records of the Past*, Vol. VIII. (*now in press*), and the *Stele of 400 Years* in Vol. IV. of the same issue, while of these two texts the latter one is considered by a competent authority to be more than doubtful. The lists of the kings as given by Manetho in Bunsen's *Egypt*, Vol. V., and again in Lepsius' *Königsbuch*, Vol. I., and the names occuring on a few scarabei and wooden objects in the British and Leyden Museums are too scattered and imperfect to be depended upon. Where all is still conjecture, Josephus *Contra Apion*, Lib. i., Secs. 25 to 34, and Lib. ii., Secs. 1 to 4, may be read over, but more as a piece of ancient special pleading on both sides than as an historical document.

With the close of the XVIIth dynasty, to a certain extent, all chronological difficulty ceases, and the materials for the history of the three great Theban or Diospolite dynasties are abundant and authentic, and they have fortunately been repeatedly translated and published. This is also the period when classic and early Jewish associations come into connection with those of Egypt, and as a consequence thereof it follows that almost every author upon ancient history has treated these dynasties in some detail; it would be proper therefore for the student to read each of the four Histories of Egypt referred to in succession, without relying upon any one of them for absolute conclusions as to matters of fact ; collaterally also should be read the first three volumes of Rawlinson's *Five Great Empires of the East;* Smith's *History of Babylonia,* contained in *Records of the Past,* Vols. III. and V. ; and to keep *au courant* with the classical Egyptology of the times ; Gladstone's *Homeric Synchronisms,* and Chabas' *Recherches sur le temps de l'Exode;* Brugsch-Bey's *L'Exode et les Monuments Egyptiens;* Lenormant's *Essai sur la propagation de l'Alphabet Phenician,* and *Premieres Civilisations;* De Rouge's *Recherches sur les Monuments;* Maspero's *Genre Epistolaire des Anciens Egyptiens;* and Ancessi's *L'Egypte et Moise* are all worth notice where they can be looked over ; but the *Annals of Thothmes III., Rameses II. and III.,* and *Menepthah III.,* and the *Travels of an Egyptian,* in *Records of the Past,* Vols. II., IV., and VI., are indispensable. If at this period of his studies the student should visit the British Museum he cannot do better than examine Dümichen's *Fleet of an Egyptian Queen* (Hat-a-su), *Bauurkunde der Tempelangen von Denderah,* and the remaining volumes of Lepsius' *Denkmäler, Neues Reiches.*

The events which characterised the XXIInd to the XXVIth dynasties, have, like those of the XIXth, been treated with nearly equal amplitude and success by Messrs. Birch, Lenormant, and Maspero ; if anything the latter author should be preferred in matters relating to the Ethiopic dynasties, and especially should his translation of the *Ethiopic Annals* in Vols. IV. and VI. of *Records of the Past,* and also Canon Cook's *Stèle of Pianchi* in Vol. II. of the same series be consulted. The maps, especially Nos. 1, 3, and 4, in Maspero's *Histoire* should be carefully looked over, and the last part of the *Palestine Exploration Reports,* April, 1876, be criticised to compare the identification of Syrian localities proposed by Lieut. Conder with those visited by the Mohar in the reign of Rameses II. Perhaps at this point also, the testimony, if testimony it can be called, of Herodotus in *Euterpe* and the first 66 sections of his *Thalia* may be considered. The edition by Rawlinson is incomparably the best, but no reliance can be placed upon the assertions of a credulous and ignorant romancist, whose *History of Egypt* is as veracious as Mandeville's *Travels in the East,* and about on a par with it for actual observation and critical belief. Another ancient fabulist, whom time and ignorance have canonised into an historian, Diodorus Siculus, comes next to be read and disregarded. Book I. of his *Historical Library* contains the romantic biographies of Sesostris and Osymandyas, or possibly Rameses III., which have neither parallel nor justification in the facts of Egyptian history, still as they have served to pass current for truth till very lately they cannot be ignored, and it is quite possible that certain incidental points may here and there be confirmed by monumental evidence.

For the scanty enough materials of the Sebennytic, Mendesian, and Saitic dynasties, the student had better again trust the guidance of Birch's *History* and that of Lenormant's, noting, wherever it is possible to do so, the parallel statements containing the same events which are given by Herodotus, and here Rawlinson's *Ancient Monarchies* will once more prove of valuable assistance. The reference books for this section of his studies the student will find in Hosking's *Ethiopia* and Gau's *Antiquités de la Nubie.*

With the XXXth dynasty, with which the record of Ancient Egypt virtually closes, a new author requires to be consulted, namely, Sharpe, whose *History of Egypt from the earliest period to the Arab Invasion* though inaccurate, to use a mild phrase, in its earlier chapters is indispensable as a guide to the latter days of the Egyptian Empire, from the invasion of Cambyses to the edict of Theodosius, or from chapters vi. to xxi. ; the indices to his work are especially admirable, as are also by the way those of Messrs. Maspero and Lenormant. Sharpe's book should however be revised by a perusal of its French predecessor, by Champollion Figeac, *L'Egypte sous les Lagides.* The works of Messrs. Birch and Smith have neither index nor headings to the pages, which makes a reference to them extremely tiresome. Another authority, once too highly esteemed and now too little regarded, the Greco-Jewish author of the first three books of Maccabees should also be read through, as in his narrative many details are related which by classical historians have been passed over. The translations of the *Tablet of Rosetta* in *Records of the Past*, Vol. IV., and that of *Canopus* in Vol. VIII. (*in press*); of Alexander Ægus in the *Zeitschrift fur Aegyptisch Sprache* for 1874, and *Der Grosse Stele aus Mendes* in the Vol. for 1875, all long Ptolemaic documents, will be most serviceable to the student ; so also will be Sharpe's *Map of Egypt under Antoninus Pius*, and that of the Delta in Bellefond-Bey's *Travaux Publiques*, of the Fayoum in Wilkinson's *Materia Hieroglyphica*, and Brugsch-Bey's *L'Exode* before referred to. A final journey should now be taken to the whole of the Egyptian collection at the British Museum, examining each period by its monumental and artistic remains in slow detail; the unique sarcophagus of Seti at the Soane Museum, if possible with the plates of Bonomi's, *Sarcophagus of Oimenepthah* in hand at the same time; the cover of that of Rameses III. at the Fitzwilliam Museum at Cambridge; and, if admission could be obtained, the Egyptian collections of the Duke of Northumberland at Alnwick, and of Mr. Tyssen Amhurst, at Didlington Park, Norfolk, should also be visited; and then, as a journey to Berlin, or Boulaq, or Paris, would be beyond the resources of an ordinary English student, the elaborate handbooks of the Louvre collection by MM. Pierret and Deveria, of Boulaq by Mariette-Bey, and that of Leyden by Dr. Leemens, all moreover inexpensive works, should be read through and their details noted, and where any object is described as deviating from its usual type, that object should be again compared by a reference to others presenting the typical form in the collection at the British Museum.

A fair general knowledge of classical history having been already assumed, such a course of reading and of reference as this which is thus proposed would result in clearing away a variety of misleading theories and romantic fable which have hitherto, for want of evidence to the contrary, been accepted as historical facts, and the student would then be the better able to judge for himself of the relative value of the various propositions which are from time to time put forth by writers upon ancient history. By such a systematic course of reading it is believed that the student would be able to gauge the depth of the wisdom and of the prejudices of Egypt, and to measure the influence of her arts and literature upon classic, mediæval, and modern civilisation.

The following are some of the incidental points which the student would do well to observe and follow up :—

The origin of the various races of Egypt.

The physical geography of early Egypt.

The change of name of various Egyptian cities.

The obliteration of the name of Amen at different epochs.

The several introductions of Set worship.

The original distinction between Set and Sutekh.

The several immigrations from Palestine into Egypt.

The revolt of Arsu.

The heresies of Khu-en-aten and Tumpesi.

The intercourse between Egypt and Nubia.

The position of maternal descent in the Old Empire.

The nature of animal worship.

The political offices held by one and the same individual.

The occurrence of Semitic names in Egyptian history.

The position of Horus-Haremhebi.

The genealogy of Her-Hor.

The rise of Greek influence in Egyptian polity.

The political change from an Icosarchy into a Dodecarchy.

The intercourse between Egypt and Phenicia.

The foundation of Greco-Egyptian cities.

The colonies of Egypt.

The mythological analogies of the Egyptian with the Semitic and Aryan faiths.

W. R. C.